The Civilization of the Middle Ages is
the most readable and imaginative
one-volume history of the Middle Ages in
the English language.

In 1963, Norman F. Cantor published his
breakthrough narrative history of the Middle
Ages. Further editions of this immediately celebrated book appeared in 1968 and 1974. Now
a thorough revision, update, and significant
expansion of the book has been made, with a
third of the text new. *The Civilization of the
Middle Ages* incorporates current research,
recent trends in interpretation, and novel perspectives, especially on the foundations of the
Middle Ages to A.D. 450 and the Later Middle
Ages of the fourteenth and fifteenth centuries, as
well as a sharper focus on social history, Jewish
history, women's roles in society, and popular
religion and heresy. While the first and last sections of the book are almost entirely new and
many additions have been incorporated in the
intervening sections, Cantor has retained the
powerful narrative flow that made the earlier
editions so accessible and exciting.

Cantor's book was innovative in 1963 because it was the first comprehensive general
history of the Middle Ages to center on medieval culture and religion rather than political
history (which was, however, dealt with, but
from the perspective of applied intellect and
social ordering). It remains a unique book in
that regard. The book also featured the high-

(continued on back flap)

THE
CIVILIZATION
OF THE
MIDDLE AGES

BOOKS BY NORMAN F. CANTOR

Medieval Lives

Inventing the Middle Ages

Twentieth-Century Culture

The Meaning of the Middle Ages

Western Civilization: Its Genesis and Destiny

The English

How to Study History (with R. I. Schneider)

Medieval History: The Life and Death of a Civilization

Perspectives on the European Past

The Medieval World: 300 to 1300

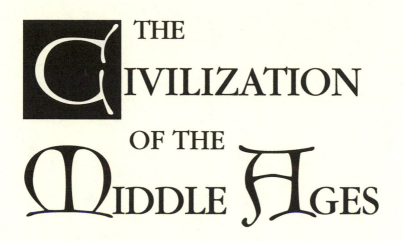

THE CIVILIZATION OF THE MIDDLE AGES

A Completely Revised and Expanded Edition of

MEDIEVAL HISTORY
The Life and Death of a Civilization

NORMAN F. CANTOR

HarperCollins*Publishers*

HarperCollins books may be purchased for educational, business, or sales promotional use. For information, please write: Special Markets Department, HarperCollins Publishers, Inc., 10 East 53rd Street, New York, NY 10022.

FIRST EDITION

Designed by Alma Hochhauser Orenstein

Library of Congress Cataloging-in-Publication Data

Cantor, Norman F.
    The civilization of the Middle Ages : a completely revised and expanded edition of Medieval history, the life and death of a civilization / Norman F. Cantor. — 1st ed.
        p. cm.
        Includes bibliographical references and index.
        ISBN 0-06-017033-6
        1. Civilization, Medieval. 2. Middle Ages—History. I. Cantor, Norman F. Medieval History. II. Title.
CB351.C24   1993
940.1—dc20   92-56237

---

94 95 96 97 ❖/RRD 10 9 8 7 6 5 4 3 2

To Sir Geoffrey Elton

CONTENTS

Preface   xiii

ONE The Heritage of the Ancient World   1
   I. POLITICS AND SOCIETY 1
   II. PHILOSOPHY AND RELIGION 13

TWO The Foundations of the Middle Ages   29
   I. FROM JUDAISM TO CHRISTIANITY 29
   II. DECLINE AND FALL 40
   III. THE ROMAN DESTINY 47
   IV. PATRISTIC CULTURE 66

THREE The Age of the Barbarian Invasions   89
   I. THE GERMANS 89
   II. THE FIRST CENTURY OF THE INVASIONS 99
   III. THE OSTROGOTHIC AND FRANKISH KINGDOMS 104

FOUR Justinian and Mohammed   123
   I. THE NEMESIS OF BYZANTINE POWER 123
   II. THE IMPACT OF ISLAM ON EARLY MEDIEVAL EUROPE 131

FIVE The Advance of Ecclesiastical Leadership   145
   I. THE RISE OF MONASTICISM 145
   II. GREGORY THE GREAT AND THE EARLY MEDIEVAL PAPACY 155

six The Making of Carolingian Kingship 161

I. ANGLO-IRISH CULTURE AND THE COLONIAL PHENOMENON 161

II. THE CAROLINGIAN ENIGMA 171

III. MONARCHY AND PAPACY 173

seven Culture and Society in the First Europe 185

I. THE CAROLINGIAN WORLD 185

II. THE FEUDAL ORGANIZATION OF SOCIETY 195

eight Ecclesia and Mundus 205

I. THE NATURE OF THE EARLY MEDIEVAL EQUILIBRIUM 205

II. THE NORMAN FEUDAL STATE 206

III. THE OTTONIAN EMPIRE 211

IV. THE CLUNIAC IDEAL 218

nine Byzantium, Islam, and the West 225

I. THE LIMITATIONS OF BYZANTINE AND ISLAMIC CIVILIZATIONS 225

II. THE RISE OF EUROPE 228

ten Europe in 1050 235

eleven The Gregorian World Revolution 243

I. THE NATURE AND ORIGIN OF THE GREGORIAN REFORM 243

II. THE DEBATE ON THE ESSENTIALS OF A CHRISTIAN SOCIETY 249

III. THE GERMAN INVESTITURE CONTROVERSY 265

twelve The Anglo-Norman Monarchy and the Emergence of the Bureaucratic State 277

I. THE TRIUMPH OF WILLIAM THE BASTARD 277

II. THE SIGNIFICANCE OF THE ENGLISH INVESTITURE CONTROVERSY 284

thirteen The First Crusade and After 289

I. ORIGINS OF THE CRUSADING IDEAL 289

II. CRUSADING MEMORIES 297

FOURTEEN The Intellectual Expansion of Europe   305

    I. THE ACCELERATION OF CULTURAL CHANGE 305

    II. THE LEGAL CONSTITUENTS OF HIGH MEDIEVAL CIVILIZATION 306

    III. A GREAT GENERATION: FIVE LEADERS OF
         TWELFTH-CENTURY THOUGHT AND FEELING 318

    IV. LITERATURE AND SOCIETY IN THE TWELFTH CENTURY 343

FIFTEEN Moslem and Jewish Thought:
The Aristotelian Challenge   357

    I. THE PROBLEM OF LEARNING 357

    II. REASON AND REVELATION IN MOSLEM AND JEWISH THOUGHT 361

SIXTEEN Varieties of Religious Experience   373

    I. MONKS AND SOCIETY 373

    II. THE DIMENSIONS OF POPULAR HERESY 384

SEVENTEEN The Entrenchment of Secular Leadership   395

    I. POWER AND CHARISMA 395

    II. THE CAPETIAN ASCENDANCY 409

EIGHTEEN The Peace of Innocent III   417

    I. THE REAFFIRMATION OF PAPAL LEADERSHIP 417

    II. THE DOMINICAN AND FRANCISCAN IDEALS 428

NINETEEN The New Consensus and Its Limitations   435

    I. THE CATHEDRAL OF INTELLECT 435

    II. THE MORAL AUTHORITY OF THE STATE 448

    III. THE INTERESTS OF SOCIETY 464

TWENTY The Search for Order   475

    I. AN OLD LAND 475

    II. THE CRISIS OF THE LATE MIDDLE AGES 480

    III. PAPACY AND CLERGY 487

    IV. THE EUROPEAN STATES 505

TWENTY-ONE Late Medieval and Renaissance Culture   529

    I. THE HARVEST OF MEDIEVAL THOUGHT 529
    II. THE ITALIAN RENAISSANCE 540
    III. MEDIEVALISM AND THE MIDDLE AGES 561

The Middle Ages on Film   567

Recommended Reading   569

    A SHORT LIST 569
    THE LONG LIST 570

Index   577

PREFACE

This book is an extensively revised, thoroughly updated, and substantially expanded version of *Medieval History, The Life and Death of a Civilization* (New York: Macmillan, 1963; second edition, 1968; revised paperback edition, 1974). About one-third of the text is now different from the old version of this book. The old book went through some fourteen printings and was a main selection of the History Book Club, which offered it to its subscribers for nineteen years. It was widely used as a college textbook. The old book was still in print in 1991. Although its core was still viable, it needed major revision, which this book achieves.

Intellectually, the main changes and additions in this version reflect the extensive publication on social structure, particularly on women's and family history and on medieval piety and heresy in the past three decades. Greater attention has now been given to the impress of the heritage of the ancient world on the preconditioning of medieval civilization, and the section on patristic thought has been extensively rewritten. The major change between the earlier version and this one is in the latter part of the book, on the fourteenth and fifteenth centuries, which is almost entirely different in this version and greatly expanded. Whereas in the old book the fourteenth and fifteenth centuries were treated as a sort of epilogue to medieval civilization, here they are given the same kind of comprehensive narrative treatment as in the rest of the book. This treatment reflects both the enormous body of new historical literature on the late Middle Ages in recent decades and my changed perception of the later centuries of the medieval era. The bibliography in this volume is completely different from the last edition of the old book. It incorporates titles up to 1992.

The first version of this book had a historiographical introduction and some further discourses on how the Middle Ages have been interpreted in the twentieth century. That material has now been rendered superfluous and thoroughly superseded by my recent book *Inventing the Middle Ages* (William Morrow, 1991; Lutterworth, 1992; Quill paperback, 1993), which is a companion volume to this book. Anyone who reads both books will have a full comprehension of both the narrative development of the Middle Ages and the course of their historiographical interpretation in this century. *Inventing the Middle Ages* was also a main selection of the History Book Club, the generous patron of humanistic history.

This revised and expanded version retains the character of the original version, namely a focus on cultural, intellectual, and religious history, considered within social and political contexts. The popular impression of the Middle Ages as the Age of Faith and one whose consciousness and sensibility were dominated by the western church is, like most popular historical images, not wrong. What is needed, however, is to articulate that impression in terms of the actual development of medieval religious culture in its interaction with social and material forces, so that the perception of the Middle Ages as a faith-centered culture will be grounded in the reality that historical research can establish. This is what this book tries to do, presenting this information in a readable narrative that highlights prominent personalities.

When I first published this book, I was teaching a hundred students a semester in the introductory course in medieval history at Columbia University and Barnard College. In spring 1992, I was teaching the same number of students in the same course at New York University. I have maintained my connection with young minds, and I draw upon this experience in this version to present to students, as well as to mature lay readers, what I think they want to know about the Middle Ages.

I wish to thank the Macmillan Company of New York for transferring its old copyright on this book; the Office of the Dean of Arts and Science at New York University for providing secretarial and technical support; my secretary, Nelly Fontanez, for immensely valuable assistance in preparing the manuscript for the press; my literary agent, Alexander Hoyt; and my wife, Mindy Cantor, for her help and advice.

New York
August 1992

Credo

This heavenly city, then, while it sojourns on earth, calls citizens out of all nations, and gathers together a society of pilgrims of all languages, not scrupling about diversities in the manners, laws, and institutions whereby earthly peace is secured and maintained, but recognizing that, however various these are, they all tend to one and the same end of earthly peace.

St. Augustine of Hippo, Algeria c.425
trans. Marcus Dodds

There are some who wish to learn for no other reason than that they may be looked upon as learned, which is a ridiculous vanity. . . . Others desire to learn that they may morally instruct others; that is love. And, lastly, there are some who wish to learn that they may be themselves edified; and that is prudence.

St. Bernard of Clairvaux, France c. 1145
trans. S. J. Eales

Bernard of Chartres, the most abounding spring of letters in Gaul in modern times, followed this method. . . . Where the subject of his own lesson had reference to other disciplines, these matters he brought out clearly in such wise that he did not teach everything about each topic, but in proportion to the capacity of his audience dispensed to them in time the due measure of his subject. . . . And he brought it about that he who imitated his predecessors became worthy of imitation by his successors.

John of Salisbury, England c. 1165
trans. C. H. Haskins

THE
CIVILIZATION
OF THE
MIDDLE AGES

CHAPTER ONE

The Heritage of the Ancient World

I. Politics and Society

Medieval history is generally regarded as extending from about A.D. 300 to 1500. European medieval civilization was not produced by any one event or series of events, but by the absorption by western Europe of certain ways of life, ideas, and religious attitudes that had prevailed for many centuries in the Mediterranean world. These ideas and values were pulled northward into western Europe—into northern France, southern England, northern Italy, and the Rhine valley—and in the process, certain aspects of Mediterranean culture were adapted and changed. (It is perhaps even more significant that many aspects were not changed.) Before the Middle Ages, then, there was a Mediterranean culture and society that was adopted and absorbed. An understanding of that civilization is essential to an understanding of the medieval world.

The culture that was eventually absorbed by medieval western Europe made its first appearance in the Mesopotamian Tigris-Euphrates valley late in the fourth millennium B.C. and perhaps a little later in the Egyptian Nile valley. That is the point where civilization began, if we define civilization primarily as structured society, organized government, and specialized economy over a large area. Men were no longer all herdsmen or all hunters; they became kings, priests, soldiers, farmers, or craftsmen.

The earliest civilized communities of the ancient Near East were dominated by a small, self-sustaining aristocracy as early as 3000 B.C. The nobility, or elite, of these Egyptian and Mesopotamian societies controlled nearly all the economic resources of these societies. One of the noble families became the ruling dynasty. From the same families and from the ranks of the bureaucrats who served the monarchy were drawn the priests who controlled the temples. Thus the ideology of the ruling religious group sanctioned the prevailing government and social structure.

In these early societies there were, in essence, only two social groups, or "classes" (to use a term that has been central to historical thought since the nineteenth century). One class was the elite: the aristocratic group that controlled both rural and urban wealth and dominated the religious institutions, the government, and the bureaucracy. The other class was a mass peasantry, who may or may not have been slaves, but in any case were bound to till the soil in the interests of the ruling elite. We have no reliable statistical information about these early societies—indeed, it is difficult to give social statistics for any period before the late Middle Ages—but a safe estimate would be that the elite comprised 5 percent of the total population. The vast majority of the population, somewhere around 80 percent, belonged to the peasantry.

In the cities of the ancient Near East, particularly in Mesopotamia, where there were few large urban centers like Babylon and Ur, an urban working class of artisans comprised perhaps 10 or 15 percent of the population of the whole state. Even in these ancient societies there was a merchant class, maybe 2 percent of the total population, whose function was to engage in international commerce and to serve as adjuncts or assistants to the aristocracy. The merchants played an important role in the economy, but they had scarcely any more political or social power than did the peasants.

It is said in the Hebrew Bible that the Hebrews were slaves unto Pharaoh in Egypt. The point here is that almost everybody was a slave (legally or empirically) unto Pharaoh and unto a small elite. It could be said, indeed, that these were one-class societies; only the aristocracy had any real consciousness of its identity, its rights, or its destiny. The aristocrats held a monopoly of power, learning, and culture, and they alone had a sense of their special and privileged place in the world.

In the long run, the existence of this intensely elitist society in the ancient Near East was of enormous importance to the history of western civilization. At late as 1700, the prevailing European social system was still one in which vast power, the greater part of landed wealth, and the prime control of political life belonged to the hereditary landed aristocracy. In the social history of premodern western civilization—whether the modern era is designated as beginning in 1500 or in the eighteenth century—a series of aristocracies perpetuated the control over the resources of society held by the ancient Near Eastern elite. It is a history in which successive challenges were made on moral and ideological grounds to the aristocratic control of society and its resources. Obviously, there is a substantial pattern of change and development in premodern social history, and these changes are highly significant and deserve close examination. Nevertheless, the factor of continuity—of the perpetuation down to the modern industrial world of a one-class social structure, or, in another phrasing, of the domination of a landed aristocracy—is one of the fundamental facts and continuing conditions of the history of western civilization.

It is natural to wonder how the Near Eastern aristocracy came to gain its dominant position, but it is not a question to which any certain answer can be given. Literacy did not begin in Mesopotamia and Egypt until the late fourth millennium B.C., and in the first written records the aristocracy had already emerged and the forms of government and social control had already been established. Historians speculate that these societies assumed their fundamental structure during the so-called prehistoric (i.e., preliterate) period—that is, somewhere around the middle of the fourth millennium B.C. However, we can only guess from archaeological evidence at the process by which the aristocracy came to dominate society, and although the evidence is substantial and has been carefully examined by scholars, it provides only an approximation of the truth at best. Archaeologists work with material objects, and the process of prehistorical social change has therefore been established according to the materialistic bias. They are bound to attribute social changes to alterations in the means of production because their evidence only discloses such alterations. Artifacts alone, without written records, cannot reveal great changes in human values or ideological upheavals that may have determined social change. Some historians have postulated a great intellectual revolution, some tremendous shift in human consciousness, behind the emergence of the first ancient civilizations, but in the absence of written records, this explanation can be no more than a happy guess.

Archaeology offers change in economic forms as the explanation of the rise of a narrow elite, with control over all the resources of the society (intellectual as well as material, religious as well as political). Whether this change was in the nature of new forms of production through the use of metal or new forms of agriculture through the use of irrigation resources, the people who initially got control of these revolutionary economic forms immediately monopolized the key economic resource of society. They could do anything they wanted thereafter, provided that they remained a relatively homogeneous and peaceful group. By and large they remained homogeneous and at peace among themselves. They decided how to divide up the power, how to divide up the wealth, who should be king, and which family should become the royal dynasty. The instability in these societies usually came not from within, but from external invasions by new people—in the case of Mesopotamia, from the north, and in the case of Egypt, from the sea or the desert—who at various times pushed into these wealthy river valleys and gained control. Their control usually collapsed or was overthrown a few generations later by the old native aristocracy or by later invaders. But all the invaders perpetuated the existing social structure, taking over the prerogatives of the old aristocracy.

The social structure of the ancient Near Eastern societies, once established, was perpetuated in the Hellenistic empires that replaced the old Near Eastern dynasties after the conquest of the Near East by Alexander the Great in the fourth century B.C. The Hellenistic empires were conquered, in turn, by the Romans in the second and first centuries B.C.; by and large, the Romans also perpetuated the Mediterranean social structure they had found.

The exploitation of serfs by their lords then, was not an invention of the Middle Ages. Medieval people inherited the rule of lords over peasants; they knew no other way of life or alternative organization of rural society. It was natural to them that a few lords should own all the land while the mass of peasants toiled their lives away—that was the very nature of society. Medieval people did not give this social structure a second thought; just as twentieth-century westerners, for the most part, take middle-class society for granted, so medieval Europeans took for granted the aristocratic-peasant organization of society.

The social system of lord and peasant was not questioned, but medieval men and women had to justify it and to organize it, and they did so in a number of ways. Variations in the social patterns of the ancient Near East and medieval Europe are not fundamental changes; they are simply variations of the methods and ideology of organization. An Egyptian lord who was mummified in 2500 B.C. and revived in France in A.D. 800 would not have been upset by the social system he found. It was a little looser, perhaps, a bit more liberal, but it was based on the same assumptions and facts. The ancient social structure was elaborated or varied in different places at different periods, but mainly it was simply perpetuated for thousands of years.

To understand medieval people, one must understand the burden of the enormous past of Mediterranean society. We do not feel such a burden today, but it was heavy upon our ancestors even in the eighteenth and nineteenth centuries. Until the twelfth century, at least, medieval people were not even conscious that it could ever be thrown off. Their way of life had always been there; to reject it was to disappear into primitivism, into the void of barbarism. Under these circumstances, it is remarkable that anything ever changed in the Middle Ages—for their heritage was extraordinary. If a Frenchman of the eighth century A.D. had traveled up the Nile and seen temples, Sphinxes, and pyramids—greater construction than anything his own people could possibly build—he would wonder at the splendid accomplishments of ancient society, and it would never occur to him to think that it was wrong. Medieval social theory, at least before the twelfth century, was entirely a justification of the existing system, and even in this respect, medieval people inherited a tradition from early Mediterranean civilization.

In the ancient world, in Egypt and Mesopotamia, the social structure was justified on religious grounds. It was God's plan for the world—God's will—and acceptance of the social forms was a religious duty. Medieval men inherited that attitude and built upon it. They had more difficulty than the Egyptians, in doing so however, because certain strains within Christianity were incompatible with the ancient system. There is an egalitarian strain in the Bible (particularly in the Hebrew prophets and in the New Testament), for example, that runs counter to the ancient traditions of exploitation and domination. Medieval people had to relate these two traditions, and they came out heavily (before the late Middle Ages, almost exclusively) on the side of the ancient, class-dominated, authoritarian society.

In a sense, then, the heritage of the ancient world set the conditions for medieval society. Although it is true that the Middle Ages (from A.D. 300 to about 1500) were a distinct and separate civilization in many respects, still medieval men were not able to create just the world that they chose: they had to work with what they inherited. They began with a definite set of social forms, political and economic institutions, and ideas and attitudes.

One of the most important patterns or conditions that medieval men inherited from the ancient Mediterranean civilization was that of political functioning, of rulership. The monarchical political system that came to exist in Egypt and Mesopotamia by 3000 B.C. did not change substantially during the Middle Ages. The social and political forms of 3000 B.C. were handed down to the Hellenistic empires that were created in the Mediterranean basin between 350 and 100 B.C. These forms were then absorbed by the Roman Empire, which took on the ancient political forms and much of Hellenistic ideology. From Rome, forms and ideology alike were passed on to the medieval world.

The first political ideology, and the most essential, was that of kingship—of monarchy, particularly of a theocratic monarchy that was God centered and God ordained. It is obvious to any student of medieval history that kings were all-important, and in the twentieth century we are apt to wonder why they were—why so much emphasis was placed on the ruler. Again, medieval men worked within the system of divine monarchy mainly because they had no clear consciousness and scarcely even an awareness of any other system. Theocratic (divinely ordained) monarchy was not only the orthodox political form, but, as far as they knew, it was the best-functioning form. The king represented God; he represented the divine forces in this world; he was the image of God on Earth. His subjects obeyed him not only because that was the useful, virtuous course of action or because his soldiers enforced his wishes, but because they believed that was what God wanted them to do. This was an essential fact of western history from 3200 B.C. down to the eighteenth century.

The beginning of monarchy is usually explained functionally, on the basis of archaeological evidence. Historians make an educated guess that in a society whose food supply and very life depended on irrigation, an autocratic system was required to maintain the irrigation system. A democracy is always fragile, perhaps too fragile for these harsh circumstances, and a dictator was needed who had the power to command the peasants to work on the dikes and canals or do whatever else was necessary to maintain the irrigation. A king in the image of God would have had enough power over the agricultural society to get the job done, while peasants in a free commune might have argued endlessly. Other systems may have been tried—we do not know—but finally one family or one group, under the leadership of a great warlord, got control of the society and organized everyone under their leadership. The belief that the king represented God on Earth began in the fourth millennium B.C. and was derived from the needs and experiences of that period.

However the system of divinely ordained monarchy came into existence, it was well established throughout ancient civilization. Medieval men knew of no form of government (certainly no successful form) except kingship, and without experience with alternatives, they could not envision any other system. By the time the Christian church came into existence and medieval culture was in its formative period (during the fourth and fifth centuries A.D.), the rare alternatives to theocratic monarchy had disappeared from the Mediterranean world. The church was the prime agent of communication between the ancient and the medieval worlds, and by the time of its formation, only the old Egyptian system remained. By the fourth century A.D.—the swing century, the gateway to the medieval world, the last ancient and the first medieval century—the old oriental system had prevailed and was well established in the Roman Empire. Constantine, the first Christian emperor in the early fourth century, was described by his friend and biographer Eusebius as the "image of Christ," God's representative in the world. This is the old Mesopotamian ideal of divine monarchy, which had driven out the various, short-lived attempts at alternative kinds of political systems.

Other systems of government had indeed existed in the ancient world. Fifth-century Athenians participated in a direct democracy, and Spartans of the same period were governed by a military oligarchy, as (for all practical purposes) were Romans of the Republic. These are well-known alternatives to theocratic monarchy, but none was long-lived or successful enough to serve as a model for the medieval world.

The republican system in Rome broke down in the first century B.C., when the aristocracy tried to use it to govern a world empire. With a vast territory to exploit, the prizes of power became enormous and the leading families could no longer arrange an equitable division of power. They began to quarrel, and the history of first century B.C. Rome is essentially the story of struggles for power within the republican oligarchy. No longer willing to share the great rewards of military command, imperial office, and control of the Senate, each family tried to eliminate its competitors. Eventually, of course, one family succeeded in attaining supremacy—the family of Augustus Caesar, the Julio-Claudian line. At first the emperors called themselves simply "first among equals," and, indeed, although the royal house controlled the army and the treasury, Rome was rich enough to allow members of all the old families to share the wealth. Over the first two centuries A.D., however, the ruling family transformed the Roman state into an imperial, oriental-style monarchy. By the third century, the emperor had come to resemble the ancient pharaohs. And it was the theocratic monarchy that was slightly modified for the Christian Roman Empire of the fourth century A.D. and perpetuated into medieval political life.

Medieval society inherited a social tradition as well as a political system from the ancient Mediterranean civilization. It is widely believed that no group is a genuine social class unless it has a sense of identity—class consciousness. Some historians describe the ancient social structure as a one-class system because other than in fifth-century B.C. Athens (always a significant exception) only one group—the ruling elite—had such a sense of identity. Only the aristocracy had a distinct life-style, justified its own existence, loved itself as a class. Not until much later did the bourgeoisie (and later still and only fitfully, the workers) begin to develop class consciousness. In the ancient world, only the elite knew things, knew how to do things; the ruling class was the only literate, conscious group in society.

Who was included in the ancient elite? Its members and size varied, of course, from place to place and time to time, but it always included governmental officials, priests, and army officers. In the great cities of the Hellenistic empires, wealthy merchants or businessmen were marginal members of the ruling class, or hoped to be: They were literate, rich, and powerful and generally were accepted into the elite. However, the most important group within the ruling class was the landlords, whose role as suppliers of food was essential. In the ancient Near East (and there, today), not much was needed in the way of shelter or clothing; with a secure food supply, the land could support a large population. Some of the subjects of the pharaohs might live miserably, but they survived as long as the food supply was maintained. Landlords were essential in preindustrial society, and as the dominant group within the elite they set the tone of the ruling class. Land was the great source of wealth until the nineteenth century; it is still a great source of wealth, and even in the twentieth century land ownership retains its mystique as a symbol and a satisfaction.

The life-style of the "one class" of the ancient world is an important part of western history because it was perpetuated in the educational curriculum right down to modern times as the only model for the good life. Until the twentieth century, the Greek and Latin classics were the staples of the educational system of the West, and these writings constituted the literature produced by and for the ancient elite. Classical literature set up a model of what the ancients believed about good living, about the right attitudes and style, and this model survived throughout the Middle Ages and grew even more influential after the Renaissance of the twelfth to fifteenth centuries. During the early Middle Ages, puritanical churchmen had serious reservations about classical culture; they disapproved of various pagan ideas and attitudes, including the eroticism of some of the ancient literature. However, the classics were never seriously threatened as educational tools, largely because no acceptable alternative curriculum could be found. After the twelfth century, and even more after the Italian Renaissance, the classic ideal and model became dominant and remained so until about 1900.

The ancient aristocratic mode was developed partly in the Greek world and partly in the Hellenistic civilization of the eastern half of the Mediterranean during the last three centuries B.C., but it was particularly a product of the Roman Empire. The Romans started out as a band of warriors bound together for conquest and exploitation, but as they conquered the world and developed a distinctive political system, the process of humanization began to operate. Roman life became more temperate and easygoing, less explosive. Conquered peoples were brought into the Roman world and given the extensive benefits of Roman citizenship; in A.D. 222, all freeborn people of the empire were made citizens.

The Roman way of life, adapted from the style of Rome's leading families, was carried over to the medieval world. It is true that the behavior of the Germanic invaders of the fifth and sixth centuries was different, but after a period of initial cultural shock, the Roman mode prevailed. Over the long run (in the Middle Ages down to the fourteenth century), the Roman aristocratic style became the dominant mode of the ruling class of Europe, and it has not yet been replaced by any lasting alternative.

The style that prevailed was that of the Roman aristocracy of the first and second centuries A.D.—the Golden Age of Rome. Our knowledge of the Roman way of life and attitudes is not based on precise ideology, on the writings of any ancient social theoretician, but on extrapolation from the works of belletristic writers, mainly rhetoricians and poets—notably Virgil, Horace, Tacitus, and Juvenal. Not even Cicero, whose work came the closest to ideology in any Roman writing, presented any consistent social theory. The Romans were intensely practical people who lived their ideology without writing much about it. A life-style, in any case, is a matter of experience, rather than theory; it is complex and existential, and political and social theory seldom comes to grips with the realities of how people think and feel.

Devotion to the family was a major aspect of the Roman aristocratic way of life, which became the upper-class European style after a brief period of Germanic predominance in the fifth and sixth centuries. The Romans had a strong sense of the importance of family and of family honor, and they worked continually for the betterment of their own families. A Roman senator or consul used his term of office to improve the fortunes of his family, to find jobs for his relatives, and to add to the family wealth, and doing so was considered natural and proper.

Another important characteristic of Roman thought was intense devotion to the state—to the *res publica,* the state as a separate entity from the individuals within it. The Romans had a deep sense of the viability and integrity of the state as an institution, as an organism with its own birth, growth, and maturity. This concept seems obvious because it became a basic element of European political thought, but the Germans had no such idea. The Germans had a concept of military kingship; they followed warlords who provided booty and protection, but when a warlord died, the loyalty of his band died with him and the members went off to find a new protector. The Germans did not distinguish between the individual king and the state. The Romans, on the other hand, believed that consuls and emperors come and go, but the state goes on forever.

The Romans assumed that their own state was eternal. Perhaps because Rome had existed for so long and had become so powerful, Rome became the world itself. *Res publica, imperium, saeculum, civilitas*—state, empire, world, civilization—these entities were coexistent with the idea of Rome by the second century A.D.

The Romans started the tradition of private splendor, and it continues still. Historians often comment on the supposed immobility of the Byzantine or Chinese ruling society, but the western aristocratic mode is also strikingly permanent—and when the bourgeoisie emerged as a class, their ambition was simply to imitate this aristocratic style. The large houses, fine clothes, and grand manners of the bourgeoisie were a continuation of the age-old aristocratic way of life.

The Roman aristocracy took great care in educating the young; they were much more conscientious in this field than was any earlier elite. It is true that the Romans learned a great deal from Athens and from the Hellenistic world, but they also believed in themselves as educators, as trainers of the next generation in a specific order of civilization. They developed a tough, aggressive educational system that took little notice of individual talents and almost none of feelings or emotional development. Children were regimented, and physical force was used to make them learn. Boys were turned over to tutors (often slaves, and frequently frustrated, sadistic men) at the age of six or seven and forced to learn their letters. There was no room for art or music within the system; all boys were forced to become little grammarians, since language and literature were, in fact, the whole of their curriculum. Higher education was simply higher studies in language. A society dominated by an aristocracy is one in which the rulers need to learn nothing but language; they do not need science or the arts, they do not need new knowledge of technology or sources of wealth, but they must communicate—they already have power, which they will exert through communication. Through narrow concentration the Romans did marvelous things with Latin—basically an awkward, inflexible language. They ignored the sciences, studied almost no mathematics and little history, but learned both written and oral Latin superbly well. Intellectual experimentation was sacrificed to rigid literary education.

The Romans were psychologically damaged by their educational system, as evidenced by their violence, aggression, sadism, hostility to women, and other unattractive characteristics. Children were treated badly, indeed, and many of them grew up to be sadomasochists. The system was modified over time, of course, but vestiges survived into the twentieth century. The educational system of the medieval church was based upon the Roman, and there were a good many neurotic educated adults within the medieval church. Later western systems were based on the Roman; educators read Cicero and Quintilian and found their model convincing and acceptable. It is a natural system for an aristocratic society, which needs to train its young people only to accept the power handed on to them—a similar system existed in Confucian China.

The Roman aristocracy had a great talent for law, which is not surprising. In an aristocratic, militaristic, landed society, the interests of the ruling class can be expressed in terms of law. Law cannot deal with perceptions and emotions—with love, beauty, joy, or sadness—but it deals well with family property, state power, class privilege, and military force. A familial, paternalistic state is rule conscious, and its inmost meaning is expressed in rules—little wonder that the Romans were the greatest lawyers the world had known. Even today, the dominant legal tradition of Europe, from Paris to Moscow, is Roman; every western country (other than England and its former colonies) has a legal system based on Roman law.

Roman law was influential because it was excellent law. On the highest (theoretical) level, law was believed to be a reflection of reason, or of "natural law," which is not the law of animal life, but the contrary. The concept of natural law (taken from Stoic philosophy) assumes that the world operates according to rational principles, that there are universal principles of reason. The law of the state was regarded as the positive, detailed implementation of natural law, and any law that was repugnant to reason had to be a bad law. The problem arose, of course, over the question of who had the authority and the wisdom to decide whether the law conformed to reason. Who could make law accord with the principles of reason? That was the great question of Roman political history.

Under the Republic, Romans believed that the people had the authority, collectively, to decide what the law of the state should be. The history of the Republic is the history of the argument over who belonged to the "Roman people"—certain leading families, all the men in the army, everyone who lived in Rome? By the first century B.C., the Romans had an awkward, cumbersome system in which everyone had some vague share in government. The system failed because the Romans of the Republic were unable to settle on a workable system of popular sovereignty, and this failure doomed the republican form of government. By the early empire, law-making power was shared by the emperor and the Senate, which consisted at that time of elder statesmen—members of distinguished families who had retired from active military or official life. As time went on, the role of the Senate became less and less important, and by the late empire, the law-making authority belonged to the emperor alone. At this point, Roman jurists proposed a legal theory, the *Lex Regia* (Royal Law), which stated that the legislative authority of the state once resided in the Roman people, but that the latter had surrendered this authority irrevocably to the emperor. Now the will of the emperor had the force of law.

The development of Roman law from an awkward kind of popular sovereignty to dictatorship or autocracy was an extremely significant fact of medieval history because the medieval world inherited the autocracy of the later empire. Roman law was codified in final form in the fifth and sixth centuries A.D., and it was codified in the form of autocratic, royal law. Subsequent European society was heavily devoted to Roman law, and that law favored the absolutism of all kings, from the absolute power of the pope to the divine right of kings.

The principle of equity is a major aspect of Roman law, and it is a logical corollary of the belief that law must conform to reason. If the law seems to work against reason in a specific case—to work an absurd injustice—then the judge must have the power to overrule the law in that instance. Roman jurists had wide powers, and judges in all Roman systems can set aside the law or make exceptions on behalf of the greater principle of justice. Equity as it developed in Rome is basically a reflection of an aristocratic system in which members of the ruling class can trust the judges (fellow members of their own group) to make decisions according to general principles of justice. In a democracy, judges may not be trusted to make law or make exceptions (they may favor one group over another), but where everyone—including the judges—belongs to one class, this system is possible.

Process is another significant aspect of law, and the procedures of Roman law were different from those of the common law that developed in England in the Middle Ages. The common law operates on the adversary system, in which opposing attorneys contend against each other while the judge acts as an impartial referee. The judge pronounces on points of law and passes sentence on the convicted criminal, but he may not impose his opinions on the jury. In Roman law the opposite is true: The court belongs to the judges, who make all the decisions. A panel (usually three to five judges) acts as an investigator whose job is to establish the truth. Pleading in common law is mostly oral, but in Roman law courts the attorneys submit long written briefs (again, this procedure is suitable for an aristocratic system in which everyone who matters is literate and skilled in the use of language) some time before the trial begins. The judges study the briefs and often are able to announce their decision without any further investigation. However, if the "truth" is not obvious from the briefs, the judges summon witnesses, interrogate them, and torture them—if necessary—to get the truth. Torture was called "putting the question," and it was part of Roman legal procedure until the eighteenth century. Vestiges of the Roman procedure of pressuring the defendant survive even today on the Continent, although the more liberal countries now have juries. The jury is a recent innovation in continental law, however, and it is distinctly subordinate to the judge; judge and jury meet together to come to a decision.

The Roman system works well, on the whole, particularly in criminal cases; the judges were often able to get at the truth through a close analysis of the facts without a jury to be swayed by popular pressures and demagogic attorneys. The Romans were extremely proud of their legal system: It provided justice, permitted the rational to operate in human affairs, and allowed men to live together peacefully. When St. Paul, the Jewish rabbi, was arrested in Asia Minor, he claimed his right as a Roman citizen to demand a trial in Rome.

The Roman legal system was, then, a beneficent aspect of aristocratic society; law is always an important part of the machinery through which a ruling class orders its affairs and perpetuates its power. Roman law perpetuated the idea of autocracy and the principle of equity, and it was responsible for the idea that there should be a legal system at all. The Germans who invaded Rome had no such system; indeed, they really had no law as we know it. The medieval idea of the necessity of a legal system, of legal education, of a legal framework for society, was part of the heritage of Rome.

II. Philosophy and Religion

Certain systems of thought within the Greek and Roman world had an enormous impact upon the medieval consciousness. Until the seventeenth century almost all western systems of thought tended to operate within the framework of Platonism, Aristotelianism, or Stoicism. These systems had an omnivorous hold upon western intellectual history, and when they finally were abandoned or rejected, it was not because they were replaced by more satisfactory systems (in fact, we are still searching for replacements), but because modern science and technology had provided new experiences or revealed aspects of human and physical nature on which these ancient systems could shed no light.

A system of thought is a group of ideas or theories with some integrating principle or basic attitude that can be worked out in every aspect of thought or life to provide a unified, integrated worldview. The modern system that best fits this definition is Marxism, which may explain its wide appeal until recently. Marxism is a subtle, adaptable system with a broad and comprehensive view of history, of society, or of human nature—in fact, of reality. It can absorb new ideas and data and keep going, and adaptability is essential to the success of any intellectual system. Attempts have been made in this century to make Freudianism into such a worldview, but they have not as yet been successful. Liberalism never developed a sufficiently wide and adaptable philosophy. It was effective in politics and in certain ethical problems, but it never really came to terms with industrial civilization and failed to develop an esthetic. Like Stoicism, liberalism was too narrow to become a successful worldview. Of the ancient systems, Platonism best fits the definition of a system of thought; it is unified and adaptable and can be applied in a wide variety of directions. Aristotelianism is too sophisticated, too abstract, and too scholarly for wide appeal; Stoicism is too narrow and not sufficiently intellectual.

The most influential philosophical system of the ancient world, then, was Platonism. More has been written about Platonism than about any other system of thought, and even today—when modern linguistic analysts reject Platonic metaphysics—it is still influential in many fields, including social anthropology (as interpreted by Claude Lévi-Strauss), literary theory (as interpreted by Roland Barthes), and linguistics (as interpreted by Noam Chomsky). Plato has been neglected and rediscovered again and again, but his influence has never vanished. He was that unusual combination: a great thinker and a great writer. Rarely visibly dogmatic, Plato was resolute in his devotion to certain basic principles, and he was one of the great masters of Greek prose—an uncommon facility for a philosopher. His style is leisurely, elliptical, and paradoxical, and his writings can be interpreted in various ways. Platonism is an entire philosophy of life; along with St. Augustine, St. Thomas Aquinas, Descartes, Hegel, and Marx, Plato produced a philosophy that could be lived. He discussed love, birth, death—all the concerns of humanity.

We know little about Plato himself. He came from a wealthy Athenian family and was well educated—a member of the elite. He was involved in the government and political life of his time, but he never achieved his ambition to be a political leader. Perhaps he was too intellectual to be successful in politics; intellectuals often suffer from their ability to appreciate complexity, to see the other side, to find a common base among arguments. Plato lived in a bad period, in any case. Athens had been defeated by Sparta in the Peloponnesian Wars, and a radical democratic bourgeoisie was taking over from the old elite. Plato was too aristocratic for that era, and he was associated—to his misfortune—with the aristocratic traitor Alcibiades. He never got a political position in Athens and may have been embittered by the failure.

Plato traveled widely, perhaps as far as the Near East. There has been speculation that he came into contact with Hebrew prophetic thought and that this contact was responsible for the strain of mysticism in his philosophy. This speculation may be true, but rationalism and mysticism are not necessarily incompatible, and Plato would have arrived at the same point without traveling to the East. He did go to Sicily, where he evidently had an opportunity to exercise some political power under one of the tyrants, or dictators, of the Greek cities there. It is generally believed that he made a bad job of it and had to leave the city. Plato went back to Athens and opened his famous Academy in the hills outside the city.

The Academy was not primarily a place for instruction or research, but a center for inquiry, for dialogue, for the pursuit of intellectual pleasures. Plato and his students (rich young Athenians) led a pleasant life and discussed such questions as: What is truth? What is beauty? How do we know anything? Is there an afterlife? Plato worked hard, and over a period of many years he molded these discussions into great works of art, affirmative philosophical statements. The *Republic*—the most important of these *Dialogues* of Plato—is one of the most significant works of western civilization.

Plato did not speak as himself in the *Dialogues,* but chose Socrates as his mouthpiece. He reported that it was Socrates' death at the hands of an Athenian jury that caused him to leave the city in outrage, but we do not know whether this account is true or whether any of what he said about Socrates is true. We do know that there was a Socrates in Athens during the fourth century, and that he was a professional nuisance, a stonemason who used to wander into the agora (marketplace) and try to involve his fellow citizens in arguments and debates. He asked such questions as, "What is justice?" and annoyed his fellows by pointing out why their answers were wrong. It was a period of speculation in the Greek world; in Asia Minor a group of philosophers (now known as the pre-Socratics) had been speculating for half a century about the nature of reality. One of them—Heraclitus—came close to a dialectic like that of Plato or Hegel. Eventually some young Athenians (of whom Plato may have been one) decided to take Socrates seriously, and because some of these young men (including the notorious Alcibiades) were involved in political life, Socrates got in trouble with the authorities. He was tried for sacrilege, or treason, convicted, and died by forced suicide. His death is described by Plato in the *Apology of Socrates,* which presents Socrates as a paragon of wisdom and virtue, although it is likely that Socrates said little or perhaps nothing that is ascribed to him.

In Plato's *Dialogues,* Socrates or someone else asks a question that is answered by a student or guest. The answer is demolished at length by Socrates, who usually turns around at the end of the argument to discover the grain of truth in his opponent's answer. Some of these *Dialogues* are short and some are long; as Plato got older, his writing got more didactic and less literary. The idea that Plato took from Socrates (if anything) is that it is necessary to analyze the real meaning of the words we use. (In this sense, Plato was the first analytic philosopher.) Terms are concepts, and to answer such questions as, "What is love?" we must find out what we mean by *love.* General terms like *faith* or *love* or *justice* predicate a concept, and in discussing terms, we are discussing ideas.

To Plato ideas, or conceptual forms, were not idle fantasies, but essential realities. When we refer to *justice* or *the state* or *love,* we are actually referring to something that has an independent existence outside our minds; this idea is translated into philosophical jargon in the phrase: "Universals have reality." A student may say, "I have a table in front of me; is it not real?" but Plato would reply "What is a table?" A table is a structure of plastic or metal or wood in a particular form, but without that particular form, there would be a shapeless mass of material—not a table. The table would not have come into existence without the idea of a table; it is the idea that gives it shape and reality. Pure, ultimate reality is pure Idea, and the physical world that we touch and see has a reality only insofar as it participates in or is formed by pure Idea. Reality requires recognizable form, and the physical world has no form unless it is shaped by Idea.

Plato believed that anything real must be eternal. He thought that reality was identical with eternity, that when we speak of reality, we mean something perfect, permanent, secure, definable—nothing transient or indiscriminate. This belief seems plausible when we realize that the concept of a table in Plato's time is still around, while the particular tables of Plato's time moldered away. In our own lives, our bodies die and decay while our ideas survive. This fundamental fact of human nature probably helped to inspire Plato's theory and certainly partly accounts for its ever-recurring popularity.

To Plato, reality is purely conceptual, and the terms used refer to eternal forms and pure, independently existing ideas. The purpose of dialogue or communication is to clarify our ideas, so we can bring them to full consciousness and refer to them with understanding. Two men refer to *justice,* but until they can agree on the meaning of the term, they cannot discuss it effectively. The purpose of education, of thought—of life, even—is to clarify our ideas so we can develop knowledge instead of opinion. Knowledge, in Plato's sense, is ideas thought out and critically examined; it is achieved only through the painful examination and rejection of unclear, unreal concepts. "The unexamined life is not worth living."

Plato's theory of knowledge is as good as any theory ever developed, but Plato was more than an epistemologist. Having concluded that reality is pure Idea and that we know it by defining and purifying our concepts—by reason and critical thinking—Plato went on to develop a whole philosophy of life and of the world, perhaps because he was forced to examine how man gets ideas in the beginning.

Is a child born an animal, in whom, as time goes on, accumulated experimental responses add up to consciousness, or mind? If so, then consciousness is created by experience. This is (roughly) the position of the modern behavioral psychologists. Plato, on the other hand, believed that the mind exists when the child is born, that experience serves only to modify and develop consciousness. There is a world of pure Ideas somewhere in the universe—a world of reality—from which the child received the impress of images and thoughts at birth. If the child is correctly educated (and Plato was the first adherent of progressive education; he realized that the childish mind could be irreparably damaged by bad education), then in adult life he will receive the fullest possible perception from the world of Ideas. We cannot get the complete perception of reality (one cannot convey a three-dimensional fact in words or images), but with a proper education and rigorous training, we can greatly better our understanding.

Plato's philosopher-king was a man whose understanding was refined beyond that of other men. In the end, a fortunate few go beyond the understanding of others. In the end the philosophers go beyond thought in words or images to "the flight of the soul"—what we may call a mystical experience, an ultimate illumination. It is possible to go beyond any particular idea to the One Idea, the ultimate of the universe—the Good, God, or X—"the source of all things beautiful and right." This does not happen to many people or often; it is a rare, beautiful illumination that comes only after an excellent education, constant thought, and fine training of the mind.

Plato wrote about death at great length, about what became of the marvelous mental equipment developed in a lifetime of thought and study. At this point Platonism can become a religion of sorts, which explains why it was attractive to the early Christians. Christianity was built as much on Plato as on the Judaic tradition, and for that matter, there has been a great deal of Platonism within Judaism since the first century A.D. Plato pointed out that the human being has two aspects. He agreed with the Greek dramatists and artists who portrayed men as half-man, half-god; half-man, half-animal. Man decays like an animal, but lives forever like a god. This recognition of the polarity of human life is the origin of the long-lived and crucial philosophical distinction between the soul and the body. The biblical Hebrews did not distinguish between the soul and the body. It was Plato who emphasized and even inaugurated the distinction. The human body is material, transient, corruptible, and therefore unreal. Bodies are usually ugly—on the rare occasions when they are beautiful, we worship them—but they are important as temporary resting places for the soul.

Plato convincingly tells us that human life is valuable because the soul grows and matures in the body, and /the soul of Socrates, the philosopher, is different from that of Socrates, the infant. Through study and insight and love and dialectic and—finally—mystical experience, the soul can ascend, can become one with the Idea. If the soul has been rightly educated, if it is beautiful and just and good, it will return to Beauty and Justice and Good after death. Obviously, this concept entered into the Christian view of immortality, of ascension into heaven at the end of a good life and descent into hell at the end of a bad one.

The Platonic philosophy leads, obviously, into a social and moral theory. Good conduct is the pursuit of the intellectual life. A man must cultivate the finer things of the mind, must study and refine his taste to get as close as possible to pure Idea. The just man fulfills as much as possible of his potential for beauty and truth, and the just state allows each individual to fulfill his potential. To Plato, the first criterion of a good society would be: What kinds of schools does it have? How does it clarify the minds of young people? How does it liberate their souls?

Plato's theory can thus be elaborated to explain much more than epistemology and educational theory; it can tell us who we are, where we are going, and how we may escape the limitations of death. His solutions to questions of knowledge, of human personality, of society, are not final answers, but they are plausible answers.

The philosophical system of Aristotle was different from that of Plato, and it had little influence until the twelfth century A.D. Aristotle himself was a brilliant, hard-working scholar who came from northern Greece and studied for a time at Plato's Academy. The two men were different in temperament—Aristotle wanted to collect data and to categorize, while Plato wished to sit still and to reflect—and eventually they parted. Aristotle founded his own school, known as the Lyceum, and his disciples are generally known as the peripatetic (walking around) philosophers. Aristotle was too busy teaching, lecturing, and advising statesmen to write down a coherent body of doctrine, and what remains of his work is generally believed to be a collection of lecture notes put together by students after the philosopher's death. The result is unattractive as reading matter because it is full of repetition, of answers to students' irrelevant questions, and of confusing and impenetrable material. Aristotle was more a pedagogue than a poet, and his best-known pupil was Alexander the Great. Philip of Macedon called on Aristotle to educate his son, and from what we know of Alexander, his tutor did an excellent job.

To understand Aristotle, we have to appreciate his temperament of mind, his belief that if one investigates, examines data, collects information, and does research, one can set out all the gathered material and come to a decision. His was the first scientific mind, and he believed that if all the data are collected and put together, a pattern will emerge. This is a different theory of knowledge from that of Plato; it assumes that the human mind is an active, conditioning receptacle for experience, that the mind interacts with its environment and receives sensory data. On the basis of that data, the mind discriminates, generalizes, and develops universal concepts. Our concepts are generalizations from experience, not necessarily parts of the divine order of the universe. This is basically a scientific, academic attitude.

Aristotle says: So you want to know something, whether physical motion or the best political constitution? Then gather exhaustive data about it. Then sit and look at the data, each piece of them—no, really look at them, thoroughly and intensely. Then organize the data in categories and examine these categories. Now a hypothesis (generalization) about the data will appear in you mind. Test the general hypothesis by seeing whether it can encompass all or nearly all the data. If so, you have a general "form" that has emerged out of particular "matter." Plato's response is that this is all foolish nonsense. You have no capacity to organize the data into categories or even know what data you are looking for unless you start with an idea in the first place.

On human behavior, Aristotle is as practical as Plato is mystical. In any given segment of human behavior, a moderate position between polarities—the golden mean—is liable to be best, says Aristotle. Good behavior is habitual; it the result of conditioning to act in a certain way over time. "One swallow does not make a summer." Education is just as important for Aristotle as it is for Plato, but for somewhat different reasons—not so much to discover ultimate truth, but to shape and condition the mind into good habits and logical thinking.

Aristotle was poorly received for many centuries after his death. His philosophy was too dry, too theoretical and abstract, not total or emotional enough to satisfy the needs of the time. It was difficult to popularize, and except for his work on logic, Aristotle's works were little considered until Arabic and Jewish scholars in Spain began to study them around the year 1000. From about 300 B.C. to A.D. 1100, Platonism was the dominant philosophical system.

Stoicism, the third influential philosophy of the ancient world, was an offshoot of Platonism diverted into practical ethics. Stoic philosophy was a day-to-day guide, rather than a theory of ethics, yet it was enormously important in the Greco-Roman and Christian worlds. It is the moral philosophy of the "inner man" and the "outer man," and its chief proponents were a Roman emperor (Marcus Aurelius) and a Greek slave (Epictetus). These philosophers urged men not to commit themselves too much to the outer world or to material things, to remain in tune with the joy and reason and harmony of the universe, and not to be swayed by the temptations of passion or the corruption of power. This became a code of privatism, of the nine-to-five man who keeps back the best part of himself for his private life of feelings, of the arts, of family, and of beauty. His real life takes place after five and on weekends, when he can concentrate on the emotional, esthetic, intellectual pleasures available to everyone. Nature, music, and family life can be enjoyed by everyone, and material blessings are not worth a great struggle.

Stoicism is well suited to a society that could not control or explain ravages of nature, such as plague, fire, war, or holocaust, and therefore convinced itself that the physical world was not important. It was well suited, too, to the Roman Empire, where political life for many years was either in the hands of a tiny autocratic group or dispersed in a violent, unstable kind of situation. Political life offered little because at one time one could not get into it and at another time it was dangerous and frightening. The reigns of crazy emperors and the murders of emperors were not reassuring. Apathy, fear, and disillusionment with public life encouraged the concentration on private life, which is a recurrent pole in human history. At the other extreme are the periods of millennial, apocalyptic fervor, times when people believe they can create a great society and make everyone happy and that they must sacrifice everything to improve society. From the time of the decline of the Athenian polis, around 430 B.C., the political life of the ancient world was corrupt and despotic or violent and unstable, and those who could retreat were glad to do so.

Stoicism is a wonderful philosophy for aristocrats or millionaires who have made their money (or inherited it) and do not need to worry about the competition for material things. They claim to find joy in simple things, in nature—a recurrent theme of this long-lived philosophy. Revolutionaries and even social reformers obviously cannot be satisfied with Stoicism, but it was a crucial element in medieval thought, and before there could be social revolution or unrest, the conservative Stoic cast of thought had to be broken. Stoicism is a powerful thread in the New Testament, in the writings of St. Paul; it was central to the medieval social ethic. The Stoic thread in medieval Christianity may account for the scarcity of social upheavals in the Middle Ages.

The alternative foundation of medieval culture lies in the Jewish tradition. Medieval culture was a culture of the Book, and in the Middle Ages, the Book was the Bible. It may be said that the primary task of the medieval universities, when they were established in the twelfth and thirteenth centuries, was the explication of the relation of biblical thought to secular culture. In fact, this was true in some sense of all educational institutions down to the late nineteenth century. The biblical tradition brought special problems, ideas, and beliefs—religious, historical, moral—to the medieval world, and these were unlike the legacy of the classical philosophers. It is not surprising that medieval scholars were able to spend their lives studying and arguing over the Bible. It is an extremely difficult book, and we can sympathize with scholars who claimed that it was beyond reason—that God's word could not be understood without faith, that belief was essential to comprehension.

Who were the Jews, and why were they unlike all other people? There is no certain answer to these questions, and perhaps the old description of a "chosen people" is as satisfactory as any explanation. Scholars used to speculate that Judaism developed an immaterial and universal god because the Jews (Hebrews) were originally a wandering, pastoral people. Egyptians and Babylonians could worship material deities who resided in special temples or palaces, but nomads needed a god they could carry around with them. It has also been said that the Jews

learned monotheism from other Near Eastern cultures. There are similarities between certain Mesopotamian religious ideas and stories and those
of Judaism: the story of the Flood, for example, is a common Mesopotamian myth, and the Jews may have originated in Mesopotamia—the
patriarch Abraham was supposed to come from Ur of the Chaldees. One
of the pharaohs (Akhenaton) evidently practiced a kind of monotheism,
but the Egyptian priests objected, and his experiments did not survive
him. The Persians worshipped a spiritual, immaterial god, but they were
not monotheists; their god of light and spirit battled a twin god of darkness and matter, and if the Jews learned their religion from the Persians,
they did not learn it thoroughly. Elements of a monotheistic, universal
religion existed in the ancient Near East, but even if the Jews had picked
up every available fragment, these fragments could not have amounted to
more than a small percentage of the religion of Moses.

The great questions of Old Testament scholarship have always been:
When was the Hebrew Bible written, and who wrote it? To put it another
way: Who founded Judaism—the patriarchs, Moses, the prophets, or
some other people? (The phrase Old Testament, which is offensive to
many Jews because it implies the existence of a later and higher revelation, is used in this context as a convenient label for the Hebrew Bible.)
In the nineteenth century, the so-called Higher Criticism began to supply
answers to these enduring questions. In the Higher Criticism, the Bible
was examined as a socioliterary document and not accepted at face value
as divine revelation. This kind of criticism was not entirely new in the
nineteenth century: The approach was used in some of the work of the
church fathers, in the Talmud, and in some medieval criticism. The first
critic to take a genuinely historical approach to the Bible was probably
Benedict Spinoza, the Dutch Jewish philosopher of the seventeenth century, who treated the Bible as a social document and eventually was
excommunicated. However, like every other kind of modern scholarship,
Higher Criticism really began in nineteenth-century Germany, where
philologists (usually Protestant ministers) applied the tools of classical
scholarship to Bible studies.

These biblical scholars concluded that the text of the Old Testament,
and Judaism as expressed therein, appeared quite late in Hebrew history
(after the seventh or sixth century B.C.): Jewish theology was a product
of the age of the late prophets and of the scribes after the First Exile.
Fragments of the pristine, early Judaism of the age of the patriarchs and
of Moses may be incorporated in the Bible, as well as in old myths and
legends and laws (especially in the book of Deuteronomy), but most of it
was written after 700 B.C. and as late as 300 B.C. The sixth century was a

period of great stress, of constant turmoil, of struggle for national survival, and eventually of exile, which provided contact with other cultures. This argument depends for proof on sophisticated literary and philological inquiries, and during the late nineteenth and early twentieth centuries, it was widely accepted among secular and Protestant scholars. Orthodox Jews never accepted this view, and Roman Catholics, until recently, tended to ignore the entire controversy.

The fundamental tenet of Judaism, as expressed in the biblical text, is the belief in an immaterial or spiritual god who created the world and is omnipotent and omniscient. God is everything good, everything great, everything true—He is everything that is. The second essential of Judaism is the belief in a god of Israel who is also a god of all people. It is true that the universal (or international character) of God is emphasized more strongly in the later books of the Bible and the writings of the prophets than in the Pentateuch, but universality was one aspect of Judaism from the beginning.

The third essential of Judaism is particularly significant to a historian: The Jewish God is a god of history, and the important things that happen in the world happen in time. The Greeks wrote history, but they did not believe in its importance: To Plato, man's excellence—or salvation or security—depended on his realization of perfect forms and his ability to unite with the timeless Idea. In the static Greek view of the universe, perfect forms had always existed and would always exist, so real change was not possible. In the Hebrew view, on the other hand, God existed before the world began (He created it), but He acts in our lives through history. God set up a drama in which men participate; He directs the course of human history—and He does all this to give man a chance to love Him. In the drama of history, which had a definable beginning and moves toward a definable end, man has the freedom to love God or to reject Him. This last point has proved profoundly mysterious to Jews and Christians alike, and many medieval thinkers struggled to reconcile the belief in human freedom with the belief in an omnipotent and omniscient God. If God is omnipotent, He can direct man to love Him; if God knows everything, then He knows whether men will love Him, and therefore men are not free. Medieval Christian theology can be regarded as a series of attempts (perhaps futile) to solve this ancient problem.

The first book of the Bible deals with Creation, the next books with "sacred history"—the history of God's actions in the world and of man's struggles to accept Him. Later books (Daniel, in particular) speculate on the end of the world. The Jews believed that the end would come when God judged all men, and the prophets speculated on its meaning—would it bring joy or terror, stress or peace, or all these things? The Jews were not certain what the end would be like, but they were confident that there could be an end—*eschaton,* in Greek: The Hebrew Bible becomes increasingly eschatological in its later books.

As a whole, then, the Bible posits a created world, with human society established as a setting for the continuing drama of the choices of various societies, particular communities, and individuals to love or to reject God. Finally, the Bible posits a definite end to human history in a time of terror and peace, joy and suffering. This is a different view from that of the Greeks, who believed that things were as they had always been and would always be. The Jews believed in perpetual change. States have come and gone, and people; even the pharaohs disappeared into dust. Man transcends his past and moves forward, and human society perfects itself as it moves through history.

The Hebrews had a continuous tradition of political and social upheaval, presumably directed by God toward some great moment in the future. The reforming spirit of the West, the western belief in change and reformation, can be understood as a perpetuation of their tradition. The ancient Jews expressed their belief that things would change, that an unjust situation or society would be made just. This was a moral attitude, based on a view of God as good and of man as the servant of God's intention to perfect society. Other ancient peoples did not develop any such attitude, and we do not know why the Hebrews did so. It is true that they never established a monolithic, bureaucratic monarchy; that there was always fragmentation and change; that no one dynasty ever got hold of all the resources of society in the style of the governments of the Near Eastern river valleys. There was always a possibility of change in Hebrew society; it was (relatively) open and democratic, and perhaps this openness made possible the development of a reforming religion.

Just as important in the Hebrews' impact on medieval culture was their idea of the covenant. Covenant theology is central to Judaism, and some scholars tell us that it was actually derived from the commercial contracts of the markets and oases of ancient Judea. However, the religious covenant was not like a commercial contract freely entered into by both participants. The Hebrew covenant was imposed by God; the Hebrews did not ask for it, and indeed they often rebelled against it (and such rebellion was a sin). God mysteriously chose the Jews for His own purposes to be His witnesses in the world, to be agents of history and of divine Providence, to proclaim His word and advance history to its end. The covenant imposed religious, moral, social, and political obligations upon the Jews, many of whom resented them—but God kept issuing commands, recalling His people and punishing them for breaking the covenant or turning away from Him. This concept had a significant impact on Christianity; medieval Christians thought of themselves as the new chosen people, the true spiritual brotherhood, the new Israel. The medieval church assumed the obligation to be God's agent for the advancement of human history, which partly accounts for both the restlessness and arrogance of medieval churchmen.

Among the Jews, God's particular spokesmen were the prophets. Modern scholars emphasize the continuous tradition of prophecy in Judaism (a tradition that goes back at least to Moses, Joshua, and Samuel, if not to the patriarchs), but it makes more historical sense to use the term to refer to the particular group who appeared in the marketplaces of Judah and Israel in the sixth and fifth centuries B.C. There is no easy political or social explanation for the appearance of the prophets, and no social category that suits them all.

No matter why the prophets appeared, their very existence and the acceptance of their writings as canonical books of the Bible were essential to medieval Christianity and to western civilization. By accepting their works, Judaism gave sacred status and moral sanction to a group of critics or rebels against authority. Rare in any society, this view was singular in the ancient Near East, with its congealed monarchies and elites in which all authority came from above. The Jewish prophets spoke from below, with the voice of the people, and they criticized the elite for their violations of the covenant and their failure to live up to their moral obligations as God's witnesses. The prophets had a strong sense of history, and they perceived the doom about to overtake Judea and Israel. (This was not much of a visionary feat: It must have been obvious that the great empires—Babylonia, Assyria, and Egypt—that surrounded the Jewish principalities must eventually swallow them up.) Their works expressed powerful social consciousness along with eschatological dreams: The prophets perceived present evil, as well as future triumphs. They denounced the existing corruption and social injustice; they foretold national defeat and dispersion, but tempered their vision with promises: *For out of Zion shall go forth the law, and the word of the Lord from Jerusalem.*

Jerusalem will be a great city again, said the prophets, and in the new Zion, God's covenant will be observed and the principles of justice fulfilled. The prophetic emphasis on individual conscience and social justice and the promise of the achievement of God's kingdom in this world became pervasive elements in medieval thought.

The Hebrew prophets had no official status; they spoke as individuals.

Despite bitter opposition, they achieved enormous influence in their own day, and the acceptance of their writings as part of the Bible had significant consequences for the medieval church. A churchman who opposed official doctrine might rebel against the established order and still feel that he remained in the biblical tradition, and many rebels named themselves God's witnesses, as part of a holy brotherhood, and spoke against the priestly hierarchy. The medieval church (and the philosophical-religious tradition of the West) owes much of its rebellious, individualistic, antiauthoritarian elements to the prophets. The prophets' successful insistence on the right to speak and to be heard gave a theological base and moral sanction to radicals within and outside the church.

A different and equally important strain in the medieval church—authoritarianism—was also derived from the Hebraic tradition. Medieval churchmen consciously modeled themselves on the teachings of the Hebrew Bible, which they accepted as the word of God. Believing themselves to be the new Israel, God's emissaries in the world, they assumed immense power over human souls and believed they had the right—even the duty—to use force against those who resisted the truth. The authoritarian, hierarchical structure of the church as an institution was inherited largely from the Roman Empire (the pope replaced the emperor, and the church, the empire), but its justificatory theory came partly from the Old Testament. Churchmen took over the biblical view of history and its tradition of positive leadership, in which religious leaders were charged by God with the duty to advance human history toward its final triumph. Their duty included the use of force against unbelievers, heretics—even Jews. The church was God's holy brotherhood, and just as ancient Israelites who resented the obligations of the covenant were forced by God to do their part, so a medieval pope was expected to force the enemies of God to join in the advance of Christianity.

Medieval Christians believed that history would arrive at its appointed end when the church became truly universal, when all men were Christians. They had little idea, at least before the thirteenth century, of the size of the world or of the number of non-Christians in the East; they believed that the triumph of Christianity was close at hand and that the use of force to complete the task was God's will—that force was justified by the immensity of the accomplishment.

Thus the hierarchy of the church, the priesthood and the papacy, based its theory and authority on the Hebrew doctrine of the covenant and the divine Providence while religious dissenters took their inspiration and justification from the Hebrew prophets. Medieval heretics, subversives, and dissenters (and there were already many of them in the fourth century) based their right to dissent on the prophets, who spoke outside the temple, who spoke because God spoke in them. These men did not uphold the right of conscience as we understand it or defend every person's right to believe as he or she chose. On the contrary, they believed that they had God's voice, that they spoke with truth, that anyone who disagreed with them was wrong. They were dissenters, not libertarians; they did not tolerate contrary opinion, they damned it. The prophets (and the medieval heretics after them) were inclined to be just as authoritarian as was the priestly hierarchy; they were religious radicals, not liberals. Their courage in resisting the elite provided those medieval Christians who opposed the power or doctrine of the pope with a biblical precedent and allowed them to see themselves as the true Israel. Medieval heretics generally regarded themselves as especially holy, as a community of saints working for the ultimate triumph of God's will in the world. Both the medieval Christian establishment and its opposition, then, derived sanction from the Hebrew Bible.

CHAPTER TWO

The Foundations of the Middle Ages

I. From Judaism to Christianity

There are obvious continuities between Judaism and medieval Christianity, but scholars differ markedly over how the teachings of Jesus fit into the story. Clearly much in medieval Christianity was not derived from the Hebraic tradition, and it is necessary to define the essence of Christian theology to find out how its various elements fit together.

The essential difference between Judaism and Christianity is the concept of the Incarnation. Christians believe that the Holy Spirit assumed human form, that spirit became flesh, that Jesus Christ was both a human being and the way to salvation—the Saviour. Man is too weak, too rebellious against God (too sinful) to reach salvation by his own efforts. This belief is not implausible if one assumes that righteousness consists of living a pure, puritanical life free of selfishness, aggression, materialism, and anger. Men could not get through one day without these sins; it is in man's nature to rebel against God, to fail to live as He wants us to live. Because man cannot live as God wants him to, he is a sinner—there is a fundamental corruption in human nature. The story of the fall of Adam is a paradigm, or model, of man's rebellion against the purity of mind and holiness of temperament that God demands.

Since it is impossible for man to be pure and saintly, how can God forgive him? In an apparently hopeless situation, man cannot escape from his own nature and must be eternally damned. The Christian solution is that God loves man so much, is so generous, that He gave some of Himself to redeem man. The divine spirit assumed human form and suffered, was punished for man—became man's scapegoat. God can forgive man because the God-man sacrificed Himself for all men; He saved men by His love because they could not save themselves. Man cannot be saved by his own efforts, but at a certain moment, God's love comes from outside to liberate him from the degradation of human nature.

That is the central message of early medieval Christian theology. Obviously it was different from the Judaism of Moses, and it was once assumed that the changes all took place with the teachings of Jesus. Scholars now realize, however, that important changes occurred within Judaism itself before Jesus ever appeared. Students of postexilic Judaism (that is, of the religious ideas of the Jews after they returned from exile in Mesopotamia in the fourth century B.C.) believe that Judaism was dramatically evolving during this period into a saviour-religion and that Jews were responsible for several important steps in the development of what eventually became medieval Christianity.

In the postexilic period, which was a time of great unhappiness and repeated foreign conquest, the Jews could see that the triumph of Zion, predicted by the prophets, had not taken place. The failure of Israel to achieve the promised independence and leadership caused disillusion and dismay, and inevitably, religious beliefs changed in response to circumstance and emotion as Jews tried to discover how Zion might still throw off foreign oppression.

Another aspect of Judaism was unsatisfactory to many Jews after their return. To those who had contact with other Mediterranean cultures through exile or commerce—mostly sophisticated, middle-class Jews—Judaism began to seem bleak and impersonal. Unlike various other Near Eastern cults, early Judaism was silent on immortality and on the afterlife. During the turbulent centuries after the Exile, Judaism did not satisfy the longings of some of the devout any more than it fulfilled the national aspirations of the patriotic people.

Judaism was founded on the concept of rewards and punishments, and this very system led educated Jews to a question that became almost a fixation in the postexilic period: Why does the righteous man suffer? It was obvious that sinners often flourished in this world, that rewards were unequal and often unjust. The puzzlement and concern aroused by this question are best expressed in the Book of Job—one of the most beautiful and skillful books of the Bible, but hardly an advertisement for Judaism. (Scholars believe that its happy ending was added by a later writer who found the book too disturbing as it was written.) Job is a good man, a thoroughly righteous man, visited with a terrible series of calamities—deaths in his family, ill health, the loss of his livelihood, and so on. His friends insist, at first, that Job cannot be the good man he seems, that God must be punishing him for some hidden sin. Perhaps his apparent philanthropy is nothing but an expression of pride, a cover for a stiff-necked, rebellious spirit. If that is not the explanation, then God must be testing Job to discover how righteous he is at heart. It is easy to be good when things are going well; the test comes with trouble, when only the genuinely good man can accept God's will. (This concept is based on the assumption that suffering is good for people, which became important in later Judaism and Christianity.) At the end of all Job's discussions with his friends, God's voice comes out of the whirlwind and orders them to be still—and it is at this point that the later writer reported that Job was rewarded by God for his patience.

The story of Job reveals many of the concerns and ideas of the post-exilic period, including the growing belief in the value of suffering. Certain thinkers began to believe that suffering is redemptive, that it purifies its victims. In the same period there developed the concept of vicarious suffering, which marked a great step toward Christian theology. In the book of Isaiah, Chapter 53, there appears a Man of Sorrows who wears a crown of thorns and suffers for others. Isaiah's Man of Sorrows represents Israel (the Jewish people) and offers an answer to those who wondered why sinful Gentiles prospered and conquered the Earth while pious Jews languished in captivity. (The so-called second Isaiah, the author of the latter parts of the book of Isaiah, was an anonymous writer who lived in exile in Mesopotamia.) Christians later applied the description of Israel to their own Man of Sorrows, claiming that Isaiah foretold the coming of Christ. Christians localized the personalized Isaiah's Man of Sorrows in Jesus Christ even while they made him into a universal saviour, whose wounds on the cross were the means of salvation for all men.

Further development toward resolving the problem of suffering emerged in the first century B.C. with the idea of a personal saviour—the Messiah. There were stories of a hero from the royal house of David, the king who would claim his birthright as a ruler of Israel, throw off the yoke of the Romans, and bring about the long-awaited triumph of Zion. This saviour was a human, personal messiah, a political and social being, rather than a metaphysical or sacramental figure. He was not the Christian Saviour, but he was sent by God, and the appearance of messianic ideals marked another step in the evolution of Judaism toward Christianity. The doctrines of the value of suffering, of vicarious suffering, and of redemption by a messiah all pointed toward Christianity, which evolved out of late Judaism and was later mixed with Greek and Roman ideas.

There has been continuous and vehement debate among scholars as to the place of Jesus himself, and of St. Paul, in the transition from postexilic Judaism to early Christianity. The debate has involved many Protestant scholars and some Jews, but until recently it was ignored by most Roman Catholics, largely because the Roman Catholic church denied the evolutionary development of Christianity. Until this century, Catholic churchmen liked to imply that the medieval (and modern) church sprang full blown from the head of Jesus. In this century, however, liberal Catholics, using an Aristotelian term, say that the modern church was potential in earliest Christianity, and Catholic scholars have joined in the arguments over origins. In this field, as in many others, the intellectual emancipation of present-day Catholicism has powered a creative burst of intellectual activity among Catholics. The Roman Catholic church is no longer an anti-intellectual institution, and biblical scholarship has shared in the benefits of the change.

There are three dominant schools of interpretation of the historical significance of the New Testament, especially of the Gospels. These schools are not necessarily contradictory, but they emphasize different aspects of the problem. Scholars of the Higher Criticism (developed in Germany in the second half of the nineteenth century) decided that Matthew, Mark, and Luke tell roughly the same story—not entirely the same, but their accounts have much in common. These three Gospels must have been derived from a common source, an account of Jesus' life and teachings by a contemporary (or contemporaries) or near-contemporary. That source has disappeared, but the later writers based the first three Gospels upon it. The Gospel of St. John is quite different; it is a reinterpretation of Jesus and of the Christian message in terms of Platonic philosophy. The interpretation of Jesus in Matthew, Mark, and Luke is a development out of and beyond postexilic Judaism, but John gives a full-fledged theology of the Incarnation, with Jesus as a divine Saviour. He begins "In the beginning was the Word"—the logos, the divine Idea of Plato. According to the Higher Criticism (and it was enormously influential), the first three Gospels were written between A.D. 60 and A.D. 90, and John, between A.D. 100 and A.D. 120.

A second school, the "liberal" interpretation of the New Testament, first appeared in Germany and flourished (particularly in the United States) in the first forty years of the twentieth century. According to this view, Jesus was a saintly, holy man who taught a philosophy of social righteousness. He was a radical social leader who preached nonviolence, pacifism, and generosity and favored the poor and downtrodden over the rich and powerful.

The third school was headed by Rudolph Bultmann, a distinguished German biblical scholar and philologist, who was a neo-Lutheran or neo-

Augustinian. Bultmann believed that the New Testament is not a historical document but a collection of legends and *midrash,* or commentary. The Gospels are a group of stories about a teacher of righteousness, stories of the kind commonly told in later Judaism about saintly men and important rabbis, and they offer little biographical information or theological principle. However, Bultmann was convinced that Jesus was firmly rooted in the eschatological tradition of postexilic Judaism, that he was out not to reform the world or its institutions but to preach its end, to warn men that their sinfulness and corruption could be overcome only by divine intervention.

The appearance in 1948 of the first of the Qumran, or Dead Sea Scrolls, aroused great excitement and curiosity among biblical scholars, who had high hopes of obtaining new information and an understanding of the life and teachings of Jesus from them. The Dead Sea Scrolls have given us some new insights into Jesus' world and his message. They show, for instance, that John the Baptist was a historical figure; that baptism was a common rite in Jewish circles; that Jesus' lifetime was a period of great millennial, apocalyptic, messianic yearnings among Jews; and that groups were gathering around various kinds of hellfire-and-damnation preachers, of whom Jesus may have been one. The scrolls tell of groups of Jews who withdrew to communities around the Dead Sea to lead a form of monastic life. These people did not withdraw entirely from the world; they contained a military group prepared to fight the Romans. One such group, called the Essenes, was much involved in apocalyptic and millennial speculations and preached a stern morality, and John the Baptist (and perhaps Jesus himself) was strongly influenced by them.

After centuries of argument and speculation about the life and teachings of Jesus, what is really known about him can be stated in a few simple paragraphs. Jesus came from the north of Judea and appeared in Jerusalem with a small group of followers who were poor men, mostly fishermen. The Jews of that time were extremely bitter and disturbed under Roman rule, and Jesus responded to their anguish, as did many preachers and teachers then at work in the streets and synagogues. Jesus proclaimed that the kingdom of God was within and advised men and women to worry about their own souls instead of social revolution or national redemption. The only good thing in the world is love—love of man for man and of man for God—and a man must find love and goodness within himself, must turn his mind from aggression and anger to peace and joy. The world was approaching its end, and this was the last moment to save oneself—to become humble and poor in spirit and to love God and condemn the world. The only revolution that mattered was the revolution of the human heart.

That was the essence of Jesus' message, and he kept repeating it, although people wanted him to say much more. When officials tried to trap him into denying that taxes should be paid to Rome, he held up a coin and showed them the likeness of Caesar, saying "Render therefore unto Caesar the things that are Caesar's, and to God the things that are God's." Again, he called himself the "Son of Man" (a phrase used by Jews to refer to the Messiah), but if he thought of himself as a messiah at all, it was in the old sense of a preacher of righteousness or helper of men, rather than of a national saviour against the Romans or the Saviour-God of later Christianity. Jesus talked about those familiar elements of Judaism that emphasized love, justice, nonviolence, joy, and brotherhood.

Jesus' teaching was simple, and his influence in his lifetime was small, but he preached at a time when the Jewish community was profoundly disturbed and its leaders were fearful of sedition and rebellion. There were active underground organizations whose members stored arms and planned assassinations, and Jesus became a victim of Jewish resistance and Roman fears. Anyone who gathered a crowd in Jerusalem was likely to get into trouble, and finally Jesus was arrested. The Roman governor, Pontius Pilate, was an unintelligent and insecure official who believed that the execution of a supposed leader of the underground would please his superiors. He offered the crowd a choice between Jesus and Barabbas (who is described in the Bible as a robber, but may have been a genuine leader of the Jewish underground), and the crowd preferred to save Barabbas. Jesus was crucified (a common Roman method of execution), and his disciples ran away.

The disciples saw visions of Jesus a few days after his death; they believed that he had risen from the dead, and certainly he stayed alive in their memories. They returned to Jerusalem after the excitement died down and began to meet regularly to share a meal and talk about Jesus. Jesus was crucified during Passover, and at the seder on the evening before the execution, Jesus (knowing that he was to die) asked his disciples to remember him when they gathered to eat the unleavened bread and drink the wine of Passover.

After his death the disciples met frequently to reenact this last supper as a ceremony of Eucharist (thanksgiving), and even in their poverty and obscurity, their evident contentment began to attract some attention. People wondered why such poor, simple men should seem happy; they annoyed the synagogue authorities and fascinated other poor men who hoped to share in their secret. The disciples told others about Jesus when they were questioned, and the story began to spread, but their answers did not add up to anything resembling a new religion. Nothing tremendous had happened: In the years immediately following the crucifixion, the Christians were a tiny group of poor men who met to remember a man who preached ancient, simple aspects of Judaism—devotion to God and purity of the heart.

The next stage in the development of Christianity came with the appearance of Saul of Tarsus—St. Paul—the creator of Christianity as it developed into a new religion. Saul was different from the disciples of Jesus. He was a rabbi from Asia Minor, a learned man who spoke several languages and had studied classical philosophy. Saul went to investigate reports of sectarian troubles in the Jewish community of Jerusalem and discovered (and harassed) a group of Christians, whose ideas were beginning to spread to other Jewish communities in the eastern Mediterranean world. Then, as for several centuries, there were many more Jews in the Diaspora than in Judea. Hearing of a Christian sect in Damascus, Saul set out to warn the Jewish community there against admitting Christians to their synagogue. On the road to Damascus Jesus appeared to him in a vision asking "Saul, Saul, why do you persecute me?"

From that day on, Saul was the most dedicated and devoted of the followers of Christ. He had never met Jesus, but had heard of him and before the vision had hated him. (There is some evidence that Saul was an epileptic, and there is speculation that his vision occurred during a seizure.) In any case, Saul (in Greek, Paul) returned to Jerusalem, where he presented himself to the Christian community. From the beginning there was tension between Paul and the disciples—between the middle-class scholar and the subliterate fishermen—and Paul soon departed to preach the Gospel to the Jews of the Diaspora. Paul was a brilliant, forceful speaker who spoke several languages, looked respectable, and was accepted in synagogues throughout the Mediterranean world. He angered and upset a great many people, but he also persuaded a large number of converts. His eloquence, power, and charisma won wide acceptance for his interpretation of the life and work of Jesus.

The response to Paul came from Gentiles as well as Jews. The slums of the cities of the eastern Mediterranean teemed with unhappy, frightened people who lived in a world of political instability, desperate poverty, and natural disasters, and these people found the message of the Gospel ("the Good News") attractive. Jesus said that what is in a man's heart is more important than his group or background, and Paul stretched that concept to include the Gentiles in his mission. Not all his converts lived in slums, however: many were wealthy, respectable men who wished to accept Christianity without becoming Jews. The great stum-

bling block to conversion to Judaism was circumcision—a major operation for an adult (especially in those days) and a source of shame and
humiliation to a Roman citizen in the public baths. However, the original
disciples, including Simon, Peter, and James (the brother of Jesus), argued
that the followers of Jesus must accept and live by the law of Moses. This
was a major controversy between Paul and the disciples, which is
reflected in New Testament writings, but in the end Paul won his point.
He had to win: He had wealth and followers, while the original disciples
materially had nothing, and he would have gone ahead with his new
Christianity even if they had not agreed with him.

By this time, Paul had elaborated the simple teaching of Jesus—part of
ancient Judaism—into a new and universal religion. Christianity, according
to Paul, was a new dispensation, a new witness (testament), a new chapter
in history—a new religion for all people. Paul preached (at least in the
beginning) that this was an inward religion of love, that the depths of the
human heart were more important than the law. To him, the Torah was a
snare because its negative approach ("Thou shalt not") promoted rebellion.
Genuine goodness was spontaneous; it arose from within and was not
encouraged by interdictions. It was Paul, not Jesus, who believed that the
new dispensation made the Torah obsolete. As far as anyone knows, Paul
remained an observant Jew until his death, but he believed that the law of
Moses was not necessary to Christians.

Paul also preached the corruption of man, that man is too wicked to
save himself by his own efforts. The prophets were wrong to demand
that man reform and simply save himself; man cannot be holy unless
God saves him. God decides who shall be saved, which men shall have
faith and righteousness and which shall fall back on their own resources
and be doomed. Paul also taught that Jesus was the divine Son of God—
God in human form—by whose sufferings men are saved. He taught that
Judaism is not enough, that obedience to the Torah cannot save men, that
salvation takes place within the human heart but comes as a gift ("grace")
from God.

After many years of travel and preaching all over the Mediterranean
world, Paul began to fear that his message of love might lead to anarchy.
In many ways he was a paradoxical figure: a stern, conservative, disciplined man whose religion was one of love and freedom from the strictures of the law. Later in his career, Paul began to stress the necessity of
leadership and authority even in Christian communities where salvation
was accepted as an inward grace. God loves everyone, but that does not
give men the freedom to indulge in all their desires. Men need leaders,
and Christian leaders must be obeyed because they know more than do

other men and are closer to God. Christians were a community, a flock, and each flock had its shepherd, or bishop, whose authority must be recognized by the faithful. Thus St. Paul became the founder of the hierarchy of the Christian church as well as of much of its theology.

The development of the church between the death of St. Paul (around A.D. 65) and the conversion of the Emperor Constantine in A.D. 312 was much affected by its status as an illegal organization. The church expanded steadily in size and influence throughout this period, particularly in the eastern, Greek-speaking part of the Roman Empire that had most of the population. After the year 200, about 10 percent of the people in the eastern part of the Roman Empire were Christians, and by the end of the third century, there may have been 15 million Christians in the Roman Empire—out of a population of about 60 million. Probably the church was a secret, hermetic organization until at least the late second century, but that was a common characteristic of the sacramental religions that flourished in the late Empire. By the late third century, the church was still underground in the legal sense—but it was also a vast and wealthy international organization whose membership included 20 to 25 percent of the people of the Roman Empire.

Obviously, the inner development of Christianity was dependent, in part, on growth and the passage of time; inevitably it was affected by its social and physical environment and cultural milieu. As new members joined the church, they introduced their own backgrounds and concerns. Also, the church accommodated itself, to some extent, to existing circumstances—that is, to the institutions of the Roman Empire. Its own organization developed along the territorial and institutional lines of the empire, and cultural and philosophical strains appeared within Christianity that were neither Hebraic nor apostolic. From one point of view, then, the church thus developed away from pure, apostolic Christianity. On the other hand, it may be claimed that only thus could the church progress, adapting itself to a changing world, to new people and new ideas.

By and large, the church of the Roman Empire adopted conservative social attitudes. Some institutions or attitudes of Rome were clearly contrary to the standards of Christian morality, but little protest was heard from Christian bishops. Romans idolized their emperors, even worshipped them as gods; at least one-quarter of the population of the empire was enslaved; scenes of unspeakable cruelty and horror took place in the Roman circus, where public executions and public torture were the major diversions of the Roman populace; perhaps 10 percent of the female urban population of the empire were licensed prostitutes. None of these things accorded with Christian morality, yet (for the most part) the church was silent. Certainly Christians did not approve of the state religious cults, and they avoided participation in them when they could. Bishops expressed disapproval of public executions, prostitution, and the mistreatment of women, but disapproval did not imply outspoken protest or rebellion. Churchmen were almost entirely silent on the subject of slavery, and even when they complained of the moral atmosphere of the empire, they apparently had no thought of forcing any changes.

One explanation for the accommodation of church and empire may be that Christianity was not primarily a religion of slaves and of the downtrodden. Many (or most) of the Christians of the Roman Empire came from the middle class, and a few came from the ranks of the aristocracy. The men who rose to be leaders of the church were apt to be of substantial family, to be well educated, to be unlikely to attack the prevailing social order. Also, of course, they were afraid: The church was an illegal institution that was tolerated just as long as it did not cause serious trouble. Most of the emperors (except for a maniac like Nero, who persecuted everyone) left the Christians alone and, indeed, Trajan established indifference as official imperial policy in the first century A.D. By keeping quiet, by making it possible for the empire to tolerate it, the church became increasingly conservative in the first three centuries.

During these same centuries, Christian doctrine was profoundly affected by classical thought, particularly by Platonism. The dualism of the body and soul entered Christian theology, and this Platonic idea became a central, persistent strain in Christian teaching. Dualism can easily be used to justify social conservatism because if the body perishes while the soul is immortal, then the life of the body is not important. The material world and how people feel is relatively trivial. Cruelty and slavery can be tolerated if men can look forward to heaven. This world is not good (Christians always noticed the evils around them), but heaven must be a wonderful place where God makes up to His people for their sufferings on Earth. The church accepted slavery on the strengths of such arguments until the Protestants took up the cause of emancipation in the nineteenth century; in sixteenth-century Spain, Christians were still arguing over whether black slaves had souls or were animal creations of the Lord.

The church developed a strict, organized hierarchy during its first three centuries that included a distinct priesthood, with priests separated from lay Christians; Christian priests became officeholders on the Roman model. Just as Roman governors exercised the power of the state apart from (and regardless of) their personal qualities, so Christian priests carried the power of the Holy Spirit. Of course, priests should lead a moral life, but their power and effectiveness was not derived from personal qualities or puritanical lives. Like the empire, the church worked out a strict system of hierarchy based on levels reminiscent of the Platonic concept of the Chain of Being, the continuous hierarchy between pure matter and pure idea. In the Christian church, obedience was due from priest up to bishop, from bishop to archbishop, and from archbishop up to the pope (father) in the West and the patriarchs in the East. Borrowing Platonic philosophy and the Roman system of government, the church developed the Christian priesthood, with its priests set apart from ordinary men and women. Jesus never made that distinction, although most modern Roman Catholics argue that the distinction was implicit—or potential—in apostolic Christianity.

Under the Roman Empire, Christianity developed a distinct and complex culture that was heavily classical, with elements of Greek philosophy, Roman law, and classical rhetoric. Christians did not develop their own language, philosophy, law, or even organization; they adapted what they found. Tertullian, the North African priest of the late second century who disapproved of the classics, thundered "What has Athens to do with Jerusalem?" Even Tertullian, however, used an oratorical style based on classical rhetoric. Some of the Christians denounced elements of classical culture, but almost all of them made use of it: They absorbed classicism in speech and thought.

Churchmen did censor classical literature for their own students; rejecting much of the eroticism of Roman prose and poetry, they simply obliterated certain passages and ignored certain books. Certainly they did not believe in freedom of thought, and they felt entirely justified in censoring what they did not approve. They set up their own schools based on Roman models and made available the study of Latin grammar and rhetoric. Obviously these were good schools because the men who ran the church in the first three centuries were able and well educated. These men made an underground religion into a successful, universal institution—an achievement requiring astute, tough, and determined leadership. One may question how well these early priests and bishops served Christianity by making the church a viable imperial institution—did they betray the ideals of Jesus when they created a conservative social organization?—but it is impossible to question their effectiveness.

Philosophically, too, the Christians of the Roman Empire made a great many changes in apostolic Christianity. The Hebrew Bible, with its stories of violence and savagery among primitive tribal peoples, was not attractive to the Romans, partly because Jews were unpopular in the later empire. Roman Christians solved this problem by allegorizing the Bible, by agreeing with Paul that the spirit and not the letter of the law (and the Bible) is important. The struggles of the obscure Jews that were depicted in the Old Testament were allegorical representations of spiritual truth, not historical facts, and if the Bible was symbolic of mystical truth, then its deeper meanings could be interpreted in accordance with Platonic philosophy.

The allegorization of the Bible was attempted first by a Jew, not a Christian classicist. Philo Judaeus, a prominent member of the Jewish community in Alexandria in the first century A.D., approached the Hebrew Bible as the allegorical expression of a deeper philosophy that could be synthesized with Platonism. Philo's writings had little influence on Judaism because the Alexandrian community had almost disappeared (through assimilation and persecution) by the fourth century, while the Mesopotamian Jewish community and its orthodox legalistic Talmud survived to become the dominant influence on the development of medieval Judaism. There was, however, an active Christian community in first-century Alexandria, and Greek-speaking Christian scholars took up Philo's ideas and applied them to the New Testament, as well as to the Old.

Christian scholars searched the Bible for deeper meanings that were compatible with Platonic philosophy, and they discovered such concepts as the dualism and separation of body and soul, personal immortality, the Trinity, and the Incarnation. It is doubtful that any of these theological bases of later Christianity were expressed in the Gospels (at least in the first three Gospels), but Christians of the later empire sought and found them. Christianity was transformed into a new religion—a mystical, sacramental, hierarchical, Platonized religion that was acceptable to Roman citizens. The simple message of love and humility was not well suited to classically educated gentlemen, so they adapted it to meet their needs. Constant growth, transformation, and adaptation is a continuing theme in the history of ancient and medieval Christianity. The institutional development of the church allowed it to meet the challenge of the fall of Rome. In 312 the church triumphed when a professed Christian, Constantine, gained the the imperial throne in Rome. At the end of the fourth century the practice of ancient paganism was proscribed. But precisely at this point of triumph, the church experienced imperial decline and disintegration.

II. Decline and Fall

The causes and consequences of the fall of the Roman Empire in the West have been inexhaustible subjects for speculation and argument. Historians have even questioned whether there was such a phenomenon as a fall—perhaps the empire just gradually disappeared. However, it is obvious that in the political-military context at least, something happened in the fifth century. For the first time, the Romans were unable to drive German invaders out of the western part of the Empire. As early as A.D. 406, large areas of Gaul, Spain, and North Africa were out of the emperor's control, and by 430, the western emperor ruled in name only. There was a semblance of imperial government until 476, but the real turning point was 430: After that date, the old Roman Empire no longer functioned. However, the eastern, Greek-speaking part of the empire (with 60–70 percent of the imperial population) survived for centuries. This "Byzantine" empire, as it came to be called (after the old Greek name for Constantinople), did not finally fall until the Turks took Constantinople in 1453, although it was temporarily in the hands of Crusaders from the West in the thirteenth century.

In the fifth century, then, the western Roman Empire could no longer defend itself against invaders. For strategic and military reasons, including the breakdown in communications, lack of resources, and bad generalship, Rome was beaten in battle and the old empire collapsed as a political entity. German rulers replaced the emperor, and the empire was divided into several German kingdoms. Despite revolutionary political change, however, it is fairly clear that the social and political institutions and the culture of the late empire did not vanish, but were replaced only gradually (and never completely) over the next two centuries. Modern historians, by and large, regard the fall of Rome not as a single military disaster, but as the consequence of long-range internal processes. Most historians believe that the collapse was not a German triumph, but merely the final chapter of the decline of Rome—that the late empire was a "hollow husk" vulnerable to anyone, even to primitive Germans.

This interpretation was first propounded by Edward Gibbon in *The Decline and Fall of the Roman Empire,* an early and still influential book on the subject. Like all eighteenth-century historians, Gibbon concentrated on narrative, rather than analysis, but he halted his narrative to append to Chapter 38 a discussion of the reasons for the fall of Rome. He offered two explanations, of which the first has been widely accepted. The Roman Empire, said Gibbon, collapsed under its own weight. It grew too vast to be supported by its institutions, communications, education, resources, and legal structure. Managing the Roman Empire was an enormous, exhausting task that demanded constant attention and hard work, and the balancing act finally toppled. The twentieth-century French historian Ferdinand Lot elaborated this thesis in *The End of the Ancient World,* in which he described various aspects of the imperial structure (government, economy, morale, and so on) and showed that each had grave functional problems. These problems expanded like snowballs until the entire structure collapsed.

Gibbon's other explanation for the decline of Rome was the success of Christianity. (He did not say that Christianity alone caused the decline, but that it was one factor.) With its otherworldly ethic, Christianity distracted the Roman elite from the problems of the empire, which could be solved only by intense and continuous application. The church was a distraction—and indeed, Christianity was indifferent if not hostile to secular pursuits. Also, the church deprived the empire of its natural leaders, as able and educated men chose to become bishops and abbots, rather than imperial governors. One may respond that this situation was not entirely the fault of the church, that these men must have been alienated from the state to begin with. By the late empire, government must have seemed a difficult and dangerous (if not hopeless) job, and many men looked for alternative careers.

There is no doubt that the Roman Empire had serious economic problems, and many historians have blamed these difficulties for its collapse. But these economic problems were not new. The empire was not a strong economic entity at any time, and although its weakness became more apparent after the second century A.D. (when the Romans stopped plundering newly conquered people), it is questionable whether they became sufficiently serious to cause the fall of Rome. There is evidence of economic deterioration (for example, of a decline of trade after the year 200), but the evidence does not include the kind of reliable statistical information that would permit quantitative conclusions. Societies always undergo economic change of one kind or another, but change does not always signify disaster.

We do know that the population of the empire declined markedly, perhaps by 20 percent between A.D. 250 and 400, primarily because of a great outbreak of bubonic plague in the third and fourth centuries. The decline in population shrank the markets, reduced the volume of trade, diminished international exchange, and thus weakened the relationship of various parts of the empire. Separate regions grew more localized, turned in on themselves, and thus weakened the political unity of the whole. Commerce declined for other reasons, too—notably because of the Romans' failure to develop any industrial technology. Without a factory production system there was no specialization, and handcrafted goods could be produced anywhere: There was no need to import pottery from Greece when it could be produced in Gaul. Between A.D. 200

and A.D. 400, partly through the decline in population and partly through the failure to industrialize, the volume of trade may have declined by 50 percent.

Did economic crisis contribute to political disunity and disaster? After all, citizens in various parts of the empire might have looked to Rome for solutions to their economic problems, thus strengthening the central government. Perhaps they did turn to Rome, but if so, the imperial government provoked greater alienation and disloyalty by its inability or unwillingness to help. Taxation was extremely heavy in the late empire, and merchants and wealthy townspeople undoubtedly resented paying large taxes when they got little or nothing in return. Undoubtedly, the combination of economic difficulties and governmental ineffectiveness caused widespread hostility to the state.

Another factor in the decline of Rome was slavery: The empire rose and fell as a slave society. It is argued that Rome's failure to develop an industrial technology caused economic disintegration and that this failure was a direct result of slavery. For the first two centuries A.D., Romans could rely on slave power for all their needs, and this reliance inhibited technological change. After 200, with the end of the wars of conquest, there was a severe shortage of manpower, but by the time this shortage became critical (in the fourth century), it was too late to industrialize. Historians speculate that it was too late because the institution of slavery had left its ineradicable mark upon the attitudes and life-style of the Roman elite. It was beneath the dignity and outside the competence of the upper classes to involve themselves in production. The upper classes lived off inherited land and slaves, contributing nothing to the economy, and concentrated on a purely literary form of education that prepared their sons only for government. Because the economic base had seemed perfectly secure, aristocrats were not trained to apply themselves to economic problems. When production, economy, and slave power declined, the Roman forms of life and education were too deeply entrenched to adjust to changed circumstances.

This seems a rather deterministic interpretation, but there is an interesting parallel in Chinese history. China had a vigorous industrial technology at the end of the first millennium A.D., a more refined system than anything in Europe even in the fifteenth century—travelers from the West (like Marco Polo) were much impressed with what they found. However, the Chinese ruling class gradually withdrew from its involvement in economic matters, and by the sixteenth and seventeenth centuries, the education and interests of the mandarins were purely literary and intellectual. The mandarins lost interest in and even knowledge of science that could be applied in technological development. By the middle of the eighteenth century, when the Chinese economy was in desperate need of revitalization (and of the application of scientific knowledge) to compete with western industrial powers—and indeed to resist western invasion—the mandarin class was so traditional, so congealed in its genteel style, that it was unable to recover what it once had. Even in the face of military threat and economic disaster, it was too unprogressive to adjust to changed circumstances.

Like the mandarins, the Roman aristocrats could not or would not recognize the changes occurring around them, and this is obvious from contemporary letters and writings. It is true that they had adjusted to Christianity, but that was a scribal religion based on a written text, and they could accept a new religion more easily than they could jettison their literary culture in favor of practical endeavors.

The problems of Rome were severe, but by no means insurmountable. All societies have problems, and often they are resolved, but the Romans suffered a failure of leadership that made it impossible to solve problems because the problems were not even recognized. The Romans let difficulties get too complex without attacking them, and the Germans took advantage of their mistakes. The empire never reached a point of total disintegration, but it was rapidly moving toward it when the Germans took over.

The disproportion between German and Roman arms has often been exaggerated by historians who imply that Rome must have been a "hollow husk" if it could not drive out the barbarian tribes with its enormous resources of men and arms. Certainly the Germans were outnumbered and inferior in arms, but the disproportion was not so great as it seems because the Romans, for a variety of reasons, were unable to bring their full power to bear. First, they were greatly hampered by their traditions of recruitment and military service. According to Livy, Rome was once a nation in arms; in the early days of the Republic, every Roman male would drop his plow or pen and rush to the defense of the state or to conquest. This may or may not be an accurate description of the republican attitude, but it certainly was never true of the empire. Even by the first century A.D., it seemed perfectly natural to the Romans that their legions be manned by mercenaries. Middle-class citizens—city people—did not want to fight, and aristocrats were not often allowed to join the army. Senators and emperors had bitter experience with aristocratic generals who built up large private followings and then marched on Rome (Julius Caesar was only one of such officers), and those whose loyalty was certain were needed as governors and officials.

With the middle and upper classes excluded, the army had to fill its ranks with freedmen, dispossessed peasants, city rabble (notoriously bad soldiers, partly because they were undernourished)—and Germans. After about A.D. 100, hundreds of Germans waited along the Rhine-Danube frontier for an opportunity to move into the Empire. Conquest would have seemed inconceivable then; these tribes wanted to settle down. The Romans made treaties with certain German chieftains, allowing them to cross the river and become mercenary allies (called federates later in the fourth century) who fought to defend Rome against their own kinsmen. This was not an ideal arrangement, but it worked fairly well for two or three hundred years. The Romans never had as many soldiers as they needed, and as the population declined they relied more and more on German mercenaries. In A.D. 200 the proportion of Germans in the army may have been 5 to 10 percent; in A.D. 400 it was perhaps somewhere between 30 and 50 percent.

There was a serious shortage of officers, too, and in the later Empire they often were promoted from the ranks. (Constantine's father, for example, was a Balkan peasant who worked all the way up to assistant emperor). These officers were able men, by and large, but they were Balkan peasants or Germans who had spent their entire lives in the army. They lacked education or training in the Roman traditions, and their loyalty was more likely to be directed toward the army than to the Roman state. They served in the army to advance themselves, and if they were not successful, they were apt to become dangerous. Certainly Virgil or Cicero or Livy meant little or nothing to these officers; they had no training in citizenship or devotion to the state. When it came to a crisis, the men on whom Rome depended (because of its system of recruitment) knew and cared nothing of Roman history, law, or tradition.

Like most empires, the Roman Empire required vast quantities of men and money simply for defense. It had an incredibly long frontier with few natural defenses (the Rhine-Danube system was a natural defense, but not a good one—it could be crossed). The empire stretched from Scotland to Central Asia, and from Austria into the Sahara—a fantastic extent. The Roman frontier was so long and open that 3 to 5 million men would have been necessary for a secure defense—and there were only 50 million citizens of the empire by A.D. 400. It might have been possible, in a society like the Republic as described by Livy, to mount such a defense, but the Romans of the empire were not interested in joining the army. The old Roman aristocracy enjoyed fighting, but their descendants—and the other classes of society—did not.

The Roman army was chronically understaffed, and its leaders continually faced the problem of where their men might be most effective. The so-called military reforms of Constantine and Diocletian (early in the fourth century) were in a sense confessions of failure, for many legions were withdrawn from the frontier and stationed in central places from which they could move into trouble spots as these appeared. The Romans abandoned the stationary defense (which they could not manage) for a more mobile policy. It was a good idea, but communications and transportation were not fast enough to move men to a battle before it was well under way, if not over. At the Battle of Adrianople in A.D. 378, the first defeat of Rome by Germans, the emperor waited for reinforcements until he became impatient enough to go ahead without them and was defeated and killed. The battle was critical even though it settled nothing politically because it showed the Germans that Romans were not invincible. Any German tribe, or *volk,* was tiny in comparison to Rome (perhaps 20,000 men at most), but even 20,000 men was more than Rome could usually put into the field at any one place or time. The late empire was not militarily feeble, but it was fatally unable to adjust its military system (in recruitment, tactics, and organization) to meet new challenges and changed circumstances.

One factor in the fall of Rome is often overlooked or misunderstood: the extent to which the empire was ever a genuine unity. In the beginning, certainly, imperial unity was artificial, and in many ways it remained so to the end. The Romans were vicious, aggressive conquerors, but as rulers they were fairly beneficent—of necessity, since they had neither the men nor the materials to run an oppressive regime. In the first two centuries A.D. the Roman rulers demanded little of the conquered people. Taxes were extremely low (almost negligible); there was no real economic control or interference; the cities had self-government; and people were allowed to speak their own languages and worship their own gods as long as they worshiped the emperor, too (a requirement that was waived for Jews). With only a few thousand aristocrats to govern its empire, Rome could not establish the kind of stern oppressive system that could enforce heavy demands. Individual aristocrats made large private fortunes out of the business of government, but they did so in an empire that was not much more than a superficial political unity imposed upon the old Mediterranean variety of cultures, societies, and economies.

After A.D. 200, when the empire began to get into economic and military trouble, the Romans began to demand much more. Heavy taxes were levied, and the emperor decided to put an end to local autonomy, partly to get more money out of the cities. Economic controls, such as Diocletian's edict on prices, were unpopular. A tough, centralized administration was attempted, and although it was never successful (because of the primitive communications system), it was totalitarian in spirit, if not in practice. Finally, when fanatic Christian bishops convinced the emperors in the late fourth century that there was only one true religion and all others must be proscribed, the empire began to try to control thought. In the end, Roman Catholicism alone could be practiced in the West and Greek Orthodoxy in the East, and there was an end to freedom of religion and culture.

The new controls made people extremely restless and unhappy and to wonder what they were getting in return for their money and their loyalty (if any). The empire was no longer providing protection in return for negligible taxes and a token allegiance; it was making severe demands on the populace. Furthermore, people had forgotten the horrors of war and foreign invasion during the long peace. The Germans did not look too frightening, and it was believed that taxes would be lower under their regime—as they were! It is often said that the Romans of the late empire lost their public spirit, but this is not to say that they had become corrupt. Indeed, in private morality they were more puritanical under Christian rule. However, the Roman Empire had become a burden, and when great demands were made on its constituents, the essential artificiality of the imperial structure was revealed. Many people had never been genuinely committed to Rome or involved with the empire, and they were not distressed at the prospect of its defeat.

III. The Roman Destiny

The character of the eastern Roman empire was largely fashioned by two emperors, Constantine in the fourth century and Justinian I in the sixth. Their social backgrounds were remarkably similar; they were both of Balkan peasant stock. Constantine's father and Justinian's uncle both rose from this humble background to be important generals and later attained imperial power. Constantine's mother Helena (St. Helena in the Greek church) had been a Balkan barmaid and probably a prostitute. Justinian married a circus dancer, Theodora, probably also a prostitute. Constantine and Justinian also resembled each other in great industry, administrative ability, and devotion to the church.

Constantine was born about 280 to Helena and Constantius Chlorus, who later became caesar, or assistant emperor, in the western empire in charge of Britain and Gaul. Constantius Chlorus' religion tended toward pagan monotheism in the form of the Unconquerable Sun. Constantine himself, sent to the Emperor Diocletian's court and traveling extensively in the eastern empire, came to know many Christians early in his life. When Diocletian retired in 306, his complex scheme for the imperial succession, consisting of a senior and a junior emperor and two caesars, or assistant emperors, immediately failed. Bitter civil war ensued until, in 310, three generals contended for supremacy. They were Licinius in the east; Maxentius in Italy; and Constantine, his power based in Gaul and Britain, the poorest and least populated part of the Roman world. In 312, although outnumbered by his rival Maxentius, Constantine risked everything in a march over the Alps and upon Rome. At the battle of the Milvian Bridge near Rome—one of the few really important battles of history—he defeated and killed his enemy. This victory made him ruler of the West and with Licinius in the east, Constantine shared the rule of the Roman empire from 312 to 324. In 324 Constantine defeated and deposed his eastern rival and became sole ruler of the Roman world.

Contemporaries wondered at Constantine's apparently miraculous victory at the Milvian Bridge; Constantine himself later claimed that it was no fortuitous event, but the result of his adherence to the Christian God before the battle. This conversion of Constantine has become a controversial subject among historians. Much of the evidence for the conversion of Constantine to Christianity comes from Lactantius, a Latin writer in Asia Minor, who, about 320, wrote the *Death of the Persecutors,* a popular book in the Middle Ages. This book is a collection of horror stories about the downfall of those rulers who had persecuted the Christians. In it, Lactantius discusses the events that led to the battle of the Milvian Bridge. He tells us that Constantine was instructed in a dream to place the Labarum (standard) of Christ—the crossed chi and rho that was the Christian monogram—on the shields of his men to bring him victory. Bishop Eusebius of Caesarea, the first great historian of the Christian church and a friend and confidant of Constantine, gives three accounts of the events leading to Constantine's great victory. In 316 he stated vividly that Constantine accepted Christianity and put the chi-rho upon the shield of his legionnaires. In 325, in the *Ecclesiastical History,* Eusebius asserted that Constantine prayed to the Christian God before the battle and later erected in Rome a statue of himself with the Christian standard. No evidence of the statue has ever been found, and the account is probably untrue. Eusebius' *Life of Constantine,* written shortly after the emperor's death in 337, presents the model for the standard life of a Christian monarch that was followed until the eleventh century. In this work Constantine and his army are said to have seen a flaming cross in the sky and the inscription "By this sign thou shalt conquer" before they crossed the Alps to Italy. This sight demonstrated to Constantine the power of the

Christian God, whose standard his army henceforth carried.

There is some numismatic evidence for Constantine's conversion, but it is inconclusive. Both the cross and the Unconquerable Sun are depicted on one coin, while another type of coin shows the chi-rho destroying a serpent, symbolizing Christianity's destruction of paganism. On yet another coin Constantine is depicted in armor with the chi-rho on the crest of his helmet. A medallion from 330, commemorating the establishment of Constantinople, has distinctly Roman overtones; it shows Victory crowning the emperor. If Constantine was a sincere Christian, it is evident that he was rather cautious about expressing his full acceptance of Christianity on his coins.

Constantine, it must be remembered, was not a well-educated man. In his anxiety before the battle of the Milvian Bridge he actually thought he could strike a bargain with God. This gamble on Christianity apparently led to his victory, and he therefore became a supporter of the church. Constantine believed in the great power of a monotheistic deity in any case, and the pressure of the period before the crucial battle concretized his beliefs in the direction of the Christian God. It is true that the emperor was not baptized until he was on his deathbed, but the baptism of infants was not general in those days; Constantine, for the last twenty-five years of his life, was a sincere Christian. His character was such that he was more active and impulsive than intellectual and spiritual, more subject to fits of temper and violence than to quiet contemplation. Clearly he was no saint, but he looked upon himself as a man with a mission. He felt that he had been called on to save the Roman state and to further the Christian church, and he thought of the two institutions as being tied together. Early in his imperial career Constantine sensed that the church could act as a backbone for the empire. Hence he made desperate attempts to preserve the unity of the church, believing that God had given him a personal commission for this task. His efforts, religious and political, preserved the Roman Empire for another hundred years and blunted the power of such divisive heresies as Arianism and Donatism. In this work Constantine proved himself a man of vision and high ideals and demonstrated his unflagging energy and administrative skill. Constantine's understanding of Christianity was never sophisticated, yet from his own point of view he was a devout Christian. He had laid the foundation and prepared the way for the Christian church of the Middle Ages.

From the beginning of his reign Constantine tried to help the church by granting special privileges to the bishops. He apparently intended to act as the representative of the church to the non-Christian population of the empire—he called himself "bishop of those outside the church"—and to allow the bishops to administer the internal affairs of the church. But Constantine soon discovered that it was not possible to do so. From all sides he was immediately called upon by the bishops to settle doctrinal disputes that were threatening to split the church apart. The church had not yet developed a system of universal authority to define dogma. Each bishop was left to decide such questions in and for his own episcopal see. This practice led to the need for some great council of all bishops of the empire to consider and settle these problems; the Council of Nicaea in 325 was the first such general meeting. Constantine presided and tried, with only momentary success, to impose a dogmatic formula to which all parties could subscribe.

The western participation in the Council of Nicaea was small because the Arian controversy, which the council was summoned to settle, was purely a Greek problem. In the first three centuries of its existence the Christian church had come to adopt the culture of the various areas in which its believers dwelled. Thus there was bound to be a doctrinal and dogmatic split between the East and West. The Christians of the eastern Roman Empire, the Greek-speaking part, desired that dogma be defined in logical, philosophical terms. The Latin world was, for the most part, free of the Christological heresies that consequently plagued the eastern church. To the western Christians their Greek-speaking fellows were trying to define the indefinable—the trinity of God, Son, and the Holy Spirit. The deeply philosophical problems that were of such overriding importance to the easterners gave way in the West to more pragmatic problems of church administration and consideration of the relationship between the deity and man. In the West it was not until the twelfth century that Abelard tried to come to grips with the definition of the Trinity, which for centuries had appeared to be beyond human reason to the Latin church. In the East, from the fourth century to the late sixth century, the leaders of the church kept unflinchingly to their self-appointed task of analyzing the godhead. The eastern insistence on philosophical and logical definitions led to numerous disputes that centered on two great heresies: the Arian in the fourth century and the Monophysite in the late fifth and sixth centuries.

Arianism, named after its originator Arius, an Alexandrian priest, insisted on a strong definition of the distinction between God and Christ (God the Father and God the Son). This view reflected the resurgence of Greco-Roman polytheistic concepts within Christianity; Arius, like the pagan Greek thinkers, tried to make distinctions and levels in the godhead. The western church was immediately anti-Arian, recognizing the danger inherent in such a retrogression to polytheism. The eastern church was badly split on the Arian question, with nationalist feeling aggravating the situation. There had been a long-standing bitterness between Alexandria and the other great eastern cities. Not only did Alexandria resent and feel jealous of the new bishop of Constantinople, but the Egyptians had never been fully satisfied with imperial rule, and in the fourth century there was a great resurgence of nationalism in Egypt. It is clear that the Arian religious controversy was based, in large part, on national and cultural differences. The upshot of the dispute was that by the late fourth century the bishop of Rome and the emperor both took the side of the patriarch of Constantinople, increasing the desire of the Egyptians to break away from the empire. The Egyptians' nationalist feeling was expressed in Arianism in the fourth century and the Monophysite heresy in the sixth century. More than two centuries of bitterness culminated in the Egyptians offering only token resistance to the conquering Moslems in the seventh century.

The Donatist heresy was more important than others to the Christians of the western church. It led to a conflict between Donatism and Catholicism that, with a long hiatus from 700 to 1050, lasted from the fourth to the sixteenth centuries. This is the fundamental doctrinal dispute in western Christianity. In the fourth century Donatism was confined to its birthplace of North Africa (the present Algeria and Tunisia), where it divided the old and militant Christian community into schismatic and orthodox churches. Donatism, named after a certain bishop Donatus, one of its founders, was an indirect outcome of Diocletian's persecutions. The governor of the North African province had been quite lenient, merely requesting the Christians to make a symbolic repudiation of their faith by handing over their scriptures. The wealthier Christians adopted this convenient course of action. But when the persecutions ended, they found themselves branded as *traditores* (betrayers) by a group of zealots, mostly from the poorer classes, who demanded that only the heroic saints who had in no way betrayed their faith should be regarded as members of the church.

The Donatist puritans claimed that the traditores had lost grace and were not even Christians any longer. They demanded that the sacramental rites be administered by priests of pure spirit and held that sacraments administered by unworthy priests were invalid. The Catholic majority maintained their belief that it was the office of the priest and not his personal character or quality that gave sacramental rites their validity. This was the pivotal point of dispute—a church of saints as against the Catholic (universal) church. At the end of the fourth century the great church father and native North African, St. Augustine, mustered all his learning and eloquence against the Donatists in behalf of the Catholic position, but neither the arguments of the Catholics nor even the persecutions waged by the orthodox emperor entirely prevailed against the Donatists. They became an underground church and disappeared only after the Moslem conquest in the seventh century. Donatism reappeared again in the West in the second half of the eleventh century. Its absence from the Christian religious scene for several centuries enabled the Catholic church to assert its leadership in early medieval Europe, a task that could not have been successful had the church followed the Donatist ideals of exclusiveness and not attempted to bring *all* men and women into the fold and tried to civilize them.

In the High Middle Ages literate and self-consciously moral laymen demanded, in Donatist fashion, higher standards of morality from members of the clergy. When they were not satisfied in this regard, certain zealots among them denied the distinction between laity and priesthood. In various parts of western Europe heretical theories, all traceable to the Donatist outlook, made their appearance. The church fought the heresies with all the means at its disposal because they struck at the foundations of Catholicism, but it was never able to root out Donatism completely. By the sixteenth century many people felt that the Donatist position was right. The Reformation, in the instance of Protestant sectarianism, showed its Donatist heritage: To be a full member of the church, you had to have a conversional experience and you had to have a conviction of reception of grace. The problem the Catholic church faced was that in absorbing society there was the chance that, just as society would be civilized and changed by its association with the church, so, too, could the church be barbarized by society. Had Christianity remained a religion of the elite, this danger from society would have been reduced, and the Donatist ideal of a church of the saints could have been realized. But a church of the saints could not at the same time be a catholic church bringing the means of grace to all mankind. There never could be a compromise between Donatism and Catholicism. Poor Constantine was bewildered by the Donatist dispute. His attempts at peacemaking between the two groups inevitably failed.

In his dealings with the church Constantine was advised by his friend and biographer Eusebius, bishop of Caesarea in Palestine. Eusebius' *Life of Constantine* is one of the most important works of medieval literature. It sets the pattern for the ideal life of a medieval king. Medieval kings were, by and large, hard, brutal, and barbarous men until at least the late eleventh century. The lives of these men were written, however, by clerical ministers of the king who wished to portray their masters as men of noble virtues called to their office by God and as great friends of the church, as well as temperate and kind.

Early medieval historical literature, like hagiography (saints' lives), was based upon the concept of presenting a fulfillment of the ideal and not the actual. This historiography followed the Platonic conception of the *idea* of what a king, emperor, or bishop should be. Medieval historical writing is full of saints performing miracles in fulfillment of the authors' conception of the ideal saint, and of kings likewise conforming to an ideal pattern. This formalist emphasis on the ideal lasted at least until the eleventh century. Early medieval literature had no room for the real personality, for individual characteristics. Following on tendencies already evident in late Roman writing, the ideal and the general drove out the real and the particular. In early medieval historiography only occasionally in contradictory passages is there a breakthrough of realism. There is a question of whether such an occasional departure was due to a weakening of the idealistic conception or simply a lessening of literary craftsmanship.

Eusebius, then, attempted to show Constantine as he should have been but probably was not. Constantine is for Eusebius the fulfillment of the lines of universal development set down when the Roman Empire (under Augustus) and the Christian church were inaugurated at the same time. According to this thesis of Eusebius, the world entered its greatest stage with the joint inauguration of the Christian faith and the Roman imperial power, both personified in Constantine. The Roman Empire would make sure that Christianity lasted forever, Eusebius believed, and God would reward the empire with yet greater glory and happiness. The deflation of this kind of optimism came only with the failure of the empire at the close of the fourth century. Then the optimism based upon the unity of the empire and the church gave way to the pessimism accompanying the realization that the empire was after all ephemeral, and the destiny of the church was independent of the rest of the empire. This was to be the theme of Augustine's *City of God*.

Eusebius has been badly treated by modern critics; it has been fashionable to compare him unfavorably with Augustine. Medieval writers, while they were deeply indebted to Augustine in many ways, of course, did not find Eusebius' historical views at all shallow. Whenever a king favored the church, he would be hailed as another Constantine, and an optimistic tone would enter contemporary accounts of the ruler. Assuredly God would bless and reward a devout Christian king with victory and glory!

Constantine's final effort on behalf of the church was the founding of a second Rome at Constantinople. Despite all his efforts in the first decade of his rule, the Roman aristocracy remained devoted to the ancient rational pagan gods, and most of the old ruling class in the Eternal City did not convert until the late fourth century. Constantine did not feel powerful enough to force the old aristocracy into the church, but hoped he could undermine the position of Rome in the world and sabotage the influential position of the pagan aristocracy. The Roman aristocracy continued to enjoy wealth and power in the West, particularly in Rome. In building Constantinople, Constantine envisioned a new imperial capital where Christianity would be supreme and unchallenged. Eusebius tells of a miraculous dream bidding Constantine to establish a new capital in the old Greek city of Byzantium on the Hellespont, where it would have the added advantage of not being liable to capture by a frontal attack because of its impregnable strategic position.

The new capital of Constantinople was, by Constantine's direction, designed in imitation of the original Rome. It was filled with the ancient artwork of many Mediterranean cities. Constantine even imported from Rome a proletarian mob, which he called "the Roman people," to give the new city the flavor and appearance of the old. In the long run, despite his efforts and great plans for his new capital, Constantinople only heightened the disintegration of the Roman Empire. The creation of a new eastern capital encouraged the division of the empire between an eastern and a western ruler, which had already been tried by Diocletian. Several times in the fourth century there were two emperors, and after 395 the Latin and Greek halves of the Mediterranean world were never politically reunited. By the sixth century Constantinople had become firmly Greek in language and culture. The new capital turned the people of the eastern Mediterranean away from Rome and encouraged their growing separation from the Latin West and its culture. The Justinian code, published in the sixth century, was the last work of Latin literature to originate in the eastern part of the empire.

But Constantinople was at least a great new fortress in the East and, in that capacity, was to serve as the savior of Christian western Europe in the early Middle Ages. In its strategic position at the crossroads of East and West, Constantinople was able to hold back the invasions of various oriental races and religions, blocking them off from the road to Rome and western Europe. The most important instance of this service was the halting of the Moslem advance at the walls of Constantinople in the eighth century. But for Constantinople's role as the fortress of Europe, the people of medieval Europe would have been overwhelmed by the religious determination and military superiority of the Moslem armies.

In the short run, the effect of the building of Constantinople did not fulfill Constantine's hopes. The prestige of Rome in the Latin world was not harmed by the new eastern capital. Constantinople was merely an alternate Rome, and there remained the real questions of whether the old Roman aristocracy could be converted to Christianity and whether the full transformation of Rome into a Christian city would be completed. This work was accomplished in the century following Constantine's death by the succeeding Christian emperors and by the bishops of Rome.

The Roman emperors' acceptance of Christianity in the fourth century raised the problem, for the first time, of the relationship between the church and the Christian monarchy. This was to remain one of the fundamental and characteristic problems of medieval civilization. It would be no exaggeration to maintain that this church-state relationship was the dominant continuing theme in European politics until the twelfth century.

Even the hardheaded Romans of the first two centuries A.D. were influenced by traditions of sacred kingship. The solar theology of the third century went much further. A full-fledged charismatic basis for the emperor's authority was developed. The idea of the emperor as the vicar of God with semidivine attributes slowly but certainly became influential in political life. The culmination of this intellectual trend was a kind of political monotheism: It was believed that there was one God in heaven and one emperor on Earth who was the representative of, and participant in, divinity.

Before Constantine the leaders of the church had perforce to reject this political monotheism because their God was not the god of the imperial propagandists. The most they could say for kings and emperors was that they were a necessary evil. Many early Christians were actively or passively disobedient to the emperor. In accordance with the early church's eschatological bent, the authority of the earthly powers (governors, kings, emperor) was regarded as temporary and limited; it would pass away with the last judgment, which the Christians expected in the not too distant future.

The advance of a Christian to the imperial throne produced an inevitable reconsideration of the church's attitude to kingship. As long as the emperor was a non-Christian, sometimes openly anti-Christian, the theoretical question of church-state relations scarcely arose; the church could take a negative attitude toward the state without any doubt or hesitation by its leaders. But the emergence of the Christian king raised a host of new problems, for which the solution was not readily apparent.

The readjustment in the church's conception of kingship was further made inevitable by the close involvement of the emperor and bishops in each other's affairs in the fourth century. Heresies, schisms, and requests for state interference in the life of the church by Christian bishops, on the one side, and what J. B. Bury aptly called the emperor's despotic instinct to control all social forces, on the other, brought about a close union between church and state.

From the time of Constantine the Christian Roman emperor played a commanding part in the life of the church. The history of the church in the fourth century was determined largely by the fluctuating policies and theological views of the various Christian emperors. We have seen how all this was already obvious in Constantine's reign, which saw the intervention of the state in church disputes, the clash of secular and ecclesiastical aims, and the antagonism of, as well as cooperation between, the emperor and the bishops. The lugubrious and at times ridiculous incidents of church-state relations in Constantine's time were repeated over and over again in the reigns of his successors to the end of the fourth century. We must remember that Arianism was not rooted out simply by being condemned at the Council of Nicaea in 325. The conflict between the orthodox bishops and the Arian party and other heretical groups continued in bitter and frequently violent fashion until the last decade of the fourth century.

The disorders caused by violent divisions in the church on questions of doctrine called for the intervention of the public authorities, and the rival Christian parties in the fourth century—the Arian and Orthodox groups and other such parties—were only too eager to obtain the aid of the government to suppress their opponents. Hence, at the very beginning of the Christian Roman Empire Constantine had been able to establish the tradition that it devolved upon the emperor to settle questions of doctrine largely at his own discretion and to summon general ecclesiastical councils, to preside at them, and to dominate their proceedings.

This situation could not but encourage a general drift to the reemergence of the third-century political monotheism in a Christian form. Constantine regarded *himself* as divinely commissioned to be emperor. Eusebius thought that the *office* of emperor itself was a divine commission on Earth and that the emperor was elevated to a position higher than the church as a whole. Eusebius applied the political ideas of solar theology to the Christian emperor and, in his panegyrics on Constantine, enshrouded imperial power with a sacred aura. Here is the beginning of the later (sixth-century) Byzantine ideal of the king-priest, in which the emperor is indeed both caesar and pope. By the sixth century the emperor conducted ecclesiastical policy in accordance with this caesaropapist doctrine, which proclaimed him the vicar of God on Earth and superior in religious authority to the patriarch of Constantinople and all churchmen.

Great benefits accrued from the Christian acceptance of political monotheism and its implications. The recovery of imperial unity and authority in the fourth century would have been impossible without the ideology that regained for the emperor the loyalty and devotion of the illiterate masses of the empire. By the time of Constantine it is difficult to see any other basis for the restoration of popular loyalty than the association of the imperial office with divinity. Political monotheism was a political necessity; it was the pressure of political and social need that lay behind the flowering of the doctrine of Christianized sacred monarchy in the late empire. Although the new ideology could uphold popular loyalty for only a century in the West, in the more heavily populated and literate eastern empire, imperial unity, founded on the autocracy of the sacred emperor, survived the barbarian invasions.

By the last two decades of the fourth century in the Latin West, the possibility that civilization would survive the empire began to enter the minds of thinking men; this made possible a more critical attitude toward the imperial ideology and prepared the way for the fifth-century rejection of caesaropapism. But by this time the bishops could afford a more independent attitude, because the Christian Roman emperors who succeeded Constantine had destroyed the two most pressing enemies of the fourth-century church, namely Arianism and organized, intellectualized paganism centered in the Roman aristocracy, and they had strengthened the church in other ways as well.

One of the chief problems facing the Christian Roman emperors after the death of Constantine was the settlement of the great Arian controversy. From the first the Arian party had been too strong to be crushed by the orthodox group without the aid of the emperor, and the orthodox bishops appealed to the Roman state to intervene in their behalf. But the church's dependence on the emperor to settle doctrinal issues and to eradicate heresy soon led to a further difficulty: What if the emperor himself should become sympathetic to the Arian party?

Constantine had been baptized on his deathbed by an Arian bishop, and his sons who succeeded him tended to be sympathetic to the Arian cause. By the fifth decade of the fourth century, the situation had become critical for orthodoxy. All the voices that could be raised in favor of the Nicene Creed or in protest against the intrusion of the prince in ecclesiastical matters were silenced by the state. Many of the great episcopacies were vacant—or occupied, if not by Arians, at least by their sympathizers. Only in the seventh decade of the fourth century did a change in the fortunes of the orthodox party occur, simply because the emperors of that period sympathized with their doctrines and became more and more hostile to Arianism.

In the early part of the eighth decade of the century, Arianism was condemned by the orthodox emperor Theodosius I (the Great) and never recovered from this imperial condemnation. Finally, in 383 and 384, Theodosius embarked on a vigorous campaign to destroy the remnants of Arianism in the eastern half of the empire, which he ruled and where Arianism had its stronghold. He promulgated laws forbidding the meetings of the Arian sect, and henceforth the survivors of Arianism formed only obscure and powerless sects in the empire.

Thus the Christian church, in the fourth century, finally settled the great controversy that had so seriously disturbed ecclesiastical life. But it did so only by subordinating itself to the will of the emperor. Furthermore, the destruction of Arianism came too late to prevent the spread of the Arian heresy to the Germanic peoples. It was the Arian, rather than the Catholic, church that sent missionaries beyond the Danube and Rhine, with the result that several of the Germanic kings of the following century turned out to be favorers of Arianism. While the Arian heresy was extinguished in the empire itself by the end of the fourth century, other Christological controversies arose in the eastern Roman Empire in the fifth and sixth centuries. The Byzantine emperor, following the precedent of Theodosius, nearly always took the side of orthodoxy. The result was that the heretical churches welcomed the Moslem invaders in the seventh century. Similarly the heretical church of the Donatists, lingering in North Africa, favored the Arabic conquest. Thus the heretical controversies of the fourth century and those that succeeded them eventually did great harm to Christianity in Syria, Egypt, and North Africa. Since the state, from the time of Theodosius at least, took the side of the orthodox party, the heretics turned to the invading Moslems for help. Hence, the will of the Roman emperor could not protect the church from all the consequences of the great doctrinal controversies that began in the fourth century.

Similarly, for the eradication of the other great threat to the peace and security of the church in the fourth century, namely, the survival of paganism, the leaders of the church also had to rely upon the power of the emperor. Here the imperial policy was even more successful than in the case of the heresies.

There can be little doubt that the emergence of Christian emperors intimidated many of the enemies of Christianity and encouraged the conversion of pagans to the new religion. Nevertheless, it must be remembered that at the time of the conversion of Constantine, no more than 10 percent of the population of the western half of the empire was Christian. Because of the Roman pagan aristocracy, Constantine had been forced to found a new Christian capital at Constantinople in 330. Throughout the fourth century paganism still had zealous followers and active sympathizers, and more than once the vicissitudes of political developments in the empire led the pagans to hope for a new turn of fortune that would be to their advantage and would once more change the situation.

Paganism found its warmest defenders among the ranks of the Roman aristocracy and the Italian and Greek academic world. In the Roman Senate and in the civil service the pagans remained strongly entrenched until the last two decades of the century. During the fourth century, pagan piety in the upper classes became more elevated, more ardent, and more mystical. Under the influence of Stoicism and Neoplatonism, many of the aristocratic pagans developed a kind of monotheism and abandoned their old lax morality for a more ardent and stern code of ethics that was reminiscent of the Roman aristocracy in the best days of the Republic. Paganism in the fourth century cannot, therefore, be conceived as a dying relic of the past that would have slowly disappeared of its own accord as Christianity advanced. Rather, this reinvigorated, monotheistic paganism had given the old religion a new lease on life, and in the West it constituted a real threat to the security of the Christian church.

The leaders of the church were unable to vanquish of their own accord this reinvigorated paganism, and they looked to the Christian Roman emperors to help them in their missionary work. Constantine and his sons who succeeded him were inclined, however, to be cautious, in view of the strength of paganism among the Roman aristocracy. The little that Constantine's successors did to suppress paganism was interrupted at the end of 361 by the succession to the imperial throne of Constantine's nephew, Julian, who immediately set about reversing the religious policy of the emperors since Constantine's conversion.

Julian is generally known as Julian the Apostate. Like his uncle Constantine, he also experienced a conversion, but in the opposite direction—from Christianity to paganism. While Julian had been brought up in the Christian religion, he had acquired a taste for Roman literature and Greek philosophy, and he finally abandoned the Christian religion for that monotheistic kind of paganism already described. As long as his cousin, Constantine's son, was on the throne, he kept his apostasy from the Christian religion to himself, but after his accession to the throne, he openly made a profession of paganism.

Julian the Apostate has aroused the interest of many scholars and students of literature, especially those who have a higher regard for classical culture than for Christianity. He was, indeed, a man whose ideas and character were formed by the best that classical culture could offer in the fourth century. He was well educated in Neoplatonic Greek philosophy and learned in the literature of Greco-Roman culture. He always led a sober, austere, and ascetic life, and he had a grand vision of restoring pagan religion and classical culture to a new, high level. He did not find the means to realize this grandiose conception. Julian actually achieved little in the way of checking the spread of Christianity and restoring paganism.

Soon after his accession to the throne, he began to rebuild and refurbish the old Roman temples, most of which had fallen into decay. He soon began to persecute the Christian clergy and finally prohibited them from engaging in education. But the non-Christian peoples of the empire were more interested in various kinds of mystery religions than in Julian's highly sophisticated and intellectual brand of Roman paganism. When the emperor Julian delivered his long-winded defenses of classical religion and culture to the mobs of the cities of the Mediterranean world, their reaction was either dumb silence or scornful derision. Before he could really do any damage to the Christian church, he was killed in 363 while fighting the Persians, and henceforth the rulers of the Roman Empire in both the East and the West were always Christian.

Julian's rule, however ineffectual, nevertheless encouraged the Roman aristocracy to resist stubbornly the advance of Christianity and left the problem of the survival of paganism in the western half of the empire even more difficult than it had been before Julian's apostasy. The emperors in the sixth and seventh decades of the century, although Christian, refused to help the church suppress paganism and adopted a policy of religious impartiality and tolerance. It was only in the eighth decade of the century that the church again succeeded in obtaining the support of the emperor in suppressing the remnant of paganism.

We have already seen how Theodosius took the side of the orthodox party and virtually destroyed the Arian party. Similarly, the leaders of the church were able to obtain his support in crushing paganism. Important steps along this line were already taken by his predecessor as emperor in the West, Gratian (375–383), who brought about the separation of paganism from the Roman state. The pagan title Pontifex Maximus was finally excluded from the list of the emperor's titles. Gratian had the altar of victory, which had symbolized the association of the Roman state with the pagan gods for centuries, removed from the chamber of the Senate in

Rome, and he deprived the college of priests of the old religion of their state subsidy. In this way the meetings of the Senate and the imperial dignity were removed from any official contact with the old traditional religion.

Gratian's removal of the altar of victory from the Senate was the occasion for a great debate between Symmachus, the leader of the pagan aristocracy, and the ablest Italian ecclesiastic, Bishop Ambrose of Milan (St. Ambrose). The debate makes fascinating but sad reading in view of the subsequent vicissitudes in the history of the freedom of thought. Symmachus was the eternal liberal with all his good and bad qualities: He was tolerant and generous, but weak and not a little naïve. This worthy Roman argued that many roads lead to God—why should the old religion of Rome, under whose aegis the Roman state had prospered, not be left in peace? Ambrose was the hard man who knew that he possessed the Truth—Christianity is the one true religion; all others must be destroyed.

Time was running with St. Ambrose, not with Symmachus. Whatever the merits of their arguments, the man they had to convince was the Roman emperor, and, in the person of Theodosius I, he sided fully with the bishop of Milan. Theodosius, who had already destroyed the enemies of the orthodox Christians within the church, went further than Gratian in the matter of paganism and sought to destroy the enemies of orthodox Christianity outside the church. In 392, after he gained control of the whole empire, he issued an official proscription of paganism, forbidding anyone in any place whatsoever, even in private, to exercise any of the rites of the ancient religion.

The grave character of this legislation led to a dangerous reaction. The remnant of the Roman aristocracy fought desperately to preserve the ancient religion of the Roman state, and they finally gathered around a would-be usurper, a general who had promised to restore paganism. For a time this usurper, this last champion of paganism, gained control of Rome, but finally, in 394, he and his army were completely defeated by Theodosius, and most of those responsible for the pagan reaction perished in the battle.

The victory of Theodosius thus marks the final defeat of paganism. After his death in 395, which followed soon after his military triumph, more laws against paganism were promulgated by his sons, who succeeded him in the East and West. All the sanctuaries and temples of the old Greco-Roman gods that still remained were ordered destroyed. Freedom of worship was no longer allowed in the Roman Empire.

After 394 the Christian church alone thus enjoyed the material and moral advantages that Constantine had conferred on the Catholic clergy to put it on an equal footing with the pagan priests. And with the granting of new favors to the church by the orthodox emperors of the last two decades of the fourth century, the church received a large number of judicial and fiscal privileges that raised it above the common law of the empire and made it a state within a state. From the time of Constantine the clergy had been exempted from the taxes imposed on all citizens. In the last two decades of the century the orthodox emperors went further along the line of fiscal exemptions to the church. They allowed men to leave the curial class, and with it all the tax obligations of the urban bourgeoisie, and to enter the ranks of the clergy, where they no longer had any fiscal obligations to the state. In this way the orthodox emperors of the end of the fourth century allowed the tax system erected by Diocletian and Constantine to break down to strengthen the ranks of the clergy.

To fiscal exemptions for the clergy were added judicial privileges. The church was allowed to have its own tribunals and to develop its own law—the canon law. Indirectly bishops could mitigate sentences passed by the imperial tribunal through the exercise of the right of sanctuary. Finally the clergy was exempted from the ordinary law courts of the empire, so that the Roman state abandoned its judicial control over the Christian church. The Christian Roman emperors of the fourth century, especially Theodosius, thus made the Christian church fully independent of the jurisdiction of the Roman state.

By the beginning of the fifth century the Christian Roman emperors in the West had freed the church from doctrinal disunity, crushed its pagan enemies, and granted it exclusive privileges that made it a state within a state.

In the long-range perspective, however, the policy of the fourth-century Christian emperors toward the Christian church was fortunate for the survival of western civilization, for in the fifth century the Roman state in the West disintegrated before the onslaught of the invading Germanic peoples. By the fourth decade of the fifth century, the Roman emperor in the West had no power outside Italy, and the barbarian kingdoms began to emerge in western Europe. In the seventh decade of the fifth century, there was no ruler left in Italy who even called himself by the grandiose, but now empty, title of Roman emperor. If the Christian emperors of the fourth century had not unified, protected, and favored the Christian church to the extent that it became a state within a state, the church might not have been strong enough to withstand the barbarian invasions of the fifth century. And thanks to the Christian Roman emperors, the church in the fifth century was still a strong-enough institution to begin the conversion of the barbarian peoples and their education in the Christian Latin culture. The Christian Roman empire in the fourth century had built up the power of the Christian church, and now the church was to supplant the Roman state.

The emperors who followed Theodosius were incompetent men. Theodosius had managed to pacify the Germans, but his sons antagonized them; in 406 the Rhenish frontiers gave way, and many tribes burst across. There was officially a western Roman empire until 476, but the last emperors had no influence on the course of events. They had even abandoned Rome for Ravenna in the early fifth century. This left the Eternal City open to the invaders, and the bishop of Rome emerged as the leader, taking the place of the absent emperor.

As the Roman state disintegrated in the fifth century, the attention of men in the West came more and more to be directed to the only institution that could provide some unity and leadership to religion and education—the bishopric of Rome, the acknowledged leader of the Christian church in the West.

The first pope who seems to have perceived the great role in western civilization that the bishopric of Rome could possibly attain as a result of the disintegration of the Roman Empire was Pope Leo I, usually called St. Leo the Great (440–461). The fourth- and early fifth-century popes were weak and incompetent men who did not take advantage of the prestige of their office. For instance, Constantine asked the bishop of Rome to solve the Donatist dispute, but the pope failed to act and lost a great opportunity to assert papal influence. We must not think of the pope (as the bishop of Rome came to be called) in the early Middle Ages in terms of the eminent position that the papacy attained during the High Middle Ages. In the early Middle Ages the papacy only slowly and painfully, after many vicissitudes and several retrogressions, was able by the latter half of the eleventh century to begin to attain the eminent position that it achieved in the twelfth and thirteenth centuries. It was Leo I who clearly formulated the doctrine upon which the papacy could make those claims to jurisdiction that came close to fulfillment in the High Middle Ages. St. Leo can therefore be said to be the creator of the doctrine of the medieval papacy.

St. Leo was born in the last decade of the fourth century and was elected bishop of Rome in A.D. 440. He was a member of an old aristocratic Roman family, which indicates that the church was beginning to draw upon members of the old ruling class of Rome for its own leadership. The most conspicuous element in Leo's personality, as in that of all the great medieval popes, is his indomitable energy. He worked hard to increase the educational and moral level of the clergy in the West and to improve the liturgy of the church, and he took a leading part in the doctrinal issues that arose in his day. At the Council of Chalcedon in 451 the Greek church accepted Leo's interpretation of the trinity. Finally, he did much to promote the development of canon law.

Twice, in 452 and 455, Leo, aware of the impending collapse of the Roman state, went out from Rome to engage in negotiations with barbarian kings who had invaded Italy and implored them to spare the city of Rome. In at least the first instance, in his negotiations with the Huns, he was successful. In 455 he had less success dealing with the Vandals, but it is significant that the bishop of Rome had taken the place of the Roman emperor as defender of the Eternal City. As a scion of the Italian aristocracy, Leo could not conceive of the end of the empire, although there were many indications in his day that imperial authority was sliding to extinction. Yet half-consciously the pope worked to make the Roman episcopate the successor to the Roman state in the West.

The way for this transformation of leadership in the West from the Roman state to the see of Rome was prepared not only by Leo's activities, but even more by the success with which he vindicated the claim of the Roman see to theoretical supremacy in the church. It was a claim that was to prevail in Europe through all the vicissitudes of the early medieval papacy and that constituted a direct challenge to the pretensions of the Byzantine emperor.

The claim made by St. Leo to the primacy of the bishop of Rome in the church was based on the so-called Petrine doctrine. This doctrine can be traced back at least as far as the second century, and Catholics, of course, find it in the New Testament, but it was St. Leo who first gave it full and forceful expression. The Petrine doctrine is based on the words of Jesus addressing His apostles in Matthew XVI, 15–19.

> But whom say ye that I am? And Simon Peter answered and said, Thou art the Christ, the son of the living God. And Jesus answered and said unto him, Blessed art thou, Simon Bar-Jona; for flesh and blood hath not revealed it unto thee, but my father which is in heaven. And I say also unto thee, thou art Peter, and upon this rock [this has been called the most important pun in history, the Greek word for rock being Petros; of course, Christ, speaking Aramaic, said Cephas] I will build my church; and the gates of Hell shall not prevail against it. And I will give unto thee the keys of the kingdom of heaven: and whatsoever thou shalt bind on earth shall be bound in Heaven: and whatsoever thou shalt loose on earth shall be loosed in Heaven.

Interpretations of this gospel text vary greatly, as may be imagined. A common Protestant view holds that Jesus was addressing all the apostles in the person of their leader, Peter. Hence all bishops—or all ministers of Christ—have this God-given power to bind and loose. It was Leo the Great who positively established the Roman Catholic interpretation, which is made plausible by the tradition that Peter was the first bishop of Rome and was martyred there. Recent archaeological work has tended to substantiate the historical accuracy of this tradition.

Leo's Petrine doctrine claims that Jesus intended Peter and each of his successors in the chair of Peter to be the primate of the whole church, the rock or foundation of the church, and to have absolute power over faith and morals as Christ's vicar on Earth. Thus the bishop of Rome alone possesses the keys to the kingdom of Heaven. He alone is the vicar of Christ on Earth. He is the chief shepherd of Christ's flock. This view was never accepted by the Greek bishops; it had, in fact, been denied by North African Latin Christians as late as the third century. In Leo's day the Latin church accepted the validity of the Petrine doctrine, and it was not to be questioned in the West until the twelfth century. But although the bishops of the western half of the empire recognized the validity of the claims made by St. Leo for the Petrine doctrine, the pope's effective power was confined to Italy. France and Spain were on their own, and there were to be great labors and struggles in these other areas in succeeding centuries as the pope tried to extend his jurisdictional influence and make himself the *real* head of the western church. This attempt to turn the Petrine doctrine into a practical reality was to be the main theme in the history of the medieval papacy.

Nevertheless, it is of the greatest importance for medieval civilization that in St. Leo's time the Petrine theory was universally recognized among the churches of the West. Through all the troubles in which the church found itself in the early Middle Ages, the doctrine set down by St. Leo served as an ideal, calling the papacy to establish an effective jurisdiction over the western church. In the Petrine theory the Roman church found an ideal that gave it the calling of supplanting the collapsing Roman state in the West as the central institution of western civilization.

We can look back over the whole period between the death of Constantine and the end of the pontificate of Leo the Great and see that, unintentionally, the Christian Roman emperors had laid the foundation for the power of the medieval papacy. During the fourth century, the bishops of Rome were a succession of weak and incompetent men who used the great traditions and inherently vast power of their office to little advantage. Fortunately, the emperors did the popes' work for them. They crushed paganism and made Rome into a Christian city, which Constantine had failed to do and which the popes by their own efforts would almost certainly have never done. The emperors destroyed heresy and assured the doctrinal unity of the western church. They endowed the church with enormous material benefits and corporate privileges.

Then in the middle of the fifth century the Roman state in the West collapsed. All that was necessary was the appearance of a great personality on the throne of Peter, a man of bold ideas and enormous energy, for the bishop of Rome to take over the leadership of the western church from the empire. St. Leo was the right man. Thanks to the work of the Christian emperors, the foundations of papal power had been laid. The edifice would take another five centuries to complete, it is true, but St. Leo now gave the papacy its mission: From the materials provided, in large part, by the Christian emperors and following the Petrine ideology of St. Leo, the work of constructing the papal authority in the medieval church could now begin.

IV. Patristic Culture

The ideas and opinions of a few great thinkers of the fourth and early fifth centuries molded the outlook of the medieval western (Latin) church. The term is old fashioned, but St. Jerome, St. Ambrose, and St. Augustine were, in a real sense, "fathers" of the Roman Catholic church of the Middle Ages. In the same period Eusebius, bishop of Caesarea, friend and adviser to the Emperor Constantine and one of the fathers of the Greek church, also exercised a strong influence on the development of western Christianity. In the late sixth century, Pope Gregory I the Great supplemented the doctrines of the earlier church fathers.

Medieval Christians did not always follow the teachings of the fourth-century church fathers (although most of them claimed that they did), but the authority of these men remained second only to that of the Bible. Among thirteenth-century scholars, for example, a reference to St. Augustine was almost as unimpeachable as a quotation from Scripture, although (like biblical quotations) it might be answered by a reference from the same source that proved the opposite. The church fathers were men of great sophistication, and their writings wove various strands of thought into the Christian synthesis. Their ideas were not always consistent: They could be arranged along a spectrum more easily than around a closed circle, but they shared a great many important assumptions.

Any society has groups that can be identified with prevailing social patterns and institutions and others that oppose or defy the Establishment. The Roman Empire of the third century had its critics and enemies, including Jews, nationalistic groups from the eastern Mediterranean, and certain Romans of ancient aristocratic families who had never accepted the rule of the Caesars. The largest and most important group in opposition to the Roman Empire (or who were at least unconvinced that it was the best of all possible worlds and the end of history) were the Christians, who had serious reservations about Roman morality and political philosophy.

The differences between Christianity and imperial Rome were implicit from the beginning of the Christian era, but churchmen tended to avoid direct confrontation with the imperial authorities—partly because they lacked the wherewithal to defy the empire and partly because they believed sincerely that the end of the world was at hand. Christ said "Render unto Caesar the things that are Caesar's," and the early Christians avoided challenging Roman ethics, believing that Caesar would not be able to enjoy his worldly possessions very long. St. Paul was concerned that Christians should have the opportunity to proselytize, to gain converts, under the empire; he did not want to risk the destruction of his infant church by a direct challenge to Caesar. *"The powers that be are ordained by God, and be ye in subjection to the higher powers."*

By the end of the second century A.D., however, Christians were no longer convinced that the end of the world was necessarily imminent and that pagan culture could be ignored. Tertullian (a North African bishop) uttered statements of serious dissent from Roman power and classical culture. Confrontations increased, and in the third century there were great persecutions of Christians throughout the empire.

Suddenly, with the conversion of the Emperor Constantine early in the fourth century, the once-persecuted became the victorious, and the religious, social, and intellectual atmosphere of the empire underwent rapid and profound transformation. Church membership was dangerous to an ambitious man in 300; by 315 (in the West at least), it was advantageous. Significant intellectual adjustment was required, as churchmen moved into positions of influence in which they were supported and protected by the emperor and the imperial family. Understandably certain clerics saw the emperor as a man of destiny who came from the North to conquer Rome and redeem the church from persecution. These men regarded the conversion of Constantine as the most wonderful event since the Resurrection, and they were not likely to criticize the Christian empire. Their attitude was one of accommodation: They believed in the identification of church and empire.

Eusebius, adviser to Constantine and chief spokesman for the newly established church, explained that Christ's birth in the reign of Augustine proved that the church and the empire were partners. Born at the same time, the two institutions would coexist in triumph until the Second Coming. Eusebius and his colleagues sanctified the empire, and they were as lavish in support of the state as the Christian emperor had been generous to the church. These fourth-century churchmen gave moral and religious sanction to imperial rule; priests and bishops preached the divine appointment of the emperor and his representatives to rule Christians. All the conservative implications in the political teachings of St. Paul were revived and stressed in the doctrine that opposition to the established authorities was religious error as well as treason: To resist the ruler was to resist God. From this turning point in the fourth century grew sixteen centuries of tradition, so that it is still the norm of priestly conduct (and of ministerial and rabbinical conduct) to support, serve, and sanctify authority. As long as the emperor was a Christian, the church was joined to the state without regard to the personal character of the emperor or his public policy, and even when churchmen like St. Ambrose quarreled publicly with the emperor later in the fourth century, they did so when the ruler hurt the church, not when he hurt ordinary people. Rapidly, then, the Christian church became an authoritarian, compromising public institution. Fourth-century churchmen became magnates of the Establishment. Their successors have followed in that tradition.

Despite its rapid and decisive transformation from a spiritual brotherhood into an authoritarian organization, the church never abandoned its doctrines of love, faith, inner spirituality, and self-sacrifice. Ambiguities appeared within Christianity and were perpetuated, as Christian ethics and theology came (at least potentially) into conflict with the church's public policy. Remnants or vestiges of the early, antiestablishment attitudes of the underground church survived in the institutional church, and that conflict has made the history of Christianity noble, agonizing, and complex. Most of the vast, prolific writings of the church fathers reflect the accomodation of the church to the Roman state, but there are fragments of dissent and rebellion that became important later on. The rebellions of the later Middle Ages took their primary inspiration from the New Testament, but they also exploited strains of antiauthoritarianism within the patristic writings.

It is complexity—or ambiguity—that gives the western church (and western civilization) its special character. Jerome, Ambrose, Augustine, and others were great men whose lives and thoughts were not simple or polarized. Their doctrines, like those of their contemporaries, tend to be conservative, to encourage compromise with the world, but the minor

strain of dissent—of liberation from the prevailing order—became important in western Europe.

Dissent existed only in the Latin church; in Greek Orthodoxy, the
emperor was the head of the church, and the church served the state.
Byzantium and its Orthodox religion became a symbolic union. Temple
and palace were one and the same, as they had been in Near Eastern
monarchies since the third millennium B.C. In the East, the only available
form of dissent was mysticism, which was of no particular benefit to society. Mysticism, like drugs, offers personal escape from intolerable circumstances. It was a strong movement within the Byzantine church, but it
was never translated into religious reform, revolution, or social change.
The Greek church opposed the state only when the emperor directly
attacked the church (as in the iconoclastic controversy of the eighth and
ninth centuries). Only in the Latin church (and only in European civilization) was there any attempt to apply morality to society, to create a new
moral order and a better world—the kingdom of God in society, as well
as in men's souls.

Unlike other important Christians of the fourth century, St. Jerome
(died 420) held no great office in the church. He was not a public man or
a bishop, but a scholar and schoolteacher, and not an impressive figure
but a pious, rather soft and timid man. Jerome came from a wealthy
Roman family, and although he was born across the Adriatic from Italy,
he spent most of the first part of his life in Rome and received an excellent education. Later he ran a school in Jerusalem, and throughout his life
he loved to engage in pietistic, moral dialogues with various wealthy
matrons about the condition of their souls.

Jerome, then, was a private man who might have been a poet or a
dramatist in another era. His life revolved around two poles: the Christian
church and the love of language. Jerome had one of the great literary
minds of all time, with enormous sensitivity to the meaning and esthetic
of words. To such a man, all beauty is literary beauty and all meaning,
literary meaning. To some extent this kind of literary sensibility must
imply a liberation ethic—or some kind of resistance to authority—if only
because authoritarian institutions, such as governments and churches, do
not use language but jargon, repetitive phrases that are not supposed to
have meaning but merely enforce obedience. Language has its own inter-
nalizing ethic; it is individualistic and thus threatening to any monolithic
system that demands a chorus or litany. Extreme sensitivity to the meanings of the words was a burden to a devout, pious Christian, and
throughout his early life Jerome struggled to find Christian justification for
the literary approach—a struggle reflected in his famous dream. Jerome

dreamed (so he said) that he was accused before the Judgment Seat of God of being a Ciceronian (not a Christian) and claimed that he was so upset by the dream that he went to live for five years as a hermit in the Egyptian desert. This claim may not be strictly true, but it is certain that he had great difficulty integrating his literary genius with the litanistic approach of the church.

Eventually Jerome found a successful compromise. He used his linguistic sensitivity and his knowledge of Latin, Greek, and Hebrew to translate anew the Bible into Latin from Hebrew and Greek—a task worthy of his literary ambitions and yet suitable for a good servant of the church. The job was colossal because he had to transform as well as translate, to communicate the Holy Book of alien Near Eastern people to the Roman world and to ordinary people as well as to scholars. Jerome wrote in something between the Ciceronian Latin of intellectuals and the vulgar language of the streets (the language that eventually became vernacular French, Spanish, and Italian). His "Vulgate" (popular version) was entirely correct and grammatical, in no way offensive to scholars, yet it could be read and understood by the masses if the masses were literate at all. (It was not Jerome's fault that the schools of the empire failed in the fifth century and that there were no literate masses to profit from his work until the eleventh or twelfth century). This was a monumental achievement: to phrase alien concepts and words within the concepts and words in Latin, and to do so in a style acceptable to scholars and accessible to the masses. Jerome's compromise between his own inclinations and his Christian piety was of inestimable benefit to the church and to western civilization.

Unlike Jerome, St. Ambrose (died 393) was the very model of a public man. He came from an old Roman aristocratic family of the military and official class; in the fourth century, the aristocracy saw which way the wind was blowing and became Christians. Ambrose was given an excellent classical education, worked his way up in government, and eventually became the governor of Milan. In the fourth century (as in the nineteenth and twentieth), Milan was a center of radicalism and upheaval. It was the second city of Italy (and remained so until the rise of Florence in the thirteenth century), but the Christian community, as well as the rest of the citizens, was constantly in turmoil. In the fourth century bishops were still elected at public meetings of all the worshippers, and there was a fierce dispute over the election of a bishop for Milan while Ambrose was its governor. Expecting a riot, he appeared at a meeting with his guard; the crowd shouted "Elect Ambrose!" and he became bishop of Milan—or so the story goes.

Ambrose became the dominant force within the Christian church in the crucial decades of the 370s and 380s. Naturally, he brought the attitudes of a Roman official to the church and to society. With his bureaucratic cast of mind, he played a large role in moving the church toward a legalistic style of ecclesiastical life and toward the establishment of canon law as a system based on punishment, duty, office, and obligation. He was deeply concerned with obedience, believing that the role of the bishop was like that of a Roman governor. Bishops had already begun to depart from their early role as pious wise men—the spontaneous leaders of the Christian flock—and Ambrose crystallized the new concept that bishops were authoritarian figures quite separate from ordinary laypeople. A bishop dictates, decrees, and pronounces edicts, and the ordinary Christian is more apt to fear than to love him. Ambrose himself (not Jesus) became the model and prototype for the average medieval churchman; most medieval bishops were aristocratic, efficient, legalistic administrators who concentrated on obedience and tax collection.

Ambrose also had a great influence on the attitude of the Christian church toward love and sexuality. This was an important, difficult question, and the early church waited a long time to take a stand on it. The earliest Christians were often accused of holding "love feasts" (although that may have been a slander), and certainly Jesus himself was free and open with women, particularly with "fallen women." He treated prostitutes as his equals—most uncommon in the Roman world—and some of his most devoted disciples were women of the streets. A censorious attitude toward women entered the Christian world of thought with St. Paul, who favored celibacy despite his admission that it is better to marry than to burn. Was sexual love a Christian experience, the fulfillment of the human personality and an expression of divine love, or an instrument of the devil? The church did not really make up its mind until the fourth century, when Ambrose (and Augustine) threw their weight on the side of Paul.

Ambrose believed that virginity was the ideal state (especially for women), even better than celibacy. This can be regarded as a somewhat progressive attitude because it is true that women were terribly abused in the Roman world. They were regarded as machines for the gratification of men, and probably it was a step forward for a woman to regard herself as a vessel for Christ, to keep herself for God. Thus Ambrose did raise the position of women somewhat above utter degradation; his ideas allowed them to be more than tools of men. However, the consequences of his stand were extremely serious in the long run.

The views of Ambrose, with the support of Augustine, on women and on sexuality had a profound impact on the medieval church, and this influence is echoed in the Catholic Church to the present day. In the late first and early second centuries A.D., in the eastern Mediterranean, a substantial minority in the church, called the Gnostics ("those who know"), appear to have granted women a high degree of dignity in the church, to the point of equality and allowing women to be priests. Ambrose fiercely endorsed the Catholic majority view that women should be excluded from the priesthood and from leadership in the church. This subsidiary role was to be accorded even to virgin nuns, who were regarded as paragons of spirituality. There is some evidence that women virgins were actively troubling to the bishops in the patristic era—these spiritual paragons tried to assert a leadership role for themselves, raising the possibility of the revival of Gnostic gender equality. This Ambrose (and Augustine) strongly rejected.

The basic argument was that woman's essential nature was too flawed and sexually vulnerable to be given freedom and high responsibility in the church. In his sermons Ambrose carried on at great length about woman's propensity to reenact the role of Eve the temptress. A woman's use of cosmetics signified for Ambrose this essential weakness in woman's nature. The patristic view of women as articulated by Ambrose was therefore a highly ambivalent one: there was no person to be more admired than a virgin nun, but this was not to result in recognition of a Christian woman's claim to equality with men within the sacerdotal and leadership stratum of the church. It might be said that Ambrose's attitude was merely perpetuation in Christian guise of the male chauvinism of the Roman aristocracy from which he came. But something else was involved—a very negative attitude to sexual love and a compulsive intention to repress human sexuality. Augustine's attitude to the erotic side of human nature is similar.

How can we account for patristic hostility to human sexuality, which still carries a heavy impress on Catholic doctrine? First, there was the legacy of St. Paul's idiosyncratic pronouncements, highly negative, on sexuality and his wish that women play an inferior role in the Christian community, as they had in the Jewish temple. Secondly, there was in patristic culture a reaction against the sex-drenched, highly promiscuous sexual behavior of the Roman world. This reaction may be rooted in Platonic dualism, separating body and soul. But it was probably given additional force by the biomedical situation in the fourth century—the increase in venereal disease and the onset of bubonic plague were frightening and inspired saving admonitions of sexual restraint and preference for total abstinence. We can see a parallel in our own society. Thirdly, there was the matter of keeping power in the hands of the male priesthood and away from the neo-Gnostic assertion of woman's equality. Making sexuality out to be a dark, frightening, and dirty thing was a useful motif of words toward this goal.

St. Ambrose is most often remembered for his attitude toward the relation of church and state; he was frequently pictured in medieval art as the stern bishop who overcame the great emperor Theodosius. Ambrose temporarily deprived Theodosius of the sacraments (excommunication is the form particularly used for rich or powerful people). This was a radical act in that it ended the deference that churchmen had shown to the state since the conversion of Constantine. Ambrose stood up to the temporal power, told the emperor to stay out of Church business, and announced that the palace belonged to the emperor and the church to the bishop. Theodosius' crime seems insignificant today: He ordered Ambrose to rebuild a synagogue burned down by a zealous Christian mob—the emperor was no lover of Jews, but he did believe in law and order. Ambrose expressed the displeasure of the church, declaring that this was not a civil matter, and he refused to allow Theodosius into the church to receive the sacraments. The emperor humbled himself, begged pardon of the bishop, and was received back into the fold.

Medieval thinkers took this episode seriously. The incident was used to demonstrate that there is a line between church and state, that neither institution absorbs the other, and that morals and religion are outside the jurisdiction of the emperor. So interpreted, the stand of Ambrose against Theodosius was the beginning of a new political theory of Latin Christianity in which the church claimed independence from the state (the Greek church made no such distinction). Departing from Eusebian subservience, Ambrose rescued the autonomy of the Latin church.

The church, of course, was just as authoritarian as was the Roman Empire. Ambrose was no liberal, and neither institution expressed any concern for the rights of individual conscience. Independence was reserved for the leaders of the church, not for individuals within the institution; it was agreed that the bishop—not the emperor—had the right to interfere in matters of morals and religion. This belief was expressed in Ambrose's famous debate with Symmachus, the wealthy and learned Roman aristocrat who was one of the remaining pagans in the Roman upper class. Symmachus made a passionate, intelligent plea for freedom of conscience, asserting that there was one God but many ways to worship Him. Ambrose replied that the church must not tolerate error, that tolerance of falsehood and evil was sinful, and that error must be rooted out. The Christians had the truth, and God gave His bishops the right and duty to persuade the world of it.

Ambrose and his colleagues made the Christian church an institutional, public, political organization; they gave it structure, a legal system, and an efficient bureaucracy. An authoritarian church was bound to demand a certain autonomy as a functioning political institution, and that requirement held the seeds of various anti-Establishment movements. Certainly these churchmen were not libertarians. They believed that just as the emperor had the responsibility to maintain order, so the bishop had the responsibility to maintain theology and morals—by force, if necessary. However, their political church did become a second authority in the world, and its very existence introduced a certain tension into western society. When the church is totally absorbed by the state (or vice versa), there is no pressure and no possibility of opposition. When the two are separate—or at least distinct institutions—there exists at least the possibility of departure from monolithic totalitarianism like that of the fourth century—not toward liberalism, but away from the inclusiveness and absolutism of Eusebius and the Christian empire. One of the most progressive factors in the Middle Ages was the continuing struggle between church and state. Both institutions were authoritarian, both wanted to control the people's mind, but because there was tension between them, there was the possibility of emancipation. Later, rebellious men could play off pope against emperor, church against state, and thus make room for intellectual freedom.

Of all the fathers of the church, St. Augustine (died 430) was the most admired and the most influential during the Middle Ages. He was well suited by background and experience to conduct a fundamental examination of the relationship of the Christian experience to classical culture. Augustine was an outsider—a native North African whose family was not Roman but Berber (today regarded as "Arabs"). His family were townsmen, once fairly wealthy but newly poor under the burden of taxation in the late empire. Augustine was forced to make his own way and to depend on others—on his parents, who struggled to educate him, and on various friends, school authorities, and officials. Not born to the imperial power elite, he could disassociate himself from the empire and its destiny.

Augustine was enormously learned. He was a genius—an intellectual giant—and he received a thorough classical education. He was not much of a linguist (his Greek was poor, and he never learned Hebrew) but he was a master of Latin rhetoric; certain passages in *The City of God* equal the writings of Cicero in complexity and eloquence. Augustine was educated to be a classical scholar. He abandoned the scholarly profession (and the avenue to political office it opened up) to become a priest, but when he entered the priesthood, he was sufficiently learned to confront the question of the relevance of classical culture to the needs of the church. Having spent almost every waking hour between the ages of fifteen and thirty-five on the study of philosophy and literature, Augustine was in an excellent position to decide what part—if any—of the classical tradition might be jettisoned in the Christian era.

Despite his scholarly achievements, Augustine was no armchair theologian. As a priest and as bishop of Hippo (a fairly poor, undistinguished, and remote town in North Africa), he was deeply involved with the lives and problems of his flock. What Augustine said about people and God came not only from his multicultural background but from his profound commitment to the needs and troubles of people. This is a rare combination at any time, particularly within the church, whose scholars have usually been cloistered from the life of the community.

Augustine presented a whole theory of man and society which drew upon classical culture even while it self-consciously opposed that tradition. Thus Augustine's philosophy epitomizes medieval culture, which drew heavily upon ancient civilization and yet fought its influence. In that sense, Augustine was the first medieval thinker, and no one in the Middle Ages quite reached his level of insight and integration.

Augustine's last twenty years were spent amid the disintegration of the Roman Empire. That was a different world from the world of Eusebius, which was a time of triumph for church and empire alike. Augustine lived in an era of dismay, pessimism, and confusion, at a time when it was necessary to evolve a philosophy that would allow the church to survive the empire—to maintain its mission and identity separate from the dissolving Roman world and from classical culture.

Perhaps the most important message in Augustine's philosophy was his view of human nature. He believed that the Platonic concept of morality and ethics was wrong, based as it was on the classical view of man. Greek and Roman philosophers believed man could be trained to be capable of rational decision making, that ignorance was the cause of evil and that properly educated men would exercise their rational faculties and do good. (That view of man was revived in the Enlightenment of the eighteenth century and became the moral basis of modern liberalism. Liberals assume that men will be good if their environment and education are good, that improving men's circumstances will improve their behavior). Augustine denied this classical concept. Men may know what is right, he said, but something prevents them from acting rightly; human nature is disfunctional.

Evil, immorality, wretchedness, and violence are defects of the will, not of the intellect. The will is the mind (or soul, as described by Augustine, or personality) directed toward an end outside itself; it is action, or active conduct, directed to a goal. Men know that hatred and selfishness are wrong, but they cannot escape from their "carnal will," or love of self. Love is will joined to the object of its desire; a man can love himself and exclude all the rest (carnal will), or love God, and through Him, humanity (excluding himself). These are the polarities of human nature.

Christian theology enters Augustinian philosophy at the point where Augustine claims that evil exists because men are inescapably selfish and bad; they cannot love outside themselves, and thus they produce all the misery of the world. Spiritual will never triumphs over carnal will unless God helps—only when God chooses men to love Him (which they cannot do on their own) can they escape their nature. God's choice is grace, and it is a free gift that cannot be bought at any price or with any amount of effort.

Augustine's understanding of humanity improved on the classical view by its recognition of the violent, hateful, and corrupt aspects of human nature. It appeals to modern theologians and thinkers because it accounts for otherwise inexplicable phenomena such as Auschwitz. Augustine realized that wealth and learning did not necessarily improve human nature, that reading the classics did not dilute the savagery of men. "Even their virtues are only splendid vices," he said of contemporary aristocrats. The Roman gentleman, as much as the peasant, had his dark side—his instinctive drive to dominate and exploit. Augustine was no democrat, but in this understanding he did achieve a kind of social or moral egalitarianism that amounted to a revolution in thought. When the accoutrements and defenses learned by the wealthy and educated man are stripped away, the brute is revealed, exposed as identical in depravity with his peasant cousin. Augustine was the supreme pessimist among Christian thinkers; he was (and is) influential because he came close to the inner reality of human life.

As well as a new and persuasive view of human nature, Augustine possessed a special social and historical vision that became extremely influential in the development of medieval thought and of the entire course of western civilization. Impressed by the circumstances of his own time, Augustine told the Christian church that it could and must survive the Roman Empire. He said the empire had never been a moral institution, that although it had established earthly peace, it had never made men good (or even better)—no political institution could to that. The best a government could do was to provide enough peace and security so that the pilgrimage to the Heavenly City could continue: Everything really important happened in the human heart and in the way men acted toward each other in their daily lives. One great empire had crashed, and others would rise and fall. Romans were no better than Germans, and political forms could not of themselves raise the level of goodness in human society. A government that established peace had done all it could; beyond this basic need, social and political institutions made no real difference.

Augustine has been called a conservative, but that is an ambiguous term: A conservative can also be a radical. Insofar as he believed that salvation did not arrive through political or social change, he was a conservative. However, it was radical to deny the state's claim to salvation—the claim that citizenship in a particular system gave man a virtuous or evil character. Augustine said that such distinctions between systems were futile and false, that Christian doctrine did not accept the absolute character or inner moral integrity of any political system.

In another aspect of his social philosophy, Augustine attacked the cyclical view of history that was fashionable in the ancient world. Greek and Roman historians believed that history kept repeating the same cycle of growth and decay, that circumstances recurred, that men stepped into the same river over and over again. In Christian theology, however, Jesus came to Earth only once. The Incarnation was a unique historical event, and so are all historical events unique. Augustine's affirmation of the Judaic linear historical concept (as against the Greek) had an enormous social impact. Belief in an inevitable, repetitive cycle must produce indifference to contemporary circumstances, but belief in uniqueness—the confidence that history is advancing to the singular triumph of the kingdom of God—produces a different attitude. Not only are men inspired to collect and record as many unique events as possible (writing more, and ultimately better history), but they are bound to adopt a meliorative philosophy. The primordial western cast of mind sees men marching toward a glorious future through the dregs of the present; belief in progress is the very heart of western thought.

To Augustine, the future triumph was religious; he perpetuated the Judaic, messianic, apocalyptic idea. He saw the Second Coming of Christ as the ineffable end of history, when men would be judged and the world that we know would dissolve in glory. Since the eighteenth century, westerners have secularized the progressive tradition of Judaism and of Augustine. They have invested social and political institutions with quasi-religious sanctions, believing that social change, political programs, and revolution will bring about the final triumph. Augustine might have deplored the secularization of his historical view, but one cannot deny his influence. The belief in progress inspired the restlessness and struggle for perfection that brought about the western hegemony over the rest of the world in the nineteenth century; for good or evil, the belief in progress and continual change had given the West its distinctive character.

The great contemporary dispute about the nature of the church forced Augustine to make a decision of enormous consequence to the medieval world. The North African Donatists of the fifth century believed in a church of the saints, a minority church whose members received God's grace before they could join the holy brotherhood. Augustine believed that everything important happened within the human heart, and he might have been expected to agree with the Donatists. However, he denied their views, insisting that the church was catholic, universal, and heterogeneous. Sinners and saints would be separated at the end of history, not by the institutional church. The brotherhood of saints was real, but it was internal; its collective group was not the Christian church but the City of God.

Augustine's church was the instrument of the Holy Spirit, and its mission was to act in this world. In Platonic terms (which Augustine often used), the church was the earthly embodiment of the Holy Spirit. Its function was to absorb, to educate, and to reform the world, and it could not do so if it was against the world or retired from the world. Augustine believed that churchmen had to work in the world and slowly, painfully transform it.

Thanks largely to Augustine, the Christian church of the fifth century made the difficult decision to be a universal institution. Had it decided otherwise, it might not have survived the next five hundred years. The church had to absorb the great lump of German barbarism into Christendom, and after five centuries of struggle it did succeed in converting most of Europe to Latin Christianity. This conversion was accomplished only because churchmen went into the world and lived and struggled with violent people. Many monks did not retire to the cloister; they carried Christianity to the frontier. Augustine did so himself, believing that the church (like Jesus) had to suffer with the world in order to save it. Those who love God also love humanity, and Christians were willing to encounter men on their own ground. This willingness has been the glory of Roman Catholicism, and Augustine was largely responsible for its tradition of service. He recognized that the empire was gone, that the barbarian world was real and pressing, and that churchmen must live with violence and misery to convert and educate and transform society—the great mission of the medieval church.

There are obvious ambiguities and contrary directions in Augustine's thought. These contradictions may have occurred partly because he was a busy man who did not have time to work everything out; at the end of his life, in fact, he published a small book that questioned some of his earlier ideas. More important, they reflect deep ambiguities within Christianity itself (and within Judaism). Christian doctrine never resolved all its tensions, which may have saved it from becoming a congealed, monolithic system like Confucianism. The conflicts themselves eventually became productive impulses toward conflict and change.

Augustine was both a radical experientialist and an authoritarian institutionalist, and both these tendencies were strong in medieval Christianity. Augustine claimed that the all-important fact was the relationship of the individual to God, that the Heavenly City was a mystical, internal, secret, spiritual brotherhood whose membership would be revealed (and whose reign begin) only at the end of history. The institutional church was different, but it was essential to the fulfillment of God's purpose. It was essential for everyone to belong to the church, to obey its leaders and to take the sacraments. The instrument of the state could and should be used to force people into the church, which must have absolute authority in this world. Augustine's ideas were used to justify the Inquisition, the persecution of Jews (although Augustine himself discouraged that), and the destruction of heretics and heresy. Membership in the Heavenly City was won only when a man's will was directed entirely toward God—and membership in the earthly church was implied as a prerequisite, although Augustine was sufficiently liberal to hint that certain good men (the Hebrew patriarchs) who had not had the privilege of church membership might still belong to the Heavenly City.

Obviously, two different kinds of Christianity were involved in Augustine's thought. One was the mystical, internal Christianity of individual religious experience; the other was Roman, legalistic, and institutional. The two concepts or doctrines can be combined (although ultimately they do not entirely mesh) in a theory that Augustine never fully stated, but that was worked out by later thinkers. These men, inspired by Augustine, saw the domination of the church in the world as a necessary, temporary condition. The church was a historical institution, and at the end it would disappear like other institutions. Only the Two Cities would survive the end—one for eternal blessing and one for eternal damnation. Until that day the church must exist to communicate God's will and love to men. It is God's chosen instrument through which He acts on the world. In this theory the church was absolute not in an ultimate sense, but only in a relative historical sense, and the ultimate triumph of God's will and of the Heavenly City was an end that justified the church's immediate control over the individual conscience.

As a radical individualist (who must have half-consciously sympathized with the Donatists), Augustine said that all that mattered ultimately was the Christian experience, not institutional membership. The church was a temporary institution—this Augustinian doctrine paradoxically allowed the medieval church to excuse its own weakness. It was not the Holy Spirit, but only the vehicle of the Spirit, in which incompetence and corruption could be expected. The church was not the City of God but only a way station to the Heavenly City, and it could afford to be less than rigorous in its demands on its leaders. This was a useful doctrine in a violent, chaotic, underdeveloped society. The church was bound to be absorbed and corrupted by society to some extent, but a puritan, Donatist church would have been destroyed in resisting its violent environment. Augustine's interpretation of the church allowed it to face its own failings, to accommodate, and to socialize, and it allowed the church to be somewhat corrupted by participation in the Germanic world. But if the church had remained aloof from the primitive world, it would have betrayed Jesus' directions to preach the good news everywhere and in the face of all obstacles. Augustine's doctrine was socially realistic and well suited to the circumstances of early medieval life.

It is difficult to categorize Augustine as a conservative or a radical. Much of what he said sounds conservative in modern terms, but in an ultimate sense, if radicalism is defined as the refusal to accept conventional solutions, as insistence on confronting issues and getting to the roots of the problems, as determination to attain the salvation of humanity and not to accommodate to power and society, then Augustine was a great radical.

St. Augustine was much less favorably disposed toward the values of classical culture than his great contemporary Jerome. Augustine was a master of the Latin language, and he had been a teacher of rhetoric before his conversion in middle life. But partly on intellectual grounds and partly because he was, like Tertullian, a dour North African, he was highly critical of some salient aspects of the classical tradition. Yet he advocated on pragmatic grounds extensive Christian adoption of the Roman system of education and classical literature. He argued forcefully that the spiritual Israel of the Christian church, setting out on its pilgrimage to the Heavenly City, should "spoil the Egyptians"—that is, take from the classical tradition whatever it found necessary and advantageous for the achievement of its ends while abandoning the useless residue. He made specific suggestions on how this program might be carried out. The Roman system and curriculum of education ought, he said, to be preserved to maintain a literate church, and he advocated the preparation of compendia of the liberal arts, textbook summaries of those aspects of classical philosophy and literature that conformed with Christian doctrine. In his theological writings Augustine drew heavily upon Platonic philosophy.

The suggestions for the right relationship between Christianity and classical culture that Augustine set down had a tremendous influence in the early Middle Ages, and from the fifth to the eighth century Christian education followed the line he had set down: the continued study of grammar and rhetoric as the staple of the educational curriculum and a drawing up of compendia of the liberal arts. Christian education followed this line not only because of the force of Augustine's authoritative influence on Christian education, but because of the general cultural circumstances of that period. In the first place, as late classical culture became more and more sterile and academic, there was a general tendency even before Augustine to reduce classical thought to easily read summaries, or compendia. But such compendia were exactly what Augustine was urging for Christian education. In the second place, the harassed and relatively ignorant world of the period between the barbarian invasions and the meliorative Carolingian monarchy of the eighth century could not assimilate the full intellectual fare of classical culture. It could only imbibe the classical heritage through the media of compendia, summaries, and encyclopedias.

Thus, both St. Augustine's influence and the circumstances of the intellectual history of the West between the fourth and eighth centuries brought about the Christian church's receiving the classical heritage through the media of summaries and brief treatises on rhetoric and the liberal arts and sciences. The defects of the treatises are more obvious than are their merits. They are meager and jejune to the extreme; the scientific knowledge they provided was frequently derived from the realms of fancy and superstition. Yet inadequate as these encyclopedias of classical thought were, they provided the bridge between the fourth century and the flourishing Carolingian schools of the late eighth century.

The first of these encyclopedists and "Latin transmitters," as they have been called, was Martianus Capella, a contemporary of Augustine and a fellow North African. It is uncertain whether Martianus was a Christian—Christianity never enters his treatise—but medieval men certainly believed he was, and his work remained popular and influential well into the twelfth century. His treatise bears the strange title *The Marriage of Philology and Mercury:* It begins as an allegorical romance and ends as a textbook of the seven liberal arts. It was indeed Martianus Capella's treatise that fixed in the early medieval mind the number of the liberal arts as seven, although, of course, this number was supported by a biblical text from the book of Wisdom: "Wisdom hath builded herself an house, she hath hewn out seven pillars." And even the universities of the High Middle Ages organized their arts course according to Martianus' division. In Martianus' treatise the seven liberal arts (which appear initially as the seven bridesmaids to Philology) fall into two groups, one of three and the other of four arts. The threefold group (which medieval writers hence called the *trivium*) were the literary ones: grammar, dialectic, and rhetoric. The fourfold division (the *quadrivium*) were the "mathematical" or, as we may say, the nonliterary or technical arts: geometry, arithmetic, astronomy, and music. It is highly significant that medicine and law were omitted from the liberal arts by Martianus and hence from the arts faculties by the high medieval universities and even our modern liberal arts colleges. Like Augustine, Martianus argued that medicine and law were not "liberal" studies because they were concerned with "earthly" things— or, as we would say, they were applied, not pure, sciences.

To Martianus' treatise was added the encyclopedic work of two Italian scholars, Cassiodorus and Boethius, in the early sixth century. These scholars were both members of old Roman aristocratic families, and both rose to high positions in the government of the Ostrogothic king Theodoric. It was Cassiodorus' first intention, in working for the preservation of the classical heritage in the Germanic kingdoms, to found a sort of Christian university in Rome. The troubled political and social conditions of the time made this goal impossible, and he therefore sought to employ the growing monastic movement for this purpose. It was Cassiodorus who founded the first monastery that was a center of scholarship, as so many other monasteries later became. Cassiodorus' summary of the liberal arts was the result of the need to formulate a program of education for his monastic scholars. Although Cassiodorus of course believed that the ultimate aim of a monastic education was the study of theology, holy scripture, and church history, he claimed, in the now traditional way among Christian humanists, that for the proper attainment of this end, the study of the liberal arts must come first. Consequently Cassiodorus prepared a sketch of the seven liberal arts, a kind of syllabus of universal knowledge, and appended to it a bibliography of classical writings that would further the monks' liberal studies. His program was the basis of the curriculum of the monastic schools of the early Middle Ages, and thus it was an important contribution to the preservation of the classical heritage in the West. To read the classical works, he suggested, the monks needed copies; hence the slow emergence of some monasteries as kinds of publishing centers in which the selected classical texts were copied either for the libraries of these monasteries themselves or to be sent to monastic houses that were not so well equipped or advanced in scholarship.

Cassiodorus' contemporary, the philosopher Boethius, undertook to translate the entire works of Plato and Aristotle into Latin. He did not live to complete this work, but his translation of Aristotle's logic was the only text of the great philosopher available to the early medieval West and was therefore an important contribution to the preservation of some semblance of Greek philosophy in the early Middle Ages. Boethius' own treatise, *The Consolation of Philosophy,* is one of the few philosophic works of the period between Augustine and the eleventh century that still has anything to say to modern readers. It was written while Boethius was awaiting execution for treason against the Ostrogothic king, and it provided a neat summary of the classical ethical theories, with a dominant theme of stoicism.

The final great contributor to the classical heritage in the West from the fourth to the eighth century was the early seventh-century bishop of Seville, Isidore, who also came from an old Roman, non-Germanic family that moved from North Africa to Spain in the sixth century. Isidore exercised a great influence on medieval learning through a twenty-book encyclopedia called the *Etymologies.* This strange title reflects Isidore's belief, common in the early Middle Ages and the result of the prevalent concern with allegory and symbolism, that the road to knowledge lay through the origin of words. Isidore's philological knowledge was inadequate for etymological inquiries, and his work is riddled with fantasies and superstitions. Yet it was immensely popular and influential because Isidore did not confine himself to the liberal arts, but attempted to survey the whole range of knowledge of the Greco-Roman world, including medicine, biology, botany, and architecture. For early medieval men his work also had the advantage of systematic arrangement and succinctness. In spite of his numerous errors, he managed to carry over to the early Middle Ages a great deal of information derived from fields outside the pure liberal arts. He is perhaps not to blame if medieval scholars for several centuries treated his work with unnecessary respect and repeated without critical reflection his fantastic opinions, which he, in turn, frequently derived from writers of the late Roman Empire.

The so-called Latin transmitters were neither original thinkers nor masters of language. They were schoolteachers and textbook writers. Almost nothing they wrote is still worth reading for its own sake. But their role in the history of culture was a most important one. To these dedicated but mediocre thinkers was given the momentous task of fulfilling the program of Christian preservation of the greater part of the classical tradition. This program evolved out of the great debate on the values of classicism, which was one of the dominant themes of patristic thought between the second and fifth centuries. The great church fathers had decided in favor of a Latin Christian culture and rejected the radical puritanism that Tertullian represented. It was left to their humble successors from the fifth to the eight centuries to put this program into practice with the limited means at their disposal. These transmitters did their work just well enough for the church to remain literate and in touch with the classical heritage. There was an enormous falling off in the level of erudition and intellectual sophistication between Augustine and Isidore of Seville. But the Latin transmitters, however inadequate themselves as writers and thinkers, made possible the cultural revival of the late eighth- and ninth-century Carolingian world that witnessed a partial return, at least, to the rich and vibrant culture of the patristic age.

On the questions of predestination and free will, the medieval church departed in practice from the strictly Augustinian position. The problem of reconciling divine omnipotence and human freedom was not invented by Augustine or even by St. Paul, whose opinions on this question greatly influenced Augustine. The problem is already raised in the Old Testament and is, in fact, bound to arise in any theistic system. Augustine contended that men were responsible for their sins but not for their salvation. He explained damnation more in terms of Adam's fall than as a consequence of individual action. Man's nature was corrupt, and all men were condemned because of that nature. Without divine assistance, no man can escape from the limitations of human nature. There is no freedom *from* anything, but only freedom *to* live according to the ways of God, and this freedom is only the consequence of God's gracious gift. In other words, the only free men are those who live in accordance with divine will, who escape from the bondage of the human will because God has chosen them for salvation. Augustine developed this stern doctrine in the course of a dispute with the British monk and theologian Pelagius, who claimed that man merited salvation because he freely chose to live the good life or merited damnation because he chose to live a bad life. Augustine could not accept the Pelagian free-will position because he thought it negated the Christian doctrine of fallen man and detracted from the majesty of God.

But the church, in its pastoral work, found it hard to accept Augustine's position, which was too sophisticated and stern a doctrine to use in converting illiterate masses, because it did not seem to make salvation readily available to most members of the church. Already in the century following Augustine's death, some French bishops argued for a semi-Pelagian position. They held that salvation was dependent upon the grace of God, but they also said that members of the church could merit that grace. They wanted to be able to promise an immediate reward for moral action. Although the church officially accepted the Augustinian doctrine at the synod of Orange in 529, in actual practice the Augustinian teaching was watered down, and the Christian ministers in the Middle Ages frequently discussed salvation in terms that their parishioners could take as implying an extensive degree of human free will.

The medieval Catholic doctrine was set down by St. Gregory the Great at the end of the sixth century. Gregory took the sensible approach that whereas salvation was a consequence of grace, the individual Christian, in fulfilling the good works that the church advocated, was demonstrating that God's grace had come unto him. In actual practice this approach meant that if church members received the sacraments and followed the moral teachings of the church, they need not worry about salvation. This was not a gross violation of Augustine's position, but, it was not fully in accordance with what Augustine had taught. Augustine would never have accepted the performance of good works as a sign of the reception of divine grace. But Gregory was more concerned with the pastoral work of the church than with precise theological definitions. He wanted to assure his audience that any who became moral and practicing Christians merited salvation. It was hard enough to get people to do so; to advocate fulfillment of the church's teachings and still not be able to ensure salvation would have placed the church in a disadvantageous position in its struggle to Christianize European society.

To provide even greater assurance of salvation, the church by the time of Gregory the Great (died 604) had worked out a scheme of penance by which forgiveness for falling away from the church's teachings could be obtained. It was assumed that between heaven and hell there was an intermediary stage called purgatory. Only saints entered heaven immediately; all others had to be purified, and purgatory was the stage and place where this purification of souls, this punishment for the sins of people, who on the whole were good and who would eventually enter heaven, could be carried out. But it was possible, so the church taught from the time of Gregory, for this purifying penance to be performed in this life, thereby making the travails of purgatory easier and shorter. Given that the church wanted to ensure its members that it possessed all the means for salvation, and given the legalistic conception of the deity, it is easy to see how this idea of purgatory and this doctrine of penance evolved.

Gregory's teaching of penance was institutionalized by the church and became an essential part of church life in the Middle Ages, as it is even today. Penance had four stages: first, a perception of sin and a dread of God's punishment; second—and of the greatest importance—regret or contrition at having sinned; third, a confession to an ordained priest, an intentional humiliation to the penitent; and finally, the actual doing of penance, "giving satisfaction" for the sin committed and confessed.

There were many varieties of satisfaction. It could be a contribution to the church, physical toil on behalf of the church, a pilgrimage, or even artistic work that had some religious purpose. It is well known that in the late Middle Ages certain controversial practices crept into institutionalized penance, such as the famous indulgences against which Luther fulminated. But by and large, penance had a sound psychological, as well as religious, purpose. It allowed a church member to obtain forgiveness for many sins, and it thereby reassured him of the safety of his soul and allowed him to look forward to the afterlife with less fear and dread. Through Gregory's doctrine of penance, the church qualified Augustine's deep pessimism about the fate of the greater part of mankind. In fact, it played a great role in making Latin Christianity into an optimistic religion that was therefore more appealing to early medieval society.

Another cultural front in which the implication of patristic doctrine were developed in the fifth century was political theory. In the last decade of the fifth century Pope Gelasius I, making use of the opinions of both Ambrose and Augustine, tried to formulate a political theory for the church. Gelasius was pope from 492 to 496. By this time it was clear that there would be a split between the pope and the emperor. The Byzantine church and emperor had adopted a heretical doctrine on the nature of Christ and wanted Gelasius to accept it. The pope excommunicated the patriarch of Constantinople and attacked the whole foundation of the power of the emperor. He went on to define the relationship between secular and spiritual authority. He said that there were figures in the Bible, such as Melchizedek and Christ, who were both kings and priests, but that since the time of Christ, authority was divided between the church and the state. There were two institutions of authority in the world: the prelates exercising sacred power, and the kings and emperors holding royal power. The authority of the church was *auctoritas* (legislative), while the authority of the secular rulers was *potestas* (executive power). In Roman law auctoritas was superior to potestas. In any good state it was thought that the legislative should be supreme over the executive. Therefore Gelasius separated church and state, on the one hand, but implied that the church was ultimately superior on the other hand. He wanted to separate the church and the state because of the immediate problem of keeping the emperor out of church affairs, but he left a loophole by implying that the legislative institution (the church) gave power to the executive (the emperor). Ambrose had said that because the pastor was responsible to God for the souls of his flock, he *must* interfere with the king if the state violated the morality of the church. In Gelasius' terms, the church ultimately had auctoritas.

At least the Gelasian theory could be used to argue, against the Byzantine system of caesaropapism, that the spiritual and temporal powers are entrusted to two different orders, each drawing its authority from God, each supreme in its own sphere and independent of the other within its own sphere. But it had further implications that allowed for its expansion into the doctrine of papal supremacy over the emperor. The Gelasian theory gave the papacy an organized doctrine whose implications could be made both moderate and radical, as circumstances permitted. Until the eighth century the papacy was content to draw only the more moderate conclusions from the Gelasian theory. Hard pressed by the Byzantine emperor, the papacy was content to claim the independence of the jurisdiction of the church from royal control. Its battle to enforce this claim was a long and hard one, and in the end it met only with limited success. But in the eighth and ninth centuries the papacy began to make use of the radical aspect of the Gelasian theory. In the eleventh century Pope Gregory VII fully drew the radical implications from the Gelasian theory, demanding not only the separation of church and state, but the supremacy of papal authority over all kings.

Can we not see in this double aspect of the Gelasian theory the two legacies of political Augustinianism? Augustine implied that the spheres of the Heavenly City (reflected in the church) and the state are entirely separate. This, too, is the view of Gelasius in the more moderate aspects of his theory. But Augustine also said that the moral sanction of the state is not intrinsic, but is derived only from the Heavenly City (reflected in the church). Thus Gelasius contended that the imperial potestas is derived from papal auctoritas in the radical version of his theory. The Gelasian theory is political Augustinianism in a simpler, more practical, and polemical form.

The foundations for the political thought of the following six centuries were laid down in the patristic period. I shall later examine in detail the long struggle between the idea of theocratic monarchy and the Gelasian theory, as well as the tension between the moderate and radical aspects of the Gelasian doctrine. Until the Aristotelian revival of the twelfth century, all disputes on church-state relations were argued along the lines of these political theories.

❧ CHAPTER THREE

The Age of the
Barbarian Invasions

I. The Germans

From the fifth century to the early part of the eighth century, western Europe and the Mediterranean world experienced invasions by various seminomadic peoples: Mongolian, Germanic, and Arabic. The effect of these invasions was three centuries of enormous upheaval and confusion, which resulted in the transformation of European government and society. The most serious invasions were the intrusions into the Roman world by the Germanic peoples—the so-called barbarian invasions—for, unlike the Mongolian and, for the most part, the Arabic invaders, the Germans settled in and determined the destiny of western Europe.

The word *barbarian* was used by the Greeks, to designate an alien, and therefore, by definition, someone inferior in culture to a Hellene. The Romans applied this in the pejorative sense to the people who came to live along the Rhine-Danube frontier. They also generically termed these people *Germani,* which was originally the name of only one of the tribes who lived beyond the Roman frontier. Another tribe was called the *Allemanni,* which later became the root of the French and Spanish terms for *German.* The Germans referred to themselves with a word that became the root of the modern *Deutsch* and *Teuton,* that is, *Theut,* which simply means "the folk" or "people."

Who were the Germans? Where did they come from, and why? What were their political and social institutions? These important questions exercised the energy and imagination of many historians, particularly in Germany where naturally the study of the *Völkerwanderungen,* or the migration of the peoples, has been encouraged by nationalist feeling. The literary sources, however, are meager, and all we know about the Germans before the first century B.C. has been derived from archaeological research. These studies revealed that the German invaders of the Roman Empire originally came from Scandinavia. Therefore, the later Vikings, whose migrations and invasions of western Europe came during the ninth century A.D., were ethnically the same people as the ones whom the Romans called the Germans. About 1000 B.C. the Germans began to move southward from their original homes in Denmark and southern Norway and Sweden. By 100 or so B.C., spreading south and west, they had reached the Rhine river, and somewhat later, perhaps in the first century A.D., they migrated into the Danube basin as well.

As the Germans began to press across the Rhine, they had an easy time pushing back the Celts, who were peaceful people given to agriculture, poetry, and song. The Germans would have conquered Gaul, as they later were to conquer Britain and to push the Celts into the Welsh mountains, had it not been for the arrival of Julius Caesar and the Roman legions in the middle of the first century B.C. After hard fighting, Caesar pushed the Germans back beyond the Rhine, and the Romans extensively colonized the southern half of Gaul. The Germans temporarily crossed the Rhine in the middle of the third century, during a period of transitory imperial breakdown, but the Rhine frontier was soon reconstructed. Until the final collapse of the Rhine frontier in 406 A.D., the only Germans who crossed the great river into Roman territory were the tribes who were allowed to become federates or mercenaries in the imperial army.

By the second century A.D. the Danube basin was heavily settled with Germans, who pressed on the imperial frontier in this region as well. The Germans along the Danube were dominated by the two great divisions of the Gothic nation: the Visigoths, who lived nearest the frontier, and the Ostrogoths. In the third century A.D. the Danube frontier also was temporarily broken, but the Goths were driven back beyond the Danube before the end of the century. It was not until 376 that any of the Goths were again allowed to cross the Danube river.

There is no positive evidence of the causes of the Völkerwanderungen. We can only surmise the causation a priori. The Germans left Scandinavia partly because of a shortage in food supply that was due to the growth of the population and partly because of continual wars between the tribes, in which the losers were driven from their homeland to seek a new place to live in the south. As the Germans approached the frontier of the empire, they came in contact with the wealth, advanced technology, and pleasant climate of the Mediterranean. They sought to get into the empire not to destroy it, but to participate in its higher standard of living.

The nature of the early Germanic political, legal, and social institutions has aroused great interest among historians, and many tomes have been published on the subject. This great interest is due not only to nationalist motivation, but to the fact that so many of the later institutions of medieval Europe seem to have developed out of, or at least are related to, the early Germanic ways of doing things. Particularly in the nineteenth century, when scholars subscribed to the organic view of political and legal development—that the fully developed institution is predetermined by the shape of the microcosmic primitive institutional form—they devoted enormous energy to studying early Germanic institutions.

The sources for the early history of the Germans are meager. The most valuable description of Germanic life by any ancient historian is the *Germania* of Tacitus, written in A.D. 98, which comes to about fifty pages in modern print. Tacitus never visited the German frontier, but as a powerful aristocrat he was able to talk to soldiers who had returned from the front, and he had access to governmental officials and documents. Unfortunately, his purpose in writing the *Germania* was not entirely the impartial dissemination of information. Rather, he wanted to present to his readers the contrast between the primitive, unspoiled, energetic, virtuous Germans and the decadent, oversophisticated, effete Romans. His idealized picture of the virtuous German *hausfrau* may be taken with a grain of salt. There is, however, enough circumstantial detail about German political and social institutions in the *Germania* to make Tacitus' work extremely valuable to the historian.

The second group of sources consists of the Germanic folk poetry. Unfortunately, of this group only the Anglo-Saxon poem *Beowulf* has come down to us in a form close enough to the original version to be usable as a historical source. The great German cycle of the *Nibelungenlied,* which inspired the libretti for Wagner's operas, has come down to us only in a thirteenth-century version heavily overlaid by ideological concerns of that era. *Beowulf,* on the other hand, was written down by a cleric in the late eighth century; the Christian overlay is superficial, and the poem graphically reveals the ideals and mores of the upper strata of Germanic society. The social picture it presents can be confirmed by comparing the Germanic way of life it depicts with the mores of Scandinavian society presented in the Icelandic sagas and eddas. Although these sagas and eddas depict Scandinavian society in the High Middle Ages, they reveal a society at a similar stage of development. This stage can also be found in the Homeric poetry, which similarly is a product of what the English scholar H. Chadwick called the "heroic age."

A third group of sources for the early history of the Germans is the so-called Germanic law codes. These are not really law codes, but merely written statements designed to amplify the greater part of Germanic law that remained oral and customary. In spite of their drastic limitations, the Germanic laws, such as those of the Burgundians, the Franks (the Salic law), and the Anglo-Saxons (the "dooms"), contribute valuable information on Germanic political and legal life.

Finally, archaeological evidence has contributed to the historian's reconstruction of early Germanic life. Archaeology not only can trace lines of migration, but it often graphically reveals.the level of technology and culture that a particular German people attained. Thus the jewelry and other ornamental work found in the Sutton Hoo ship burial in eastern England in 1939 confirms *Beowulf*'s description of the ship burial of a great king and demonstrates the Germanic skill in metalwork. On the other hand, it must be admitted that the results of archaeological work on medieval history are often difficult to interpret, partly because the investigations of archaeologists of medieval civilizations, unlike those of Egyptian and Mesopotamian civilizations, are limited by the fact that the sites of medieval estates, towns, and roads are still usually very much in use, and therefore systematic excavation is usually precluded.

The picture of the early Germans has undergone great changes in the past four decades. In the 1920s and '30s it was fashionable to emphasize the similarities of German and Roman life and the continuity of institutions through the fifth and sixth centuries, with the result that the effects of the Germanic invasions on European government and society were viewed as relatively minor. The leading proponents of this view were the Austrian scholar Alfons Dopsch and the famous Belgian economic historian, Henri Pirenne. Dopsch, in his massive *Economic and Social Foundations of Western Civilization,* by means of dubious archaeological evidence, tortured misreading of texts, and special pleading, concluded that there was little difference in the level of culture and economy of the Germans and the inhabitants of the Roman world. The Germans in Dopsch's work appear as good Austrian burghers who were ready to sit down for a bit of Wiener schnitzel and Löwenbrau with their fortunate Roman hosts. Likewise, Pirenne contended that the German invasions did not mark a cataclysmic break in the economic and social development of western Europe. He attributed cataclysmic proportions not to the Germanic invasions, but to the expansion of Islam in the eighth century.

Since the Second World War, not surprisingly due in great part to the work of French scholars, the Dopsch-Pirenne interpretation of the early Germans has been seriously undermined, and we have returned to the earlier view of the disastrous consequences of the Germanic invasions.

E. Salin presented archaeological evidence that directly contradicts the material marshaled by Dopsch in favor of his thesis. P. Courcelle, in his brilliant *Literary History of the Germanic Invasions,* convincingly argued that we ought to take seriously the lugubrious views of contemporaries on the significance of the invasions and the actions of the Germans. R. Latouche, relying on the research of other scholars as well, presented a synthetic view of early medieval economic development that restores the central importance of the German invasions; he also wrote the best general history of the barbarian migrations and settlements.

From the limited written and archaeological evidence that we have about the development of Germanic society from the time the Germans came to settle along the Rhine-Danube frontier to the establishment of the Germanic kingdoms in western Europe—let us say from 100 B.C. to A.D. 500—two fundamental facts emerge that must be realized if one is to understand correctly the Germanic society in the time of the invasions. The first fact is that the degree to which the Germanic peoples across the Rhine-Danube frontier had been influenced by Roman civilization differed markedly from one tribe to another. Some had reached about the same stage of civilization as that which they saw across the frontier along the border of the empire. They devoted themselves to agriculture, engaged in extensive commerce with Roman merchants, and accepted Christianity, although by chance it was actually Arian Christianity—they were converted by Arian missionaries in the fourth century. Such Germans only wanted to enter the empire as federates and participate in the life of the Mediterranean world. They greatly respected Roman power and had no intention of bringing harm to it. This level of civilization was reached especially among the Goths living in the Danube basin, who were in contact with the richest and most heavily populated part of the empire.

On the other hand, it appears evident that other Germanic peoples had been little affected by Romanization and were fierce, ignorant, and barbarian in every sense of the word. Most, though not all, Germans who invaded the empire from across the Rhine appear to have belonged to this category. The reasons for this situation are not clear. It would seem, however, that these Germans remained in closer contact with their Scandinavian homeland, which was, of course, nearer. In addition, there were a greater number of German peoples stacked up against the Rhine frontier, so that those who were farther back from the frontier tended to be progressively less affected by contact with the empire. Thus the Franks were more violent and less civilized than some of the early invaders, such as the Burgundians. And the Anglo-Saxons, who came directly from the North Sea area, were untouched by Romanization.

Thus it is not easy to generalize about the Germanic peoples. Some were at a social and cultural level equivalent to the peasants of the empire; others indeed impress us as primitives, in spite of attempts by modern German historians to portray them as quite civilized.

The second fundamental fact that should be borne in mind in regard to the Germans of the period of the great invasions is that their political and social institutions did not remain static between 100 B.C. and A.D. 500, but underwent profound changes. Like many primitive peoples Germanic society was first organized according to blood ties—the family and kindred. Although these ties were preserved to a considerable extent up to and through the period of the invasions (as shown by the blood feud in criminal cases), another form of social organization was slowly emerging, and it became central in the period of the invasions (400–600). During this period, the bonds of kinship were weakened, a process that shows itself in the prevalence of strife between relatives. The binding force formerly wielded by kinship was increasingly transferred to the relationship between "lord" and "man," between whom no bond of blood relationship was necessary, only the bond of loyalty. Thus during this period the importance of kinship decreased and the use of the bond of allegiance, or loyalty, greatly increased.

This great change in social organization went along with, and facilitated, a change in political organization, the growth of an irresponsible type of kingship resting not upon the folk but upon military prestige. To the war leader who could provide booty went the allegiance of his followers, but these followers might not even belong to the same kindred or folk as their "king."

Thus, during the period of the Germanic invasions, and at least partly the result of the circumstances of a people on the move and engaging in conquest, there was a social and political transformation within Germanic society itself. Many of the able-bodied fighters were emancipating themselves from the tribal obligations and bonds by which a society of primitive peoples is usually governed. Furthermore, the princes who emerged among the Germans during this period were freeing themselves, to a large extent, from any public control by the tribe or community. As long as they could feed and enrich their soldiers, they retained the allegiance of these warriors, and neither the king nor war band had any social or political obligation to the folk as a whole. We shall see this situation appear many times among the Germans during the Germanic invasions; the Frankish kingdom of the sixth century arose out of this social and political context.

The basic German political institution at the end of the fourth century can therefore be said to be the *comitatus,* or *gefolge,* consisting of the chief or king and his war band, who accorded him their loyal service in return for his protection and largess. A chief who reigned for a long time or who achieved great military success was able to create a royal dynasty. The dynasty would claim descent from Woden, put on sacred airs, and possess the kingship as its private property. But succession to the kingship could not be by primogeniture; this was not an early Germanic idea and was restricted by the original power of the war band to give or refuse loyalty. At the death of the king, the leaders of the folk would come together and choose that member of the royal family who was most "throne worthy," that is, the best fighter. While strict hereditary succession appeared rapidly in the new Germanic kingdoms of the fifth and sixth centuries, the right of election by the folk remained a strong medieval political tradition for many centuries, especially in areas where the original Germanic institutions remained influential. The election of the king by the leaders of the community was operative in England in the late ninth century in the case of the elevation of the famous King Alfred to the English throne, and as late as 1199 the infamous King John owed his crown, in part, to the electoral principle. The Germanic electoral principle played havoc with dynastic continuity in the medieval German empire and survived to the nineteenth century. The perpetuation of this aspect of early German institutions was due, at least in part, to the fact that it found favor with the church, which recognized in the principle of throne worthiness a way of exercising a veto on royal accessions.

The comitatus was an extremely weak nucleus for the medieval state. In fact, it can be said that the Germans had no concept of a state, no idea of public authority, and no understanding of loyalty other than the personal loyalty to a chieftain. With some exaggeration, it may be said that the Germanic political theory was not above the level of that held today by marauding street gangs. The distance from the sophisticated Roman idea of public authority and office and of loyalty to an impersonal emperor who represents the state was vast, and the decline in the level of political thinking was precipitous. To understand the disastrous histories of all early medieval kingdoms, it must be remembered that the medieval state had to develop from this abysmal and crude level. Early medieval political construction was constantly challenged and inhibited by the inability of the Germans to conceive of public, as distinct from personal, loyalty. It is not surprising, therefore, that the medieval state did not begin to take shape until the eighth and ninth centuries and did not experience its first era of greatness until the middle years of the eleventh century. And even this late and partial success was made possible only by the addition of ecclesiastical (in part, Roman) conceptions of authority and loyalty to the primitive Germanic political tradition.

The Germans' original legal conceptions were scarcely more advanced than their political ideas. The purpose of the Germanic law courts and forms of procedure was not to establish justice, which the Germans had no way of determining or even of defining, but simply to stop a fight. Rather, the aim was to inhibit the blood feud, to find an alternative for an aggrieved kin or family seeking vengeance. There were various ways of doing so, and the purpose of the law courts was simply to put these alternatives into operation. The first alternative was the payment of *wergeld* (man money), a monetary compensation to a family for the killing of one of its members or a smaller payment to an individual who had been maimed. The so-called Germanic law code consisted mostly of tables of wergeld: so much to be paid for the slaying of a nobleman, so much for a freeman, so much for a serf, so much for an arm, so much for an eye, etc. The compensation required was often heavy, and even then the aggrieved kinsmen or individual did not always have to accept it and might prefer to gain satisfaction by vengeance. It was the court's duty to convince the plaintiff to take the wergeld and thereby preclude the outbreak of a blood feud. Nevertheless, blood feuds were frequent in early Germanic society. Such a feud in England as late as 1060 decimated whole families. Anyone who reads early medieval legal records knows that life then was nasty, brutish, and short. It was a violent society in which drunken brawls ending in homicide were extremely common, and the resulting blood feuds were a constant possibility.

Early medieval men did not think of a brawl resulting in homicide as murder. Their legal conception resembled that of the American frontier, at least as represented in popular literature and entertainment. To kill a man in a fair fight meant that you had to reckon with his kinsmen, but it was not murder. Murder was killing someone by stealth—a homicide in which the killer was not known for certain. Such a situation put heavy pressure on the Germanic law court, for if the court did not designate the murderer, the slain man's kin would take justice into their own hands and exact vengeance from whomever they suspected. It was therefore necessary to hold a trial and prove the guilt or innocence of the suspect. But neither the methods of proof and assessment of evidence devised by Roman law, which involved a thorough inquiry by a panel of judges, nor the later common-law jury system were available to the Germanic law court. The leaders of the Germanic court would not have known how to assess the evidence even if it were presented to them. This left two methods of proof: the ordeal, involving divine decision, and compurgation, involving the swearing of oaths.

In proof by ordeal the odds were weighted heavily against the defendant. In the ordeal of hot iron the defendant was required to grasp a red-hot piece of metal. His hand was then bandaged, and if after three days the burns were on the way to being healed, the defendant was innocent; otherwise he was guilty. The ordeal of hot water worked similarly: The defendant was made to put his arm into a caldron of boiling water and lift a stone from the bottom; his arm was then bandaged and in three days it was inspected to decide his guilt or innocence. The ordeal of cold water was a favorite in England, where there were numerous rivers and brooks. The defendant was tied hand and foot and thrown into the water; if he sank he was innocent, and if he floated he was guilty, on the premise that water, a divine element, would not receive a guilty person. In the feudal period an additional ordeal, trial by combat between the accuser and the defendant or their "champions" (representatives), was instituted. Because guilt or innocence was decided by the strength of the champion, trial by combat did not leave the question sufficiently to divine judgment; a wealthy man could hire the biggest thug in the country and systematically get rid of his enemies by bringing false accusations. Hence, trial by combat was severely limited by the powerful monarchies of the twelfth century, although technically this method of proof was not abolished in England until 1819. Although the three common ordeals were rough on the defendant, it must be emphasized that they were intended to be biased in this direction. For the defendant who was put to the ordeal—in England this was called "making his law"—was either someone who was reputed to be a criminal by his neighbors or was a person of low social status. A wealthy or highborn person of good reputation in his community was seldom put to the ordeal. The ordeal, therefore, was a method of providing divine support for popular prejudice. Through the ordeal each folk court was able to cleanse the community of the ill famed, who sooner or later were bound to be accused of a crime and put to the ordeal.

The church was initially hostile to the Germanic ordeal, but if it was to influence the early medieval legal process, it had to accept this common method of proof. After the Germans were converted, the church imposed a religious sanction on the ordeal: Before going to the ordeal, the defendant appeared in church and swore on the Bible or a holy relic that he was innocent, while the priest admonished him to confess his guilt so as not to damn his soul and lose eternal as well as mortal life. We think that in many cases this brainwashing resulted in confession and that thereby an element of rationality was added to the crude legal process. A defendant convicted by the ordeal was hanged on the spot, hanging being one of the Germanic contributions to civilization. At times in the early Middle Ages the church succeeded in having kings substitute maiming for the death penalty. Medieval medicine being what it was, the loss of a limb frequently amounted to a slow death in any case. It is also doubtful that the community courts actually followed those humanitarian pronouncements.

Compurgation was a privilege of a defendant who had popular opinion on his side, and this usually meant that he was wealthy or highborn. It greatly favored the defendant, for by this method of proof the defendant simply denied his guilt under oath and produced a certain number of oath helpers, preferably of high social status, to swear that his oath was a true and good, or "clean" one. Although the church warned about the perils of perjury, we know that it was common in proof by compurgation. A guilty man who had important relatives or a powerful lord who were willing to lie for him would never be convicted. The conditions of compurgation further attest to the underlying fact that the Germanic criminal process was class biased. The poor, the unfree, the lordless were lucky if they did not end on the gallows, whereas the rich and well connected could come to this end only through the most flagrant and repeated crimes, and even then usually only when their victim was from the upper strata of society.

It is apparent that little can be said in favor of the early Germanic legal process. Yet German law made one great contribution to western civilization in its political implications. Roman law found its origin in the will of the despotic emperor and favored political absolutism. The king had no control over Germanic law; his only legal function was to see that the community courts met and decided cases, and even in this regard his contribution was often negligible. Germanic law was based on the principle that law resided in the folk, that law was the custom of the community, and that the king could not change this law without the assent of the community. Because of this difference between Germanic and Roman law and because England, even in the High Middle Ages, remained relatively untouched by Roman law, the Victorian historians found the origin of English parliamentary institutions and the idea of the rule of law in the forests of Germany. Although it has been fashionable among twentieth-century writers to scoff at this interpretation, there is an element of truth in it. The Victorians, with their organic conception of institutional development, erred in thinking that the great oak of English liberalism grew *inevitably* out of the acorn of German law. There was nothing inevitable about this development; in 1200 England appeared to be going in the direction of absolutism, and it took centuries of experience and political strife before the legislative supremacy of Parliament triumphed. But it is true that from German law England received a heritage of the legal supremacy of the community over the king. All western European countries could have drawn upon the same legal tradition. But after 1100 the Roman principle of legal absolutism slowly won out on the Continent, whereas England alone preserved the early Germanic idea that law resides in the folk, rather than in the will of the king.

II. The First Century of the Invasions

From a simple comparison of the population of the empire and the number of Germans, it would be hard to explain why the Germanic tribes were successful in establishing themselves on Roman soil in the hundred years that followed the Visigothic crossing of the Danube in A.D. 376. The population of the empire at this time was 50 to 70 million people. Comparatively, the Germans were few in number. The largest tribes, such as the Visigoths, had only about a hundred thousand people, including women and children, and could not have put more than twenty thousand fighting men into the field. The total number of Germans who came into the empire during the first century of the invasions could not have equaled more than 10 percent of the population of the Mediterranean world.

It must, of course, be remembered that the Roman government faced a great variety of political, economic, and military problems. The Roman army consisted mostly of proletarians and Germans, and the German generals in the service of the western emperor turned out to be unreliable in many cases. Furthermore, the empire had an extremely long frontier to defend, so that in any one place (west of Constantinople, at least) the German armies were substantial in number compared to the Roman defenders. A large army had to be maintained in the East to hold back the Persians, who steadily threatened the eastern defenses from the third to the seventh centuries. It must also be remembered that those regions of the western empire that were more distant from the Mediterranean coast were thinly populated, and hence German settlement in many regions of the Latin-speaking world had a strong impact on the demographic situation.

The impetus for the German invasions came in the 370s from the invasion of the West by Mongolian tribes called the Huns (known as the Hsiung-hu in their Asiatic homeland). Until the seventeenth century, western Europe was to be periodically threatened by nomadic Asian invaders; the Turks were the last of these invaders, and the Huns were the first. It is believed that in the second or third century A.D. the Huns lived in what is today northern China or Mongolia. Certain internal changes in the Chinese political situation forced them to move westward. They tried to invade India, but were repulsed. They then moved with great rapidity westward and passed north of the Caspian and Black seas and down through southern Russia into the Balkans. About the middle of the fourth century they broke into the Danube basin and easily defeated and subjugated the Ostrogoths. They struck terror into the hearts of the Germans, who as yet made only limited use of cavalry and were unable to withstand the Hunnish armies, which apparently fought entirely on horseback. A contemporary Roman historian described the Huns as invincible devils who not only fought but even lived on horseback; he claimed, no doubt on the basis of stories he got from the Germans, that the Huns did not even dismount to eat, but warmed raw meat under their saddles and kept going.

The terrified Visigoths, who lived closest to the Danube frontier and who desperately sought a way of avoiding the fate of their Ostrogothic kinsmen, begged the eastern emperor to allow them to cross the river and find refuge on Roman soil. The emperor granted this request, and the first large-scale migration of a German folk into the empire took place peacefully in 376. Almost immediately there arose all those problems involving the settling of displaced persons with which we are familiar in the twentieth century. The Visigoths claimed they were being cheated by the Roman governors and businessmen, and the Roman population in northern Greece was scarcely overjoyed by this influx of barbarian immigrants. After two years of bickering, the desperate Visigoths revolted and fought against the emperor. The overconfident emperor entered battle with insufficient preparation and without bothering to bring up his cavalry; in consequence his army was soundly beaten, and he was killed. This battle of Adrianople in A.D. 378 can be said to mark the real beginning of the German invasions, for whereas the Visigoths were pacified soon after by Theodosius I and the immediate damage was slight, they had demonstrated that a Roman army could be beaten by a Germanic tribe.

After the death of Theodosius I in 395 the Visigoths again became restless. They were dissatisfied with the lands in Greece that the emperor had given them, and they doubted the good will of Theodosius' sons toward them. The great emperor was succeeded, in the East and West, by his two sons, who were immature and stupid and who were surrounded by venal courtiers who were incapable of dealing with the explosive situation that was bound to develop. The Visigoths meanwhile had chosen as their king a certain Alaric the Bold, one of the most aggressive and competent of the early Germanic leaders. Alaric had no intention of destroying or even impairing imperial power; he simply wanted good lands for his people. The Visigoths, it may be said, did not want to destroy the empire; they wanted a homestead act, and all the trouble they were to make for the emperor in the following quarter of a century, which had the effect of shattering imperial power in the West, could have been avoided had the emperor initially granted their modest requests. But the silly and ill-advised emperor refused to make any concession whatsoever, and Alaric was left only with the recourse of waging war against the Roman authority that he, in fact, greatly respected.

The Visigothic invasion of Italy, which followed in the first years of the fifth century, was more in the nature of a picketing demonstration than actual warfare. The Visigoths were reluctant to inflict any damage on the Roman power, while, the head of the western imperial army, the German general Stilicho, was lackadaisical in his dealings with the Visigoths. Stilicho prevented the Visigoths from marching down into Italy, but he made no effort to drive them from the empire or even to push them back beyond the northern boundaries of the Italian province. The terrified emperor fled to the impregnable fortress of Ravenna, which was, however, off the main road into Italy, and hence played little role in the calamitous events that were to follow. In A.D. 406 Stilicho withdrew his armies from the Rhine frontier to bolster the Italian defenses against the Visigoths. A motley group of German tribes poured across the Rhine into France, Spain, and North Africa, and within thirty years these provinces were lost to the emperor. Therefore, the year 406 marks the most important turning point in the first century of the Germanic invasions.

It is not easy to determine what was in Stilicho's mind, but in any case he was murdered in 408 by jealous aristocrats with the approval of the incredibly stupid emperor, and henceforth the road to Italy lay open to the Visigoths. In 410 Alaric's army took Rome and held it for several days in an attempt to blackmail the emperor into accepting the Visigothic demands for a homeland. It was this famous "sack of Rome" that so exercised the imagination of contemporaries, including St. Augustine; as Augustine pointed out, the Visigoths actually inflicted little damage on the city. It was Alaric's intention to march his people to the foot of Italy and then to cross over and settle in the rich province of North Africa, but on the Visigoths' march beyond Rome their great king died. He was succeeded by his brother-in-law Ataulf, who announced the reconstruction of the empire under Gothic leadership, a policy that was later put into practice by the Ostrogothic king Theodoric. To symbolize his policy, Ataulf kidnapped and married Theodosius' daughter, a vivacious and brilliant woman who enjoyed herself immensely as a German queen and who played a leading role in the confused diplomacy and politics of the following three decades.

Ataulf marched his people back into northern Italy and across into Gaul. Finally, in A.D. 418, the emperor granted the Visigoths their request and allowed them to settle as allies and dependents of the empire in western Gaul, from where they also spread across the Pyrenees into Spain. The Visigothic kingdom in Gaul was conquered and absorbed by the Franks in the early sixth century. In Spain Visigothic rule lasted until the Arab conquest in 711. The story of the Visigothic invasion of the empire is a mixture of farce and tragedy. Its disastrous effects could easily have been avoided, for at no time did the Visigoths wish to harm imperial power. That in the end the Visigothic migrations opened the door to a host of other German invaders was largely the fault of the imperial government.

Of the many German tribes who broke across the Rhine frontier in 406, the most important were the Burgundians and the Vandals. The Burgundians settled in the Rhone valley and contributed their name to French geography. They were a peaceful people, apparently quite adept at poetry. The thirteenth-century poetic cycle of the *Nibelungenlied* was ultimately derived from stories that originated in fifth- or sixth-century Burgundy. The Burgundians were absorbed into the Frankish kingdom in the early sixth century.

A much more fierce and primitive people were the Vandals, who, led by their king Gaiseric the Lame, marched across France, through Spain, and into North Africa. The awesome Vandals were besieging St. Augustine's city of Hippo when he died. By the fourth decade of the fifth century the rich province of North Africa had become the Vandal kingdom. The Arian Vandals mistreated the Catholic clergy and never gained the loyalty of the North African population. As a consequence North Africa was easily reconquered by the Byzantine emperor in the 530s, and the Vandals' influence on North African development was ephemeral and negligible. Nevertheless, the Vandals' conquest of North Africa was an important turning point in the process of imperial disintegration in the West. The Vandals turned out to be good sailors; almost as soon as they invaded North Africa, they formed piratical fleets and cut off the sea communications between Italy and the rest of western Europe. This action made it impossible for the imperial government to reinforce the imperial armies in Gaul and Spain, and it accelerated the establishment of new Germanic kingdoms on Roman soil. Already in the 420s the Roman legions had been withdrawn from Britain, leaving the native Christian Celtic population there prey to invasion by savage and heathen German tribes from across the North Sea.

The last victory in western Europe of an army carrying the imperial standard occurred at Chalons in Gaul in 451. At this battle the Hunnish invasion of western Europe, led by their terrifying king Attila, was repulsed, and the Hunnish empire disintegrated soon afterward. But even this last triumph of Roman arms was misleading because while the army that defeated Attila was led by a Roman general, most of his soldiers were Visigoths. After 451 the imperial destiny in the West moved steadily toward extinction. In 455 the last descendant of Theodosius died, and for the next twenty years the western emperors were merely the puppets of various German generals and chieftains who contended for mastery in Italy.

The victor in this struggle was a German general named Odovacar, who deposed the reigning emperor in 476 and chose not to replace him. When Odovacar realized that he could not take the imperial title for himself, he ruled the Italian population as the viceroy of the eastern emperor, but he called himself king of the Germans in Italy. Odovacar made use of an old Roman law on the quartering of soldiers to force the Italian landlords to give up part of their estates for the settlement of his heterogeneous German army on Italian soil.

During this first century of the Germanic invasions, what was the attitude of the Roman population to these great upheavals in government and society? Many people, disgusted with the despotism and heavy taxation of the later empire, were either indifferent to the invasions or actually welcomed the invaders. It was hoped that the primitive Germans would not be able to preserve the imperial taxation and police system, and, with few exceptions, their hopes in this direction were fulfilled. Letters written by Roman aristocrats in the early fifth century in Gaul show how hard they tried to ignore the momentous changes occurring outside the walls of their estates. But there were aspects of the invasions that immediately struck fear among the ruling class of the empire. There are contemporary reports of the atrocities inflicted on the Roman population, especially by the Arian Vandals in North Africa. Furthermore, when the prospects of imperial collapse became real, the indifferent aristocracy in some instances experienced a revival of patriotic feeling. The same types of Gallo-Roman nobility who had looked upon the early stages of the invasions with smug indifference suddenly, about the middle of the fifth century, formed armies of their own and maintained pockets of resistance until they were finally crushed by the Franks at the end of the fifth century.

The fact that the Goths and Vandals turned out to be Arians made the invasions a particularly difficult problem for the church. While Augustine interpreted the invasions as being the result of a providential plan for the eventual assimilation of the Germans into the Catholic church, St. Ambrose and St. Jerome looked upon the invaders with horror. Another Catholic bishop denounced the Germans as vermin who ought to be exterminated.

By the second half of the fifth century the Augustinian view was beginning to prevail, as pessimism and lamentations of disaster were giving way, among the leaders of the church, to growing hope. The work of Pope Leo the Great demonstrated the new opportunity for leadership that had come to the church as a consequence of imperial disintegration. It was becoming apparent that the end of the empire did not mean the end of the world or even the end of the Latin church.

The mood of the Roman population of the Germanic kingdoms in 480 was therefore one of watchful waiting. What attitude would the German kings finally take toward the church? Could they be converted to Roman Catholic Christianity? And there was always the possibility of reconquest by the eastern emperor, still waiting in the wings and declaring that his war of reconquest was only a matter of time. The Latin churchmen contemplated this possibility with mixed feelings: The emperor would be better than Arian German persecution, but they knew that he would attempt to subordinate the pope to his authority and dictate to the western church on doctrinal questions as he was doing in the eastern empire. Hence the formulation of the Gelasian doctrine at this time, as we have seen. Might not a German king, uncouth and violent but nevertheless a loyal Roman Catholic, be a better ruler for the Eternal City? These were the vital questions at the end of the first phase of the Germanic invasions circa 480. The answers to these questions would appear in the following century, during the second phase of the Germanic invasions, and would determine the destiny of western Europe.

III. The Ostrogothic and Frankish Kingdoms

By A.D. 480 three German kingdoms had been established on the continent of western Europe on the ruins of the Roman Empire, but none of them was destined to survive beyond the early eighth century or to have any significant impact on medieval civilization. The kingdom of Odovacar

in Italy was an ephemeral institution and collapsed under the force of the
Ostrogothic invasions in 489. In the Rhone valley the Burgundian kingdom was absorbed by the Franks and incorporated into their domain in
the 520s. The kingdom of the Visigoths stretched through western France
and all Spain. In the early sixth century the Franks also drove the Visigoths out of France.

The Visigothic kingdom in Spain affected Iberian history and culture
very little. The Visigoths were originally Arians, but converted to Catholicism in the late sixth century. The seventh-century Catholic bishops tried
to glamorize the Visigothic monarchy in Spain and to strengthen it with
the powers and sanctions of religion. In the eighth century the church
adopted the same policy with regard to the Frankish monarchy, with far-
reaching effects. But the Visigothic kings were so weak and incompetent
that not even the support of the church could save them. Despite the
efforts of the church, the Visigothic kingdom yielded instantaneously to
the Moslem invaders in 711. Until the eleventh century the Spanish Christian princes survived only in pockets of the far north of the Iberian
peninsula. The sole cultural legacy of the Visigoths is found in the work
of Bishop Isidore of Seville, who was not even a Visigoth but a scion of
the Italian aristocracy.

After the successive failures of all the initial German kingdoms the
question arose whether any permanent German kingdom could be established in western Europe. In the last two decades of the fifth century two
new kingdoms were created, and it appeared that the political destiny of
Europe would be determined by the shape and fate of these two new
entities. The Ostrogoths erected their kingdom in Italy, and the Salian
Franks became the masters of Gaul. To anyone who lived in western
Europe in the year 500, it would have appeared certain that the future lay
with the Ostrogoths. Theodoric, the king of the Ostrogoths, wanted to
revive Roman culture and reinvigorate Roman administration under his
aegis, and at the beginning of the sixth century it seemed that Theodoric
would realize this traditional Gothic policy of synthesizing Gothic and
Roman institutions. The Frankish kingdom did not appear to have an
equal opportunity for success, for its ruler, Clovis I, seemed to be a barbarian with no appreciation of Latin culture or of Roman government.
Clovis compared most unfavorably with the great Ostrogothic king as a
worthy heir of the Roman emperors. Yet the kingdom of the Franks did
survive perpetually while the Ostrogothic state collapsed soon after the
death of Theodoric in 526. With Theodoric gone, Italy was reconquered
by the Byzantine emperor Justinian, and the Ostrogothic kingdom disappeared from history. The leadership of western Europe therefore passed

by default to the Franks. Consequently, Ostrogothic failure and Frankish success were crucial for the development of early medieval Europe, and the causes of these decisive events deserve special consideration.

The Ostrogoths came into the empire from the Danube basin. They had been conquered and enslaved by the Huns in the 370s, but after the death of the Hunnish leader Attila in 453, they gained their freedom. Theodoric, whose name means "leader of the people" and who was one of the Ostrogothic royal family, had been sent while a young boy as a hostage to Constantinople, where he learned to appreciate Roman culture, law, and government. In the 480s he became king of the Ostrogoths through election by the folk.

At the end of the eighth decade of the fifth century Theodoric's policy of establishing a union of Roman and Gothic interests found favor with the emperor in Constantinople. The Ostrogoths had begun to threaten to invade the Byzantine empire. Instead, the wily emperor convinced Theodoric that he should lead his people into Italy, where Odovacar was beginning to assert his independence of the eastern empire. Thereby the emperor could rescue Byzantium from the Ostrogothic peril. At the same time he could bring Italy more firmly under the official jurisdiction of the eastern empire than was the case in Odovacar's reign, for Theodoric went to Italy with the understanding that the rights of the emperor in Italy would be preserved. The emperor considered the Ostrogothic king his lieutenant, and he expected that the Ostrogothic invasion would do nothing to decrease imperial sovereignty there, but would increase its strength.

In four years, between 489 and 493, Theodoric and the Ostrogoths destroyed the kingdom of Odovacar and conquered Italy. Theodoric set up his capital in Ravenna, in northeastern Italy, where several of the fifth-century emperors had already taken up residence. What was the legal position of Theodoric in Italy? It was substantially a continuation of the same system under which Odovacar had ruled. Theodoric's authority consisted of a delegation of imperial power to conduct the general affairs of the government and included a royal title to preserve his prestige over his own people. The Roman people were becoming habituated to a ruler who was the representative of a distant emperor in Constantinople and who was the head of the Germanic people quartered on their soil. Thus they came to accept the notion of a barbarian kingdom exercising general powers of government.

For over a decade Theodoric was satisfied with his role as representative of the emperor and as chief of the Germanic federates. Then he began to adopt a new policy, disquieting to the Byzantine emperor. He began to contemplate the eventual establishment of a Germanic kingdom led by the Goths, comprising both Gaul and Italy, perhaps even Spain. He inaugurated a policy of diplomatic marriages, which eventually could have resulted in such a great kingdom. In 493 he married the sister of Clovis and then gave one of his daughters in marriage to the Burgundian king. He also became the guardian of the Visigothic king, who was a minor. Theodoric seemed, little by little, to be emancipating himself from the distant emperor in the East.

The Byzantines had never renounced Italy because the Roman Empire without Rome was an inconceivable thing to them. Now the emperor became concerned that Theodoric would become too strong, and to counterbalance Theodoric's power, he recognized Clovis' hegemony over Gaul and established an alliance with the Frankish king. This was one of Theodoric's greatest errors. His attempt to make the Ostrogoths a Mediterranean power with influence in France and Spain as well as supremacy in Italy brought about the hostility of the Byzantine emperor and the recognition of the legal hegemony of the Franks in Gaul. This situation proved disastrous for the Ostrogoths when the Byzantine empire, under Justinian, regained enough military strength to attack Italy.

If we ask why Theodoric dared to undertake such a hazardous foreign policy, which in the end united the Franks and the Byzantine emperor against the Ostrogothic kingdom and resulted in its destruction, the reason for the great risk he took is evident. By the 520s, as a result of his internal policy, he thought he had obtained the loyalty of the Italian people and at least the neutrality, perhaps even the support, of the pope and the Catholic church.

From the beginning of his reign Theodoric declared that it was his intention to restore the vigor of Roman government and Roman culture and bring benefits to the Italian people. Such a policy was not new among the Goths; Ataulf, the second Visigothic king, had professed similar intentions. The novelty was that Theodoric had the opportunity to carry out this aim and that he took great pains to do so. His shrewdest move was the preservation of the bureaucratic system of the later empire, which had lingered on, in form at least, through most of the fifth century while the worthless last emperors were holding out in Ravenna. Now Theodoric made Ravenna his capital, completely restored the bureaucratic hierarchy, and recruited officials from the ranks of the Roman aristocracy. By 500 he had found the man to implement his internal policy— Cassiodorus, a scion of an old Roman family, a skilled rhetorician, an able administrator, and a great "press agent" for the Ostrogothic kingdom.

Cassiodorus advised Theodoric on how he might win over the Italian people and set about writing various works of propaganda, including an official *History of the Goths,* which would make Theodoric appear in the best possible light to the Italian people.

It was Cassiodorus who coined the slogan for the new regime—*civilitas*—which was stamped on the royal coins and proclaimed in numerous royal letters written by Cassiodorus. It was claimed that the Goths were not the enemies of civilization, but that the aim of the new government was to further and preserve Roman civilization. Nor in Cassiodorus' writings are the Goths ever referred to as "barbarians." In fact, in his *History of the Goths* Cassiodorus identified the Goths with the Scythians, a people mentioned in Greek mythology. Cassiodorus' *History of the Goths,* which has come down to us in Jordanes' abridgment, portrayed the Goths as being "almost equal" to the Greeks in culture. This gross historical misinterpretation was the result not of Cassiodorus' ignorance, but of his ideology. Similarly, the extremely rhetorical style of the letters that Cassiodorus wrote on behalf of Theodoric was the result of a conscious attempt to demonstrate that the Ostrogothic ruler was a defender of the classical tradition.

The program of civilitas was given considerable semblance of reality by Theodoric's domestic policies. An extensive program of public works was undertaken, and strict measures against brigandage were enforced; the resulting peace encouraged a return of prosperity in Italy, probably to the level of the late fourth century (or at least so we are told by the contemporaries). The Italian population continued to live under Roman law, while only the Ostrogoths used Germanic law. To his court Theodoric summoned the leading scholars of Italy and gave them his patronage—not only Cassiodorus but Boethius, another Roman aristocrat who became a high governmental official and began to translate Plato and Aristotle into Latin. Even a Byzantine court historian admitted that Theodoric treated the Italian population with laudable moderation and generosity.

There were two aspects of Theodoric's policy, however, that could not seem admirable to the Italians and that he was forced to maintain by his position as leader of the Ostrogothic war band: expropriation of Italian land for the Ostrogothic army and Arianism. The Germans were legally federates and were to be quartered on the land of the native Italian population according to the Roman law of "hospitality." Thus we find Odovacar ordering the Italian landlords to surrender one-third of their land to his soldiers, and Theodoric used the same policy. How else could he provide for his soldiers? We have little information that allows us to determine how the Italian landlords regarded this policy. Some historians have suggested that, in any case, many estates were vacant by this time as a result of the disorders of the previous century, so the amount of land that Theodoric had to expropriate was small. But the fact that Cassiodorus worked hard to justify this act on the grounds that the Goths were the Roman army indicates that the expropriated landlords must have felt some resentment.

On the question of the continued loyalty of Theodoric to Arianism, we historians are also perplexed by the meager quality of our sources. What did Arianism really mean to Theodoric? Theodoric built Arian churches; then who were these Arian priests? Presumably they were native Ostrogoths. About this we know nothing. All we can say is that Arianism had become the folk religion for the Goths, and they could no more give up their customary religion than they could give up their customary law. Theodoric did the next best thing; although he remained an Arian, he did everything he could to appease the Catholic church short of his own conversion. He allowed absolute freedom of religion; he went through a ceremony that implied that he recognized the authority of the pope not only over the Catholic church but over the city of Rome. By 520 it appeared that the pope had been appeased and that the church would continue to support the authority of the Ostrogothic king even after Theodoric's death. Hence his hazardous foreign policy would succeed because of his skillful domestic policy.

But in the last few years of Theodoric's reign the delicate balance of forces that he had created swung against him, and it was already apparent before his death in 526 that the collapse of the Ostrogothic kingdom could not long be delayed. Unfortunately, here again our sources are meager, but the dim outline of the changes that occurred is distinguishable. The key to the situation appears to have been the policy of the emperor. Through most of Theodoric's reign the emperor had been quarreling with the pope; these quarrels produced the denunciation of imperial authority made by Gelasius I in the last decade of the fifth century. The pope believed that the emperor had fallen into heresy and was trying to impose his errors on the church. An Arian who allowed freedom of religion was much to be preferred to the Byzantine emperor as a ruler in such instances. Then, in A.D. 518, there was a change of dynasty in Constantinople. The great aim of the ambitious new ruling house was the reconquest of the West. For this end all else must be sacrificed. The emperor Justin I declared his acceptance of the theological dogmas held by the pope (even though he thus alienated many of his subjects), and the emperor and pope appear to have come to a secret understanding while the pope was acting as Theodoric's ambassador in Constantinople. A considerable number of Roman aristocrats threw in their lot with the pope and Byzantine emperor, including the leading official Boethius. Probably they were worried that Visigothic kinsmen of Theodoric, who were still vehemently anti-Catholic, had become leading courtiers at Ravenna.

Theodoric discovered the conspiracy, and his reaction was violent. For some time he had been worried about the succession to the throne (untimely deaths in his family had left only a woman and a child as possible successors), if there was not to be a contest for the throne by the leading Ostrogothic generals. In the last two years of his reign Theodoric abandoned civilitas. He imprisoned the pope and executed Boethius and several leading members of the Roman aristocracy. But his kingdom was doomed. In the decade following his death the Byzantines began their reconquest.

In his personal qualities Theodoric was the greatest German king before Charlemagne, and his policy of civilitas parallels in many ways the aims of the Frankish monarchy in A.D. 800. Theodoric's failure to establish a permanent kingdom was therefore of the greatest consequence to medieval Europe. Theodoric was able to establish in his lifetime a de facto supreme power in Italy, but he did not destroy the continuity of Roman political ideas and political institutions in Italy; indeed, he had no intention of doing so, for he himself had the greatest respect for the glory of Rome. He wished to reconstitute the empire in the West, but under the rule of a Gothic king.

His policy turned out to be mistaken. He aroused the fear of the Byzantine emperors that the Ostrogothic kingdom would become so powerful that the reassertion of Byzantine authority in Italy would become impossible and that the Ostrogothic kingdom would emerge as a great Mediterranean power to compete with Byzantium for domination of the Mediterranean world. At the same time, because of his respect for Roman institutions and ideas, Theodoric made no attempt to break the continuity of Roman civilization and political organization in Italy. He allowed the Ostrogoths to remain an alien band of Germanic soldiers who played no part in the political and religious life of the country. As powerful as the Ostrogothic monarchy seemed to be in his day, he left his successors in an impossible position. They were left prey to a counterattack by the revived military power of Byzantium under Justinian, but Theodoric had not gained for the Ostrogothic kingdom sufficient loyalty among the Italian people to withstand the Greek reconquest.

The early history of the Franks exhibits marked contrasts in every way with the Ostrogothic development. The Franks were much less in-fluenced by Roman culture—their kings were markedly inferior to Theodoric the Ostrogoth—yet the Frankish kingdom survived the confu-sions of the fifth and sixth centuries. It became the largest and most important kingdom to be created on what had been Latin soil, and there-fore until the tenth century the political development of western Europe, and to a considerable extent its cultural and ecclesiastical history, was determined by the destiny of the Frankish monarchy.

There were at least two important branches of the Frankish people; the one that was to play the important role in history was the Salian Franks, whose original homeland lay in what is today west central Ger-many. The Salian Franks lived far beyond the Rhenish frontier and had little contact with the Romans, either economically or culturally. Unlike the Visigoths, they had not been converted by Arian missionaries, and when they entered the empire they were heathens. In Frankish society the independent free peasant predominated; a class of nobility, if there was one, was not powerful, and even in the early sixth century the Frankish army consisted mainly of peasant infantry, with little use of cav-alry. The only civilized aspect of early Frankish society was an interest in agriculture. Because of this interest and because, like all Germans, they wanted to get closer to the wealth of the empire, the Franks obtained from the emperor Julian the Apostate, in the middle of the fourth century, the right to settle along the northern border of the empire in Flanders. Here the outstanding characteristic of Frankish migration immediately became apparent: Unlike the other Germanic invaders, the Franks inten-sively colonized their new homeland. They devoted themselves to agri-culture and left a strong demographic, economic, and linguistic impact on the region.

Our only important literary source for the early history of the Franks is the comprehensive and detailed work of Bishop Gregory of Tours, written in the late sixth century. Gregory's information was naturally fullest on the period closest to his own day, but from oral traditions he was able to provide fragmentary information on fifth-century Frankish history. Gregory's *History of the Franks,* in spite of certain weaknesses in style and the author's vehement prejudices, is the fullest account we have of any Germanic people. We also have the benefit of place-name evi-dence for the early history of the Franks. The study of the linguistic roots of the place names of Flanders and northern France allows us to con-struct the pattern of Frankish migration southward from Flanders into Gaul.

As Roman power disintegrated in the early fifth century, the Franks began to move slowly southward into imperial territory. Here again their settlement consisted not merely of a military occupation, as was the case with other Germanic peoples, but of extensive colonization. It is probably at this time that one family began to exercise leadership in the Frankish folk and was elevated to the privileged position of a royal dynasty. Until the middle of the eighth century the Frankish monarchy was regarded as the private property of this one family, irrespective of the personal inadequacies of many of its scions. The Frankish royal family, as was common among the Germans, claimed descent from the gods, and in tradition they ascribed the founding of the family to a certain mythical hero named Merovech. The fifth-century Merovingians varied in quality; some of them appeared to have been quite inadequate as warriors and leaders, but what characterized all the early Frankish rulers as late as A.D. 500 was their intense hostility toward Roman civilization. It is probable that for a decade or so in the mid-fifth century, the Franks came under the domination of one of the last Roman generals in Gaul. This "very hard yoke of the Romans," as it is described in the prologue to the Salic law, when combined with the native savagery and barbarism of the Franks, accounts for their hatred of the Romans. This negative attitude finds no parallel among any previous Germanic invader of the empire, as R. Latouche emphasized.

By the eighth decade of the fifth century the Franks had intensively colonized the northern part of Gaul, stretching north from the old Roman city of Paris. As they moved into the central and southern regions, they encountered a relatively dense Gallo-Roman population, and the Frankish influence on language and institutions was consequently small in this part of the country. Because the Gallo-Romans greatly outnumbered the invading Franks, the native vulgar Latin continued to be the language of the whole country, and even the Franks themselves rapidly adopted the Roman tongue.

With the disorganized condition of fifth-century Gaul, the Franks needed only a strong leader to advance from their northern stronghold to conquer the whole country, and this leader was found in the greatest of the Merovingian kings, Clovis I (481–511), whose long reign established Frankish hegemony west of the Rhine. In the pages of Gregory of Tours, Clovis' crude and savage qualities are painfully evident; at the same time, he appears as a formidable war leader and a shrewd strategist. After crushing the Gallo-Roman armies for the last time, Clovis subdued other Germanic peoples who had been living along the west bank of the Rhine. He then prepared for further conquest by receiving baptism, along with his whole army, at the hands of the archbishop of Rheims. Although later shrouded in legend of one sort or another, the reason for Clovis' conversion in 496 was simple: He saw that if he would accept the Catholic religion, he would be the only orthodox Germanic king in Gaul—in fact, in all western Europe. Thereby, as the Catholic champion, he would find it easier to gain the allegiance of the Gallo-Romans as his conquests proceeded. Furthermore, by his conversion he would gain the support of the episcopate, the only political, economic, and moral power that still existed throughout Gaul. The enthusiasm of Gregory of Tours, the spokesman for the Frankish church in the sixth century, shows not only that Clovis guessed rightly, but that he succeeded in surrounding himself with an aura of sanctity. In Gregory's account the savage leader of the Frankish war band is suddenly transformed by his conversion into a new Constantine.

His power reinforced by the support of the church, Clovis proceeded in his conquests. First he moved into the northwest, the land between the Seine and the Loire, and brought it under his allegiance, although this area remained separatist throughout the greater part of medieval French history. Finally Clovis was ready for his great enterprise: the conquest of Visigothic Gaul, Aquitaine. First he neutralized the Burgundians in the year 500, making a treaty of alliance with them. He left it to his sons to conquer Burgundy in the third decade of the sixth century. Although the Visigoths had established a vast kingdom stretching from Spain to Brittany and centered in Toulouse, their kingdom was vulnerable for many of the same reasons that brought down the Ostrogothic kingdom: They were merely military occupiers, not colonizers, and they were Arians. Clovis' victory over the Visigoths was quick and decisive, and the church gave him full support in his conquest. In Gregory's account the Frankish conquest of Toulouse is portrayed as a holy war. About the same time, Clovis effected an alliance with the eastern emperor against the Ostrogoths. In 507 the Frankish conquest of Gaul received the sanction of the emperor, who accorded Clovis the titles of consul and Augustus. These titles were purely honorary; they were meant to consecrate under a solemn form the alliance of the emperor and the Frankish king against the Ostrogoths and to recognize the supremacy of Clovis in Gaul. Thus, even though Clovis had no respect for Roman institutions and ideas, he was able to obtain imperial approval for his conquests.

One step remained in the foundation of the Frankish kingdom: the designation of Paris as the capital. Paris was within the area that had been heavily colonized by the Salian Franks. But the new Gallo-Roman-Frankish church was able to find a greater glory for Paris. At the beginning of the sixth century the tradition that St. Denis, the disciple of St.

Paul, had been the first bishop of Paris and had been martyred there took on a new importance. Clovis and the episcopate encouraged this legend; Paris became one of the holy cities of Christianity, and Montmartre the site of a popular shrine. By associating Paris with St. Denis, Clovis emphasized his position as the Germanic champion of Catholic Christianity. He well knew that this role had greatly facilitated the Frankish conquest of Gaul.

It was one thing to conquer Gaul, another to govern it. And the Merovingians turned out to be much less effective as rulers than as leaders of the Frankish war band. Under any circumstances the Merovingian dynasty was bound to run into trouble, given the inadequate political conceptions of the Germanic people. Furthermore, the Merovingians' kingdom, which included not only what is today France but a large part of the southern half of western Germany, covered far too much territory for the limited institutions of the sixth century. But the mistakes made by Clovis and his successors and the personal inadequacies of most of the Merovingian rulers served to make the situation much worse, with the result that by the early seventh century political power in France was in the hands of the provincial aristocracy, while the royal family held the crown and not much else.

Certainly the Merovingian ruler started out, in Clovis' reign, in a position of apparent strength—even, it could be said, of autocracy—and with enormous material resources. Clovis and his successors regarded the whole country as their personal possession. As a result, whenever a king had more than one son, he decreed that the royal fisc (property) simply be divided among his heirs and that the crown be similarly divided. The Merovingian rulers, holding the crown and its resources as their private property, further decided to rule without consulting anyone. The result was an almost incredible combination of primitive autocracy and anarchy. The Merovingian rulers did nothing for the people except to lead an occasional military expedition. They spent their time satisfying their gross desires and enriching their relatives and dependents. When there was more than one king, as was frequent in the century following Clovis' death, the rulers' chief interest was in fighting and killing each other, so the history of the Merovingian family in the sixth and early seventh centuries is mostly a bewildering tale of carnage and dishonor.

Almost no attempt was made by these primitive chieftains to maintain the Roman administrative system; almost no governmental documents survive from Merovingian France except a few badly drafted charters, and apparently the work of monarchy, so far as there was any, was carried on almost without literacy. The only aspect of Roman government that the

Merovingians tried to maintain was the taxation system, but they lacked sufficient loyal and able administrators, as well as any public feeling that taxes were worth paying. By 600 the vestiges of Roman taxation had all but disappeared, and a Merovingian king who wanted to get rid of one of his officials simply sent him out to collect taxes; the man would never be heard from again.

The Frankish and Gallo-Roman nobility, who were rapidly coalescing, were unanimous in their hostility to a monarchy that contributed nothing to their welfare and that presented a miserable spectacle of greed and incompetence. The Merovingians tried to win over some of the nobility to their service by granting them offices accompanied by benefices (benefits), that is, property attached to the offices to ensure the loyal service of the holders to the king. The favored nobility rapidly made these offices and benefices their private property and established themselves as provincial dynasts. Thus the title of duke, originally the king's local military representative, and count, originally a royal legal representative, were transformed into aristocratic titles that were inherited along with the accompanying benefices in the great aristocratic families.

By the early seventh century the monarchy was being robbed blind by the provincial aristocracy, and the Merovingians were left with only a shadow of their original power and only a small part of the enormous royal fisc of the time of Clovis I. Merovingian France presented a picture of an intensely disorganized kingdom politically, with all loyalty going to the local big shots and none to the king. The sixth-century kings, given to fratricidal war, made possible the aristocratic usurpation of the governmental power and wealth of the Merovingian family. Nearly all the seventh-century Merovingian rulers were either children, women, or mental deficients. Such "unthrone-worthy" rulers always signified the death of royal power during the early Middle Ages.

The church, or rather the bishops of Gaul who provided all the leadership in the church, was greatly disappointed by the Merovingian decline. The episcopate had established an alliance with Clovis, and great hopes were held out for mutual benefit from this union of the royal family and the Catholic bishops. But Clovis' successors turned out to be so incompetent and savage that by the end of the sixth century the bishops had taken their stand with the great nobility against the monarchy. One of the last of the Gallo-Roman bishops, Gregory of Tours, revealed the outlook of the late sixth-century episcopate in his *History*. Although Gregory was better educated than any of his episcopal colleagues, his perspective was nevertheless limited and selfish. He turned away from Clovis' successors in revulsion at their crimes and stupidity and bewailed the breaking up of the alliance between the monarchy and the church of the early sixth century. If only Clovis' grandchildren would emulate the Frankish "new Constantine"! But since Gregory saw little hope of the happy reconstruction of the old alliance between the royal family and the episcopate, he devoted himself mainly to building up the wealth and prestige of the church of Tours, just as any duke or count would devote himself chiefly to the interests of his own family.

Thus, by the end of the sixth century the political future of the Frankish kingdom, with its effects of localism and provincialism, had driven the episcopate to throw in their lot with the nobility. The church, by separating itself from Frankish kingship in the sixth and seventh centuries, made more certain the ever-increasing impotence of the Merovingian dynasty. Only the church could have provided sufficient leadership and literacy to have created an effective royal government in France. But the bishops, in pursuing this policy of separation from the monarchy, however justified they may have been in view of the gross personal inadequacies of the Merovingian family, had taken a step that harmed the church itself. The old Gallo-Roman church, which was renowned for its learning and devotion in 400, was notorious for its ignorance and lack of energy in 700. A major reason for this development was the tendency of Gregory of Tours and his colleagues to identify their interests with those of the nobility, whose selfishness and provincialism became characteristic of the seventh-century French episcopate. If the Merovingians had produced a few rulers of the caliber of Theodoric the Ostrogoth, the decline of the French church, as well as of the French monarchy, in the later sixth and seventh centuries would certainly have been averted.

The Merovingian monarchy played only a small part in influencing the great social changes that occurred in France in the sixth and seventh centuries. Although royal and ecclesiastical leadership between 500 and 700 did little to establish permanent institutions, the coalescing of Frankish and Gallo-Roman society during this period provided the social context with which later leaders had to contend. Frankish society in the early fifth century was organized along simple lines. The royal family and the nobility made up no more than 10 percent of the population of the Frankish folk. At the bottom of the Salian social scale was a group, constituting perhaps 20 percent of the population, in various stages of dependence, including personal slavery. The largest group in early Frankish society, taking in as much as 70 percent of the folk, consisted of the free peasants and soldiers. Under the pressure of the invasions and wars of the fifth century this large central group was polarized. A small part emerged as war leaders and joined the ranks of the nobility, while many were pushed down into unfree status.

The coalescence of the native Gallo-Roman population with Frankish society gave added impetus to the decline into dependence of many of the original Frankish freemen. As the Frankish nobility associated themselves with the Gallo-Roman aristocracy, they naturally attempted to force the Frankish peasant soldiers into a servile status that somewhat paralleled the bottom groups of the Gallo-Roman society. About half the population of Gaul in A.D. 400 consisted of people in an unfree status; at least 30 percent were slaves outright, and another 20 percent were the semi-servile *coloni*. At the top of the social scale were the wealthy landlords, from whose ranks also came the bishops and other important churchmen. This lordly class constituted somewhere around 15 percent of the population, and free peasants and the lower clergy made up another 15 percent. Finally, in 400, especially in the south of France where the Gallo-Roman population was most dense, there were many townsmen who were separate from both the landlord group and the various classes of peasants; these bourgeois, who engaged in trade and industry, probably constituted 20 percent of the population of Gaul.

By 600 the Gallo-Roman and Frankish societies had thoroughly mingled, and a new French social structure had appeared. Intermarriage between Frankish and Gallo-Roman families was both rapid and extensive. Gregory of Tours was the last bishop in Gaul who could claim descent entirely from the old Gallo-Roman aristocracy. The new French society was marked by a large group of dependent serfs at the bottom of the social scale, perhaps as much as 60 percent of the entire population consisting of the unfree of both the Gallo-Roman and early Frankish societies, as well as many depressed free Frankish peasants. The serf was not a personal slave to his lord; rather, he was bound to the land and retained certain legal and economic rights. The lord was supposed to protect him and to provide him with the means of economic sustenance, although frequently the lord neglected to do both. What he wanted of the serf was labor on his own estates and/or a share of the serf's own crop. There was great gradation within the serf ranks; some serfs were prosperous, while others were perpetually on the verge of starvation. Yet, if there was economic heterogeneity among the servile class, there was also legal uniformity: The serf and his family could not leave the lord's estate—the manor, as it came to be called; he owed the lord servile dues and labor, and he was subject to the jurisdiction of the lord's manorial court.

The serf was probably better off than the slave on the Roman estates;

he may often have had less to eat, but he had much greater personal freedom. Hence some historians have talked about the process of "social amelioration" in sixth-century France as the Roman slave system gave way to medieval serfdom. This judgment may be justified; total misery was replaced by partial misery. But the transformation of the economic and legal status of the peasantry did not raise the largest and lowest social group above an animal existence. At least until the twelfth century the lives of medieval peasants differed little from that of beasts of the field. They toiled, they bred, and they died. In the sixth century they even lacked whatever comfort and inspiration a local curate could provide because there was as yet no parish clergy. The religious needs of the peasantry were met by a priest who was occasionally sent out from the cathedral clergy of the nearest episcopal center. If a sixth- or seventh-century peasant saw a priest and received the sacraments once a year, he was doing well. Under these conditions it is not a surprise that the Christianity of the serf class was frequently nominal. Whether the peasant was baptized, he continued to worship the forces of nature, as he had always done. And even when he thought himself a Christian, his religious outlook was dominated by superstitions and fertility cults. The Christianity of the early medieval peasant was a hodgepodge of saints, relics, and demons.

This is what anthropologists call a religion based on *magic,* one that uses material things and tribal rituals to connect with the godhead. The more intellectual among the clergy in the sixth century challenged the high magical component of Frankish (and other Germanic peoples') religion for a time. But under the aegis of Pope Gregory I the Great, a subtle Roman aristocrat, the church relaxed its opposition and came to cultivate the popular religion of saint worship, relics, holy places, and incessant miracles. Gregory recalled St. Augustine's teaching that divine providence had sent the German peoples into the Roman Empire to be converted to the Christian faith. How was such a conversion to be meaningful, how could the episcopate and the missionary monks communicate with the masses except in terms of their own culture? There were ample precedents in the ancient church for a magical religion. For one, the church in the Roman Empire certainly had its share of holy men and women; now it had many more, some perhaps not quite as elevated and ethereal as in earlier days. In addition, the sacramental nature of the Christian faith was itself a kind of magical religion. To go from there and absorb a wide array of popular practices and a full-fledged culture of saints and relics was not difficult, and the clergy soon sensed that along this route lay power, influence, and social leadership for themselves in Frankish society.

By 600 the numbers of the middle group of both early Frankish and Gallo-Roman society had greatly declined. Probably no more than 10 percent of the peasant population including the lower clergy, had managed to maintain a free status. With the economic decline of France and the rapid deurbanization that took place following the Frankish invasions, the bourgeois class all but disappeared. Certainly not more than 3 percent of the French population were townspeople in 600.

At the top of the social scale was a small group of people who possessed great private wealth and power. This group consisted of the royal family and the great provincial aristocracy—the dukes and counts, with their vast estates and territorial authority. This class of great lords, in which the bishops and more important abbots may be included, could not have constituted more than 2 percent of the population. In addition to this great aristocracy there was a large group of modest lords and ordinary free soldiers, who made up as much as 25 percent of the population of France in 600. Some of this group were wealthy landlords, but others were merely hired thugs who made up the armies of kings and aristocrats.

The social structure that had emerged in France, the most important kingdom created on the ruins of the western Roman Empire, was dominated by lords and serfs. Urban life had almost entirely disappeared, and all leadership had passed to a small group of royal princes and great aristocrats. These men were interested mainly in building up the wealth and power of their own families. Most of their lives were spent in warfare, they were ignorant of the arts of government, they were blind to the ideals of justice and peace, and they had no understanding of economic problems; for them, Christianity was a system of magic, miracles, and hagiography. A comparison of these leaders of French society at the beginning of the seventh century with men of the quality of Theodosius I, Ambrose, Augustine, and Symmachus must lead to the conclusion that the collapse of the western Roman Empire was a political, economic, and cultural disaster of the greatest magnitude.

Yet there is one important exception in this gloomy picture. An important way in which Frankish society differed from that of the later Roman Empire was the greater degree of freedom enjoyed by women, at least of the nobility and class of freemen and soldiers and landlords. Women in Frankish society were more independent of their fathers and brothers, more capable of making decisions about their lives, and allowed to hold landed property and to play a role in political life than in Roman times. A feature of narratives of the Frankish monarchy in its first two centuries is the intrigues and manipulations that women of the

Merovingian family engaged in. That their intrigues seem just as volatile and violent as those of the men in the family may be regarded as another sign of the women's freedom and equality.

This liberated condition of women conflicted with Roman family, legal, and political practice, and some bishops regarded it as conflicting with St. Paul's myognyic view of women, whom he wanted, in Jewish fashion, to keep quiet and take a back seat in the churches and contemplate their divine dispensations to be chaste and perfectly celibate vessels of the Lord.

One of the intriguing aspects of medieval social history is to watch the tension between the Roman male chauvinist and the Frankish more egalitarian and liberated view of women. The more the Frankish nobility became Romanized and Christianized, the more the traditions of Roman law came into play and the more the status of women declined into subservience. But even in the eleventh century in frontier places like England or northern Germany there were still survivals of the independent German condition of at least wealthy high-born women that characterized Frankish society before 700.

Among Latinized countries of the West—France itself by 900—the autonomous figure of a woman of the lay nobility did not endure, but high-born wealthy Frankish women nonetheless created a viable legacy that persisted in the society of the High Middle Ages. The sisters, widows, and daughters of Frankish kings, dukes, and counts chose not to marry (or remarry again) and urged by their confident priestly confessors, took the veil and became nuns. In many instances these women brought with them to the nunneries they entered their private wealth in the form of land or treasure, which became part of the endowment of the convents. Frequently such a wealthy and aristocratic woman, if she entered the convent at a mature enough age, became the abbess of the community or succeeded to it eventually. It was considered good conduct in the ecclesiastical perspective for a widow or unmarried daughter or sister of a king or duke to found a convent, bringing with her other women of her class to establish a new community. The high-born abbess provided a substantial part of the nunnery's endowment and got her father and other relatives to provide additional support. The nunnery would thus become a favorite family charity. It would not only receive women from the same family into its community in later decades and generations, but gain further gifts from the family.

It was women of the Frankish nobility, building on some Roman precedents, who created a familiar-model institution on the medieval scene, the well-endowed nunnery with a community heavily populated by daughters of the rich and powerful, leading to an ambience that combined quiet devotion, moderate learning, and disciplined spiritual exercises with a kind of remote aristocratic fastidiousness. The nunnery was as much a facet of the culture of the nobility as a variety of religious experience.

A majority of the Benedictine nunneries of the twelfth century in France and elsewhere in western Europe exhibited this profile. The women of the early medieval Frankish nobility played an important role in getting this tradition started. It was the most continuing, least controversial, and universally admired form of medieval feminist spirituality. It is much admired by women medievalists today who trek the route of the backwaters of the Loire or Rhine seeking frail manuscripts and other memorabilia that recall this lost world of well-born and comfortable sublimity.

Justinian and Mohammed

I. The Nemesis of Byzantine Power

Western government, law, society, and economy had been transformed by the Germanic invasions. In the sixth and seventh centuries, however, western Europe was not left alone to work out the effects of these great changes. The life of the Mediterranean world was again to be disturbed during these two centuries by the ambitions of Greeks and Arabs. The Byzantine and Moslem impact on western Europe was less important than was the Germanic influence. But the aims of the Byzantine emperor Justinian I and Mohammed, the Prophet of Allah, played significant roles in the shaping of the new European civilization.

The eastern Roman Empire was the first to be invaded by the Germans who initially had broken the Danube frontier, which was defended by the ruler in Constantinople. The first great defeat of Roman arms at the hands of the Germans, at the battle of Adrianople, was suffered by the eastern emperor. Yet it was the western Roman Empire that disintegrated in the fifth century. Why, then, did the Byzantine empire survive the German invasions? In the first place the population of the eastern empire was much greater and much more urbanized than was the Latin-speaking part of the Mediterranean world. The Germans were not so ignorant as to be unable to realize that they faced an immensely more difficult task if they turned eastward after they crossed the Danube. Second, the eastern Roman Empire found the focal point of government, culture, and economy in the impregnable fortress of Constantinople. It took the Arabs, who were militarily far superior to the Germans, seven centuries to take Constantinople. Even in the second decade of the twentieth century a military and naval onslaught on the great fortress of the Dardanelles ended in total failure. Obviously the Germans would have had no chance against Constantinople, and they realized it. Yet there was no other way for the Germans to enter the wealthy part of the Byzantine empire except through Constantinople. The fifth-century western emperors also had an impregnable fortress at Ravenna, but the Germans easily bypassed this city and pushed on unhindered into Italy.

The third reason for the survival of the eastern Roman Empire was the ability of the fifth-century Byzantine rulers. These rulers introduced governmental reforms, such as the reduction of the heavy taxation imposed in the preceding century, to gain popular support. They encouraged education and inaugurated the first large-scale codification of Roman law. Following on the work of third-century jurisconsults, the Byzantine legists produced the initial extensive Roman law code in about A.D. 425, which is named after the emperor Theodosius II. Also, the Byzantine rulers were wise enough not to surrender their military powers to German generals, as did their western colleagues. Finally, it must be seen that the invasions had a cumulative effect on the power and wealth of the western emperor that was avoided in the East. As the empire lost its territory, it lost its income from taxes, which meant that the government found it harder and harder to maintain the army, and the shrinking military resources brought about the loss of even more territory, which further reduced imperial income. The government in Constantinople, avoiding this downward spiral, maintained steady tax resources throughout the fifth century. The position of Constantinople as a great center of East-West trade further contributed to the emperor's wealth.

In the fifth century the emperor took great pains to husband resources; he was preparing for the great day of reconquest. Since no emperor remained in the West after 476, the eastern emperor claimed that the Latin countries had reverted to his domain. He maintained that the *imperium* was inalienable, and he looked forward to the time when his resources would be sufficient to restore his effective authority at Rome. In the early sixth century the Ostrogothic attempts to create a pan-Germanic Mediterranean empire appeared to endanger the realization of Byzantine claims. Consequently, in 530 the emperor Justinian the Great launched the reconquest for which his predecessors had been preparing for a century.

Justinian I (527–565) had a greater influence on the development of Byzantium than any other emperor between Constantine and the tenth century. Justinian's uncle was a Macedonian general who had seized the throne. Justin I (518–527) carefully trained his nephew to succeed him on the imperial throne, and of all early medieval rulers Justinian was the best educated and possessed the greatest degree of native intelligence. If destiny had not called him to the imperial purple, he would have had a great career as either a lawyer or a theologian. He was a stern, puritanical individual, the hardest-working man in the empire and greatly devoted to the state. His wife Theodora, formerly a circus dancer, turned out to be an intelligent and vigorous woman who helped her husband considerably. The crowd in the Byzantine circus had organized itself into a strange combination of sport-fan clubs and political associations. Early in Justinian's reign, during riots between such rival circus groups that the emperor could not control, he felt compelled to abdicate the throne. Theodora, however, having risen from prostitute to empress, would not let her husband forsake his imperial eminence, and Justinian managed to regain control of the situation. His rule turned out to be both long and memorable on many grounds.

Two monuments of Justinian's reign still survive: the cathedral of St. Sophia (Holy Wisdom) in Constantinople and the *Corpus Juris Civilis,* the Justinian code. St. Sophia is the greatest achievement of Byzantine architecture. Its style is a perpetuation of the church architecture of the later empire, which, in turn, is modeled on the Roman basilica, but its size and massive quality make the cathedral of Constantinople one of the outstanding examples of medieval art and engineering. The inside of this magnificent structure is adorned with great mosaics that depict the emperor as the representative of God on Earth and thereby proclaim the ideology of imperial rule. Only in recent decades has the covering that the Turks placed over the mosaics been removed so we can at last fully appreciate the skill and resources that went into the creation of the great church commissioned by Justinian. The church of San Vitale in Ravenna, also constructed by Justinian, is likewise remarkable for its splendid mosaics.

Of all the emperor's work, the making of the *Corpus Juris Civilis* is the best known and most important in its impact on civilization. The Justinian code is perhaps the outstanding accomplishment in the history of jurisprudence. It consists of nothing less than the codification into a few volumes of the legal life of a great world empire over many centuries. It could only have been commissioned by an emperor who firmly believed that "there is nothing to be found in all things so worthy of attention as the authority of the law" and who was willing to devote all the necessary resources of his state to the inauguration and realization of this enormous enterprise. For the making of his *Corpus,* Justinian recruited the greatest legists of his empire and carefully set down for them a program of preparing a code of all Roman law on the grounds of rationality, coherence, equity, and the furtherance of imperial power. The Justinian code greatly favors absolutism: The emperor is considered the living law, and his will has the unchallenged force of law. "The emperor alone can make laws [and] it should also be the province of the imperial dignity alone to interpret them." In this autocratic doctrine, as well as in its rationality and organization, its overriding principles of equity, its adherence to a system of legal procedure in which the authority of the judge as the representative of the emperor dominates the court, the Justinian code stands in boldest contrast to Germanic folk law.

Although the Justinian code was not studied in the West in the early Middle Ages, after the middle of the eleventh century it slowly became the basis of the legal systems of all the European countries, with the exception of England. It is true that this reception of the Roman law brought unfortunate consequences politically in that it provided a juristic basis for the absolutism of the later Middle Ages and early modern times, but the other characteristics of the Justinian code are so much in line with enlightenment and rationality that it deserves to be recognized as an unsurpassed legal system. Furthermore, it must be remembered that if the Justinian code propagated the Roman-Byzantine doctrines of imperial autocracy, it is unlikely that any but an absolute ruler would have had the power and resources to carry through such a monumental work of codification to its conclusion. A comparison with the other great legal system of western civilization, the English common law, bears out the truth of this statement. Even at the present time the extent of codification of the common law is insignificant when contrasted with the work of legal synthesis and rationalization effected by Justinian I thirteen centuries ago.

St. Sophia and the *Corpus Juris Civilis* would have been monuments enough for most rulers, but they were not enough for Justinian. Partly because of the autocratic tradition of imperial rule; partly because of the febrile atmosphere of the court that adored the emperor as the deputy of Celestial Majesty; and partly, no doubt, because of his own unbounded ambition, he could not rest until he was the ruler of the Eternal City. He never questioned whether an exhausting war of reconquest was in the interests of the welfare of his people; that is not the way Byzantine emperors thought. Justinian did not even consider whether Byzantium really possessed sufficient resources to undertake a costly war of reconquest. He ignored the threats to Byzantine security represented by the Germans, Slavs, and Mongolians, who pressed on the Balkan frontier, and the powerful Persian empire to the East. Aroused by the ambitions of the Ostrogoths, Justinian determined, at his accession, to restore his authority "over the countries which the ancient Romans possessed, to the limits of both oceans, and lost by subsequent neglect." An emperor who could proclaim himself "pious, fortunate, renowned, conqueror, and triumpher, ever Augustus" in his great law code was not a man to consider the possibility of failure. Placing his "sole reliance upon the providence of the Holy Trinity," he despatched his army and navy to invade North Africa only three years after the beginning of his reign.

Even before Justinian exhausted the military and economic resources of his empire on Italian battlefields, he had, by his religious policy, dug the grave of Byzantine power. Since the fourth century the eastern empire had been troubled by religious problems. Theodosius the Great had extinguished the Arian heresy, but novel unorthodox theological doctrines again won wide support in Egypt and Syria in the fifth and sixth centuries, inspired, in part, by Platonic philosophy and, in part, by nationalistic feeling that found its expression in religion. Large masses of the Egyptian and Syrian populations abandoned the traditional doctrine of the Incarnation and, following the tenets of Platonism, subscribed to the Monophysite heresy that claimed that Christ had only one spiritual nature. This view was an anathema to the Latin church, which held that in the one person of Christ there were two natures, human and divine. This doctrinal dispute between the Latin church and the Egyptian and Syrian Christians placed the emperor in a difficult position. If he was to retain the pope's loyalty, without which he could scarcely hope to regain his authority in Italy, he could not afford to agree with the Monophysites. Consequently, at the Council of Chalcedon in 451 the emperor forced the Greek bishops to accept the Latin doctrine on the nature of Christ held by Pope Leo I. This did not, however, settle the issue. In the last decade of the fifth century the emperor went over to the Monophysite position, which brought down the wrath of Pope Gelasius I. In the 520s Justin I, preparing for the Byzantine invasion of Italy, reverted to the Latin position to gain papal support against the Ostrogoths.

Justinian continued his uncle's policy, but not just for political reasons. As a trained theologian he decided that the Monophysites were wrong on doctrinal grounds, and he launched a severe persecution of the Monophysites that lasted throughout his reign and was continued by his successors. The result was widespread disaffection in the great cities of Egypt and Syria, which, next to Constantinople, were the most valuable parts of the empire. By the end of Justinian's reign the persecuted Monophysites had been forced into a position of disloyalty to the Byzantine state, and Egypt and Syria were easy prey for any invader who would provide toleration for the heretical churches of the eastern Mediterranean. Whatever might be said of Justinian's doctrinal views on purely theological grounds, they turned out to be disastrous for the unity and security of the empire. As J. B. Bury, the great historian of the Byzantine empire, commented with respect to Justinian's religious policy, "a theologian on the throne is a public danger."

The long-range effects of Justinian's disputes with the Monophysites were thus most unfortunate for Byzantine power. In the short run they made possible the invasion of Italy, with papal support for the imperial army. In fact, in the early part of his reign, Justinian went so far as to issue a decree acknowledging the separate spheres of jurisdiction of the *sacerdotium* and the *imperium* to placate the pope. Of course, he later abandoned this acceptance of the moderate aspect of the Gelasian doctrine and returned fully to the traditional Byzantine caesaropapist position. But in 530 he was prepared to risk everything for the success of his great venture. To regain Rome, he was willing to hazard all the military and economic resources of his state, to antagonize large groups in the greatest cities of his realm, and even to swallow papal political doctrines. With so much at stake, the future of both Byzantium and western Europe hinged on the success of this great gamble.

The initial stage of the Byzantine invasion of the Latin world went well for the Greek armies. Under the command of Belisarius, a military genius, Justinian's forces easily conquered the Vandal kingdom in North Africa. In 533 Belisarius was ready to cross to Italy, pursuing the same invasion route as was to be followed by the allied armies in World War II. The bishop of Rome welcomed the Byzantine invaders, and, following papal leadership, the Italian population abandoned their Arian Ostrogothic rulers. The Ostrogoths had lost their great king, Theodoric, and they were not well led, but unlike the Vandals they had not forgotten how to fight. A quick Byzantine victory in Italy would have seen the fulfillment of Justinian's plan and turned the clock back to the fourth century. Instead, it took the Byzantines nearly three decades to destroy Ostrogothic resistance. This Gothic war, as it has been called, ruined Italy economically. Italy suffered a devastating blow from which it did not recover until the tenth century. By the middle of the sixth century a noticeable deurbanization had taken place; the great cities, such as Rome, Naples, and Milan, had suffered a catastrophic loss of population, and great Mediterranean cities were transformed into sleepy provincial towns. A contemporary wrote in about 550 that "Nothing remains for the inhabitants of Italy but to die." The Gothic war is the decisive dividing point in the economic and social history of early medieval Italy, a far more important break than the Germanic invasions of the fifth century. Italy declined rapidly from her traditional position as the cultural and economic leader of Europe and did not begin to regain this place until the late tenth century.

The long Gothic war was as great a disaster for the Byzantine state as it was for Italy. To carry through his grandiose policy of reconquest, Justinian was forced to revive Roman financial oppression in its worst form and to exhaust the resources of his empire. By the time his reign finally came to an end in 565, he was hated not only by the persecuted Monophysite groups in Egypt and Syria, but even by members of the imperial court who, at the beginning of his reign, had acclaimed him the greatest emperor. This widespread disaffection is expressed in the libelous *Secret History* of Procopius, who had been Belisarius' secretary. The emperor who had built St. Sophia and commissioned the *Corpus Juris Civilis* is portrayed by Procopius as "deceitful, devious, false, hypocritical, two-faced, cruel, . . . a faithless friend . . . a treacherous enemy, insane for murder and plunder." Procopius' censures reflect the inevitable reaction of an exhausted and ruined people against the leader whose excessively ambitious policies have led them to disaster.

While undertaking great campaigns in Africa and Italy, Justinian had done nothing to diminish the power of enemies closer to home. His successors were left to struggle desperately against the Persians on the eastern frontier and a host of Mongolian, Slavic, and German tribes pressing on the Balkan defenses of the empire. Finally the emperor Heraclius I (610–641) decided that a new policy had to be adopted to save Constantinople. He allowed the Bulgars, a Hunnish tribe, and various Slavic peoples to settle in the Balkans and in Greece, asserting only a nominal suzerainty over them. The emperor retained under his own authority only the fringe of the peninsula around Constantinople itself, and the ethnic composition of the Balkans changed even more radically than that of western Europe. Heraclius devoted all the remaining resources of his empire to saving Constantinople and Asia Minor from the Persians. In this he was successful. He inflicted a decisive defeat on the Persian empire, which had threatened Rome for several centuries, and the Persian state disintegrated.

Heraclius I was one of the greatest, but also one of the most unfortunate, of the Byzantine emperors. He rescued the empire from destruction and even inaugurated a revivifying organization. It could be said that he also saved Europe from the Persians, for if Constantinople had fallen to its eastern enemy, there was nothing to prevent a Persian advance into Italy. But already at the time of Heraclius' death in 641 a new and even more powerful menace had made its appearance: the Moslems from the Arabian desert. By the end of the fourth decade of the seventh century, the Arabs had conquered Syria and were in the process of invading Persia and Egypt. Three decades later they had swept on along the Mediterranean coast and conquered the whole of North Africa.

Thus, within a century of Justinian's death, the richest and most heavily populated parts of the empire had been lost to the new masters of the Mediterranean world. It is necessary to agree with J. B. Bury's hard judgment that "if any man can be regarded as responsible for this dismemberment of the eastern empire, it is the great emperor Justinian." As a result of his religious policies, the East was irrevocably disunited on religious issues. Egypt and Syria were alienated from Constantinople and were disinclined to resist the new invaders, who tolerated their religious beliefs. Furthermore, Justinian had so exhausted the resources of the Byzantine state that his successors did not possess sufficient men and money to maintain the eastern frontier. First the empire had to abandon the Balkans to the Bulgar and Slavs, and then it lost to the Moslems everything else except Constantinople and Asia Minor.

In Italy the reversal of Justinian's work was not as complete and catastrophic as it was in the East, but it came even more rapidly. Italy had hardly passed under Byzantine administration—in fact, Justinian was only three years in his grave—when a new Germanic people broke across the Danube frontier and invaded northern Italy in 568. These were the Langobardi, or the Lombards, one of the crudest and most primitive of all the Germanic invaders. The Lombards established a domain very different from the kingdom of Theodoric the Ostrogoth.

The Lombards never ruled the whole of Italy. They dominated the country north of Rome, except for the fortress of Ravenna, which remained in Byzantine hands until the middle of the eighth century. Most of the territory south of Rome continued to be ruled by Constantinople, although the Lombards had some outposts in the south as well, and Sicily was conquered by the Moslems in the seventh century. In this way Italy came to be divided among four rulers—the Byzantines, the Lombards, the pope, and the Moslems—and was not to be reunited under one ruler until the latter part of the nineteenth century.

The Lombards organized themselves into two or three large duchies and a few smaller principalities. Like the early Franks, they condemned Roman culture and government, with the result that the Roman administrative and legal systems disintegrated. The Byzantines had not had enough time to make the Justinian code well known in Italy. Roman law survived in its homeland only as the customary law of the native Italian population and was mixed with the miserable hodgepodge of Lombard folk law. In addition to their political and legal decrepitude, the Lombards remained Arians (for the most part) for a century after their conquest of northern Italy and thus were completely out of touch with the church and the papacy. In fact, even in the eighth century the pope looked upon the Lombard dukes as his bitter enemies. Perhaps no Germanic people had so little to offer to European civilization as did the backward Lombards. They contributed to Italian life only their name and their blood; the former affected the political geography of northern Italy, and the latter made the physical makeup of north Italians different from the Mediterranean physiognomy of the southerners. These were meager boons in exchange for Theodoric's policy of civilitas. Of course, Justinian had not intended to replace the Ostrogothic with Lombard rule in Italy. But as in his policy in regard to the eastern part of his empire, the risks that he took were so great that failure was bound to result in a worse condition than had existed at the beginning of his reign.

The emperors after Justinian never possessed the strength to attempt the reconstruction of the Roman Empire. Placed on the defensive by the Moslem armies, Byzantium drifted farther and farther away from Europe into a culture of its own. The Justinian code is the last great product of Byzantine letters to be written in Latin. Henceforth the civilization of the eastern Roman Empire consisted of a distinctive blending of Greek, Balkan, and oriental qualities.

Justinian's failure demonstrated to the men of the West that, as a result of the barbarian invasions, the Roman Empire could not be effectively reunited. Justinian, the greatest Roman emperor since Constantine, was the nemesis of Byzantine power. In the late sixth and seventh centuries Europe turned away from Constantinople, and the European peoples no longer looked to the hard-pressed Byzantine emperors and the essentially alien Byzantine culture for leadership and guidance. Hence, the most important consequence of Justinian's work for sixth- and seventh-century Europe was to bring to center stage the West's own men and institutions. The West was thrown back upon its own resources and had to find leadership in its own ranks: the church, led by the papacy and the monastic orders, and the Frankish monarchy. The short-lived alliance between the papacy and the Byzantine emperor had in the end created only a new disaster for Italy. It remained to be seen whether an alliance between the papacy and the Frankish monarchy could be effected with more fortunate consequences.

II. The Impact of Islam on Early Medieval Europe

The expansion of Islam was a decisive factor in medieval history. It divided the Mediterranean world into three civilizations and power blocks: the Byzantine, the European, and the Islamic. One of the major themes in medieval history from the seventh to the twelfth centuries was the relationship and interaction among these three cultural, economic, linguistic, and religious groupings. In various degrees each of these civilizations was an heir of the late Roman Empire. Byzantium exemplifies the most direct continuation of Roman law, administration, and thought. Western Europe also inherited many Roman traditions, and Islam absorbed some aspects of Roman imperial organization and the better part of the philosophy and science of Greece and Rome. However, Islam was also heavily indebted to oriental traditions, particularly those of Persia and Egypt. Oriental culture had also influenced the later Roman Empire, but Islam was the medieval civilization most directly in touch with the eastern heritage.

The triumph of Islam on the eastern and southern shores of the Mediterranean in the seventh century was the consequence of the final and successful attempt made by Arabic tribes to break into the Mediterranean world. There was nothing novel in an Arabic invasion of Egypt and Syria; there had been periodic invasions of the Fertile Crescent by nomads from the Arabian desert since the second millennium B.C., and the appearance of the Hebrews in Palestine may have been the consequence of one such northward thrust. The organization of the Mediterranean world under Roman rule had, however, put a stop to large-scale Arabic incursion, and the Byzantine empire, until the early seventh century, was successful in blocking the northward migration of the Arabian peoples.

What difference, then, can be seen in this new Arabic invasion that accounts for its success on a great scale? In the first place, the attack on the Mediterranean world came at a time when the two empires that could have blocked the path of migration and conquest were either dead or exhausted. Heraclius I had just destroyed the Persian empire, but Byzantium's military resources had been fully expended, and the imperial armies were able to offer only token resistance to the Arabs. Furthermore, great masses of the population of Egypt and Syria had been alienated by the religious policy of the orthodox emperor. Not being satisfied with this disaffection, Heraclius had undertaken a large-scale persecution of the Jews, who made up substantial portions of the population of Alexandria, Antioch, and other great eastern cities. Under these circumstances, the Arabic invaders could not but have succeeded, provided that they possessed a modicum of unity and organization.

And for the first time the warlike peoples of the Arabian desert had been united by a common faith and by religious authority. In this way Islam contributed the vital factor that made possible the rapid Arabic conquest of the richest provinces of the eastern Roman Empire. The old myth that the Arabs burst forth with the sword in one hand and the Koran in the other, offering the Mediterranean peoples either conversion or death, has long been discredited. In fact, the Arabs tolerated the religious practices of the Christians and Jews they conquered, only placing a head tax and limitation of political rights on those who would not recognize Mohammed as the Prophet of Allah, and therefore they had a vested interest in not hurrying the conversion of their subjects.

We should also forgo the assumption that Arabia was an impoverished desert. On the contrary, there were several important commercial cities, of which Mecca was the largest and most prosperous, and extensive commerce was carried on with the lands to the east. Great caravan routes stretched across the peninsula, and the picture we build up of Arabia at this time must include areas where urban and agricultural life flourished.

The Prophet was himself a city dweller. Mohammed was a poor member of one of the most prominent families in Mecca, and he made his living as the caravan manager for a wealthy widow many years his senior, whom he subsequently married. We know little about Mohammed that would serve to explain his teachings. He had a substantial acquaintance with Judaism and Christianity, which he picked up in his business relations; he was given to epileptic fits in which he experienced visions and received the word of Allah from the archangel Gabriel that he set down in the Koran; and, unlike Jesus of Nazareth, he was an extremely able political organizer and military leader. In his early career, while he was building up his authority, Mohammed did not refrain from following the principle that the end justifies the means. He relied for early support on Jewish tribes in the neighboring city of Medina, but when he no longer needed them, he turned against them. On one occasion he organized bandit attacks on passing caravans to finance his religious enterprises. Although many legends have been preserved in Arabic literature about the great Prophet, what we know of his personality comes mainly from the meager facts of his biography and Koranic doctrine. These accounts reveal him to have been an austere, devout, strong man with a smattering of learning and a moderate level of intellectual sophistication, and great personal courage.

Mohammed may not have been the most sophisticated and learned of religious thinkers, but no spiritual leader has ever founded a faith which has so rapidly appealed to such an enormous number of people. Of all the great religions of mankind, Islam is most suited to serve as a universal religion. The theology presented in the Koran is simple and easily comprehended. It envisions an omniscient deity who makes severe ethical demands on mankind, but who at the same time promises certain reward of eternal life in return for fulfillment of the divine precepts. The all-powerful and all-knowing Allah is a purely monotheistic deity; the Christian idea of the trinity is as much an anathema to the Moslems as to the Jews. Mohammed brings to mankind the word of God, but Mohammed is only the last and the greatest of the prophets, "the seal of the prophets," and he is not in any way a partaker of divinity. In the Koranic view Christ, like Abraham, is one of the great prophets who prepared the way for Mohammed, but the Christian theology of the Trinity, with its heavy debt to Platonism, is rejected by Mohammed in favor of pure monotheism.

"Islam" means "submission" to the will of Allah, and Allah demands from His adherents among mankind, if they wish to enjoy the great rewards which He promises, the fulfillment of a stern and puritanical code of conduct. The Moslem is to pray several times a day, and he is to make an attempt to go on a pilgrimage to the fountainhead of the true faith at Mecca at least once in his life. The Koran sets down a long series of regulations on the daily life of the Moslem. The Moslem is to refrain from drinking and gambling, he is not to practice usury in business, and generally he is to deal with his fellow humans according to the highest precepts of justice and mercy. The Moslem is to exercise charity toward his fellow men, and he is to be most generous in assisting the unfortunate and downtrodden of mankind. The Koran emphasizes the value of family life, and while, for the Moslem who can afford it, four wives are allowed, the most rigorous precepts of sexual morality are enjoined upon all members of the Islamic faith. Finally, the Moslem is required to give his life, if necessary, to further and protect the true faith, and for those Moslems who suffer such martyrdom the rewards of eternal life will be the most assured and the greatest. Holy war is one of the pillars of Islam.

The Koranic doctrine presents the most explicit theory of merits among any of the great religions of mankind. Those who follow the word of Allah and who serve God with sincerity and devotion are assured of eternal life and eternal happiness. The agonizing problems raised by the Pauline-Augustinian stream in Christian thought are completely avoided in the Koranic teachings. And even the occasional doubts that creep into Hebraic thinking on the question of merits and reward, such as are found in the Book of Job, are largely absent from Islamic thought. Furthermore, whereas the Hebraic concept of heaven is extremely vague and the Christian concept of heaven is purely ethereal and spiritual, the Koranic picture of heaven is both specific in detail and highly attractive to human desires. In fact, the Moslem is promised a heaven in which he can partake of pleasures denied him in this world; he may drink; gamble; and enjoy the company of beautiful black-eyed maidens, who are mentioned several times in the Koran as rewards promised to the most worthy members of the faith. The Islamic religion, then, is an optimistic one. It conceives of an omnipotent and omniscient God who requires a high and generous level of conduct, and for those who fulfill these precepts it promises the certainty of reward in a heaven that turns out to be a most attractive oasis. It is no mystery why this religion proved to be most popular among the Arab warriors, but its theology is austere enough and its ethic certainly rigorous enough to appeal also to men of the greatest education and sophistication, both in the medieval period and today.

In the eighth and ninth centuries the great majority of the Christian populations who lived along the eastern and southern shores of the Mediterranean went over to this new faith founded by Mohammed. It was a great blow for Christianity that its oldest and most intensive centers were lost to Islam. Yet, from the point of view of the history of human values, when the high quality of Islamic theology and ethics is taken into account, it cannot be said that a great disaster occurred. It is obvious that the Christians were eager to accept the faith of their conquerors and to free themselves from the civil disabilities that were imposed upon those who remained outside the Islamic faith. But the disabilities were not severe, and it is both sad and strange that the great churches of Syria, Palestine, Egypt, and North Africa so quickly collapsed before the attractions of conversion to Islam. It is true that the Christian churches did not entirely disappear and that fragmented Christian groups continue to exist in the Islamic countries to the present day, but two hundred years after the death of the Prophet, the influence and number of the great churches of the eastern and southern Mediterranean had become negligible. And it was not only the orthodox eastern church and the various heretical Greek churches that lost the majority of their followers to Islam; by A.D. 900 the Latin church in North Africa had all but disappeared, and the Spanish Christian church had suffered enormous losses. A Spanish Christian writer of the tenth century tells us that many of his younger contemporaries were converting to Islam not only because of their political ambitions but because of the attractions of Arabic literature and culture.

The effect of the expansion of Islam on the eastern and southern shores of the Mediterranean may be gauged from the fact that these regions are thought of today as the heartland of Islamic civilization, with attendant distinctive political, economic, and intellectual qualities. Long before Mohammed received the word of Allah from the archangel

Gabriel, the intellectual life of the eastern and southern coasts of the Mediterranean was dominated by St. Paul, Philo, Eusebius, and St. Augustine. Yet so complete and irrevocable was the effect of the Arabic expansion and domination that St. Augustine's North African homeland is thought of as profoundly Moslem and Arabic in language and culture.

The expansion of Islam occurred over exactly one hundred years— from the death of the Prophet in 632 until the battle of Tours in 732, when the Arabic armies penetrating into France suffered a defeat at the hands of the Frankish ruler. Many Arabic tribes became violent and restless after Mohammed's death, and the caliph, the "successor" of the Prophet, urged them to resume their marauding expeditions toward the Byzantine empire. By 638 Jerusalem had fallen to the Arabic armies, and in the following three decades the armies swept on through Syria and Persia and even reached northern India. Other Arabic armies went into Egypt; conquered Alexandria; and then moved rapidly across the Libyan desert into North Africa, which they easily took from the Byzantine governor. In 711 the Arabic armies, assisted by the fierce Berbers of the North African desert who had rapidly been converted to Islam and Jews who has suffered persecution in the hands of the Spanish church and monarchy, inflicted a complete defeat on the Visigothic king and became masters of Spain. The Christian princes managed to hold out in the Pyrenees until the tenth century, when they began the slow reconquest of the Iberian peninsula from the Moslems, which was not completed until the fifteenth century. Until the twelfth century the Moslem position in Spain was secure, and they were masters of the greater part of the peninsula; until the tenth century, in fact, nothing was heard from the petty Christian lords who barely managed to survive in the mountains.

It may be that the Arabs had now fully expended their resources and that they would not in any case have conquered France, but their defeat at the battle of Tours in 732 put a stop to their further advance to the north, and they remained satisfied with Spain. Meanwhile, in 717 the Arabs made their last great assault on Constantinople before the fifteenth century and were unable to take the great fortress on the Bosporus. The Arabs quickly became masters of the Mediterranean and conquered Sicily and Crete, and they attacked Constantinople from the sea. But the citadel on the Dardanelles was able to withstand the Moslem onslaught in part because of a new weapon that the Byzantines had developed: the so-called Greek fire, a form of incendiary bomb that the Greeks used to inflict great damage on the Moslem fleets. Constantinople thus managed to survive the Arabic attack and thereby saved western Europe from Moslem conquest via the soft underbelly of the European peninsula. Yet, of all its great and wealthy eastern provinces, Byzantium had managed to hold on to only Asia Minor. The harassed emperor was now forced on the defensive, and there was no possibility of the exhausted Byzantine state undertaking a war of reconquest against the Arabs for another two hundred years.

Until the middle of the eighth century, the extensive territory that the Arabs had conquered was under one rule. The caliph made his capital in Damascus and ruled these vast territories and peoples with an autocratic government modeled on the oriental monarchy of Persia. In the eighth century the non-Arabic peoples who had been conquered and had converted to Islam became dissatisfied with their subject position and demanded a share of the government of the vast Arabic empire and equal citizenship with the warrior caste that had come from Arabia. Finally, in the middle of the eighth century the subject peoples revolted against the caliph of the Omayyad dynasty, who ruled from Damascus, and a new dynasty, the Abbasids, who were mainly Persian in background seized the title of caliph and set up a new capital in Baghdad.

The supplanting of the Omayyad by the Abbasid dynasty was a signal for revolt and political decentralization throughout the Islamic world, and by the end of the ninth century, instead of one great Arabic empire, the Islamic world was divided into several states. The rulers of these states continued to respect the caliph as the successor of the Prophet, but the political power in the Islamic world had now fallen into the hands of various despotic princes. Among these princes was the ruler in Spain, where the Omayyad dynasty alone had managed to prevail. The Mediterranean world was now united by the Arabic religion and language, and it formed a great international economic system, but the Arabic civilization was no longer a political entity. From the eighth century the term *Arabic* identifies a great civilization on the eastern and southern shores of the Mediterranean to which many peoples—Greek, Persian, Syrian, Egyptian, Jewish, and Berber, as well as Arab—contributed.

The caliph's position as the religious leader of Islam became a purely nominal one. By the end of the ninth century three distinct traditions and groups had emerged within the Moslem religious community, which by and large still prevail. First of all, there was the orthodox position, which had an overwhelming superiority in the size of its following. The orthodox tradition depended strictly on the Koranic revelation; the Traditions of the Prophet, which were additional doctrinal pronouncements attributed to Mohammed; and a vast complex of religious, moral, and social law derived from the Koran and the semicanonical Traditions. The caliph was supposed to be the defender of orthodoxy, but this task was actually assumed by a group of religious teachers whose attitude and professional status closely resembled that of the Talmudic Jewish rabbis, who, indeed, they may have originally emulated. There was actually no overriding central authority in the Moslem religious fellowship; there was no pope in Islam. In each Moslem country the orthodox teachers banded together to proclaim the truths of revelation and religious law, and the extent of their power and influence depended largely on whether they could obtain the support of the state. Until the eleventh century the Arabic princes were frequently much more liberal and secular in their attitudes than were the leaders of orthodoxy, and hence the latter, while they had great influence, generally lacked the power to persecute those who dissented from their doctrines and legal precepts.

The two other traditions in medieval Islamic religion were the messianic and the mystical. The messianic form of Islamic thought involved the belief in a continuing revelation expressed by new prophets who claimed to be descendants of Fatima, the daughter of Mohammed. The supporters of these successor prophets (Shiites) were naturally bitterly opposed by the orthodox Sunnis, who regarded Mohammed as the ultimate prophet. But occasionally, in the Middle East and northern India, messianic leaders succeeded in transforming their theocratic claims into actual political power and thereby provided isolated areas in which the supporters of a continual revelation found refuge.

The mystical tradition in Islam, as in medieval Judaism, was a reaction against the stultifying confines of orthodoxy. The Moslem mystics (Sufists) sought a direct personal relationship with God and an intense religious experience as an escape from the heavy legalism of orthodoxy.

Before the end of the twelfth century, there was a very rich current of secular thought in the Islamic world, which made Arabic scholars of the tenth and eleventh centuries the greatest philosophers and scientists of their age, from whom the Europeans in the twelfth and thirteenth centuries were to derive a considerable part of their knowledge in these fields. The Greek philosophic and scientific writings, including the whole of the Aristotelian corpus, which was unknown in Latin Europe before the twelfth century, were translated into Arabic in eighth-century Syria with the assistance of Greek scholars who belonged to heretical Christian sects. The Aristotelian and other Greek scientific writings moved westward through the Islamic world and reached Spain by the end of the ninth century. Tenth-century Cordoba was famous even in hostile Latin-Christian countries as a center of thriving scholarship and science. A nun, writing in distant Germany in the late tenth century, referred to Cordoba as "a fair ornament" of culture, renowned for its seven streams of knowledge. As late as the twelfth century Arabic medicine was far superior to the western variety, and only the opposition of orthodox religious leaders to dissection prevented the Moslem physicians from achieving the medical discoveries that came in the sixteenth and seventeenth centuries in western Europe. In the tenth and eleventh centuries mathematics was almost exclusively an Arabic science, as the perpetuation of the terms *algebra* and *Arabic numerals* in western languages indicates. The Arabic mathematicians were heavily indebted to Chinese scholarship, but they made many original contributions. In the Arabic world before the twelfth century philosophy and science were in the hands of scholars who made their living in secular professions, such as medicine, education, and government. Religious and intellectual leadership was separate, and intellectual life was dominated by scholars who had little to do with orthodoxy. This situation contributed to the vitality and boldness of Arabic science, although in the long run it made rational inquiry and speculation vulnerable to attack and subversion on doctrinal grounds during the orthodox reaction of the twelfth and thirteenth centuries.

The Arabic world of the early Middle Ages was renowned not only for intellectual achievements but for its agricultural wealth and commercial prosperity. Compared to the Moslem countries, western Europe appears as an underdeveloped area. The Mediterranean world under Moslem rule at the zenith of its power and prosperity in the early eleventh century resembled the Hellenistic and Roman empires in the size and grandeur of its cities. Medieval Islam in its best days was a commercial economy held together by long-distance trade between great cities.

The favorable economic situation of the Arabic world was, of course, scarcely an Arabic creation. A multitude of ancient populations were involved—Syrian, Egyptian, Persian, North African, as well as Jews and Arabs. The Arabs, however, did have the good sense during the early Middle Ages to preserve the irrigation systems of the Mediterranean countries, which had been in existence since Roman times and even much earlier in many places, and to perpetuate international trade in the Mediterranean, which had hitherto been dominated by Byzantine merchants. The Arabs themselves had originally nothing to contribute to the economic life of the Mediterranean world, but they learned commercial and industrial techniques rapidly from the peoples they conquered. They turned out to be remarkably good sailors; they built large fleets and in the eighth and ninth centuries almost completely controlled the Mediterranean. The Moslem princes provided a sound coinage, which became the medium of exchange for important commercial transactions not only in the Mediterranean world, but in many parts of western Europe as well. After the Latin-speaking peoples stopped producing their own gold coins in the eighth century, they continued to use Arabic gold coins in international trade, and archaeologists have discovered these coins all over western Europe. It must always be remembered, however, in considering Arabic commerce, that the ubiquitous figure of the Arabic merchant in the early medieval world was often only Arabic speaking; ethnically he could be an Egyptian, a Syrian, a Jew, or one of the many other peoples who were brought together under Islamic rule.

The impact of the expansion of Islam on the economy of western Europe has been the subject of enormous controversy among historians. There can be little doubt about the impact of Islam on the political and intellectual development of early medieval Europe; it was negligible in both cases. The impact was negligible not because western Europe had nothing to learn from Islamic civilization; on the contrary, both in government, in which the Arabic countries had absorbed the Roman-Byzantine traditions of bureaucracy, and in philosophy and science, the western Europeans could have benefited greatly from Arabic instruction. But during the early Middle Ages there were no Moslems living under Latin-Christian rule, and, because the western peoples looked upon the Moslems as perverse and pernicious heretics, they closed their eyes to the benefits they could derive from association with the Arabic peoples.

The Latin-Christian peoples deprived themselves of the benefits of Moslem civilization through their self-imposed political and cultural isolation. Only at the end of the tenth century did the hatred that the Christians felt for Mohammed's teachings begin to take second place to the obvious advantages that could be gained through study at Cordoba. The greatest Latin scholar of the age, the Frenchman Gerbert of Aurillac, who eventually became pope, went to Moslem Spain to study philosophy and mathematics. The education he received from Arabic teachers made him so intellectually superior to his Christian contemporaries that for many centuries Gerbert was regarded as the possessor of mysterious powers of sorcery and black magic. It was not until after 1100 that the iron curtain between Latin Europe and Moslem Spain was effectively breached; the result was the importation of the Aristotelian corpus from Spain and Sicily into western Europe, inaugurating an intellectual revolution.

The economic effects of the expansion of Islam are by no means so clear, and the question of the effect of the emergence of the new power block in the Mediterranean in the seventh and eighth centuries on the economic relations between East and West is still debated. This controversy was the result of the last work of the influential Belgian economic historian, Henri Pirenne, entitled *Mohammed and Charlemagne* and published posthumously in 1936. Pirenne was a rarity—an able and learned scholar who was also an original thinker and the master of a vivacious and persuasive literary style.

What was Pirenne's thesis? Briefly, it was that the expansion of Islam brought about the economic disintegration of the Mediterranean world. The advance of Islam produced the final separation of East from West and the end of the Mediterranean unity that, Pirenne claimed, had continued to exist all through the period of the Germanic invasions. Africa and Spain, which had always been part of the Latin world, belonged henceforth to a culture centered in Baghdad. "The western Mediterranean became a Moslem lake; the west was blockaded and forced to live upon its own resources. For the first time in history, the axis of life shifted northward from the Mediterranean." Cut off from Mediterranean life, western Europe reverted to a natural (that is, rural) economy and developed the new institutions of the feudal state and manorial society. The attractions of this clear, incisive, and cosmic thesis are obvious, and Pirenne was able to advance it with a considerable show of evidence. But several scholars writing after 1950 contended that the *Mohammed and Charlemagne* thesis is a gross exaggeration and oversimplification of the course of early medieval civilization.

Two distinct aspects of Pirenne's thesis must be sustained if his interpretation is to remain valid: first, that the Germanic invasions were *not* a turning point in economic history and second, that the expansion of Islam *was* the cataclysmic turning point.

Pirenne contended that in spite of the Germanic invasions, the economic unity of the Mediterranean world was preserved in the fifth and sixth centuries and Merovingian France remained part of Mediterranean civilization. This view depends on a misreading, intentional or otherwise, of the picture of Merovingian society provided by Gregory of Tours. According to Gregory, there had not been a complete break with Mediterranean trade and culture, but there had been a marked decline of Mediterranean influence. In the economy of sixth-century Gaul trade and monetary transactions were not important; Merovingian France was dependent to a large degree on landed wealth alone. The cities depicted in Gregory of Tours' history were political and episcopal centers, not commercial centers. The Roman *curiales* class had disappeared; the trade with the eastern countries was carried on by easterners—Syrians and Jews. Merovingian France, compared with Byzantium, was already an underdeveloped area in which agriculture was the basis of the economy and in which commerce was of little importance. This picture of the

Merovingian economy, furthermore, has been substantiated by archaeological evidence. Obviously then, the economic decline of France and the disintegration of the economic unity of the Mediterranean world were well under way before Mohammed.

This is not to say that the Germanic invasions were a sudden catastrophe that alone produced this economic decline. The economic unity of the Mediterranean, and with it the volume of international trade, was declining from the end of the second century. Although it is still not completely certain to what degree the Germanic invasions marked a sharp turn in economic history, it definitely appears that "the meeting of German primitivism with Roman decrepitude," as Robert Lopez described it, markedly accelerated the economic disintegration of the Mediterranean world, whose first symptoms were evident as far back as the second half of the second century A.D.

Toward the end of the sixth century there was a partial restoration of international trade in the Mediterranean under Byzantine auspices. The Syrian merchants in Gregory of Tours' time are evidence of this fact. By the middle of the seventh century there is evidence of a partial restoration of the tin trade between England and the eastern Mediterranean. There is also fragmentary evidence that Ireland and the Baltic countries, which had never been touched by Roman civilization, were now drawn into the nexus of Mediterranean trade.

The second part of Pirenne's *Mohammed and Charlemagne* thesis now remains to be examined: To what extent did the Moslem expansion terminate this partial revival of east-west trade? Pirenne argued that the Moslems and Christians hated each other, and since Moslem sea power dominated the Mediterranean in the eighth and ninth centuries, the continued economic relations between western Europe and the Mediterranean became, a priori, impossible. He pointed to the moving of centers of European life to northern France and the Rhine valley, the decline of the Mediterranean French ports, and the increasing tendency to a purely rural economy in eighth-century France and concluded that they must have been due to a breakdown of east-west trade as a result of the Arab advance. He also offered some specific and empirical evidence for his thesis. In the late seventh century the western church stopped using Palestinian wine in the Eucharist and published its documents on parchment, no longer on paper imported from Egypt.

Perhaps for half a century or a little longer east-west trade was almost completely cut off, but certainly from the middle of the ninth century there is ample evidence of a continued trade between western Europe and the Islamic countries. The staple western exports to the Islamic countries consisted of slaves, furs, metal products, and timber. In return, the Moslem merchants offered oriental luxury goods to make the harsh life of the European nobility a little more comfortable. It seems strange that Pirenne, who was a great authority on medieval commerce, completely overlooked the significance of the thriving slave trade between western Europe and the Mediterranean countries. Jewish merchants initially played an important part in this exchange, and by 900 the Venetians and other Italian merchants had suppressed their religious zeal sufficiently to become the middlemen of east-west commerce. Certainly at all times in the early Middle Ages Mediterranean trade was hampered by Arabic pirates, and this situation made international commerce a risky business and kept the cost of transportation high. But the European merchant got a high return on whatever goods did not fall prey to piracy or shipwreck, and since the goods involved were luxury items and raw materials intended to satisfy the tastes of the ruling classes and were not for mass consumption, the necessarily inflated cost to the buyer was not a prohibitive factor.

It may be conceded that the expansion of Islam encouraged the commercial disintegration of the Mediterranean world and that it was a factor in the progressive ruralization of the European economy and the transference of the centers of European life to northern France and the Rhine valley. But the actual cutting off of Europe from Mediterranean trade was only momentary, if it ever occurred. The expansion of Islam represents but one stage in an economic process of autarky and deurbanization that had been going on since the end of the second century A.D. The civil wars of the third century, the Germanic invasions, and finally the Arabic military triumph were the events that accelerated the process and helped to produce the feudal and manorial world of the ninth century. Pirenne contributed greatly to our understanding of medieval history by calling attention to the economic consequences of Islam, but he exaggerated its cataclysmic significance and underrated the impact of the Germanic invasions. Mohammed did not determine the world of Charlemagne, as Pirenne believed; the institutions of eighth- and ninth-century Europe would not have been substantially different had the expansion of Islam never taken place. Nothing is more fundamental in early medieval history than the self-sufficiency of western Europe after Justinian failed to reconstitute the Roman Empire and the working out in isolation of the destiny of western civilization, with its own institutions and its own leadership.

CHAPTER FIVE

The Advance of Ecclesiastical Leadership

I. The Rise of Monasticism

The leadership that was so badly needed by the disorganized western society of the sixth century could come initially only from the church, which had in its ranks almost all the literate men in Europe and the strongest institutions of the age. The church, however, had also suffered severely from the Germanic invasions. The bishops identified their interests with those of the lay nobility and in fact were often relatives of kings and the more powerful aristocrats; the secular clergy in general was ignorant, corrupt, and unable to deal with the problem of Christianizing a society that remained intensely heathen in spite of the formal conversion of masses of Germanic warriors to Christianity. Heathen superstitions and magic were grafted onto Latin Christianity: The religiosity of the sixth and seventh centuries was infected with devils, magic, relic worship, the importation of local nature deities into Christianity in the guise of saints, and the general debasement of the Latin faith by religious primitivism. There was no parish churchman who could go out into the countryside and counter these crudities; at most, a member of the cathedral clergy would occasionally journey out from the episcopal see to administer the sacraments. The secular clergy were neither interested in nor capable of undertaking extensive missionary work. No one even cared about attempting the formal conversion of the German tribes within the Merovingian kingdom who lived east of the Rhine, and these tribes remained heathens until the eighth century. By the beginning of the seventh century church discipline in Gaul was in a state of chaos, and the problem was the most basic one of preserving the sufficient rudiments of literacy to perpetuate the liturgy and doctrines of Latin Christianity. Many priests literally did not know what they were saying at church services, but uttered mumbo-jumbo that vaguely resembled Latin as a magical incantation to impress their near-savage parishioners.

The Latin church was preserved from extinction, and European civilization with it, by the two ecclesiastical institutions that alone had the strength and efficiency to withstand the impress of the surrounding barbarism: the regular clergy (that is, the monks) and the papacy. Of all the institutions in western Europe, only monasticism and the papacy were able to provide leadership for European society, and out of their joint efforts were eventually to come the amelioration of Germanic kingship and its transformation into an additional creative force in early medieval society. But although the papacy and Germanic kingship were ultimately to provide the most dramatic and effective direction to the people of western Europe, it was the monks who were the most continuous force for education, organization, and social amelioration between the sixth and twelfth centuries and a determining factor of the most fundamental kind in the formation of medieval civilization. How did the regular clergy, that is, the clergy living under monastic rule, come to assume these indispensable social obligations? The structure of the new civilization that was created in the early Middle Ages was determined by the answer to this question.

Monasticism is a form of religious asceticism, which, in turn, involves the disciplining, limitation, or abnegation of the material and physical aspects of human life to assure a saving relationship with a deity conceived of as a purely spiritual being. Asceticism is therefore intended to secure salvation, and this end can be achieved either by the withdrawal of the ascetic from society and its corrupting temptations and distractions or by the severe control of social life to make the environment suitable for the ascetic to continue to live in the world. The former manifestation of asceticism is called monasticism, and the latter may be termed puritanism. It is obvious that in the circumstances of the early Middle Ages, with a violent, disorganized, and fundamentally un-Christianized society, the puritan control of society to make the world safe for asceticism was out of the question. The ascetic had to withdraw from the world to ensure the triumph of his spiritual will and the salvation of his soul. But the nature of early medieval western monasticism in its ultimate form was such that this flight from the world did not succeed very well; instead, the monastery became a social institution of the utmost importance. The more outstanding monks came to render the greatest services both to the church and monarchy and to give new vitality and leadership to both institutions.

Monasticism is by no means exclusively a western or medieval institution. There are Buddhist monks even today. And there were Jewish monks in Palestine before the Christian era—the radical sect of Essenes, who are believed to have been the authors of the Dead Sea Scrolls; St. John the Baptist was influenced by the messianic and eschatological doctrines of this sect. John certainly practiced the most astringent kind of ascetic life, and Jesus can be said to have supported such a life as the most ideal one when he told his followers that to enter the fellowship of the kingdom of God, they ought to dissolve all bonds that bind men to the material world, even the love for their own parents. Jesus' warning that "you cannot serve God and Mammon" and the example of his life, in which he never married and rendered obedience to his Father even to death on the cross, were inspirations to all subsequent generations of Christian ascetics to separate themselves from the world and to lead a purely spiritual life as far as is humanly possible. The heavy infusion of Platonist philosophy into Christian thought in the early centuries after Jesus, with its body-soul dualism and its denigration of the material world, engendered the common belief that the soul was most assured of salvation when the spiritual aspects of humanity were cultivated to the exclusion of the physical. Some of the more devout members of the church in the second and third centuries, who interpreted the Gospel in this heavily dualistic manner, sensed a grave danger to their souls from living in society and ran away to wild places to pursue purely spiritual exercises.

A favorite place of retreat for these holy and contemplative people was the Egyptian desert. But the fathers of the desert, once they had achieved a great reputation for sanctity, found that the world would not let them go; they were literally hounded through the Egyptian desert by admirers seeking to obtain their assistance in entreaties to the deity. Thus, almost from the beginning of Christian monasticism, the monks found themselves pursued by the world they had just abandoned in disgust and implored by society to act as its intercessor with God. The tension between the world and the monastery was in evidence from the inauguration of the ascetic movement in Christianity.

The figure of the hermit-saint was a particularly prominent and popular one in the Greek church, and Greek monasticism never entirely overcame the pattern established by its anchoritic origins. The ideal hermit type was established by Athanasius' *Life of St. Antony,* the most famous of the fourth-century desert fathers. Greek anchoritism was liable to go to extremes as the populace confused holiness with extreme physical privation. Such was the case with the early fifth-century Syrian saint, Simeon

Stylites, who was reputed to have spent the last thirty years of his life sitting on top of a pillar seventy feet high. The more sensitive and cultured minds in the Greek church discouraged such extreme asceticism. The great fourth-century Christian humanist and Greek church father, St. Basil, contended that the monks ought to obey the commandment to love one's neighbor as well as God. St. Basil was the leader in the creation of a communal type of monasticism in the Greek church that gradually came to predominate over the old anchoritic form. But the Greek cenobitic form of ascetic life remained loose, and the individual monk retained most of his independence. The characteristic Greek monastery was a large community where monks lived together for convenience, but the abbot (*abbas,* father) had little control over them; he was merely a revered and senior religious.

The development of western monasticism also began with the anchoritic form. The failure of nerve of western society during the last century of the Roman Empire induced some who had lost their faith in civilization but not in God to assure themselves of salvation by undertaking the hermit life in caves and other wild places. Such men frequently achieved great celebrity as saintly miracle workers. The relics of St. Martin, one of these Latin anchorites, were deposited at Tours, which became a popular shrine for pilgrims and accounted largely for the wealth of the bishopric, as Gregory of Tours proudly tells us. Yet extreme anchoritic asceticism never attained the importance that it did in the East, and in the fifth and sixth centuries it gave way to various kinds of cenobitism—that is, communal monasticism—partly for climatic and partly for social reasons. It was a different matter to try to be a hermit in the cold climate of northern Europe than to survive by oneself in Egypt. Furthermore, extreme asceticism only appears as a reaction to a wealthy urbanized society. There is no point in dramatically renouncing worldly fleshpots when nearly everyone is finding it hard to get enough to eat, which was a common situation in early medieval Europe. Anchoritism became a powerful movement in western religious life only with the emergence of an urbanized society in the eleventh and twelfth centuries. Until then, western monasticism was distinguished for its attachment to cenobitism.

The earlier kinds of communal monasticism in western Europe closely resembled the loose structure of the Greek religious communities. It was this kind of monastery that the Greek churchman St. John Cassian established in Marseilles in the early fifth century. Cassian's *Collations,* his account of conversations with the Egyptian desert fathers, is an important contribution to the development of the western monastic ideal. His work demonstrated both the sanctity of the desert fathers and the dangers that came from the isolation of the hermit life. His book, therefore, became required reading in early medieval monasteries.

The most thriving monasteries of the fifth and sixth centuries were those in Ireland. The Irish monasteries closely resembled the Greek in their form, and this similarity may have been the result of direct influence from the eastern Mediterranean; there is some evidence that Greek churchmen may have come to sixth-century Ireland, presumably following trade routes between Ireland and the East. The Irish monks were exceptionally well educated and zealous; they made excellent missionaries and pioneered the conversion of the heathen Anglo-Saxons and attempts to reform the church in Gaul. But the abbot in the Irish monastery had no authority over the brothers, who were free to come and go as they pleased. It was not this loose kind of cenobitic life but a much more strictly controlled and, in fact, corporate monastery that became the institutionalized form of asceticism in western Europe until the eleventh century.

By the end of the ninth century the basic rule for all western monasteries, with the exception of those in Ireland, was the one set down by St. Benedict of Nursia (died 543) for his own monastery of Monte Cassino near Naples. Western monasticism became identified with the Benedictine order, and because of the indispensable contributions of the black monks (as they were called from the color of their habits) to religion, education, government, and economy, the period from 550 to 1150 has often been called the Benedictine centuries. St. Benedict certainly did not intend to establish an institution that would provide leadership in medieval society. There is even some debate as to whether he intended his rule to be applied universally to all Latin monasteries, but assuredly he hoped that others would imitate the form of the religious life he established at Monte Cassino. He arrived at the final form of his *Rule for Monks* only after many years of careful consideration of the ideal religious life and some painful experiments. St. Benedict was a scion of the old Roman aristocracy, and he brought to the monastic life the Roman corporate sense of order, discipline, and authority. He turned in revulsion from the school at Rome to which his parents had sent him and fled to a wild region to become a hermit, but he found the lonely anchoritic life unsatisfactory and psychologically dangerous. He then became the abbot in a prevailing Greek kind of loose cenobitic community, but he was chagrined by the laxity and disorder he found there. Out of these experiences he derived the severe criticisms of the older forms of monasticism that he presented in the introduction to his *Rule*.

The purpose of the Benedictine community was to assure salvation for the souls of its members. It was a completely self-contained community, economically and politically as well as spiritually, and was not to rely upon the world for anything, except in the extreme case of the notorious corruption of the monastic community. Only when the abbot and the monks were obviously living scandalous lives was there a provision in the Benedictine Rule for outside interference; only then were the bishop or pious laymen of the neighborhood expected to intervene and restore regular life. Except for this unusual situation, the Benedictine monastery was to be a completely self-contained, self-supporting, and self-governing world. The abbot was to be elected by the monks for life, and he was to have absolute authority over the lives and souls of the brothers, who were to take unmitigated vows of chastity, poverty, and obedience to the abbot for life. The abbot's absolute authority was predicated on the hierocratic principle: He would be called to account before God for his performance as the divine minister in the monastery, and this superior obligation was the sanction for his absolute rule in the community.

The abbot had unchallenged authority to regulate the daily life of the monastery, to assign monks to various duties, and to punish them when necessary. The monks were never to leave the monastery, except under the most unusual circumstances and then only with the abbot's permission, and they were to obey whatever order the abbot gave them, even if they considered it to be wrong; the responsibility for a wrong act would lie with the abbot, not with the monk, who was obeying the regulations set down for him by his hierocratic superior.

The monastic life envisaged by the Benedictine Rule was characterized by a communal life of absolute regularity, with the strictest discipline and unvarying routine. The Rule was not remarkable for extreme forms of asceticism. Benedict had a Roman sense of balance and a keen psychological insight into the possibilities and limitations of human nature. Mortification of the flesh was not to be the rule in his monastery. On the contrary, the abbot was responsible for preserving the health of the brothers: He was to make sure that the monks had two solid meals a day and that the sick, the young, and the old received special care. It is obvious that Benedict did not care much for the extreme forms of asceticism, such as flagellation, hair shirts, or prolonged fasting. He believed in the discipline of the physical appetites, but not in self-abnegation and self-destruction.

The order of the monastic day, as envisaged by the Benedictine Rule, depended somewhat upon the season of the year, but taking an average over the whole year, the twenty-four hours in the daily life of the monk were to be divided into four parts. Four hours of every day were devoted to the *Opus Dei* (divine service), that is, communal liturgical prayer in the chapel. Four hours were provided for individual meditative prayer and the private reading of religious literature. Six hours were to be given to physical labor; the monastery was to provide its own food and to be completely self-supporting. This left ten hours for eating and sleeping, which indicates Benedict's moderation and common sense. The black monks were to live in a constantly devout atmosphere of silence and abstraction from the world. Absolute silence was not required, but needless gossip was prohibited. At mealtimes one of the brothers would read aloud from a religious book—the Psalms, or Cassian's *Collations*—while the other brothers ate in silence.

Benedict realized that some men of even pious inclinations would not be able to endure a life of such strict discipline and routine. Consequently he provided strict entrance requirements for admission to the monastic community. The candidate for monastic life was to undergo a year-long novitiate before he took his final vows, during which the abbot was to consider carefully the candidate's temperament. St. Benedict regarded his monastery as a microcosm of society and included all classes and age groups: the rich and the poor, the old and the young, the educated and the illiterate, both priests and laymen. The Benedictine Rule allowed for the receiving of children into the monasteries as oblates to God. By no means did Benedict expect that all his monks be educated men and priests. He wanted the brothers who were illiterate or ignorant to be educated, but he certainly did not regard his monastery as a center of learning. His community was to have nothing to do with society and was to perform no services to civilization, not even to the church. This corporate selfishness was justified on the grounds that it provided a refuge where the devout could pursue the highest end of man, the pilgrimage to the City of God. The Benedictine monastery was a kind of self-contained religious spaceship.

In the three centuries after Benedict's death the kind of monastery he created underwent important transformations and became absorbed into society as an institution of the first importance. This was neither what Benedict had wanted nor would have liked, but as David Knowles suggested, in a sense he had made this development inevitable by the effectiveness of the institution he had created. Early medieval society, so pitifully lacking in workable institutions, had to impose social obligations on the monks. Nor could western society afford to lose the services of literate men and able leaders who were found within the monastic communities; it drafted them out of their religious establishments to render services of the greatest importance. The self-contained nature of the Benedictine monastery made it an institutional unit that was eminently suited to the circumstances of the early Middle Ages. Only actual physical destruction could disperse the self-supporting and self-governed Benedictine community. In the new world that was coming into being after the Germanic invasions, social and political life was atomized, and the local units in society were the most effective ones. The estate, the village, and the province were rapidly replacing the state and the city as the centers of civilization. The Benedictine monastery fitted in completely with the tendency toward localism, and because of its efficiency and self-perpetuating nature it came to assume several important functions: educational, religious, economic, and political.

Even in Benedict's day the Roman aristocrat and scholar Cassiodorus had envisaged monasteries as the most suitable places for the educational and literary centers of the new society. Cassiodorus tells us that he wanted to found a Christian school of higher study in Rome similar to the rabbinical schools he knew existed in the Middle East, but that under the circumstances of the time he found this to be impossible. Instead of such an institute of higher studies, what he devoted himself to was the creation of a more elementary kind of educational institution. He therefore established a large monastery with the conscious purpose of using it as a center for Christian education and scholarship, and in his *Introduction to Divine and Human Readings* he carefully outlined a program for the monastic school. The monks were to cultivate the Biblical-patristic tradition, but to obtain the necessary knowledge of Latin for this Christian scholarship, they were also to preserve and study certain classical texts. This educational work, Cassiodorus pointed out, presupposed that the monastery would have a good library of Christian and classical texts, and this supposition, in turn, involved the creation of a monastic *scriptorium* that would prepare copies of the works to be studied in the monastic school.

In the two centuries after the founding of Cassiodorus' educationally oriented monastery, Benedictine communities all over western Europe similarly established schools, libraries, and *scriptoria*. This learned enterprise was not due so much to Cassiodorus' influence and the impact of his educational treatise, although these were of great importance, as to social need. With the collapse of the Roman state and the deurbanization of western Europe, the state and municipal schools disappeared. The episcopal schools in the early Middle Ages were only occasionally effective institutions because they were completely dependent on the patronage of the bishops, who were rarely interested in the life of the mind.

Even when a flourishing episcopal school was established, the next bishop was liable to be a semiliterate who would disband the teaching staff and sell off the library. The Benedictine monastery alone, during the early Middle Ages, had the continuity, the dedication, the library, and the substantial supply of teachers to serve as an effective educational institution. The monks had to undertake this educational task if Christian literature was to be preserved, and all over western Europe by 800 the more important Benedictine monasteries had flourishing schools, large libraries, and scriptoria for the production of manuscripts. At a conservative estimate 90 percent of the literate men between 600 and 1100 received their instruction in a monastic school.

It cannot be said that the Benedictine monasteries were ideal educational institutions. Their attitude to learning was almost entirely functional; they were interested in teaching the Latin language and the dissemination of the Biblical-patristic tradition to preserve a literate church. With few exceptions, the early medieval monastic scholars took a severely functional, Augustinian attitude toward the classical heritage. They were interested in the Latin literature only as a means of educating their students to write serviceable Latin. Such an attitude precluded the monastic school from becoming a center of creative thought. But in any case, early medieval society scarcely had the leisure for intellectual creativity; all literate men were needed for the service of church and monarchy. And although the early medieval monastic scribe usually did not have a deep aesthetic appreciation for the classical texts he was copying, he did preserve nearly all that was valuable in the Latin writings of the ancient world. The earliest manuscripts of all the surviving classical texts are the work of early medieval Benedictine monks.

Although St. Benedict had envisaged liturgical prayer as only one distinct part of the monastic day, by the early ninth century the *Opus Dei* had become the major function of many Benedictine monasteries, and service at the altar occupied nearly all the waking hours of the monks in such communities. This development was a consequence of the continued esteem and awe with which ascetic and saintly men were regarded by lay society. Just as the populace of Alexandria had begged St. Antony to pray in their behalf, so the much-admired Benedictine monks were made into the official intercessors with the deity on behalf of early medieval society. Kings and nobles endowed monasteries with lucrative manors in return for monastic masses for the souls of their relatives. By the ninth century many monasteries had become extremely wealthy as a consequence of this endowment of their liturgical function, and the abbots found themselves lords over large estates worked by dependent peasants. Even in this regard the Benedictines made a contribution to medieval society. Their estates were run more efficiently and intelligently than were most of the manors of the lay nobility, and they were the pioneers in whatever rudiments of agrarian science the early Middle Ages possessed. By the tenth century the black monks owned a considerable part of the best farmland in western Europe.

This development made many abbots into local powers, and they, like the lay nobility, were given political and judicial functions over the people in their domains. Because of their wealth and influence the abbots of the more important monasteries of northern Europe were also drawn into the developing feudal nexus in the ninth and tenth centuries and were required to become vassals of some king or duke and to send knights to the armies of their lords. The Benedictine abbot of the feudal era was frequently a royal vassal of the greatest importance. The abbot of Bury-St. Edmunds in the twelfth century ruled more than half the county of Norfolk. There are even a few instances of French abbots in the tenth and eleventh centuries buckling on armor and going off to fight at the head of their knightly contingent.

The political influence of the abbots also emerged as a result of the monastic monopoly of learning. Outstanding Benedictine scholars were recruited in the service of the church, and they became bishops and popes. But others staffed the chancery of a king or duke. They became royal chancellors, the advisers and confidants of rulers, and from the ninth to the middle of the twelfth century there were several instances of monastic statesmen who were in effect the chief ministers of western monarchs.

The heterogeneous and onerous social obligations undertaken by the Benedictine monasteries only two centuries after Benedict's death could not but affect the internal life and composition of the religious communities. By 800 most monasteries were no longer self-sustaining units, nor did the black monks perform physical labor. The monks were supported by the labor of serfs on their estates, while they devoted themselves to educational and liturgical work. Nor did the membership of the ninth-century Benedictine community represent any longer a cross section of society: The monks were drawn almost exclusively from the class of the nobility, and the Benedictine abbots, by the tenth century, were usually men of the highest aristocratic and frequently princely origin. The Benedictine convents for women, which had begun to be founded soon after Benedict's day, became particularly homogeneous in their social composition. The nuns of the ninth and tenth centuries were all high-born ladies, and it was almost impossible to be admitted to these convents without being a widowed or maiden relative of an important lord. Although the majority of the monks remained in their monasteries and abided by their vows, the ablest Benedictine monks from the eighth century on frequently left their communities to become missionaries, churchmen, and royal secretaries. This was not the monastery as created by St. Benedict, but it was an institution that was an extremely effective ameliorative force in early medieval society. Monasticism, which had begun as a flight into the desert from the civilized world, became in early medieval Europe not only an integral part of society, but a saving force of the greatest significance in the disorganized civilization that followed the Germanic invasions.

II. Gregory the Great and the Early Medieval Papacy

The contribution of Benedictine monasticism to the leadership of the early medieval church may be gauged by the fact that several of the most outstanding popes from the middle of the sixth century to the twelfth century were black monks. In the year 590 the first of these monastic popes, Gregory I the Great (died 604) ascended to the throne of Peter. His pontificate marks one of the most important turning points in the history of the medieval church, not because Gregory was able suddenly to overcome the disastrous impact of the Germanic invasions upon the culture and discipline of the Latin church; it was to take five centuries to achieve this end and complete the Christianization of Europe. Gregory I's importance lies in his clear formulation of the program that the papacy was to follow over the next two centuries. He clearly perceived that the historic destiny of the papacy lay in western Europe and that the way to assert papal leadership in European society was through an alliance with the monastic orders and the Frankish monarchy.

Immediately after Gregory's election as pope he sent out letters announcing that he had not wanted the throne of Peter and that he would have preferred to have lived the contemplative life of the monk. Although such modest statements became traditional with later popes, even with those who had campaigned for the office for many years, in Gregory's case it was a sincere avowal. He knew that the church at his accession was in a very bad way and that the problems involved in asserting papal leadership in western Europe were almost insuperable. He compared the Latin church of his day to a ship that "creaked shipwreck." Actually the papacy had exercised no effective leadership since the pontificate of Gelasius I almost a century before. The sixth-century popes had done nothing to deal with the consequences of the transformation of European government and society that followed the Germanic invasions. The bishops in Gaul had completely identified their interests with the Merovingian dynasty and then with the provincial aristocracy. In the outlook of even the best of them, Gregory of Tours, there had been a tremendous shrinking of vision, in comparison with the worldview of Ambrose and Augustine, toward a narrow parochialism.

The situation of the church in Visigothic Spain was not much more promising. The Visigoths had abandoned their Arianism for Catholic Christianity, and the Spanish bishops closely identified themselves with the Visigothic monarchy. In so doing, they had associated the destiny of the Spanish church with a decrepit institution whose sole strength was derived from the moral support given it by the church. This support was not to be enough to save Visigothic Spain from Moslem conquest in the early eighth century.

The situation of the Roman church itself at Gregory's accession was most precarious. The pope was beset by enemies on all sides. To the north of Rome the primitive Lombards persisted in their devotion to tribal Arianism, while in Ravenna and to the south of Rome the forces of the Byzantine emperor were a constant threat to the security of the pope. The alliance between Rome and Byzantium that had brought about the destruction of the Ostrogothic kingdom in the first half of the sixth century had long since collapsed, and in view of the mutually exclusive claims to be the vicar of God on Earth made by the pope and the emperor, the best relations that could exist between them was an uneasy peace. The one bright spot in this picture of the church at the beginning of the last decade of the sixth century was Ireland, but Gregory could not rejoice over the high cultural level of the Celtic monks. Since the Irish church had not been created under Roman direction, the Celtic church-men not only had peculiar practices that differed from the Latin church, but they seemed to adopt an indifferent attitude toward the Petrine doctrine. This was at least the conclusion that Gregory had to adopt when he received letters from the great Irish missionary in Gaul, St. Columban, haranguing the pope in a severe and not altogether respectful tone on the proper management of ecclesiastical affairs. When Gregory became pope, the Irish missionaries already were penetrating northern England, inaugurating the conversion of the heathen English and, in Gregory's eyes, threatening to foment a schism between the Latin and the Celtic churches.

Gregory by no means fully overcame any of these problems that the church faced at the time of his accession, but he set down the policy that his successors were to follow in struggling to resolve them, and he set in motion the chain of events that began the amelioration of the Latin church and European society. Gregory is the only pope between the fifth and the eleventh centuries whose correspondence and other writings have extensively survived, and we have sufficient documentation to write his biography and assess his character. He need not be for us a faceless man, as is the case with nearly all other early medieval churchmen. His character strikes us as an ambiguous and enigmatic one. On the one hand, he was an able and determined administrator, a skilled and clever diplomat, a leader of the greatest sophistication and vision; but on the other hand, he appears in his writings as a superstitious and credulous monk, hostile to learning, crudely limited as a theologian, and excessively devoted to saints, miracles, and relics.

This apparent ambiguity can be explained only in terms of Gregory's background and milieu. Late sixth-century Italy reveals the catastrophic effects of the long Gothic war and Lombard invasion. Its culture was marked by the decline of cities and literacy, the progressive ruralization of the economy, and the advance of ignorance and superstition. Gregory came from an old Roman family, and he had received a good classical education, but his primary concern as he grew to manhood was the salvation of his soul by a flight from the world. He founded a monastery in which he lived as a humble monk, and while he greatly admired St. Benedict, whose biography he wrote, his own attitude to monastic life lacked Benedict's moderation and respect for human nature. As a monk Gregory gave himself over to severe austerities that permanently affected his health, and even as pope his outlook exhibited traces of fanaticism and a lack of common sense side by side with the traditional efficiency and effective governance of the Roman aristocrat. At one time Gregory heard that a bishop in Gaul had established a school for the study of liberal arts. Instead of congratulating the Frankish churchman on his effort to improve literacy, the pope castigated him for engaging in a frivolous enterprise! A similar limitation of vision is revealed in Gregory's neglect to learn Greek while he was a papal ambassador for several years in Constantinople. Gregory's personal culture reveals the disastrous consequences of the vicissitudes through which Italy had passed during the sixth century; in his writings there are traces of the pettiness, parochialism, and self-defeating intransigence that mark the work of his contemporary, Bishop Gregory of Tours. Fortunately, Gregory the Great was not allowed to pursue his inclination to become an obscure and ignorant monk. The church needed a man of his education, intelligence, sincerity, and political experience. He was recruited out of the monastery into the papal service, becoming a prototype for many Benedictine monks in the following centuries who undertook similar careers, and against his will was elevated to the throne of Peter. His work as pope falls into three parts: his contribution to the papal office, his attitude to monarchy, and his use of monastic missionaries in the service of the church.

Pope Gregory was first of all conscious of the fact that he was a member of the episcopate, and in his *Book of Pastoral Care* he delineated for his episcopal colleagues their duties as pastors of the Christian flock, contrasting these duties with the privileges they enjoyed as ecclesiastical princes and nobles, which tended to be their primary concern. It cannot be said that Gregory's treatise on the episcopal office persuaded his colleagues to take a more zealous attitude toward their offices, but at least it served for later centuries as a definitive statement of the nature of the episcopal office. Gregory, however, was conscious that he was more than just a bishop; as bishop of Rome he was the vicar of Christ on Earth. He did not contribute anything new to the evolution of papal ideology, but he carefully summarized the Gelasian doctrine and Leo I's Petrine theory. This view of papal office was summed up in the term *servus servorum Dei,* "servant of the servants of God," which he used as an official appellation and that still appears as a subtitle on papal documents. Gregory thereby expresses the papal authority in terms of the hierocratic principle that St. Benedict had already used to justify the absolute authority of the abbot over the souls of the monks in his monastery. The hierocratic principle found its biblical support in Christ's statement in the Gospel of Mark: "Whoever is the chief is the servant of all"—that is, he who has the most responsibility has the most power. Since the pope was responsible before God for his ministry as the leader of the Christian church, he required unlimited authority to carry out the divine work entrusted to him.

It was one thing to state the papal ideology, but it was a different matter to assert papal leadership in western Europe. Gregory saw that the first necessity was for the pope to secure his position in Italy itself, and he labored to expand the territory under papal rule beyond the confines of Rome and to build up the "patrimony of St. Peter," the papal state. He was also conscious of the need for a steady income to effect his administrative work in the church, and many of his letters are devoted to telling his agents how to manage effectively the papal estates in southern Italy.

Even if the pope achieved an independent and secure position in Italy, he had to establish a relationship with the territorial churches in the Germanic countries if he was actually to assert his position as the leader of Christendom. Gregory was far more conscious of this fact than was any other previous pope, and herein lies a claim that may be made for him as the real founder of the medieval papacy. He realized that Europe was not just a matter of geography but a distinct culture and spirit contiguous with Latin Christianity, with whose destiny the papacy was ultimately to identify itself. Gregory was respectful toward the emperor in Constantinople, but not because he thought that the bishop of Rome had any longer something to hope for from the Roman emperor; he was merely concerned with maintaining the uneasy peace with Constantinople and leaving the papacy free to pursue its aims in western Europe.

To achieve the creation of a European civilization, Gregory saw with a prophetic clarity that the papacy would somehow have to ally itself with the Frankish monarchy, which, while it was a most unpromising institution in Gregory's day, would inevitably dominate the political future of Europe. Because the Frankish kings ruled, at least nominally, the heartland of Europe and because their kingdom was by far the largest and wealthiest in Latin Christendom, leadership in European society would have to come from the Frankish monarchy working under the direction of the church and revivified by this association. Gregory could not see how it could come in any other way. It was because of his understanding of this fundamental fact in European life that Gregory wrote highly deferential letters to the Merovingian king, Childebert II. Gregory was not blind to the gross inadequacies of the Frankish kings, but he envisioned an alliance between the papacy and the Merovingian dynasty that would transform Germanic kingship into an effective and ameliorative institution.

Gregory's letters to the Merovingian king had no consequences in his own day. It was not until the eighth century that the Frankish rulers were sufficiently intelligent to understand the possibilities for the growth of their own power in an alliance with the papacy. The surprising consequence of Gregory's missionary work was the bringing into existence of a group of churchmen who, in the eighth century, fomented the Frankish-papal alliance on which the new European civilization was to be founded. Shortly after his accession, as a consequence of the challenge from the Celtic church, Gregory felt the need for the conversion of England. As a monk who had been recruited into the service of the church, it was natural for him to employ Benedictine monks as his missionaries to England. He instructed the leader of this mission, Augustine, to begin his work in the kingdom of Kent in southeastern England because its ruler was known to have married a Frankish Christian princess. At the time of Gregory's death Augustine's mission had achieved its initial success with the conversion of the king of Kent and his nobles and the establishment of the first Latin church at Canterbury (literally, "Kent town").

In the half century after Gregory's death the Latin monks, advancing northward from Canterbury, and the Celtic missionaries at work in the north contended for the adherence of the English people. Finally, in 664, a synod of the English churchmen decided to bring the whole country under Roman rule. This decision not only precluded the schism in the western church that Gregory had struggled to avert; it had much more important consequences. The English Benedictines had the most flourishing schools in late seventh-century Europe, and in the eighth century they sent out missionaries to the Continent, inaugurating the transformation of the Frankish church and monarchy. It was an English Benedictine who, in the middle of the eighth century, played a leading role in establishing the Frankish-papal alliance that Gregory regarded as the necessary foundation for achieving a new European civilization.

The Making of Carolingian Kingship

I. Anglo-Irish Culture and the Colonial Phenomenon

Historians have discovered many of the causes of decadence and decline of a civilization; as yet they have done little to explain the principal factors leading to the rise and efflorescence of a civilization. We have only empty tautologies about responding to a challenge. Assuredly, it is easier to explain failure than success; it is easier to account for the lassitude and failure of nerve involved in cultural collapse than for the novel energy, intelligence, and leadership that mark the beginning of a new civilization. After centuries of disintegration and disorder the first Europe took shape in the eighth and ninth centuries; it was an incipient and imperfect civilization whose leaders overreached themselves and attempted to create a political structure, the Carolingian empire, that was too ambitious for their resources. They suffered bitter disappointment and fell prey to deep disillusionment, but a great many characteristic institutions and ideals of medieval civilization were defined during these two centuries and served as the basis for more successful political experiments in the following two centuries.

In accounting for the formation of the first Europe, we can discount economic determinism. The improvements in political, ecclesiastical, and intellectual life were actually contemporary with the acceleration of both the decline of commerce and the ruralization of the western economy. The moving force in the rise of European civilization in the eighth century came from the church. Anglo-Saxon monks and the papacy willed the creation of the first Europe. Working together, they transformed the Frankish church and the nature of Frankish kingship and awoke political and intellectual capacities in the continental peoples, which led to the Carolingian empire and the improvement in educational and intellectual life that distinguished the eighth and ninth centuries.

The origins of this great historical change are to be found in the culture of sixth- and seventh-century Ireland and seventh- and eighth-century England. It may seem strange that the Irish, who were never part of the Roman world, and the English, who in 590 were savage heathens and similarly out of touch with the traditions of the Mediterranean world, should have played such a great role in the creation of the first Europe. This role can be explained as a manifestation of the colonial phenomenon in world history: The people on the fringes of an empire or civilization, the frontiersmen or colonials, are frequently the greatest partisans of the system or culture to which they choose to belong. By their hothouse enthusiasm, their conscious efforts to identify with the civilization whose center is so far away, they make their claim to equal citizenship with the people in the heartland of the civilization. The latter often take their world for granted and do little to perpetuate or improve it. The Irish and English monks exhibited the typical zeal of colonials struggling to identify themselves with the center of the civilization. The Irish, who never enjoyed the benefits of Roman civilization, took pains to establish great libraries of classical texts and even became proficient in Greek. The English scholars of the late seventh and early eighth centuries, who were only two or three generations removed from heathenism, became fanatical supporters of the Roman church. Their great historian, Bede, was such a fanatical Romanist that he even tried to disguise the contributions of Irish missionaries to the conversion of England.

The beginning of Latin-Christian culture in Ireland is shrouded in obscurity, and presumably it will always remain so. It is probable that in the late sixth and early seventh centuries three groups of churchmen came to Ireland and brought with them the Christian religion and learning. The first group consisted of British priests fleeing before the Anglo-Saxon invasions; among them, likely, was a certain St. Patrick. The second group consisted of churchmen who fled from Gaul during the Germanic invasions of the fifth and sixth centuries and sought refuge in Ireland. A third group may have consisted of Greek churchmen from the eastern Mediterranean, who, during the late sixth and early seventh centuries, followed the trade routes to Ireland and brought with them their language and certain texts that were not found anywhere else in early medieval Europe. These groups may help to account for the Irish scholars' singular knowledge of Greek; in the seventh, eighth, and ninth centuries, if a churchman in western Europe knew Greek, he was assumed to be of Irish provenance.

Irish Christianity was distinguished by an intense devotion to learning and missionary zeal. Since it had developed in isolation from Rome, it was also remarkable for certain peculiarities that separated the Celtic and Roman churches. The Celtic church celebrated Easter on a different date than did the Roman church, and the clergy was exclusively monastic. The Irish church was not organized into dioceses, and since Ireland had never been part of the Roman Empire, there was no reason why the Irish should have developed the diocesan clergy. The leaders of the Celtic church were not the bishops but the abbots of their large and flourishing monasteries. The Irish monastic schools established great libraries and intensively pursued the study of the trivium and quadrivium. In the early seventh century the Irish monks had the best centers of learning in western Europe, but after 800 they ceased to play an important role in European cultural life, and the Celtic church rapidly declined.

Why did the flourishing and enlightened Celtic church decline after 800? Three reasons can be suggested. By their reluctance to accept the decrees of the Roman church, the Irish cut themselves off from medieval western Christendom when it was entering its first creative phase and thereby condemned themselves to intellectual isolation. This decision proved to be particularly disastrous when Scandinavian invaders destroyed many of the Irish monasteries in the ninth century. Finally, the continued political disunity of Ireland as a result of the perpetuation of primitive tribalism could not but have a long-range deleterious effect on the ecclesiastical and intellectual life of the island.

The Celtic monks found an outlet for their missionary zeal during the late sixth century across the Irish channel, where the Anglo-Saxons remained heathen before Augustine's mission and out of touch with Latin Christianity. Following the withdrawal of the Roman legions from Britain in about A.D. 425, Germanic war bands came across the North Sea from the Low Countries and penetrated the river estuaries of eastern Britain. They defeated the British Christian princes, possibly including a certain Arthur, subjugating many of the native populace into a slave status and slowly driving the remaining Celts back into the mountains of Wales and Cornwall and across the English channel to the part of northern France that came to be known as Brittany.

The slow and piece-meal nature of the English conquest of Britain was reflected in the fragmented political structure of sixth-century England. The leaders of the war bands established small kingdoms—traditionally seven in number, but the number fluctuated—and contended for hegemony against each other during the next three centuries. In the late sixth century the king of Kent was a prominent lord in southern England; in the seventh century the rulers of Northumbria were powerful for a time; and in the eighth century the king of Mercia, in the rich agricultural midlands, established his ascendency over many of the other chieftains. But even by the eighth century the political and social structure of Anglo-Saxon England had scarcely advanced beyond the institutions described in Tacitus and *Beowulf.* The king's power was dependent upon his effectiveness as a war leader and the extent to which he could reward his *gesiths,* or warrior-companions, and the social structure was characterized by large masses of free peasants.

The Celtic missionaries who began the conversion of northern England in the late sixth and early seventh centuries brought with them their deep learning, and the Anglo-Saxon schools of the seventh and eighth centuries were partly indebted to the contributions of Irish scholarship. But the efflorescence of Anglo-Saxon culture was mainly the result of continental influence. Following the decision of the English churchmen to join the Roman church in the 660s, the pope sent to England, as archbishop of Canterbury, an extremely learned scholar, Theodore of Tarsus, who had originally come from Asia Minor. Theodore established at Canterbury a great school whose students went out to become abbots of Benedictine monasteries in southern England. At about the same time, a native Anglo-Saxon churchman from the noble class, Benedict Biscop, founded the great monastery of Jarrow in Northumbria (Yorkshire). Benedict had traveled extensively on the Continent, and he is said to have brought with him to England the nucleus for a library at the monastic school at Jarrow and even some continental art objects.

Jarrow became the center of learning in northern England, as Canterbury and its satellite monasteries provided leadership in the south, and it produced in Bede (died 735) the greatest Anglo-Saxon scholar. It is a tribute to Northumbrian scholarship, and again evidence of the operation of the colonial phenomenon, that the most learned scholar of the early eighth century spent his whole life as a monk at Jarrow and never left his bleak and thinly populated homeland. Finding the most learned monk of the eighth century in the frontier society of northern England is roughly comparable to locating the greatest scholar of mid-nineteenth century America in the backwoods of Missouri.

Bede regarded himself first and foremost a teacher, the head of the monastic school at Jarrow, and a perpetuator of the biblical-patristic tradition. He used his learning in an empirical way to serve the needs of the church, and he was not interested in philosophic speculation. He applied his knowledge of mathematics and astronomy to deal with the problem of reckoning the date of Easter. He produced a compendium of scientific knowledge that was derived largely from Pliny's natural history. His original scholarship was in the field of history. It was Bede who took up Isidore of Seville's suggestion of a Christian chronology according to the Incarnation, and it was Bede who made it the common European way of reckoning historical time. Bede's great historical effort was the *Ecclesiastical History of the English People,* one of the few works of the early Middle Ages that is still attractive to the educated public. It is a carefully organized and subtly argued book that gives to the Roman church the decisive role in the making of English civilization. Bede had a more scholarly attitude toward historical writing than did any medieval writer between Gregory of Tours and the eleventh century. While in his hagiographical works he is inclined to be as credulous as the authors of most medieval saints' lives, his history is remarkably free from miraculous fantasies. Its tone is factual, restrained, and dry. He took pains to gather whatever information about the Anglo-Saxon invasion that survived in popular memory, and for his account of Augustine's mission he sent a monk to Rome to search the papal archives for Gregory the Great's letters concerning England, which he published extensively in his history.

The quality of Bede's thought differs markedly from that of the other great Anglo-Saxon scholar of the eighth century, Alcuin, who in the 780s was summoned from his position as head of the school of York to become a prominent assistant to Charlemagne in the reform of the Frankish church. Whereas Alcuin was imaginative, emotional, and personally involved in the political affairs of his time, Bede appeared to be an austere and cautious thinker who was involved to a limited degree with monarchy and the general problems of society.

At the end of his *Ecclesiastical History* Bede made some lugubrious remarks on the decline of the vitality of Anglo-Saxon culture, and while these remarks may simply have been the traditional pessimism of the old commenting on the new generation, the subsequent history of the Anglo-Saxon church confirms his concern about the continued progress of the church to which he was devoted. The later development of Anglo-Saxon England, after the eighth century, is by and large a disappointing story, especially in view of the preeminence of the English Benedictines in European culture in the age of Bede and Alcuin. After 800, Anglo-Saxon churchmen were never again to be the intellectual leaders of Europe, and during the tenth and eleventh centuries the English church was indebted to the Continent for guidance and inspiration. By the year 1000 there is no doubt that England was an intellectual backwater of Europe. The ubiquitous Scandinavians are traditionally blamed for this decline of Anglo-Saxon culture. Jarrow was destroyed by Viking marauders at the end of the eighth century, and for the next 250 years there was only occasional respite for the English people, whose energy was dissipated in struggles against successive waves of Scandinavian invaders.

There are two additional reasons for the decline of early medieval England. The Anglo-Saxon kings turned out to be singularly inept. They remained primarily warriors and failed to develop effective royal institutions. By the last quarter of the ninth century, as a result of the Danish invasion, only King Alfred of Wessex remained of all the Anglo-Saxon princes. Although Alfred, who was originally intended for the church, was a good scholar, fought the Scandinavians to a draw, and divided England with them, he made no contribution to the growth of royal leadership in Anglo-Saxon society. His successors in the tenth century established their hegemony over the Danelaw, as the area conquered by the Scandinavians was called, but they were unable to stem the rise of lordship and the passage of real power in society to the earls and thanes who constituted the local nobility. The most effective king in Anglo-Saxon history was the early eleventh-century Danish conqueror Canute. The English clergy of the ninth century tried to buttress the ineffective Anglo-Saxon monarchy with moral and sacred qualities, but with no more effect than that achieved by the bishops of Visigothic Spain. The weakness of Anglo-Saxon kingship and the passage of the leadership in society into the hands of the local nobility contributed to the decline of the Anglo-Saxon church from the flourishing and preeminent position it had enjoyed in the age of Bede. The final cause that can be discerned for this development is relatively simple: The zealous and dedicated English church of the eighth century sent so many of its outstanding missionaries and scholars to work on the Continent that it lost its best potential leaders and dissipated its resources. The devotion of the Anglo-Saxon church to the bishop of Rome was such that it served the interests of the papacy far better than its own.

The Anglo-Saxon missions to the Continent began in the last decade of the seventh century. The monastic missionaries began their work among the heathen Frisians in the Low Countries, from where most of the English tribes had originally come. They wished to bring the benefits of salvation to heathens whom they regarded as their kinsmen. Almost immediately Anglo-Saxon missionaries came in contact with the Carolingians, the new dominant family in France. They worked under the direction of Pepin II, the head of the Carolingian family, who wished to extend his influence over the Low Countries and regarded the Anglo-Saxon missionaries as the vanguard of Frankish expansion. The leader of the English mission in the Low Countries also worked under papal aegis and went to Rome, with Pepin's permission, to be consecrated bishop of Friesland. This was the first instance of any kind of definitive relationship between the papacy and the Frankish rulers, and it set the pattern for their increasing association in the first half of the eighth century as a result of their joint support of the efforts of the Anglo-Saxon missionaries.

The rise of the Carolingian family to prominence in France was the ultimate outgrowth of the aristocratic usurpation of royal power in the seventh century. The Merovingian rulers after the 630s were all either women, children, or mental defectives, which meant that they were unable to prevent the seizure of royal property and authority by the provincial aristocracy. The process of disintegration went so far that the Merovingian kings were left with no effective power outside their own private estates. And by the middle of the century they had even lost control over their estates to the "mayors of the palace," their household officials. In this anomalous situation, however, lay the origins of the revival of royal power in France. The mayors of the palace, having usurped what remained of royal power and property, found it in their interest to regain whatever they could of the royal fisc, which had been usurped by the provincial aristocracy. By the eighth decade of the seventh century, an Austrasian, or eastern, family, later known as the Carolingians, were using their control over the office of mayor of the palace to establish their ascendency not only over the aristocracy in the Germanic eastern part of the Merovingian kingdom, but over the dukes and counts of the more Romanic west.

The Carolingians constantly sought ways to reconstruct the royal power in France, which was in their hands. They welcomed the activities of the Anglo-Saxon missionaries along the frontier of the Frankish realm in the late seventh and first half of the eighth century. The Carolingians' sympathetic attitude toward the Anglo-Saxon missions was motivated by their desire to appear friends of the church, whose moral support could be especially useful, in view of their own doubtful legal right to dominate the French monarchy, and because they believed the Christianizing of the frontier Germanic tribes would make their effective absorption into the Frankish monarchy much easier.

Among the Anglo-Saxon missionaries in Friesland in the 690s was a young Benedictine named Wynfrid, better known by his later Latin name of St. Boniface, who came from a prominent noble family in southern England. He was one of the truly outstanding creators of the first Europe, as the apostle of Germany, the reformer of the Frankish church, and the chief fomentor of the alliance between the papacy and the Carolingian family. After working for many years as a missionary in the Low Countries, he decided to inaugurate the conversion of the Germanic tribes who lived within the Merovingian kingdom east of the Rhine, in what was to become southwestern Germany. Boniface returned to England, recruited several companions from Benedictine monasteries, and in 718 set out for the Continent, where he was to work as a missionary, bishop, and papal envoy until his death in 754.

Boniface's work was carried out with the support of both the Carolingian family and the papacy, as had been the case with the Anglo-Saxon missionary work in the Low Countries. But since Boniface was engaged in bringing a large territory that lay within the Merovingian kingdom into Latin Christian civilization, the significance of this joint direction was much greater in his case. Most of Boniface's missionary work in Germany was accomplished in the reign of Charles Martel, a rough warrior who became the hero of Christian Europe in 732 by his victory over the Moslems. Charles was cautious in his attitude toward Rome and was not prepared to enter into a close alliance with the papacy, but by allowing Boniface to carry out his work directly under papal authority, he opened the way for the entrance of papal influence into the Frankish kingdom and for the league with the papacy that his son, Pepin III, created in the 750s. In his letters Boniface made very clear the extent to which he depended on Charles Martel's assistance. "Without the protection of the prince of the Franks, I can neither rule the people of the church nor defend the priests and clerks, monks and nuns; nor can I prevent the practice of pagan rites and sacrilegious worship of idols without his mandate and the awe inspired by his name."

Boniface made three trips to Rome during the course of his missionary work in Germany, which lasted until 739. On his first visit he received a papal commission to convert the German people and was given his Latin name to symbolize his new position as the representative of the Roman church in Germany. On his second visit to Rome Boniface was made a bishop, and his final interview with the pope resulted in the organization of the German church with the English monk as the archbishop of the primatial see of Mainz.

Boniface's conversion of Germany was a tremendous undertaking. It brought a whole new area of western Europe into Latin Christian civilization and ended with the creation of the German church, which, in the tenth century was already remarkable for the intensive quality of its religiosity. Boniface achieved the inauguration of German Christianity through the building of great monasteries, such as his own establishment at Fulda, which became centers of learning and provided the personnel for the new German church organized in the 730s. Even in the tenth and eleventh centuries the great monasteries that Boniface and his assistants had established were the vital centers of German ecclesiastical life. Since the time of Benedict Biscop, in the previous century, all the Anglo-Saxon monks had been Benedictines, and it was the Rule of St. Benedict that Boniface now imposed on the great monasteries he founded in Germany. The constitutional form of his own monastery of Fulda had special significance; for it Boniface obtained a *privilegium* of exemption from episcopal control, thereby subordinating it directly to the papacy as the head of Christendom. This kind of special jurisdiction had been developed by Gregory the Great to bring certain Benedictine monasteries into direct association with the papacy, but it had been rarely applied. Fulda and the other German monasteries became famous for their great libraries and scriptoria. Some of the greatest works of Carolingian art, in the form of illuminated manuscripts, were the product of the Fulda monastic school.

The effecting of this enormous missionary undertaking required all the resources of the Anglo-Saxon church of the eighth century. In a letter that Boniface addressed to all the bishops and clergy of the English church, seeking their assistance in his missionary work he said: "We humbly beseech you . . . that the word of God may go forward and be glorified. We beg you to be instant in prayer that God . . . may turn the hearts of the heathen Saxons to the Catholic Faith . . . and gather them among the children of Mother Church. Take pity on them, for they themselves are now saying, 'We are of one blood and one bone with you'. . . . Be it known to you, moreover, that in making this appeal I have the approval, assent and benediction of two pontiffs of the Apostolic See." This letter shows the peculiar attitude of deep consciousness of their own Germanic background and at the same time a fervent loyalty to the papacy that distinguished the Anglo-Saxon clergy in the seventh and eighth centuries. Boniface's appeals to his countrymen led to a remarkable exodus of priests, monks, and nuns from England to the Continent, resulting in the establishment of a large Anglo-Saxon religious colony in Germany.

Boniface's appointment as archbishop of Mainz made him the primate of the church in the eastern half of the Frankish kingdom, and after 739 he turned from his work as the apostle to the Germans to begin the reform of the Frankish church. In this work he received the support of the two sons of Charles Martel, Pepin III and Carloman, who ruled the western and eastern parts of the Frankish kingdom, respectively. Carloman was the first of a new type of saintly king, more interested in religious devotion than in royal power, who frequently appeared in the following three centuries and who was an indication of the growing impact of Christian piety on Germanic society. In 747 he abdicated to become a monk at Monte Cassino; in the previous eight years he and Boniface began the reform of the Frankish clergy. A synod of Frankish churchmen declared their loyalty to the pope. This declaration did not signify the effective papal jurisdiction over the French bishops, but it at least was indicative of a new spirit and attitude by the French clergy, for they had never made such a profession of loyalty to Rome before. Boniface inaugurated the revitalization of the French monasteries, their acceptance of the Benedictine Rule, and the establishment of the first important monastic schools in the Merovingian kingdom. Among the greatest needs of the Frankish church was the creation of a secular clergy on the local parish level, outside the episcopal cities. If the Christianization of Europe was ever to be a reality, the faith would have to be taught by educated priests in each village. The dim beginnings of the medieval parish system, which we can perceive to be a real institution in some parts of ninth-century France, can be traced back to the work of Boniface.

After Pepin III became the ruler of the whole Frankish kingdom in 747, the same kind of reform that Boniface had inaugurated in his own ecclesiastical province was extended to western France with Pepin's assistance. Pepin's relations with the church were not characterized by the deep personal piety that had distinguished his brother. He had discerned in Boniface's work the opportunity and means to transform the Frankish kingship and to gain the crown from the Merovingians through an alliance with the papacy, for which Pepin prepared by accepting Boniface's program of church reform in his realm. In Rome, at the same time, the results of Boniface's work were believed to open the way to a realization of the papal ideology that had developed from the time of Gregory the Great. In the 750s the consequences of long centuries of confused development were coming into sharp focus at last, and the outlines of the first Europe began to take on definitive form. The 750s constituted one of the momentous turning points of medieval history. This decade was characterized by the final emancipation of the papacy from the framework of the eastern Roman Empire, the supplanting of the Merovingian dynasty by the Carolingians, the penetration of the idea of theocratic monarchy into western Europe, and the legal founding of the papal states. Only a half century later was to come the revival of the imperial title in western Europe, which was a direct outgrowth of the events of the 750s. The necessary background for all these decisive achievements was the contributions of St. Boniface and his assistants to the Christianization of Europe.

In 754 Boniface returned to the Low Countries as a missionary, taking up the work he had left four decades before, and he suffered martyrdom at the hands of the savage and ungrateful Frisians. In terms of medieval hagiography, his life of service to the church thus had a perfect ending. His biographers proclaimed him the "Apostle to the Germans," and the zealous, Benedictine-dominated German church of the early Middle Ages was the worthy monument of his service to Latin Christianity. But the Carolingian monarchy of the eighth and ninth centuries was also, to a considerable extent, a consequence of his work. Carolingian kingship was, however, a monument he would not entirely have appreciated or have wanted to take credit for. The English Benedictines' heroic struggle for the Christianization of the West had set in motion a complex of ideas and institutions that formed the civilization of the first Europe, and this was to be a world whose tensions, ambiguities, achievements, and disappointments were far beyond the ideals and expectations of the English missionaries.

II. The Carolingian Enigma

The course of Carolingian history was enigmatic. Carolingian history was full of paradoxes, sharp contrasts, and cyclic extremes between idealism and barbarism, intelligence and ignorant violence, apparently rapid achievement and equally rapid collapse. Many historians have found the main theme of the period in its ideological struggles, in the working out of certain sophisticated ideas, which loom large in the documentary sources of Carolingian history. Others have dismissed these ideological pronouncements as the wishful thinking of monks who produced all the literature of the period, and they have emphasized instead what appears to them to be the realities of social and political life: lordship, an intensely rural economy, and the usual disorders of Germanic society. Out of this interpretation comes a picture of Charlemagne not as the great Christian emperor of a united Europe, but as a typically violent and inept Germanic warrior-king, so that the sharp distinction between the Merovingian and Carolingian worlds is replaced by the common pattern of the "barbarian West" before the tenth century.

The solution to the enigmatic character of Carolingian history lies in perceiving that eighth- and ninth-century Europe belonged to the general form of an underdeveloped, preindustrial society that was only beginning to benefit from intelligent leadership. Because in such societies power is vested in a small elite group—in the case of the Carolingian world, the king, the leading churchmen, and a few great aristocrats—it appears that great improvements can be made quickly. In such a situation the ideology of the elite group is inevitably an extremely important causal factor in the inauguration of social change. If a few top leaders are won over to the cause of progress and enlightenment, a great reversal of the previous conditions of localism and disorder seems to take place immediately. And while this social amelioration rarely conforms to the high ideals of the elite group, real improvement can be effected in a relatively short time because the leaders have under their control all the intelligence and literacy available in their society. The situation, however, remains a precarious one in view of the deep traditions of disorder, localism, and violence in the underdeveloped society.

The death of only a few enlightened leaders, or even the sudden loss of one great personality, can cause the whole system to collapse and open the way for an equally rapid reversion to chaos and barbarism. Surrounding the enlightened group of leaders in such a preindustrial society are a mass of wild warriors and bovine peasants who lack any comprehension of what the leaders are trying to do. Consequently, as the central direction falters, there is an immediate backsliding into barbarism.

The vicissitudes of the Carolingian world become comprehensible in terms of the pattern of an underdeveloped society. The ideals of the elite group, centered in the royal court and the church, were extremely important causal factors in political and social change. At the same time it must be remembered that this group worked in an intensely ruralized and localized society and that even the great majority of the Frankish lords had no understanding of the greater part of the sophisticated ideology of the ecclesiastical theorists, and they disliked the implications of most of what they could dimly understand. The elite group of kings, bishops, abbots, popes, and dukes were by no means unanimous in their view of the ideal Christian society. But there was a further underlying and irreconcilable conflict between the general attitude and expectations of the leaders of society and the grim realities of political and economic life. This is why Carolingian history is marked by the emergence of sophisticated and complex ideologies, on the one hand, and the increasing vitality of lordship and manorialism, on the other hand. It explains why Charlemagne appeared both as a Christian emperor and a barbarian overlord. It accounts for the soaring aims, the short-term triumphs, and the disappointments of the leaders of the first Europe.

The most significant aspect of Carolingian history, however, was not the perpetuation of Germanic institutions and their inhibiting effect on the realization of the high ideals of the churchmen of the period, but the expression of these ideals and the great efforts made to establish a Christian society. These are the novel factors that distinguished the first Europe from the world that immediately followed the Germanic invasions. Although the great expectations of the Carolingian kings and churchmen were not immediately fulfilled, the greater part of their ideology and institutions was perpetuated even after the collapse of the Carolingian empire, and it formed a considerable portion of the more successful social order of the tenth and eleventh centuries.

III. Monarchy and Papacy

A great part of the history of eighth- and ninth-century Europe is centered on three ideologies, their expression, encounters, and interaction: the concept of papal authority; the doctrine of theocratic monarchy; and the imperial ideal or, more accurately, ideals. The leaders of the Carolingian world were strongly motivated by one or more of these ideologies, and the development of royal and papal policies was largely determined by attempts to turn them into practical programs.

The doctrine of papal authority was formulated between 730 and 760, and its expression was partly a consequence of the iconoclastic controversy in Byzantium. In the late 720s the emperor condemned the use of pictures and other representational art objects (icons) as idolatrous and ordered their removal from the churches under his rule. The result was a violent and schismatic quarrel that absorbed the energies of the Greek state and church for two centuries until the iconodules, the defenders of religious images, finally triumphed. The motivation of the emperors who fomented the iconoclastic controversy have been variously interpreted. The emperors who condemned religious images came from Asia Minor, where the Byzantine army was now recruited, and their iconoclastic attitude has been viewed as a consequence of the rise to power in the eastern Roman Empire of men influenced by the religious traditions of Middle Eastern peoples, such as the Arabs and Jews, who forbade pictures in their houses of worship. This interpretation regards the iconoclastic controversy as the result of the increasing orientalization of Byzantine civilization. Another view finds the origin of the iconoclastic controversy in eighth-century emperors' attempts to increase the power of the Byzantine state. The emperors considered as an obstacle to this end the fanatical popularity of the Greek monks, which they concluded was a result of a popular belief in the miracle-working propensities of icons kept in monastic establishments. The emperors, therefore, believed that their iconoclastic policy was a necessary foundation for the revival of imperial power.

Whatever may have been the emperor's motivation in issuing his iconoclastic decrees, they could not be obeyed by the pope, whom he had ordered to conform to his new policy. In the first place, the pope could not concede that the emperor had the right to legislate on such an important doctrinal question. Second, the western church was strongly opposed to the iconoclastic attitude. Its attitude on images in the church had been clearly enunciated by Gregory the Great, who defended their use as a means of education and edification in religious instruction.

The pope in 730 was Gregory II; his name was significant, for it was the custom of popes at their accession to assume the name of the previous pope whom they most admired. Gregory II wished to emulate Gregory the Great, and he put into practice his program of papal leadership in Europe. The papacy had not been able to do so during the seventh century, partly because of the weakness of the Frankish monarchy and partly because of its oppression at the hands of the emperor and his army in Italy. The iconoclastic controversy brought matters to a head and gave Gregory II the opportunity to carry out the policy of his namesake. He sent an angry letter to Constantinople denying the right of the emperor to intervene in doctrinal matters and asserting that if the emperor again intended to use force against the bishop of Rome, the whole of the western world stood ready to help the pope. Gregory had no way of knowing if this was true, and when in 739 the papacy asked Charles Martel to go to Italy to protect it against the emperor and the Lombards, he refused. Charles undoubtedly thought that he had enough to do at home, and in any case the Franks had been on good terms with Constantinople since the time of Clovis. But Gregory II unquestionably believed that the time had come for the papacy to declare its independence of the Roman emperor and to associate itself with the western world and therefore with the Carolingian family, who ruled by far the largest territory in Europe.

In 751 the policy of the two Gregorys came to fruition when Pepin III turned to Rome for assistance in gaining the Frankish crown. The Merovingian king in the eighth century was a complete nonentity. He had no power or property and rode around in an oxcart like a peasant, but he still had the royal title, and by Frankish law there was no way that the Carolingian mayor of the palace could take it away from him. He needed ecclesiastical support, particularly papal authority, to usurp the French crown, and Pepin III was clever enough to do so as soon as possible because while the Merovingians had been physical and mental defectives for a century, they might still produce another Clovis. The work of Boniface in the Frankish kingdom, the increase of ecclesiastical influence in

Frankish society, and the new respect with which the papacy was regarded by the Frankish clergy indicated to Pepin the course of action that he ought to follow. Church law and papal sanctions would be brought in to overrule Frankish traditions. Consequently, he had Boniface transmit to Rome the question of whether the man who actually exercised royal power ought to be king.

The papacy had waited a century and a half for this moment, and the pope could not but give Pepin the answer he wanted. But as a matter of fact, the papal decision that Pepin had the right to displace the reigning Merovingian and assume the French crown was in accordance with the traditions of political theory of the early medieval church. The ecclesiastical theorists had never been impressed by the claims of inheritance. They had always advocated that succession to the throne was contingent on suitability, that is, on the candidate's qualifications to be an effective and just ruler. Pepin seemed eminently suitable in papal eyes. While the Germanic principle of throne worthiness was similar to the ecclesiastical doctrine of suitability, Pepin was not able to take advantage of it because in France the principle of throne worthiness had died out in the fifth century and had been replaced by the tradition of the exclusive right of the Merovingian family to the throne. The origin of this transformation of the basis of Frankish kingship probably lies, in pre-Christian times, in the Merovingian claim to be descended from the gods. This claim was reinforced in the early sixth century by Clovis' conquest of Gaul and his claim that the whole kingdom was the private property of his family. It is apparent that only the decision of the vicar of Christ on Earth could break the Frankish primordial attachment to the Merovingian house, attested to by their toleration for over a century of a line of royal idiots.

The elevation of Pepin to the Frankish throne in accordance with ecclesiastical law and papal sanction was effected through an elaborate, symbolical, and religious ceremony. St. Boniface, as the papal representative in France, annointed Pepin with holy oil in the same manner as bishops were elevated to the dignity of their offices and then crowned him king of the Franks. This sacring of the Carolingian ruler had the desired effect of impressing not only the Frankish churchmen but also the lay lords with Pepin's right to the crown. The last Merovingian was sent off to a monastery, and Clovis' dynasty became extinct. Boniface's anointment of Pepin marked an important turning point in the development of early medieval kingship, for it involved the introduction of the idea of theocratic monarchy into western Europe. There is evidence that the seventh-century Spanish bishops experimented with a similar ideology and ceremony in an attempt to give some moral and religious sanction to the feeble Visigothic monarchy, but this experiment ended with the Moslem conquest of the Iberian peninsula and does not appear to have served as a precedent for the sacring of the Carolingian ruler.

Why did the papacy introduce royal anointment into western Europe and with it the ideology of theocratic monarchy, against which, in its Byzantine form, the papacy had struggled bitterly since the fifth century? In the long run it must be asserted that the papacy erred in making this innovation; theocratic monarchy became even more troublesome a doctrine to the church in its western form than in its Byzantine form. This was something which could not be seen in the 750s. The fault of Germanic kingship, in ecclesiastical eyes, had been that it was too weak and could give no leadership to society and no protection to the church, not that it was an engine of despotism and a threat to the moral leadership of the church in society. The papacy in 751 finally had the opportunity to put into practice Gregory the Great's programs and to place the Frankish king in debt to Rome. But to do so, it had to overrule strong Frankish traditions and secure the crown for its Carolingian allies. The most certain way of achieving this aim was by the full application of religious sanctions, thereby elevating the head of the Carolingian family to a sacred office. It appeared to be a symbolic, dramatic, and glamorous ceremony that would achieve the desired end of securing the Frankish throne for Pepin but that seemed to offer no threat to papal leadership in western society. Ecclesiastical theorists knew about the implications of theocratic kingship and the royal anointing, but the papacy in the 750s did not expect that illiterate German kings would make use of them in a way that would be disadvantageous to the interests of Rome or even clearly perceive all the implications of the sophisticated doctrines involved.

The papacy was furthermore not concerned about the introduction of theocratic monarchy into western Europe because it had formulated its own ideology of the papal suzerainty over the kings of western Europe, and it obtained from Pepin the apparent recognition of the validity of this doctrine. The idea of papal authority in the western world was formulated in the famous medieval document, the Donation of Constantine, the best-known forgery in history. There is some doubt about the date of the authorship of the Donation of Constantine in the form in which it has come down to us. It is probable that the surviving version was drafted in the middle of the ninth century, but there is ample evidence that the original Donation of Constantine, substantially the same document that has come down to us, was drawn up in the papal chancery in the 750s, personally presented by the pope to Pepin at Paris in 754, and accepted by the Frankish king as a true statement of the valid powers of the papacy.

The papacy thought it necessary to express its ideology through the medium of a forged document attributed to the emperor Constantine because of the nature of legal concepts in the early Middle Ages. The good law was the old law; law was virtually equivalent to custom, and new claims had to have some customary or historical basis. Given also the respect that men in a largely illiterate society accorded written documents, it is easy to understand the propensity of churchmen in the early Middle Ages to forge documents to establish a legal basis for their claims. The forged character of the Donation of Constantine does not convict the eighth-century popes of moral turpitude; the document was merely a legal way of expressing papal ideology. It is furthermore probable that the papacy actually regarded as true the peculiar interpretation of the history of Constantine's reign upon which the Donation was predicated and that is summarized in the prologue to the document. The papal court in Rome was not able to find a copy of the document that they really believed Constantine had issued, so they forged their own version in much the same way as many medieval monasteries forged new copies of genuine charters that had been lost.

The author of the Donation of Constantine drew upon the legend of St. Sylvester, which Gregory of Tours referred to in his *History of the Franks* and which probably originated in late fifth-century Italy, contemporary with the formulation of the Gelasian doctrine. The legend presents in historical-legal form the radical aspect of Gelasius I's concept of the relationship between papal *auctoritas* and royal *potestas*. According to the legend upon which the Donation of Constantine is based, Pope Sylvester I had cured the Roman emperor of leprosy. In gratitude Constantine not only made the bishop of Rome the head of all the priests in the Roman world, but resigned his imperial crown and all his power to the pope. As an example of his servility to Sylvester the emperor nominally performed the office of the papal groom. The generous pope, in turn, restored the imperial crown to Constantine. The emperor, however, abandoned Rome, Italy, and the western world to the pope and took up residence in Constantinople. The doctrine behind this charming story is a radical one: The pope is supreme over all rulers, even the Roman emperor, who owes his crown to the pope and therefore may be deposed by papal decree. The pope has the absolute legal right not only to Rome and the patrimony of St. Peter, but to Italy and the whole western world if he chooses to exercise his claims.

The boldness and radicalism of the Donation of Constantine may be explained by the papacy's success in realizing the policy of Gregory the Great. The popes of the first half of the eighth century had secured their independence from Constantinople, effected an alliance with the French monarchy, and apparently gained the moral leadership of western Europe. The prospects for papal power seemed endless in the 750s. Furthermore, the papacy was encouraged to express its ideology by the fact that the Frankish king officially performed the services of papal groom— he led the pope's horse a few paces in accordance with the Roman emperor's role in the Donation of Constantine. A great ceremony was then held at the church of St. Denis, the royal monastery of France, which, by its dedication to the disciple of St. Paul, symbolized the association between Rome and Paris. The pope anointed not only Pepin but his wife and children and gave the Frankish king the additional title of *patricius Romanorum,* protector of the Romans (that is, of the Roman church), and in fulfillment of this new office Pepin vowed to restore to the papacy the exarchate of Ravenna. The latter territory had fallen to the Lombards in 751, but Pepin swore to return it, not to the Byzantines to whom it had recently belonged, but to the patrimony of St. Peter, in accordance with the Donation of Constantine's grant of all Italy to St. Sylvester and his successors.

In the following year the Carolingian king fulfilled his promise to the pope. He invaded Italy, took Ravenna from the Lombards, and against the futile protests of the Greeks handed it over to the papacy. Before he returned to France in 756, he deposited on the tomb of St. Peter in Rome a document that has been known as the Donation of Pepin, confirming the independence of the patrimony of St. Peter. Thus, by the end of the 750s the papacy had good cause to believe that it had secured the leadership of the first Europe and that the revitalized Frankish monarchy would be a deferential and useful supporter in the creation of a Christian world order.

Yet within three decades of these momentous events in the 750s, it became apparent that the first Europe was taking shape in a way that did not conform to the papal ideology expressed in the Donation of Constantine. Leadership in western Europe was in the hands not of the bishop of Rome, but of Pepin's son, Charlemagne (768–814). The pope more and more found himself taking second place to the Carolingian king. Nor did Charlemagne actually maintain the Donation of Constantine. He had begun by confirming his father's donation, but in the 770s he destroyed the Lombard kingdom and took for himself the title of king of the Lombards. By laying claim to northern Italy, Charles directly contravened the Donations of Constantine and Pepin. Furthermore, the pope was alarmed to find Charles taking seriously the implications of his anointment; Charlemagne's court scholars addressed him as King David, who was the prototype of a sacred king. It appeared that the ideology of theocratic monarchy was emerging in the Carolingian kingdom for much the same purpose as it had developed in Byzantium.

Where the eighth-century papacy had miscalculated was in not understanding that the reformed Frankish church, in spite of its formal professions of loyalty to Rome, would not inevitably be subservient to the papacy. Rather, the bishops and abbots would just as well ally themselves closely with the Carolingian ruler, who could offer them important positions in his government at court and at least provide them with patronage and security, and if the Frankish king now held a sacred office, if he was *rex et sacerdos,* so much the better; it provided a pretext for the Frankish ecclesiastics' involvement with the monarchy. The papacy had assumed that an educated and thriving Frankish church would look toward Rome; this was its fatal mistake.

The pope had also miscalculated in not making allowance for the rise of a strong personality in the Carolingian family. And no more impressive a figure appeared in the early Middle Ages than Charles the Great. He was a prodigious warrior who spent his reign trying to extend the boundaries of his kingdom on all sides. He incorporated northwestern Germany into the Frankish kingdom and, in the course of his conquest, slew thousands of heathen Saxons in a single day without flinching. The nature of Germanic kingship was such that whatever other admirable qualities a king might have, his ability as a great warrior would gain him enormous admiration and loyalty among lay lords who could respect no other qualities except proficiency on the battlefield. But Charlemagne did have other qualities that gained him the fanatical loyalty, devotion, and service of the ablest churchmen not only in his own vast kingdom but even in England and northern Italy. Altogether, as he appears in the description of his clerical biographer and secretary, Einhard, Charlemagne was an impressive personality. If Einhard occasionally cribbed a line from Suetonius' *Lives of the Twelve Caesars* to describe his master and hero, it is in a certain sense justified, for Charlemagne deserves to stand next to the greatest of the Roman emperors. Although only modestly literate—he did not read Latin well and could barely scratch his name—he had a keen intelligence that he applied to all problems of government. He was the great warrior of the age, but he also took pains to continue the work of Boniface to improve church discipline and further education in the monastic schools of his realm. He recruited the most renowned scholar of the day, the Englishman Alcuin, to improve the Frankish monastic schools, and at his court he surrounded himself with learned and zealous churchmen whose advice he sought and followed.

The primitive German chieftain occasionally breaks through the façade of civilization. Charlemagne had a large number of concubines and bastards, he mistreated his daughters, and like the crudest of the Merovingians he planned to divide up his kingdom among his surviving sons as if it were a piece of real estate. But there is enough in Charlemagne's application of intelligence and idealism to government to signal a profound transformation in Germanic kingship. He was the first Germanic king since Theodoric the Ostrogoth who consciously and consistently aimed at social amelioration. The churchmen of his day fully realized that he did and consequently hailed him as the hero of Latin Christianity, leaving the pope in a respected but decidedly inferior position. Charlemagne, unlike the Byzantine emperor, made no claim to be God's prime representative on Earth or to legislate doctrinal matters. But he had a strong sense of his own destiny, and he fully agreed with the churchmen at his court who hailed him as the leader of the new European society.

The papacy had one weapon left in its spiritual armory by which it could assert its authority over the Carolingian monarch. According to the Donation of Constantine, the emperor had resigned the imperial title and given it to the pope, who had returned it to him. Henceforth, went the papal argument, the imperial title was the pope's to give and to deny. Beginning in the 780s there is evidence that the papacy was preparing to "translate" the imperial title from Constantinople to the Carolingian realm. The pope stopped dating papal documents by the Roman emperor's regnal year and substituted Charlemagne's, and in the 790s the pope sent the official announcement of his election to the Frankish king instead of to the Byzantine ruler, as was the custom. The granting of the imperial title to Charlemagne as a means of reasserting papal authority in western Europe was a desperate expedient, but the only recourse open to the papacy. The imperial coronation of Charlemagne would give a new validity to the Donation of Constantine, and since the pope had the right to remove as well as grant the imperial title, it would give the papacy a powerful sanction against the Carolingian king. Of course, Charlemagne would understand the implications of the imperial coronation by the pope. This presented an obstacle to the realization of the pope's plans. At the end of the eighth century the papacy was forced to accelerate its program of translating the imperial title to the West.

A new menace had come to threaten the security of the bishop of Rome, namely, the Roman nobility, who struggled to secure the election of one of their scions to the throne of Peter. As a consequence of this internal squabble, Pope Leo III was beaten up by a Roman mob and charged by his enemies in the Roman nobility with moral turpitude. He fled northward to gain the assistance of the official "protector of the Romans," who was engaged in his long war against the Saxons. On the advice of Alcuin, Charlemagne acted deliberately and slowly in his reply to Leo's entreaties. He sent the pope back to Rome under guard and kept him in protective custody until he himself could cross the Alps toward the end of the year 800. On December 23, at a trial at which Charlemagne presided, Leo finally purged himself of the accusations against him in the German manner. This course of events had signified a dreadful humiliation for the pope and his abnegation before the Carolingian ruler, and he determined to try to regain the prestige and authority of his office by carrying out the imperial coronation of Charlemagne.

On Christmas day, 800, as Charlemagne rose from prayer before the tomb of St. Peter, Pope Leo suddenly placed the crown on the king's head, and the well-rehearsed Roman clergy and people shouted, "Charles Augustus, crowned great and peace-giving emperor of the Romans, life and victory!" Charlemagne was so indignant and chagrined that, according to Einhard, "he said he would never have entered the church on that day, although it was a very important religious festival, if he had known the intention of the pope." Charlemagne did whatever he could to mollify the outraged Byzantines, who claimed that their imperial title had been stolen from them. He hardly ever used the title emperor of the Romans, which the pope had given him, but satisfied himself with the phrase, "Emperor, king of the Franks and Lombards" to indicate the real and effective basis of his power.

The imperial coronation of Charlemagne has engendered considerable controversy among historians, many of whom have dismissed Einhard's statement as excessive modesty on Charlemagne's part. The fact is that Charlemagne did not want to be crowned emperor of the Romans because first, "Roman" meant "Byzantine" to him, and he had no desire to emulate the ruler in Constantinople, and second, because he understood the constitutional implications of papal coronation and had no intention of placing himself in a position of debt or weakness to the bishop of Rome. What makes the situation more complex, however, is that an imperial ideal was coming to the fore among the churchmen of the Carolingian realm, but it was not the same concept of the empire that prevailed either at Constantinople or at Rome. The letters of Alcuin in particular are full of references to the "Christian empire" and to "Europa," the area contiguous with Latin Christianity whose leader was Charlemagne. In view of Charles' contributions to the welfare of Europe and in view of his position as the greatest king in Europe, Alcuin and other court churchmen were beginning to think that Charlemagne ought to take the title of emperor. This view, however, had little to do with emulation of the old Roman emperor or the ruler in Constantinople; rather, it was intended to be the apotheosis of Charlemagne's position as the leader of Christendom. It is likely that an imperial coronation of Charlemagne would have taken place had not the pope forestalled the Frankish king and his advisers on Christmas day 800. Certainly Charlemagne would not have allowed himself to be crowned by the pope; the coronation ceremony that Charlemagne preferred was the one used in 813 when he crowned his son and heir, Louis, emperor.

Having been crowned by the pope, Charlemagne chose to interpret his imperial title in the way delineated by Alcuin. He refused to think of himself as a Roman emperor, ignored the sanctions that were implied in his coronation by the pope, continued to call himself king of the Franks and Lombards, and regarded the title of emperor as the expression of his position as Christian war hero, theocratic monarch, and leader of the Frankish church.

The imperial idea played a much more important role in the policies of Charles' son and grandson, Louis the Pious and Charles the Bald, and it became a concept whose content was much more heavily influenced by the original papal ideology. The ninth-century Carolingian churchmen moved away from the Christian empire of Charlemagne and in the direction of a political antiquarianism that sought the full revival of Roman imperial ideas by imitating the ornate court ceremony of the Byzantine emperors and by using the full title, emperor of the Romans. Already in 816 Louis the Pious allowed himself to be anointed by the pope with this title. To the ninth-century Carolingian rulers and their ecclesiastical supporters, emphasis on the imperial title and the association of the Carolingian ruler with the Roman emperors were a buttress against the progressive decline of royal power after Charlemagne's death. Ideology became a substitute for Charlemagne's fame as a Germanic war leader. But ideology could do nothing to stem the advancing tide of localism and the rise of feudal lordship. The ninth-century bishops composed treatises on the glories of empire and kingship and the Carolingian emperors elaborated their court ceremonial, but they were unable to maintain effective leadership in their kingdom.

The papacy, over the long run, gained no more than the Carolingians from the revival of the imperial title in the West and from the acceptance by the Carolingians of the Romanist ideology. The mid-ninth-century pope Nicholas I aggressively asserted the radical doctrine of the Donation of Constantine, and the popes were adept at using their control over the imperial title to harass the later Carolingians, but this did not save the papacy from disaster in the late ninth century. For the popes needed a strong Carolingian ruler to protect them from the gangster Roman nobility. With the decline of Carolingian power, the papacy entered one of its darkest periods, in the late ninth and first half of the tenth century, in which it became the puppet of the ruling Roman nobility and completely lost its position as a leader in European society.

If the history of the ninth-century empire is one of failure on all sides, it should not blind us to the fact that a new element had been introduced into the political life of western Europe. In the latter part of the tenth century the title was taken up again by the German monarchy, which rose out of the ruins of the east Carolingian kingdom. The German kings were to make the imperial title an essential part of their policy until the middle of the thirteenth century, and their successors were to preserve the title until 1806.

Culture and Society in the First Europe

I. The Carolingian World

The literary sources and documentary evidence for the Carolingian period are much more voluminous than they are for any era since the fourth century. Whereas our knowledge of sixth-century France is drawn heavily from the information supplied by Gregory of Tours, and the sources for the seventh-century Merovingian kingdom are extremely fragmentary, there survive from the period 750 to 900 hundreds of pages of chronicles, letters, government documents, and treatises. The improvement in literacy is indicative of the advance of civilization, of the partial overcoming of the effects of the Germanic invasions and the expansion of Islam, and of the emergence of a new distinct culture and society in western Europe. In A.D. 400 western Europe was merely a geographic expression. Roman civilization was centered on the Mediterranean, and France, England, and the Rhine valley were mere adjuncts of the Mediterranean world. In 800 Europe signified a new civilization that was coextensive with the area of Latin Christianity and created by the confluence of Germanic traditions and Latin-Christian culture. Compared to Byzantium and Islam, Europe was still poor and backward, but it had developed particular ideas and institutions of its own, had found leadership within its own ranks, and had become conscious of its own distinct existence and destiny.

The first Europe included France, England, western Germany, Ireland, central and northern Italy, and the mountain regions of northern Spain. The vital centers of civilization were not on the Mediterranean coast, but in the river valleys of northern France and the Rhineland. The culture of the first Europe was unified by the universal language of churchmen, kings, and the aristocracy—Latin. Latin was the language of both ecclesiastical and secular governments and the tongue in which all intellectual matters were discussed or written down. In all cases, whether on behalf of monarchy, church, or duke, the Latin writing was actually executed by clerical scholars who were nearly all products of the flourishing monastic schools of the Carolingian empire. The everyday language of ordinary people, including most of the nobility, varied from region to region. In England Anglo-Saxon was spoken, and in the eighth and ninth centuries it even became a literary language. In Ireland the Celtic tongue was perpetuated. On the Continent the north and east were German-speaking areas, while the south and west contained a variety of dialects derived from the vulgar (that is, popular) Latin, the language actually spoken by ordinary people in the Roman Empire. These derivatives of vulgar Latin were the precursors of the Romance languages. By the middle of the ninth century German and French were emerging as distinct languages. In the Oath of Strasbourg of 842 the kings of the eastern and western parts of the Carolingian empire subscribed in what were recognizable French and German dialects. Thus, by the middle of the ninth century there was a growing separation of vernacular tongues between the eastern and western parts of the Carolingian empire. The emergence of French and German contributed to the disintegration of the Carolingian empire, whereas Latin was a strong force in uniting the various regions of the first Europe in a common higher culture.

In 400 the church was under the domination of the Roman emperor. By 800 it was freed from the last vestiges of Byzantine control, but the clergy in western Europe were strongly under the influence of the Carolingian rulers and identified their interests with those of the Frankish kingship. The Carolingians did not interfere in matters of doctrine, but they were concerned with the improvement of church discipline and aimed to use the intellectual and even the financial resources of the church in the service of the monarchy. The Carolingians recognized the Petrine theory and the more conservative aspects of the Gelasian doctrine. They conceded that the church belonged to the bishops, but they thought that the bishops belonged to the Carolingians. The clergy of the Frankish realm, in view of the Carolingian ruler's position as anointed king, Christian emperor, and patron of the church, was inclined to agree with this attitude. Typical of the ninth-century higher clergy was Archbishop Hincmar of Rheims (died 876), who was the friend, adviser, and chief propagandist of Charles the Bald, an expert on government and court ceremonial, and an aggressive advocate of the privileges of his see and of the episcopal office in general. The secular obligations and interests of the Carolingian clergy and the spiritual claims of the eighth- and ninth-century kings signified the interpenetration of the church and the world, which was to be the distinguishing quality of medieval civilization over the next three centuries.

Urban life was still important in A.D. 400, but it played no part in the first Europe. The Carolingian world was an underdeveloped, thinly populated, intensely rural society. Communications were almost incredibly bad, far worse than in the Roman Empire, and at least 80 percent of the population never moved more than ten miles from the place where they were born. Famine was a constant danger, violence a fact of everyday life, and the average life expectancy no more than thirty years. The people of the Carolingian world had little knowledge of science and hardly any knowledge of medicine. Under these conditions it is not surprising that magic proliferated among the populace and that the miraculous powers of local saints were the only recourse that ordinary people had against the ravages of nature and physical illness. The educated clergy struggled to moderate superstition and tried to limit the continual emergence of new cults of local saints by requiring episcopal canonization, but to little effect.

The centers of Carolingian life were the castle, the cathedral, and the monastery. Even the so-called cities of the Frankish kingdom, such as Charlemagne's capital at Aachen or the cathedral city of Rheims, consisted only of a governmental edifice surrounded by a few houses and encircled by a wall. There were remains of great Roman cities in northern Italy, such as the Eternal City itself, but many of the streets of the Italian towns were deserted, the houses falling into ruin, and the great Roman systems for water and sewage abandoned. Even the governmental, military, and ecclesiastical buildings of the Carolingian world were extremely modest. The Carolingian castle was usually a wooden stockade, and the churches and other buildings erected in stone were low and squat, modeled ultimately on Roman bathhouses.

At least half of western Europe in 800 either was covered with dense forests or consisted of swampy land unsuited to agriculture. The topography of the agricultural regions and the form of rural economy had been determined by the heavy-wheeled plow, drawn by oxen, that the Germans had brought with them. The furrow driven by the German plow was much deeper than that made by the light plow used in the Roman world. A day's work for the Carolingian peasant would consist of a single long, narrow strip. Consequently, the countryside came to be dominated by large open fields, divided into the strips driven by the heavy plow. Because of the lack of fertilizer, it was necessary to leave each field fallow every two or three years. By no means all, or even a great majority, of the peasants of the first Europe were dependent serfs, bound to the land and subordinated to the manorial lord. Especially in Germany and in eastern England, villages of free peasants, who held the open fields in common, sharing the strips, were the rule. Here the original Germanic social structure persisted, characterized by a large mass of free peasants.

In the Frankish kingdom west of the Rhine and in the wealthy agricultural midlands of England the medieval manor was already the basic unit of the economic system. In manoralism, the lord would retain part of the arable land of the village as his demesne, which would similarly be divided into strips. The peasant-serfs were given strips in the open fields in return for working the lord's demesne. They were bound to the land and subject to the lord's judicial authority and various servile dues, such as an inheritance tax called the *beriot*. The open field divided into strips was to remain the basis of the economic system of a great part of rural Europe until the fourteenth century. It was an unprogressive agrarian system of meager productivity, but it was the only one possible in terms of the technology available.

Of necessity, the manor was a self-sufficient economic unit in view of the overwhelming difficulties of transportation in the period. International trade was carried on only to serve the demands of the wealthy, and it was largely in the hands of aliens—Greeks, Jews, Moslems. Local society made almost no use of money. To the extent that local exchange was carried on, it was conducted by barter. The small amount of international trade precluded the need for gold coinage. The Carolingians minted only silver coins, which were all that was usually necessary when the smallest silver coin could buy a cow. When gold coins were needed, Byzantine and Moslem currency was used.

The poverty and localism characteristic of the first Europe made it appear insignificant in comparison with the Roman Empire and the contemporary civilizations of Byzantium and Islam. But the Carolingian world was marked by the beginnings of the application of intelligence to the problems of society, and although relatively the achievements in this connection may not appear to be great, this development was of the greatest importance in medieval civilization, for it marked the starting point for the political and intellectual growth of later centuries.

The work of the Carolingians secured a substantial literate class in Germanic society to do the work of church and monarchy. The leader in this great educational movement was the Englishman Alcuin (died 804), whom Charlemagne had brought from England to improve the monastic schools of his realm and to continue the work that Boniface had begun.

Alcuin was eminently successful in accomplishing the tasks that Charlemagne set for him. He established and expanded schools, libraries, and scriptoria in monasteries all over France. He wrote textbooks, prepared word lists, and made the trivium and quadrivium a firm part of the curriculum of the Carolingian school. The impact of his work can be seen in the great increase of literary and documentary materials surviving from the Carolingian period. It can be seen in the number of classical texts whose manuscripts are in the Carolingian hand. It can be seen in the spread of Roman liturgy to the French church and in some original contributions made by the Frankish churchmen themselves in this field. It can be seen by the fact that the earliest large collections of canon law, albeit not systematic and containing many forged decretals, date from the middle of the ninth century.

The educational work of Alcuin was decisive for the ninth and tenth centuries. Never again would Europe face the perils of barbarism, illiteracy, and the possible extinction of Latin culture that had been the danger in the seventh century. Alcuin completed the work that Boniface began: Latin Christianity became identical with western Europe not only in theory but in practice. An important test of the deep penetration of Latin Christianity into the life of the Carolingian world is the effect that the disintegration of the empire and the Viking invasions had upon education. There was some effect—a decline of some monastic schools because of disturbed local conditions or Viking marauders—but by and large the monastic schools continued their work successfully during this difficult period. Where the Vikings did not penetrate, in the eastern part of the German kingdom, the schools flourished increasingly and took over cultural leadership from the more western monasteries.

We can see, through the ninth century, as one generation of monastic scholars succeeded another, a steady increase in the extent and depth of their learning. Alcuin had been fighting to impose a basic literacy on the Carolingian church; by the middle of the ninth century this was no longer a problem, and with the first line of culture having been gained and secured, the monastic scholars could go on to more profound studies. What they consciously sought to achieve was the recovery of the whole biblical-patristic tradition of the fourth century, and they achieved this aim by the end of the ninth century. In a dozen or more great monastic schools in all parts of the Carolingian realm, especially in communities that had been founded or at least invigorated by Anglo-Saxon or Irish monks in the seventh and eighth centuries, there were extensive and active writing offices that preserved and spread the texts of the Bible and all the patristic writers. Augustine, especially, was carefully studied. The care and devotion that the ninth-century scholars gave to Bible study are indicated by the magnificent illuminated manuscripts they prepared. The influence of Byzantine iconography is evident in the Carolingian illuminations. But their artistic style is marked by a greater degree of classical naturalism and less of the disembodied symbolism of the Byzantine models.

The Carolingian monks' motive for the study of Latin literature was at first exclusively pragmatic, as had been the case with Alcuin following the programs of Cassiodorus and Augustine. By the second half of the century, in isolated cases the monastic scholars went beyond a utilitarian attitude to the classical texts and developed something of a humanist attitude: They admired the style and even the ideas of Cicero and especially Virgil for their own sakes. Such monastic scholars, it must be emphasized, were always a small minority, but the fact that they appeared in the ninth century attests to the degree of the penetration of Latin culture into the life of the French church.

The small currents of humanism that occasionally rose to the surface in the monastic schools joined with what was in the beginning a different stream of culture in the Carolingian age. Charlemagne had gathered around him in his "palace school" a group of eminent scholars, including several from Italy. Alcuin was the leader of this group. They devoted themselves to turning out reams of Latin poetry and playing little court games with the emperor. There were similar groups of court scholars in the reigns of Louis the Pious and Charles the Bald. A note of conscious antiquarianism and imitation of classical motifs runs through their work. This movement has been called the Carolingian Renaissance. The Carolingian court scholars were a small group of educated men who gave an aura of Roman culture to the Carolingian court and were well rewarded for their services. They included only one thinker with any important degree of originality—John the Scot, an Irishman who worked at the court of Charles the Bald. John translated the Neoplatonic philosophy of the fifth-century Syrian monk who wrote under the name Dionysius and added some Neoplatonic speculations of his own. But he did not inaugurate a philosophic movement; he had no one to continue his work, and his importance is limited.

Yet, if many of the most learned Carolingian scholars devoted themselves to literary exercises and did not try to deal with the problems of society, we can nevertheless see in the Carolingian period the beginnings of the application of intelligence to social problems. Charlemagne and his clerical advisers were not content to rely upon Germanic political tradition; they consciously set out to improve the institutional and technical aspects of government. After three centuries of disorder and drift the Carolingian world exhibited sharply contrasting instances of planning and ingenuity. Carolingian script itself is an example. Merovingian handwriting is almost impossible to read, but anyone who can read Latin can read most Carolingian documents after a couple of hours' instruction. The Carolingian script is so sensible and clear that it was used by the first book publishers of the fifteenth century for their type and is therefore substantially in use today. In a sense Carolingian script is even an improvement over the Roman, which employs only capital letters. The Carolingian scribes invented minuscule script, that is, lower-case letters.

The same intelligence is revealed in the operations of the Carolingian monetary and legal systems. After three hundred years of numismatic confusion, the Carolingian government established a new and reliable currency based on the simplest principles. They instructed their minters to take a pound of silver and divide it into 240 pieces, out of which the Carolingian coins were manufactured. The name *denarius* was given to this kind of coin, after one of the units in Constantine's monetary system. The Carolingian coinage worked so well that it was imitated by the English, who retained it as the basis for their monetary system until recently. A similar element of rationalization enters into the Carolingian impact on the development of the Germanic law. As a way around the inadequacies of Germanic methods of proof, the Carolingian courts devised the inquest, by which a panel of sworn men from the neighborhood gave their opinion in disputes about the possession of land. The inquest was perpetuated in tenth- and eleventh-century Normandy and was carried to England in the latter part of the eleventh century by William the Conqueror, where it developed into the jury of English common law.

The Carolingian government reveals in many ways the application of intelligence and rationalization to the problems of Germanic kingship. Charlemagne in particular was not satisfied with his position as either warlord or theocratic monarch, so he attempted to establish an effective administration, and he had the best bureaucracy since Theodoric the Ostrogoth. The first step in the reform of the Carolingian government involved the establishment of a chancery staffed by monastic scholars and the issuing of documents on several aspects of the life of lay and ecclesiastical society in which the king was interested. The Carolingian royal documents take the form of capitularies, each dealing in turn with various problems of government; the capitularies are reminiscent of Roman imperial decrees. A capitulary on the church ordered ecclesiastics to undertake educational obligations and to live up to the discipline and rule required of them. Another capitulary addressed to the stewards of the royal manors instructed them on the management of the estates under their responsibility; this instruction was necessary in view of the fact that the Carolingian king's domainal lands were his chief source of income. Still another capitulary applied intelligence to the problem of raising an army. The military system of the Frankish empire was still based on the principle of the Germanic folk-in-arms; when the king, as war leader, summoned them, all able-bodied men were supposed to join the royal army. Charlemagne and his ministers sensed the wastefulness and general unsatisfactory nature of this system. Hence the king published a capitulary allowing villages to band together to support one knight on horseback who would be much more useful than a motley mob of peasants carrying sticks and scythes.

Perhaps the most important of all Charlemagne's decrees dealt with the problem of local government. When the king, with his chancery, court, and army, was in a given area, there was no problem of obtaining the loyalty of the local population. But given the bad communications and the atomized nature of social relations, the problem was to maintain royal influence in areas beyond the possible impact of the king's personality. How were the duke (the local military official) and the count (the king's local representative in matters of law and finance) to be controlled in the areas away from the immediate influence of the royal court? This question had bedeviled the Merovingians, and their inability to solve it greatly contributed to the collapse of royal power in the sixth and seventh centuries. It remained a stumbling block to the Carolingians. Indeed, it may be said to be the most continuous, difficult problem of medieval monarchy. The Carolingian solution was to send representatives from the royal court, the *missi,* on periodic tours of inspection in the provinces in the hope of maintaining control over the local royal officials and preventing their integration into the provincial aristocracy.

The system of the missi was a highly intelligent and plausible innovation in Carolingian government and a tribute to the administrative skill of the ecclesiastics, such as Alcuin and Einhard, who served Charles the Great. But already in Charlemagne's later years, the central government was having trouble preventing the rise of a new provincial aristocracy. Nobles might be sent out from the royal court to act as dukes or counts, and they would be carefully chosen from among loyal men, but once they got to Aquitaine or some other distant province, they tended to strike roots in the local society and turn their title and the royal estates that were bound to it into hereditary property. This process of political disintegration was greatly intensified after Charlemagne's death, and the missi or any other expedient could not have countered the new factors that brought about the decline of Carolingian power in the ninth century.

Charlemagne's surviving legitimate son and successor, Louis the Pious (814–840), was an intelligent and well-meaning man, but unable to serve as the leader of a Germanic society. He was completely inept as a soldier, and this lost him the respect of the lay nobility, who felt themselves free to do what they wanted and so set about expanding their patrimonies. The situation was made worse by the bitter struggles of Louis' children for the royal title, which were well under way before his death. It was in many ways a repetition of the worst moments of the Merovingian monarchy. Finally, in 843 the three sons of Louis the Pious decided on the partition of the empire by the Treaty of Verdun. There were to be three Carolingian realms: the western, the eastern, and an anomalous middle kingdom that stretched a thousand miles from the Low Countries, along the Rhine, and over the Alps to include northern Italy. The middle kingdom almost immediately collapsed, leaving a maze of petty principalities from Flanders to Lombardy. Remnants of the middle kingdom along the Rhine were to be incorporated into the German empire in the tenth and eleventh centuries; their conquest was to be attempted by the powerful French monarchy of the thirteenth century, and they were thence to be the cause of frequent wars between France and Germany well into the twentieth century.

The Carolingian line did not end in Germany until 911, and in France the Carolingians held on until 987, but from the last quarter of the ninth century the Carolingian king was a nonentity. The power in Germany was in the hands of tribal chieftains whose position had been strengthened by the Carolingians, who gave them the title of dukes. In France the power of the central government had been usurped by the dukes and the counts, who were to remain the leaders of French society until the middle of the twelfth century.

The situation in the west Carolingian kingdom was acerbated by the incursion of Viking marauders up the Loire and Seine valleys. The Scandinavian attack on western Europe was the consequence of obscure struggles in Denmark and Norway that resulted in the expulsion of the defeated war bands. The latter either escaped into Russia or took to their long ships and pillaged the river valleys of western Europe. Some went through the straits of Gibraltar and attacked ports in Italy. But it was northern France that, except for the British Isles, felt the brunt of the Viking invasion most heavily. The Scandinavians had nothing to contribute to western European civilization. Their level of culture was no higher than that of the more primitive tribes among their German kinsmen who invaded western Europe in the fifth and sixth centuries. The unit of Scandinavian society was the same kind of war band that is depicted in *Beowulf.* The bounty-giving chieftain alone could gain the loyalty of these savage warriors. The Danish and Norwegian kings had little authority; in fact, the Scandinavians had a penchant for drowning their rulers in wells. The Northmen were untouched by Latin Christianity until the tenth century; they were heathens who were particularly fond of sacking great monasteries, which they soon discovered were very wealthy.

The later Carolingians were incapable of dealing with these new invaders. These descendents of Charlemagne were pious and frequently sophisticated men but nearly always cowards as well. In most cases they did not even attempt to engage the Vikings in battle, but offered the invaders bribes, which only satisfied them for a short while. The Scandinavians who attacked France in the ninth century were small in number, and their incursion did not represent a cataclysmic event comparable to the Germanic invasions. But their attacks produced fear and disorder, which further encouraged men to look to the most powerful lord in their own neighborhood for protection and to offer him loyal service in return for security. The Scandinavian invasions further emphasized what had been apparent since the 830s—that the Carolingians were no longer great warriors and that the provincial aristocracy need not concern themselves any longer with obeying the royal capitularies.

The Frankish churchmen who witnessed these lugubrious events were deeply chagrined and disappointed. The literature of the last three quarters of the ninth century is extremely pessimistic and bitter in tone, not because of the complete collapse of the social order, but because the world that the bishops found coming into existence was so strongly at variance with their high ideals. The bishops had dreamed of the political unity of Christian Europe under the Carolingian empire, in which a sacred and beneficent king, in accordance with their understanding of Augustinian teaching, would establish earthly peace and dispense justice with the advice of ecclesiastical leaders. This dream had been shattered. The empire was divided, real power had passed into the hands of the aristocracy, and the Carolingian kings were less and less able either to maintain control over government and law within their realm or to withstand the incursion of savage invaders from without who pillaged churches with impunity. The disillusioned and embittered churchmen of the ninth century resorted to desperate expedients. Some tried to gain new prestige for the monarchy by heightening its sacred qualities and by elaborating the ceremonial aspects of kingship. Others turned in disgust from the impotent Carolingians and threw in their lot with the papacy. They published a vast compendium of canon law, including many forged decretals attributed to St. Isidore, exalting papal authority over the kings and metropolitans in accordance with the Donation of Constantine. This expedient was of course no help to the Frankish clergy, in view of the growing domination of the Roman nobility over the papacy.

After 900 the ecclesiastics' despairing and bitter tone subsided. The churchmen of what had been the east Carolingian realm associated themselves with the creation of the new German monarchy and found in the Ottonian dynasty worthy successors to Charlemagne. The bishops and abbots of France in the tenth century turned away from imperial dreams and came to terms with the new feudal order.

II. The Feudal Organization of Society

The great English legal historian F. W. Maitland was wont to amuse his classes at Cambridge by remarking that feudalism was introduced to England in the eighteenth century. By this he meant that the word *feudalism* was not a medieval term; it was invented by English and French lawyers in the seventeenth and eighteenth centuries and was popularized by the political philosopher Montesquieu. At the time of the French Revolution the word was often identified with the ancien régime and the privileges of the French aristocracy, which aroused the wrath of the French bourgeoisie. The term *feudalism,* therefore, was frequently used in the late eighteenth century in a pejorative sense. From the French radicals it was adopted by Karl Marx, who used the term to signify precapitalistic economy. In the late nineteenth century medieval scholars, particularly in France and Germany, began to define feudalism with reference to western Europe in the Middle Ages and tried to work out its history. In view of the fact that feudalism was not a medieval term and that it had already been given certain meanings by modern social philosophy, it might have been wise for medieval historians to avoid using the term and to substitute medieval words, such as *vassalage* and *lordship.* They were not, however, able to be so reticent on this matter; the educated public demanded a scholarly definition of feudalism, and a host of authorities came forward with their interpretations.

In the vast scholarship of the past half century on the nature of feudalism, there have been sharply conflicting interpretations. One school regards feudalism as a group of political and legal institutions, as a system of decentralized government—"public power in private hands," in J. R. Strayer's excellent phrase. It maintains that feudalism emerged in the second half of the ninth century with the disintegration of the Carolingian empire. This school does not believe that feudalism was necessarily bound up with any specific kind of economic system. It points out that there were still feudal institutions in the expanding money economy of the thirteenth century and that instead of being rewarded with real estate, vassals received *fief-rentes,* or money fiefs, that is, pensions. This view sharply distinguishes feudalism from manorialism. It points out that feudalism was a system of political and legal relationships involving freemen, while manorialism was an agrarian system involving dependent peasants. The advocates of the political-legal interpretation of feudalism, or the strict interpretation, as it may be called, tend to be skeptical about the use of the term *feudalism* with reference to non-European history. Feudalism is a specific kind of decentralized government that prevailed in western Europe from the ninth century into the thirteenth.

The alternative prevailing interpretation of feudalism was largely the work of Marc Bloch and his *Annales* disciples in France. As a product of the French School of Sociology and Anthropology, Bloch was not prepared to define feudalism purely in political and legal terms. He regarded it rather in terms of a whole system in which all aspects of life—not only political but economic, ecclesiastical, and cultural—were centered on lordship. Feudalism was a political system, an economic system, and a system of values. We can speak of feudal economy, a feudalized church, and a feudal literature in much the same way as we can use the term *capitalism* to refer not only to a certain kind of production and exchange, but to government, thought, and culture. Those who lean toward Bloch's broad definition of feudalism are inclined to regard it as a stage in social development that has existed at various times in non-western European parts of the world, such as Japan, Byzantium, and Russia.

Lordship is the indispensable element in feudalism, which is a form of social organization in which most, or at least a great part, of the political, economic, and military power is in the hands of a hereditary nobility. The economic power of the nobility is based primarily on their lordship over large estates and a dependent peasant class. The political and military power of the nobility is based on the control that they gain over freeman soldiers and decentralized governmental and legal institutions. This is the form of social organization that was characteristic of France from the late ninth to the late twelfth century. It did not appear in England until the late eleventh century and not in Germany until about 1100, and it never emerged in Italy. This does not mean that in the nonfeudal areas of western Europe there were no lords, but it does mean that the lords did not gain an almost exclusive control of political, economic, and military power. Nor does the definition imply that the hereditary nobility was no longer important in Europe after 1200. On the contrary, the nobility continued to be important in political, economic, and military life, and in the fourteenth and fifteenth centuries the great aristocrats throughout Europe enjoyed an enormous amount of political influence. But the power of the nobility was no longer based primarily on its lordship over serfs and manors and its control over decentralized governmental and legal institutions. In medieval history feudalism existed at certain times and in certain places. It is plausible that feudalism has existed in other areas of the world, but the validity of this hypothesis must be based on empirical evidence assessed by the historians of these civilizations.

How did feudalism as we have defined it come to exist in tenth-century France? In the classical feudalism of tenth- and eleventh-century France three elements can be distinguished: the personal element (lordship and vassalage), the real or property element (fief), and the decentralization of government and law. The development of feudalism until the tenth century involved the process by which the latter two elements were associated with lordship and vassalage. In addition feudalism came to comprise a system of social ideals and values.

Nineteenth-century historians wasted a great deal of energy and paper debating whether feudal institutions were German or Roman in "origin." Most scholars today would say that this is a badly conceived, and essentially false, problem. The nexus of feudal institutions of the tenth century developed out of certain political, legal, and economic forms, in some cases German, in some cases Roman, in response to social need after the collapse of the Roman Empire in the West.

Lordship was the basic social and political institutions in Germanic society. The *comitatus,* or *gefolge,* the Germanic war band as described by Tacitus and in *Beowulf,* was based on the loyalty of warriors to their chieftain in return for the latter's protection and generosity; it was the embryo of medieval feudalism. The perpetuation of this kind of loyalty in the fifth and sixth centuries was made easier by the existence of a similar institution in the later Roman Empire, the *patrocinium* (clientage). In the disturbed conditions of the late empire, certain aristocrats gathered around them young men of fighting age whom they rewarded and protected in return for their loyalty and service. The vassals of the sixth and seventh centuries were simply the perpetuation of the German gefolge and the Latin patrocinium. They were freemen who voluntarily subjected themselves to some prominent warlord in their locality, but otherwise their only quality was their fighting ability. The term *vassal* comes from the Celtic word meaning "boy." As is implied by the etymology, the vassals of the sixth and seventh centuries were simply "the boys," gangs of thugs who fought on behalf of certain big men in the neighborhood, beating up people and destroying property at the behest of their warlord in return for protection, maintenance, and a share of the booty. They were as far removed as possible from the chivalric knights pictured in the romantic literature of the twelfth and thirteenth centuries. The social status of the vassals, beyond the basic fact that they were all freemen, depended on the lord they served. Those, for instance, who comprised the personal bodyguards of the Merovingian kings had greater prestige and wealth and were dignified by the special appellation of *antrustiones*.

As yet, vassalage had nothing to do with holding land; the vassals lived in a stockade provided by the lord and were fed, clothed, and armed by him. The next stage in the emergence of feudal institutions involved the association between vassalage and landed wealth, which was intended to reward the vassals for their service and support them. It is a fact of the greatest importance that this "realization of the feudal relationship," as it has been called by F. L. Ganshof, was an extremely slow and far from uniform development. Even in the tenth century the majority of vassals in France held no land and continued to live in their lord's household, and even in the early twelfth century, in the intensely feudalized areas of northern France and England, there were many landless vassals, although by this time they were definitely in the minority. In Merovingian times it appears that the only vassals who received estates were very prominent men in society. The Frankish dukes and counts were given "benefices" (benefits), gifts of land, by the Merovingian rulers to secure their loyalty and maintain them while they performed their services to the royal government. But the great aristocrats who received these benefices proceeded to treat them as hereditary estates. This practice was the beginning of the association of hereditary estates with loyalty and service to the lord. The system of benefices was imitated on a smaller scale in the relationship between some of the great aristocrats and their more important vassals.

A slow but fundamental change in military methods between the fifth and eighth centuries increased the necessity for associating vassalage with the benefice, or the fief as it came to be called after the eighth century. The Germans had used mostly infantry, and they had followed the military principle of the folk-in-arms, with the king summoning the mass of free peasantry to come to his aid in war. But the superiority of the armed cavalry, which had already been employed during the period of the Germanic invasions by the Roman emperor, the Huns, and some of the Germanic tribes, became more and more evident. By the eighth century more enlightened warlords in western Europe were seeking to build their armies around the mailed and mounted soldier—the *chevalier,* or *cniht* (knight). The introduction of the stirrup into western Europe from the Mediterranean world in the early eighth century markedly increased the effectiveness of the cavalry. But the knight's equipment was a heavy expense, and a lord who wanted a formidable army of knights among his vassals found it expedient to enfeoff (invest) his chevaliers with manorial estates from which they might obtain the income necessary to array themselves for battle.

The granting of a fief did not involve giving the vassal complete property rights over the estate. The vassal had the use of the income of the land as a reward for service and to make it possible to outfit himself as a knight. But technically the ultimate ownership of the land was still the lord's, who could recover it if the vassal ceased to be loyal, and when the vassal died, the fief automatically reverted to the lord. It is believed that the precedent for feudal tenure was a system of landholding called the *precarium,* which existed especially on church lands in the seventh and eighth centuries. By this precarious tenure an abbot or a bishop who had more land than he could profitably manage himself allowed laymen to have the use of such lands, usually on the payment of a rent and with the understanding that the estate was recoverable at will.

With their accustomed intelligence and ingenuity, the Carolingian family early realized the military advantages accruing from the enfeoffment of their vassals. Thus, when Charles Martel raised an army to encounter the invading Arabs in the fourth decade of the eighth century, he sought to obtain as large a knightly contingent as possible. He succeeded in carving out fiefs for his vassals from church lands, probably on the basis of precarious tenures. During the second half of the eighth century, the Carolingian ruler was rewarding his aristocratic vassals with large fiefs granted from the royal demesne itself. And the great lords of the western part of the Carolingian realm were quick to imitate the king and transformed some of their own vassals into enfeoffed knights. This growing association of fief and vassalage had the effect of generally elevating the social status of the vassal. From the hired thug, the vassal was himself becoming, in many instances, an important local lord, enjoying control over one or more manors. There was, of course, a great disparity between the duke or count, who was the vassal of the king, and the common run of knightly vassals, who were, for many centuries to come, violent and uncouth people.

The increasing involvement of vassalage and fief inspired a land hunger on the part of all vassals in feudal society that persisted well into the twelfth century. Whereas previously the fief was regarded as a reward for loyalty, now vassals sought out lords who were prepared to offer them landed estates. Those vassals who already had fiefs set about obtaining more and sought to assure the hereditary character of the land that they held of their lord. Although technically the fief was not inheritable and reverted back to the lord at the vassal's death, by the middle of the tenth century the fief had already become a hereditary patrimony for all practical purposes. On payment of an inheritance tax called the "relief," the deceased vassal's son professed his loyalty to the lord and took possession of the fief. The land hunger of the ninth- and tenth-century vassals is well illustrated by the great feudal epic *Raoul de Cambrai,* which, although it has come down to us in a twelfth-century version, dimly reflects a true incident that occurred in the ninth century and admirably mirrors the mores of the feudal class of that period. In the poem the emperor neglects to give Raoul the fief that his father had held, whereupon Raoul takes up arms against his lord in an attempt to force him to grant what he considers his rightful inheritance.

The final stage in the development of feudalism was the passing of governmental and legal authority to the king's great feudal vassals, who, in turn, passed some of this authority on to their own vassals. This stage is the product of the ninth century and was the consequence of the inability of the later Carolingians to maintain control over the dukes and counts who usurped the royal power over their duchies and counties and turned them into enormous hereditary fiefs. Lordship over manorial estates had always involved political and legal control over the dependent peasantry, but this authority was negligible compared to the passing of public power into private hands in the ninth century. The feudal princes won from the feeble monarchy the right to collect taxes and to hold courts to hear important pleas—the right of "high justice," the power to hang criminals—in their duchies and counties. Similarly, all lesser lords strove to gain pieces of public power and to exercise some political and legal authority within their own fiefs. By the middle of the tenth century in France, the powers of the Carolingian king had been swallowed up in the private feudal courts, which exercised overlapping and conflicting jurisdictions in a crazy patchwork of decentralized authority.

The emergence of the feudal kind of social organization was followed by the refinement and rationalization of several aspects of lordship and the entrenchment of a group of social values based on the ideal of loyalty. An involved ceremony by which the vassal declared his loyalty or homage to the lord was worked out. The candidate for vassalage knelt before the lord, who clasped his hands around the vassal's. The church added the usual Christian façade in the appended ceremony of fealty by which the vassal made a sacred vow of loyalty to his lord.

In enfeoffing his vassal, the lord usually handed over a symbol of the estate, such as a stalk of grain or a knife. It became customary (in a society where literacy was increasing) to attest to the grant of land by a deed called simply a "charter" (document). The medieval charter generally had five parts: the salutation, usually addressed to the leading men of the neighborhood in which the fief lay; the harangue, which gave the reason for the grant and was often elaborate if the grantee was an ecclesiastic; the dispository clause, which listed, often in great detail, the location and boundaries of the estate or estates granted; then the curse, which inflicted an ecclesiastical anathema on anyone who dared to contravene the terms of the charter, again very elaborate if the beneficiary was an ecclesiastic; and finally, the witness list, to which those who had witnessed the grant attested their private seals. In royal charters the scribe frequently wrote down the names of everyone present at court until he came to the end of the parchment. The medieval charter was thus an impressive document that, at least until the twelfth century, was apt to be decisive evidence in a lawsuit over the possession of land; it is not surprising that ecclesiastics frequently forged charters to help their claim to an estate. It is surprising how negligent lay lords were about preserving charters. They rarely could produce them when they had to, which encouraged interminable lawsuits over the possession of estates.

By the end of the tenth century the respective rights and duties of lord and vassal had been fully worked out. The vassal owed military service to his lord, not to exceed forty days a year. If he was an important vassal who held a large fief, he owed in addition the military service of a contingent of knights to his lord's army. Furthermore, the vassal owed suit at court—that is, he had to turn up at the lord's private court to participate in lawsuits between his peers, the other vassals of the lord, and to give the lord advice if the latter asked for it. In addition, the vassal was subject to feudal taxation—the relief, the money obtained from the vassal's property through wardship when the vassal died leaving no male heirs of age, and the regular "feudal aids," which the vassal had to pay the lord when the latter knighted his eldest son, married off his eldest daughter, or had to be ransomed from captivity. In return the lord was to maintain his vassal, but by no means did he have to give him a fief, and he was not to "disparage" the vassal by insulting him in one way or another. When the vassal failed to fulfill his vow of loyalty to the lord, he was subject, after trial in the lord's court, to forfeiture of his fief. If the lord acted improperly toward the vassal, the latter had the right of *diffidatio,* the dissolution of the feudal bond, usually inaugurated by the breaking of the symbolic stalk of grain or knife that represented the transfer of the fief. The former eventuality usually, and the latter always, meant war, but war was in any case a fact of everyday life in feudal society.

By the end of the tenth century subinfeudation—the process by which a vassal enfeoffed part of his own fief—had become common and had been frequently carried down through several degrees in the feudal scale from king or duke to lowly "vavasour," as the humblest subvassal was called. It was a question of whether the subvassals owed loyalty to the ultimate lord or only to their immediate overlords. There was no general answer to this question; it was a matter of whether the original lord was sufficiently strong and energetic to compel the subvassals to take oaths of homage and fealty to him as their liege, or chief, lord. A similar problem arose out of the fact that land-hungry knights became the vassals of two or more lords to gain additional fiefs. The anomaly might be solved by one of the lords asserting his rights to be the liege lord. If he did not and if the vassal's two lords should go to war against each other and summon the vassal to render them military service, the vassal would solve his predicament by joining the lord who seemed most likely to win.

The Carolingian churchmen had initially been bitterly critical of the advance of lordship, which they believed, with justice, to be a cause of the disintegration of the Christian empire. But they were not long in coming to terms with the new social order by integrating themselves within it. The bishops and abbots became lords and vassals like the lay nobility and were involved in all aspects of the life of feudal society, except personal participation in feudal warfare. The churchmen did their best to pacify feudal society and to Christianize and idealize the feudal relationship. They added the religious ceremony of fealty to the act of homage and became adept at enumerating the mutual obligations of lord and vassal in terms that presupposed a level of conduct far more civilized and moral than the rough fighters who still composed 95 percent of the feudal class were capable of achieving. The church tried its best to limit war in feudal society during the eleventh century by the spread of the Peace of God movement, by which the feudal nobility were to form leagues to preserve the peace and to promise not to fight on certain days. Generally the peace movement was a failure; it was successful only when a strong ruler got behind it because he saw in it advantages for himself.

As a general rule feudalism was antagonistic to royal power. As we have seen, it involved decentralized government and the passing of public power into private hands. The king of France in the tenth and eleventh centuries was indeed the nominal lord over the great feudal princes, but he had no real power over the dukes and counts who were his vassals because he was not the liege lord over their subvassals. As long as he could not defeat the duke of Normandy or the count of Toulouse, the king in Paris had no control over them, although he had a right to their formal homage. The duke of Normandy had a much better army than the king had, and the Norman knights did not recognize the king as their overlord in any way. For all practical purposes, the monarch of France, whether he was a Carolingian or, after 987, of the new Capetian house, was only the duke of Paris. A similar situation prevailed in the feudal organization of Germany in the twelfth century.

Where the feudal pyramid with the king at the pinnacle actually did operate was in England after the Norman Conquest in 1066. It did so because the Norman duke in the tenth and the first half of the eleventh centuries learned how to use feudal institutions in a special way—to increase the power of the central government, which was not the way feudalism had worked in the later Carolingian empire.

All social systems are founded upon a set of assumptions about what is good and what is bad in human relationships, and these assumptions tend to be perpetuated and adhered to long after the precise social needs they served have ceased to operate. The values that served feudalism and the feudal lords were these three: first, that military prowess is a social good because only the strong man can provide peace and protection; second, that the bonds of personal loyalty are the sinews of the social order and only the relationship of one man to another can give sanction to political and legal obligations; third, that these bonds of loyalty are arranged in an ascending and descending order, stretching through society and on to heavenly regions.

The third assumption allowed feudal relationships to receive the approval of ecclesiastics who were trained in the old doctrines of hierarchy. Indeed, it is likely that churchmen placed a much greater emphasis on this feudal value and made hierarchy both more central and more rigid in feudal society. Although French ecclesiastics were initially wary of the growth of feudal lordship, by the end of the tenth century, they were often ideological advocates of feudalism as part of the divinely ordained hierarchical order of the world.

The second assumption, that of loyalty, was useful to ambitious kings and dukes who sought to impose a sovereign power over the landed society in the eleventh and twelfth centuries. The ideal of loyalty also inspired, to a degree, a new sensitivity to personal relationships, a sentimental view of the attachment of one human being to another; it became a constituent of the medieval idea of love and an inspiration for the romantic movement of the twelfth century.

The first assumption, on the social value of military prowess, became transmuted into the ideal of aristocratic leadership in society and the belief that the man on horseback was the natural leader, whereas others stood and served. Feudal recognition of the intrinsic goodness of physical strength was perpetuated in the moral sanction of the stronger over the weaker that became essential to the operation of the European states system from the twelfth to the twentieth century.

CHAPTER EIGHT

Ecclesia and Mundus

I. The Nature of the Early Medieval Equilibrium

By 900 it was certain that the ideal of the political unity of the new Latin Christian civilization could not be realized. The European peoples would have to be satisfied with more limited political structures. During the tenth century these states began to take shape; the political decentralization and social chaos of the late ninth century was reversed, and two successful examples of political leadership appeared in northwestern France and in Germany. The feudal duchy of Normandy and the Ottonian German empire were, to a considerable degree, founded upon strongly contrasting kinds of institutions. But they had in common a fundamental quality of new European civilization: Ecclesiastical and secular political ideas, leadership, and resources were inextricably joined together in the creation and progress of these states. The same interpenetration of *ecclesia* and *mundus,* the church and the world, can be seen at work all over tenth-century Europe, even in the disappointing later Anglo-Saxon monarchy with its ineffective central government and in the even weaker Capetian monarchy.

This equilibrium between the church and the world was the outcome of the long struggle to achieve the Christianization of European society. Gregory the Great and St. Boniface had been the founders of this movement, which in the later eighth and ninth centuries had been greatly advanced by the Carolingian kings and higher clergy. The failure of the Merovingian monarchy had demonstrated Germanic kingship's great need of the moral and religious sanctions and other assistance that the church could provide. The efforts made by the leaders of the Carolingian world to create a world order in which church and kingship worked together had resulted in a bitter and painful failure. The same interpenetration and identification of the church and the world was used, however, by the Norman dukes and German emperors to create more limited political structures, but ones that exhibited outstanding qualities of strength and endurance and that gave European civilization its first examples of successful political leadership.

The power of both the German emperors and the Norman dukes of the tenth and eleventh centuries was founded, to a substantial degree, on the control they were able to exercise over the church in their territories, especially the Benedictine monasteries, and by the aid and support the church gave them in the form of revenues, knights, administrative personnel, and the fostering of popular veneration for the pious ruler who affected to be a friend of the church. On its side the church gained its patron's protection against the unruly lay nobility, the endowment of monasteries and bishoprics with great estates and magnificent Romanesque religious houses and cathedrals, the raising of the higher clergy to the front rank of the nobility, and frequent opportunities for the leading ecclesiastics to attend the courts and councils of the ruler and thereby to influence his policy.

This kind of relationship between ecclesiastical and secular leaders was supported by the learned doctrine of the identification of the ecclesia and mundus that was popular precisely at the period when the early medieval equilibrium came to fruition. Since the ninth century there had been a growing tendency for ecclesiastical writers to describe the church, regarded as the mystical Body of Christ, as embracing the whole world. In this view there were not separate spheres for the ecclesia and the mundus; rather, the church was one, indivisible, universal Body of Christ encompassing the whole world. By the eleventh century this theory had become commonplace among the leading thinkers and even less prominent writers of the Latin church. "The church" and "the world" were treated as identical and synonymous terms, and hence empires and kingdoms had to be regarded as entities not outside the church, but within its universal bounds. This theory of the absorption of the secular into the spiritual realm was inspired by the actual prevailing relationship between church and kingship in western Europe in the tenth and first half of the eleventh centuries.

II. The Norman Feudal State

In 987 the Carolingian line finally lost the royal title west of the Rhine. The descendants of Charlemagne had exercised no effective control over the great feudal princes for a hundred years, and the monarchy had no resources of its own. But the persistence of the Germanic and Christian traditions of kingship made the French crown still a prized possession, and the most powerful lord in the Ile-de-France, Hugh Capet, pushing aside the Carolingians, took pains to secure his elevation to the French throne by the formal Germanic process of election. The church legitimated his rule by anointment, and the abbot of the royal monastery of St. Denis was as devoted to Hugh as he had been toward the Carolingians. With clerical support Hugh Capet was able to pass the royal title on to his son, and, in fact, the Capetian family was to hold the French throne by direct line of hereditary succession until the fourteenth century. As far as the tenth and eleventh centuries are concerned, nothing important had happened; one weak dynasty had merely been supplanted by another. Before the twelfth century the Capetian kings were famous for only two things: extreme piety and sexual promiscuity. This somewhat paradoxical combination of qualities may be due to the fact that all we know about the earlier Capetians comes from the description of monastic chroniclers whose judgment of character was based on severely limited criteria. But it is significant that the tenth- and eleventh-century Capetians attracted notice only by their devout exercises and adulterous scandals. These are purely personal enterprises; the Capetians had no effect on the government and society of France. The great feudal princes who were nominally their vassals acted independently and gave them no support. In fact, these kings were not even secure in their own domain of the Ile-de-France, which was infested with the castles of robber barons. It is true that the Capetians did have the royal title and, with the aid of the abbot of St. Denis and the archbishop of Rheims, they cultivated the traditions of sacred kingship. Although these traditions would eventually be useful to the later Capetians, they availed the kings of France in the tenth and eleventh centuries very little. Theocratic monarchy could be an extremely powerful moral force, but only when combined with power derived from effective institutions, and of these the earlier Capetians had not a shred.

Among the leaders of feudal France of the tenth century the count of Flanders and the duke of Aquitaine stand out for their effective control over the vassals of their principalities. The counts of Champagne, Toulouse, and Anjou were also figures of prominence in the new feudal society, but it was the dukes of Normandy who stand preeminent among the vassals of the king of France. In the late tenth century and first half of the eleventh they made of the hitherto backward frontier, Neustria, in northwestern France, a country renowned for its great monasteries and schools, and they manipulated feudal institutions in an unprecedented manner to create the strongest state in Europe west of the Rhine.

Normandy came into existence as a feudal duchy in 911 when a certain Rollo, the savage leader of a group of Viking war bands, wrested from the terrified Carolingian king the area contiguous with the ecclesiastical province of Rouen. Rollo became the vassal of the French king and received the title of duke, but he proceeded to act in an entirely independent manner and to expand the original size of his fief. The size of the Scandinavian settlement was small, and the Northmen rapidly intermarried with the native population and adopted the French language. Rollo and his companions allowed themselves to be received into the church by the archbishop of Rouen, but their conversion no more altered their way of life than it had that of Clovis and his companions. For seven decades Normandy was the scene of interminable wars and blood feuds among the Norman lords, and the power of the early dukes was simply dependent on their ability as warriors. There is nothing in the history of Normandy before 980 to account for the subsequent development of Norman institutions. How, then, did the Norman dukes create the most powerful feudal duchy in western Europe between 980 and 1050?

Three stages can be distinguished in the creation of the power of the Norman dukes. In the 980s the dukes helped place Hugh Capet on the French throne, and as a consequence the Capetians did not attempt to interfere in the affairs of the duchy during the crucial period of Norman state building. By the time the Capetian king finally realized the significance of the rise of a new kind of feudal state in the duchy contiguous to the Ile-de-France in the 1030s, it was too late to remove this danger. The second and most decisive stage in the emergence of Normandy involved the relationship between the Norman dukes and the church in their territory. The dukes of the late tenth and early eleventh centuries were much more sophisticated men than were their predecessors. They were aware of Normandy's cultural backwardness, and they brought into the duchy from the Rhineland and northern Italy outstanding monastic scholars to inaugurate the improvement of the Norman church. The dukes built and endowed monasteries, supported the monastic schools, and allowed these able scholars to establish some of the most thriving centers of learning in western Europe. Their relationship with the church was not, however, confined to this worthy patronage; they proceeded to use the ecclesiastical resources and personnel to advance their effective power in their territory. It is probable that the leaders of Norman monasticism gave them valuable advice and encouragement in this connection. For these churchmen had come to Normandy in most cases from areas that lay within the confines of the German empire, whose rulers were using the German church for a similar purpose. Certainly the higher clergy in Normandy did not question the kind of church-state relations that the dukes proceeded to establish before 1035, but rather consciously accepted it.

The dukes' plan was to impose heavy feudal obligations on the higher clergy and to use the knights who were enfeoffed on ecclesiastical lands as the nucleus of an army that could overcome the unruly lay nobility. By the middle of the eleventh century the Norman duke could, in fact, obtain the military service of more than three hundred knights from his ecclesiastical vassals, which was more than sufficient to destroy the power of the lay nobility. Certain advantages accrued to the duke from his inauguration of the feudalization of Normandy by imposing vassalage on the clergy and only then turning to the lay nobility. The clergy could not legally marry; though many had children, these children were bastards who could not inherit fiefs under feudal law. Hence no bishop or abbot could pursue a dynastic interest with regard to his fiefs. The fiefs, in any case, were attached to the ecclesiastical office and were not the personal possession of the bishop or abbot. Furthermore, the duke had control over the election of the higher clergy. He was the venerated patron of the Norman church, whose opinion would be sought before the monks or cathedral clergy proceeded with the election of an abbot or bishop. The duke had in addition a veto power over the selection of the higher clergy because unless he was willing to receive the bishop or abbot-elect as his vassal, the latter could not take possession of the lands associated with his office.

The final stage in the rise of ducal power began in the 1020s with the imposition of vassalage and feudal obligations on the lay nobility. This work was made easier by land hunger and overpopulation among the knightly class in Normandy. A few of the restless Norman lords had already departed for southern Italy in the second decade of the eleventh century to carve out domains for themselves in that wealthy land. The landless knights who remained at home could obtain fiefs from the duke only if they were prepared to undertake onerous feudal obligations. The greater lords in Normandy, who already were substantial landowners, found themselves driven to the wall by the dukes' military power and forced into vassalage. This successful final stage in the building of the Norman feudal state suddenly stopped when one of the dukes, in a fit of piety, departed on a pilgrimage to Jerusalem and died en route, leaving as his heir a child whose legitimacy was clouded by the fact that he had been born before his parents' marriage. The early part of the reign of William II, the Bastard (1035–1087), was marked by a desperate attempt by the enemies of ducal power—namely, the Capetian king and the lay nobility—to undo the work of the previous half century. The alliance between the ducal family and the Norman churchmen remained firm, however, and the union of the strength of the ecclesiastical vassals with William's precocious military ability resulted in the complete victory of the duke over his enemies by the end of the 1040s.

William then set about continuing his predecessors' policy, establishing the strongest feudal power in Europe by the end of the 1050s. He not only imposed vassalage on all the lay nobility, but was able to demand from them military service of a particularly well-defined and onerous kind. He overcame the debilitating effects of subinfeudation by making himself the liege lord of every vassal in the duchy. In Normandy the amount of feudal service that the tenants-in-chief owed their lord was specifically set down, proceeding in multiples of five knights to as large a feudal contingent as 120 chevaliers, according roughly to the amount and value of land that the vassals held of the duke. By 1060 the Norman duke could command an army of one thousand knights, which was by far the largest available to any ruler west of the Rhine. William prohibited the building of castles without his license on pain of forfeiture, and he was strict in demanding suit at court from his vassals. His local official, the viscount, was effectively employed to draw the jurisdiction of law and taxation away from the feudal lords and into the ducal authority.

The moral sanction for this effective military and administrative power was provided by the support that William received from the church. Like his predecessors, William was a great patron and endower of monasteries, and the Norman schools continued to attract some of the finest minds in Europe. Among them was Lanfranc, a former teacher of law at Pavia in northern Italy, who became a monk in Normandy and won renown as one of the foremost theologians of the mid-eleventh century. Lanfranc became one of William's strongest admirers. The Norman duke gained the plaudits of churchmen all over Europe for taking seriously the Peace of God movement. William saw in it a way to give religious sanction to centralized ducal authority and to limit still further the traditional indiscriminate warfare of feudal society, which had no place in his conception of a feudal state. He made himself the president of the Peace of God movement in Normandy and forced its vows upon his vassals. By 1060 a Norman lord who thought of revolting against the duke faced the prospect of ignominious defeat and forfeiture, as well as ecclesiastical condemnation.

The completion of the structure of ducal power gave William the freedom to look for new fields of conquest and triumph. He had behind him a magnificent army and an aggressive nobility who sought a satisfactory outlet for both their love of fighting and hunger for land. Consequently, in the 1050s William began to turn his attention to events across the channel and to scheme for the eventual gaining of the English throne. The situation in England offered a dramatic contrast to that which existed in Normandy. The power of the later Anglo-Saxon monarchy was in the course of being drained by the rise of lordship in a manner that paralleled that of the ninth-century Carolingian monarchy. The great earls had gained for themselves not only enormous estates, but control over royal legal, administrative, and financial institutions in their regions. Compared to England, Normandy was a small, thinly populated, and poor country. But the Norman dukes had succeeded in bringing all the resources of their land under their own control, whereas in England public power was rapidly passing into private hands and the authority of the king was on the verge of extinction. Compared to the Anglo-Saxon king, who was an offspring of the house of Wessex, which had ruled part or all of England for five centuries, the Norman duke was an upstart. Nor could the Norman duke make use of the doctrine of theocratic kingship that had been popular in England since the middle of the tenth century. He had, however, what the Anglo-Saxons, like the later Carolingians, lacked: effective institutions, a strong personality, and military ability. This combination marked a new departure in the development of medieval monarchy.

III. The Ottonian Empire

East of the Rhine, as compared with France, feudal institutions were not the basis of social organization. The political and social structure of the east Carolingian kingdom was still dominated by pristine Germanic traditions. Each of the various tribes, or "stems," as they were called—the Franks, Saxons, Swabians, Bavarians, Lotharingians, and Thuringians—recognized the leadership of a great warrior chieftain who in the Carolingian period had acquired the administrative title of duke and had made it into a sign of his superiority. Below the stem dukes on the social scale there was a small group of great nobles and a large mass of free peasants. In the south and west both manorialism and feudal lordship were making their appearance, but in a degree too limited and embryonic to have any effect on political authority. The leaders of Germanic society were the stem dukes, the great nobles, and the bishops and abbots of the German church. The latter were influential because they controlled all the literacy and a considerable part of the landed wealth of the country. In a sense the German church had existed before there was any effective royal leadership in Germany because the great abbeys that Boniface and his disciples had established in the river valleys of what is today western

Germany had been the vanguard of Carolingian expansion. Only after the monks had converted the people, established centers of learning and civilization, and created the German church did the Frankish kings begin to exercise effective rule east of the Rhine.

By the end of the ninth century the Carolingian kings had become nonentities and could offer no leadership to the tribes in their struggles to hold back invaders along their borders. To the west the Scandinavians offered a threat. To the east the incursions of Magyars (Hungarians)—another invader of Europe from Central Asia—and Slavs were dangerous to the survival of the German duchies. In 911 the last of the Carolingians died, and the stem dukes, asserting the German electoral principle, chose Conrad I, duke of Franconia, as king. This choice cannot be said to have marked an important change in the history of the German monarchy. Conrad was unable to exercise any authority over the other stem dukes, who remained independent. At Conrad's death in 918 the dukes elected as king his chief tormentor, Henry I, the Fowler, the duke of Saxony. Henry's family, which later came to be known as the Ottonians, was to rule in Germany for more than a century, and consequently the beginning of his reign has frequently been said to mark the real beginning of the German monarchy. But he was not much more successful than his predecessor, and at the accession of his son Otto I in 936, the German monarchy had found neither the institutions nor the ideology to give it any control over the great dukes. In fact, the duke of Bavaria was attempting to join his duchy with Lombardy, which would have made him more powerful than the Saxon dukes and would have demolished whatever unity the German realm possessed.

The creation of the German monarchy was the work of Otto I the Great (936–973), who consciously symbolized the policy he intended to follow by the manner of his coronation. By insisting on being anointed and crowned by the archbishop of Mainz, the primate of the German church, at Charlemagne's old capital of Aachen, he thereby signified that he regarded himself as the successor of the great emperor and that he intended to associate himself with the powerful German church and to make use of the ideology of theocratic monarchy. His father had feared the powerful bishops and abbots and had refused even to be crowned by an ecclesiastic. Otto determined to dominate the church and to use its resources and personnel in the interests of establishing the institutional basis of royal power in Germany. There was no other way by which the German monarchy could obtain the wealth, military support, and the administrators it needed to overcome the entrenched power of the stem dukes. The German clergy were willing to cooperate with the king, who offered them protection against the nobility, rich endowments for ecclesiastical establishments, and the opportunity to serve in his chancery and act as royal ministers.

A threefold institutional basis for the Ottonian control over the German church can be distinguished. Most important was the institution that came to be called "lay investiture" by its critics in the late eleventh century, but until then was simply referred to as the royal investiture of churches. The king asserted the right to invest bishops and abbots with the symbols of their office, finding theoretical support for this claim in his sacred quality as an anointed king. Without royal investiture, the bishop and abbot-elect could not assume office; the effect was to give the king control over the election of the higher clergy. To make the king's control of ecclesiastical appointments even more secure, ecclesiastical homage was joined to lay investiture, so the bishop or abbot could take possession of the property belonging to his office only after he became the king's vassal. Under these conditions clerical election became a mere formality in the Ottonian empire, and the king filled up the ranks of the episcopate with his own relatives and with his loyal chancery clerks, who were also appointed to head the great German monasteries.

The Ottonian domination over the church was aided by the persistence of the Germanic legal ideas of property that form the background to the institution of proprietary churches (*Eigenkirchen*). This institution was by no means exclusively confined to Germany; it existed all over Europe and still exists in the Anglican church in the form of the advowson. But it was in the German empire of the tenth and eleventh centuries that the proprietary church system assumed its greatest importance, for it became one of the foundations of royal power. German law held that any structure, including a church, that was erected on a proprietor's land legally belonged to the proprietor. Thus, whoever owned the lands on which churches and monasteries were built could act as the lord over them and appoint the ecclesiastical officials. This was not important if the church was a parish church, but it was significant if a monastery with great estates was involved. The Ottonian house, partly because of its benefactions to the church and partly by more violent means, gained proprietary rights over many of the German bishoprics and abbeys, thereby acquiring the right to appoint important members of the higher clergy and the control of the ecclesiastical revenue.

The third institutional basis of the Ottonian control over the German church was the system of "advocacy." The advocate was a secular manager of the estates belonging to a cathedral or monastery who thereby gained a large share of the revenues and lordship over the people on the ecclesiastical estates. The Ottonian family was adept at gathering the majority of advocacies in Germany into their hands.

By the middle of the tenth century the wealth and military power of the German monarchy was steadily on the increase as a result of these ways of establishing close control over the church. It is known that almost half the army that Otto II used in Italy in 981 came from monastic lands. The higher clergy were also used extensively as royal administrators, not only in the royal chancery; the abbots were granted the power of counts in many cases and given onerous tasks of local administration on behalf of the monarch. With the political, military, and economic support of the church, Otto did not find it difficult to beat the stem duchies, including Lorraine, into submission. By 955 he had begun to meddle in the chaotic affairs of northern Italy through his marriage to Adelaide, an Italian "queen," and his claim to the Lombard crown.

That year marked the turning point in Otto's reign. He inflicted a crushing defeat on the Magyars at the Battle of the Lechfeld and became the hero of western Europe. To the German nobility he appeared to have fulfilled the claim he made at his coronation to be the successor of Charlemagne. On the field of his victory over the Magyars the great lords raised him on their shields in the Germanic manner and proclaimed him emperor. A few years later, in 962, Otto went to Rome and had himself crowned emperor by the pope.

Otto wanted to bring remnants of the old middle kingdom under his control, particularly Lorraine and northern Italy, and he needed the imperial title to provide the legal basis for such claims. He was especially concerned with northern Italy, whose political condition was chaotic, and he wished to preclude further attempts by the south German dukes to conquer Lombardy. Another motive for Otto's imperial coronation was his need to emulate Charlemagne as much as possible to strengthen the legal foundation for his control over the German church. A third reason for Otto's taking the imperial crown was the potential danger of the renovation of the imperial title outside Germany by the French king or a French duke. Another thesis, strongly favored by German historians in the 1930s, is that Otto wanted the imperial title to be the moral leader of a German drive into the Slavic lands beyond the Elbe. All or most of these motives were involved in Otto's imperial coronation, but whatever special reasons Otto had for reviving the imperial title, it was the natural consequence of his position as the most outstanding ruler in Europe. He commanded the greatest military power since Charlemagne, he was a theocratic monarch who dominated the church in his territory, and he was the warrior-hero of Germanic society. These qualities made Otto appear, both to himself and to contemporaries, as the worthy successor of Charlemagne, and if the great Frankish king was an emperor, then Otto had to be also. His imperial title was simply the apotheosis of his rule over Germany and northern Italy.

There was nothing Roman in Otto's conception of the imperial title. The nineteenth-century *Kleindeutsch* historians blamed the Saxon king for getting the German monarchy involved with the fatal and debilitating charms of Italy, which they believed to have been the source of all the later troubles of the medieval German monarchy. But Otto hardly spent any time there and did not even make any effective contribution to rescuing the papacy from its subversion by the Roman nobility. Otto the Great was a hard, tough soldier and administrator; he was intelligent enough to make use of ideology, but he was not the kind of man who was actually inspired by ideas. He did, however, fall prey to the proclivity of the *arriviste* to obtain social recognition for his heir. And the only recognition that seemed suitable for the son of the German emperor was marriage to a Byzantine princess. The Greeks initially dismissed Otto as a barbarian upstart, but after a change in dynasty, the new Byzantine emperor finally allowed the Ottonians to have one of his distant relatives. Otto II's marriage inaugurated a kind of political antiquarianism that had marked the Carolingian empire after Charlemagne. Under his Greek wife's influence he directed his attention to establishing effective authority south of the Alps. Otto II allowed the Slavs to destroy the German settlements east of the Elbe, while he used his army to undertake an expedition into southern Italy, where he was killed fighting the Moslems in 983.

During the reign of Otto II's son, Otto III (983–1002), the association of the German empire with Rome became predominant, and the policy of Otto I was abandoned in a fundamental way. It is a tribute to the strength of the institutions that Otto the Great had created that the German monarchy did not completely collapse during his grandson's reign. Otto III succeeded to the throne as a child, and until 995 the empire was ruled first by his Byzantine mother Theophano, and then by his grandmother Adelaide. During the seven years of his own rule Otto was rarely in Germany, but devoted himself to the achievement of a far-flung imperial plan centered on Rome. This program was a consequence of the influence exerted on the youthful Otto III by his teacher, the French churchman Gerbert of Aurillac, who had studied in Moslem Spain and who had become the greatest western scholar of his age. Gerbert and other churchmen who predominated at the court of Otto III talked about a "renewal of the Roman Empire." Gerbert easily won over the young and impressionable Otto to his plans for a new empire, with Rome once again the center of the western world. Accordingly Otto took up residence in Rome and set Gerbert on the papal throne as Sylvester II. It was intended that this would be the most important moment in the history of the Roman Empire since the time of Constantine. The coins, illuminated manuscripts, and poems coming from Otto's court proclaimed an involved and sophisticated imperial ideology going far beyond the political antiquarianism of the later Carolingian empire.

To the Ottonian court theorists the city of Rome symbolized both the political unity of the world and the unity of the church. One of Otto's documents begins, "Otto, slave of the Apostles and according to the will of the Lord Savior, august emperor of the Romans. We proclaim Rome capital of the world. We recognize that the Latin church is the mother of all churches." These ideas are depicted in the extremely well-executed Ottonian illuminations. One picture shows Otto seated on his throne and flanked by the Apostles Peter and Paul. Another shows the countries of Europe bringing him gifts of homage.

Gerbert's plans were confined not only to ideology, art, and court ceremonial; Rome as the head of the world and as the head of the church implied some specific policies that, if they could have been executed, would have had a profound impact on the development of Europe. The first policy involved the creation of a great federal empire embracing east central Europe to obviate a renewal of the struggle between Germans and Slavs. Otto, in fact, made a trip to Poland to grant the Christian duke of Poland an honorary title and to receive him within the renovated Roman Empire. A similar kind of federal arrangement was made with the king of Hungary. The second policy that Gerbert induced Otto to support was in the area of papal-imperial relations. For almost a century the papacy had played no part in European life because of its subjection to the Roman nobility, and as Pope Sylvester II Gerbert was conscious of the conflicts that might arise between the German emperor and a revived papacy. In his view the papacy ought not to assert temporal claims, but should become a purely spiritual institution. Gerbert did not believe that the Donation of Constantine was genuine, and he persuaded the emperor to condemn it as "lies forged by certain popes and attributed to the name of the great Constantine."

Otto III died in 1002 and Sylvester II one year later, and their ambitious program expired with them. Already in the last years of Otto's reign the Saxon nobles were beginning to rebel against him on the grounds that Otto's imperial ideology neglected Germany and went against their interests. Otto's successor, his cousin Henry II (1002–1024), abandoned Otto's plans and confined himself to maintaining the royal power in Germany. This was certainly a more realistic approach to the problems of the German monarchy than those adopted by Otto II and Otto III, and it is doubtful if the institutions created by Otto the Great could have sustained another reign like his son's and grandson's. Nevertheless, it is remarkable that Gerbert had foreseen two of the bitterest conflicts that marked later medieval German history: the struggle of the Germans against the Slavs and the conflict between empire and papacy. Many aspects of the renewal of the "Roman Empire" appear as useless and as empty of real significance as the political antiquarianism of the later Carolingians. But in these two respects Gerbert and his disciple Otto had exhibited a keen perception of two fundamental problems that were in their incipient stage.

The Ottonian empire has sometimes been interpreted as merely a continuation of Carolingian kingship. It has been pointed out that the Ottonian kings relied for their power on their association with the church, that they made use of the doctrine of theocratic monarchy, that they cultivated the imperial ideology; all these ideas and institutions can be found in the age of Charlemagne and his successors. It is true that the Ottonians were not great innovators, as were the Norman dukes. It is true that the essentials of Ottonian government were already delineated by the Carolingian monarchy. But the Ottonians used these precedents to establish a successful and long-lived monarchy, whereas the Carolingian efforts resulted in bitter disappointment. The Ottonians did not have to deal with such a large area, nor were they as troubled by the decentralizing effects of lordship. In addition to these initial advantages, the success of the Ottonian empire must be attributed to the firm hold over the resources of the church that Otto the Great established and that served as the foundation of effective royal power even when the presence of a strong royal personality was wanting in Germany during the two successive reigns. The Salian rulers of the second and third quarters of the eleventh century were able to build on the achievements of their Ottonian kinsmen, to go beyond Carolingian precedents, and to strengthen the institutional foundations of the German empire.

The Ottonian period, which inaugurated German history, sets the tone and in some ways acts as a microcosm of all the later vicissitudes of German civilization. In the Ottonian empire we see that peculiar combination of aggressive, ruthless efficiency and the expression of a childlike, lyrical idealism or, as the German writers call it, that union of *Macht* and *Geist* that so often distinguishes the later history of the lands between the Rhine and the Elbe.

IV. The Cluniac Ideal

The interpenetration of ecclesia and mundus that characterized the institutional foundations of both the Ottonian empire and the Norman duchy depended heavily on the resources and activities of the Benedictine order. The relations between church and kingship in the tenth and eleventh centuries and the contemporary theory of the identification of ecclesia and mundus were, in effect, founded upon the ubiquitous Benedictine cooperation with the leaders of the lay society. The monastic order was the keystone of the early medieval equilibrium.

This equilibrium, as it came to be firmly established in the late tenth and first half of the eleventh centuries, was particularly identified with the ideals and activities of the Burgundian monastery of Cluny and her dependencies and affiliates. As the ideal of the acknowledged leader of western monasticism in the first half of the eleventh century, the Cluniac program became the intellectual expression of the prevailing world order. The abbot of Cluny was the elder statesman of mid-eleventh-century Europe. Cluniac monks were closely involved with the government of the German Salian dynasty, which succeeded to the German throne in 1024, and they played an important role in the creation of the Norman church. The monastery of Cluny itself was the largest, best endowed, and most prestigious in Europe. It held the admiration of churchmen and the devotion of laymen, and the kind of religious life it inculcated was at the heart of early eleventh-century piety.

The monastic life as envisaged by Cluny was, on the whole, not original; it was a perpetuation and intensification of the Benedictine form as it had come to exist by the ninth century. Carolingian monasticism had been given official form in the monastic constitutions of 817, which had been drawn up by St. Benedict of Aniane, who had been placed at the head of all the Carolingian monasteries by Louis the Pious. The aim of the second Benedict was to supplement the rule of the first Benedict and to acknowledge the changes that had taken place in western monasticism over the previous three centuries as the communities of the black monks had come to undertake their indispensable social duties. Benedict of Aniane recognized that the monks no longer supported themselves with their physical labor; instead, they acted as official intercessors for lay society with the deity through liturgical prayer and performed educational, political, and economic functions. This was the kind of monastic life that came to be identified with Cluny during the tenth and eleventh centuries.

The actual beginnings of the monastery in 910 were extremely modest. The monastery was founded in an obscure corner of Burgundy by a duke of Aquitaine on the site of his hunting lodge, and for a while the duke even neglected to remove his hunting dogs to make room for the monks. Yet within a century Cluny had become the leading monastery in Europe and had formed a loose kind of special order of its own. Several monasteries were directly subject to the abbot of Cluny, particularly daughter houses founded by Cluny itself, and other Benedictine communities, many of which were much older than Cluny, were loosely affiliated with it and recognized the leadership of its abbot. Cluny exercised a strong influence over the great monastery of Gorze in Lorraine, the Cluniacs reformed and then dominated the important French royal monastery of Fleury on the Loire, there was a strong Cluniac influence at work in the revitalization of English monasticism undertaken by St. Dunstan in the late tenth century, and it was a Cluniac abbot from Dijon whom the duke of Normandy brought to his duchy in the early eleventh century to inaugurate the expansion of the Norman church.

Cluny's success must be partly attributed to the fact that it had obtained immunity from both lay and episcopal interference and was directly subject to the pope, and since the papacy was in a condition of complete decrepitude until the middle of the eleventh century, the monks of Cluny were free to work out the destiny of their community. They chose a succession of extremely able abbots, usually men with the highest aristocratic, or even princely, backgrounds, who led the Burgundian religious house to its position of eminence in the affairs of Europe. This was particularly true of the two abbots who between them ruled Cluny for most of the eleventh century: Odilo (died 1049) and Hugh the Great (died 1109). Cluny demanded of its own brothers and of dependent and affiliated monasteries the full observance of the Benedictine Rule as amended by Benedict of Aniane. The monks at Cluny became famous for the extent and beauty of their liturgical devotions. Kings and nobles all over Europe who had come to take seriously the teachings of the church and who were concerned for the salvation of their own souls and those of their relatives were eager to give Cluny rich endowments to be named in Cluniac prayers. But neither its enforcement of monastic discipline nor its association with popular piety accounts for Cluny's leadership in the world order of the early eleventh century. While Cluny was free of any lay control, its abbots did not make this a requirement for Cluny's daughter houses or affiliates. On the contrary, the Cluniac monks, who worked all over western Europe, exhibited the greatest eagerness to accept kings and dukes as the patron lords of their establishments. The abbot of Cluny looked with respect, gratitude, and admiration on the friends of the church who ruled in Germany, the Ile-de-France, Normandy, England,

and other states in western Europe. The Cluniac monks were eager to offer their services to royal chanceries and were not loath to receive the usual rewards for this work—appointments to bishoprics. The Cluniacs readily accepted, and certain of them even encouraged, the entrenchment of the doctrine of theocratic kingship in Germany, and they took the lead in spreading the veneration of the ruler as the patron and friend of the church even in Normandy, where such traditions had hitherto been lacking.

The Cluniac movement entered Germany from Burgundy and Lorraine at the beginning of the eleventh century, and the attitude of the German rulers was *from* the first sympathetic to the spread of this movement. The first ruler of the Salian dynasty, Conrad II (1024–1039), was a harsh soldier and administrator who exploited the German clergy severely, but he favored the spread of the Cluniac movement in his realm. But the great advance of Cluniac influence in Germany came during the reign of Conrad's son, Henry III (1039–1056), who acted as the patron and protector of the order in his realm. Henry had married the daughter of the duke of Acquitaine, whose house had founded Cluny in the early tenth century, but Henry's affinity for the Cluniac order was based on much deeper motives than his wife's special association with the leading monastery in western Europe. In the character and ideals of Henry III can be seen what appears also in the outlook and conduct of the rulers of France, England, and Normandy in the middle of the eleventh century—the completion of the Christianization of Europe.

The leaders of western society, nearly all the rulers of the period, and many of the ordinary nobility themselves had come to take seriously the teachings of the church and to allow these teachings to govern their lives. Contemporaries sensed that Henry III of Germany was a monk in worldly garb, and Edward the Confessor of England, as his appellation implies, later was canonized as a saint. All over Europe in the middle of the eleventh century kings, dukes, and nobles were building churches and endowing monasteries. The regular clergy in particular had come to receive fanatical devotion and respect from the leaders of the lay society. Monastic intercession was deemed to be almost indispensable for achieving heavenly grace, and nobles, when they felt mortality creeping on, got themselves off to the nearest monastery to die clothed in the monastic habit. Gifts were made to monasteries not only to secure the salvation of certain named relatives, but, in more general terms, for the welfare of all believers living or dead. It is during the eleventh century that the holy day of All Souls was fixed in the church calendar.

The spread of lay piety did not, however, imply the willingness of kings and dukes to subject themselves to ecclesiastical authority. On the contrary, it provided a further intellectual basis for royal control over the church, for it made kings feel as spiritual as churchmen. In no case was this situation more marked than in that of the great German emperor Henry III, who was not only a great patron of the Cluniac order in Germany, but was inclined to adopt monastic attitudes. His greatest delight was participating in the translation of relics to a new shrine. He was fond of making speeches in which he declared that he forgave all his enemies. At the same time, however, he believed that he had received a sacramental office at his coronation and that he had full spiritual authority to bestow the symbols of ecclesiastical office on bishops or abbots and to order the affairs of the church. He believed that Christ was working through his royal power just as He did through a priest at the celebration of the mass. As the representative of Christ on Earth Henry felt compelled not only to govern the German church but to order the affairs of the papacy, which had been in a scandalous condition for more than a century. In 1045 there were no fewer than three rival popes in Rome, corrupt scions of the gangster Roman nobility. The synod of Sutri of 1045, which Henry called and presided over, marked the first step in the reform of the eleventh-century papacy. In two years Henry appointed three German bishops to the throne of Peter, and the pontificate of the last of these, Leo IX (1049–1054), who was the emperor's kinsman, became the turning point in the development of the eleventh-century papacy.

Henry's piety and ecclesiastical interests by no means precluded his continuing the work of the Ottonians and adding to the institutional foundations of royal power in Germany. As a strong personality, able warrior, theocratic monarch, and great administrator, Henry III represents the apotheosis of early medieval kingship in that he brought together all the qualities that made for successful medieval monarchy. Henry realized that the German monarchy was still short of strong and permanent institutions and that it still relied too exclusively on the personnel, resources, and doctrine of the church. He discovered a new kind of royal soldier and administrator in the institution of the *ministerialis*. The latter was a serf-knight, a soldier who was given the best training and equipment of the day but did not have the legal status of a freeman. The ministerialis did not voluntarily enter into vassalage, but was entirely dependent on his lord. Serf-knights were by no means exclusively a German institution, but they never played any important role in feudal societies outside the Salian empire. It appears that German churchmen were the first to recruit serfs from their estates and to train them as knights, but it was Henry III who made the ministerialis into an important royal institution. He used ministeriales to garrison the castles that he was building all over northern Germany. It was his plan to join Saxony to Franconia, the homeland of the Salian dynasty, and to make these duchies into the permanent crown lands of the German monarchy. Thus Henry had discovered a new kind of personnel for his army and local government, and in his concern to build up the German crown lands he had laid the foundations for a policy similar to that which the Capetian kings were to pursue with enormous success in the late twelfth and thirteenth centuries. He set up his capital at the great fortress of Goslar in Saxony, which was situated close to the silver mines discovered in Otto I's reign, and he proceeded to use his ecclesiastical knights and the new ministeriales to bring the recalcitrant Saxon nobility and free peasantry under the full authority of the Salian dynasty.

In 1050 it appeared that the political destiny of Germany, as much as that of the feudal duchy of Normandy, would be marked by the ever increasing power of the central government. The world in which Cluny was the leading spiritual force was marked not only by the final stage in the Christianization of Europe, but also, in Normandy and the German empire, by the achievement of a degree of political and social order that western Europe had not known since the collapse of the Roman Empire.

Early eleventh-century ideals of church and kingship were given monumental form in the style of architecture that modern art historians have chosen to call Romanesque. In the river valleys of western Germany, France, and northern Spain, many stone churches had been built to serve the needs of the monarchical, feudal, and ecclesiastical elite by the middle of the eleventh century. The churches that have been designated as Romanesque in style exhibit strong regional and local differences in their structures. They have, however, certain things in common. First, these ecclesiastical structures tend to be small compared with the grandiose churches of the twelfth and thirteenth centuries. The Romanesque churches were chapels for the lay and sacerdotal hierarchies, whereas the later Gothic churches were designed to bring in the masses for public worship. Second, the Romanesque churches were ecclesiastical fortresses; they were built by the same architects and artisans who erected the feudal fortresses of the eleventh century. The Romanesque church was God's fortress, and it reflects a view of Jesus as head of the feudal hierarchy and the prototype of theocratic kings. Third, the Romanesque churches tend to be dark inside; the walls have few windows to let in the light. The absence of windows is a consequence not only of technological limitations in architectural engineering, but of the elitist and private character of this kind of house of worship. Finally, the Romanesque style is marked by a richness in ornamentation and sculpture, often individual in character and much less universal in style than the Gothic of the thirteenth century. This quality again reflects the elitist and private character of Romanesque art, but it also reveals the increasing self-consciousness and confidence that prevailed in the Cluniac world of the mid-eleventh century. Considered as feats of structural engineering, the Romanesque stone churches mark a tremendous advance upon Carolingian churches. In the Rhine valley, southern France, and northern Spain, many of these imposing buildings still stand as monuments to the increasing rationality, piety, wealth, and public power that marked the age of Henry III and the leadership of Cluny in European culture.

CHAPTER NINE

Byzantium, Islam, and the West

I. The Limitations of the Byzantine and Islamic Civilizations

In the 960s the German emperor Otto I sent a Lombard bishop, Liudprand of Cremona, as his ambassador to Constantinople to obtain a Byzantine princess for his son. The embassy was not successful, but Liudprand left an account of his experiences that offers an illuminating insight into the relations between the still new European civilization and the old and wealthy culture of the Mediterranean world. The Greeks regarded the Germans as impoverished barbarian upstarts, and Liudprand was conscious of the fact that there was nothing in the West that even distantly resembled the wealth and luxury of Constantinople. He had to compensate for his sense of inferiority by depicting the Greeks as effeminate and corrupt and living off the glories of a vanished age. His hero, Otto, was bold and honest, the Byzantine emperor cowardly and devious. Liudprand's report of his embassy to Constantinople reflects the encounter of the old and the new, the meeting of a civilization just beginning to develop its characteristic form and one that had reached its ultimate limits. Compared to Byzantium and the other Mediterranean civilization, Islam, western Europe was indeed impoverished and backward in the middle of the tenth century. A hundred years later Byzantium had begun to enter its long eclipse—the Arab world had reached the limits of its cultural, political, and economic growth—while medieval Europe was at the beginning of its greatest period of creativity and improvement, and the Latin peoples had begun their economic and political penetration of the Mediterranean world. This fundamental change in the relative situations of Byzantium, Islam, and the West marks the conclusion of the early Middle Ages.

In the middle of the tenth century Byzantium entered its last golden age under the wise and aggressive Macedonian dynasty, particularly during the reign of Basil II (963–1025). The government, economy, and cultural life of the east Roman Empire exhibited its greatest vigor since the reign of Justinian in the sixth century. The Macedonians finally brought the divisive iconoclastic controversy that had intermittently raged since the first half of the eighth century to an end by subscribing to the orthodox view on images. They protected the peasant class against the depredations of the wealthy landlords, who aimed to achieve a decentralization of political authority similar to that which had ruined the Carolingian empire. Basil II destroyed the power of the Asiatic Bulgars, who had pressed on the Balkan frontier of Byzantium, and he undertook a counterattack against the Islamic power in the Middle East, bringing back Antioch, Cyprus, and Crete under Greek rule. The emperor benefited from his control over the commerce of Constantinople, which in the tenth century was probably the wealthiest city in the world. These political and economic achievements were paralleled by a cultural efflorescence that art historians, at least, have called the Macedonian Renaissance. The magnificent illuminated manuscripts that were produced in the Byzantine court and monasteries during Basil's reign are marked by a greater degree of classical naturalism in their depiction of the human figure.

But the Macedonian age turned out to be the last achievement of Byzantium before the long twilight of Byzantine civilization set in. The rise of lordship after the first quarter of the eleventh century weakened the power of the Byzantine state from within, and in the middle of the eleventh century a new Asiatic invader of the Mediterranean world, the Moslem Seljuk Turks, again forced the Greeks to engage in a bitter struggle for survival. By the beginning of the 1070s the conquests of Basil II had once more been lost to the Moslems, and the desperate emperor was forced to appeal to the pope for aid in preventing the fall of Constantinople.

The history of Byzantium is a study in disappointment. The empire centering on Constantinople had begun with all the advantages obtained from its inheritance of the political, economic, and intellectual life of the fourth-century Roman Empire. Except in the realm of art, in which the Greeks excelled, Byzantium added scarcely anything to this superb foundation. The east Roman Empire of the Middle Ages made no important contributions to philosophy, theology, science, or literature. Its political institutions remained fundamentally unchanged from those that existed in the reign of Theodosius the Great at the end of the fourth century; while the Byzantines continued to enjoy an active urban and commercial life, they made no substantial advance in the technology of industry and trade developed by the cities of the ancient world. Modern historians of the medieval eastern Roman Empire have strongly criticized the tendency of nineteenth-century scholars to write off Byzantium as the example of an atrophied civilization. Yet it is hard to find, outside the field of art, any contributions by way of either original ideas or institutions that the medieval Greek-speaking peoples made to civilization. Perhaps the unprogressive nature of medieval Byzantium was precisely the consequence of the vast legacy of the Roman world that the Greeks received inviolate. The Byzantine world apparently had already answered for it all problems of government, economy, and higher thought, and therefore the task to which the Byzantines dedicated themselves was merely one of preserving the satisfactory and comfortable existence they had inherited. The limitations of Byzantine civilization must also be attributed, of course, to the tremendous pressures that were exerted almost incessantly on the frontiers of the empire from the sixth century onward. The Byzantines had to apply all the resources at their command to hold back the Arabs and their other enemies, and in so doing they dissipated their best energies and allowed their culture to become more and more rigid.

The penetration of the Mediterranean world by the Seljuk Turks was by no means a boon to eleventh-century Islamic civilization. The level of Turkish culture was much more primitive than that which prevailed among the sophisticated Arabic-speaking peoples of the eastern Mediterranean. The Turks' attempt to seize political power in the Middle East deeply divided the Moslem world for more than a century. At the western end of the Mediterranean a similar incursion took place in the eleventh century by nomadic Berber tribesmen from the North African desert, who crossed the straits of Gibraltar and gained control of Moslem Spain. At both ends of the Mediterranean Moslem world by the middle of the eleventh century, political authority was passing to unsophisticated, fanatical puritans who cared nothing for the great achievements of Arabic thought and who were willing to listen to the hysterical strictures of the orthodox against philosophy and science. After the tenth century the weakness of the Arabic political tradition became more and more evident. The political institutions of Islam were strictly those of oriental despotism, and the later political history of medieval Islam is marked by the irresponsibility of the rulers toward the welfare of the people and the recurrent palace revolutions that are endemic to this kind of political system. The political instability that began to distinguish the Islamic world in the first half of the eleventh century caused the increasing neglect of the Mediterranean irrigation system, which had been in existence in some cases for three millennia and upon which the prosperity of the Arabic countries was ultimately based. The Islamic world had not yet entered its deep decline in 1050. Some of its greatest military and intellectual achievements were yet to come, and the Moslem merchant was still a dominant figure in Mediterranean life in the eleventh century, but by and large the greatest days of Islam had ended, and the strength of Islamic civilization was leveling off from its pinnacle of creativity. These limitations of Islamic civilization account for the inability of the Arabs to prevent the political and economic penetration of the Mediterranean by the European peoples in the tenth and eleventh centuries.

II. The Rise of Europe

Compared with the Byzantine and Islamic worlds, tenth-century western Europe was still an underdeveloped area, impoverished, intensely ruralized, and thinly populated. But whereas the Greeks and Arabs had reached the ultimate extent of their economic development, western Europe was just beginning a demographic and technological revolution that was to bring the Latin world, within two centuries, to a commercial and industrial level surpassing the economic achievements of any area and period of the early Middle Ages and probably also of the ancient world.

The new European political and social order, the improved degree of peace and good government, the Christianization of Europe, and the increase in literacy and social intelligence created an environment that encouraged optimism, enterprise, improved communications, and technological innovation. There was still a great deal of violence in European life, but there was sufficient peace and order in many areas to allow men to use their energies for something beyond the war of all against all—improvement in their material condition.

In the tenth century the European people adopted improvements in technology that had been available in the Mediterranean world for centuries. The importation of the horse collar and stirrup gave them a much greater use of available horsepower. Some historians have said that the stirrup made possible the emergence of the knight who was able to stand up in the stirrups and tilt a lance against his adversary, but this advanced form of military horsemanship did not actually appear until the twelfth century. Until then, as contemporary illustrations demonstrate, the medieval knights threw their metal-tipped wooden lances in the manner of nineteenth-century Comanche warriors. The innovations in the control of horsepower were mainly useful in improving transportation in tenth-century

Europe. Europeans also began to make use of waterpower in the tenth century on land and wind power, to a greater degree than before, on the sea. The introduction of watermills greatly facilitated the grinding of grain and contributed to an increase in the food supply. Waterpower was also used to operate sawmills, which contributed to an increase in the amount of good lumber available for construction. The development of the lateen sail made it possible for ships in the Atlantic and Baltic coastal trade to tack against the wind, which the old square sails did not permit. For naval warfare and long-distance commerce in the Mediterranean, where the winds were unreliable and inadequate, the Italians employed a Byzantine-type galley that was the descendant of the oared ships of antiquity.

These social and technological changes go a long way toward explaining the steady growth in the population of Europe from the middle of the tenth century. There was no alteration in the extremely primitive conditions of European medicine and no apparent improvement in the pitifully short average life expectancy, but the increased food supply must have resulted in a marked decrease in infant mortality. For all classes in society there was a greater hope of controlling the physical environment and greater expectations of a better life. Greater confidence in the future, joined with the impress of Christian teachings on all classes, increased respect for the value of human life and created a favorable milieu for raising larger families.

Nothing demonstrates more dramatically the impact of social and technological change in western Europe than the eagerness of the more numerous younger sons of lords, knights, peasants, and other people who were dissatisfied with their too meager lot to move around in search of a better life. The scions of aristocratic families could establish large domains of their own in areas where central authority was weakest inside Europe, or they could move to the frontier regions or even overseas and try to carve out fiefs for themselves. The young knights competed with each other to become the vassals of some established great lord, and, failing this, they could follow enterprising nobility in their freebooting new ventures. The opportunity for the younger and poorer peasants was similarly promising and probably greater in the tenth century than either before or after, at least for another four hundred years. The tenth century was the great age of the internal colonization of Europe, turning some of the immense stretches of forest and swamp into agricultural regions. The peasants learned how to clear wooded land, reclaim marshes, and make greater use of field rotation, leaving one of the two or three open fields of the village fallow each year to restore its fertility and thereby increase the yield. In Germany the more robust sons of the peasants had a special kind of opportunity for improving their condition; some became royal ministeriales and ended up as the captains of royal castles.

In many parts of Europe in the tenth century some of the poorer knights and more intelligent peasants followed an unprecedented avenue of economic advancement. They took up residence in towns and became merchants and craftsmen. The process of the rise of urban life in tenth-century Europe has been somewhat obscured by the categorical thesis that Henri Pirenne presented in his brilliant essay, *Medieval Cities*. Pirenne, in this and other well-written and highly plausible works, insisted that the origin of the tenth-century cities lay exclusively in international trade. He contended that the merchants who engaged in this large-scale enterprise gathered for protection under the walls of a "burgh," a fortress belonging to some lay or ecclesiastical prince, and such "burghers" proceeded to make their town into a center for international trade. Eventually, as the bourgeois grew in number, they built a wall around themselves. As the suburbs developed, a new wall became necessary fifty or a hundred years later. Thus Pirenne, measuring the surviving walls of his native Belgian cities, was able to demonstrate their growth in concentric circles, which served as indices of ever-expanding commercial activity. This neat pattern of medieval urban growth existed in Flanders and the Rhineland, but there were cities in other parts of Europe whose beginnings and nature were different. Most of the cities of Italy had been there since Roman times, but they had been neglected and underpopulated for centuries. In the tenth century people from the surrounding countryside moved into the cities to engage in commerce and industry, making them again into centers of urban life instead of mainly centers for ecclesiastical and political administration. Many towns in England and northern France began as burghs and ended as centers of only local trade. And all over Europe there had appeared, by 1050, towns that were merely overgrown villages, places in which a few wealthy and enterprising peasants set up a market for the immediate neighborhood. There are many small towns in England whose main street is still called the Corn Market.

An English churchman of the late tenth century distinguished three classes in society: those who fought, those who prayed, and those who worked. He did not mention the bourgeois, for whom there was no place in the traditional social structure. The burgher did not even have a *wergeld* in Germanic law. Was he a freeman or unfree? Was he subject to the bishop or lord whose fortress or cathedral he nestled against for protection? In northern Europe there was no clear answer to these questions, and it was to take three centuries before many cities would gain the right to administer their internal affairs and the bourgeois would achieve the full status of freemen in royal and ducal law courts. These rights were usually obtained by purchase, at exorbitant prices, of a charter of urban liberties from king, lord, or bishop.

The dominant class in society looked with suspicion upon a group of men whose provenance was frequently humble and obscure and who made their living in ways that hitherto had been associated with social outcasts and aliens, such as Jews and Arabs. The landed class enjoyed the benefits of commercial exchange and industrial production that the burghers provided. But kings, dukes, bishops, and lords did not regard even the wealthiest burghers as their social equals, and they refused to give the city people their freedom. The burghers of the tenth and eleventh centuries were ruthlessly harassed, blackmailed, subjected to oppressive taxes, and humiliated. This drove the bourgeois back upon their own resources, and it accounts for the intensely corporate and excessively organized character of medieval cities. The city people living in their dark little houses in their crooked and dirty streets, surrounded by an indifferent and frequently hostile world, began in the tenth century to regulate every aspect of urban life with a compulsive efficiency.

In the late tenth century there were already guilds of merchants and craftsmen in Italy and even along the Rhine that carefully regulated commerce and industry. The merchant guilds were corporations of entrepreneurs who engaged in international commerce. The craft guilds were dominated by the master craftsmen who regulated the standard of industrial products, fixed prices, and strictly controlled the journeymen and apprentices who worked in their shops. In the first half of the eleventh century the Italian cities took up the institution of the commune—a sworn association of men banded together for some purpose—which had existed in rural areas, and used it as the legal basis for turning their cities into self-governing corporations. By 1050 another common characteristic of medieval life had appeared in the commercial centers of Flanders and northern Italy: The real power among the bourgeois was in the hands of a small oligarchy of great entrepreneurs who controlled the merchant guilds in each city and dominated the town government. In the old episcopal center of Milan there was a bitter feud not only between the bishop and the bourgeois, but between the wealthier people and those of more modest means, "the rag-pickers." The class struggle in Milan already indicated what would be a common characteristic of the medieval townsmen: They hated each other even more than they hated everybody else.

The economic growth that Europe was experiencing between 900 and 1050 involved the processing of some natural resources for export. It was the Flemish cities that discovered the first staple of medieval European international trade. Having drained the marshes of Flanders, the late tenth-century peasants found the recovered land unsuitable for agriculture and used it for raising sheep. They obtained enough wool to make cloth for export, and it was on the basis of this commerce that the Flemish weaving towns of Ghent and Ypres prospered in the eleventh century. By 1050 the first internal trade routes had come into existence, stretching from Flanders across the heart of Europe to northern Italy, whose merchants were willing to exchange Mediterranean luxuries for Flemish textiles. The meeting ground for the Flemish and Italian merchants was the county of Champagne, whose ruler in the twelfth century was to sponsor an annual international fair in his territory.

The north Italian cities had initially become wealthy as interlopers in Byzantine and Moslem trade. The Venetians, who were technically part of the Byzantine empire in the tenth century, were given special trading privileges at Constantinople that allowed them to become the intermediaries between Byzantium and Europe. Not satisfied with this enormously profitable commerce, the ruthless Venetians established relations with all the important Moslem commercial centers of the Mediterranean world. In the later decades of the tenth century Genoa and Pisa, on the west coast of Italy, also sought a share of Moslem wealth, which they attained by a subtle mixture of commerce and piracy. It was the Genoese and Pisan merchants who brought the Rhone valley back into the Mediterranean orbit and who inaugurated the use of the Alpine passes for trade with northern Europe.

The revival of western Europe's participation in Mediterranean economic life was followed, during the first two decades of the eleventh century, by political and military penetration. The more enterprising or land-hungry French knights followed the lead of the Italian merchants in trying to gain a share of the fabulous wealth of the Moslem lands. Norman free-booters appeared in Sicily in the second decade of the eleventh century and began a long struggle to carve out domains for themselves in southern Italy, a country wealthy beyond the dreams of feudal avarice. Similarly, Norman and other French adventurers joined the struggle against the Moslems in northern Spain. This advance of the western European nobility was to culminate, at the end of the eleventh century, in the first crusade of 1095.

Bourgeois, nobles, and peasants were not the only people who were seeking new opportunities in the late tenth and early eleventh centuries. The churchmen, who in any case had always had a much more international outlook, also exhibited a greater degree of mobility. A Frenchman and several Germans went to Italy to become the bishops of Rome, and a Norman Frenchman was for a time archbishop of Canterbury in the 1050s. The leaders of the Cluniac order moved around Europe, founding monasteries and advising rulers. What was unprecedented in the early medieval church was the emergence of a new kind of itinerant scholar, who traveled great distances to find a suitable intellectual milieu and to study under renowned teachers. The great monastic schools of Normandy drew a steady stream of outstanding Italian scholars. Others, however, were making their way to cathedral cities in northern France and Lorraine to study theology and canon law. A few intrepid souls had even dared to cross over into Moslem territory to study mathematics and science at Cordoba. These usually obscure and impecunious scholars were preparing the ground for a tremendous upheaval in European intellectual life.

In the year 1050, in every country in western Europe, there were groups of people engrossed in some kind of novel enterprise. Europe no longer lagged far behind Byzantium and Islam in any way, and in some respects it had surpassed the greatest achievements of the two civilizations with which the Latin-speaking peoples now competed for hegemony in the Mediterranean. In all areas of human activity new aims were being pursued and new methods tested in the western Europe of 1050. The civilization formed out of the union of the Latin Christian and Germanic cultures was entering an era of unprecedented creativity and achievement. The question that remained to be answered was whether the social order of the early medieval equilibrium, which had provided the background for political, economic, and cultural success, could prevail in the changed world that was at the dawn of its existence.

Europe in 1050

What was Europe like in the year 1050? What were the remarkable sights and sounds of the age? What would have caught the eye of the traveler through Europe in this year? We may get some insights into the answers to these questions by accompanying an Anglo-Saxon monk on a journey from his monastery in bleak and distant Yorkshire to the Eternal City in the year 1050. It was now only half a century since the end of the first Christian millennium in the year 1000. At the time there had been speculation, especially among some nervous French monks, that at the end of the millennium the world would melt in fire and the Second Coming of the Lord would occur. After a year of watchful waiting in some quarters, the calendar moved to 1001 and nothing exceptional happened. By 1050 these momentary concerns were long forgotten and there was buoyancy and optimism in the European ambience. Not until around 1200 did speculation resume on when the world would end.

One day, while our monk was at work in the scriptorium of his monastery, copying manuscripts, he was summoned by his abbot and told that he had been chosen to go on a journey to Rome for two purposes. First, he was to pay the abbot's respects to the great Pope Leo IX, who was making far-reaching changes in papal administration and greatly increasing the prestige of the papacy, which had been very low for two centuries. Second, the abbot wanted the young monk to obtain a divorce, or technically an annulment, for the abbot's cousin, a great earl, and for this a papal dispensation was necessary. At this time annulments could be obtained on the grounds of consanguinity within the seventh degree (changed in the thirteenth century to fourth degree), and since many of the European nobility had married relatives within the proscribed degree, it was not hard to obtain a divorce provided the pope gave his approval.

Our young monk set off on the old Roman road southward through the wild frontier province of Yorkshire, where most of the thriving religious settlements of the eighth century now lay in ruins as a result of the Viking invasions. When he reached the more southern part of England, he was impressed by the amount of construction and building going on. In fact, throughout Europe in the year 1050 the manmade sounds that one heard most often were the sounds of an axe chopping down trees or hammers and saws at work on new buildings. In a few places, particularly in the great cathedral cities on the Continent, buildings of stone were replacing the customary wooden structures, although European craftsmen were still inexperienced in handling stone construction. In 1050 Europe was still heavily forested, many times more than it is today, with a steadily expanding population and a growing pressure on the food supply. It was necessary to clear the forests and colonize new lands. In any case, the timber provided by the deforestation was greatly needed for building homes, castles, and churches in both urban and rural areas.

The young Yorkshire monk, after several days' journey, arrived at Canterbury, which had been the first Roman church in England and whose bishop was consequently the primate of the English church. When our monk arrived at the cathedral of Christ Church, Canterbury, he was not surprised to find a great assemblage of people, including the king, Edward the Confessor. Edward, as his name implies—he was later canonized—was an extremely saintly and pious man although, as was common with saints on the throne, a weak and ineffectual ruler. The monk from Yorkshire found Edward in his favorite occupation—installing new relics in the cathedral of Christ Church. The monk could not help but notice the contempt with which the English nobility regarded the king because of his disinclination to fulfill the Germanic kingly function of war leader. As he had traveled south he had also noticed the disorder and petty wars among the English nobility, which gave evidence of a kingdom on the verge of disintegration.

The Yorkshire monk crossed the channel and landed in Normandy. Here he found a world remarkably different from England, especially with regard to governmental organization and cultural vitality. Normandy was ruled by a man who was by no means a saint, Duke William the Bastard, although he affected to be a great friend and patron of the church and was on good terms with the papal court. In strong contrast to his kinsman Edward the Confessor, William exercised strong control over the nobility of his duchy and used feudal institutions to enhance the ducal power and to unify the territory under his jurisdiction. In Normandy the Yorkshire monk was greatly impressed by the building under way, particularly the construction of great cathedrals and monasteries. The monk was quick to notice that many of the leading churchmen in Normandy were of Italian or Rhenish descent; in either case they had come from regions that were, at least nominally, under the rule of the German emperor. They had been recruited by the duke himself, or by his predecessors, to improve the intellectual and moral qualities of the Norman clergy and to assist him in administrative and legal work. The monk was accustomed to wooden churches in England, and to the extent that there were any stone churches in his homeland, they were squalid little things. He was somewhat taken aback by the attempts to put up ecclesiastical buildings of considerable height and with a new emphasis on the perpendicular line. Certainly this was something new in church architecture in northern Europe, and nothing like it existed in England, although similar architectural styles could be seen in northern Italy, from where many of the leading Norman churchmen had come.

The English monk encountered in Normandy a clerk who had just returned from southern Italy, where he had gone as the chaplain of a Norman baron. The baron had joined a freebooting expedition some years before and was now engaged in conquering this fabulously wealthy land. From the Norman chaplain the Anglo-Saxon monk heard about an alien world, the distant and unfamiliar Mediterranean lands, inhabited by the feared and hated Moslem infidels and the wrong-headed Byzantine Greeks and distinguished by a comfortable urban way of life beyond the dreams of northern greed. Now, in A.D. 1050, the Moslem and Byzantine control over these fabled lands was being challenged for the first time by the uncouth race of the Franks. It was also known that the Christian princes were beginning to push back the hated Moslem foe even in Spain, where for so long the cross had ruled over only tiny principalities in the mountains, while the stiff-necked followers of the archheretic Mohammed had enjoyed the riches and comforts of Cordoba and the other golden cities of Iberia.

From Normandy the English monk crossed into Flanders, where he visited several great monasteries. While he was in Flanders, he became aware for the first time of the existence of a kind of people he had not known before, people who lived in walled towns and who were called bourgeois. These people were neither adjunct to the cathedral clergy nor the servants of the lords; in industrial cities, such as Ghent and Ypres, they constituted a new group in medieval society. The English monk had known of only three social classes—those who fought, those who prayed, and those who labored—but these bourgeois made their living from the manufacture and sale of woolen cloth, some of which was taken by merchants to fairs in Champagne, where it was sold and exported to Italy and other distant countries. The background of many bourgeois was obscure, some came from the lower ranks of the knightly class, while others were said to be of servile origin. The bourgeois were not a pleasant people. They were insecure, fearful, and at the same time clever and determined. Their psychological and intellectual makeup was much more complex than that of the old nobility and knightly class and even of most churchmen. They appeared avaricious and not a little dishonest, but at the same time extremely devout and pious in an intense, individual way that puzzled the simple monk from Yorkshire. These bourgeois, who stood outside the whole traditional social structure, had no political power, and their precise standing in the law courts was still not settled. One thing they did have was an enormous amount of hard cash, and they used this money not only to build strong walls around their urban enclaves, to erect municipal churches, and to build moderately comfortable houses in the crowded, narrow, and filthy streets of their cities, but to buy from the count of Flanders extensive rights of self-government.

The English monk realized that he still had a long way to go on his journey to Rome, and it was time to leave the comfortable monasteries and curious cities of Flanders. Even if he could follow the most direct route to Rome via central France—which he could not do because the central part of the country was a no man's land infested with robber barons—the journey would take him two months. He headed from Flanders to Paris with the intention of eventually following the Rhenish route southward via the great ecclesiastical center of Lyons.

What impressed him now as he pursued his journey was the number of lords, merchants, and churchmen whom he encountered on the road. Eighty percent of Europe's population still did not move more than twenty miles from their places of birth in their whole lifetimes, but the European upper classes were becoming mobile, and a surprising number of ordinary people were on the road, making religious pilgrimages. Any travel was still dangerous; the roads were incredibly bad, and robbers and brigands might be encountered around almost any bend. But in a civilization in which the pace of life was accelerating, men, and occasionally even women, found it necessary to travel considerable distances. The harnessing and shoeing of the horse one or two hundred years previously had greatly facilitated this travel.

Paris was in some ways a strange city, reflecting the peculiar condition of the French monarchy. As close as ten miles to the city the countryside was dominated by the castles of robber barons, and it is said that the Capetian king feared to go outside the walls of his own city. What impressed the Yorkshire monk most on his visit to Paris was the great royal abbey of St. Denis, which was even more closely associated with the destinies of the Capetian monarchy than its cross-channel counterpart, Westminster Abbey, was with the fortunes of the Anglo-Saxon kings. At St. Denis were kept the regalia, the symbols of office of the French crown, which signified the sacred qualities of the Capetian monarchy. But although the magnificent ceremony of anointment and coronation convinced the Capetian king of his obligation to the church, it had no influence on the great feudal princes of France, who went their separate ways and recognized the hegemony of Paris only in the emptiest, most formal way.

The abbot of St. Denis urged his English visitor to stop on his journey to Rome at the great monastery of Cluny, near Lyons. The abbot himself had originally been a monk of Cluny, as were many of the ecclesiastics in Normandy. Indeed, the English monk had already heard wonderful reports about Cluny, which was the largest monastery of the time and which came to represent the outlook of the whole church in the middle years of the eleventh century. The English monk was not disappointed; Cluny was all that it was supposed to be, and he, like other visitors, came away impressed by the splendor of the buildings, the sophistication of the liturgy, and the discipline and devotion of the monks. It is true that these monks lived much more comfortably and ate much better than the rustic Benedictines of Yorkshire. The Cluniac monks did not undertake any kind of physical labor, nor did they even devote much effort to education and scholarship. They were content to live off the estates and endowments they had received from the admiring rulers of Europe, such as the contemporary German Salian emperor, Henry III, who was particularly devoted to the Cluniac order. Was it not time that the life of the regular clergy reflected the monastic leadership in society? Were not the Cluniac monks truly the princes of the church? Indeed, many of the Cluniac monks were of princely and aristocratic lineage, and did they not deserve even more princely accoutrements as leaders of the church? The Cluniacs answered these questions in the affirmative, and even monks who were devoted to simpler and more rigorous lives were for a long time inclined to agree with them. The Cluniacs were content with the world as it was; it was apparently a perfected world, one in which religious like themselves exercised strong political influence and the German, French, and English rulers fulfilled the implications of their anointments to the office of theocratic monarchy.

The one manmade sound that the English monk had heard most often on his journey, next to the sound of peasants' axes in the forest, was the sound of the bells ringing from the rapidly increasing number of monasteries and churches. Everywhere he had gone the English monk had seen new parish churches erected on their own lands and endowed by great nobles. Piety was taking hold in society; it was delightful to find everywhere not only dedicated churchmen, but nobles, bourgeois, and even peasants who understood and regarded with utmost seriousness the doctrines of the faith that had so long ago been carried to the frontiers of Europe by the intrepid disciples of St. Benedict.

These happy musings of the Yorkshire monk were interrupted by his arrival at the great city of Milan after his journey through the Alpine passes. As in the time of St. Ambrose, Milan was dominated by its bishop, but new elements had entered into the life of the great cathedral center that the English monk found surprising and not a little disturbing. Here there existed not only a large bourgeois class, hostile to the traditional political prerogatives of the bishop, but a disaffected industrial proletariat seething with bitterness against all constituted authority and easily transformed by millennial and apocalyptic doctrines into a revolutionary mob. Here the English monk found the same individualistic and intense lay piety that he had encountered among the Flemish city dwellers, but in Milan this piety was magnified to the point of becoming a grave problem for the church. The literate bourgeois looked with contempt upon many of the cathedral clergy, who indeed were often corrupt and unworthy men, and the general religious atmosphere of the city was one of deep spiritual yearning running off at the edges into rebellion and heresy and not to be easily satisfied or turned aside.

The simple English monk was glad that he did not have to minister to the pastoral cares of the Milanese bourgeois and the proletariat; he was relieved to hear that the reformed papacy of Leo IX was hastening to give attention to such explosive situations. But when he finally arrived in Rome and traversed its ruined and deserted suburbs and passed along its dirty, stinking streets, coming ultimately to the basilica of St. Peter, the northern monk found even more disturbing ideas in circulation. Leo IX was a kinsman of the great German emperor Henry III and was devoted to the reformation of the papacy under the imperial aegis, but the young cardinals whom he had brought to Rome seemed to be men of a different outlook. They not only spoke in scathing terms of the decadence and corruption of the secular clergy and questioned the ultimate authority of the emperor over the papacy, they even made occasional critical remarks about the validity of the Cluniac approach to the religious life. Here was a new and disturbing tone that seemed to run contrary to everything that the English monk had admired in his journey southward. He found in the speech and attitudes of the young cardinals a note of intensity and recklessness that in some ways was similar to the lack of restraint of the Milanese and Flemish bourgeois. The simple Yorkshire monk was happy to plead his suit as quickly as possible and to obtain the annulment on behalf of the earl. He was eager to begin the long journey homeward— through a Europe whose perfected state was not acknowledged by all and whose felicity and contentment seemed transient.

CHAPTER ELEVEN

The Gregorian
World Revolution

I. The Nature and Origin of the Gregorian Reform

The eight decades from the middle of the eleventh century to the end of the third decade of the twelfth constitute one of the great turning points in European history. It was one of those periods during which vitally important changes in all aspects of life occur simultaneously and with such great rapidity that no contemporary could foresee the far-reaching consequences of many of them.

Such a period of fundamental and, at the same time, rapid change was the age of the Gregorian reform and the investiture controversy that the Gregorian reform precipitated. The Gregorian reform gets its name from Pope Gregory VII (1073–1085), the most visible leader of the reform movement. The term *investiture controversy* is derived from the crucial issue of whether kings and other great lords had the right to invest bishops and abbots with the symbols of their office, that is, whether laymen had the right to appoint church officials. The period from 1050 to 1130 was the period of enormous commercial expansion, of the well-known rise of urban communities, of the first expression of political influence by the new burgher class. It was an age in which the first really successful medieval monarchy was created in Anglo-Norman England on the basis of the feudal institutions and administrative methods and personnel created by the energetic and far-seeing Norman dukes. It was an age in which the long separation of the new western European civilization from the life of the Mediterranean world came to an end. This isolation, in existence since the eighth century, was now replaced by the political and economic penetration of the western European peoples into the Mediterranean basin to the detriment of the Moslems and Byzantines, who had long ruled the Mediterranean lands and controlled Mediterranean trade without a challenge from the north. It was an age of tremendous intellectual vitality that witnessed the most important contributions to the Latin Christian theology since Augustine and the slow transformation of some of the cathedral schools of northern France and the municipal schools of northern Italy into the universities of the following centuries. It was an age of great vitality in legal thought, in which Roman law came to be carefully studied for the first time since the German invasion of the fifth century, and great strides were made in the codification of the canon law.

But as in the eras of fundamental change in modern history, these achievements must be accorded second place by the historian in favor of an ideological struggle. Out of a far-reaching controversy on the nature of the right order to be established in the world the pattern of civilization of the following centuries was to emerge. The period from 1050 to 1130 was dominated by an attempt at world revolution that influenced in highly effective ways the other aspects of social change. It seems, in retrospect, that it was almost necessary for a revolutionary onslaught to shake the order of the early Middle Ages to its foundations, so that the new political, economic, and intellectual forces could be given the opportunity to develop in the face of the old institutions and ideas.

It has been characteristic of the history of the West that its destiny has been shaped by world revolutions in which previous tendencies culminated and from which new ideas and systems emerged. A world revolution is a widespread and thoroughgoing revolution in worldview, the emergence of a new ideology that rejects the results of several centuries of development organized into the prevailing system and calls for a new right order in the world. The investiture controversy, which the Gregorian reform engendered, constitutes the first of the great world revolutions of western history, and its course follows the same pattern as the well-known revolutions of modern times.

Each world revolution has begun with some just complaint about moral wrongs in the prevailing political, social, or religious system. In the investiture controversy the leaders of the revolution, who have been called the Gregorian reformers, complained about the domination of the church by laymen and the involvement of the church in feudal obligations. This system had led to severe abuses, especially that of simony, which came to be defined in its most general sense as the interference of laymen with the right ordering of church offices and sacraments. In their condemnation of simony as heresy, the Gregorians had a perfectly valid complaint.

It has been characteristic of all the world revolutions, however, that while each has begun by complaining about abuses in the prevailing world order, the ultimate aim of the revolutionary ideologists has been not the reform of the prevailing system but its abolition and replacement by a new order. In the case of the investiture controversy, the complete freedom of the church from control by the state, the negation of the sacramental character of kingship, and the domination of the papacy over secular rulers constituted the ideal new order.

As in all other world revolutions, the ideology of the Gregorians called forth violent opposition from both vested interests and sincere theoretical defenders of the old order. After many acrimonious disputes and a flood of propaganda literature, bitter and protracted warfare resulted. The polarization of educated society into revolutionary and conservative left a large group of uncommitted moderates, including some of the best minds of the age, who could see right and wrong on both sides.

As in all other world revolutions, the ideologists of the investiture controversy were only partially successful in creating the new order. They succeeded in destroying the old system, but the new world was not the revolutionary utopia. Rather, it was a reconstruction of the political and religious system that took into account both old and new elements and left room for the human limitations of greed and power. The church gained a large measure of freedom from secular control, and there was a noticeable improvement in the moral and intellectual level of the clergy. But the church itself, from the time of the investiture controversy, became more and more interested in secular affairs, and so the papacy of the High Middle Ages competed successfully for wealth and power with kings and emperors. The church itself became a great superstate that was governed by the papal administration.

As in all other world revolutions, the ideologists during the investiture controversy were themselves united only upon the most immediate and more limited aims of the revolution. As the revolution proceeded, the Gregorians divided into a moderate and a radical wing, each led by eminent cardinals. The radicals were headed by Humbert and Hildebrand, the moderates by Peter Damiani. As in the modern world revolutions, the radicals were in control of the Gregorian reform movement, a period that was long enough to destroy the old order. But as the conservatives and moderates of various complexions at last perceived the real aim of the radicals and their reckless disregard for consequences, the radicals lost their leadership and were unable to realize their utopian ideals.

As in the modern world revolutions, the radicals lost their leadership not to the moderates of their own group, whom they had earlier swept aside, but to the politicians, the practical statesmen who called a halt to the revolution and tried to reconstruct from the shattered pieces of the old system and the achievements of the revolution a new and workable synthesis that would again make progress possible. This tendency is already evident during the pontificate of Urban II in the last decade of the eleventh century, and it became dominant in the papacy during the 1120s.

Like all world revolutions, the investiture controversy never reached a final and complete solution. New ideas in a new generation made former issues less meaningful, and the men of the new generation turned to other interests and new problems. In the 1130s many educated churchmen could not understand why popes and kings should have quarreled over lay investiture only two or three decades before.

The age of the investiture controversy may rightly be regarded as the turning point in medieval civilization. It was the fulfillment of the early Middle Ages, because in it the acceptance of the Christian religion by the Germanic peoples reached a final and decisive stage. On the other hand, the pattern of the religious and political system of the High Middle Ages emerged out of the events and ideas of the investiture controversy.

The Gregorians revolted against the medieval equilibrium and hence against many things that eleventh-century Cluny and its allies represented. What, then, were the origin and cause of the Gregorian reform movement that brought about the decisive turning point in medieval history?

The Gregorian reform movement was the logical outcome, but by no means the inevitable and absolutely necessary outcome, of the early medieval equilibrium itself. As the church in the late tenth and eleventh centuries penetrated more and more into the world, imposing its ideals on the lay society, it began to face the dangerous possibility of losing its distinctive identity and hence its leadership in western society. For as the lay piety steadily increased throughout western Europe, the special qualities of the clergy stood out less clearly. No longer did a devout attitude toward dogma and ritual and the veneration of the saints and their relics suffice to distinguish the outlook of ecclesiastic and layman. By the middle of the eleventh century it was apparent that lay piety had in many cases attained the level of religious devotion hitherto exhibited only by the more conscientious among the clergy. Cardinal Peter Damiani, whose writings so frequently served as a sort of barometric indicator of eleventh-century attitudes, observed that every faithful Christian was a microcosm of the whole church: "Each of the faithful seems to be, as it were, a lesser church." If the Holy Spirit raised some of the faithful to the ministry of ecclesiastical dignity, Damiani asserted, it was to be expected that these ministers of God would reveal their special divine gifts by a superior form of religious life. Above all, the monks, who had professed the most perfect religious life, should at least act as the militia of Christ.

The great increase in lay piety created a new problem for the church, and its own traditional hierocratic doctrine, reflected in Damiani's statement, made the problem particularly urgent. The power of the priesthood and the papacy had been built upon the principle that "him to whom more is given, from him more will be demanded." Previously there was no doubt that more in the way of the spirit was demanded from the clergy; hence the justification of sacerdotal powers in the popular mind. Now doubts were arising on this issue. To many eleventh-century churchmen it seemed that only a greatly improved morality and heightened religious fervor among the clergy could continue to justify the exclusive powers of the sacerdotium. Otherwise the ecclesia would be absorbed into the thoroughly Christianized mundus, and the clergy would lose its distinctive position in society.

By the middle of the eleventh century churchmen everywhere in western Europe were encountering this new, critical problem. They knew that kings such as Henry III of Germany and Edward the Confessor were monks in worldly garb, always eager to lead the procession in a translation of holy relics. They found many nobles who took seriously the Peace of God, who endowed monasteries and cathedrals, undertook arduous pilgrimages, and hoped to be accorded the privilege of dying enshrouded in the monastic habit. Even the scurvy bourgeois gave glimpses of falling in with this new tendency, with their support of municipal churches and their devotion to religious festivals. Such laymen would expect a clergy to be still as morally superior to themselves as it was in the old days when society was savage and heathen, save in the most nominal sense. The hold of the church over lay society, the universal respect that the monks especially received from laymen, could be maintained only by a greatly enhanced piety and morality among the monks themselves.

The Benedictine order provided the greater part of the leadership for the eleventh-century church, and consequently the regular clergy was most sensitive to the consequences of the rise of lay piety. The origins of the Gregorian reform movement lay in novel tendencies that developed in eleventh-century monasticism, in a new spirit that made many monks dissatisfied with the prevailing Cluniac religious life and led them to advocate different and more stringent monastic ideals. The roots of Gregorianism are therefore to be found in the eleventh-century crisis of western monasticism.

The first stirrings of a new attitude toward monastic life (or, perhaps more accurately, an old attitude that was revived) came in northern Italy about the year 1000. For the first time, at least since the fourth century, the eremitic form of monastic life made its appearance to an appreciable degree in western Europe. It is not surprising to find that these hermits appeared first in northern Italy. Extreme asceticism is not a characteristic of an underdeveloped agrarian society in which the general standard of life is marginal and frugal in any case. Asceticism must have a wealthy society, the fleshpots and temptations of urban economy, to revolt against. This was true of the eastern Mediterranean in the fourth century, where the fathers of the desert flourished, and it was true of northern Italy at the beginning of the eleventh century, where for the first time in the development of medieval western Europe an urban society existed. North of the Alps new ascetic movements made their appearance in the second half of the eleventh century. Particularly in northern France, Flanders, and the Rhineland devoted monks turned away from the comforts and security of the Cluniac type of monasticism and went into frontier regions in small groups to form new, strongly ascetic communities. These isolated new monastic establishments coalesced in the twelfth century into the great Cistercian movement and other new religious orders. In northern Italy, however, while new and more stringent cenobitic communities also appeared, the figure of the itinerant hermit-saint remained a powerful catalytic force in religious life into the thirteenth century, culminating in the Franciscan movement.

Whether cenobitic or eremitic in their inclinations, the leading spirits of the new ascetic movement within western monasticism were vehement in their criticism of the prevailing Cluniac type of religious life. They believed that Cluny and the other great Benedictine monasteries of the day were sadly deficient in observing the rule that the founder of their order had set down and that they were professing. Far from applauding the worldly influence and possessions of the great Benedictine communities, the ascetic leaders complained that the abbeys' wealth and power were a source of temptation to their members, leading them away from the realization of the monastic ideal. The solution then for the hermits of the new, more ascetic communities was a strict subjection to the vow of poverty: They must live as the monks in Monte Cassino had lived in the time of St. Benedict, or, expressed in its full doctrinal form, they must return to the spiritual ideal of the apostolic church. In this respect, as in most others, Peter Damiani spoke for the new generation of puritanically inclined churchmen: "We not only abandon nobler occupations and worldly gain, but we have made profession of a perpetual renunciation of these things." Only by adopting this great reform of the regular clergy, it was thought, could the monks preserve, and deserve to maintain, their position of leadership in Christian society.

How did these critical changes in monastic life result in the Gregorian revolution and the monumental struggle over the right order in the world? It was not inevitable that one should have led to the other, but under the circumstances of the era it was a natural progression. The men who came to prominence in the papal court in the 1050s were all monks, and it was natural for them to carry their ascetic and purifying interests one step beyond the monastery and apply it to the whole church. Thus Damiani devoted many years attempting to reform the corrupt clergy in northern Italy. The final step, logical though not inevitable, was to carry over the ascetic and purifying impulse into the world itself. This was the origin of the radical Gregorians' attack on the whole prevailing Christian world order, and is explained by the circumstances of the medieval equilibrium itself—the interpenetration of the ecclesia and the mundus. If the church and the world were identical and synonymous, as many contemporaries said, then how could asceticism and reform stop within the limits of the church? For the church had no limits, or at least its limits were those of the world itself; the Gregorian radical felt compelled to apply his puritan ideals to all aspects of social life and to establish a unified Christian world system—*Christianitas,* Gregory VII called it. The Gregorians accepted the common eleventh-century identification of the church and the world with complete seriousness, and their ideology therefore required them to carry the ascetic, reforming, purifying impulse from the hermitage and the new monastic community into the most vital aspects of contemporary life outside the monastery. The institutional structure of their world confirmed the lessons of ideology. The regular clergy was so central to the life of the eleventh-century church that it was hard to conceive of a critical change in monastic life that would not affect and reform the whole church. Similarly, in most parts of Europe church and kingship were so involved with each other that radical church reform necessitated political and social revolution.

II. The Debate on the Essentials of a Christian Society

By the 1050s the chief assistants of the pope were organized into the "college" (corporation) of cardinals. The term *cardinal* comes from the Latin word for the hinge of a door; the cardinals were the hinges on which the great papal door moved. The term *cardinal* was singularly appropriate for the men who dominated the papacy in the second half of the eleventh century and attempted to carry out the Gregorian reforms. They were remarkably few in number—not more than a dozen all together over a period of more than half a century were important in the Gregorian movement. Actually, for only two pontificates, that of Gregory VII himself (1073–1085) and Paschal II (1099–1118), was there a real radical on the papal throne. The other two prominent Gregorian reformers were the cardinals Peter Damiani (died 1072) and Humbert (died 1061). The latter is often called Humbert of Silva Candida, after the small church in Rome whose pastorate he nominally held in conjunction with his cardinalate, as was customary.

The four leading Gregorian reformers were as remarkable a group of men as ever appeared in European history. They not only dominated the life of the eleventh-century church, but they participated in, and in many ways contributed to, the leading intellectual currents of the period. In every case the doctrines they propounded did not die with them or even with the eleventh or early twelfth centuries, but rather entered into the mainstreams of medieval thought. The implications of the Gregorians' thought-world reach out in many directions and by no means only within the bounds of orthodox Catholicism. The Gregorians inaugurated a great debate on the nature of a Christian society. Their doctrines were challenged by other learned and devout churchmen, and out of this intellectual conflict emerged at last the outlines of almost every ideological position that was to develop more fully in the following five centuries. Many of the arguments propounded during the Gregorian reform period are still relevant to our experiences and problems.

Of the men we call the Gregorian reformers the one who was most universally loved and respected and least controversial in his own day was St. Peter Damiani. Nevertheless, the inspiration, the pattern, and the implications of his doctrines are in some respects the most difficult for us to grasp of any of the Gregorian reformers' because of their diffuse nature and because they penetrated and affected almost the whole culture and literature of the High Middle Ages. With justice did Dante, in his *Divine Comedy,* place Damiani in one of the highest circles of heaven and regard him as the predecessor of St. Francis. It might be said, in fact, that St. Francis was only the ultimate development of a religious movement of which Damiani was the most outstanding and identifiable originator.

Damiani's voluminous writings reflect the spiritual conditions of northern Italy in the first half of the eleventh century, from where he was brought to the papal court. Damiani was born in about the year 1007. He was an orphan of a poor family, but was adopted by a priest and received a good education in both theology and canon law. He found the prevailing Cluniac life, while in some respects admirable, too much involved with the world, and he became one of the leaders of the new eremitic movement in northern Italy. His vehement denunciation of the corruption of the secular clergy in the Italian cities brought him to the attention of Leo IX, who made him a cardinal and tried to channel his energies in the service of Rome. Damiani was never happy as a cardinal; he was more an itinerant hermit-saint and preacher than an institutional reformer. Damiani was sent to Milan to try to reform the church there, but his success was not great. He found himself at odds with Hildebrand (later Gregory VII) and Humbert, his colleagues in the college of cardinals, whom he admired but considered reckless and dangerous. He was the kind of man who inspired revolutionaries, but his saintly and charitable disposition precluded his being a revolutionary himself. His death the year before Hildebrand became pope is significant, for it removed from the scene the one man who could have restrained Gregory.

One of the prime items in the Gregorian program, as enunciated by Peter Damiani, directly affected the personal lives of the bishops and priests—the Gregorians' strenuous efforts to implement the long-standing but hitherto scarcely enforced prohibitions against clerical marriage and in favor of clerical celibacy. Following the prescriptions of St. Paul, the early western Church had advocated that neither bishops nor priests should have wives and raise families or cohabitate with women or have occasional sex with women. Damiani devoted a whole book to exposing the clergy's sexual scandals. The Byzantine church allowed ordinary priests to be legally married; Greek bishops were supposed to be celibate, and it was expected that a priest's wife would do the right thing and enter a convent if her husband was promoted.

The Gregorian view that the Latin clergy should be fully celibate was predicated on the theory that bishops and priests, as well as monks, were married to the Church as the Bride of Christ. But what lay immediately behind the incessant pressure of the Gregorian papacy on behalf of sacerdotal celibacy was the practical belief that if bishops and priests did not have families, they would be more likely to devote themselves selflessly to their offices, rather than use their offices to get property and jobs for their children. The purpose, then, was to untangle the secular clergy from its involvement in the feudal order.

At the accession of Gregory VII, bishops commonly cohabitated with women, fathered children by them, and looked after the interests of their "nephews." The cathedral clergy's children were a significant segment of urban populations. The parish priests were generally married and heads of households. There was strong opposition to the Gregorian view of clerical marriage and sacerdotal celibacy, but the Gregorian papacy made a huge fuss about it and started a slow trend toward the rejection of wives and families by bishops and priests. Damiani was merciless in denouncing the clergy's sexual practices. Of course a lot of bitter personal hostility against the Gregorian papacy was stirred up by this severe application of canon law.

From the twentieth-century point of view, the Gregorian papacy was engaging in negative eugenics—the best educated and, in many instances, most intelligent component of the population was told not to produce offspring (compared with the opposite in the Jewish community, where rabbis were instructed by the Talmud to marry young and procreate freely). If Damiani and the other Gregorians could have understood this Darwinian argument, they would have rejected it because of their eschatalogical and messianic inclinations. By purifying the clergy, they were preparing for the imminent Second Coming; a few more or less intelligent children made no difference because historical time was running out.

Damiani was the leader of the more moderate group in the college of cardinals who tried to avoid a final break between the reforming papacy and the German emperor. But his teaching was revolutionary enough, in the sense that it reached to the foundations of the medieval religious experience and helped bring about a transformation of spiritual values. A great change was under way in the eleventh century in the medieval conception of the relationship between the deity and humanity. The judging, wrathful, distant God of the Old Testament, which predominated in early medieval religiosity, was coming to be replaced by the loving, self-abnegating son of the New Testament, with his weeping and charitable mother. Religion was becoming less a matter of formal worship and obedience and much more a personal experience. It was in the ascetic and eremitic monasticism in northern Italy and the intense religious experience of the Italian urban communities that this new spiritual outlook made its first appearance. By the middle of the twelfth century the new piety, as it has been called, had spread throughout Europe, had penetrated into the inmost reaches of the European consciousness, and had spilled over and enriched and ennobled the art and literature of medieval civilization. St. Peter Damiani was the first writer to express this new piety clearly. He was the founder of that mystical strain of personal identification of the self-abnegating, loving deity and the hopeful, ascending human spirit that sharply distinguished the religion of the High Middle Ages from what had gone before.

If Damiani thus played a primary role in the enrichment and fulfillment of medieval Catholicism, he must also be seen as an originator of an uncontrollable emotionalism that is not so praiseworthy as this new conception of the deity nor in the long run easy for the church to control. The new intense emotional religiosity brought with it an irrational fanaticism that if inculcated in the masses, could produce violent manifestations that no public authority could control. The popular reaction to the first crusade was to be an early example of this problem. It is not surprising to find that the massacre of Jews in 1096 as a popular response to the crusading appeal found its ultimate authority in the writings of Damiani himself. Even in the opinions of the great saint and mystic of the early eleventh century, fanaticism made its appearance as the reverse side of the new personal, intense religiosity that he did so much to foment. The great increase of anti-Semitic literature in the late eleventh century began with two pamphlets written by Damiani himself, whose passionate charity did not extend to those outside the Christian church.

The ultimate ambiguity and tension of Damiani's doctrine lay in the fact that while he was the most orthodox defender of the validity and necessity of the sacraments as the means of divine grace and the authority of the priesthood alone to administer them to the laity, the central mystical inclinations of his teachings tended to lessen the indispensability of both sacraments and priesthood. For if personal identification is ultimately possible between the human soul and the loving Christ (at least in the popular mind, if not in theological argument), an alternative route to the deity has been opened up. The implications of this underlying dilemma were not seen in the eleventh century, but in the following two hundred years they were to become more and more a source of confusion, doubt, and agonizing conflict in Christendom. Considered against the whole structure of medieval culture, the doctrines of Damiani, who was in his personal inclinations the least radical of the Gregorian reformers, were potentially as revolutionary as anything ever said or done by Humbert or Hildebrand.

Damiani's competitor for the intellectual leadership of the Gregorian papacy was Cardinal Humbert of Silva Candida, a thinker fully as learned and forceful as the great Italian mystic and in some ways more subtle, original, and complex. Humbert came from Lorraine, where Leo IX had been a bishop. It has been established that Humbert had been a monk at Cluny and came to feel strongly that Cluny had betrayed the ideals of its founder. Otherwise his early biography is obscure. Like nearly all the Cluniacs, Humbert of Lorraine was probably a product of the high nobility; this class background would help to explain his consistent hatred of the German monarchy that had asserted its authority over Lorraine against strong local opposition. It is certain that Humbert had studied in the new schools of the canon law that flourished in Lorraine and that he had obtained a vast knowledge of theology and church history. He was likely an intellectual prodigy—he had a good knowledge of Greek, which was unusual in western Europe at the time—and in spite of his acidulous and critical disposition and his extreme intellectual arrogance, which are revealed in almost every page he wrote, the church could not afford to dispense with his services. Leo IX was glad to have him in the papal service, where his erudition and daimonic energy made him an outstanding figure. Only his premature death—he could not have been much more than fifty in 1061—kept him from the throne of Peter.

Humbert's knowledge of Greek fitted him for the role of papal ambassador to Constantinople. The revitalized and aggressive attitude of the papacy was leading to a reconsideration of papal relations with the Greek church, and the age-old conflicting claims of pope and emperor were again becoming an important issue. The Norman conquest of southern Italy, where many Greek Christians lived, also served to remind the papal court of the problems of Latin-Greek relations. Humbert was not the man to be either cautious or subservient in his negotiations with the Greek church. He ended his legation in 1054 by excommunicating the patriarch of Constantinople, thereby officially declaring a schism that had been developing since the fifth century. This schism has not been ended to the present day, although several attempts at reconciliation have been made over the centuries.

On his return to Rome Humbert became the theoretician of the reform movement and the leader of the radical wing in the college of cardinals. The crucial date, when the effects of his planning and theorizing became evident, was 1059. In this year he was responsible for the publication of two works that signaled the beginnings of the Gregorian revolution. The first was the papal election decree, setting forth the legal manner of electing popes. It placed the election fully in the hands of the cardinals and excluded the interference of both the German emperor and the Roman people. In view of the fact that less than twenty years before Henry III had made popes with almost annual regularity, it marked a great change in the relations between Rome and the German emperor. But Henry IV (1056–1106) was at the time a minor, and his family was fighting off the rebellion of the German nobility; Humbert was able to carry out his coup d'état with impunity, as he had expected. The second work that Humbert published in 1059 was his great treatise on church-state relations, *The Three Books Against the Simoniacs,* the ideological formulation of the Gregorian revolution. It is suffused with violent hatred of the German emperor and calls forcefully for the complete freedom of the papacy from secular control. But there is much more to Humbert's masterpiece than this; it is essentially an attack on the whole early medieval equilibrium between the church and the world.

Just as Damiani's work reflects one of the leading intellectual currents of the time, the new piety, so does Humbert's book reflect the new logic, or dialectic—the new emphasis on the formulation of argument according to the strict canons of whatever was known of Aristotelian logic at the time. Humbert was a pioneer in this controlled manner of debate, which contrasted markedly with the shapeless, or at least purely rhetorical, kind of didactic prose in the early Middle Ages. And he used this new intellectual tool in combination with his vast erudition to undermine the existing world order. He argued that simony is not merely the buying and selling of church offices; it is any interference by laymen in the affairs of the church. By this definition much of the prevailing institutional organization of western society—lay investiture, proprietary churches, royal influence over ecclesiastical appointments—stood condemned as errors in the faith. By Humbert's argument no king or nobleman in western Europe, and not many churchmen, were at that moment free from participating in acts that condemned their souls.

This was strong medicine, but Humbert was not content to stop at even this radical position. The fatal charms of dialectic, which were to lead so many other brilliant medieval minds into the uncharted swamps of heresy in the following three hundred years, claimed Humbert as an early victim. His puritanism compelled him by logical steps to the conclusion that if the clergy could be reformed in no other way, then the people should examine the moral character of their priest, and if they found it unsatisfactory, they should refuse to take the sacraments from him. Thus was Humbert led to a revival of the Donatist doctrine that the ministration of the sacraments by an unworthy priest was invalid and to its corollary that the laity had a right to judge the priesthood. It was against these very principles that St. Augustine had labored so hard more than six centuries before, with the outcome that the church had proclaimed Donatism the most dangerous of errors. It had been decided that the priest, in administering the sacraments, acted as the representative of God, that the efficacy of the sacrament was not dependent upon the personal qualities of the priest but upon the divinely constituted office that he held, and that the laity could not sit in judgment on the priesthood. Humbert's revival of Donatism must be seen as an indirect consequence of the development of lay piety. It is apparent that he had greater respect for the opinion of many laymen than he had for the views of their official pastors.

Humbert had clearly fallen into doctrinal error, and the effect of his teaching, if widely accepted, could only be the undermining of the authority of the priesthood and the negation of the Catholic concept of the predominance of the office over the individual moral character of ecclesiastics. Put simply, it would lead to the substitution of a proto-Protestant church of the saints for the Catholic church. Damiani was quick to point out the Donatist tendencies in Humbert's treatise; to him it was a lesson in the dangers of dialectic, whose value to the church he greatly doubted. Yet others in the papal circle, fired by puritanical fanaticism and no doubt not a little influenced by Cardinal Humbert's strong personality and tremendous intellectual force, were not so quick to see the dangerous and explosive consequences of Humbert's argument. Hildebrand, who was strongly under Humbert's influence and who derived a great part of his ideology from Humbert's writings, was slow to reject Humbert's neo-Donatism and came around to condemning it only in the latter part of his pontificate.

Although it was finally again denounced by the papacy as the severest of errors in the faith, a position that the Catholic church has not altered to the present day, the revival of the Donatist ideology by Humbert, a prominent cardinal and the most subtle theoretician of the eleventh century, was a momentous event in the development of the medieval church. Never again was Donatism to disappear completely from the medieval thought-world. In the second half of the twelfth century it was to be the fruitful source from which heretical movements and doctrines were to evolve into the sectarian Protestantism of the sixteenth century. No scholar has yet established the precise line of continuity between Humbert's treatise *Against the Simoniacs* and the Donatist heretics who appeared in large numbers in northern Italy in the last half of the twelfth century. It seems not too much to postulate, however, that Humbert's teachings, while eventually condemned by the papacy, were taken up into the intense religiosity of the north Italian urban communities and played a leading role in turning the new lay piety in the direction of popular heresy.

In comparison with Damiani and Humbert, Hildebrand was not an original theoretician. He was, however, unsurpassed as an ideologist, which is not necessarily the same thing. He pulled together, from many sources, the novel and radical ideas of his day and synthesized them into a formidable, total program of revolution. As Pope Gregory VII he attempted to implement these doctrines, and in so doing he inaugurated the great struggle between pope and emperor that shook western society to its foundations. Whatever the judgment on the merits of his ideology and the achievements of his pontificate, Gregory VII must be regarded as one of the three greatest medieval popes. Among all the holders of the throne of Peter before the sixteenth century, only Gregory I and Innocent III are comparable in stature. And no pope was ever as controversial as Gregory VII. No one in Europe in the 1070s and '80s could hold for long a moderate and neutral opinion of him. He was greatly admired and loved by some, and at the same time he aroused more hatred and contempt in his own time than probably any other bishop of Rome.

Gregory's controversial quality makes it difficult to establish some of the key facts of his biography and the salient aspects of his character. So many stories and legends, favorable and unfavorable, were told about him that his personality remains somewhat obscured. He was a native Roman who literally grew up in the shadow of the basilica of St. Peter's, took monastic vows, and entered into the service of the papacy in early manhood. Even before Leo IX became pope in 1049, Hildebrand was already an important man in papal circles, and although for a quarter of a century he was passed over for less able candidates in papal elections, he was a dominant force in the college of cardinals and the effective chief of the papal administration. Hildebrand's attitude to the Roman see can be termed almost nationalistic, or at least parochial. Irrespective of the ideological questions involved, he detested the German emperor as an alien interloper who had no business interfering in Italian affairs, let alone in papal policy. Hildebrand's last words when he died in southern Italy in 1085, after being driven from Rome by an imperial army, are highly significant: "I have loved justice and hated iniquity; therefore I die in exile." Any place outside the Eternal City was exile to this native Roman.

It is difficult to establish Hildebrand's family background. It is probable that he was of bourgeois background and that there were Jewish converts to Christianity in his family. His background would help to explain his almost paranoiac hatred of the established order. Beyond doubt, Hildebrand was a hard man to get along with. His prodigious ability as an administrator, his puritanical zeal, and his fantastic energy made him a great leader but a difficult colleague. Even the charitable Damiani referred to him as the "holy Satan." Abbot Hugh of Cluny, the fastidious elder statesman of the eleventh-century church, detested Hildebrand on sight, regarded him as a crass careerist, and did everything he could to block the implementation of Gregory's programs.

Without being either a great scholar or a systematic thinker, Hildebrand was well versed in canon law, theology, and church history. Lacking the true scholar's interest in knowledge per se, he was nevertheless quick to make use of the new learning of the eleventh century to support his point of view. Even before he became pope, Hildebrand had directed some leading Italian scholars to undertake the collection and organization of the canon law, a scholarly work that was being pursued at the same time in northern France and Lorraine. The canon law was such a vast, unorganized body of contradictory propositions that he wanted to make sure that its codification was worked out in directions favorable to papal power. If he had done nothing else, Hildebrand would thereby have made a great contribution to the rise of papal authority, for when the codification that he inaugurated came to fruition in the mid-twelfth century, it resulted in a canon law that emphasized papal absolutism and rejected alternative early-medieval traditions.

Immediately after his elevation to the throne of Peter, in 1073, Hildebrand drew upon this papal-oriented research in canon law for the propositions that he published as the *Dictatus Papae,* a statement of papal power. The *Dictatus Papae* asserted that the Roman church was founded by God alone; that only the papal office was universal in its authority; and that the pope alone could depose bishops, reinstate them, or transfer them from one see to another. No church council was canonical without papal approval. No one could condemn an appellant to the apostolic see, which was the supreme court of Christendom. No decree or book was to be considered canonical without papal assent. Furthermore, the pope was said to be beyond the judgment of any human being; his actions were to be judged by God alone. The Roman church, by which is presumably meant the papacy, had never erred, and according to the Scriptures it never would err. The Roman pontiff was sanctified by the merits of St. Peter. No one could be a true Catholic unless he agreed with the pope. A final group of propositions in the *Dictatus Papae* dealt with church-state relations. It was asserted that only the pope could use the imperial insignia, implying that the pope was the true successor to Constantine. The pope had the power to depose emperors, and it was lawful for subjects to bring accusations against their rulers to the papal see.

The *Dictatus Papae* was a sensational and extremely radical document, and it is inconceivable to think that Hildebrand was so naive as not to realize that it would make this impression. It was a statement of the revolutionary program that Gregory intended to implement: the creation of a new world order for Christian society founded on the principle that papal authority alone was universal and plenary, while all other powers in the world, whether emperors, kings, or bishops, were particular and dependent. This idea of the plenitude of papal power was by no means novel. It could be found in the radical aspects of the Gelasian doctrine; in the Donation of Constantine; and in the pronouncements of the ninth-century pope, Nicholas I. Gregory could claim with justice that every proposition in the *Dictatus Papae* was merely a quotation from one or another early medieval canon-law text. But the revolutionary quality of a program is not lessened by the fact that at distant points in the past other people had said the same thing. The *Dictatus Papae* was a revolutionary document in view of the comprehensiveness and intransigence of its assertion of papal absolutism and its contradiction of the prevailing world order. For two hundred years papal power had been in abeyance and the great bishoprics and abbeys of western Europe had flourished with little or no assistance from Rome, and certainly with no effective papal jurisdiction over their affairs. The great ecclesiastics of northern Europe could not but feel greatly disturbed by this unmitigated assertion of their absolute subservience to Rome, which went so contrary to common experience. They could not deny the legal, and perhaps even the theological, basis for Gregory's claims, but they would have been less than human if they had not felt that Gregory's program was unnecessary and imprudent and a threat to their whole way of life. The church in Germany, France, and England had done well enough for two centuries without the benefit of papal assistance. To many, and probably to most, of the great churchmen of Europe the *Dictatus Papae* appeared to be the shrill assertion of long-forgotten and rarely exercised theoretical papal authority in the interests of the personal ambitions of Hildebrand.

To the kings of western Europe the *Dictatus Papae* necessarily seemed even more revolutionary and upsetting. It claimed a papal supremacy over monarchy that had never been practiced in European history. Granted that the Donation of Constantine made such claims, no important medieval ruler had ever allowed a pope to interfere in the affairs of his realm. The assertion of this supreme papal monarchy in the world seemed all the more shocking in view of the successful leadership in western society and the unchallenged authority over territorial churches that the great western kings had exercised since the days of Charlemagne.

The churchmen and kings of western Europe were to learn rapidly that Gregory intended to carry out the program he enunciated in the *Dictatus Papae* at the beginning of his pontificate. They were also to learn that his ideology was, if anything, more radical than was evident from the simple legal propositions of his initial programmatic statement. Drawing upon Augustinian theology, tapping the emotional resources of the new popular piety, and strongly influenced by the teachings of Humbert, Gregory proceeded during the stormy twelve years of his pontificate to refine and formulate his revolutionary ideology. Almost every letter of his voluminous official correspondence contained some part of this doctrine, but his ultimate theory of a Christian social order was drawn together and presented with tremendously persuasive force in his famous *Letter to Hermann of Metz* in 1082. Ostensibly a reply to certain questions put to him by the bishop of Metz, the *Letter* was actually a public pamphlet. It was published in many copies and sent to royal courts and important churches all over Europe.

Since the ninth century political Augustinianism had been on the wane. The social amelioration effected by the government of Charlemagne, Otto I, and Henry III visibly contradicted the bishop of Hippo's strictures on the moral quality of the state. The theocratic kings of the tenth and eleventh centuries were, in the eyes of the churchmen who assisted them, not the pirates whom Augustine had talked about but, rather, divinely commissioned leaders who did the work of the Lord. The common identification of the ecclesia and the mundus was a different attitude from Augustine's sharp distinction between the heavenly and earthly cities. The Augustinian view that the state had no moral sanction in and for itself but derived its sanction only from its position as a servant of the church was a meaningless and irrelevant proposition in a world in which there was no clear line of distinction between church and state. But it was this political Augustinianism that Gregory VII now revived in its fullest and most intransigent form. In his *Letter to Hermann of Metz* he contended that royal power was originated by murderers and thugs and that the state continued to bear the stamp of Cain. In the whole history of the world, he said, there were scarcely half a dozen kings who had avoided the damnation of their souls, and these, such as Constantine and Theodosius the Great, had saved themselves from the fatal temptations of secular power only by their subservience to the church. Many simple and ordinary Christians, he said, were more certain recipients of divine grace than were the mighty and powerful holders of royal power, who were in most cases really the instruments of the devil.

Continuing in the Augustinian vein, Gregory concluded that the only legitimate power in the world resided in the priesthood, particularly in the bishop of Rome as the vicar of Christ on Earth. Only those who subjected themselves to this divinely constituted authority could hope to be included in the Heavenly City. Strongly emphasizing the Pauline-Augustinian conception of liberty, he boldly asserted that the freedom of the Christian man consisted in the subjection of his selfish will to the divine ends that the papacy pursued in the world. Only a world order in which these doctrines were realized could be called just and right. Justice, Gregory insisted, was a matter not of custom or tradition or usage but of fulfillment of the Christian ideal as he saw it. No claims of convenience or custom could be made against his doctrine. He reminded his critics that the Lord had not said, "I am tradition," but rather, "I am the Word." With an apocalyptic zeal he demanded a new right order that would fulfill the ideals of Christian justice and liberty as he had defined them. Nothing less than this total *Christianitas* was acceptable; there could be no compromise with the devil.

The new piety and emotional religiosity of the eleventh century influenced Gregory VII's outlook almost as much as Damiani's. His writings are full of references to the Virgin and to the *pauperes Christi,* "Christ's poor ones," whose assistance he summoned and whose welfare he sought. In Gregory's view this Christian poverty was not an economic or class matter—or at least it was only incidentally so. He was on the side of the poor in spirit, the meek, the humble, and the downtrodden of whatever class or group, and he was the enemy of the rich, the proud, and the powerful, whoever or wherever they might be. His hatred of the most powerful men in Europe was based upon a psychological and emotional sympathy for the underdog and hostility to their lords and oppressors. Gregory's conception of Christian poverty was thus in part an attempt to read the Sermon on the Mount to the class-stratified society of the eleventh century. At the same time, his violent hatred of the leaders of contemporary society and his highly emotional concern for the *pauperes Christi* were probably symptoms of a paranoiac hysteria and manifestations of a deep neurosis.

Whatever the roots of Gregory's emotionally charged concept of Christian poverty, he was opening up an important, but as yet tenuous and hitherto almost unknown avenue in medieval thought. With the minor exception of the sermons of St. Ambrose, social criticism and a Christian social gospel had not yet made an appearance in medieval civilization. They were not to be expected in the agrarian society of the early Middle Ages, in which all literate forms of expression were the preserve of the landed classes. The emergence in the eleventh century, especially in northern Italy, of new bourgeois and proletarian groups, affected as they were by the new emotional piety, was bound to change all this. Whatever Gregory's intentions in his emphasis upon the spiritual superiority of the poor Christians, his teachings were bound to give encouragement to the underprivileged and ambitious classes of the European cities. Given the religious orientation of all forms of thought in the eleventh century and the pietistic outlook of the city dwellers, their social disaffection was bound to be expressed in millennial and apocalyptic doctrines.

They, the underprivileged, were the poor who deserved to inherit the Earth, or at least much more of it than the established landed classes were willing to allow them. Gregory's emotional attitude toward Christian poverty therefore found a fertile seedbed in the social disaffection and millennial yearnings of the new urban classes.

The ambiguous meaning of poverty, referring to the lack both of wealth and spiritual qualities, was encouraged by the Gospel itself, for the first Christians, the members of the apostolic church, the original disciples of the Lord, were poor in all senses of the word, both spiritually and economically. Was this a necessary relationship? To achieve that ideal state of poverty of the soul, that humility which was a sign of Divine Grace, was it necessary to divest oneself of worldly goods? This question was to become an agonizing dilemma for the church in the High Middle Ages. Gregory's enthusiasm for Christian poverty accentuated the central importance of this problem in medieval thought without doing much to resolve it.

The last of the four Gregorian reformers, Pope Paschal II, the only radical Gregorian aside from Hildebrand to obtain the papal throne, carried the debate much further and provided a definite answer, although one unpalatable to the great majority of the leading churchmen of his time. Paschal had been a monk in the monastery of Vallombrosa, near Florence, one of the new ascetic and reform communities. He entered the papal service as an ardent disciple of Gregory VII and remained to the end of his days, long after the high tide of revolutionary ardor had begun to ebb at Rome, an intransigent high Gregorian. After serving as papal legate in Spain, where the fanaticism of the warrior Iberian Christians engaged in the *Reconquista* gave him no cause to lessen his puritanical zeal, he was elected pope in 1099. The nineteen years of his pontificate were marked by his stubborn continuance of the struggle with the German emperor Henry V, by a conflict over church-state relations with the English king, and by his support of a reckless and bootless scheme for a crusade against Byzantium. In 1111 he startled Europe by announcing that he had arrived at a concordat with the German emperor, ending the long conflict between empire and papacy. But when the terms of the peace treaty were published, his rebellious and angry cardinals forced him to repudiate the settlement.

Paschal's solution of the debate over church-state relations was both simple and radical. Since the origin of the controversy lay in the question of the relative jurisdictions of *regnum* and *sacerdotium,* he proposed to the emperor that the German churchmen surrender to the imperial crown their lands and secular offices and constitute themselves a purely spiritual church. In return, Henry V promised not to interfere with the affairs of the German bishops and abbots; of course, the delighted emperor could afford to do so in view of the tremendous accretion of landed wealth and public offices he was given by Paschal's proposal.

Paschal's concession was neither the unaccountable act of an eccentric old man nor the consequence of *force majeure* by the emperor, as the papal court later claimed in repudiating Paschal's treaty. The Concordat of 1111 was fully in accord with Paschal's ideological position, which was, in turn, an offshoot of radical Gregorianism. Just as the new ascetic monastic orders had taken inflexible vows of poverty in imitation of the apostolic church, so Paschal, who was a product of this puritanical movement, had moved in the direction of the idea of the apostolic poverty of the whole church and the doctrine of a purely spiritual church "poor" in every sense of the term. This may be said to be a logical development of Gregory VII's emotional, if ambiguous, advocacy of Christian poverty.

The provocative doctrine of the apostolic poverty of the church thus made its first clear appearance in the policy of the last of the Gregorian popes. Rejected by the high medieval papacy, looked upon with horror by the wealthy and powerful ecclesiastics of western Europe, this doctrine was to find favor with the popular heretical movements of the twelfth, thirteenth, and fourteenth centuries. It was to be advocated at the end of the thirteenth century by the radical wing of the Franciscan order, whose own religious heritage derived ultimately from that same north Italian asceticism of the eleventh century that produced Paschal II. The doctrine of apostolic poverty was condemned by the papacy as a heresy in 1323, but it continued for many decades thereafter to be a source of debate and confusion in the life of the medieval church. Frequently, in the indistinct thought-world of medieval popular heresy, the doctrine of the apostolic poverty of the church was to be held jointly with that millennial social gospel whose roots were also in the teachings of Gregory VII.

The intellectual consequences of the Gregorian reform must be seen as extremely heterogeneous and complex. The Gregorians propounded doctrines that built up papal authority, the centralized organization of the church, and the power of the sacerdotal office—and at the same time undermined them. The doctrines of plenitude of power, papal infallibility, and subservience of the monarchy to the priesthood were Gregorian. But from the teachings of the Gregorian reformers also came those ideas that eventually played a leading role in the dissolution of the medieval world order: religious individualism, Donatism, the millennial social gospel, and the doctrine of the apostolic poverty of the church.

In their own day the Gregorians by no means had the forum of public debate to themselves. On the contrary, their discussions of the nature of a Christian world order called forth a variety of comments, critiques, and treatises reflecting almost every shade of opinion. It is indicative of both the intense feelings that the Gregorian reform aroused and the increased literacy in the eleventh century that the surviving treatises of the period on church-state relations fill more than two thousand pages when printed in modern folio. It is not much of an exaggeration to say that it seems that around the year 1100 almost every monk in western Europe was writing a pamphlet on church and kingship.

Three representative and typical expressions of the criticisms directed against the Gregorians may be considered. First, there was the reactionary position expatiating on the early medieval tradition of theocratic kingship and asserting that the king was the anointed of the Lord, "and through Grace he is God," as the Norman churchman who wrote the treatises that are commonly called the *Anonymous of York* tractates contended in the year 1104. Second, there was the conservative Cluniac position exemplified by the *Treatise on Royal and Sacerdotal Power* by Hugh of Fleury, the French royal abbey allied with Cluny. Hugh directly attacked Gregory's denigration of the moral sanctions of kingship and concluded that, for the sake of right order in society, monarchy must continue to be superior to priesthood. The final position, and one of the most interesting and important of the period, was taken by the great canon lawyer, Bishop Ivo of Chartres. This wise and shrewd scholar expressed his doubts that the prevailing social order was actually contrary to the canon law and the demands of church dogma. But even if it were, he said, the sanction of social custom had to predominate even over the exigencies of written law and theology. Since the prevailing order had such wide support among the laity and even among the clergy that it could not be abolished without a schism, Ivo concluded, the reformers had better be content with a discreet protestation and hope for slow reform. The ideologists of the Gregorian papacy, however, were no more willing to listen to the moderate opinion of Ivo of Chartres—who was told by Rome to keep silent—than to the fulminations of royalist reactionaries and the bitter protests of Cluniac conservatives.

To many contemporary churchmen, sincere and devout in their calling, the Gregorians were not so much doctrinally wrong as imprudent, naive, and provincial. In countries where kingship was strong, especially in Anglo-Norman England and the German empire, the higher clergy had come to respect monarchy, in whose presence they literally stood with great frequency as royal councilors and ministers. The Gregorians, in contrast with such churchmen, were indeed naive and provincial. Nearly all of them came from Lorraine and northern Italy, where royal power was weak and disorganized and where no one, least of all a monk, could gain much respect for kingship. None of them had the opportunity to work in a royal chancery and to become acquainted with the personality of a Henry III or a William the Conqueror or to gain insight into the tremendous problems of eleventh-century government. Kingship was an idea for the Gregorians, something to be studied in Augustine or Gelasius; it was neither a brutal fact of everyday life nor a glorious sentiment (as it was to the higher clergy of England and Germany). The Gregorians were learned, devout, brave, and even intellectually brilliant men, but they were profoundly lacking in the wisdom and moderation that came from years of intimacy with power and majesty—knowledge that could not be gained in patristic literature, in canon-law collections, by devotions in a monastic oratory, or even by drawing upon the rich intellectual resources of the new piety and the new logic.

III. The German Investiture Controversy

In 1075 the Salian German emperor Henry IV was the most powerful ruler in Europe, at least east of Normandy. Yet the "holy Satan," Gregory VII, setting out to implement his program of justice and liberty, did not fear to demand that the German king immediately give up the institution of lay investiture by which he controlled the appointment of the great churchmen of his realm, and the pope threatened to depose Henry if he did not obey this decree. Gregory's attack on the institutional basis of Salian power came at a crucial time in the development of the empire; it precipitated a fifty-year struggle that, in the opinion of many German historians, decided the fate of Germany.

Henry IV had ascended to the throne of his father's premature death in 1056, but for nine years he was a minor, and until he attained his majority in 1056 his hold on the crown was insecure. The aggressive policy of centralization that Henry III had pursued had frightened the German nobility, and they determined to take advantage of the sudden reversal of fortune of the Salian house to strip the crown of its powers. Following along the lines set down by the tenth-century Ottonians, Henry had based his power on his control of the resources and personnel of the church, exercised through the doctrines of theocratic monarchy and the institutions of lay investiture, the proprietary church system, and advocacy over the great monasteries of the realm. In addition, Henry III had made use of royal ministeriales to garrison the crown castles that he had built all over the realm and especially in the northern duchy of Saxony, whose nobility and free peasantry had continued to exhibit a strong separatist tendency. It appears to have been Henry's intention to incorporate the recalcitrant Saxon duchy into the family possessions of the Salian house, adding this territory to the native Salian duchy of Franconia to form extensive crown lands. The fulfillment of this dynastic policy would have placed the Salian monarchy in a position of overwhelming superiority with reference to the German nobility and would have been the capstone in the building of royal authority in Germany that had begun with the work of Otto I in the middle of the tenth century. It was through the expansion of their crown lands that the Capetian monarchs were able to ascend to supreme authority in France in the twelfth and thirteenth centuries.

The German nobility, led by the recalcitrant Saxons, determined to take advantage of the sudden death of the great emperor Henry III in 1056 and the succession of a minor. The result was nine years of rebellion and civil war in Germany, in which the duchies exhibited the traditional centrifugal tendencies. But the German episcopate, even in Saxony, remained loyal to the monarchy and saved the throne for the young Henry IV. The wisdom of Otto I's alliance with the German church thus received fresh confirmation.

When Henry IV became king in fact in 1065, he brought this decentralizing tendency to an immediate halt and set about continuing the work of his father. Henry was perhaps the ablest and wisest German ruler of the Middle Ages. Certainly no other German king exhibited more cunning, energy, and inflexible determination in advancing the cause of royal authority. Henry believed that the key to the problem was the duchy of Saxony, where he continued his father's building of castles and embarked upon a policy of not only stripping the nobility of their autonomous privileges but pushing down the mass of free peasantry into a status of manorial serfdom completely dependent upon the crown. The inevitable consequence was another great rebellion in Germany, in which the aroused nobility and peasantry of the north were supported by dissident aristocrats in the rest of the realm and even by a few disaffected bishops. The struggle, however, was an unequal one, for on the king's side were the great majority of the bishops, the royal ministeriales, many of the lower nobility, the wealthy monasteries under royal control, and the new burgher class of the Rhenish cities. By 1075 Henry IV had won a complete victory. The rebel leaders of the aristocracy had been humbled, and the Saxon peasantry had lost great numbers in battle and had come to feel that they had been betrayed by the nobility. The way now appeared to be open for the creation of a strong and unified state in Germany, paralleling the degree of central authority in the lands under the rule of the duke of Normandy and anticipating the French monarchy of the thirteenth century.

At this critical juncture the German king received the papal decree against lay investiture with the accompanying threat of deposition if he did not obey immediately. Henry had not been unaware of the great changes taking place at Rome. During his minority the papal election decree of 1059 had divested him of the prerogative of dominating the papal elections that his predecessors had enjoyed for a century. But, engaged as he was in pressing domestic concerns, he had been prepared to let Italian affairs take their course, at least until he could give them his undivided attention. Henry's natural disposition toward Rome appears to have been cautious and moderate, and it is likely that, if let alone, he would not have interfered with the new independence of the papacy. But given the aggressive policy that Gregory undertook from the beginning of his pontificate, it was impossible for Henry to avoid a conflict with Rome. The initial dispute between the pope and the emperor was over a relatively minor issue, but one indicative of a much deeper underlying conflict. Shortly after Hildebrand became pope, the episcopal see of the febrile community of Milan fell vacant, and Henry and Gregory each maneuvered to secure the election of his own candidate. Gregory regarded this as an indication that the German king had not given up his claim to dominate the affairs of northern Italy, and perhaps it caused Gregory to accelerate his attack on the institutional basis of imperial power—its alliance with the German church—by means of the papal ultimatum of 1075. Flushed with his great triumph over the nobility, Henry decided to take the strongest possible line in replying to Gregory's demands, and he found enthusiastic support for this policy among the German churchmen. For a long time these churchmen had been more aware than the king of the revolutionary course of the Hildebrandine papacy, and they were no more eager than Henry himself to abandon the prevailing system of church-state relations in Germany.

Consequently, at the beginning of 1076 the clerical scholars at the royal court prepared a letter to be sent in the king's name to Rome in reply to the papal decree on investiture, damning "Hildebrand, at present not pope but false monk," in the strongest possible terms. One of the outstanding examples of medieval Latin rhetoric and reflecting the learning and literary skill of the Salian chancery, Henry's letter constituted nothing less than a defense of the prevailing world order and a declaration of war on the pope who had presumed to dissolve this beneficent system. Henry informed Gregory that his conduct as pope had brought confusion and malediction upon the church; that he had dared to rise up against the royal power conferred on Henry by God; and that he had threatened to divest the Lord's anointed of his kingdom, which Henry had received from the hand of God. Gregory, it was claimed, had usurped the apostolic chair; he had practiced violence under the cloak of religion and betrayed the teachings of St. Peter. The letter concluded with the stirring peroration that Hildebrand was now called upon by Henry, king by the Grace of God, and by all the imperial bishops, to come down from the throne of Peter. Some of the surviving copies of the letter add an eternal damnation for the pope.

Henry IV's letter to Gregory VII was the desperate cry of self-justification upon the part of early medieval kingship, which had reached its culmination in the Salian empire of Henry III and his son. But Hildebrand seems to have anticipated such a reply. He was not afraid of the imperial army because in the preceding two decades the papacy had found powerful allies in Italy to serve as a balance of power against the great northern king—namely, the new Norman rulers of southern Italy and Sicily. At first the papacy had been hostile to the Norman invasion of the territory south of Rome, but by the end of the 1050s the papal court had come to realize that the Normans could be made into a counterweight against the troublesome Roman nobility and ultimately even against the German emperor, whose vague claims to hegemony in Italy the Normans as well as the papacy could be expected to oppose. The Norman-Italian rulers in turn needed papal sanction to give an aura of legitimacy to their naked seizure of the south Italian realms, which had previously been held by a motley crew of Moslem, Byzantine, and Latin princes. This recognition was gladly given by the papacy to cement an alliance with the Norman rulers, whose armies provided the necessary military support that the papacy hitherto lacked. In addition to this southern support Gregory could look for assistance in the north to the wealthy and powerful countess Matilda of Tuscany, a pious widow on friendly terms with Gregory himself. Matilda is the earliest example of that new type of independent aristocratic lady of great power and prestige who was to play an occasionally significant role in the politics and society of the High Middle Ages. Although she was a distant relative of the German king, the pope apparently felt that Matilda could be relied upon to protect him from Henry IV's wrath if the occasion arose.

Acting with characteristic speed and determination, Gregory deposed Henry on receipt of his contumacious and insulting letter and sent papal agents into Germany to stir the ashes of the recent rebellion into a new flame of civil war. Every dissident element in Germany was now accorded a new and unprecedented pretext for attacking royal authority, and rebellion in self-interest was given divine sanction. It is likely, however, that Henry could have weathered this storm if Gregory had not taken the precaution of trying to preclude the continuance of the traditional support given by the great German ecclesiastics of the crown.

The bishops and abbots were informed by the papal agents and by letters sent directly from Rome that on pain of excommunication they were no longer to recognize Henry IV as their king. Excommunication was still a powerful instrument in the spiritual armory of the papacy; Europe was a long way from the time when the force of this weapon was to be blunted by excessive use. Furthermore, there was a real possibility that Gregory would triumph in his struggle with the German king, and the ecclesiastics of the empire, fearing for their own security, hesitated to risk their offices and status by openly siding with Henry IV. The immediate effect, of the papal decree of deposition, therefore, was a stunning collapse of royal power. Since at least two-thirds of Henry's army came from ecclesiastical lands, he had lost the greater part of his military power without a blow being struck. By the end of 1076 the king found himself almost completely isolated, as the bewildered and frightened German ecclesiastics withdrew their support of the Salian house. The German nobility exulted in this unexpected reversal of their fortunes, and reasserting the old electoral principle in the German monarchy at papal suggestion, they set in motion the constitutional process of electing a new king from outside the Salian dynasty.

The court clerics convinced the king that only his surrender to Gregory and papal forgiveness of his purported sinful acts could save his throne. Henry determined to go to Italy and personally seek absolution from the pope. It was necessary for him to do so as quickly as possible, for Gregory had announced his intention of going to Germany to preside at the assembly of the German nobility that would formally divest Henry of his crown and elect a new king.

A contemporary German monastic chronicler of royalist sympathies has given us a probably romanticized account of how the desperate Henry IV rushed southward, accompanied by only a handful of retainers, through lands infested with his enemies. At the same time Gregory, traveling in a slower and more ceremonial manner, had set out from Rome with the intention of getting into Germany before the king could seek an audience with him. This melodramatic race, which held the attention of all Europe, was won by Henry. He encountered the pope at Matilda of Tuscany's castle of Canossa, in northern Italy, where Gregory had been received as a guest by the countess.

The events that occurred at Canossa in the winter of 1077 constitute one of the great dramas of European history. Contemporary royalist chroniclers described, with pardonable exaggeration, how Henry stood in the snow for three days until at last the pope was willing to give him an audience and receive his penitent pleas for forgiveness and absolution. Actually, the events that occurred at Canossa were not only high drama but a crucial political encounter of great consequence for the subsequent development of the German investiture controversy, as both the king and the pope well knew. Henry needed papal absolution if he was to hold his throne, and Gregory was unwilling to grant it at the very moment of the collapse of Henry's power, when the pope was on his way to attend a great assembly that would elect a papally approved candidate as the German king. By the tradition and law of the church, however, no priest, let alone the vicar of Christ on Earth, could refuse the comforts of absolution to a sincerely penitent and confessed sinner. Gregory very much doubted, and with good reason, that Henry was genuinely penitent, but it was difficult for him to proclaim his opinion publicly in view of Henry's great show of remorse. Consequently, the pope ignored the king's plea for an audience for three days. Matilda of Tuscany interceded with the pope on behalf of her kinsman; no ruler or great lord, at least outside Germany, enjoyed seeing the continued humiliation of one of the great anointed kings of Christendom.

Probably not even Matilda's entreaties would have moved Gregory in his moment of triumph. It was only the unwelcome appearance at Canossa of abbot Hugh of Cluny and his unrelenting intercession on Henry's behalf that forced Gregory's hand. Abbot Hugh was the most widely respected and beloved churchman of his day. He and Hildebrand had always disliked each other, and the Gregorian and Cluniac worldviews strongly clashed, but Gregory could not afford to ignore the advice of the revered and saintly abbot. To have done so would have endangered his own position in Europe, for Gregory well realized that the crowned heads of Europe stood aghast at such novel events as were transpiring at Canossa. He knew that the active opposition of the Cluniac elder statesman of the church would have sufficed to turn public opinion against him and bring about the alignment of the other kings and rulers of Europe alongside the now vanquished Salian monarch. Hence Gregory finally gave Henry the audience he sought, heard his confession, and absolved him; he then made him promise to obey the papal decrees and restored him to his royal status.

In the pope's eyes, if not in the opinion of the disappointed German nobility, there was now no need for electing a new king. Gregory abandoned his planned transalpine journey and dispatched a triumphant letter to the German nobility informing them of the events that had transpired at Canossa and of his peace with the penitent king, who had vowed to be henceforth a loyal servant of the papacy. But Henry, returning to his kingdom, also departed from Canossa in a victorious mood. He had saved his throne and had been given time to reestablish his power. It is most unlikely that he ever intended to observe the oath he had taken at Canossa, and within a year, when he made his intentions public, he was again deposed by the pope. But Henry was never again to be in the helpless position in which he had found himself at the end of 1076, and in fact, in the half century of the German investiture controversy, the papacy was never again to be anywhere as close to total victory as it had been on the morrow of Gregory's initial attack on the German monarchy. After Canossa some German ecclesiastics had second thoughts and once again threw in their lot with the Salian house. For example, the abbot of the great monastery of Fulda, founded by St. Boniface, was in Henry's later years the head of the royal chancery. With some ecclesiastical support and with the aid of the royal ministeriales and armies raised from the crown lands, the German king held his own in the long and bitter war with the German nobility. In 1085 Henry was momentarily powerful enough to take vengeance by driving his papal archenemy from Rome to refuge among his Norman allies in southern Italy, a humiliating exile from which Gregory did not return. Henry IV's last years were embittered by the rebellion of his son, who joined the German nobility against him, but this was mainly a personal and dynastic matter. On his succession to the German throne in 1106, Henry V continued the war against the papacy and its allies in Germany.

Both contemporaries and many modern writers have debated whether it was the pope or the emperor who gained the most from the dramatic confrontation at Canossa. It was clear that both parties gained and lost something and that neither won a total victory. Canossa restored the German crown to Henry, but considering his abnegation before the pope, it also dealt a fatal blow to the ideology of theocratic kingship, upon which the Salian dynasty had relied so extensively. Furthermore, in being forced to obtain papal absolution, Henry gave substance to the Gregorian claim that the papacy had the right to judge and depose even the most prestigious ruler in Europe. Certainly Gregory had cause to exult that the moral power of the papacy had been demonstrated when the greatest ruler of the West was literally forced to become a penitent at his feet.

Canossa signified that the bishop of Rome, who had played an insignificant role in the political affairs of Europe for two centuries, would now be a central figure in the affairs of European states.

Gregory's triumph, however, was not unmitigated. Canossa sowed those seeds of doubt and concern about the good intentions and moral standards of the papacy that were to grow rapidly in the following century. The kings of western Europe had been put on their guard and were reluctantly forced to undertake a careful reappraisal of their relations with the church. Canossa made archaic the equilibrium of the early eleventh century. Even conscientious and devout churchmen now had to ask themselves why as sincere and able a ruler as Henry should have been put in such a miserable position. In discussing Canossa a century later, the church historian and imperial prince bishop Otto of Freising refused to see absolute right or wrong on either side. He thought that Gregory had gone to extremes, and he doubted the pope's prudence and, by implication, his good intentions. Thus the magnificent demonstration of papal authority at Canossa had a far-reaching and complex influence on the moral consciousness of medieval society. It signaled the sudden resurgence of Roman leadership in Europe and at the same time set in motion that long chain of disillusionment and controversy that was to end two centuries later in another little Italian town with the demise of the medieval papacy.

After Canossa Gregory and Henry fought each other with relentless hatred and all the resources, both moral and physical, that they could summon. The pope again announced the deposition of the Salian ruler and joined with the rebellious German nobility in setting up an antiking. Similarly, Henry found a north Italian bishop who was willing to take the gamble of being installed as the antipope. These maneuvers had little or no effect, and the investiture conflict turned out to be a draw. After Gregory's death in 1085, and particularly during the pontificate of the former Cluniac monk Urban II (1088–1099), the papacy's determination began to slacken. While officially asserting his loyalty to Gregory's policies, Urban began to seek a way out of the war of attrition in which the papacy had become involved. He tried to unite Europe behind the Roman pontiff through the preaching of the first crusade. Urban's departure from Gregorian ideology was indicated by his willingness to grant the Norman rulers of England and southern Italy the same domination over their territorial churches that Gregory had condemned in the case of Germany. But the ending of the German investiture conflict had become a most difficult matter involving the necessity of saving face on both sides, and Urban was not able to find a way out of this impasse. It need hardly be said that no supporter of the German king joined the first crusade.

Urban's successor, Paschal II, renewed the struggle, but after a decade even this intransigent high Gregorian wanted to call a halt to the seemingly endless conflict. His radical solution, as we have seen, while it pleased Henry V, was unacceptable to almost everyone else. By the latter part of the second decade of the twelfth century, a new generation of cardinals had come to dominate the papal government. Their experience in law and administration conditioned them to view the world from the standpoint of careful bureaucrats, not that of aggressive ideologists. To these new men the all-or-nothing policy of the Gregorian papacy seemed both dangerous and unnecessary. They envisioned the enhancement of papal authority through the institutional means of legal and administrative centralization of the church, rather than by a desperate war with the rulers of Europe. The new leaders at Rome agreed in general with Gregory's ultimate aims, but emotionally they were not inclined to adopt the means he employed. What they wanted to preserve in Gregory's program was the institutional reforms he had inaugurated: the increase in the bureaucracy of the papal court; the sending of legates, or papal ambassadors, to all parts of Europe; and the establishment of the Roman Curia as the effective high court of the church. But they were willing to work slowly for the fulfillment of these ends; to come to terms with the kings of western Europe, when necessary; and to bargain hard and continuously for limited concessions, rather than dare to risk all on a fundamental conflict. It is this moderate, bureaucratic, legalistic spirit, contrasting markedly with the apocalyptic frenzy of Humbert and Hildebrand, that distinguished the papacy of the twelfth century from the Gregorian revolution.

The new generation of cardinals regarded the German investiture controversy as an embarrassing vestige of a now-vanished age, and they were willing to make extensive concessions to achieve a compromise with Henry V. The principle upon which the short-lived English investiture controversy of 1103–1107 had been terminated was consequently resurrected and embodied in the Concordat of Worms of 1122 between Calixtus II and Henry V. The emperor abandoned the institution of lay investiture with its overtones of the now-discredited doctrine of theocratic kingship. But he was allowed to require the homage of bishops and abbots in his domains before they were invested with the symbols of their offices. Thus the papacy granted to the German king the right to exercise a veto over the appointment of German ecclesiastics and, by implication, to maintain the decisive voice in their selection.

This compromise had allowed the English king to maintain his practical control over the affairs of the church in his realm. But the effect of the Concordat of Worms was by no means a simple return to the *status quo ante bellum* because the half century of the investiture controversy had brought about such vast changes in the German political and social structure that the king was unable to take full advantage of the papal concessions. In many parts of the realm the great dukes had gained a semiautonomous territorial sovereignty, and it was they, not the king, who benefited from the Concordat's grant of jurisdiction over ecclesiastical appointments in their duchies. In still other parts of Germany, particularly in the Rhineland, the great bishops themselves had become territorial princes whom the monarchy could no longer dominate. Thus, as far as Henry V and his successors were concerned, the Concordat of Worms in effect gave them the right to control the appointments of bishops and abbots only in the territories belonging to their own families.

This cataclysmic decline in the German crown's traditional domination over the resources and personnel of the church was paralleled by its losses in other directions. Many of the royal ministeriales on whom the eleventh-century German monarchy had so heavily depended proved unreliable. They took advantage of the confusions of the long civil war to usurp control over the royal castles they were guarding and to bargain for their legal freedom with king or antiking, thereby becoming lords in their own right. By the early twelfth century some of these former ministeriales were marrying into the old noble families, and not a few of the great aristocrats of modern Germany are descendants of Salian serf-knights. This weakening of royal institutions was contemporaneous with the advancing power of the territorial princes. In Germany history the period of the investiture conflict signified a tremendous growth in the territorial sovereignty of the dukes and other great lords and the creation of provincial autonomy, which was not overcome until the second half of the nineteenth century. It is therefore with considerable justice that many German historians claim that the period between 1075 and 1122 determined the German fate.

The growth of territorial sovereignty and aristocratic power in Germany was greatly abetted by the extensive feudalization of the country for the first time. Vassalage was not unknown in Germany before the investiture conflict, but the feudal pattern was fragmentary and relatively unimportant, especially in the northern half of the land. Fifty years of civil war produced far-reaching political and social changes. The great lords imposed homage on their knights and placed themselves at the head of feudal armies. By the 1120s the bonds of vassalage had proliferated among the landed classes. This extensive feudalization of German society was a catastrophe for the monarchy because the feudal pyramid in Germany, as in France before 1150, was truncated. The feudal bonds did not ascend to the king's level; they terminated in the suzerainty of the great aristocrats. The vassals of the great lords were bound by no feudal relationship to the king, and their loyalty was henceforth given to the territorial princes, who now had large and well-trained armies to use against the monarchy. The king's military power was derived only from his position as feudal overlord in his native family duchy. But circumscribed as he now was by the virtually independent territorial princes, his private resources were inadequate to restore the shattered structure of central authority. Many great lords, taking advantage of their new autonomy, usurped the king's former control of ecclesiastical property by assuming the advocacy of the great monasteries and the lordship over proprietary churches. Thus the nobility adopted for their own benefit and to the detriment of royal power some of the favorite Ottonian-Salian institutions.

To ensure the continued weakness of the monarchy, the nobility perpetuated the electoral nature of German kingship. Although, in constitutional theory, the electoral principle had never entirely died out and the Ottonian and Salian rulers had taken the precaution of having their sons elected before the royal deaths, in actual practice the tenth and eleventh centuries witnessed the substitution of hereditary succession. But under the urgings of the Gregorian papacy the nobility revivified the electoral idea. The clerical theorist Manegold of Lautenbach produced a treatise presenting a purely functionalized view of the German monarchy in which the king was compared to a swineherd, employed for a specific purpose, who could be dismissed if he displeased his employer. This radical Augustinian view of the German monarchy pleased the territorial princes, who naturally saw the king as a functionary with limited powers, whom they would chose and, if necessary, remove from office. For a quarter of a century following Henry V's death in 1125 the German monarchy conformed to Manegold's swineherd principle. The king was chosen by the princes, given no resources outside those his own duchy, and prevented from exercising any real authority or leadership in the realm. The royal title was furthermore passed from one family to another to preclude the development of any dynastic interest in the German crown.

Thus, when Frederick I of Hohenstaufen was chosen king in 1152, the royal power had been in effective abeyance for a quarter of a century and, to a considerable degree, for eighty years. The only untapped resources of the crown lay in northern Italy, over whose wealthy cities the emperor had a nominal claim of suzerainty. As a consequence of the investiture conflict, any king bent on regaining the authority that the

Salians had exercised had to look to Italy. But the age of the investiture conflict had also witnessed great changes in northern Italy, which made any attempt at the real exercise of imperial power there highly problematical. Since the time of Henry III the Italian cities had experienced no effective rule by their nominal German overlord. And this was precisely the period of their tremendous expansion in wealth and population and the development of their communal institutions. The northern Italian cities, by the middle of the twelfth century, were dominated by narrow oligarchies of merchant and industrial entrepreneurs, ready and able to fight for the preservation of their status and power. They were the natural allies of the papal court, which greatly feared the reappearance of the emperor in Italy. The emperor could see no way of restoring royal authority in Germany except by conquest of northern Italy, but the pope thought that if the emperor should triumph in Italy, he would destroy the independence of the papacy. The investiture controversy, by decimating the resources of the German crown, paradoxically brought the papacy into inevitable conflict with the first ambitious and able prince to come to the Roman throne after the Concordat of Worms. The transformation of northern Italy during the period of the investiture controversy, however, made the success of such an imperial venture unlikely.

To these catastrophic political consequences of the struggle between pope and emperor may be added a cultural disaster: Germany's loss of the intellectual leadership of western Europe. In 1050 the German monasteries were great centers of learning and art, and the German schools of theology and canon law were unsurpassed and probably unmatched anywhere in Europe. The long civil war and the acrimonious disputes between church and state seem to have syphoned off the energy and diverted the attention of the German churchmen. The churchmen were assiduous in producing treatises on church-state relations, but they ignored the tremendous advances in philosophy, law, literature, and art that were taking place during the same period west of the Rhine and south of the Alps. Thus German intellectual life fell out of step with the times and slowly became backward and archaic. At the beginning of the twelfth century French and Italian scholars were in the process of creating a new institution for higher thought and education that was to play the central role in the intellectual life of the High Middle Ages, but the first such university was not established in Germany until the fourteenth century. Culturally as well as politically the Germans fell behind during the investiture conflict and never quite caught up during the Middle Ages.

CHAPTER TWELVE

The Anglo-Norman Monarchy and the Emergence of the Bureaucratic State

I. The Triumph of William the Bastard

In his later years Gregory VII seems to have wondered at times whether he had undertaken to fight the real enemy. He became concerned with the ecclesiastical policy of the new Anglo-Norman monarchy, but he was not able to diminish in any way the authority of William the Bastard, now usually called the Conqueror, over the English church. With the decline of the Salian monarchy, the Anglo-Norman ruler's position as the most powerful king in Europe was unchallenged. William and his sons were able to advance English royal institutions to a point of perfection and efficiency hitherto unknown in medieval Europe. They ended by developing a new kind of medieval kingship that relied upon administration and law to unify the realm, allowing them to dispense with the traditional ideological basis of monarchy. At the very time that the Gregorian revolution was undermining the old religious foundation of kingship, the Anglo-Norman rulers were fashioning a most effective substitution that was relatively invulnerable to papal condemnations. The Norman Conquest, therefore, is of the greatest significance for medieval civilization because it made possible the creation of a new kind of state, initiating the movement toward the secularism and absolutism that was to mark the twelfth and thirteenth centuries.

In 1066 England was what the economic historian Reginald Lennard has called an "old land." Although the northern part of the country, being unsuited for agriculture, was sparsely settled, the southern half, particularly the fertile central region, was intensively colonized. The total population of England at the time of the Norman conquest was a million people, which made it a rather thickly settled country; five centuries later the English population was still less than four million. In 1066 London was already an important commercial city, and other ports in the south and the east were carrying on extensive trade with the Continent. Later Anglo-Saxon England appears to have been a wealthy country. The Anglo-Saxon coinage was among the best in Europe, and the Danegeld, a tax levied by the English king to fight the Scandinavian invaders, brought in enormous amounts of specie. The Anglo-Saxons were furthermore a devout and intelligent people. They had renowned saints, good poets, and skillful artists working on illuminated manuscripts and jewelry.

In spite of all these promising conditions, England was ripe for foreign conquest in the middle of the eleventh century. The Anglo-Saxons offer a prime example of a people who were good at everything except government and warfare, and this lack was the undoing of the Anglo-Saxon monarchy. The local English shire and hundred courts, which were a continuation of the old Germanic folk moots, were reasonably effective, but the central government's administrative institutions were weak and primitive, and the great lords, or earls, easily usurped the legal and financial prerogatives of the crown. This political backwardness was accompanied by military weakness. Whereas the armed and mounted knight had become the mainstay of continental armies, the English in 1066 had still not learned to fight on horseback. For thirty years in the early eleventh century England had been part of a great Danish empire, and it was the Scandinavian ruler Canute who was probably the most effective king in Anglo-Saxon history. After Canute's death his great northern empire disintegrated, and the English lay and ecclesiastical nobility found in a continental monastery a surviving member of Alfred's line and placed him on the English throne. The resulting reign of Edward the Confessor (1042–1066) was marked by the incipient political disintegration of the kingdom in the face of the advancing territorial power of the great earls. The childless Edward's death precipitated a succession crisis, and the king of Norway prepared his fleet for the invasion of England. The Anglo-Saxon nobility, in line with the old Germanic electoral tradition, chose the most powerful of the earls, Harold Godwinson, as king of the English folk. But William the Bastard, the ambitious duke of Normandy, claimed the throne by right of succession through his great-aunt and maintained that both Edward and Harold had promised him the throne on the Confessor's death.

The American historian of Norman institutions, C. H. Haskins, called the Normans the supermen of the eleventh century. A more judicious description is that of Ordericus Vitalis, a contemporary Anglo-Norman writer who said that the Normans were a good and able people when ruled by a strong man, but inclined to a natural violence and disorder when their ruler was weak. William the Bastard had been able to channel the aggressive characteristics of his people in a constructive direction. Following lines already set down by his predecessors and with the advice and support of experienced and learned churchmen, many of whom came from territories at least nominally within the Salian empire, he had created the most centralized feudal state in Europe and succeeded in winning an enviable reputation as a friend and patron of the church, which stood him in good stead at Rome.

William was able to make good use of both of these feudal and ecclesiastical foundations of his power in preparing for the invasion of England. He summoned almost the whole feudal army of the duchy, which constituted a thousand knights. The continued rise in population among the landed classes in the duchy, which had not been significantly diminished by the departure of Norman freebooters to southern Italy, meant a shortage of fiefs in Normandy and made the warrior class extremely eager for foreign ventures. In addition, William recruited mercenaries from among the landless knights of Flanders and Brittany, and he was able to cross the channel with an army of as many as 1,500 knights, together with the necessary bowmen and supporting infantry. By eleventh-century standards it was an enormous military force.

The probability of William's success was enhanced by the moral support that he received from Rome. At the urging of cardinal Hildebrand, the supreme pontiff had sent the duke a papal banner, which he carried with him to England. Why did the papacy support William's conquest? The Norman duke had a hereditary claim to the throne, which Harold lacked, and it might be argued that he was more throne worthy than the English earl, that is, more able to provide effective rule. But such traditional reasons were only peripheral papal consideration. The Roman Curia was dissatisfied with the condition of the Anglo-Saxon church, which it believed had conducted its affairs too independently and held to be retrograde and corrupt. In fact, in 1066 a scandalous situation prevailed in the see of Canterbury; the papacy claimed that the incumbent archbishop had not been canonically elected and deposed him, but Harold Godwinson was reckless enough to refuse to carry out the papal decision. The papal administration under Hildebrand's direction expected that William's conquest of England would bring about the reform of the English church and its close association with Rome. This turned out to be an only partially correct assumption as a consequence of Hildebrand's failure to assess realistically the ecclesiastical policy of the Norman duke. Hildebrand had been greatly impressed by William's reputation as a pious friend and supporter of the church, but he did not take into account the nature of church-state relations in Normandy, which were markedly similar to those that prevailed in the Salian empire. Hildebrand's pardonable error in judgment opened the way for the establishment of the Norman system of church-state relations in England.

The pictorial account of the Bayeux tapestry and the vivid, if somewhat confused, details given by contemporary writers depict the Battle of Hastings, which decided the fate of England. They showed that the Anglo-Saxons put up a good fight—better than could be expected under the circumstances, for Harold's army was exhausted after having just defeated the invading Norwegians in the north and having been forced to march the length of England to encounter the formidable Norman forces. William won his great victory through more advanced armaments and superior tactics. The Anglo-Saxons fought with their accustomed bravery, and the Battle of Hastings was a bloody encounter by medieval standards. A great many of the Anglo-Saxon nobility were killed on the field, and most of those who survived were deposed from their lands and probably made serfs. Thus the Norman conquest, although it did not affect the status and condition of the English peasantry, resulted in the elimination of the English ruling class and the substitution of French lords. The Anglo-Saxon bishops and abbots did not fare much better than the lay nobility. William made his friend and adviser, the Italian-Norman monastic leader and scholar Lanfranc, the archbishop of Canterbury, and the latter was not loath to bring probably trumped-up charges against the Anglo-Saxon higher clergy and replace them with Norman and other French churchmen.

For four decades after the conquest the Normans exhibited an unmitigated contempt for all Anglo-Saxon culture. During this period some of the greatest works of Anglo-Saxon art were probably destroyed; some of the best Anglo-Saxon illuminated manuscripts survived only in continental libraries, having been sent as gifts to rulers or churchmen across the channel. The cosmopolitan Norman nobility spoke French and were representatives of French culture and civilization. The Anglo-Saxon language became a peasant dialect, and it was revived in literary form only in the fourteenth century. For at least a century and a half after the Norman conquest, England was culturally a province of France. In spite of the losses to native vernacular literature and art, the Norman conquest was a great benefit to England, which in any case was bound to lose its independence in the 1060s. England was on the verge of political disintegration, an easy prey for foreign conquest. It was bound to become an adjunct either of Scandinavia or of France. The Norman invasion produced the political unification of the country and allowed England to participate in the thriving intellectual, religious, and artistic life of eleventh- and twelfth-century France. Scandinavian conquest would have cut England off from all these achievements.

With characteristic political skill William salvaged whatever was viable in the Anglo-Saxon institutions. He preserved the local shire and hundred courts and the Anglo-Saxon royal writ, the official written communication sent out by the royal chancery to its local agents, and the Anglo-Saxon coronation order with its stirring overtones of theocratic kingship. But this religious ideology was only a peripheral matter, for the Anglo-Norman monarchy established its power upon a whole new framework of institutions borrowed from Normandy. Even the preconquest institutions that were continued were given a new vitality and importance by their place in the comprehensive political and legal system.

The complete feudalization of the realm was undertaken by the Conqueror and for the most part completed by the end of his reign in 1087. As the supreme lord of every fief in England by right of conquest, he was able to work out a careful scheme of feudalization that centered in the king as the liege lord of every knight in the realm. As in Normandy, the bishops and abbots were first placed under heavy feudal obligations, and then the lay nobility was enfeoffed. With the exception of the frontier lords, who were given special privileges and large blocks of territory, the estates of any particular great lord were spread over two or more counties to preclude the development of provincial autonomy. As in Normandy also, the precise amount of knight service was established for every royal tenant-in-chief, proceeding in multiples of five to a maximum of sixty knights owed to the royal army. The feudal military service owed by vassals to the Anglo-Norman king amounted to five thousand knights, a vast number for the period. No castles could be built in the country without royal permission, and at least three times a year the royal vassals had to come to the *Curia Regis,* the king's court, to hear the king announce his plans, to advise him on policy, and to participate in important law suits involving the royal tenants-in-chief. The day-to-day affairs of the government were conducted by a small group of lay and ecclesiastical nobles and monastic clerks who staffed the chancery. The local agents of the Anglo-Norman monarchy maintained the old English title of sheriff ("shire reeve"), but he was actually the Norman viscount, by which title he is often referred to in official royal documents. He was no longer the weak and ineffective royal agent of preconquest times who had been dominated by the great earls, but the leading voice in the government and law of the shire. A middling landholder in his private capacity, the sheriff was given enormous influence and authority by his status as the representative of an efficient and determined royal government that brooked no recalcitrance by even the greatest lords in the country. The sheriff presided over the shire court, and he was the local agent of the royal treasury.

William the Conqueror and his sons amazed continental contemporaries by the extent of their financial resources. Their financial resources were great not only because of England's wealth, for certainly, taken as a whole, the kingdoms of France and Germany were much richer, but because the Anglo-Norman king was able to tax the resources of his realm to a degree far exceeding that of any ruler in Europe. Money was needed to support the king and his family, his central administration, his local representatives, and his military establishment. The relative effectiveness of English royal taxation inaugurated by William the Conqueror is an important key to the political history of the Middle Ages. It helps to account for the fact that as late as the fifteenth century the king of England was able to inflict crushing defeats upon French kings, who ruled a country with three times the population of England and whose landed, commercial, and industrial wealth, if we could estimate it precisely, would be even greater. In the Middle Ages, no less than in the twentieth century, wars cost money, and the power of any particular king was greatly dependent upon the comprehensiveness and efficiency of his taxation system. In this regard the Anglo-Norman king was at least a century ahead of the Capetian monarchy, and no German ruler of the twelfth and thirteenth centuries ever had any comparable command of the financial resources of his country.

The chief source of income of early medieval kings had been their own estates, and William naturally drew a substantial part of his income from the royal demesne, whose administration was the sheriff's responsibility. The law courts were also a lucrative source of income, but it was their clever and unrelenting use of the feudal possibilities for taxation that accounts for the great financial resources of the Anglo-Norman rulers. Like any other feudal lord, William enjoyed the prerogatives of relief, wardship, and the regular aids, and his treasury found that these old institutions could be made to produce great sums. Not only the lay vassals but also the bishoprics and abbeys that owed feudal obligations to the crown, were subjected to this kind of taxation. In addition to all these sources of royal income William inaugurated the practice of allowing his vassals the option of not sending their knights to serve in the feudal host on payment of a certain sum per knight's fee; the practice came to be called scutage (literally, "shield money") in the early twelfth century. William's tenants-in-chief were glad to be freed of the burden of keeping their knights trained and equipped for war, and William preferred to use the income he obtained from scutage to hire mercenaries for his continental wars. Paradoxically, the same king who brought feudal institutions to their highest refinement and used them most effectively for enhancing royal power was the earliest to realize the inefficiency of the feudal method of raising armies. By feudal law the vassals were required to serve only forty days a year, which was a tremendous nuisance in a long campaign; the knights who were provided to his feudal host were not always adequately prepared and armed; it was advisable to leave most of the English army at home in case of another Scandinavian invasion, which threatened during most of the Conqueror's reign; and William had the special problem of transporting the knights and horses across the channel, which was both expensive and risky. He preferred to hire mercenaries among the landless knights of Normandy, Flanders, and Brittany for his frontier campaigns against various French princes. The Anglo-Norman monarch's envious continental enemies were not slow to realize the significance of this military innovation. A chief minister of the French king in the first half of the twelfth century referred to the English ruler as "that wealthy man, a marvelous buyer and collector of knights." William initiated the slow substitution of mercenary forces for feudal armies, which is one of the central military developments of the High Middle Ages.

The enterprise and ingenuity of William's government is demonstrated by legal as well as political and military innovations. For the settling of land disputes among the great barons he commissioned the shire courts to empanel inquests of sworn men of the neighborhood, or juries as they later came to be called. The Anglo-Saxons had occasionally used similar juries to bring criminal accusations in the folk courts, but the pre-conquest kings were so politically incompetent that they did not realize the value of this institution, and it died out before the eleventh century. The inquest, which can be traced back through Norman legal development to its origins in Carolingian times, was introduced anew into England by the Conqueror, who was not aware of the abortive Anglo-Saxon experiments with it. In the second half of the twelfth century the sworn inquest, or jury, came to be used in criminal as well as civil suits and became the central institution in English legal procedure.

The intelligence and energy of the Anglo-Norman monarchy was magnificently revealed in the last year of William's life by a complete survey of the property and proprietors of England as they existed before the conquest and in 1086. No other government in Europe before the thirteenth century could have carried out such an investigation, the results of which were summarized in two huge volumes that came to be known as the Domesday Book. The Domesday Book provided the royal government and law courts with a complete record of the wealth and landholders in England for purposes of taxation and litigation. It was put together by royal commissioners working with information derived from the testimony of literally hundreds of local juries. It provides the most detailed record of medieval social and economic life that had yet been made, and its value as a source of statistical information was not surpassed in Europe until the nineteenth century. It remains the most remarkable monument of the work of William the Conqueror and his clerical assistants, who in two decades transformed England from one of the most backward states to one of the most advanced in Europe.

II. The Significance of the English Investiture Controversy

Even disgruntled Anglo-Saxon churchmen admired and stood in awe of the achievements of William the Conqueror, but Gregory VII found little cause to rejoice in his protégé's success. As the power of the German emperor declined under papal attack, a new secular leader of much greater potential emerged on the European political scene. Gregory was not blind to the significance of this development. In the long run here lay a greater threat to the achievement of the new world order he envisioned than even the Salian emperor could have offered. Furthermore, the Anglo-Norman church-state system bore disquieting similarities to the situation in Germany on the eve of the investiture controversy. William did not bother to emphasize the traditions of theocratic kingship, but through lay investiture and the vassalage of bishops and abbots he completely controlled the affairs of the English church. And yet, as in Germany, the churchmen were completely loyal to the monarchy, and the king was not only feared but respected and admired by them. The literate work of his government was in the hands of passionately loyal monastic clerks who were promoted for their valuable service through royal appointments to vacant episcopal and abbatial offices. The archbishop of Canterbury, Lanfranc, who was renowned throughout Europe as a theologian and canon lawyer, strongly approved of this close association between the king and the church, and as William's confidant and adviser he seems to have been responsible for many of its refinements.

The Norman conquest brought about a great improvement in the moral and intellectual level of the higher clergy of England. Under royal patronage the monasteries prospered, canon-law collections of a conservative, pre-Gregorian kind were introduced and studied, great monastic libraries were established, and liturgical studies and historical writing were actively pursued. Impressive new stone churches in the Norman perpendicular style were erected, of which Durham cathedral is an outstanding example, and the number and quality of the parish clergy were augmented.

But Gregory discovered that the English church after the Conquest was no more in contact with Rome than before. William issued a decree forbidding any of his clergy to go to Rome, to receive papal legates, or to appeal to the papal curia without his permission. Such provisions were in flagrant violation of the policies of the Gregorian papacy, yet Gregory was powerless to intervene. England lacked a rebellious nobility that he could use as a lever against the monarchy, the widely esteemed Lanfranc of Canterbury clearly lacked enthusiasm for the Gregorian reform, and Gregory was not so foolish as to come to an open break with the English king while Henry IV was not yet vanquished. However, the pope could not resist trying to assert his authority over the English king and archbishop. Gregory claimed that William's conquest of England under the papal banner and the general provisions of the Donation of Constantine required that the Conqueror become his vassal. William, of course, would not hear of it. The pope then demanded that Lanfranc come to Rome and personally make his subservience to the supreme pontiff, but the archbishop prevaricated, refused to leave England, and as a precaution entered into secret negotiations with the imperial antipope. Gregory was thus unable to influence the English situation in any way.

The monolithic alliance between the monarchy and the church in England began to show signs of strain after the Conqueror's death in 1087 and Lanfranc's in 1089. William's successor in England, his second son William II, Rufus (1087–1100), used the feudal prerogatives of the crown to tax the church mercilessly. He furthermore exhibited homosexual qualities and a strange sympathy for Jews, which made him unpopular. The new archbishop of Canterbury, the elderly St. Anselm, another Italian-Norman monk and the greatest theologian of his day, was much more sympathetic to the Gregorian-reform program than his teacher Lanfranc had been. A bitter dispute between the king and Anselm ensued in which the English higher clergy sympathized with the venerable archbishop personally but would not support him, partly because they feared Rufus's wrath and partly because they were hostile to the introduction of the Gregorian-reform program in England. Anselm was left with the sole alternative of going to Rome to appeal for papal intervention. Gregory VII would have jumped at the chance, but the occupant of the throne of Peter was now the moderate and wily Cluniac monk Urban II, who had no taste for bitter conflicts. Urban had just completed an agreement with the Norman ruler of Sicily that gave the latter effective control over the church in his domains, and to Anselm's chagrin the pope proceeded to complete a similar concordat with the English king. It was a simple *quid pro quo;* Rufus recognized Urban instead of the antipope, and Urban gave papal sanction to the Anglo-Norman church-state system.

The accession of Rufus's younger brother, Henry I (1100–1135), who resembled his father in every way, and of Paschal II changed the situation radically. By 1103 the pope and king were embroiled in a bitter dispute over lay investiture. A Norman count who was Henry's chief adviser was excommunicated by the pope, and the excommunication of the king was threatened as the next step. Not even the bewildered Anselm's appeal for moderation seemed to be able to head off a long and protracted struggle. The resourceful Anglo-Norman king commissioned his chief ecclesiastical supporter, Archbishop Gerard of York, to dredge up the traditions of Anglo-Saxon theocratic kingship in defense of the royal investiture of ecclesiastics. The resulting *Anonymous of York* treatises are a delight to students of early-medieval political theory, but they in no way typify the outlook of the Anglo-Norman monarchy, which had substituted the secure foundation of administrative and legal bureaucracy for outmoded religious ideology. In case of a long struggle with the papacy, however, Henry considered that even the antiquated traditions of theocratic kingship might prove useful.

The English investiture controversy proved to be short-lived, however. Anselm withdrew into exile to let the pope and king fight it out between them, and the English bishops and abbots remained steadfast in their loyalty to the prevailing church-state system. Paschal's attention was diverted in 1106 by a projected crusade against Constantinople that he was supporting and in which he vainly hoped Henry I would participate. He agreed to the king's proposal for a compromise based upon the principle, which the Anglo-Norman government had long followed, of making a distinction between the religious and the feudal-political capacities of the great churchmen. By the Concordat of London in 1107, which was the model for the later Concordat of Worms, Henry made the token surrender to Rome of abandoning lay investiture, but he maintained inviolate his authority over his bishops and abbots through ecclesiastical homage.

The English investiture controversy was by no means without consequence. It warned Henry of the dangers implicit in the English monarchy's
alliance with the church, which could be threatened by papal intervention,
and encouraged him to expand his purely secular power through the continued building up of the administrative bureaucracy. After the investiture
controversy Henry abandoned his father's policy of using monastic scholars in his administration because the regular clergy had proved to be
most infected by Gregorian ideas and influenced by Rome. Instead he
employed secular clerks, who, while nominally churchmen—no other
kind of literate men were available in England—pursued the king's interests with the attitude of dedicated professional bureaucrats. Such harsh,
ruthless, but extremely able servants the king rewarded with appointments to lucrative bishoprics. Henry expanded his father's practice of scutage to make the Anglo-Norman monarchy even less reliant than before
on knight service from church lands. The effectiveness of the English
treasury was increased through the founding of a controlling accounting
body called the exchequer, which borrowed from the Continent the system of reckoning with a variant of the abacus. The exchequer kept the
extensive annual records of the income and expenditures of the crown,
which came to be called the pipe rolls; nothing like this sophisticated
accounting system existed in the Capetian realm until the early thirteenth
century. The effectiveness of the law courts and the increase of royal
jurisdiction over the shire courts was achieved by sending out, on circuit,
panels of itinerant justices from the *Curia Regis* to preside over the
county courts. By 1135 the institutions of the English monarchy were so
far ahead of the continental kingdoms that royal clerks could plausibly
attribute to Henry I the qualities of the emperor in Roman law "from
whom law and power [likewise] radiated through the whole kingdom."
The same situation existed in Normandy, which Henry had conquered
from his incompetent brother Robert.

At a time when the nobility of France and Germany were in the heyday of territorial sovereignty, the English barons found themselves completely circumscribed by the expanding royal institutions, and their feudal
privileges were evaporating before the advance of crown bureaucracy.
The only possibility of interrupting the expansion of royal power seemed
to be in a succession crisis that would allow the English lords to play off
one candidate against another, and, to Henry's great disappointment, this
prospect became a real possibility through the early death of his only
son. His only other legitimate heir was his daughter Matilda, who had
once been married to the German emperor Henry V and was now the
wife of the count of Anjou. There was no principle in English law that

excluded a woman from ascending to the throne, but Matilda was an arrogant and foolish woman who offended everybody, and in any case the nobility was determined to take advantage of this rare opportunity to stem the tide of advancing royal power. After Henry's death many of the ambitious barons resurrected the Germanic electoral principle from desuetude and gave their allegiance to Henry's nephew (a son of the Conqueror's daughter), the feckless adventurer Stephen of Blois, who appeared in England to assert his claim. The two decades of desultory civil war that followed have sometimes been called "the anarchy," which they certainly were not, because the central political, legal, and financial machinery of the monarchy, although weakened by the removal of strong direction, in no case disappeared. By the end of the 1140s the lesser nobility in England, who were coming to be called the knightly class, could see no point in perpetuating a struggle that benefited only the private interests of the great baronial families, and even many of these more prominent lords longed for peace and the security of royal justice. A compromise was reached that brought Matilda's son to the throne as Henry II, the first of the Angevin line, when Stephen of Blois died in 1154.

Henry II and his administrators had to work hard to recover the ground that had been lost in the previous two decades, but in this work of reestablishing the royal institutions of his grandfather's day and then extending the power of the royal bureaucracy, the king was aided by the lessons of the civil war itself. After more than six decades of increasing centralization, the English landed classes had been given a taste of continental feudal disorder. By 1154 they were firmly convinced of the benefits that William the Conqueror and his sons had brought to England and prepared to acquiesce in the Angevin refinements of the Anglo-Norman state.

CHAPTER THIRTEEN

The First Crusade and After

I. Origins of the Crusading Ideal

In the popular historiographical conception, medieval civilization is virtually identified with the crusades. The only event of the eleventh century known to the average graduate of American universities would be the first crusade of 1095, which he would visualize in terms of gigantic warriors dressed in burnished plate armor and riding magnificent steeds, following the standards of the cross to victory over the swarthy hordes of pusillanimous Arabs. No aspect of this picture is quite accurate. The average stature of the late eleventh-century knight, because of insufficient nourishment in infancy and a generally bad diet and medicine, was not above five feet three inches. The knights of the first crusade still, for the most part, wore chain mail rather than plate armor, which did not come into general use until the latter part of the twelfth century. Their horses, by modern standards or even by those of the thirteenth century, were distinctly puny; it was increased crossbreeding with the superior Arab strains that improved the western breed in the following two centuries. It is true that the knights of the first crusade followed the cross, but by no means entirely for religious purposes. Finally, the Arabs were every bit as valiant and skilled in combat as were the western knights, and it was the internal political weakness of the Islamic world, not the personal inadequacies of the Arab warriors, that accounted for the success of the first crusade.

It is necessary to look for the idea of the crusades in the struggle between Christians and Moslems in Spain and consider how the Latin idea of a holy war emerged from this background. When the Moslems conquered the Iberian peninsula in the eighth century, a few of the Spanish Christian princes and their followers fled into the northern mountains, from which they launched the *Reconquista* in the tenth century. In the eleventh century these Spanish Christians, greatly assisted by the growing political disunity of the Spanish Moslems, gained their initial successes, and by 1100 they held somewhere between a fifth and a quarter of the whole country. The tide of reconquest crept slowly and relentlessly southward, and while the final expulsion of the Moslems was achieved only in 1492, the greater part of the peninsula from the middle of the thirteenth century was ruled by Christian kings. The Reconquista was the dominant, almost the exclusive, theme of medieval Christian Spanish history, and some historians have seen it as the determining factor in the molding of the peculiar Spanish character. All Iberian society originated in a grim war of five centuries against Islam, and the Spanish institutional structure was organized around the warlord and the necessities of aggressive warfare. The Spanish Christians eventually, and probably unconsciously, imitated the Moslem *jihad,* or holy war, with its doctrine that the highest morality was to die fighting on behalf of the deity. Religious fanaticism and military valor became the dominant socially approved values in Spanish society, and it has been said that herein lies the key to the enigmas of Spanish history. The Christian ruling class never learned to do anything but fight, and while this pugnacious energy and military skill led directly to the great overseas Iberian empires, Spain lacked the political and economic experience, the institutions, and arts of peace to take long-range advantage of these initial triumphs.

The Gregorian papacy, through its legates, maintained a careful watch on the progress of the Reconquista and for several reasons, both intellectual and strategic, found it worthy of more general imitation. The doctrinal validity of a holy war and the shedding of blood on behalf of the Lord was a moot question. Apostolic Christianity had exhibited strong pacifistic tendencies, but St. Augustine of Hippo had justified the use of force in the church's interest, and we have seen that Hildebrand's outlook was strongly neo-Augustinian. Carl Erdmann emphasized that the strongly militant quality of eleventh-century Christianity, which is reflected in the attitudes of the leaders of the reform papacy, made a war against Islam an attractive proposition. These are the intellectual factors that inspired Gregory VII to project an oriental expedition, directed by the papacy, against the Moslem heretics. There were, however, other motives involved. Such a crusade would be an expression of the supreme pontiff's moral leadership of the western world (which was one of Gregory's cardinal doctrines) and would bring the peoples of the north into closer relations with Rome. Finally, the Latin invasion of the Orient could be expected to take a long step toward the assertion of papal hegemony in Greek Christian lands. The Roman curia was deeply concerned by the continuation of the schism of 1054 and regarded a crusade as an effective instrument for affirming the long-claimed papal supremacy over the Greek church.

The situation in the Middle East in the 1070s provided an excellent opportunity for this Latin intervention. The Byzantine state was weakened by the rise of feudal lordship and proved unable to withstand the advancing armies of the Moslem Seljuk Turks, the latest wave of Asian invaders to penetrate the long-suffering Mediterranean world. The Turks had regained Antioch from the Greeks, and they inflicted a crushing defeat on the Byzantine armies at the Battle of Manzikert in 1071. They now advanced deep into Asia Minor, and the highly intelligent but rather timid emperor, Alexius Comnenus, feared that Constantinople itself was in imminent danger. The extent of the emperor's panic may be gauged by the fact that he appealed to the traditional papal enemy to send him military aid. If Gregory could have vanquished Henry IV, he would have undoubtedly tried to turn Alexis' plight to the immediate advantage of the papacy by dispatching an army designed to serve the Latin cause more than the Greeks. But the perpetuation of the German investiture conflict precluded the organization of a crusade during Gregory's pontificate. It was left for the more moderate, but no less ambitious, Urban II to do so.

To Urban the crusade served four ends in addition to the obvious one of regaining the Holy Land for the cross. First, it would help to reunite Christendom after the bitter and divisive disputes over the Gregorian reform, and second, it would increase papal prestige at a time when there were supporters of the German emperor even in the city of Rome. Third, it would work toward ending the schism between the western and eastern churches. Urban had tried to bring the Greek church in southern Italy under papal authority, but his plan had foundered on a theological dispute about the relationship between the Son and the Holy Ghost (the so-called *Filioque* controversy). A crusade might go to the heart of the matter by making the Byzantine emperor dependent upon, or even subservient to, a Latin army. The fourth value that Urban saw in a crusade was a consequence of his own French background. He well knew that the Germans would not join his enterprise and that the powerful Anglo-Norman ruler would not be inclined to participate. The backbone of the crusading army, aside from a contingent of Norman Italians, would have to come from the French feudal principalities, and Urban realized that an eastern expedition would fit in with the needs of many French lords and knights and at the same time would employ their energies in the service of the church. By the end of the eleventh century the boundaries of the French duchies and counties had become stabilized, and a primitive balance of power existed among them. The great French feudal princes, therefore, had little opportunity for conquest at home, and many were restless and potentially eager for foreign ventures. Furthermore, the rising population curve meant that an ever-increasing number of landless knights in France were ready to cast their lot in an expedition that would allow them to gain domains in the Middle East. In addition, Urban well knew that lay piety was having its effect on the French nobility. The nobility's devotion to at least the external accoutrements of the Christian faith indicated that the idea of a holy war would appeal to them.

The pope planned his proclamation of the crusade with great care. He summoned a council at Clermont in central France for 1095 and urged the French bishops and abbots to bring with them the prominent lords of their provinces. Before he arrived at Clermont, he already knew that one of the leading French princes, Raymond of St. Giles, count of Toulouse, would take the cross. As Urban began his highly emotional appeal to the "Race of the Franks" to join the crusade, he already anticipated a favorable response. His speech was one of the most skillful and effective examples of rhetoric in European history. He touched upon every motive that a French knight might have, both religious and otherwise, for taking the cross. Urban expatiated on the sufferings of Christians in the Holy Land at the hands of the Seljuk Turks. He mentioned the imminent danger to Byzantium of the Moslem advance. He reminded the French knights of their reputation for courage and piety and called upon them to rescue the Holy Sepulchre from infidel hands. He offered his listeners the prospect of carving out kingdoms in Palestine, "a land flowing with milk and honey." He promised papal protection for the property and family of any crusader, and finally, as the keeper of the keys to the kingdom of heaven, he promised the crusaders plenary indulgence for their sins.

This last inducement closely resembled the Koranic assurance of heaven for any Moslem warrior who died fighting for the faith. The crusading indulgence was to be abused greatly in later centuries, and its ultimate form was attacked in the sixteenth century not only by Martin Luther but by the Council of Trent. In the twelfth century the church developed the institution of indulgence for vicarious crusading, that is, for supporting crusaders through monetary assistance. By the fourteenth century the papacy allowed the outright selling of indulgences without even this crusading pretext, as is vividly described in Chaucer's *Canterbury Tales*. But there was nothing abusive in Urban's original idea of a crusading indulgence. In his view it was merely an exemplary form of penance, and, of course, its effectiveness was dependent upon genuine contrition. However, he left these theological aspects of the crusading indulgence rather vague, and it is likely that many French knights were led to believe that taking the cross by itself would secure their heavenly reward. While self-interested motives played a considerable role in launching the crusading movement—and Urban by his speech in fact encouraged them—it was nevertheless true that many took the cross for primarily religious reasons. We are told by eyewitnesses that at the conclusion of Urban's speech at the Council of Clermont a great shout of *Deus Vult* ("God wills it") arose from the assembly, and many lords and knights came forward to take the cross. Red cloaks were cut into strips that were sewn in the form of crucifixes on the fronts of tunics.

This emotional scene was repeated all over France and southern Italy in response to the spreading of Urban's message by papal legates. Indeed, it seems that Urban had underrated the effect of his proclamation at Clermont. He was not prepared for the immediate organization of the various groups of knights now clamoring to set out for the Holy Land, and it was not until the following year that the first crusade began. Certainly no one at the papal court anticipated the explosive effect of Urban's appeal at Clermont on the Rhenish cities. Before the French knights could set out on their expedition, a "people's crusade," consisting of unruly mobs from the slums of the Rhineland urban communities, blindly set out in the general direction of the Holy Land. Led by popular preachers, such as Peter the Hermit, they committed pogroms on the prosperous Jewish populations in their own cities and then moved through Germany and the Balkans like a plague of locusts until they arrived at the gates of Constantinople. The frightened emperor immediately transported them across the Hellespont, where they were exterminated by the Turks.

This popular reaction was one of the most significant aspects of the first crusade because it demonstrated the millennial and apocalyptic outlook of the lower and middle classes of European cities. The papacy had already encountered this millennial feeling in Milan, where social disaffection had also sought an escape through emotional religion. To the participants in the people's crusade, Urban's preaching had a significance that the pope himself did not understand. They yearned for release from the frustration and poverty of their unhappy lives, and they found in the pope's pronouncements apocalyptic and eschatological overtones that were beyond the worldview of the sensible Cluniac pope. The people's crusade offers a remarkable glimpse of the highly emotional and revolutionary forms that the new piety was taking in urban areas, out of which the popular heresy of the late twelfth century and the papacy's policy in the face of this mass religiosity were to emerge.

The papacy, however, dismissed the momentary social earthquake of the people's crusade with a bewildered shrug and set about organizing the French feudal princes and knights into a crusading army. The varied motives of the leaders of the first crusade indicate the growing sophistication of the European nobility that distinguished their attitudes from the brutish outlook prevailing among this class in the tenth century. Genuine piety inspired most of them, but they also had other reasons for setting out for the Holy Land. Some, such as Raymond of Toulouse and Godfrey, duke of Lorraine, were bored by the lack of opportunity for valor and adventure at home. Others, such as Robert Curthose, duke of Normandy, the incompetent eldest son of William the Conqueror, wanted to restore the prestige they had lost at home by winning a great victory in the East. Count Stephen of Blois joined the expedition because his wife, the ambitious daughter of William the Conqueror, made him go. The Norman Italians were motivated by their genuine hatred of the Byzantine empire and a desire to carve out territories for themselves in the Middle East at the emperor's expense. They looked upon the first crusade more as an expedition against Constantinople than as a war against Islam. Their most outstanding leader, Bohemund, had already led an abortive expedition against the Greek empire, and he was to attempt a similar unsuccessful venture, with papal encouragement, in 1106. The north Italian mercantile cities, especially Venice, were enthusiastic for the crusade, and not primarily for religious reasons. They regarded it as another step in their economic penetration of the Mediterranean world. They hoped to gain seaports in the eastern Mediterranean to compete more effectively with the Arabic merchants. And the Venetians were awarded the lucrative work of supplying the crusaders once they had reached Syria and Palestine.

Although no European king joined the first crusade, its leaders were, on the average, able and valorous princes. Their great weakness was an inability to agree upon a single leader, mainly because they were of the same social status. The pope finally appointed a French bishop as the nominal leader of the expedition, but from the beginning to the end the first crusade was marked by bickering among the princes and their vassals. Another, and pardonable, deficiency in the direction of the crusade was the leaders' gross ignorance of the geography, climate, and political organization of the Moslem countries, but it is remarkable how quickly the crusaders adjusted to their novel environment. Alexius Comnenus gave them some valuable information, and more was furnished by the Venetians.

The crusaders finally set out in 1096 on the land route through Germany and the Balkans to Byzantium, the jumping-off point for their attack on Islam. This route had already been traversed by the people's crusade, and the Franks, as the Greeks and Arabs called all the crusaders, acted similarly. They massacred Jews in the Rhenish cities and abused and robbed the Balkan peoples whose lands they crossed. Alexius Comnenus greeted them with apprehension. He was glad to receive Latin support, but it was certainly not the kind of aid he had envisaged, and he feared that the crusaders were just as keen on the dismemberment of what remained of the Byzantine empire as they were on attacking the Moslems, especially when he saw his old enemy Bohemund in their midst. He transported them across the straits to Asia Minor as quickly as possible. The Frankish reaction to Constantinople was not different from the attitudes of Liudprand of Cremona a century and a half before. When they came face to face with the wealth and military forces of Byzantium, the leaders of the crusade realized that they would have little chance of taking the golden city on the Hellespont. They would have to content themselves with carving out feudal domains in Syria and Palestine and thereby humiliate the emperor by establishing Latin principalities on territory claimed by Constantinople and by providing a foothold for the Roman church in the eastern Mediterranean.

In the face of Byzantine grandeur and culture the Franks had a strong sense of inferiority, and they compensated for their rusticity and crudeness by condemning the Greeks as effeminate and corrupt. Actually the mannered Greek courtiers rightly found the Frankish princes boors in comparison with themselves. There was merit in each party's criticism of the other, but the Franks were representatives of a still youthful and extremely vital civilization, while Byzantium was sterile and decadent and had to rely on its western enemies for salvation from the more pressing Arabic foe. This fascinating encounter between the Byzantine imperial court, the citadel of oversophistication, and the uncouth but enterprising French feudatories was thus highly significant, for it symbolized the meeting of the dawning and the dying day.

The naïveté of the leaders of the first crusade prevented them from realizing the magnitude of the task they had undertaken. The whole western force could not have numbered more than five thousand people,

probably fewer, and the united Moslem world would have had little difficulty destroying the invaders. But the advance of the Seljuk Turks into
the eastern Mediterranean had upset the prevailing political order and
had brought about bitter internal disputes among the Arabic princes. The
crusaders showed unsurpassed bravery and considerable military skill,
and at a critical moment, when their spirits flagged, the discovery of what
was purported to be an important relic rallied them to pursue their invasion. But the fact remains that it was the temporary disunity of the
Moslems and their inability to present a united front that played the indispensable role in the triumph of the crusaders. The crusaders marched
through Asia Minor into Syria and took Antioch after a long siege. Bohemund usurped authority over the city and made himself, for a short time,
prince of Antioch; one other crusading leader also fell away from the
expedition to carve out his own Middle Eastern fief. But the others
pressed on, and after a bitter struggle, they took Jerusalem and characteristically massacred the Moslem and Jewish civilians in the Holy City.

The success of the first crusade was the end result of the penetration
of the Mediterranean world that had been initiated by the north Italian
cities in the tenth century and furthered by the Norman conquest of
southern Italy. It was the consequence, but scarcely a cause, of this and
other important changes in European civilization. Although the first crusade undoubtedly increased European awareness of the riches of the
Middle East and enriched European taste for spices and other oriental
products, it certainly did not bring about the opening of economic relations between West and East; that development had already been effected
on an extensive scale in the previous century. Nor did the first crusade
play a part in establishing the intellectual and cultural relations between
the Islamic and Latin worlds that brought about the revolution in western
philosophy and science in the twelfth and thirteenth centuries. None of
the Latin translations of the writings of the Greek thinkers and their Arabic interpreters was made in the crusading states; they made no contribution whatever to western learning. The translations were carried out in
the old centers of Latin-Arabic intercourse in Spain and Sicily. The only
long-range impact of the establishment of a Latin outpost in the Middle
East was slowly to teach the European peoples a tolerance for men of
another culture and religion. The Latin knights who lived in the crusading
states found that their Moslem neighbors were at least as intelligent and
moral as themselves, a discovery that inevitably undermined their original
fanaticism and hatred for peoples they had known only as stereotyped,
monstrous infidels. The lords of the crusading states quickly adopted the
dress, food, and many of the private mores of the neighboring emirs. It

was not, however, until the second half of the thirteenth century that these more realistic and tolerant attitudes toward the Moslem people penetrated the consciousness of western Europe.

II. Crusading Memories

The first crusade of 1096 created the Latin Kingdom of Jerusalem, a small Palestinian principality centering in Jerusalem and Acre and tightly organized along feudal lines. Godfrey of Lorraine was its first ruler, although without calling himself king, and he was succeeded by his brother Baldwin, who was allowed by the clergy and other crusaders to use the royal title. From the beginning of its days the Latin Kingdom was threatened by Moslem reconquest, and in the following two centuries its territory suffered slow but irreversible attrition. Periodically the papacy and other important churchmen inspired European rulers to undertake expeditions in aid of the Latin Kingdom, none of which were ever successful and several of which were disastrous. Actually, the western outpost in the eastern Mediterranean achieved its greatest size at the beginning of its history. By the start of the thirteenth century it had been shrunk, by counterattacks of the great Egyptian ruler Saladin, to a slim belt of territory. Jerusalem itself was lost to the Moslems in 1187, and the Latin Kingdom was finally extinguished in 1291. The lugubrious history of the later crusades of the twelfth and thirteenth centuries—traditionally consisting of six, although there were a few smaller expeditions—raises the important question of why western Europe was apparently unable to preserve the Latin Kingdom of Jerusalem.

It was more a matter of lack of interest than of inability. There is no doubt that if at any time in the twelfth and thirteenth centuries the total resources of the papacy and the European monarchies had been applied to the crusading movement, a crushing defeat could have been inflicted on the Moslem armies that encircled the Latin Kingdom. The fact remains, however, that the leaders of western society had many other, more pressing interests, and the crusading movement, however worthy they deemed it in their public pronouncements, was to them a rather peripheral matter. Many of the kings and the great feudal princes of western Europe took the cross during the twelfth and thirteenth centuries, but only a fraction of them actually departed for the Holy Land. Frequently the papacy did not mind this backsliding because it placed the vowed crusader in a spiritual debt to Rome and allowed the pope to demand some other form of service to the church as the price of dispensation from the crusading oath. Even when a great king actually went on a crusade, he more often than not simply went through the motions of fighting the Moslems, taking only a small part of his army with him, staying only a few months in the Holy Land, engaging in only perfunctory skirmishes, and finally reaching some face-saving treaty with a sultan to appear back home as a hero of the Christian faith. Paradoxically, the crusading leaders of the twelfth and thirteenth centuries who took their tasks most seriously were the worst soldiers and accomplished nothing except the massacre of their knights at Arabic hands. The crusading ideal during the twelfth and thirteenth centuries was a popular outlet for the intense and widespread piety of the period, but it was only one form among many. To the kings and princes of western Europe, taking the cross was a necessary duty encouraged by the pope and other important churchmen. It was something they had to do as an expression of their status in society and to appease public opinion, but nearly all of them took it as a formal matter that required only a small part of their energy and resources.

The second crusade of 1144 was preached by St. Bernard of Clairvaux, the moral leader of the mid-twelfth-century church, in response to urgent entreaties from the Latin Kingdom of Jerusalem for aid against the resurgent Arabic power. St. Bernard succeeded in inducing two of the crowned heads of Europe, Louis VII of France and Conrad III of Germany, to take the cross. The inclusion of the two kings provided more prestige than the first crusade had enjoyed but no more military prowess, for Louis and Conrad were not renowned for their skill on the battlefield or the size of their armies. They never reached Palestine, their forces being cut to pieces in Asia Minor. The sole consequence of the second crusade was the strain it placed on the relations between Louis and his queen, Eleanor of Aquitaine, who accompanied him on the expedition and whom Louis accused of infidelity with one of his generals. The resulting divorce of the Capetian king and the duchess of Aquitaine and her subsequent marriage to Henry II of England had an important effect upon the political development of twelfth-century Europe.

The mixture of tragedy and farce that characterized the second crusade was repeated in the third crusade of 1190, the most ambitious, at least in its inception, of all the Latin expeditions to the Holy Land. The power of Saladin was to be challenged by a crusading army that, at least on paper, commanded the greater part of the military resources of Europe. The three greatest rulers of western Europe at the time, Richard the Lion-hearted of England, Philip Augustus of France, and Frederick Barbarossa of Germany, set off for the Holy Land with formidable armies. Barbarossa drowned en route, and the Germans ended by participating only in a token manner. It soon appeared that the cynical Philip Augustus intended only to go through the motions of fighting the Moslems; he was eager to get back home to continue his plotting against the English king. Richard Coeur de Lion took the expedition and himself with great seriousness. He was renowned for his gigantic stature and strength, being six feet tall, and was eager to demonstrate both his individual valor and prowess, which were undoubtedly great, and his skill as a general, which was another matter entirely. An overgrown and spoiled child, Richard had antagonized almost every ruler in Europe by the time he got to the Holy Land, and once there, he not only succeeded in increasing the hostility of the French king toward him, but incurred the hatred of the Germans. The expedition rapidly disintegrated, and after the English king had satisfied his vanity in a few battles, the wily Saladin accepted a peace treaty that simply preserved the status quo. Then Richard discovered that he had no way to get home because every route he could possibly take was blocked by his enemies. Characteristically, he chose the most roundabout route, via Germany, and was imprisoned and held for ransom by the emperor Henry VI. These dramatic events enhanced Richard's stature as a chivalric knight, but they indicate the steady decline of a genuine interest in the crusading movement. The European kings were too busy pursuing their dynastic and territorial interests to give more than perfunctory support to the Latin Kingdom.

The fourth crusade of 1204 was undoubtedly the most successful of all the later oriental expeditions, but it was directed against Byzantium, rather than the Moslem world. Pope Innocent III, who preached the crusade, did not originally intend it to take this form. But the Venetians, who provided the fleet for the crusading army (a motley collection of French knights), insisted upon this change of plans, and since they had advanced loans to the crusaders, they were able to extract compliance from them. Innocent readily aquiesced in this change of plans as a means of asserting papal authority over Constantinople. The anti-Byzantine tendencies of the crusading movement, which had been evident from its inception in the eleventh century, came to fruition in the fourth crusade. Constantinople had withstood Moslem armies for five centuries, but it now fell to the Venetians and the French knights, who pillaged the city, abused the Greek churchmen, and set up the Latin Kingdom of Constantinople with papal blessings. For six decades Latin princes ruled in Constantinople, and the papacy used this opportunity to try to bring the Greek Christians under the authority of Rome. In 1261 a Greek prince finally regained the imperial throne, with the schism between the Latin and Greek churches not yet healed. Imperial power never recovered from the disaster of the fourth crusade, and while Constantinople did not fall to the Moslems until

1453, it henceforth played a negligible role in the affairs of the Mediterranean world.

The fourth crusade demonstrated to the papacy how the crusading movement might be used for other purposes than the succor of the Latin Kingdom of Jerusalem. In the thirteenth century crusades were directed more against the enemies of the pope within Europe than against the Moslems. The older kind of crusading venture was perpetuated in two crusades led by the saint-monarch, Louis IX of France, and one expedition conducted by the German emperor Frederick II of Hohenstaufen. None of these three last crusades helped the declining Latin Kingdom of Jerusalem. St. Louis boldly attacked the Moslems in their strongholds, first in Egypt and at the end of his reign in Tunisia. In both cases he was defeated. Frederick II's crusade was a perfunctory exhibition with farcical qualities, since he was actually under papal excommunication at the time of his crusade. Insofar as the crusading movement played a significant role in the life of thirteenth-century Europe it was in the novel and perverted form of wars against papal enemies. The first instance, the crusade against the Albigensian heretics of southern France preached by Innocent III, was generally approved of in western Europe, although the way in which it provided a pretext for the invasion of Toulouse by the avaricious nobility of northern France was reprehensible. But the further uses that the papacy made of the crusading movement discredited it as a spiritual force by flagrantly contradicting its original ideals. In the 1240s Frederick II was branded a heretic on questionable grounds, and the French army, which was invited to seize his south Italian territories, was given the status of crusaders. By the 1280s the crusades had become a purely political institution. The crusading label was granted to Philip III of France for his attack on the king of Aragon, who by no stretch of the imagination could be called a heretic, but whose conquest of Sicily had displeased the papacy. This purely political use of the crusades occurred at the very time when the Latin Kingdom of Jerusalem, lacking reinforcement from western Europe, was sinking to its extinction.

The fact was that in the second half of the thirteenth century the leaders of European society were not enthusiastic for new wars against Islam. In part their lack of enthusiasm was due to a more tolerant and enlightened attitude. They had come to share the discovery of the residents of the Latin Kingdom of Jerusalem that the Arabs were an intelligent and able people. By 1200 there was a greater interest in converting than fighting the eastern peoples. The Franciscan order took the lead in this missionary work. They were especially concerned with the attempted conversion of the Mongols, the latest Asian horde to threaten the eastern

Mediterranean. By heading off the Mongols' conversion to Islam and by getting them to accept Latin Christianity, the Franciscans, with the support of the papacy, hoped to destroy Moslem control of the Holy Land. But the European peoples did not devote much energy even to this peaceful endeavor. The sending of two Franciscan friars to the court of the khan scarcely indicates that much attention was devoted to this abortive scheme. The western European peoples should have been greatly interested in converting the Mongols, but the fact remains that the ruling class of Europe, including the pope, was too concerned with pressing domestic matters to give much thought to the conversion of eastern peoples. The meeting of East and West was a worthy ideal, but it is not one that greatly appealed to the men of the High Middle Ages. The problems of European government, economy, and culture absorbed all their energy, and what little was left of crusading fervor in the thirteenth century the papacy directed against its enemies inside Europe.

The crusading movement was a legacy to the twelfth and thirteenth centuries of the fanaticism and zeal of the age of the Gregorian reform. It was bound to become outmoded, to undergo great vicissitudes, and ultimately to decline as European civilization itself experienced profound changes.

Nevertheless, the crusading ideal, as distinct from the crusades as a military and political venture, had a profound and not altogether fortunate impact on medieval life. The crusades gave an absolute moral and religious sanction to the union of military force and religious devotion. An important legacy of the crusades was the lesson that it taught Europeans—that it is right and fitting to kill and destroy in the service of Christian ideals. The immediate sufferers from this belief during the twelfth and thirteenth centuries were Jews and heretics. The long-range sufferer was European society as a whole. For righteous militarism was taken over during the thirteenth century by the new European bureaucratic states.

In addition, although the history of the crusades to the Holy Land after 1100 is mostly a story of failure and incompetence, there are three ways in which the crusades can be viewed as an important chapter in medieval history. First, they involved a tremendous expenditure of human and material resources. This fact doesn't strike home from reading contemporary narratives and records because the crusades are not well documented and perhaps much of the written material has been lost. The way to understand the energy and wealth expended in crusades is to go to Acre, thirty miles north of Haifa, and to look at the huge crusading castle overlooking the water that was for the most part excavated by Israeli archaeologists in the 1970s. The crusaders' castle is one of the most impressive monuments of the Middle Ages. The thickness of its walls—impregnable before gunpowder and perhaps not easy to demolish even today—are incredible, as is the vastness of the underground storage chambers for food and other supplies. Indeed, Acre never fell to the Moslems. In 1291 the French knights who garrisoned it decided that their homeland had forgotten them and that the siege of many years to which they had been subjected would never be relieved. They arranged with the Arab general to surrender the castle and left with their honor intact and their crucifix-laden pennants flying high.

Acre shows what a massive investment the Near Eastern venture of medieval Christendom was and why it was abandoned. After St. Louis fought the Arabs in their Egyptian strategic heartland and lost, there was no hope for the crusading movement. It would have needed the maximal commitment of human and material resources by the European societies, and this the kings and nobility were unwilling to provide. Even if the largely fortuitous success of the first crusade could have been repeated, that would have only been the end of the beginning. The Arabs would never have stopped their war to recover the Holy Land. Ask the Israelis.

The second long-range significance of the crusades involves the strategic situation of the Mediterranean. In 1000 the Moslems were close to completely controlling all shores of the Mediterranean. After the first crusade that possibility never again loomed. The Arab hegemony was permanently dissipated.

The third important outcome of the crusades was the character of the Spanish civilization, which was powerfully shaped by the Reconquista. In the eighth century, the Moslems, with the aid of the Jewish population who had suffered severe persecution under Visigothic Christian rule, won a devastating victory, and the tiny Christian kingdoms surviving in the rocky north seemed of no importance. By 1050 the Spanish kings and nobility had made major inroads into Moslem power. In 1212 at the battle of Las Navas de Tolosa they won as total a military victory as the Moslems had gained in 711. By the middle of the thirteenth century only Moslem Granada in the south remained outside Christian rule, and that outpost was finally taken in 1492.

Meanwhile in the twelfth century the Jews suffered a reversal of fortune under Berber rulers in the Moslem lands of Iberia. These Berber princes were committed to a narrow Moslem fundamentalism, and the Jews departed for more liberal Christian realms in Spain and prospered until the late fourteenth century under Christian rule. When pressured to convert after 1391, the great majority of the Jews joined the church in massive numbers. The outcome of all this crusading venture of the Spanish people was a multiethnic and culturally diversified society drawing upon Latin, Germanic, Jewish, and Arabic sources. In the end it was a missionary society devoted to ambitious programs and great undertakings, and therefore it was Spain and Portugal that inaugurated the great age of European imperialism in the late fifteenth and sixteenth centuries and created the new civilization of Latin America that could very well be the most dynamic culture of the early twenty-first century. The year 1095 leads directly to 1492, and the Iberian peoples bear the stamp of the crusading culture—its violence, its ambitions, its mobility, and its energy.

The Intellectual Expansion of Europe

I. The Acceleration of Cultural Change

The ending of the divisive and exhausting investiture conflict allowed medieval scholars and thinkers to concentrate their energies on the tremendous changes that were already taking place in higher culture. This acceleration of cultural change and creativity and improvement in all facets of medieval civilization involving the life of the mind has often been called "the Renaissance of the twelfth century."

What was supposed to have been reborn in the twelfth century? If it is the European contribution to philosophy and science that is being considered, it would be more correctly described as a birth, rather than a renaissance, since many intellectual movements of the twelfth century created something new; they did not simply recover an older tradition. The twelfth-century thinkers were also not concerned with the simple recovery of the classical style in literature and art. Insofar as they drew upon the classical heritage, it was to provide a starting point for new directions and dimensions in all facets of civilized life: religion, law, government, economy, ethics, and education, as well as in art, literature, philosophy, and science.

The manifestations of twelfth-century creativity deeply affected all aspects of social life in which some intellectual endeavor was required; it was not merely a movement supported by a group of littérateurs or the advocates of a certain type of artistic style, but it was as broad, complex, and heterogeneous as medieval civilization itself. The cultural growth was not limited to one country. Although France provided the leadership, England; Italy; and, to a lesser degree, Germany participated in the achievements of twelfth-century thought. John of Salisbury, one of the great figures of the twelfth century, was born in England, educated in France, worked in Italy, later returned to England, and ended his career in France as bishop of Chartres. The intellectual creativity of the twelfth century was an international movement. It had very little national feeling and no sense of divisions by political boundaries.

The cultural changes of the twelfth century were responsible for the introduction of Aristotelianism—the best science available at the time— into European thought, and the twelfth century also witnessed the intensification of the new popular piety and the fulfillment of the trend toward an emotional religion, which brought with it new theological insights and enhanced the western consciousness of the dignity of man.

The vitality and boldness of the intellectual leaders of the twelfth century could scarcely be surpassed. They exhibited a marvelous desire to experiment with new intellectual systems, to investigate new problems, and to follow new methods and avenues of thought, and they had an extremely optimistic belief in their ability to do new things in a short space of time. A prime example of this vitality is the invention and extensive spread of a new architectural style within a single generation. Not since the fifth century B.C. had the history of architecture seen such inventiveness, and not until the twentieth century was it again to reveal such a rapid proliferation of a new style.

The optimistic and bold characteristics of twelfth-century culture are reflected in the attempt to apply intelligence to the problems of society. Learning and higher thought reached out from an exclusive concern with theology and literature to a concern for the amelioration of the contemporary political and social structure. The most outstanding instance of this development is the transformation of European law during the twelfth century, which had momentous consequences for the medieval state. Because it was concerned with social need, because it drew upon but was not enslaved by the classical heritage, because it was involved with the institutionalization of higher education, and because it produced a distinctive new group in society, the growth of law typifies the most important aspects of intellectual creativity and improvement during the period and is probably the best introduction to understanding the characteristics of cultural change in the twelfth century.

II. The Legal Constituents of High Medieval Civilization

The twelfth century contributed to western civilization the central and ubiquitous figure of the professional lawyer. In the ancient world lawyers

were no more than semiprofessional; their training was mainly in rhetoric, and only a few great jurisconsults were masters of legal science.
Customary Germanic folk law knew no professional lawyer; the legal tradition was declared by the old men of the folk, and even the judges were
laymen in the sense that they had no special training. Only at the end of
the eleventh century did there appear the professional lawyer, trained by
a rigorous education in legal science, ready to apply his knowledge and
discipline to the rationalization of human relationships, suited to engage
in public life and to do the work of government. At least until the emergence of the professional scientist in the nineteenth century, the law was
the most socially valuable learned profession in European civilization,
and the lawyer still plays a great role in our contemporary way of life. By
1200 lawyers had become indispensable to the work of both the western
monarchies and the church, and the course of medieval political development was strongly conditioned by the attitudes and ambitions of this new
group of social leaders. Also during the twelfth century, the legal systems
of the various European states and the Roman Catholic church began to
take on institutional forms that have been largely perpetuated to the present day and that became powerful determinants of their characteristic
political attitudes.

The twelfth-century innovations in legal institutions and personnel
were a consequence of the new, more peaceful conditions of medieval
European society. A greater degree of political order and stability allowed
the European governments to consider the morass of confused and contradictory legal traditions that was the heritage of the upheavals of the
early Middle Ages. In no European country in 1100, and not even in the
church, was there anything approaching a comprehensive and organized
legal system. In attempts to assert their authority in society and to provide
a measure of order and justice, the secular governments of western
Europe were hampered by limitations of and conflicts among the various
German customary legal traditions. In Mediterranean countries Germanic
legal procedures and principles further clashed with debased fragments
of the much more sophisticated Roman legal system. In northern France
and England feudal law presented yet another group of competing juristic
traditions. Political and social progress could no longer tolerate this legal
anarchy. A new political order and the slow shift toward a money economy demanded legal rationalization and codification. The task involved,
however, was enormous and bound to strain the resources of legal scholars and royal servants. In the reign of Henry I the skill and intelligence of
the Anglo-Norman monarchy, the most advanced secular government in
western Europe, was directed toward the beginnings of English legal cod-

ification. The results were not encouraging, for even Henry's scholars were unable to synthesize a comprehensive system out of the welter of Germanic, feudal, and ecclesiastical traditions.

The social need for legal reform and codification, and the enormity of the task, made the beginnings of the study of the Justinian code in northern Italy a momentous event in the history of European government and law. It accounts for both the dedicated zeal with which the northern Italian scholars pursued their study of the civil law and the rapid spread of this Roman law revival north of the Alps. At the beginning of the twelfth century the work of legal scholars was considered to be as socially useful and as much in the interest of the state or the church as the discoveries of the atomic scientists are held to be socially valuable in the twentieth century.

Historians of medieval law are uncertain as to the precise way in which the Justinian code was discovered in northern Italy and its study begun. It has been suggested that the legal studies on behalf of papal authority that were commissioned by Gregory VII led to the accidental discovery in some Italian library of a long-forgotten copy of the *Corpus Juris Civilis*. On the other hand, it is obvious that the merchants of the northern Italian cities, where the study of Roman law was centered, could have imported a copy of the Justinian code directly from Constantinople. It is of course possible that there was more than one source for the civil law text that scholars in the northern Italian cities first began to study intensively in the 1070s. It is not important how they came by the text; it was not hard to come by, and it had been ignored in western Europe for five centuries because it was irrelevant to the circumstances of early medieval society. What is significant is the great social value that these pioneering legal scholars of the late eleventh century attributed to the Justinian code and that impelled them to begin its intensive study. The codification of the legal system of an advanced civilization into a summary that was written, systematic, comprehensive, and rational suited ideally the legal needs of western Europe at that time. The strong governments toward which European political development was moving were supported by the absolutist doctrine of the Justinian code. In addition, the commercial leaders of the Italian cities were attracted by the law code of an urbanized society that dealt with areas of life unknown to the rural primitivism that lay behind the Germanic customs. The fact that the Justinian code was a summary of the law of the great Roman emperors enhanced its attraction for certain groups, particularly scholars who were conditioned by a strong sense of the classical heritage and enthusiasts for the Holy Roman Empire. But the intensive study of the

Justinian code that began in northern Italy in the second half of the eleventh century was not primarily the consequence of either literary or political antiquarianism, but rather the direct result of the pressing needs of European society.

The *Corpus Juris Civilis* was the greatest legal code ever devised. It envisaged the law of the state as a reflection of natural law, the principle of rationality in the universe. The absolute power over the promulgation and operation of the law was held by the Justinian code to reside in the will of the emperor. The law, it was claimed, originally resided in the Roman people, but by the so-called *lex regia,* "the royal law," the people surrendered their legislative power to the wise and beneficent emperor. The aim of the law is the achievement of equity, or justice, and to attain it, the law court may alter or suspend the prevailing statutes in a particular case and proceed to decide the issue by abstract ethical principles. The Roman law court is judge centered. The jurists are supposed to be learned and experienced men, above corruption and even above sentiment. Their power is derived from their position as representatives of the emperor, "the living law," who appoints them. To get at the truth, the judges request and receive written depositions from the prosecuting and defense attorneys; they interrogate witnesses themselves; and, if necessary, they employ torture—"put the question," in the terminology of the civil law. Aside from this debatable use of torture, the Roman legal system has only two weaknesses. No provision is made for the incompetence or bias of the judges; they are always assumed to be men of the highest wisdom, probity, and goodwill. Such paragons of legal virtue are hard to come by. The final and greatest weakness of the Roman legal system is the position of the court and the judiciary as the instruments of the state. In questions involving ordinary criminal matters Roman law is liable to work well, but defendants who are charged with sedition and other crimes against the state are not likely to receive impartial treatment from judges who are civil servants. In other words, the Roman law system is at its worst in matters of conscience, and the Roman law court is easily turned into a engine of despotism.

At the end of the eleventh century the weaknesses of the civil law were scarcely evident when compared with the great services that its reception could render to European government and society. It appeared to be enormously superior to the Germanic legal system, which had no concept of equity, no rational canons of evidence, and no professional judiciary, and that was an uncodified and largely unwritten body of confused traditions. Hence the discovery of the text of the Justinian code inaugurated immediately its intensive study in the cities of northern Italy.

This study was carried out under municipal auspices, for the wealthy businessmen who dominated the governments of the urban communities perceived in the *Corpus of the Civil Law* that same devotion to rationality and order that informed their existence. By the last decade of the eleventh century a great school of law had been established in Bologna, which remained the dominant center for education in the civil law through the High Middle Ages. The *universitas,* or corporation of masters and students, at Bologna was a pioneer in the institutionalization of higher education, one of the most important aspects of twelfth-century intellectual development.

The synthesized and rational qualities of the civil law made it a suitable subject for academic study. In turn, the academic nature of Roman legal study profoundly affected the outlook of the lawyers of continental Europe in the Middle Ages. To become a member of the legal profession in a country that had received the Roman law, it was necessary to devote many years to formal academic study under a strict regimen. This long, strict regimen helps to account for the fact that the young lawyers of medieval Europe tended to be cut from the same cloth: They were all well educated and zealous, but also generally impecunious, somewhat inhuman, and eager to sell their services to the highest bidder. They made ideal bureaucrats. At the very time that the governments of Europe were beginning to require the services of professional civil servants trained in law, a school had been established in Bologna that commenced the production of a new species of bureaucratic man. The rise of secular administrative governments in western Europe and the emergence of a new class of civil lawyers are thus contemporaneous and intimately related developments. It was not until the second half of the twelfth century that the University of Bologna and the new law schools founded north of the Alps produced enough graduates to satisfy the needs of the European monarchies. But by 1200 the administrations of the powerful continental states were being regularly staffed with faceless *magistri,* the civil lawyers.

The academic presentation of the Justinian code followed educational lines long used in the study of the Bible. The professors read the text to their students and added their comments and explanations by way of marginal glosses; hence the twelfth-century commentators on the Justinian code are called the Glossators. Eventually the glossed text was published and became an authority that all who wished to be expert in the civil law had to study carefully. The most famous pioneer of this method of legal study was the Bolognese scholar and teacher Irnerius (died 1125), who drew students from all over Europe. Irnerius's glosses were empirical as well as scholarly, for he was not satisfied merely to explain the meaning of the text under discussion, but attempted to apply the law to contemporary situations. The leading disciples of Irnerius, commonly called the Four Doctors, continued this integration of the civil law into twelfth-century civilization. By the time of Irnerius's death, students from France, England, and Germany were streaming to Bologna to acquire the new legal science that offered them not only a rigorous intellectual discipline, but entry into a new profession.

Frederick I Barbarossa, the German emperor in the 1160s, was the first important transalpine ruler to take advantage of the recovery of the civil law and the availability of the new professional lawyers. Civil law was attractive to him for two reasons. He could use the lawyers in his government and administration, and the Justinian code provided him with an ideology to replace the old sacred kingship that had been undermined during the investiture conflict. By laying claim to the legal prerogatives of the Roman emperor, Barbarossa justified political absolutism and the enhancement of his authority in Germany; in addition, he could use the evidence of the Justinian code to assert his sovereignty over the Italian cities. When he first entered Italy on his great expedition of reconquest, he summoned an assembly at which civil lawyers in his service presented the juristic basis of his claims to absolute authority over the Italian community. Naturally the northern Italian oligarchs were not happy at the use that the German emperor was making of the revival of Roman law, the study of which had been originated with their support. But Frederick's enthusiasm for the Justinian code indicated how the work of the Glossators might be turned to the advantage of the monarchies of northern Europe. Although the strong native traditions of Germanic law in the empire precluded the immediate application of the Roman legal system on the local level, by the end of the fourteenth century the reception of the civil law was well under way in Germany, and its procedure remains the basis of the German legal system to the present day.

Because of Barbarossa's early association of the revival of Roman law with his own policies and ideology, the Capetian kings of the late twelfth century were wary of introducing the civil law into France. But by 1200 the king of France had discovered that the civil lawyers were the most suitable personnel for his expanding administration. As, during the thirteenth century, the civil lawyers came to dominate the French government, the introduction of the civil law into France was not long delayed. An important law school was established at the University of Montpellier. The civil lawyers who dominated the royal judiciary slowly wore down local vestiges of feudal and Germanic law and made the Justinian code more and more the foundation of the expanding jurisdiction of the royal courts. By the middle of the thirteenth century Roman procedure had been adopted by the French courts, which still retain a strongly judge-centered character. The Capetian monarchy overcame its initial distrust of the Justinian code as its value in the legal unification of the kingdom became more apparent. Furthermore, the French king discovered that he was able to use the principles of the civil law in support of his absolutist political doctrine in much the same way that the German king had. The French legal scholars interpreted the imperial office of the Justinian code in a generic way and arrived at the conclusion that every "king is an emperor in his own kingdom," that is, he possesses the prerogatives of legal absolutism that the *Corpus Juris Civilis* attributes to the Roman emperor.

The revival of the Justinian code profoundly affected the nature of the legal systems not only of France and Germany, but of the church itself. The canon law of the church in its formative period in the first half of the twelfth century was strongly conditioned by the concepts and procedures of the civil law. In the middle of the eleventh century church scholars had begun to try to systematize and eventually codify the canon law out of the disorganized mass of pronouncements and traditions left over from the early Middle Ages. The originators of this difficult work were two northern bishops, Burchard of Worms and Ivo of Chartres. In 1050 the law of the church consisted of a heterogeneous group of pronouncements made by the Bible, patristic writers, church councils, popes, and bishops. In the early Middle Ages various unofficial collections of canon law were made, of which the most famous was the one falsely attributed to St. Isidore of Seville and hence known as the Pseudo-Isidorian Decretals. The first generation of canon lawyers encountered an enormous body of material put together according to no critical or rational principle, containing legal propositions that contradicted each other and even some flagrant forgeries. The pioneering northern canonists of the eleventh century were, however, extremely able and dedicated scholars, and there is no doubt that they could have carried through the codification of the church law to a successful conclusion. But they were not allowed to do so by the Gregorian papacy. Hildebrand and his colleagues in the college of cardinals were apprehensive that the synthesizing of the ecclesiastical law by northern scholars would not be entirely favorable to the kind of papal absolutism they advocated, but would instead draw upon early medieval usage to give the episcopate considerable autonomy. The papacy therefore directed its own codification of the canon law, and by the beginning of the twelfth century this work was largely carried on under papal auspices by Italian scholars who were strongly inclined to the doctrine of papal plenitude of power.

The progress in the study of the civil law helped the Roman canonists to complete their work. The canonists envisaged the legal position of the papacy in the church as being identical with the emperor's in the state. All legislative power in the church was deemed to reside in the will of the supreme pontiff, and the Roman curia was held to be the supreme court of the church, with full appellate jurisdiction over any other ecclesiastical court in Europe. From the first decade of the twelfth century, the canon lawyers were all trained extensively in the civil law, and they were inclined to see the pope as an absolute emperor in his own international, ecclesiastical kingdom. The intensive work of codifying the canon law came to fruition in the *Decretum* of the Italian, papally commissioned legist Gratian, published in 1140. Gratian drew upon the synthesizing of the canon law that had been in progress for a century, upon the principles of the civil law, and upon the new dialectical method that was being developed by the philosophers in the French universities. The alternative title of his treatise, *The Concordance of Discordant Canons,* indicates the method Gratian employed. He placed one contradictory principle next to another, that is, thesis against antithesis, and then argued toward a logical resolution of the conflicts. In every instance of disagreement in his sources, he decided in favor of the plenitude of papal authority. The *Decretum* was given canonical status by the papacy, and it remains the foundation of the canon law to the present day. It was supplemented during the ensuing century by the commentaries of the Decretists (as the Glossators on Gratian's text were called), by the pronouncements of Popes Alexander II and Innocent III, and finally by the *Collections* of Pope Gregory IX, an additional textbook of canon law published in 1234.

The creation of a comprehensive and systematic code of church law facilitated the creation of a great international, ecclesiastical, judicial system centered on the papal court during the twelfth and thirteenth centuries. The support that the canon law afforded the doctrine of papal plenitude of power was bound to be helpful to the papacy in its relations with the great transalpine churchmen. It would, nevertheless, be an error to assume that every statement in a canon-law textbook or a Decretist's gloss was fully in accord with medieval reality. The canon lawyers were inclined to engage in wishful thinking and to describe as the inflexible, universal law and custom of the church what was only an ideal and potential. In countries such as England, where the great ecclesiastics were closely associated with powerful monarchies, many provisions of the canon law remained largely inoperative. It has become fashionable with some historians in recent years to accept all the pronouncements of the canon lawyers as fully reliable accounts of medieval life. This doubtful methodology can lead only to the creation of fanciful myths about the real position of the church during the High Middle Ages.

In two special ways did the civil-law revival affect the church in the twelfth century. First, it gave the canon lawyers the procedure they used in ecclesiastical courts. The church so fully adopted the practices of the Roman imperial courts, as set down in the Justinian code, that historians now frequently talk about the Romano-canonical procedure of the twelfth and thirteenth centuries as a single system. The fact that the civil law advocated a judge-centered court with absolute powers given to the juristic representatives of the emperor appealed to the canonists, with their inclinations toward papal absolutism. There was nothing, therefore, novel about the procedure used by the famous papal Inquisition of the thirteenth century. The Inquisition was a special ad hoc court commissioned by the papacy to deal with heretics. It basically followed civil-law procedure, and there was certainly nothing original in its use of torture as far as the history of Roman law is concerned.

The second special contribution of the Roman-law revival to the development of the high-medieval church was its provision of trained personnel for the growing papal administration. The papacy required men who were educated in law to staff its courts and bureaucratic offices, and the new schools of civil law provided this personnel in the same way they staffed the growing administrations of the European monarchies. A graduate in law from a medieval university could therefore enter the service of a secular ruler, or he could, in effect, undergo postgraduate training in canon law and enter the service of the church. If he followed the former course, he might someday become the chief minister of a powerful king in conflict with the papacy; if he pursued the latter course, he might end his career by ascending to the throne of Peter itself. The original choice of the young law-school graduate was usually made on simple professional grounds. By the second half of the twelfth century the papacy was recruiting nearly all its administrators from among the products of the European law schools, and with scarcely an exception every pope from 1150 to 1300 received his initial training in canon law. The papal administrators of the twelfth and thirteenth centuries were well trained and skillful, but the homogeneous legalistic background of the leaders of the papal curia also had less fortunate consequences. Their homogeneous background partly accounts for the great difficulty that the high-medieval papacy experienced when faced with the problem of channeling and controlling the new popular piety. The lawyer-popes of the twelfth and thirteenth centuries were far more successful in fulfilling the administrative than the spiritual responsibilities of their office. Their juristic education and bureaucratic experience did not tell them how to cope with the emotional religiosity and heretical inclinations of the urban communities.

England was the only country whose legal system did not come heavily under the influence of the Justinian code. While the civil law was beginning to penetrate into the juristic systems of Germany and France in the twelfth century, English law went off in another direction, developing both institutions and principles that were remarkably different from the theory and procedure of Roman law. This departure had a profound effect on both the later government and law of England, and it constitutes one of the outstanding ways in which the intellectual changes of the twelfth century influenced the subsequent course of European history. Therefore, no study of the twelfth century can avoid the question of why England developed its own non-Roman legal system. Many English historians have ignored this problem, simply assuming that the channel sufficed to cut England off from the great changes that were taking place on the Continent. This is not, however, a safe assumption, because twelfth-century England was a cultural satellite of France. English art, literature, and religious development in the twelfth century were heavily under French influence; then why was English law excluded from this general cultural impact?

It is simply not true that the Justinian code was unknown in England. One of the outstanding Bolognese scholars was teaching in England as early as the 1140s, and many of the royal administrators from the latter part of the reign of Henry I received their education in France and Italy. Most of Henry II's judges were churchmen who had been given the usual indoctrination in Romano-canonical procedures and principles, and they certainly were sufficiently familiar with Roman law to introduce it into England. It was assumed by liberal English historians of the nineteenth century that the Germanic legal tradition, descending from the Anglo-Saxon period, was so pure and powerful that Roman law had no chance to overwhelm it. There is some merit in this view, but it does not take into account the real facts of the situation. While Roman vulgar law was obliterated by the Anglo-Saxon invasion and the Germanic legal system exclusively dominated English juristic practice and doctrine during the preconquest period, the Anglo-Norman rulers had no vested interest in preserving it. No English king after 1066 had reason to be enthusiastic about the political implications of Germanic law, which was biased in the direction of the power of local communities and against strong central governments. The legal absolutism and centralism enshrined in the Justinian code were far more in conformity with the policy of the Anglo-Norman and Angevin monarchs than was the old Germanic system. On a priori grounds Henry II should have eagerly imposed the civil law on England; it was as amenable to his general inclinations as it was to Barbarossa's or the Capetian monarch's. It must finally be pointed out that the existence of pristine Germanic law in the empire did not discourage or ultimately prevent the German rulers from introducing the civil law into their country. Henry II's power over England was far greater, and he certainly could have effected the imposition of the Justinian code on his kingdom; yet he did not do so, and the question remains: Why did England, for all practical purposes, remain outside the area of the Roman legal system?

The answer emerges from the historical timetable of the twelfth century. Precisely because the Anglo-Norman monarchy was at least half a century ahead of every other government in Europe in the development of strong centralizing institutions, it ultimately refrained from adopting the Roman law. During the founding period of English royal power, between 1066 and 1135, the text of the Justinian code and the new personnel for administrative bureaucracies that the law schools were to provide were not yet available north of the Alps. The aggressive royal government had to make do with whatever was at hand, although it was by no means as suitable for establishing royal centralism and absolutism as the materials that the Capetian monarchy could draw upon at the end of the twelfth century. The Anglo-Norman rulers allowed the shire and hundred courts, the descendants of the old Germanic folk moots, to stand with their procedures and juristic principles fundamentally unchanged. The domination of the court by the prominent men of the neighborhood or county, the strictly oral pleading, and the use of the ordeal as a prime method of proof in criminal proceedings were perpetuated. The royal government sought to exercise a general supervision over the workings of the local courts by dispatching panels of itinerant justices to preside during the court days. But the function of the justices was merely to see that the correct procedure was followed, to impose a sentence and to collect the fines and amercements. The local English courts remained community courts, and their procedures preserved the Germanic principle that law belonged to the community and that it could not be changed without the assent of the political nation, the important classes in society.

The feudal law followed by the central Curia Regis reinforced this Germanic tradition. The king presided at and dominated the royal court, but did not exert absolute control over it. Changes in the law were made with the consent of the magnates, conforming to the Germanic tradition of the legislative power of the people, and in suits between the king and one of his vassals the decision was rendered by the assembled lords. William the Conqueror ameliorated the archaic and inefficient Germanic procedure by introducing the Frankish-Norman inquest into England and by commissioning his justices to use it in civil suits, but here again the fundamental doctrine of Germanic law only received reinforcement. The institution of the inquest required the justices to place an even greater reliance on the opinions of the leading men of the community, for it was they who made up the juries and whose testimony was instrumental in deciding the lawsuits in civil matters. The success of the inquest in strictly legal matters encouraged the royal government to use it for purposes of administration as well. If juries could give testimony on such matters as the income of local landlords, which was needed for tax purposes, the government would be freed from the necessity of assigning royal agents to these tasks. In the days before the European law schools began turning out their flood of graduates, reliable administrative personnel were hard to find. Thus, by the 1130s the English monarchy became accustomed to using unpaid representatives of the local communities for a great part of the work of both law and administration in the counties.

When Henry II became king in 1154, he found a legal system in operation composed of Germanic, feudal, and additional elements that had been fused by the royal justices after half a century into a common law for the whole realm. This peculiar system had certain deficiencies. It still relied exclusively on oral pleading, which made it archaic in relation to the civil-law systems that were spreading throughout Europe. It had no concept of equity; no way of suspending the law in a particular case in the interests of abstract justice; and although it was devoted to peace and order, it had no idea of justice. In criminal proceedings common-law procedure was strongly biased against the defendant, especially if he came from the lower classes in society. The man who was "ill famed" in his community had little chance when the opinion of the neighborhood was the determining factor in criminal proceedings and when the investigation of evidence by the court was unknown. As a cosmopolitan Frenchman and one of the best-educated kings of the twelfth century, Henry II was fully aware that the common law compared unfavorably in several respects with the Roman system, nor were his justices, trained in Romano-canonical procedures, blind to this fact. Yet the government of Henry II decided to leave the common law in operation and not to undermine it by the introduction of civil-law institutions and principles. The common law was already in existence; it worked smoothly enough and was popular. Above all, it found favor in Henry's eyes because it was cheap. It required few judges in comparison with the Roman system and yet returned a steady profit to the crown. Furthermore, the use of the jury for administrative purposes at the local level allowed the English government to operate with a minimum of bureaucratic personnel and, instead of an expensive host of royal agents, to make use of the unpaid services of the local nobility. One historian called this system "self-government at the king's command." If these peculiar English institutions had not already been in operation in 1154, there is no doubt that Henry II would have introduced the Roman kind of centralized law and administration that the Capetian monarchy established at the end of the twelfth century. Henry satisfied himself with improving English legal procedure by expanding the use of the jury in civil suits and introducing the indicting grand jury in criminal pleas. Ordeals were still used as proof in criminal cases, but they were terminated by the Fourth Lateran Council of 1215, and in the thirteenth century the English common law assumed its full recognizable institutional form with the development of the jury of verdict.

The preservation of the common law, with its strong Germanic overtones, was thus a consequence of simple convenience to the government of Henry II. Henry and his ministers were not unaware of the fact that the political theory of the common law was much less favorable to royal absolutism than was the Justinian code. But the general advantages of the common law more than compensated for this absence of a theoretical foundation for royal power. Henry believed that he could achieve a practical absolutism through the effective exploitation of existing English institutions. Although he was to succeed in this aim to a remarkable degree, the common law preserved for future generations in England the idea that the law of the land resided in the legislative power of both the king and the community and that it was not simply an expression of royal will. Thus, whereas "the will of the emperor has the force of law" in the Justinian code, in English juristic theory the king was as much subject to the law as any member of the community. A thirteenth-century English jurist, Henry of Bracton, remarked that in England law rules and not will. For England, as well as for France, Germany, and the Catholic church, the effect of the heritage of twelfth-century law is felt to the present day.

III. A Great Generation: Five Leaders of Twelfth-Century Thought and Feeling

A student at the embryonic University of Paris in the year 1140 would have encountered directly or indirectly the five great leaders of European thought and expression at the high tide of twelfth-century cultural creativity. There is a peculiar rhythm in intellectual history that, after long ages of gestation and merely derivative thinking, brings together several creative geniuses in a single, marvelously creative generation and that connects their most vital work to one center of civilization. Periclean Athens, Shakespeare's London, and the Paris of Voltaire and Diderot spring immediately to mind. It is a lesson of history that genius does not appear in either physical or intellectual deserts, but requires the challenge and protection of an appreciative environment and the fellowship of other great minds and personalities. Medieval civilization exhibited such a creative moment and place in the Paris of the fourth and fifth decades of the twelfth century. Five masters of thought and feeling crossed one another's paths along the banks of the Seine, and between them they represented and dominated every aspect of important cultural change in the period. The subsequent history of medieval thought could be viewed with considerable plausibility as the working out of their immensely rich cultural legacy. The two later critical periods of medieval intellectual development, 1240 to 1270 and 1300 to 1325, were largely concerned with meeting the challenge of ideas and emotions that the great twelfth-century leaders imparted into the mainstream of medieval thought. Four of these twelfth-century intellectual leaders—Suger, Abelard, Otto of Freising, and St. Bernard—died in the 1140s or 1150s, and they may be regarded as belonging roughly to the same generation. The fifth, John of Salisbury, was of a younger generation and lived until 1180, but he did most of his important intellectual work before 1160 and can therefore be viewed as the intellectual contemporary of the other four. Three of the men were French, one was German, and one was English, but a student at Paris would have discovered their physical and intellectual tracks all around him, and he would have experienced that rare, intoxicating satisfaction that comes with the sense of having been privileged to study in the vital center of an emerging cultural era.

Through the narrow, crooked streets of Paris, where wolves still sometimes appeared in winter, students from all over western Europe were making their way in 1140 toward the diocesan cathedral in the "Latin Quarter," where under the patronage and protection of the bishop of Paris, a school of higher studies had been established. Out of this cathedral school and others, such as Chartres, which was probably the first to be organized, the universities of northern Europe were to grow in the twelfth century. In a technical sense a cathedral school required only the incorporation of the masters into a universitas, or guild, to make this advance. The scholars who had been licensed by the bishop of Paris to teach in his school dealt with subjects that had no place in the circum-scribed intellectual world of the monastery. Using the new intellectual tools of dialectic, which they derived from the part of Aristotle's logic that had been translated by Boethius into Latin in the sixth century, they were prepared to analyze and resolve the persistent problems of western thought: the nature of the world; of man; and above all, of the deity and the relations among them. Little of such speculation had been undertaken since patristic times; a world that was fighting for physical survival, in which the preservation of literacy itself was a constant struggle, or even, as was the case in the ninth and tenth centuries, a world that was estab-lishing the foundations of social order had to concern itself with more immediate problems and could not release its best minds for speculative thinking. In the late eleventh century Europe could afford the luxury of higher thought, and under the protection of the wealthy and sophisti-cated bishops of northern France, first at Chartres and then at other places, such as Laon and Paris, the great intellectual quests of western civilization resumed. For two or three decades the debates over the nature of a Christian world order diverted the attention of many of the best minds from philosophy, science, and theology, but the termination of the investiture conflicts freed the surplus mental energy of Europe for speculative ratiocination.

It was difficult to slake the intellectual thirst of the generation that came to maturity about 1100. From the obscure corners of France; Eng-land; Italy; and, to a lesser degree, Germany, young clerical scholars took to the road in pursuit of some famous teacher whose reputation had dimly penetrated their homelands. In the 1060s a certain Bérengar of Tours appeared as the first of a soon-to-be-familiar type of intellectual master who drew the most brilliant of the younger generation to him by the magnetic quality of his mind and personality. Bérengar's fall into doc-trinal heresy confirmed the suspicions of anti-intellectuals, such as Dami-ani, and more cautious theologians, such as Lanfranc, that dialectic could easily be put to dangerous and irresponsible uses, but his fall in no way impeded the spread of the new intellectual movement or the proliferation of Bérengar's imitators. In a world growing more ordered, wealthy, popu-lated, and literate, mastery of the well-tilled biblical-patristic tradition of the early Middle Ages could not satisfy the best minds of the rising gener-ation. This generation's restless intellectual quest shattered the framework within which Alcuin, Bede, and even Augustine had worked and reached back across silent centuries to seek the guidance of Greek philosophy and science.

No one in 1100 or even 1140 was sure of the ultimate tendencies of the new learning; no one could clearly perceive the reconstruction of the Christian thought-world that would result from the new investigations into philosophy, science, and theology. Yet no one, not even those who doubted the validity or social usefulness of the new pursuits, could afford to ignore the new investigations undertaken by the masters and students in the cathedral schools of northern France. In the early twelfth century it was becoming more apparent every day that knowledge was power; without much consideration of the enormity and difficulty of the task they had assumed or even to what specific use they could put the new learning, many of the most brilliant minds of the new generation that came to maturity about 1100 set off for the new cathedral schools to participate in the intellectual revolution. Outstanding contemporaries who found the new dialectical methods temperamentally unpalatable and who were concerned about their long-range effect on the traditional Christian thought-world came forward with alternative systems drawn from extensions of the early-medieval neoplatonic tradition, from classical humanism, or from the emotional resources of the new piety. These other approaches did not stem the intellectual upheaval in which the universities were engaged; rather, they added other facets to it, enriching and intensifying its impact. These other approaches helped make the intellectual expansion of the twelfth century a more comprehensive and complex movement, affecting all important aspects of higher culture, and helped increase the variety and magnitude of the problems with which later generations of medieval thinkers had to deal.

On their way through Paris to the cathedral school, many students in the 1140s had to pass the great abbey of St. Denis, the royal abbey of France. They were astonished at the results of the reconstruction of the old Carolingian church of St. Denis that had been carried out under the close supervision of abbot Suger. The abbot had dared to make a radical departure from the church architecture of northern Italy and Constantinople, whose style, the so-called Romanesque, had hitherto dominated western art. Students who came to Paris from England or Normandy thought they saw in the abbot's work the influence of the Norman cathedrals, which had begun to shift from the Romanesque emphasis on the horizontal lines to the perpendicular plane and had introduced ribbed vaulting. But many aspects of Suger's reconstruction could not be paralleled anywhere; here was a new French style, as novel and startling as the new ideas discussed in the cathedral schools. Over the entrance to the church of St. Denis had been placed a stained-glass rose window, whose manufacture had taxed the ingenuity and skill of the craftsmen employed by the abbot. The sides of the church had been raised to emphasize the perpendicular lines, and, in sharp contrast to the solid masonry wall of the Romanesque church, large windows had been cut through the stone to allow a uniform light to suffuse the hitherto obscure interior and to illuminate the altar.

At first look Suger seems a most improbable candidate for the role of inaugurating the first really new architectual style in 1,700 years. Superficially he appears to have been a typical figure of the early Middle Ages, more at home in the Cluniac culture of the tenth century than in the revolutionary intellectual world of twelfth-century Paris. His whole life was spent in the monastery of St. Denis, which had been associated with the French monarchy since the seventh century. As an affiliate of Cluny and the keeper of the regalia of the French crown, the monastery of St. Denis was intimately involved in the affairs of the royal dynasty. The close association of St. Denis with the Capetian family is symbolically rendered in the sculptured façade of Suger's church. Abbot Suger became the chief minister and then biographer of Louis VI, and until the abbot's death in 1151 he continued to render extremely valuable services to young Louis VII, whom he had tutored. While Louis was absent on his ill-fated crusade, Suger served as his regent and capably directed the Capetian government. Thus it can be said that the abbot of St. Denis was the last of the great monastic statesmen of the Middle Ages, the successor of St. Boniface, Alcuin, and Lanfranc of Canterbury. Certainly his background sharply distinguished him from the chief servants of the French monarchy in the thirteenth century.

Suger's culture also seems to mark him off as an early-medieval man, a conservative thinker out of touch with the intellectual currents of his day. His philosophy of art, by which he justified the style of the reconstruction of his church, was expressed entirely in the neoplatonic terminology of the early Middle Ages. He was heavily indebted to the mystical writings of Pseudo-Dionysius, the anonymous fifth-century Syrian monk whom he identified with St. Denis, the disciple of St. Paul, and the apostle of France to whom his church was dedicated. For Suger, the Dionysian neoplatonic philosophy had canonical authority; he used its mystical identification of the deity with light to explain that the function of the new windows in the clerestory of his church was to illuminate the altar with divine emanation.

These aspects of Suger's career and doctrines, which appear to be archaic survivals of an earlier age, were balanced by other qualities that reveal him as one of the leaders of a great generation of innovators. Although certainly more conservative than the lawyers who came to dominate the Capetian administration in the following half century, he resembled these magistri in his application of critical intelligence to the problems of medieval government. Although French kings were still crowned and anointed in the old Carolingian manner, Suger did not urge upon his royal masters the continued assertion of theoretical claims that had resulted in humiliation for the early Capetians and even for Louis VI. Instead he advocated the more sensible and realistic policy of the careful building up of royal power in the Ile-de-France. The concentration upon the resources of the royal domain as the starting point for the expansion of royal power, which became a fundamental policy of the Capetian monarchy in the later years of Louis VII, seems to have been first adumbrated by the abbot of St. Denis.

Suger's quotations from the Pseudo-Dionysian writings should not preclude us from understanding the radical significance of his artistic innovations. The purpose of his architectural reconstruction was to create a more inspiring place of worship. He regarded St. Denis not merely as a chapel for the monks, but as a church where the populace of Paris could feel emotionally closer to the deity than they could in the dark and squat ecclesiastical buildings of the early Middle Ages. Behind the austere exterior of the monastic statesman can be perceived a devout but shrewd intelligence who was keenly aware of the new popular piety and the yearning of zealous laymen for a more intimate relationship with the Lord. In his treatise on the reconstruction of the church of St. Denis, Suger described in detail his plans for enriching and beautifying the interior of the church. His account of his search for magnificent liturgical vessels and jewels for the altar, together with his architectural innovations that illuminated the interior of the church, reveals a profound sense of the popular educational function of religious art.

Suger's work made him a worthy contemporary of the masters and students of the Paris school in yet another way. With almost no precedent he had conceived and executed a new style of ecclesiastical architecture. This innovating spirit involved a bold departure from the intellectual attitudes of the early Middle Ages, which sought the preservation of the best traditions of the past. Suger's confidence in the validity of his own judgments and his boldness in pursuing the consequences of these judgments distinguish him as one of the new kind of self-reliant and progressive thinkers of the twelfth century. The work and care involved in effecting the reconstruction of the church of St. Denis were enormous. Suger had to risk spending a great part of the accumulated wealth of his abbey. He had to recruit and consult with master masons and masonic architects and to find and supervise scores of stonemasons, glass cutters, and common laborers to get the kind of building he wanted. After all this expenditure of money and time there was no certainty that, when completed, the rose window and clerestory would not go crashing down onto the heads of the congregation. Suger's intellectual self-confidence and organizing skill were far more important as the background to the new style than was his neoplatonic philosophy of art, which had been in existence for nine hundred years without producing anything that even remotely approximated Gothic architecture. There is an obvious parallel between Suger's work and the philosophical and theological investigations that were being pursued in his day a few miles from St. Denis at the cathedral school of Paris. In the embryonic university the masters and students were also applying an old doctrine to new ends; like abbot Suger, they were optimistically creating a new structure such as had never existed before and whose feasibility and permanence could not be determined for certain before its completion. The audacity, enterprise, and pragmatic intelligence of the mid-twelfth century has no more outstanding representative than the abbot of St. Denis.

Suger was an old-fashioned social type who unself-consciously created an artistic revolution. John of Salisbury was in every respect the type of new man whom the intellectual and educational revolution was producing. He was painfully conscious of the growing separation of contemporary culture from the early medieval thought-world. He tried to preserve the older values in the face of the rapid change and sought the means of controlling the effects of the new learning and power of the twelfth century. John was an English cleric of obscure and probably modest social background who came as a young man to study in the new schools of Chartres and Paris in the 1130s. He sat at the feet of the great dialecticians and theologians of the day, and his vivid accounts of his teachers and fellow students provide us with some of the most valuable information about the beginnings of the French universities. In the early 1150s, he went to Rome in search of employment and became the secretary of the English pope Adrian IV (Nicholas Breakspear), whose educational background was the same as John's. It was the only time in history when Englishmen conducted papal affairs; Cardinal Robert Pullan, also an English product of the French schools, was another prominent servant of Adrian IV. In 1153 John returned to England to become the secretary of Archbishop Theobald of Canterbury. He inevitably became a close associate of Thomas Becket, yet another English cleric who had studied in France, who was the head of the archbishop's chancery. John witnessed the advancing power of the English state in the early part of Henry II's reign, and on one occasion he seems to have incurred the wrath of the king, who regarded him as a papal agent. In the 1160s John experienced at first hand the struggle between Henry II and Thomas Becket, by now archbishop of Canterbury after having served the king as his chancellor. John was Thomas's secretary and accompanied Becket into exile. He wrote the Canterbury martyr's biography, but he was not blind to the faults of his master's character. As a widely respected churchman and writer, John was summoned back to France to spend his last years before his death in 1180 as bishop of Chartres, where he had gone almost a half century before as an unknown cleric to study in the cathedral school. No other twelfth-century figure was personally involved with so many and such a variety of important developments. Yet John of Salisbury was much more a thoughtful spectator of these events than a leading participant in them. His disposition, contemplative rather than active, compassionate rather than critical; his enormous erudition; and his solid common sense fitted him ideally for the task of observing and considering the implications of the great changes of his era.

John was well educated in the new logic, philosophy, and theology of the French schools, but he became one of the most prominent critics of the new intellectual trends. He considered the work of the teachers at Paris and Chartres to be at best useless—he described how, after returning to Paris after several years' absence, he found the masters and students pursuing the same debates with no appreciable progress except an increase in arrogance—and at worst dangerous to the foundations of the Christian thought-world. In this respect John agreed with the anti-intellectual attitudes of Damiani and his own great contemporary St. Bernard. But he did not go along with their substitution of a mystical for a dialectical road to the deity.

The fact is that John of Salisbury's mind was that of a moralist; he was temperamentally unsuited for either the scientific or emotional approaches to life. In his view there was no need to discover truth, for that was already known; the question was how to inculcate it in the rising generation. Everywhere around him he could see the corrupting effects of the new learning, wealth, and power—the undermining of the old values. John of Salisbury is therefore, if not the originator, at least one of the most eloquent spokesmen for one of the primary educational doctrines of western civilization: The function of education is not intellectual, but moral. The purpose of the schools, he claimed, should be to preserve and teach the traditional values, to counter the corrupting effects of intellectual, financial, and political power, to teach men how to live rightly.

John was deeply grieved to see the liberal arts declining in importance and taking a secondary place in the new universities of the arrogant and irresponsible masters of dialectic. He believed that it was precisely in the great literature of the classical heritage, which was being neglected in favor of its philosophical and scientific aspects that the means could be found for teaching men the principles of right conduct. Virgil, Livy, Cicero, and other great Latin belletristic writers had presented to their contemporaries the principles of human decency and self-restraint which were more and more ignored in the twelfth century. John of Salisbury's teaching was the purest form of Christian humanism that had yet appeared. More clearly than any of his contemporaries he realized the corrupting influence of power, and the use made of the classical heritage in conditioning the moral outlook of the European ruling classes from the fifteenth to the twentieth centuries plausibly demonstrates the great utility of his proposed educational remedy. But his contemporaries, engrossed by the prizes that learning, wealth, and power appeared to offer, were not willing to listen to him. The liberal arts steadily declined in importance in the universities, and the Christian humanism of John of Salisbury found its disciples not in the twelfth- and thirteenth-century thinkers, but in the late medieval Italian Renaissance. John's moralistic outlook resembles the doctrines of the Renaissance humanists in every way, both in its primary emphasis on the preservation of humane values in society through classical education and in its failure to understand the possibilities and advantages of science and speculative thought.

The evil in contemporary society that most concerned John of Salisbury was the corrupting effect of political power—the degradation of the human spirit resulting from the authority that one man or group of men held over large groups of people. He was by no means blind to the emergence of this condition within the church. He bitterly criticized avaricious and venal ecclesiastical lords, and on one occasion he frankly told Adrian IV that he was disturbed by what he had found at Rome: evidence of a self-sustaining and arrogant bureaucracy impervious to growing criticism. It was only when he returned to England in the 1150s and encountered the secular engine of the Angevin state, however, that the consequences of power were first fully brought home to him. The result was the publication in 1159 of the *Policraticus,* a treatise on the right ordering of the political life. Few works in the history of political theory have so frequently been misinterpreted. What has impressed most students of the *Policraticus* is its general support for the traditional political theory of the church. John viewed the whole society as a body and gave the church the position of the heart and the state that of the head. Thereby he restated the traditional hierocratic theory: The state must serve the church, which, as the spiritual organism, is superior. This recapitulation of the old doctrine is hardly significant; John had spent his whole life in the service of the church and had just returned from several years at Rome, and he knew no other political theory. What is significant are his quiet hesitations and his qualifications of the hierocratic doctrine in the face of contemporary political experience in Angevin England.

No dispassionate observer of England at the end of the 1150s, such as John was, could deny the fact that the leader of English society was not the church but the monarchy. The royal government, through its legal and financial institutions, was coming more and more to impose its will on the people and to obliterate the effectiveness of any competing jurisdictions. Lord, bishop, knight, and peasant—all were steadily being drawn into the nexus of royal power. These realities of social life cast grave doubts on the empirical value of the old political Augustinianism, and John's sensitivity drove him to try to integrate the existence of secular power and leadership with the old political ideals of the church. The *Policraticus* is an interior dialogue; John was trying to tell himself that the emergence of the state had not shattered the framework of the old order. He was not very convincing in his arguments, and the resulting ambiguity of his work is evident. Along with the traditional hierocratic theory, he admitted that the end of the state is the perception of truth and the rewarding of virtue, with the implication that when the state pursues moral ends, it has a sanction in and of itself. This is a subtle but highly significant departure from political Augustinianism; John's modification of hierocratic doctrine would have infuriated Gregory VII. It is the earliest example of the shift from a pessimistic to an optimistic view of the state, which was to be the fundamental theme of political thought for the next 150 years. John was the first ecclesiastical political theorist to face the consequences of the political changes of the High Middle Ages, and his exasperation and quiet desperation are reflected on almost every page of the *Policraticus*. He could neither abandon the traditional hierocratic theory nor, as an intelligent and extremely sensitive observer of the mores of his time, ignore the new leadership exercised in society by the state. The only solution was to ascribe moral qualities to the state, thereby preserving, in theory, the ethical foundations of the social order. But to do so was to give the state moral sanctions and implicitly to increase its authority. John was not blind to radical implications of his doctrine. He tried to resolve the problem by emphasizing the distinction between king and tyrant, and to give his discussion a tone of plausibility, he speculated on the possibility of justifiable tyrannicide. He fully realized, however, the dangerous consequences to the social order of such a principle and came to no definite conclusion on the question. John's treatise is the result of a painful and reluctant adjustment of a moralist and traditionalist to the realities of political life; what is most significant is not his pain and reluctance, but his adjustment at all. It marks the beginnings of an upheaval in European political thought.

John's contemporary, Bishop Otto of Freising (died 1158), carried this transformation in the political consciousness of Europe considerably further. In Otto's writings the dichotomy between the old and the new is sharper and the movement from pessimism to optimism more explicit, and cautious recognition of contemporary reality is replaced by an ominous, almost hysterical celebration of the moral potentialities of secular leadership.

Whereas John of Salisbury's social origins were modest, Otto was a scion of one of the most aristocratic families in Europe, the princely German house of Hohenstaufen. The heterogeneous appeal of the new learning and new piety is dramatically demonstrated by the fact that Otto studied in the Paris school from 1127 to 1133 and then became a Cistercian monk and abbot. He was elected bishop of Freising in 1137 and applied his vast erudition and considerable literary skill to two historical works of a highly sophisticated and philosophic nature. The first of these works, *The Two Cities,* published in 1146, is an extremely pessimistic survey of world history written from the standpoint of Augustinian theology. Otto undertook to demonstrate the conflict between the earthly and the heavenly cities on the stage of world history, which Augustine believed was fully apparent to God alone. Nevertheless, the early fifteenth-century writer Orosius, in his immensely popular *Seven Books Against the Pagans,* had presumed to see the particular working of divine providence in history, and the common historiographical inclination of the Middle Ages was to pick out the course of the heavenly and earthly cities on the plane of world history. Although Otto did not fully subscribe to Augustine's doctrine of meta-history and attempted to reveal the actual development of the two cities in world history, his general world view was conditioned by Augustinian pessimism, particularly with regard to secular power. In *The Two Cities* the bishop of Freising saw almost no good in the history of earthly kingdoms whose lugubrious annals, he thought, were almost exclusively a record of sordid crime, and the history of the earthly city, in Otto's view, is virtually identified with the development of monarchy. *The Two Cities* is a historiographical presentation of the Augustinian pessimism and hatred for secular power that looms in the doctrines of Gregory VII. The experience of his own day gave Otto no cause to mitigate his harsh judgment of the propensities of secular power; writing in Germany two decades after the investiture conflict, he could see no moral value in the imperial office.

The contrast between *The Two Cities* and Otto's other important historical work, *The Deeds of Frederick Barbarossa,* on which he was working at the time of his death and that was completed by his secretary, Rahewin, is startling. It is difficult to believe that these two works were written by the same historian. We pass suddenly from the Augustinian denigration of the state to an extremely optimistic, highly emotional celebration of the moral and messianic potentialities of imperial authority. The fact that Frederick I Barbarossa, who ascended the imperial throne in 1152, was Otto's nephew and confidant cannot be discounted. But *The Deeds of Frederick Barbarossa* is not simply dynastic propaganda; Otto was far too austere and independent a man and too dedicated to the welfare of the Christian world order to prostitute his learning in such a way. He sincerely believed that Frederick's policy of reconstructing the imperial power inaugurated a new and better era for Christian society. The interests of the Heavenly City were now to be furthered by secular power. Augustinian pessimism could not long withstand twelfth-century civilization's disposition to creativity and improvement. The spirit of the age was constructive, forward looking, bold, and optimistic. Augustinian pessimism could not resist the pragmatic claim made by success and achievement, in government no less than in architecture, for the moral approval of society. Hence Frederick Barbarossa appears in Otto's history as the charismatic hero who will not only rebuild the authority of the German crown, but will bring closer the triumph of the Heavenly City. The devout church scholar and Cistercian monk relegates the papacy to a secondary position in this heaven on Earth that Barbarossa was establishing. The bishop of Rome is regarded in Otto's work as an alien official, respected but remote.

What appears, therefore, in John Salisbury's *Policraticus* in an inferential and implicit way emerges with startling clarity in Otto's outlook: The twelfth-century state is absorbing into itself moral, emotional, and even divine qualities to buttress legal absolutism and administrative power. These additional sanctions were all that the new monarchies of western Europe needed to establish themselves as self-sustaining and irresponsible entities. Otto's history inaugurated the reversal of the effects of the investiture conflict—the regaining of moral and quasi-sacred attributes by royal power. John of Salisbury reluctantly admitted the moral sanction of the state; Otto of Freising advocated it. The next 150 years were to witness an ever-increasing repetition, by the churchmen of northern Europe, of Otto's attitude to monarchy and the papacy. Hence Otto was the prophet of the morally shrouded, self-righteous, sovereign state of the thirteenth century.

Suger, John of Salisbury, and Otto of Freising are important, but not the most central and seminal figures in the intellectual expansion of twelfth-century Europe. That accolade belongs jointly to Peter Abelard and his self-appointed antagonist, St. Bernard of Clairvaux. It would be an exaggeration, but not an entirely implausible one, to assert that the subsequent history of medieval thought and feeling constitutes a series of appendixes to the work of Abelard and Bernard.

The reputation of Peter Abelard (1079–1142) has undergone many vicissitudes among historians. In the nineteenth century he was hailed as a forerunner of Protestantism. In the first half of the twentieth century it was the fashion to underrate and ignore much of the significance of his work. In recent appraisals of medieval thought his crucial importance has begun to be perceived, but a comprehensive study of his work is still lacking.

Abelard was the son of a minor lord in Brittany, a wild frontier region that was accustomed to produce savage warriors but not scholars and philosophers. The tremendous social impact of the new learning may be gauged by the attractions it presented to this obscure nobleman. Abelard made his way to the new schools of philosophy and theology at Chartres and Paris. He was recognized from the beginning as an exceptionally brilliant student, and he mastered the new dialectical methods rapidly, but he was also a difficult person, entirely inner directed, arrogant, disagreeable, hypercritical, and gauche. After completing a course, it was his custom to set himself up as a lecturer on the subject in competition with his former teacher. He was not the kind of scholar who makes a pleasant academic colleague; such a type was as bound to get into trouble in the twelfth century as in the twentieth. Nevertheless, it was a personal scandal that, by his own account, if it may be believed, got him into trouble. He seduced a certain Héloise, the niece of a prominent cathedral canon in Paris. He tells us that her family punished him by "cutting off those parts of my body with which I had done that which was the cause of their sorrow." The rest of his career was a series of unhappy crises. He assumed the office of abbot of a Breton monastery, but gave it up when he discovered that the monks were all thugs. He entered the monastery of St. Denis, where, as might be expected, he was miserable and restless. He was denounced by St. Bernard for publishing heretical doctrines, and he was subsequently summoned before a church council, where he was forced to recant. Abelard spent the last year of his life in retirement at Cluny, where he was well treated. The Cluniac monks, like all true aristocrats, did not hold grudges.

Beyond all doubt Abelard was a genius of the first rank. Everybody who met him was impressed by the force of his personality and the power of his intellect. His stormy career may reflect a psychological instability resulting from his failure to find a suitable environment in which he could fully exercise his unusual talent. Abelard's personal troubles seem to have stemmed largely from the fact that he lived a century too soon, as it were. He was a pioneer in the rigorous use of the Aristotelian dialectic and the ruthless pursuit of rational truth. Other men were doing the same thing, but far less effectively, and Abelard's preeminence made him the obvious scapegoat for those who suspected the consequences and implications of the new logic. As a contemporary of Thomas Aquinas he might have aroused some concern, but he would have appeared far less singular or peculiar. In the thirteenth and fourteenth centuries he would have been able to follow a normal academic career, to have held a professorship in a great university, and to have avoided the unhappiness and personal misery that marked his life.

The two most important aspects of Abelard's thought were his rediscovery of personality and his views on the problem of universals. In both cases he was undermining the Platonic structure of early medieval thought. From the third century on there had been little or no recognition of individual personality. The real person, with his unique characteristics, had been obliterated by the Platonic concern with ideal types. Early-medieval culture had little appreciation for personality; only the representative type seen under the aspect of eternity and religion was portrayed in literature. Autobiography disappeared because literate men found their lives significant only to the extent that they conformed to an ideal pattern. The description of personal idiosyncracies would be regarded as proud, sinful arrogance. Augustine's *Confessions* was the last autobiography written before the twelfth century, and even it is not strictly an autobiography, for the bishop of Hippo was concerned with revealing himself only as Everyman. In the early Middle Ages there was little biographical writing worthy of the name. A mass of hagiographical literature followed conventional patterns, forcing its subjects into preconceived molds and turning them into plaster saints. Kings were generally portrayed by their secretaries in accordance with the ideal pattern of a Christian monarch set down in the prototype *Life of Constantine* by Eusebius of Caesarea. When the characteristics of a real personality did break through in these royal biographies, it was the result of a failure in artistic consistency; the writer was unable to sustain his typological motif.

Twelfth-century creativity produced a new appreciation of individual accomplishment and with it the beginning of the attempt to describe the details of particular lives. It came to be doubted that depicting men as merely conforming to an ideal type fully captured the significance of lives known for singular achievement. Thus the secretary of St. Anselm, the theologian and archbishop of Canterbury, produced two biographies of his master early in the second decade of the twelfth century. One was a piece of conventional hagiography; the other gives many details of Anselm's episcopate. In the former work Anselm appears as a conventional saint, but in the latter, he appears as a real person who occasionally loses his temper, becomes discouraged, suffers anguish, falls ill, etc. In the 1120s a French monk undertook to write his autobiography, and the Anglo-Norman historian, William of Malmesbury, published two collections of biographies, one of the English kings and the other of the bishops and abbots of his day. The latter book is so circumstantial in its account and contains so many unflattering details that William was forced to publish an expurgated edition. In the following half century a radical change in attitude toward personality occurred, and European writers discovered the art of biography. By the 1180s this development had reached the point where a Welsh clerk filled four volumes with accounts of his experiences and reminiscences, giving us a vivid and at times hilarious account of the court of Henry II, the crooked intricacies of ecclesiastical politics, and the uncouth customs of the Irish.

Abelard's autobiography, *The History of My Calamities,* was the critical turning point in the twelfth-century rediscovery of personality. It goes to the opposite extreme from early-medieval typology. Abelard revels in his idiosyncrasies and delights in revealing to the world the peculiar facts of his life, even those that could not be socially approved. In fact, like so many later biographers, he may have made his experiences appear more dramatic and startling in retrospect than they actually were. His account of his affair with Héloise does not always ring true. It was certainly his intention to titillate and shock his readers, although it is unlikely that he made up the story out of whole cloth. The important point is that Abelard wished to reveal himself to the world as a unique individual whose biography could not be confused with anyone else's. It is not the universal and ideal that he wished to portray, but the particular and individual. *The History of My Calamities* is thus a direct attack on the Platonic absorption of the individual into the universal.

Abelard's iconoclasm and individualism were a reflection of the fact that he was an urban personality, a city man. One of the most important aspects of medieval universities was their emergence in urban areas. Monastic schools had existed in rural society, isolated and without much occasion for the personal exchange of ideas. In rural society, with its strict class lines and conventional pattern of life, there was little or no opportunity for unique and original ways of life. Men were born into a certain class and followed the mores suitable to their status. But "city air made men free" not only in the legal sense meant by the nineteenth-century German historian who advertised the phrase, but in the sense of providing the environment for the creation of an original personality and pattern of thought. This was even truer of the academics than of the businessmen. The masters and students in the embryonic universities lived in an extremely competitive society. If a teacher did not appear interesting and important, he would lose his students, and if a professor was successful, it was due to the impression made on his audience by his mental and other qualities. Even in the more organized universities of the thirteenth and fourteenth centuries, an excellent teacher was a celebrity who attracted students from all over Europe to his crowded lecture hall. In Abelard's day the academic lived entirely by his own wits; if he could not attract students, he had nothing to fall back on, and his career would terminate in miserable failure and poverty. When a great scholar such as Abelard found students from every corner of Europe pondering his every word, he could not help but be greatly impressed by the quality of his own mind and become a strong egoist. It is true in any case that self-love and grandiose self-esteem are the most general psychological characteristics of an outstanding teacher. In the peculiar circumstances of Abelard's academic world the teacher was bound to conceive of himself as a charismatic individual. The awe with which he was regarded by his students was transferred to his conception of himself, until he felt that every aspect of his life, even his calamities, were worthy of revelation to the world. The extreme individualism and egoism that were to be the peculiar characteristics of the artistic temperament in later centuries appeared in Abelard's day as a quality of academics. Although the great architects and artists of the twelfth century, men worthy in every way to be ranked with Michelangelo and da Vinci, were still faceless men about whom we know next to nothing, the Paris masters thought of themselves as great personalities.

Abelard's contribution to the debate on the nature of universals was as important in shaping the intellectual tendencies of his age as was his emphatic revelation of himself as a distinct individual. In fact, these two aspects of his thought are related, for in both instances he was challenging the Platonic doctrine that the general and universal are everything, while the particular and individual are nothing, which had dominated western thought since the third century A.D. The debate on the nature of universal concepts or abstract ideas began in the late eleventh century and continued intermittently, now quietly, now acrimoniously, into the fourteenth and fifteenth centuries. The debate was carried on in academic institutions and in a highly technical philosophical language that requires the knowledge of logic and metaphysics for complete understanding. This does not mean, however, that the debate had no relevance to the general problems of medieval civilization; on the contrary, the stability of the Christian thought-world depended on the outcome of this philosophical controversy. The outcome of this philosophical debate profoundly affected the medieval conception of man's relation to the deity, the nature of the church, the sacraments, and the priesthood and the relationship between science and dogmatic faith.

The dispute on the nature of universals was the form taken in the Middle Ages by the most persistent problem in western philosophy, which still commands the attention of some of the most acute minds in the world today. The problem is, Do the general concepts in our minds, such as justice, truth, beauty, God, church, and the state, or even simpler ones, such as the generic idea of tree, chair, and horse, have a reality outside our own minds? Are they purely mental images and convenient terms, or are these images and terms expressive of a metaphysical reality outside individual minds? When men speak of the idea of justice or the idea of chair, are they merely using vague terms, or are they describing a self-subsisting universal that has an existence apart from human speech and thought? In the early Middle Ages there was no debate on these questions because before the eleventh century all medieval thinkers subscribed to Platonic philosophy. Plato's system was founded on the belief in the reality of universal ideas. Plato claimed that our idea of justice or chair was but a vague reflection of a pure, self-subsisting, eternal, metaphysical form. In fact, he contended that we have a knowledge of justice or chair only because of these eternally existing metaphysical realities outside our own minds. This is one of the two fundamental extreme forms that the answer to the problem of universals can take. In modern philosophy the followers of Plato are called idealists because they believe that ideas are real; in the medieval schools, taking the other end of the same proposition, they were called realists. The realists believed that ideas are *res,* things and, therefore, that universals have an independent reality outside individual human minds.

At the beginning of the twelfth century the validity of Platonic realism was questioned for the first time. If early-medieval men had the metaphysical writings of Aristotle available to them, they would have found Plato's doctrines seriously challenged by the other master of Greek thought. But Aristotle's metaphysics was not translated into Latin until the second half of the twelfth century; until then, only that part of his logic that was translated into Latin by Boethius was known in Latin-Christian Europe. This intellectual tool, fully taken up and used by the vigorous and critical minds of the late eleventh and first half of the twelfth centuries, was sufficient to provide a method for scrutinizing the merits of Plato's doctrine. The new logicians were not satisfied to accept Platonism as the canonical philosophy divinely inspired, but they wished to put it to the test of rigorous dialectical inquiry. From the first, this endeavor aroused concern and uneasiness in more conservative minds. It was not simply that the prevailing biblical-patristic tradition was heavily influenced by Platonism; even more important was the relevance of the question of the reality of the universals to Christian knowledge. It had been comforting to believe that human reason could arrive at the same universal concepts of God, immortality, justice, and the church that had been initially revealed by the Bible and dogmatic faith. If philosophers concluded that it was impossible for human reason to maintain the reality of those concepts, however, then faith would have to stand alone as the source of Christian knowledge, and its alliance with rational thought, which Platonism made possible, would be dissolved. As early as the 1060s Peter Damiani had well understood the dangerous implications of the new logic. He sensed that the reckless inquiry into the reality of universals could end in a growing separation and eventually a dichotomy between the world of reason and the world of faith, between the new learning and revelation, that was bound to result in disparagement and humiliation for the latter.

Damiani's warning about the course that philosophical thought was taking failed to impede the inquiry into the validity of the Platonic doctrine of universals. The great cardinal's suspicion of dialectic appeared to be groundless because the initial consequence of the pursuit of the new logic strongly confirmed the validity of Platonism. In the first decade of the twelfth century St. Anselm of Canterbury maintained that it was possible for "faith to seek understanding" through rational philosophy and science. He showed how realism could be used to prove the existence of God. His so-called ontological argument for the existence of God (which was rejected by Thomas Aquinas in the thirteenth century but later revived by Descartes and Leibnitz) contended that since ideas are res and since we have in our minds an idea of "that which nothing greater can be thought," or God, then God must exist. Anselm's immense prestige as a scholar and saint gave additional weight to his argument and momentarily indicated that realism would not be threatened by the new philosophical inquiry.

The emergence of a contrary philosophical doctrine was not long in coming, however. In the second decade of the twelfth century one of the most outstanding teachers in the French schools, Roscelin, took a position diametrically opposed to the realist view and negated Anselm's assumptions. He declared that universals were not res but merely *voces,* words, or *nomina,* names. Universals were terms used for convenience in human intercourse, but they had no independent existence outside individual human minds. This fundamental position came to be known as nominalism, the doctrine directly contrary to realism. The corollary of Roscelin's teachings was that although universals might indeed exist, they do not necessarily exist because we think about them. In other words, the reality of universals could not be established by reason, but was only known to us through revelation. On the surface there was no cause for alarm at the nominalist position; the early nominalists' skeptical attitude toward the potentialities of reason increased the exclusive importance of faith. Only through revelation could the universal concepts of the Christian faith be known. By negating the power of reason, Roscelin's and his followers' nominalism ended in extreme fideism. It was hard for anyone to deny Roscelin's orthodoxy, for, if anything, he had enhanced the importance of revelation, which was, in his view, the only source of Christian knowledge. Against the background of the Platonic tradition of the early Middle Ages, which had offered rational support for dogmatic faith, however, the nominalist view signified the disappointing radical diminution of the foundations of Christian knowledge.

In the 1130s an intense debate raged in the French schools between the realist and nominalist positions, between the supporters of Anselm and Roscelin, while sensitive and well-informed churchmen throughout Europe looked on with apprehension as to its outcome. The position that Abelard would take was of the greatest moment and was bound to cause a sensation. As the most outstanding teacher of his day, as both the most brilliant mind and most forceful personality in the new schools, his opinions were bound to be influential. Abelard had been a pupil of Roscelin, but he had also listened to the lectures of those who took the realist side. He was fully conscious of the importance of the debate and his contribution to it, and in stating his views he avoided his accustomed extremism. Abelard concluded that universals were "confused general images," that is, they were general images developed in the mind through extrapolation from particular impressions. Therefore, in his view universals were neither things nor terms; they were conceptions, useful but not necessarily real. It was a moderate position, but it leaned toward the nominalist side, and it certainly cast doubt upon the validity of rational support for the teachings of revelation, although it did not absolutely deny this possibility.

If Abelard had not towered above contemporary philosophers and if he had not been an aggressive and unusual person with a great following among the students, his moderate nominalism would not have attracted much attention. As it was, he seemed to be leading the attack on the Platonic foundations of traditional Christian thought, and, beyond doubt, to a considerable degree the implications of his philosophy were in that direction. Even when Abelard expressed his conclusions in a qualified and moderate way, the general tendency of his worldview to conflict with the biblical-patristic tradition was immediately evident to sensitive observers. Abelard was not helped by the radical and volatile propensities of his students, who were eager to criticize all sorts of long-standing traditions and aroused widespread fears that Abelard was leading the younger generation to overthrow the Christian order. One of Abelard's students, a certain Arnold of Brescia, later fomented a social revolt in Rome and was executed by Frederick Barbarossa. Such notorious disciples could only serve to enhance Abelard's reputation among the leaders of society as a monstrous subverter of Christian ideals and a devilish corrupter of the younger generation.

Abelard was a marked man, and his fall was not long in coming. He seems to have had a perverse inclination to give his enemies everything they needed to destroy him. He undertook to publish a work on the nature of the Trinity, a subject that western thinkers had always avoided because of the heresies into which Greek-Christian theologians had stumbled when they tried to define philosophically the relations between God the Father, God the Son, and God the Holy Spirit. When Abelard's book appeared, the worst fears of conservative churchmen were confirmed. Abelard had already antagonized them by the publication of an earlier book, *Sic et Non,* which placed in dialectical juxtaposition, for and against, the opinions of various church fathers on theological problems. Gratian employed this same method in his *Decretum,* as did the standard mid-twelfth century orthodox textbook on theology, Peter Lombard's *Sentences,* and Thomas Aquinas's *Summa Theologica* was also to use this dialectical manner of argument—with the important difference that they resolved the contradictory propositions, whereas Abelard allowed them to stand without resolution. Abelard seemed to be mocking the church fathers and questioning the validity of the greatest Christian mystery. His condemnation as a heretic and the ruination of his academic career inevitably followed. His subsequent personal miseries prevented him from carrying his investigation into the nature of universals further. In any case, the reception into western thought in the half century after his death of the Aristotelian corpus broadened and somewhat altered the terms of the realist-nominalist debate as it existed in the first half of the twelfth century.

Abelard's doctrine was inevitably outmoded by the tremendous impact on western thought of Greek and, to some extent, Arabic philosophy. This fact does not substantially diminish his central position in the higher culture of the Middle Ages. He was the most important spokesman of the movement away from the Platonic realism that had cemented the thought-world of the early Middle Ages. The next two centuries of Christian thought were devoted to struggling with the implications of this intellectual upheaval.

The prosecutor at Peter Abelard's trial for heresy was St. Bernard, abbot of Clairvaux, the self-appointed conscience of the mid-twelfth-century church. From the first Bernard had been hostile to the work of the Paris school. He suspected those who learned "merely in order that they may know"; "such curiosity," he said, "is blamable." He accused Abelard and men like him of wishing "to learn for no other reason than that they may be looked upon as learned, which is ridiculous vanity." As the great successor in medieval culture to Peter Damiani, he had no appreciation for the utility of the new learning. The only secular knowledge to which he was willing to ascribe any value was the liberal arts, and even then only for the traditional, limited, functional purpose of service in clerical education. Bernard claimed that literacy and learning offered no road to God. All that was needed for salvation was a "pure conscience and unfeigning faith." These pronouncements seem to mark Bernard as the conservative leader of his generation, and he liked to think of himself in this way. But when his ideas are examined as a whole, they appear to be no less a radical challenge to the early medieval thought-world than were the doctrines of Abelard, although, of course, from a different direction. Bernard was the spokesman for the new piety of the twelfth century, as Abelard was the protagonist of the new rationalism. Far from being conservative, the Bernardine vision looms as the most potentially revolutionary doctrine of the twelfth century.

As a thinker, Bernard built upon new trends in medieval religious thought that had been articulated by Peter Damiani and by St. Anselm of Canterbury around 1100. *Cur Deus Homo* was the title of Anselm's most influential book, still read today in Christian seminaries—"Why does God become man?" And the answer according to Anselm, is not only sacramental, to provide the means of salvation through divine grace, but educational, to show men and women how to live. The life of Christ is a role model for mankind, a revelation of a life of love. Anselm was articulating the transformation of early medieval sacramental Christianity into a more experiential, personal faith. Bernard followed up this trend and developed and popularized it. He also followed Anselm in the Canterbury archbishop's enthusiasm for the cult of the Virgin. The focus on the Madonna and the contemplation of Jesus not only as the Lord but as the infant of Mary's breast was the way to refocus Christianity into an experiential, highly personal religion.

This is the road that Bernard sought to go intellectually. But his message at times was clouded by his aggressive and domineering personality. He had a strong leadership capacity and an obsessive tendency to tell people what to do in an outspoken fashion. This tendency did not always mesh well with his aim to be a preacher of a highly personal and emotional kind of faith.

Bernard was the product of one of the higher ranks of the French nobility. His young manhood was devoted to the life of the aristocractic warrior, but, as was later the case with St. Francis and St. Ignatius Loyola, whose social backgrounds were similar, he was repelled by the mores of his class and underwent a powerful conversion experience that drove him toward the religious life. In medieval parlance, he became "a soldier of Christ," a monk. He joined the new Cistercian order, the leader north of the Alps of the new ascetic tendencies in western monasticism, taking some of his noble friends with him. Eventually Bernard was appointed to the abbacy of the Cistercian monastery of Clairvaux. He was by far the most famous member of his order, and his reputation contributed greatly to the rapid expansion of the Cistercian movement. In actuality, however, Bernard had erred in his calling; he was temperamentally unsuited to the contemplative life. He was too complex and vital a man to be a twelfth-century monk, and his bad temper and querulous disposition were largely the consequence of his inability to remain under the restraints of the Cistercian rule and the feelings of guilt that developed when he spent the greater part of the last two decades of his life away from his monastery.

Bernard's reputation as the leader of the much-admired Cistercians, his dynamic personality and eloquence, and his position as the unofficial spokesman of popular piety gave him the opportunity to play a great role in society. From 1125 to 1153 he seems to have dominated the western church. He made popes, harangued kings, preached crusades, advised churchmen, condemned Jews and then prohibited pogroms, and generally made a nuisance of himself. An example of his conduct was the papal election dispute of 1130, which was the consequence of a split in the electoral college. A slight majority elected Anaclete II, but the more prominent cardinals chose Innocent II. Bernard announced that votes should be weighed, not counted, and secured the papal throne for Innocent II, one of his own followers. While this view of majority rule was common in the twelfth and thirteenth centuries, contemporaries were not blind to the fact that he had scarcely acted in a disinterested way, for Innocent II was one of his disciples.

A careful reading of Bernard's voluminous correspondence reveals many similar instances of arbitrary judgment. Bernard was particularly severe in criticizing the older Cluniac monasticism. He took it upon himself to castigate the architecture of Cluny, which he found too ornate and not sufficiently austere, and he did not refrain from lecturing abbot Suger of St. Denis, whom he accused of associating with bad company and thereby endangering his soul. Many churchmen were secretly delighted when the second crusade, which Bernard had preached, ended in disaster. Bernard wondered why God had humiliated him in this way, but it did not stop him from continuing to act as the arbiter of Europe. It has sometimes been said that he was the leader of Christian Europe during his lifetime. He certainly had great influence, and he undoubtedly viewed himself in this way, but his control over the lay and ecclesiastical princes was more apparent than real. Kings, popes, and bishops came to feel that a letter or lecture from St. Bernard was a regular ordeal that they had to endure, but they did not often do what he bid them, at least for any length of time.

What Bernard wanted was the moral reformation of Europe, the strict ordering of life according to Christian teachings. No less than Humbert and Hildebrand, he was a puritan who wished to create the City of God on Earth, but he was accepted because, unlike them, he confined himself to using moral persuasion to achieve this end. This is why the leaders of society were willing to tolerate him: He was a great religious, universally respected, and an extremely eloquent preacher who had assumed the role of the moral conscience of Europe. But he had no official authority, he was not the pope, he excommunicated no one, and he had no power to depose kings. Consequently kings and churchmen were willing to listen to his harangues because he interfered in no substantial way with their endeavors to increase their power or to pursue their normal policies.

It was not for his appeals to the leaders of society that St. Bernard was really important, but rather for his religious doctrines and his tapping of the vast emotional resources of the new piety to accelerate the transformation of medieval Christianity. He bitterly criticized the masters of the French schools for trying to establish a rational avenue to divine knowledge, but no more than Abelard was he satisfied with the single approach to the deity through the traditional means of revelation and the sacraments. He believed in a direct religious experience, the union between the loving, self-abnegating God and the Christian soul. The end of religion, he said, is "to know Jesus, and to know Jesus crucified"—not Christ in majesty, but in self-sacrifice. Bernard's theology clearly makes love greater than faith. In Bernard's view the union between God and man is greatly abetted by the intercession of the Divine Mary, "the Virgin that is the royal way, by which the Savior comes to us." She is the "Flower upon which rests the Holy Spirit." St. Bernard played the leading role in the development of the Virgin cult, which is one of the most important manifestations of the popular piety of the twelfth century. In early medieval thought the Virgin Mary had played a minor role, and it was only with the rise of emotional Christianity in the eleventh century that she became the prime intercessor for humanity with the deity. She was held to be the loving mother of all, whose infinite mercy offers the possibility of salvation to all who seek her assistance with a loving and contrite heart. St. Anselm had made an important contribution to the rapid expansion of the Virgin cult at the end of the eleventh century, but it was St. Bernard who popularized Mariology, a cardinal doctrine of the Catholic faith and one that passed beyond the dimensions of strictly religious teaching to enrich deeply the artistic and literary vision of the High Middle Ages.

In Bernard's teaching the Virgin Mary thus becomes an additional aspect of the deity and aids the Son and the Holy Spirit in uniting men to God. But a more direct approach to the deity is possible: the mystical way of the beatific vision. The Bernardine doctrine fulfills the mystical tendencies of Damiani's theology. The abbot of Clairvaux was by no means the only spokesman for the mystical way to union with God in the mid-twelfth century. In the emotionally charged religious atmosphere of the age, the idea of the direct experience of divine will was bound to become prominent. In Bernard's day certain writers at the monastery of St. Victor at Paris were producing an extensive mystical literature, but Bernard was the most powerful advocate of the mystical approach to the deity between Damiani and Francis. With his usually acute perception, Dante, in the final cantos of the *Divine Comedy,* made the abbot of Clairvaux the representative of the beatific vision in medieval Christianity. The mystical union with God was for Bernard a far more possible human attainment than it was for Augustine and the church fathers. He said that if anyone is so filled with an earnest longing for union with Christ that he "desires it vehemently, thirsts for it ardently, and without ceasing, dwells upon the hope of it," then he shall feel himself inwardly embraced by the bridegroom and "shall receive a sweet inpouring of the Divine Love." His soul shall "die the death which belongs to the angels." He shall escape not only from the desire for things corporeal but even from their haunting ideas and images and shall attain the contemplative ecstasy; he shall enter into pure relation with "the image and likeness of purity."

This mystical doctrine constitutes the most profound revolution in Christian thought, for if the soul can thus escape from its human bondage in the present life, what is any longer the necessity and utility of the church and the sacramental way to salvation? The church and sacraments are still necessary as a preparation for the beatific vision, Bernard would reply, and for those who are incapable of the pure life of the spirit. But those who have followed the spiritual exercises that Bernard proposed have in effect dispensed with the necessity of the ecclesiastical means of grace; they have entered into a direct relationship with the deity; they have died the death of the angels; they have become the heavenly pure. And when these angelic saints have momentarily descended from their spiritual Sinai—when they have, for the moment, left the embrace of the Divine Bridegroom—who is to tell them what is the truth, who is to exercise authority over them? Is it to be the official ministers of Christ, the ordained priesthood? How many of the latter have attained the beatific vision and experienced the heavenly embrace? Can such as these presume to govern angels? These are the momentous questions raised by the Bernardine vision, and not only by implication. St. Bernard, whose only office in the church was that of the abbot of a small Cistercian monastery, presumed himself to judge the church and the ministers of Christ of his day. He discovered "a contagious corruption creeping through the whole body of the church," the more desperate of cure because it was universal and the more dangerous because it was so deeply seated. "The plague of the church is inward, and it is incurable," proclaimed Bernard from his angelic standpoint. The churchmen of his day, with their "meretricious splendor" and "infamous traffic" in offices, have betrayed the Lord. "They are advanced to honor upon the goods of the Lord, and to the Lord they render no honor at all." The great bishops are "ministers of Christ and they are serving Antichrist." The church has become the province of "the Demon of noonday," the Antichrist, who "has without question swallowed up the rivers of the learned and the torrents of those who are powerful." Only the final apocalyptic age remains when the Lord Jesus will destroy the Antichrist "with the brightness of his coming."

Compared to these ominous pronouncements by the abbot of Clairvaux, the most extreme statements of Abelard appear moderate in their import. In Bernard's sermon on the church the new piety becomes uncontrollable and turns upon the established order. No one ever thought of accusing Bernard of doctrinal error, but his writings are the most obvious and prestigious source of many of the doctrines disseminated by the movements of popular heresy in the latter part of the twelfth and again in the fourteenth century. In all these movements the power of the angelic saint is placed over and above the official authority of the church hierarchy, and individual morality overrules sacerdotal office. Without intending to subscribe to Donatism, St. Bernard opened the way for the proliferation of Donatist principles in the late twelfth century. His doctrines prefigure in every way the radical teachings of the south Italian monk and archheretic Joachim of Flora a half century later. Bernard never said that the pope is the instrument of the Antichrist, but he denounced every other rank of the hierarchy in the church from archbishop to archdeacon as the servants of the "Demon of noonday." Joachim only had to add that the Vicar of Christ is really the vicar of Antichrist to arrive at his full-blown revolutionary theory. Even the eschatological idea that the world had entered the age of Antichrist, soon to be followed by the coming of the Lord, upon which Joachim developed his theology of history, is already fully explicit in Bernard's writings.

The ambiguous character and many-sided consequences of the intellectual expansion of Europe are vividly illustrated in the Bernardine vision. An archconservative in some respects and an anti-intellectual, he saw the dangers of the new learning and fully understood the ominous implications of Abelard's personality and philosophy, but on his side Bernard directed the new piety in directions that the church of the late twelfth century could not control. By raising the puritan saint above the ministers of Christ and by his presumptuous moral judgment of the priesthood as instruments of Antichrist, he enunciated the doctrines that were to form the common ethos of the popular heresies. Bernard gave to medieval Catholicism a new emotional dimension that enriched and revitalized it, but at the same time he must be regarded as the gravedigger of sacerdotal authority.

IV. Literature and Society in the Twelfth Century

The intellectual expansion of the twelfth century involved belletristic literature as much as other forms of thought and feeling. The century witnessed an enormous increase in literacy, the development of important new literary motifs that exercised a powerful influence on European belles-lettres until the twentieth century, and the creation for the first time on any large scale of vernacular literatures. No early-medieval writer, with the exception of St. Augustine, possibly Boethius, and a few Anglo-Saxon poets, is read today for any purposes except purely historical ones. The twelfth century, however, produced French, Spanish, and German poets whose works are still celebrated by literary critics and command a substantial audience. These works, most of them in the vernacular languages, present a vivid picture of the ideals and mores of European society, particularly the landed classes. No aspect of the acceleration of cultural change in the twelfth century is more difficult to assess than the intellectual and social implications of the new literary forms.

What kind of people wrote the literature of the twelfth century? The great majority of writers, even in the vernacular languages, were still churchmen. But instead of the predominance of monastic authors, which characterized the period before 1100, the twelfth century exhibits prolific writing by secular clerks, most of whom were attached to cathedral chapters. A novel group of writers were the university students, who, north of the Alps, were at least nominally churchmen. In addition to the clerics, who produced the bulk of the twelfth-century literature, secular people were making contributions to European literature for the first time in the Middle Ages. Many of the nobility, particularly in northern Italy; southern France; and, by the end of the century, also in western Germany, were highly literate, and some French and German aristocrats became productive authors in their vernacular languages. The exigencies of their work required many bourgeois to be able to read and write, to do accounts, and engage in business correspondence. It was only about 1200, however, that a distinctly bourgeois literature began to appear.

In the late twelfth century, Latin was still the exclusive language for technical and intellectual subjects: philosophy, theology, law, and the documents of church and state. It remained the international academic language until the eighteenth century, and the affairs of the Catholic church are still conducted partly in the Roman tongue, but after 1200 the vernacular began to be employed in the administrative work and law courts of the developing national monarchies. In the twelfth century there was still an extensive belletristic writing in the Latin tongue, and some of the greatest Latin poems were produced after 1100. The Catholic liturgy received a rich heritage from the twelfth century, for instance, the Gregorian chant in the form we know it today and the devotional lyrics and hymns of St. Bernard and the Paris Victorines.

The twelfth century also saw the appearance of what has been called "secular Latin poetry," that is, lyrics that deal with themes that are, to a considerable extent, nonreligious. They were mostly poems written by the so-called wandering scholars, by which is meant university students. This poetry expressed the typical *Weltschmerz* of the undergraduate of any era: his frustrated ambitions, his superficial cynicism, his amorous affairs, and his drinking bouts. The best of the surviving poems by students were actually written by two middle-aged alumni: the Archpoet, a cleric in the entourage of Frederick Barbarossa's chancellor, and the Primate, a prominent canon of Orleans cathedral. These lyrics are often referred to as Goliardic poetry because many are dedicated in jocular fashion to a certain Golias, or Goliath, presumably a synonym for the devil. These "devilish" poems, urging the attractions of dissolute life, have sometimes been interpreted (especially in the early decades of this century) as accurate accounts of the life and ideals of medieval university students. This view is no more valid than would be a similar interpretation of the contents of contemporary American undergraduate journals. Wine, women, and song, even less than today, were only a peripheral part of twelfth-century student life.

The cynical attitude toward the church hierarchy that is prevalent in the Goliardic poems has some significance, but it must be remembered that the authors themselves were frequently church officials. Obviously the Goliardic poems are more secular than are Bernard's hymns to the Virgin, but their youthful pessimism does not preclude an underlying deep devotion to the traditional faith of the Middle Ages. In assessing the social significance of the Goliardic and similar student poetry of the twelfth century, it must be emphasized that the same writers who declared that it was their resolution to "drop down dead in the tavern" also listened in rapt attention to the lectures of Abelard and the sermons of St. Bernard. After the Archpoet has finished describing his dissolute life as a toper, gambler, and woman chaser, he implores God to grant him grace and absolution and looks forward to greeting "angels without measure/ Singing requiems for the souls/ In eternal leisure." The Goliardic poetry expressed the variety and complexity of twelfth-century life, but it can scarcely be taken as evidence of a genuine secularist attitude. On the contrary, this literature shows how the new piety blunted and inhibited the effects of undergraduate rebellion and how it helped to transform the young bohemians of the Latin Quarter into responsible men of affairs, whose student escapades survived only in the form of romantic nostalgia.

The achievements of twelfth-century Latin literature have been overshadowed by the prolific vernacular works of the period. Lay society in the early Middle Ages commonly used vulgar tongues in ordinary conversation. But the only vernacular literature written before 1100, or at least 1050—there is great difficulty in dating the earliest work—consisted of Anglo-Saxon poetry, of which *Beowulf* is the greatest example. The French language, which had distinctly appeared as early as the ninth century out of the *lingua romana,* the debased popular form of classical Latin, produced its first literary works two or three decades before or after the year 1100. The Iberian romance dialects began to be used for literary expression at about the same time or probably a little later. German vernacular literature made its appearance at the end of the twelfth century, and in Italy, where Latin naturally exerted the strongest hold on popular letters, the vulgar tongue began to be used by writers in the second half of the thirteenth century. The cultural effects of the Norman Conquest and the subsequent transformation of England into a cultural appanage of France precluded the development of English vernacular literature until the fourteenth century. In fact, as late as the early fifteenth century, a bastardized French was still used in English legal and governmental records.

The most important vernacular literature of the twelfth century, both by the criteria of the number of its works produced and the seminal importance of its motifs and techniques, was produced in the northern and southern French dialects. Any reader of the prolific French literature of the twelfth century will instantly see mirrored therein some important facets of intellectual and social change, but there is great disagreement among scholars as to the degree of immediacy and accuracy in this reflection. Literary historians often take the accounts in their sources at face value and accept them as accurate pictures of the ideals and mores of the ruling class of twelfth-century society; the older political historians did their best to ignore the literary accounts, regarding them as at best a distorted view and at worst so distant from the realities of medieval life as to be useless as historical evidence. Recent historical scholarship, more attuned to a broad social perspective and as sensitive to states of consciousness as to institutional forms, has found in twelfth-century literature indications of profound changes in feeling that affected important groups in the medieval world.

The mass of French vernacular poetry of the twelfth century falls into three distinct categories: the *chanson de geste;* the troubadour lyrics; and the romantic epic, which is a result of the confluence of the first two forms. The chansons de geste were long epic poems indigenous to northern France that portrayed deeds of heroism and other aspects of the life of the feudal nobility. They were certainly meant to entertain aristocratic courts, and they were probably stories that had circulated orally and been slowly expanded over three centuries before being written down at the end of the eleventh century or in the early twelfth century. They were based upon incidents, some of them known from historical sources, that occurred in Carolingian times. These epic poems, written for the entertainment of the French feudal nobility, presumably portray the great lords of northern France in the way they liked to think of themselves. The result is an idealized picture of feudal life, but one that is recognizable from, and in many instances vividly confirms, what we know about feudal life from nonliterary sources. Iberian-Christian literature began about the middle of the twelfth century with the great Spanish epic *The Cid,* an account of the deeds of a famous eleventh-century Spanish warrior. The ideals and attitudes expressed in *The Cid* are the same as in the French chansons de geste.

The chansons de geste portray the feudatories as the leaders of society: The emperor-king is at best distant and at worst appears as weak and crooked, churchmen are merely assistants to the feudal nobility, peasants are a negligible social force who have no other function except to toil for their lords and be massacred during feudal wars, and the bourgeois are hardly mentioned. The cohesive force in the world of the chanson de geste is loyalty, and the theme around which the poem is built is always some question of vassalage, its fulfillments or its violations. Thus, in the *Song of Roland,* the earliest work of French literature through which so many generations of modern students have had to toil, the hero is a count who fulfills his oath of loyalty to Charlemagne even though it involves his certain death. *Raoul de Cambrai,* which is the most valuable of the epic poems for the social historian, is built around the troubles and violence that result when the emperor does not reward one of his leading vassals with the fief he claims by inheritance. In *Raoul* the bellicose disposition of the feudal nobility is starkly revealed; the wronged hero engages in bloody rebellion and the massacre of innocent churchmen and bourgeois. Apparently the aristocratic audience enjoyed such incidents, and, in certain backward frontier regions such as Brittany and the Massif Central, such violence was still common, even in the year 1200. These manifestations of feudal disorder are intertwined in the same poem with reflections of the new popular piety. A poem whose subject is the career of a certain lord called Robert the Devil describes how the hero, after several years of banditry and pillaging of monasteries, suffers remorse, goes to Rome and obtains papal absolution for his sins, and ends up as a saintly monk himself. The combination of violence and piety in the chanson de geste is confirmed by our general knowledge of the mores of the twelfth-century nobility. There is, however, an additional element, a certain mawkish sentimentality in the poems that does not fit in with our general historical picture of the northern French nobility at the beginning of the twelfth century. Thus when Charlemagne informs Roland's betrothed of the hero's death, she immediately faints and dies of a broken heart, and we are told that the tragedy causes the great nobles in Charlemagne's court to weep profusely. This effeminate sentimentality conflicts strongly with the rough masculinity of the landed classes of northern France at the time the chansons de geste were written. If it has any historical base, it indicates only that within the narrow confines of some feudal courts a new sensibility had made its appearance by the early twelfth century.

Sensibility, emotion, and effeminate sentiment are not, however, generally characteristic of the chansons de geste. The intrusion of these romantic attitudes into the outlook of the European nobility, insofar as it ever did become important, which is a moot question, originated not in the northern feudal principalities, but in the different social environment of southern France. In Provence, Aquitaine, and Toulouse, the culture looked southward toward the Mediterranean world and was little affected by the north in the twelfth century. The military vigor of the southern nobility was diminished and their way of life fully altered by several factors working together. The boundaries of the feudal principalities in the south were well settled, and there was scarcely any opportunity for baronial wars. Many of the nobility of Languedoc, the country of the southern dialect, took up residence in the cities, and their attitudes were slowly transformed by bourgeois animadversions on violence and disorder. The new piety had a profound effect on the worldview of the southern nobility; their new enthusiasm for the saints and the Virgin made the old code of the warrior class no longer satisfactory to the more intelligent members of the nobility.

The social life of the southern French nobility came to center in the court of the count or duke, and its confining circumstances gave the great aristocratic ladies the opportunity to educate the nobles in genteel and sentimental mores. The term *court,* whose meaning heretofore was almost exclusively legal and governmental, began to take on the additional connotation of an aristocratic social center, and *courtly* became a synonym for "refined" and "sophisticated." Finally, romantic attitudes that had long existed in the courts of Moslem princes, such as are described in the *Arabian Nights,* may have penetrated southern France from the neighboring Arabic-Spanish principalities. All these elements have been used to explain the sentimental ideals that are found in the troubadour lyrics of southern France in the late eleventh and first half of the twelfth centuries. Some of the troubadours were professional poets and minstrels at princely courts. Others were members of the nobility, including some of the powerful dukes of Aquitaine. The troubadour ideals are the first clear expression of what has been called the code of chivalry. The term is not a good one; the ideas and sentiments involved were too loose and vague even to be as clearly defined a code as vassalage, and the term *chivalry* is ambiguous, for it really means nothing except the way of life of the chevalier, or knight. But whatever the term used, it is possible to perceive something new in the outlook of the aristocrats of southern France in the early twelfth century.

Chivalry has both a broad and a specific meaning. The broader sense of the term implies that the customs of a warrior class were coming to be replaced by the mores of aristocratic gentlemen. In the long intervals between wars the southern nobility engaged in various pastimes at court that could not be imitated by any other class in society, and these expensive and intentionally impractical recreations—ceremonies, dinners, hunting, falconry, tournament jousting, singing, troubadour recitals, etc.—served to preserve the identity of a class that had, for the most part, lost its military function. In a more limited and specific way, chivalry has been identified with the ideals and practices of courtly love. In the troubadour lyrics ladies are addressed in a sentimental and gentle manner unknown to the rough lords of the early Middle Ages, who looked upon women as instruments for physical pleasure and the breeding of children. Carried to the northern court of Champagne from Aquitaine in the middle of the twelfth century, courtly love developed a whole special code of its own, which was written down by a certain Andreas Capellanus (Andrew the Chaplain). This code was based on the principle of romantic love, that is, love involving a man and woman of the aristocracy who are not married and never can or even want to be, for love is presumed to exist only outside marriage. The romantically entwined go through elaborate rituals of exchanging encouraging messages, vows, and tokens. The woman becomes for the nobleman the ideal lady who symbolizes for him all virtue and beauty and in whose name he performs valorous and other worthy deeds.

Historians of medieval civilization have had a difficult time interpreting the significance of the courtly love of Aquitaine and Champagne. It has been viewed as a central motive in aristocratic life throughout western Europe, having, supposedly, been carried to the Ile-de-France and then to England by the ubiquitous Eleanor of Aquitaine. It has been viewed as a dangerous heresy imported from the Moslem world, which undermined traditional Christian morality. It has also been interpreted as the secularized form of the Virgin cult and the Bernardine vision of divine love, and as such it is believed to have made an outstanding contribution to western culture by raising the dignity of women and enriching European literature with a new romantic strain. It has also been regarded as a nebulous factor in European life, existing only in the minds of a few idle court poets who were heavily influenced by Ovid's *Art of Love,* a popular book in the twelfth century. It has even been suggested that Andrew the Chaplain's handbook of courtly love was meant as a joke or as a clever satire.

It is clear that many more people talked about courtly love than really practiced it, and even those who talked about it consisted of a handful of aristocratic ladies and their literary sycophants. But courtly love does represent, in its most extreme form, the new sentimentality and gentility that the European aristocracy came to adopt whenever and wherever its traditional military functions were atrophied. Not many of the European nobility of the twelfth century, even in Champagne and Aquitaine, were passionate, courtly lovers, but more and more the members of the aristocracy acted in a civilized and restrained manner, and if they still thought nothing of assaulting peasants or insulting bourgeois, they were "courteous" to each other and especially to the women of their own class. This slow transformation in the social attitudes of the nobility was greatly encouraged by the growth of the European monarchies, whose governments placed severe limitations on violence and thuggery and thereby forced the nobility to develop a more pacific way of life.

The average member of the twelfth-century landed class took seriously the teachings of the church and exhibited the accoutrements of popular piety. He attended church services; adored the saints and the Virgin; respected monks; contributed to ecclesiastical endowments; and joined pilgrimages and sometimes, when called upon, crusades to the Holy Land. But a small minority of the nobles of the higher ranks were influenced more strongly by sentiment and sensibility than was normal in this typical behavior of the feudal class. For them a romantic code of honor replaced the old code of loyalty. Such genuine chivalric types did not fare much better in the twelfth century than they would today. The sentimental Robert Curthose lost his duchy of Normandy to his more rough-minded brother, Henry I of England, and the extremely generous Stephen of Blois, who tried to gain the English throne in the 1130s, was singularly inept as a soldier and statesman. The most famous chivalric knight of the twelfth century was the English king Richard the Lion-hearted. The dramatic incidents of his career were celebrated by troubadours and minstrels, but he was easily made a fool of by the distinctly unchivalrous king of France; the greatest service he rendered his long-suffering people was to remain out of England for almost his whole reign, and nothing became his life so much as his manner of leaving it. He had no sooner returned to England from captivity in Germany than he dashed off to France, pennants flying, to besiege the castle of a minor vassal who refused to surrender a negligible treasure trove to the king. A stray arrow dispatched from the besieged castle wall by an idle bowman prematurely cut off the flower of European chivalry.

We may gauge the more normal outlook of the European aristocracy of the twelfth century by the character and career of Richard's contemporary, William Marshal (died 1223), the most universally admired nobleman of his day. William's family thought him so worthy of general emulation that they hired a cleric to write his biography; it is the Horatio Alger story of the twelfth century and provides illuminating insight into the actual code of conduct of a twelfth-century chevalier. William was a landless knight who began his career without even a horse and armor. His only possibility for advancement lay in his kinship to a wealthy nobleman in Normandy, who outfitted him as a knight and sent him out on the tournament circuit. As described in his biography, the tournaments of the late twelfth century did not usually involve individual combats by valorous knights who were dedicated to the service of fair ladies; they were simply war games. Two groups of knights in full armor lined up on opposite sides of a large field, charged into a general melee, and hacked away at each other. Each knight's object was to unseat as many of his opponents as possible so he could hold them for ransom. William Marshal proved to be particularly adept at these disordered combats, to which he took a highly mercenary attitude. He even had a clerk accompany him to the tournaments to keep an accurate record of the sums that his defeated opponents owed him. His many victories made him wealthy and gained him his reputation as a great fighter, which won him a position in the household of Henry II as military tutor to the royal heir. He was eventually rewarded for his services to the Angevin family by being married to the richest heiress in England, who was a ward of the crown, and he thereby became the most powerful earl in the realm. In the last years of his life he was the regent of England, admired and respected by all members of the English ruling class. Assuredly William was a civilized character, shrewd and capable in government and administration, and undoubtedly courteous to ladies, but there is no evidence that he had either the time or the inclination for the complex code of courtly love. His biography shows that in 1200 the ideal nobleman was neither a robber baron nor a chivalric knight. The European feudal lords were being transformed by many pressures—political and religious, as well as intellectual and economic—into the European aristocracy in the form it was to maintain until the nineteenth century. This class enjoyed certain privileges and entertainments that were forbidden the bourgeois and peasantry, but they also had heavy responsibilities and obligations—in the case of the ordinary nobleman, toward his family and patrimony, and in the case of a few great aristocrats, such as William Marshal, toward society as a whole.

The troubadours of Aquitaine and Champagne ultimately impinged on the style of life exhibited by an aristocrat like William Marshal by contributing to the formulation of a new system of values that gave much greater primacy to individual feelings and needs. And this individualism and self-consciousness were absorbed in muted form into the aristocratic way of life. The prime medium of the education of the aristocracy in this system was a new form of vernacular literature that developed after 1130, first in England and France and then in Germany.

The romantic motifs of the troubadour lyrics impinged on the northern chanson de geste in the second half of the twelfth century and transformed it into the adventure-romance, an extremely sentimental, idealized, and imaginative epic poem. The "affairs of France," the Charlemagne cycle, did not offer the authors of the adventure-romance sufficient opportunity to exercise their remarkable inventive powers; consequently they experimented with stories based on the Trojan War or on the legendary exploits of Alexander the Great, but even these stories did not allow them full play of their romantic imaginations. They found the subject they needed in the "affairs of Britain," the King Arthur cycle.

The inaugurator of the Arthurian legends, to whose refinement so much of the literary ingenuity of the later twelfth and thirteenth centuries was devoted, was a secular clerk, Geoffrey of Monmouth, writing under the patronage of the bishop of Lincoln. In 1136 Geoffrey published his *History of the Kings of Britain,* which he claimed, perhaps facetiously, to have discovered in an old manuscript at Oxford, but which obviously consists of tales that had circulated for a long time in Geoffrey's Welsh homeland. Arthur was probably a real historical figure of the fifth century, a British Christian prince who died fighting the invading Anglo-Saxon heathens. His compatriots, hiding out in the Welsh mountains through the long cold centuries, transformed Arthur into a Christian hero of superhuman prowess. The Arthurian legend spread eastward through Europe almost as fast as a medieval plague, growing more complex and sentimental as it went. The most important contributions to the expansion of the Arthurian cycle were made by Chrétien de Troyes, a contemporary and compatriot of Andrew the Chaplain, of courtly-love fame. It was Chrétien who highlighted the subsidiary characters in the Arthurian legend, such as Lancelot, and introduced the motif of the search for the Grail.

From Champagne the Arthurian cycle reached western Germany at the end of the twelfth century—the creative period of vernacular German literature, the age of the *minnesingers,* as the German troubadours were called. The most famous minnesinger was the extremely versatile lyric poet Walther von der Vogelweide, who worked under the patronage of the royal Hohenstaufen dynasty. The German poets, such as Gottfried of Strassburg, who was a bourgeois, and Wolfram von Eschenbach, a nobleman, produced adventure-romances in which the Arthurian cycle is suffused with religious mysticism and, in the opinion of many critics, carried to its highest art form.

The Arthurian romances, like the poems of Chrétien de Troyes and Wolfram von Eschenbach's *Parzifal,* have as their theme the two forms of love, religious and secular, which are closely related. The romantic yearning of the hero for his unattainable beloved appears as the earthly counterpart of the mystic yearning for the unattainable union with the deity, and the exertions of the chivalric knight are the mundane counterpart of the spiritual exercises of the holy mystics. The knight's lady is as mysterious, distant, and gracious as the Virgin Mary herself. The blending of the sacred and secular worlds also appears in the motif of the Holy Grail. A young romantic hero, inspired by high idealism, undertakes a quest for the Grail and cannot be turned aside by any kind of physical or social obstacle. In mundane form, the Grail was the chalice from which Jesus drank at the Last Supper. But in the subtle imagination of the romantic poets, it came to symbolize the ineffable ideal, the perfected and unattainable condition of human happiness whose quest was the purpose and joy of life.

The Arthurian cycle opened up a whole dimension for European literature, that of romantic love, which only intermittently appeared in the literature of the ancient world and was, by and large, an original contribution of the twelfth century to western civilization. This romanticism received its highest social significance in the formulation of a liberation ethic that expressed a profound revulsion against the existing feudal-ecclesiastic complex and its ideological counterpart, the hierarchical view of the world that ignored and suppressed self-consciousness and individual feelings. Romantic love is an intensely personal and individual attitude that proclaims a value system based on emotional needs against inherited status and bureaucratic political power. The romantic hero's quest for the Grail gives primacy to the individual's quest for self-realization and rebels against the static nature of the feudal and ecclesiastical hierarchies. In general, the courtly and aristocratic authors of these poems wanted to liberate the individual human personality from the stultifying subjection to authority and tradition. The new romantic literature demonstrated the uncompromising dissatisfaction with the traditional ecclesiastical culture by highly sensitive and literate minds. And the ramifications of the long-range impact of the romantic rebellion on European thought and higher culture are inestimable.

It is hard to believe that the nobility who formed the audience for these adventure-romances clearly understood the extremely subtle interweaving of religious and mundane love and the other romantic symbolism. What they got out of the poems was mostly—but not only—the involved and imaginative plot into which the extremely perceptive and skillful authors wove their emotional doctrines and symbols. If the original audience of the adventure-romances missed some of the finer shades of meaning, none who read or heard the poems could fail to glimpse the new horizon in human experience that the Arthurian cycle opened up. The romantic literature taught the late-twelfth-century aristocracy that personal feelings and individual quests were values that deserved to be recognized and reconciled with the individual's obligations to the demands of the social order.

The romantic literature also instructed the aristocracy that the sensibility that had hitherto been regarded as a mark of feminine inferiority was now made into a virtue practiced by heroes, such as Lancelot, Parsifal, and Tristan. By making feminine qualities heroic, the romantic poets enhanced the dignity of woman and made her a being with distinctive and valuable qualities. The teaching of the fourth-century church fathers on sex and marriage was the first and very modest stage in the emancipation of women in western civilization. The romantic ethos of the twelfth century marked the second and more important stage.

But if the adventure-romances contributed to the partial emancipation of women, they also laid the intellectual foundations for the double standard of sexual morality that existed in western civilization until the twentieth century. The chief basis for the double standard was not intellectual but social and legal. In a society in which landed property and title descended by primogeniture and in which illegitimacy was the bar sinister to inheritance, there were inevitably different standards of sexual conduct for husbands and wives. The lord could have as many mistresses and bastards as he wished or could afford because the consequences of his promiscuity were evident to the world, but the opposite was true of his wife, whose adulterous behavior could not so easily be detected. The mere suspicion of promiscuity in the lady of a feudal household, and the doubts about the legitimacy of her children that therefore arose, could result in interminable lawsuits and destroy a great patrimony. It was therefore necessary for the noble to keep his wife under close surveillance to preclude any suspicions of bastardy in his line. The romantic conception of women fomented by the troubadour lyric; the notion of courtly love; and, above all, the adventure-romances provided an intellectual justification for the double standard and the seclusion of women. Noblewomen were held to be frail, sentimental creatures who could not be allowed the freedom accorded the male sex. They had to be both protected and virtually imprisoned.

The growth of vernacular literature in the twelfth century thus profoundly affected the dimensions of higher culture and had some effect on the conditions of social life. It had also played a part in the development of the national monarchies. For the proliferation of rich vernacular literatures in the twelfth century secured the place of the vulgar tongues in European society, and this entrenchment of the vernacular tongues made the European peoples more conscious of being separated from each other; decreased the cosmopolitan attitudes of the European nobility; and encouraged xenophobia, which became common in the thirteenth century. This linguistic, intellectual, and social Balkanization of European society, which was well under way by 1200, was the necessary precondition for the emergence of nationalism in the thirteenth and fourteenth centuries.

The liberating implications of twelfth-century romanticism would take many more centuries to attain full realization. The frustration of the efforts of women in aristocratic courts to assert their identity and to gain a large measure of personal freedom—the inconclusive outcome of the medieval women's liberation movement that is reflected in the development of romantic literature—parallels the condition of nuns in traditional Benedictine convents. In these convents daughters and widows of the aristocracy were cloistered by their families and removed from noble households, sometimes for exalted religious reasons, sometimes to suit mundane convenience of their families. These aristocratic nuns chafed under severe discipline and control by men, such as the bishop who exercised discipline over them and the priest-confessor who was assigned to take care of their souls.

The resulting tensions are powerfully reflected in the writings of Abbess Hildegard of Bingen (died 1179), a Benedictine nunnery located in the Rhine valley. Hildegard came from the middle rank of the German nobility. During her long life she poured out a series of Latin writings (possibly translated from German with the aid of secretaries) that combined philosophy, science, and astrology with a series of elaborate apocalyptic visions that came to her while she was seized by severe migraines. Hildergard's visionary formulations, unsurpassed in medieval literature for their graphic detail and mystical expressiveness, were a form of women's revolt against the male-dominated society. Confined and frustrated, in both a disciplinary and sexual sense, she single-handedly created an alternative culture in her imagination, shaped by subconscious well-springs, that reached but did not overstep the bounds of traditional ortho-doxy. The central theme in her writings is that nuns are brides of Christ. The Church is the Bride of Christ. Therefore religious women have a spe-cial claim to articulate God's word in the world. As long as this feminist doctrine remained at a metaphorical level, it was barely tolerable to the hierarchy of the church.

CHAPTER FIFTEEN

Moslem and Jewish Thought: The Aristotelian Challenge

I. The Problem of Learning

Learning, piety, and power, through their great expansion in the twelfth century, all came by 1200 to challenge the leadership of the church in western society. The implications of the great intellectual, religious, and political changes of the twelfth century required the church to reconsider and readjust its policies and institutions to deal successfully with the consequences of European creativity and improvement. The destiny of medieval civilization after 1150 was predicated first on the implications of learning, piety, and power; then on the ways in which the church reacted to these implications; and finally upon the effectiveness of the church's readjustment.

The strongest challenge that the old order faced from the side of the new learning consisted of Aristotelian philosophy and science. The work of Abelard in the 1130s had already demonstrated how new modes of thinking derived from Aristotelianism could act as a powerful solvent of the early-medieval thought-world, with its heavily Platonic basis. Abelard had available to him only a small portion of the vast Aristotelian corpus: that part of the peripatetic logic that had been translated by Boethius. But Aristotle had also produced not only other works on dialectic but the most comprehensive scientific philosophy of the ancient world, involving cosmology, metaphysics, ethics, psychology, and political theory. In the second decade of the twelfth century the onerous work of preparing Latin translations of the Aristotelian knowledge had been inaugurated, and by the middle of the century it was well under way. Yet only at the end of the twelfth century, after an initial period of considering and digesting the Aristotelian doctrines, did Latin scholars begin to try to integrate this vast new body of science with the biblical-patristic tradition. It was a formidable and momentous undertaking, and one that many conservative churchmen believed would end in disaster for the traditions of the church. If Abelard could cause such trouble with only a small part of the Aristotelian logic, then how much more dangerous and revolutionary would be the effect of the reception of all Aristotelian science! It was a turning point in the history of western thought—a genuine "crisis of conscience"—paralleled only by the later impact of Newtonian science and Darwinism.

The Aristotelian corpus and other works of Greek science became available in the West through the medium of translations prepared in Spain; Sicily; and, to a lesser degree, Provence. Until the last quarter of the twelfth century the translations were made from Arabic versions of the Aristotelian writings, not from the original Greek. A Christian scholar worked together with a Moslem translator in Spain and Sicily or, in Provence, sometimes with a Jewish translator. In view of this awkward procedure, producing translations twice removed from the original, it was amazing how accurate were the final versions. In the first three quarters of the twelfth century scarcely any western scholars knew Greek, and they had to seek the assistance of the Arabic-speaking translators. By 1200 a new set of translations of the Aristotelian writings, directly from Greek into Latin, was under way. Thomas Aquinas, in the middle of the thirteenth century, was the first Christian philosopher who had access to the completed new translation. The new translation was, of course, more accurate than were the original secondhand Latin versions of the Aristotelian corpus, but the differences between the two translations were not remarkable.

The work of the twelfth-century translators was not organized by any central authority. A few translators enjoyed the patronage of bishops and princes, but by and large individual scholars, inspired by their training in the universities, undertook the arduous and thankless tasks of translation so that the philosophy and science of western Europe could be greatly enriched by the new material. It is indicative of the new dimensions of European thought that it was only in the twelfth century that a concerted effort was made to obtain from the Arabic world the Greek science and philosophy that had been available there for several centuries. Translation is generally a self-sacrificing endeavor; the translator makes knowledge available to others, who use it in their own intellectual work. But the twelfth-century translation of the Aristotelian corpus was a particularly heroic undertaking. The translators received little or no remuneration and enjoyed scarcely any fame; there was no other motive for their work than devotion to truth and knowledge. Their work was made harder by their isolation from one another, which occasionally resulted in the same work being independently rendered into Latin by two or three scholars.

Aristotle was by no means the only Greek author translated into Latin in the twelfth century. Every Greek contribution to philosophy and science that the Latin scholars could find in the Mediterranean world was translated. By the end of the century an enormous amount of information about natural science, medicine, and cosmology, which had heretofore been unknown, had flooded the universities of western Europe. In a sense the translators did their work too well, for they made available such an amount and variety of material that the philosophers of Christian Europe were too busy reading Aristotle and the other Greek writers to engage in critical, original, and systematic speculation. This is assuredly one reason why close to a century went by before western Europe again produced thinkers of Abelard's stature. Yet European scholars could no more afford to reject the opportunity of acquainting themselves with the intellectual riches of Greek civilization than legal scholars could have turned their backs on the Justinian code. Greek philosophy and science were the best products of the western mind in these fields; before continuing to work out their own systems, it was first necessary for medieval thinkers to absorb and comprehend the best that previously had been thought and said in the world.

Sicily was the important center for the translation of works on more technical subjects: medicine, the natural sciences, and mathematics. The heterogeneous culture of Sicily, with its mixed Greek, Moslem, Italian, and Norman population, made it an ideal center for transmitting knowledge from the Mediterranean to western Europe. Spain was the provenance of the translations of Greek philosophy and ethics. To carry out this work, Christian scholars had to take up residence in Cordoba and other Moslem cities, which, in view of the almost continuous wars between the two faiths on the Iberian peninsula, involved some risk to their personal safety. Provence was the third and least prolific center of the transmission of knowledge. The work there seems to have been effected largely through the cooperation of Christian and Jewish scholars.

When the Aristotelian corpus was made available to western thinkers in the second half of the twelfth century, they discovered that it had come from the Arabic world trailed by clouds of Moslem and Jewish commentaries. The western thinkers discovered that they were not original in trying to deal with the problem of the relation between science and revelation. Some of the greatest minds in the Moslem world, such as

Avicenna and Averroes, and Jewish scholars, such as Maimonides, had either already dealt with the consequences of Aristotelianism for their traditional faiths or were in the course of doing so in the twelfth century. The ways in which the greatest minds of the Moslem and Jewish cultures met the challenge of Aristotelian philosophy is significant in two ways. First, some of the doctrines proposed by the Moslem and Jewish commentators influenced the positions taken by western thinkers; Averroism, for example, is an important stream in thirteenth- and fourteenth-century Christian thought. Second, the doctrines of the Moslem and Jewish scholars are worthy of consideration because they offer interesting parallels and contrasts with the western reactions to the intellectual crisis engendered by the introduction of Aristotelian science and thereby provide an illuminating background to the intellectual history of thirteenth-century Europe.

Islam, Judaism, and Christianity were all theistic and providential religions. Because of their common nature, the challenge that Aristotelian doctrines offered to one was bound to be repeated with respect to the others. The difficulties that Aristotelianism presented to any believer in Islamic, Jewish, or Christian revelation were threefold. Instead of the theistic and providential God whose will constantly determines the course of the universe, Aristotle posits a mechanistic God who is simply a prime mover. He inaugurates the course of universal events, but He does not participate actively after He has inaugurated the long chain of being. The Aristotelian conception of the deity tends to preclude a belief in providence and to make prayer useless. These views seemed to conflict sharply with the teachings of the Bible and the Koran. The second stumbling block that Aristotelianism offered the scholars of the three faiths was its denial of the creation of the world *ex nihilo*. Instead, Aristotle assumed the eternity of matter, and this assumption contradicted the Judeo-Christian and Moslem belief that in the beginning there was nothing but God. The third difficulty that Aristotle presented to those thinkers who wished to show the compatibility of science and revelation was his failure to support the doctrine of the immortality of the individual soul. Plato had argued eloquently for the existence of personal immortality, which is one reason why Platonism had been so acceptable to Christian thinkers before the twelfth century. But Aristotle leaned toward a doctrine of general rather than individual immortality, that is, he indicated that the individual human intelligence survived after death through the union with the general intelligence of the universe. It was difficult to establish a compatibility between Aristotle's view and the traditional dogma of personal immortality. The Aristotelian conflicts with the teachings of revelation thus occurred at crucial points. The Moslem and Jewish thinkers of the eleventh and twelfth centuries, like their Christian successors in the thirteenth and fourteenth, had the choice of rejecting Aristotelianism in its entirety, of separating the world of science from the world of faith, or of trying to prove the ultimate compatibility of reason and revelation.

II. Reason and Revelation in Moslem and Jewish Thought

The pattern that Moslem and Jewish thought took in meeting the challenge of Aristotelianism was determined, as it was in Christian Europe, not only by the achievements of certain great minds, but by the general social environment in which they had to work. In sharp contrast with both the Christian and Jewish worlds, Islam had always maintained a dichotomy between the religious authorities and the teachers and scholars in the fields of philosophy and science. The leaders of the Islamic religion were either fundamentalists and religious legalists, who derived all their knowledge of theology and ethics from the Koran and the Traditions of the Prophet, or mystics (Sufists), who through direct religious experience discovered an additional road to knowledge and divine truth. But the leaders of the Islamic religion had never attempted to construct a rational theology by taking into account the implications of Aristotelian science. The speculative thinkers of the Islamic world were independent men who made their living as physicians, civil servants, lawyers, or professional teachers. Their peculiar social background meant, on the one hand, that these speculative thinkers could afford to be especially bold, since they were not inhibited by having to worry immediately about the compatibility of reason and revelation or about whether they would lose their jobs for preaching heresy. On the other hand, there was a grave threat to the long-range development of Islamic philosophy in this separation between the religious and intellectual leadership. If the fundamentalists and mystics felt that the traditional religion was actually in danger of subversion by the speculative thinkers and if they could obtain the cooperation of the state, they would simply silence the expression of rational thought. This is, in fact, what began to happen in the latter part of the eleventh century, and after 1200 scientific thought in the Islamic world was dead. This unfortunate development offers an illuminating contrast with the course of speculative thought in the Christian world. Because all the important philosophical work in high-medieval Europe was carried on in educational institutions that were subject to ecclesiastical authorities and because all the important western philosophers were at least in a nominal sense churchmen, the western thinkers were at first more conscious of the painful conflict between reason and revelation, and they moved more slowly than did the Arabic writers, but their work was, on the whole, protected from destruction at the hands of fanatics precisely because it was carried out under church auspices.

The Aristotelian corpus was translated into Arabic in the eighth century in Syria by Moslem scholars relying extensively on the assistance of heretical-Christian clerics. The text of the translations spread slowly throughout the Moslem world and in the tenth century reached Spain, where it was intensively studied in the great schools of philosophy and science in Cordoba and other cities. The first of the two greatest Arabic commentators on Aristotle was a Persian whom the Latins called Avicenna, but whose Arabic name was Ibn Sina (died 1037). Avicenna was an extremely prolific writer, and his contributions to medicine were popular in western Europe in the twelfth and thirteenth centuries. In philosophical thought he represented an older tradition in which Aristotelianism had not yet entirely pushed out neoplatonism, resulting in a peculiar system that drew elements from both traditions. Avicenna believed that God does not concern Himself with individuals, but creates an Intelligence, a sort of Platonic idea that engenders all other things. The result is a combination of the hierarchical universe of Plato and the mechanistic cosmos of Aristotle. It is an extremely ingenious philosophical system, but one that runs contrary to some of the fundamental precepts of Islam. Avicenna's philosophy destroyed the omniscience of God and with it, the efficacy of prayer. He further negated the creation of the world and denied personal immortality, contending that the human soul found an afterlife only through reunion with the universal Intelligence.

Substantially the same conclusions were arrived at by the greatest of the Moslem philosophers, a Spaniard named Ibn Rushd (died 1198), whom the western church called Averroes. Although he did not know Greek, Averroes imbibed the whole Aristotelian system from translations and became the leading interpreter of Aristotle to the Arabic world and, to a considerable extent, to the Latin Christian world. Thomas Aquinas referred to him as "the commentator" on Aristotle. Averroes did not flinch from the prospect of the separation of the world of science, represented by Aristotle, and the world of revelation, represented by the Koran. He believed that science inexorably demonstrates that God is the mechanistic mover of the universe; He is a machine entirely removed from interference in human life. Science upholds the eternity of the world and denies the Islamic doctrine of creation. Finally, Averroes was explicit in denying personal immortality and in upholding the doctrine of general Intelligence, or the universal soul. The adoption of this completely Aristotelian system did not imply for Averroes the abandonment of his Islamic religion. He professed himself to be a devout Moslem and met the contradiction between science and revelation by the frank recognition of the existence of a "double truth": There is one truth for science and another for revelation, and it is beyond the powers of the human mind to establish their compatibility. The ignorant must have their faith; the learned have knowledge of this double truth. Averroes's teachings infuriated the champions of Moslem orthodoxy. Although he certainly never denigrated the validity of Koranic doctrine, his conclusion that it was contradicted by science and his placing rational knowledge alongside revelation seemed to be an attempt to insult and undermine the faith. Since the eleventh century the political power in Moslem Spain had passed to groups who had emigrated from North Africa and who exhibited a fanaticism and puritanism new to the Moslem principalities in the Iberian peninsula. It was not hard for the defenders of the traditional avenues to truth by way of revelation and mystical experience to convince the Moslem princes to take measures against the continuance of free speculation. The great schools declined, Averroism was condemned, and the Arabic mind passed under the long tyranny of fanaticism and ignorance. But the teachings of Averroes, brought into the West along with the translated text of the Aristotelian corpus, were to live on, having a long history in Latin Europe and exerting a powerful influence on the course of Christian philosophy in the thirteenth and fourteenth centuries.

The relation between reason and revelation in medieval Jewish thought in some respects offers a closer parallel to the intellectual history of Christian Europe than does the Moslem experience. The dichotomy between the world of science and the world of faith was not as evident among medieval Jews as among the Moslems. The great majority of rabbis were as narrowly fundamentalist and legalistic as were their Moslem counterparts. But the best minds in medieval Jewry, who were also in many instances leaders of their religious communities, tried to establish a compatibility between science and revelation and work out a rational theology. They exhibited the same concern with bridging reason and faith that exercised the intelligence and imagination of Latin thinkers, and Maimonides' thought foreshadowed Thomism.

At the beginning of the Christian era there were already large Jewish communities outside Palestine in the cities of the eastern Mediterranean and in Mesopotamia. The destruction of the Jewish community in Palestine, which followed unsuccessful rebellions against Roman rule in the second half of the first century A.D., augmented the size of these Jewish communities in the Diaspora, as the Jews called all the lands outside their homeland. The two most important communities were the so-called Babylonian, or Mesopotamian, and the large Jewish population in Alexandria. They represented sharply contrasting approaches to the question of the relationship between Judaism and secular culture. The Alexandrian Jews found their spokesman in the great philosopher Philo, who demonstrated the compatibility between Judaism and Platonism and advocated a kind of Jewish religion that resembles twentieth-century reform Judaism in every way. The Babylonian rabbis pursued a diametrically opposite tendency. They shut out secular culture from Jewish life and preserved Pharisaic Judaism by building a vast wall of religious and moral law around the Jewish believer. This traditional and legalistic approach to Judaism was expressed through the Talmud, an enormous commentary that drew upon the precepts of biblical Judaism to provide a legalistic system that completely cut off the Jews from intellectual intercourse with the gentile world. Every aspect of the daily life of the Jewish believer was regulated by the Talmud; the effect was to make the Jewish community a world within a world, and the only intercourse that the Talmudic Jew was allowed to have with his gentile neighbors was in indispensable economic relations. This conflict between diametrically opposite conceptions of Jewish life, first presented by Alexandrian and Talmudic Judaism, constituted the main internal theme of Jewish history until the latter part of the nineteenth century.

The Jews of western Europe came gradually under the influence of the Talmudic form because of the decline of the Alexandrian Jewish community under Christian persecution between the time of Philo and the liberating Moslem conquest in the seventh century. The Jews prospered in early-medieval Europe because of their position as merchants and bankers in an agrarian society. They played an important role in whatever international trade still existed between western Europe and the Mediterranean after the sixth century. They suffered occasional persecution, particularly in Visigothic Spain, but, by and large, the Germanic kings found their services as merchants and moneylenders too useful to allow fanatical bishops to foment pogroms against them. The Jews especially prospered under the Carolingian rulers, who appreciated the economic services they rendered to the underdeveloped society of the ninth century. It is by no means true that the Jews in early medieval Christian Europe made their living exclusively as merchants and moneylenders. In some places they were allowed to become landlords, and by the early eleventh century some of them held extensive estates in the wine-growing regions of southern France.

The dividing line in the history of the Jews in Christian Europe comes in the mid-eleventh century. The new militancy of Latin Christianity and the growth of popular piety contributed to a tremendous increase in Judophobia, which was dramatically expressed in the pogroms committed by the crusaders in the 1090s. Furthermore, changes in economic and political life resulted in the deterioration of the Jews' position. The proliferation of feudal institutions made it difficult for them to hold land because they could not enter into the necessary oaths involved in vassalage. The growth of the merchant guilds, which came to control international commerce, resulted in the exclusion of Jewish entrepreneurs from business by their gentile competitors. By the early twelfth century their main economic recourse was usury. The Jewish rabbis took the biblical injunction against usury to mean that it referred only to relations between members of the Jewish community and that usurious practices were permitted between Jew and gentile. Christian ecclesiastical leaders, in effect, arrived at the same conclusion. They interpreted the same biblical statements as prohibiting usurious practices among the brotherhood of Christians (although in reality this prohibition was violated with great frequency), and they legalized usurious relations between gentiles and Jews. It was not really a doctrinal question, but a social and economic one. The Jews had capital, and they had no other way of making a living except through lending money. The developing European commerce and industry needed their services, as did profligate nobles; bankrupt churchmen; and, above all, the expanding royal governments. The Jewish usurers charged enormously high interest rates—as much as 50 percent of the principal—not because they were a tribe of Shylocks, but because enormous risks were involved. It was difficult for them to collect on their loans, since their debtors had status in the law courts that they lacked. They were lucky if they could secure a return on half the money they lent. Non-Jewish moneylenders charged rates of interest that were just as high. Nevertheless, the Jews' activity as usurers increased.

Incessant and violent anti-Semitism stems from the age of the Gregorian reform and the first crusade. By the middle of the twelfth century the appearance of the blood libels—the myths which held that the Jews had a propensity for engaging in the ritual slaughter of Christian children—and other manifestations of popular hatred led to repeated pogroms. The only protection that the Jews had against massacre came from kings and princes, and it was dearly bought. By 1200 the Jews in western Europe were in effect the slaves of royal and ducal governments. They were allowed to engage in usurious practices and to preserve their religion and were protected from mass murder, but in return they were mercilessly taxed by royal treasuries that used them as parasites to draw money out of the outraged populace.

Even before the great deterioration of their economic and social position, the internal life of the Jewish communities in Christian Europe was gradually coming to be conducted according to the precepts of Talmudic Judaism, but it was not until the end of the eleventh century that Jewish thought was completely severed from the classical heritage and general secular culture. By this time the Jewish communities in Christian Europe had assumed a common pattern. The community was governed by a small elite of rabbinical and capitalist families who governed the mass of the Jewish population, which consisted of artisans and small tradesmen. Excluded from Christian society and culture, the elite sought to strengthen the corporate nature of the Jewish community by the systematic application of Talmudic law. The outstanding and representative thinker of this Jewish elite was Rashi (Rabbi Solomon ben Isaac, died 1105), who was head of the Jewish community in Troyes. Rashi worked entirely within the Talmudic tradition, adding another commentary on the Pentateuch to relate its moral and legal precepts to contemporary Jewish needs. Rashi's biblical commentary still has canonical status for orthodox Jews, and his marginal glosses are still commonly printed alongside the Hebrew text of the Bible. His commentary is distinguished by an empirical and commonsense attitude that contrasts strongly with the highly allegorical interpretation originated by Philo and extensively used by Christian scholars. For this reason some Christian scholars in the twelfth century found Rashi's work curious and illuminating. Rashi's mind was urbane and shrewd, and he was obviously aware of the problems of daily life that his coreligionists faced. He tried to show them how they could maintain the moral and legalistic precepts of the Bible in the midst of rapidly deteriorating circumstances. He thus performed a valuable service to the European ghettos of the next eight centuries. But as an intellectual document Rashi's commentary on the Bible is mediocre and insignificant. It is distinguished neither by mysticism and deep piety nor by any attempt to relate Judaism to science and philosophy. It demonstrates all too clearly the intellectual poverty of the Jews who lived in medieval Christian Europe.

The Jewish situation in Christian Europe steadily deteriorated during the twelfth and thirteenth centuries. The Fourth Lateran Council of the Church of 1215 prescribed their absolute ghettoization and decreed that all Jews should wear a yellow label as an emblem of their pariah status. With the emergence of Christian financial institutions, the services that

Jewish capitalists could render steadily declined. The orthodoxy promulgated by the rabbinical elite was increasingly fundamentalist and hostile to philosophical thought. Under these conditions it is not surprising that there was considerable apostasy to the Christian faith. Whereas in the twentieth century persecuted Jews could not escape from the trammels of anti-Semitism, in the Middle Ages they were offered their freedom through conversion. Before 1400, the number of Jews who escaped from bondage and persecution by conversion represented a minority for three reasons. First, the Jews' sense of providence and eschatology led them to believe that the age of persecutions heralded the coming of the Messiah and their imminent redemption. Second, the pluralistic, corporate nature of medieval society left converts who had forsaken their families and communities with a bleak prospect once they had left their social group and gone into the Christian world. Third, although the church welcomed Jewish converts and even rewarded them, the lay population was generally hostile to them, since they feared economic competition from Jewish converts.

In the 1290s the kings of both England and France expelled the Jews from their territories, partly to satisfy the demands of popular hatred, and partly to enrich their treasures by seizing Jewish property. Many of the Jews who were expelled moved eastward into Germany, where there was a substantial Jewish population in the fourteenth and fifteenth centuries. Here the Jews acquired the German language, which with the addition of Hebrew words and written in the Hebrew script, became the modern Yiddish. And here also they again suffered the ravages of pogroms. The pogroms in Germany precipitated a further eastward Jewish migration into Poland and Russia, where yet further agonies awaited them.

The Jews were undoubtedly the most literate ethnic or linguistic group in medieval society. Their separation from the general European culture after the eleventh century, partly in response to persecution and ghettoization, and partly the result of dictates of narrowly orthodox rabbis, represents an incalculable loss to the intellectual life of the medieval world and a substantial impediment to the progress of western civilization. The magnitude of this loss can be shown by comparing the meager Jewish contribution to culture in the rest of Europe with their achievements in Moslem Spain.

The position of the Jews in Moslem Spain until the end of the eleventh century was more favorable than in any other part of western Europe. The Arab princes virtually accepted them as equals, and Jews rose to high positions in government and prospered in commerce and in the learned professions, particularly medicine. During the tenth and eleventh centuries, a highly cultured, secularized Jewish court aristocracy flourished in the centers of Moslem rule. For the only time between Philo's Alexandria and the eighteenth century a large community of Jews was accepted into society and given the opportunity to participate in all aspects of life. As a consequence, the Jewish scholars of Spain became attracted to secular culture and made the only important contributions of any members of their faith to the general culture of the High Middle Ages. There was almost as great a variety in the Jewish approach to learning and knowledge as there was in the Christian world. Some of the Jewish thinkers held to a strict neoplatonism; the most outstanding spokesman of this school was Avicebrol (Solomon Ibn Gabirol, died 1058). Avicebrol's most important work, *The Fountain of Life*, was translated into Latin and widely read in Christian Europe. His neoplatonic thesis is purely philosophical, and there is nothing in it to identify its author as a Jewish scholar. In fact, the authorship of this treatise was not established until the nineteenth century; medieval Latin scholars assumed it was written by a Christian.

Another aspect of Spanish-Jewish culture was represented by the greatest Hebrew poet of the Middle Ages, Judah Halevi, who died around 1140. Halevi's earlier work is concerned with themes of secular love similar to those that inspired the Provençal troubadours and the Arabic poets of the period. A homosexual motif is common in these poems. The tone of Halevi's work becomes, however, steadily more anti-intellectual, didactic, and nationalistic in outlook. Living in a wealthy society in which many Jews had become completely assimilated into the mores and ideals of their environment, he became concerned with the preservation of the identity of the Jewish people. Halevi became an eloquent spokesman for the moral grandeur of traditional Judaism and the implacable enemy of a secularized Jewish culture. He was too much of a humanist, however, to adopt the legalistic outlook characteristic of Talmudic Judaism. Halevi's greatest book, *The Kuzari*, was inspired by a kind of romantic nationalism, a distinctive proto-Zionism that celebrated not only the Jewish law and religious tradition, but the moral superiority of the Jewish people. *The Kuzari* was the favorite reading of nineteenth- and twentieth-century Zionists, and for good reason: "If we bear our exile and degradation for God's sake, as is meet, we shall be the pride of the generation which will come with the Messiah, and accelerate the day of deliverance we hope for. . . . The gentiles merely serve to introduce and pave the way for the expected Messiah, who is the fruition, and they will all become His fruit. Then, if they acknowledge Him, they will become one tree. . . . Jerusalem can only be rebuilt when Israel yearns for it to such an extent that they embrace her stones and dust." Not only was Halevi's style powerful and attractive, but the ideals propounded in his later work offered that distinctive tone of intense romanticism and aggressive nationalism that inspired modern Zionism. It may be said, however, that Halevi came eight centuries too soon. His death on a pilgrimage to the Holy Land ended the attempt to establish not a Talmudic or a Philonic but a third new force in Jewish life.

Neither Avicebrol nor Halevi nor any other Spanish-Jewish writer gained so much attention from his contemporaries and so much posthumous fame as did Maimonides ("Rambam," Rabbi Moses ben Maimon, 1135–1204). Maimonides, the scion of a prominent rabbinical family in Spain, was the greatest Talmudic scholar of his day and, in the opinion of many, of all time. At the same time, he had early become interested in Greek philosophy and science and was concerned with examining the relationship between Aristotelianism and Judaism and with demonstrating that his faith was compatible with the highest precepts of reason. He set out, therefore, to bridge the gap between Talmudic knowledge and Aristotelianism. It was a difficult undertaking, and his enterprise gained the full attention of Jewish scholars. Maimonides was an extremely vigorous and independent man and nothing could dissuade him from carrying out his chosen task, not even personal misfortune. In the twelfth century Jews were suffering persecution at the hands of Moslem fanatics who had come to power in the Iberian principality. The religious militancy that had hurt the Jews so much in the Christian world was now beginning to attack them in Moslem countries as well. Maimonides and his family escaped to North Africa, where the learned rabbi formally made obeisance to Islam while secretly maintaining his Judaism. In later years he could see nothing wrong with his conduct, painful as it is for his modern biographers to contemplate. From North Africa his family emigrated to Egypt, where Maimonides became a prominent court physician. This position did not prevent him from continuing his work of commentary on the Bible or from trying to establish the relationship between Aristotelianism and Jewish revelation.

The result of Maimonides' work was a new, massive commentary on the Old Testament and, much more important for the general pattern of medieval thought, *The Guide for the Perplexed*. The latter work was intended to assist educated Jews who were faced with the contradictions between the teachings of science and revelation. Maimonides, like Thomas Aquinas after him, rejected the Averroist double-truth doctrine. He claimed that behind science and revelation there was one single God-given truth. It was a noble sentiment, but Maimonides had a hard time maintaining it; his book seems to have perplexed more Jews than it guided. To arrive at the conclusions he wanted, he had to water down Aristotle's doctrines and engage in the kind of allegorizing of the Bible that Philo had used to show the compatibility of Judaism and Platonism. Maimonides contended that God was indeed a prime mover, but that the Aristotelian conception of the deity dealt only with part of His nature; He is also the theistic God of Judaism who interferes continuously in human affairs. Maimonides tried desperately to show that the creation of the world could be supported by reason, but he had to admit that his proofs were only probable and not certain. This admission was enough to arouse bitter criticism from the leaders of traditional Talmudic Judaism. It was when he came to discuss immortality, however, that he got himself into the greatest difficulty. Ironically, Maimonides had played a leading role in making the immortality of the soul a cardinal principle of the Jewish faith. There is no such doctrine in the Jewish Bible. It had been imported into Judaism in the first century B.C. from Persia by the Pharisees and had always been cautiously regarded by Talmudic scholars. But after making immortality an article of faith, Maimonides became involved in the question of personal, as against general, immortality, which had bothered the Moslem Aristotelians. In the end he seemed to support the Averroist doctrine of immortality through the union with universal Intelligence. His specific teachings and the generally rationalist attitude he adopted in *The Guide for the Perplexed* roused the ire and fears of the leaders of rabbinic Judaism. He was denounced as a heretic, and while his compendium of Jewish law became authoritative, his philosophical works were prohibited and not studied by Jewish scholars until the nineteenth century. Some of his critics in Provence, where there was a great school of Talmudic Judaism, opposed him so bitterly that they asked the Inquisition to burn his philosophical treatises, a request with which the inquisitors gladly complied. In defense of the Provençal rabbis, it can be said that they feared that the dissemination of Maimonides' Aristotelian treatise would allow the inquisitors to blame the Jews for instigating Christian heresy.

Instead of the rational—philosophical and scientific—road to divine truth in supplement of biblical revelation and Talmudic exegesis, the rabbis in southern France in the early thirteenth century developed an elaborate mystical culture that is called the Kabbalah. The Kabbalah drew heavily upon ancient neoplatonism, as well as on the popular astrological speculations current in the Mediterranean world since Hellenistic times. Just as Maimonides thought that Jewish rationalism should be a special pursuit of the learned and was not for general dissemination, so the Kab-

balah was a quasi-secret faith and a complex body of theosophical literature open only to those who were already steeped in traditional rabbinical culture. By and large the hermeneutic character of Kabbalistic mysticism was preserved until around 1600, when it spilled over into a more
general movement of Jewish spiritual reformation.

In both Moslem and Jewish thought, the attempts of great thinkers to
deal with the relationship between revelation and the new Aristotelian
science thus ended in defeat and disaster at the beginning of the thirteenth century. Islam turned away from science because it was considered heretical by religious leaders who were able to obtain the assistance
of fanatical princes to destroy rational speculation. The general decline of
vigor in Islamic civilization undoubtedly also played a part in the termination of the great scientific and philosophical movement in the Arabic
world. Judaism at the same time turned its back on science and secular
thought, partly again because of the hostility of orthodox religious leaders
and partly because of the ghettoization of European Jewry which began
in the twelfth century.

In later Islamic culture and in Judaism only mysticism was allowed to
stand as an addition to the prime avenue to truth found in revelation.
After 1200 only the thinkers of Christian western Europe were afforded
the opportunity to establish a new intellectual system that would take
into account the challenge of Aristotelian science.

By the early thirteenth century most of Spain was back in Christian
hands, and the large, wealthy, and highly intellectual Jewish community
in the Iberian peninsula found itself transferred from Moslem rule to the
governance of Christian kings. The Spanish Jews did not regret this reversal of fortune because their situation in the previous century of Moslem
rule in Sefard (as they called Spain) was precarious. The fierce fundamentalist Berber tribes who came over from North Africa and took over the
Moslem states ended the easygoing treatment that the Moslem emirs had
accorded the Jews.

Until the late fifteenth century, Jewish experience under renewed
Christian rule in Spain was generally favorable. The Jews were not only
prominent in banking and commerce, but held high posts in the royal
administrations, usually on the fiscal side. But the great Jewish Sefardic
tradition in philosophy and science that had culminated in Maimonides
steadily subsided. Rather, it was to the development of Kabbalistic mysticism that Spanish Jewish learning devoted itself in the thirteenth and
fourteenth centuries.

At the same time, there was a growing trend toward the assimilation
of Jews into the Latin Christian culture and aristocratic society, with a

mass apostasy to the Christian faith in the late fourteenth and early fifteenth centuries, when a hostile environment for Spanish Jews developed that was even worse than they had experienced in the twelfth century, the last era of Moslem rule. Part of the hostility was popular and spontaneous, arising from the jealousy of the affluent condition of the Jewish community among all classes in the Christian society. Part of it came from a rigorous effort by the late medieval Spanish state to exercise tight, unified control over the society. By the time Judaism was proscribed in the Iberian peninsula—in Spain in 1492 and in Portugal in 1497—the great majority of Jewish families had already converted. Their conversion improved their legal and judicial status and enhanced their business and governmental opportunities, but aroused a new wave of hatred based on racism more than on religion. Increasingly historians believe that the claim by the Spanish Inquisition around 1500 that the Jewish New Christians (Marranos) were secretly practicing their old religion was mostly untrue. Most of the Sefardic Jews became normal Christians in the fifteenth century, and today, one third of the modern Spanish nobility is descended from Jewish converts. The flowering of Spanish literature, Biblical learning, and philosophy in the early sixteenth century owes much to these Jewish New Christians

CHAPTER SIXTEEN

Varieties of Religious Experience

I. Monks and Society

By the end of the eleventh century the church had achieved the imposition of its ideals on society. Christianity was taken seriously by the landed classes; by the bourgeois; and even, on a much lower level of intelligence, by the peasants, into whose villages the Christian faith was at last being actually carried by the spread of the parish system. The problems of religion were ever-present realities to the people of western Europe, and since they took God seriously, they tried in various ways to conform to Christian ideals. Their search for the satisfactory expression of their devotion profoundly affected many facets of medieval civilization. The architecture, pictorial art, Latin poetry, and liturgical music of the twelfth century were monuments to this profound piety. But the channeling of religious feeling into controllable forms became more and more a cause of grave concern to the leaders of the late eleventh- and twelfth-century church. The expression of the new piety had been a relatively simple matter before 1050. Devout men and women who felt a strong call to live a regular religious life and who were able to dissociate themselves from their families became members of the ever-growing Benedictine community. Those who were not able to become monks assisted the Cluniacs and other Benedictines with various kinds of services and gifts. But after the middle of the eleventh century the forms of religious experience become much more varied. The Cluniac form of monasticism did not satisfy the ascetic impulses of many people who were inspired by the new piety, and they sought new institutional expressions for their ascetic impulses. The result was the tremendous proliferation of new monastic orders in the late eleventh and twelfth centuries. Many devout people who did not participate in this new wave of ascetic withdrawal from the world, especially among the urban population of western Europe, found satisfaction in an intense religious individualism whose doctrines were disseminated by popular preachers. By the end of the twelfth century ecclesiastical leaders were faced with the unprecedented and dismaying tasks of controlling the proliferation of new religious orders, of directing the ascetic impulse into the channels that would make it useful to the church and the society, of finding new ways to satisfy the spiritual yearnings of devout laymen, and of overcoming the schisms fomented by popular heresy.

Northern Italy at the end of the tenth century was the scene of the first stirrings of a profound revolution in western monasticism in which new ascetic concerns and eremetic tendencies came to the forefront of religious life. The hermit had never been as important a figure in Latin monasticism as he had been in the Greek Christian world. Extreme ascetic practices had not been a quality of Benedictine life in the original Rule, and were even less so in its Carolingian and Cluniac forms. The emergence of an urban civilization in northern Italy in the late tenth century, with the attendant opportunities for wealth and comfort, provided Europe with the first temptation of luxurious living against which the ascetic hermit could revolt. About the year 1000 hermit-saints made their appearance in northern Italy; they withdrew from the world to escape spiritual degradation attendant upon life in princely courts and wealthy cities, but they periodically returned to preach a moral and spiritual revival to the urban populace. These strongly ascetic and eremetic impulses and the ubiquitous hermit-saints were to be a central current in north Italian religiosity over the next three centuries.

By the middle of the eleventh century the new monasticism had assumed the character of a widespread spiritual movement in the area between Rome and the Alps, and some of these ascetics had formed monastic communities that strongly contrasted with the prevailing Benedictine life. The order of Camaldoli founded a monastic community of hermits who lived in individual cells. The monastery of the order of Vallombrosa, near Florence, consciously revolted against Cluniac life and aimed at the strict observance of the pristine Rule of St. Benedict. To fulfill this aim, Vallombrosa included within its community uneducated lay brothers, as well as clerics who could perform liturgical offices. This separation of the order into clerical and lay brothers, giving uneducated men from the lower ranks of society the opportunity to assume the monastic habit, was a radical departure that was to be imitated by several of the new religious orders of the twelfth and thirteenth centuries.

North of the Alps a similar ascetic impulse appeared in the middle of the eleventh century, although it never went as far as Italian monasticism in accentuating the eremitic life. The first significant change appears to have been the founding in 1043 of "The House of God," not far from Lyons, by a former Cluniac monk who was dissatisfied with the religious life in western Europe's leading monastery. During the following half century, there were several such rejections of the Cluniac model in favor of a more rigorous religious life within monastic communities that were less involved with society and its attendant obligations and temptations than had been the case for several centuries. The spread of the internal colonization movement in Europe undoubtedly played a part in encouraging men of ascetic inclinations to establish little cells in frontier regions and to live entirely on their own resources. In the Rhineland and southern France the ominous figure of the itinerant saintly preacher also appeared before the end of the eleventh century, as is fully attested to by the history of the people's crusade of 1095.

The vicissitudes of the Gregorian reform movement strongly contributed to the growth and influence of these new tendencies in western monasticism. The Gregorians had drawn their initial inspiration and all their leadership from the new ascetic impulses and movements of the eleventh century. In the Gregorian reform, asceticism adopted its puritanical form; it tried to create a world that would be a suitable environment for the undisturbed pilgrimage to the City of God. The reform movement's failure showed clearly that asceticism could not hope to impose its ideals on society, to turn the world into a monastery with a universal abbot demanding obedience from all rulers. The Hildebrandine papacy had brought to the church not peace but a sword, not greater strength but deep divisions, confusions, and doubts. Hence, many of the best spirits of the first three decades of the twelfth century turned from the world and sought their peace with God in new communities and orders whose aimed was complete withdrawal from the world. Many of the older monasteries, even Cluny during the abbacy of Peter the Venerable in the second quarter of the twelfth century, were influenced to some extent by this new impetus toward withdrawal.

These critical changes within western monastic life were made possible by the decline of the regular clergy's usefulness to society. In the late eleventh and first half of the twelfth centuries the services that the Benedictine monks had rendered to European civilization for centuries were no longer required. The first, and ultimately the most decisive, development along these lines was the monks' loss of control over higher education. The monastic school had admirably served the compelling educational need of society before the eleventh century—the preservation of a basic literacy through the cultivation of the liberal arts and the biblical-patristic tradition. But the monastic school was too limited in its interests and too restricting in its organization to be a suitable haven for the new intellectual elite of the early twelfth century or to be the center for the tremendous achievements in speculative thought and in law during the following decades.

The monks' loss of leadership in education contributed to the decline of their importance in political life. The municipal schools of northern Italy and the cathedral schools of northern France, which provided homes for the new higher learning, began to turn out shrewd, well-educated, and frequently ruthless secular clerks and civil lawyers who displaced monastic scholars as the literate servants of the European monarchies during the twelfth century. Simultaneously, with the decline of the monks' importance in education and their displacement as royal ministers by a new kind of professional bureaucrat, the great religious houses were becoming less useful in another way to the more powerful monarchs. In the latter half of the eleventh century the Norman and German rulers' dependence on the military resources of the monasteries declined markedly as these able and aggressive rulers found new sources of recruitment for their armies. The imposition of new knight service on the Norman monasteries ended by 1050 and stopped in England by 1080. Not only was the knight service from lay fiefs now available in sufficient amount, but the Norman rulers, using the proceeds from feudal taxation and later from scutage, extensively employed mercenaries. Similarly, the Salian kings relied heavily on their own ministeriales for military forces. By the second quarter of the twelfth century the main social obligation of the Benedictine monk was to act as an intercessor for lay society with Christ, the Virgin, and the saints. This obligation sufficed in the twelfth century to continue to make the Benedictines popular with laymen, although they were bitterly criticized by the cathedral clergy, who coveted the black monks' centuries-old privileges and possessions. But even in the religious sphere the importance of the Benedictine community markedly declined. The cathedral and the parish church became more and more the centers for expressing the religious devotion of the populace in town and country, and the fervent admiration that the Benedictines had evoked in the early Middle Ages was accorded to the new religious orders in the twelfth century.

The increasing tendency after 1100 to dispense with the educational; political; military; and even, to some degree, religious services of the regular clergy to society gave impetus to the emergence of new religious orders that were devoted to ascetic withdrawal. Among the many obscure French monasteries founded in the late eleventh century was that of Cîteaux, whose leading spirit was a saintly Englishman named Stephen Harding. Cîteaux rapidly attracted outstanding young men of strongly ascetic leanings, among them Bernard, the greatest religious mind of the twelfth century. Cîteaux was soon able to establish daughter houses and to absorb independently founded communities. By the 1130s the Cistercians had become the major new monastic order, second in size only to the Benedictines. The Cistercian way of life was from the first consciously and stridently at variance with the prevailing Benedictine pattern, and this variance was signified by the wearing of a white, instead of black, habit. The Cistercians asked their secular patrons to grant them rights of settlement only in uninhabited regions because they were especially eager to avoid the privileges and obligations that had come to the great Benedictine houses from their possession of cultivated and settled domains. The white monks claimed that manorial estates worked by dependent serfs encouraged monastic avarice and luxury and precluded the apostolic poverty that was a necessary aspect of the true religious life. By the 1120s St. Bernard, the most eloquent spokesman for the new order, although by no means a typical Cistercian, was violently criticizing Cluny's wealth, comforts, and even artistic beauty, and similar open attacks were made on the Benedictines by other leaders of the white monks. The harassed Benedictines replied in an equally bitter vein. They contended that it would be unjust to expect the faithful to endure the privations that the Apostles had suffered in the midst of heathen hostility and persecution now that the church had vanquished its enemies. They pointed out that the Cistercians, in their ostentatious self-righteousness, had not escaped the snares of pride, and they claimed that among the many white monks who had a genuine contempt for the world there were also "many hypocrites and seducing pretenders."

Both the religious and social circumstances of the twelfth century favored the triumph of the Cistercians and the rapid expansion of their order. All over Europe devout and serious young men were concerned for the safety of their souls in a world that was steadily growing more urbanized and wealthy, and hence one that, in their eyes, was fraught with ever greater danger to the achievement of the spiritual life. The desire to assume the Cistercian habit was virtually a mass movement in the twelfth century, and after 1150 the order also established convents for women of similar calling. By the late thirteenth century there were no fewer than seven hundred Cistercian establishments in Europe. Landlords everywhere greeted the Cistercians with the greatest enthusiasm, and they were eager to allow the white monks to settle in previously uncultivated lands within their domains to open up these frontier areas for later settlement. All over Europe in the twelfth century the Cistercians acted as pioneers in the colonization movement. They were particularly active in this respect in eastern Germany, where they played an important part in developing the new method of working the land in large blocks instead of in strips. It was the twelfth-century Cistercian monasteries that developed sheep raising in the hitherto unproductive hilly wastelands of northern England. This innovation was immediately imitated by the secular landlords of Yorkshire, and it opened up this frontier region. In the thirteenth century the export of wool to the Flemish weaving cities was the staple of English foreign trade.

The enormous popularity that the Cistercians gained with all classes of twelfth-century society still left room for the creation of several smaller orders with similar aims and attitudes. The Carthusians were a small, highly selective, austere order that eventually won renown for two things: their order of Chartreuse never experienced the vicissitudes of other Catholic orders, so that the Carthusians were later able to claim that they never had needed to be reformed, and they played an important part in the invention of brandy, the first European hard liquor, during the thirteenth century. The order of Fontrevault, which had forty houses by 1200, was designed primarily for nuns, although it included an attached group of monks to perform religious service and to do hard physical labor. Fontrevault was sharply different from early medieval nunneries (which were high-toned aristocratic places) in that it accepted women from all classes and was a particular refuge for fallen women, destitute widows, and the like, of whom there were an inordinate number in medieval Europe. The emergence of these and other smaller orders alongside the Cistercians indicates the ubiquity of piety in twelfth-century Europe and the increasing tendency to organize religious movements into distinct corporate orders. The early medieval Benedictines had by no means been homogeneous in their outlook, but the varying groups among the black monks had not considered it necessary to constitute themselves into separate orders. Even the Cluniacs had not been, in a constitutional sense, a separate order. The legalistic spirit and organizing impulse of the twelfth century affected even monastic life and encouraged the proliferation of several distinct orders.

All the new ascetic orders were involved with romanticized and highly emotional forms of Christianity, particularly the Virgin Cult. The tendency of the new forms of monasticism was away from an intellectualized Christianity and toward an intensely personal kind of religious experience. This tendency further separated the new monastic orders from the achievements in philosophy and science that were being pursued by secular clerks in the universities. But it brought their religious attitudes into conformity with the main trends in lay piety and gained for the Cistercians and their imitators a still higher degree of social approval. Yet by 1200 it was becoming apparent that the Cistercians' withdrawal from the world had not altogether succeeded, and the extravagant praise that the white monks had received in the first half century of their existence was frequently replaced by sardonic criticism, such as the black monks had already experienced.

The Benedictines steadily lost social approval during the second half of the twelfth century, and it is easy to see why. Ensconced behind the walls of their comfortable establishments and living off their vast income, they no longer contributed anything to society. They were simply there, and they continued to attract new members, but by no means many of the finer spiritual minds of the age. Their importance in liturgical prayer was on the decline, and they no longer had any other social functions. Here and there a Benedictine scriptorium would still produce a valuable illuminated manuscript, or a black monk would, as in times past, devote himself to writing the history of his times. But by and large, by the late twelfth century, the Benedictines were no longer making any contributions to European civilization, and in view of the fact that they did not attract the more devout religious, it is not surprising that many black monks were beset by the terrible sin of *accidia*—simple boredom. We have a graphic and detailed account of one of the largest, oldest, and wealthiest English Benedictine abbeys, Bury St. Edmunds, in the *Chronicle* of Jocelyn of Brakelond, the abbot's secretary. Abbot Samson appears in Jocelyn's description as a hard-working and sincere administrator, but one who completely lacked a real interest in the contemplative life. Jocelyn remarked that the abbot "commended good officials more than good monks." Yet Jocelyn regards his abbot as an outstanding monastic leader!

The Cistercian order did not suffer as much from ossification as from corruption. The later history of the Cistercians is one of the most disillusioning themes in medieval history, and by 1200 contemporaries were well aware of it. The Cistercians seemed to have demonstrated the truth of the aphorism that nothing fails like success. They had taken the lead in the monastic withdrawal from the world, but the world followed, and they were unable to resist its temptations. The Cistercian monasteries had been established in uninhabited frontier regions. But by 1200 these areas were among the most flourishing in Europe. The Cistercians' laborious improvement of their lands had made them prominent landlords. They technically abided by their vow not to use the labor of serfs, but they got around its spirit by leasing their estates to secular lords for high rents. Many Cistercian houses built up large amounts of capital, and their abbots used it to become moneylenders to the local nobility and less fortunate churchmen. By the early thirteenth century the Cistercians had become notorious for their business acumen and their similarity to Jewish usurers. The order of the white monks became sharply divided into a more zealous group, who wanted to return to the original ideals of Stephen Harding, and the more moderate majority, who were prepared to accept their prosperity as the grace of God. The later history of the white monks was marked by bitter internal controversies; in the seventeenth century the radical ascetic wing broke away and formed the Trappist order. The failure of the Cistercians to provide a satisfactory institutional form of piety was partly the result of inadequate government. The order grew far too fast and was too modest in its admission requirements. The abbot of Cîteaux was supposed to supervise carefully the affairs of the daughter houses, but this became a practical impossibility because of the vast number of Cistercian monasteries. This inadequate administration and lax discipline allowed the intrusion into the ranks of the white monks of men who betrayed the ascetic ideals of the founders of the order. In addition, the Cistercians had the misfortune of choosing a way of life that perfectly satisfied the economic needs of the twelfth century. They had been organized as a religious order that engaged in complete withdrawal from society, but the Cistercian program was such that they opened up the frontier regions, and society followed. The Cistercians had neither the organization, the experience, nor the leaders to deal with the situation in which they had become landlords and capitalists in what had once been their areas of ascetic retreat. The white monks had no traditions of either learning or worldly sophistication; they were anti-intellectuals who lacked the Benedictines' familiarity with government and lordship. They were inevitably overwhelmed by their involvement with the world, and their withdrawal from society, which had been such a glorious chapter in twelfth-century religiosity, ended in a mixture of tragedy and paradox.

The failure of both puritanism in the eleventh century and monastic withdrawal in the twelfth century to achieve their aims encouraged the increasing prominence of a new kind of religious order that was a compromise between the two extreme variants of asceticism. This new institutionalized form of asceticism allowed its adherents both to undertake a regular religious life and the traditional vows of chastity, poverty, and obedience and to work in the world and to make a direct personal contribution to the welfare of society. Various experiments with this new kind of religious order provided the background for the emergence in the thirteenth century of the Franciscan and Dominican friars, which marked the most important stage in the development of the Catholic orders since the Rule of St. Benedict. These new orders eventually constituted the institutional means by which the ascetic impulse was used to meet the challenge of the intensive religiosity of the urban population of Europe.

The primary twelfth-century experiments with the new kind of religious order were undertaken by the regular canons and the military orders. The cathedral canons in the early Middle Ages had been notorious for their lack of devotion to their calling. The early twelfth-century development of the additional institution of the prebend, by which each cathedral official was given a fixed endowed income, only acerbated this situation. It made the cathedral canons financially independent of the bishop, and their offices particularly tempting for the younger sons of the nobility. The founding of the order of Prémontré in France in the 1120s was an attempt to remedy this situation. Its aim was to establish an order that was open to both men and women, who would take monastic vows but who would be free to work in the world, as did cathedral canons and other secular clergy—hence the designation of "regular canons." In some ways the Premonstratensian order was inspired by the same ideal that influenced the early Cistercians. Prémontré, the original establishment of the order, was built in a desolate place that had been "shown out" by the Virgin. But whereas the white monks fled from the world, the regular canons were active in their philanthrophic, charitable, and hospital work and as parish clergy in the growing urban areas. In the twelfth century another group of monks working in the world, the Austin (Augustinian) canons, achieved prominence, particularly in England.

The regular canons foreshadowed, both in their institutional form and in their aims, the great orders of friars founded in the thirteenth century. But they did not have the impact that the Dominicans and Franciscans exercised on thirteenth-century civilization. The value of religious orders working in society, particularly in the urban areas, was not sufficiently perceived by the papacy until the beginning of the thirteenth century. The regular canons could have had much the same impact on twelfth-century Europe as the friars were to have a little later, but there were simply not enough of them for this purpose. The twelfth-century popes were able and sincere administrators, but they were remarkably insensitive to the currents of lay piety, and they offered no organized program to counter the more revolutionary implications of urban religiosity. The regular canons were forced to work with little assistance from the leaders of the church, and it was not until the pontificate of Innocent III in the first decade of the thirteenth century that the significance of their new institutionalized form of asceticism was fully perceived at Rome.

It would have been fortunate for the church and for European civilization in several respects if some of the energy and wealth that were given to supporting the crusading military orders in the twelfth century had been accorded instead to the regular canons. The military orders were the consequence of an attempt to apply the spirit and institutions of corporate monasticism to crusading ends. They are the most extreme expression of the militant stream in twelfth-century Christianity. It seemed to all kinds of people in the twelfth century in Europe that it was not only appropriate but desirable that men who had taken vows dedicating themselves to divine service should accomplish this aim by killing infidels. The military orders were particularly attractive to those members of the nobility who wanted to assume the monastic life but who wanted to continue to make use of their military skills. There had always been a psychological affinity between monastic and military discipline, and the regular clergy were commonly referred to as the soldiers of Christ. In the military orders this term took on a more than metaphorical significance.

The earliest crusading orders were initially founded as welfare agencies, to provide secondary services for crusaders and pilgrims, but they rapidly formed themselves into effective and powerful paramilitary organizations. The Knights Templars (the Poor Brothers of the Temple of Jerusalem) originated around 1120 in the efforts of a few French knights to protect pilgrims on the way to the Holy Land. St. Bernard formed these knights into a corporate religious order dedicated to fighting in the Holy Land. There was a threefold division within the ranks of the Templars: the aristocratic soldiers, the clergy, and the lay brothers of lower-class background who assisted the highborn knights as squires and grooms. The Knights Hospitalers (Order of St. John of Jerusalem) were the great rivals of the Templars. The original aim of the Hospitalers was to serve as the medical corps of the crusaders, but they rapidly became a military order and competed with the Templars for prestige and influence in the affairs of the Latin Kingdom of Jerusalem. The internecine feuds of the monastic soldiers contributed to the weakness of the crusading state in Palestine.

The later history of the Templars exhibits that same yielding to the temptations of Mammon that corrupted the Cistercian order. In the midst of the twelfth-century economic expansion, it was difficult for any effective corporate group *not* to make money, and if the corporation was also dedicated to divine service, it received endowments from all sides. As a result of the great success of their fund-raising drives, the Templars became involved with the techniques of the accumulation and transfer of capital, and by the thirteenth century they were the greatest bankers in Europe, with the papacy and the French kings as their clients. The thirteenth-century Templars did not kill many Moslems, but they were expert at increasing their capital, and they set up the headquarters of their bank in Paris. The popular attitude toward the Templars changed from fervent admiration to cynicism and jealousy, but the leaders of the order did not seem to mind. They insisted that their banking activities were ultimately in the service of God and pursued them with ascetic dedication. The history of the Templars constitutes one documented case of religion playing a part in the rise of capitalism.

If, in the case of the Templars, institutionalized asceticism ended in the creation of a bank, the Teutonic Knights, founded in 1190, provided what the nineteenth-century German nationalist historian Heinrich Treitschke called the origins of Prussianism. At the time of the third crusade some German lords formed a military order to fight in the Holy Land. But within thirty years they had transferred their area of operations from the Middle East to Germany's eastern frontier, and they came to play a leading part in the *Drang nach Osten,* the eastward movement into the Slavic lands that had begun a century before. The original spiritual ideals of the order were subordinated to political ambitions. The Teutonic Knights indiscriminately attacked Christians and heathens in eastern Europe. They were fundamentally a state in the guise of a religious order. But their monastic form imbued them with corporate efficiency and fanatical zeal and greatly contributed to their long string of victories. They conquered Prussia from the Slavs and ruled it until the late fifteenth century. They pushed into Lithuania, Estonia, and Russia, where their advance was finally stopped shortly after 1400. In a sense the Teutonic Knights constituted one of the most successful variants of the institutionalized piety of the twelfth century. They remained dedicated to their vows and firm in their organization and were great soldiers and administrators for nearly three centuries after their founding.

By the late twelfth century, as a result of the work of the regular canons and the military orders, the idea of monks working in the world had become a familiar and popular one. In the last decades of the century there was, in fact, a proliferation of obscure orders based on the principle of serving society while pursuing the ascetic life. The Order of Bridgebuilders, for instance, was organized in France in 1189 to contribute to human welfare by improving communications. The Roman curia was disturbed by the dispersion of the ascetic impulse into so many distinct orders, and at the Fourth Lateran Council of 1215 it decreed that the licensing of new orders by the papacy should cease. But almost immediately the church found it necessary to constitute the new orders of friars to meet the challenges of urban piety and popular heresy. The original contribution of twelfth-century institutionalized asceticism was its compromise between the puritan and monastic extremes and its direction of spirituality toward service to Christian society. Out of this background emerged the religious orders that were to be indispensable in the church's struggle to maintain its leadership in European civilization.

II. The Dimensions of Popular Heresy

Anticlericalism and antisacerdotalism were the two modes of thought that threatened to undermine the traditional position of the church in medieval society in the second half of the twelfth century and forced the papacy, under Innocent III and his successors in the early decades of the thirteenth century, to undertake a desperate struggle for the reaffirmation of ecclesiastical leadership. Anticlericalism prepared the ground for the rise of antisacerdotalism, but they are distinct attitudes and doctrines. Anticlericalism is criticism of the clergy for not fulfilling the duties of their office and, as such, is not an error in the faith. Antisacerdotalism denies to the clergy the power of their office and claims that the sacraments that they administer have no efficacy. This view, of course, is the Donatist heresy and contradicts the fundamentals of Catholicism.

The common tendency of medieval thinkers to vulgarize St. Augustine's conception of the City of God and to identify the heavenly community with the church provided an intellectual basis for the growth of antisacerdotalism. For if the church is the City of God, then assuredly its leaders are the most saintly men and the ministry of Christ ought to be founded on personal holiness, rather than on the impersonal, official authority of the priesthood.

Anticlericalism can, and in the twelfth century did, contribute to the growth of antisacerdotal movements. Constant and protracted criticisms of the personal qualities of the church hierarchy and the insistence upon a discrepancy between their ideals and their practices eventually raised doubts in the minds of some devout people whether the priests were the ministers of God in the first place. But it must be emphasized that criticism of the clergy as lazy and corrupt in and of itself does not constitute heresy. In fact, such criticism may be the necessary precondition for reforming and revitalizing the church. Thus it is possible to have two men speaking unfavorably about the clergy, but whose attitudes are fundamentally different. One wants the clergy to exercise the full powers of its office in accordance with the highest ideals of the church, while the other holds that the church hierarchy has no religious authority. The former represents an act of criticism, the latter of denial. The second half of the twelfth century was marked by a thunderous chorus of attacks on the clergy, and the papacy was faced with the difficult task of evaluating the merit of these criticisms and distinguishing between those who wanted a better Catholic hierarchy and those who wanted to destroy the Catholic church and substitute new kinds of sectarian religious communities.

With each passing decade of the twelfth century, criticism from all quarters of the conduct of the clergy became more intense. Some of the severest criticism came from within the church itself. Monks attacked the cathedral clergy as corrupt and materialistic, the canons claimed that the monks were useless and selfish, and competing religious orders made derogatory remarks about each other. St. Bernard and his disciples denounced the soft living of ecclesiastical princes in the severest terms, and Pope Innocent III castigated the higher clergy of southern France as "dumb dogs who can no longer bark." In the later decades of the century it was fashionable for poets, university students, and courtly writers to produce clever satires depicting the clergy as greedy and corrupt. The circle of any king who was in trouble with Rome, such as the German Hohenstaufens, attributed the grossest motives to the pope and cardinals. The German minnesinger Walther von der Vogelweide supported his Hohenstaufen patron by denouncing the papacy as a ravenous wolf, and he did not refrain from dragging up old legends that Sylvester II had been a sorcerer. Since the twelfth century almost everyone who had lost a case in the Roman court was inclined to attribute this loss to the cardinals' love of gold; the secretary of the angelic St. Anselm of Canterbury had made such a claim as early as 1095. Papal legates were fair game for all satirists and critics north of the Alps, since they were frequently alien Italians who interfered in the affairs of the territorial churches of northern Europe. The Italian legates were deemed to be devious, mendacious, and unprincipled; one English writer, for good measure, asserted that a cardinal legate had a penchant for consorting with prostitutes. The picture of the clergy as ignorant, stupid, and lecherous given in Boccaccio's fourteenth-century stories can already be found in the bourgeois literature of the thirteenth century, which, in turn, reflects the impressions that many of the educated townsmen had of their bishops and priests before 1200.

From all this literary evidence it is possible to build up the blackest image of the late twelfth-century clergy, as was done in the 1920s in the work of the fiercely anti-Catholic historian G. G. Coulton, who indicted the medieval clergy for a sordid failure to live up to its profession. There is certainly plausible evidence for the truth of such an indictment, and the records of bishops' inspections of their dioceses, which were required after 1215, provide documentation for almost every conceivable kind of wrong-doing by members of both the regular and secular clergy. On the other side of the case, however, is the fact of the magnificent achievements and vitality of the twelfth-century church and the hundreds of churchmen all over Europe, from bishop and abbot to the humblest monk and parish priest, whom we know to have been capable and zealous and even self-sacrificing in the fulfillment of their duties. In the assessment of the cause of the sharp rise in anticlericalism in the late twelfth century, the evidence points much more strongly to social and intellectual change than to a decline in the morality and quality of the clergy as the key to the problem.

In 1200 there were more dedicated members of the ecclesiastical hierarchy than ever before, but the standards the laity expected of their clergy became ever higher from the middle of the eleventh century, and the church simply did not have sufficient personnel to meet these demands. Particularly in urban areas, where there was an unprecedented degree of literacy and an intense piety among laymen, the church was pressed to provide clergy of the greatest learning and dedication, and a limited number of such men were available.

The twelfth-century merchant or craftsman necessarily had a strong sense of calling. He knew that if he did not fulfill the possibilities of the vocation he had chosen, he would be condemned to miserable poverty. This knowledge made him jealous of other groups in society who did not have to rely entirely on their own efforts—not only nobles, but the churchmen. The medieval bourgeois was obstreperous and intolerant, and he tended to judge other people by the criteria of his own way of life. He thought that every clergyman should work for a living and that the cleric should not enjoy the powers and privileges of ecclesiastical office unless he demonstrated by his personal life that he was truly a minister of Christ. The burgher should be a businessman and the priest a saint; everyone should fulfill the obligations of his calling in life. But when the burgher applied this iron standard of rationality to the world around him, he discovered that many clergymen were not doing a good job and were perhaps less worthy of their offices than the burgher himself would be. This discovery made him angry and disillusioned with the priesthood.

The fault of the twelfth-century papacy was not that it permitted monstrous scandals with impunity, but that it did not adjust with sufficient rapidity and energy to the consequences of far-reaching social change. The church at the end of the twelfth-century was still primarily organized for a rural society, and its attempts to satisfy the religious needs of the urbanized areas of Europe were halfhearted at best and perfunctory at worst. This situation left the bourgeois, particularly in the numerous and wealthy cities of northern Italy and southern France, to work out their own resolution of their religious problems. They wanted a faith that could provide an intense personal experience and involve them emotionally with Christ, the Virgin, and the saints. They had contributed to the building of magnificent municipal cathedrals all over Europe because they wanted a place to worship where they could feel a close association with the divine spirit. But a great many of the priests who worked in urban areas could not or would not pursue this intensely personal approach to the Christian faith. The old kind of cathedral cleric or parish priest believed that his function as a Christian minister should be confined to administering the sacraments, hearing confession, and performing the traditional liturgical offices. He was not prepared to give long and inspiring sermons, which were both the staple of the bourgeois's religious diet and their chief source of diversion amid the ruthless, overregulated, and cramped life of the medieval cities.

The social and religious milieu of northern Italy, the Rhineland, and southern France had already in the eleventh century produced itinerant preachers of saintly reputation who offered to the bourgeois the sermons and other accoutrements of personal religious experience they could not find in ordinary church services. After 1150 this kind of popular spiritual leader began to exercise a greater and greater influence and to command formidable followings. The church was slow to perceive the dangers inherent in such an unfamiliar situation. The new preachers appeared to be merely perpetuating and disseminating the new piety as expressed by Damiani and Bernard. But with each passing decade it became more evident that many of these popular religious leaders were going beyond it. They were advocating antisacerdotal and antisacramental doctrines that the fourth-century church had condemned as the Donatist heresy and that, although revived momentarily by Cardinal Humbert in 1059, had been again anathematized by the church after 1080.

Bored and disappointed by their dull clergy, many of the townsmen had come to doubt the value and efficacy of the sacraments and offices of the church. They were eager to listen to the itinerant saints who claimed that holiness of life and personal devotion to God determined the members and leaders of the fellowship of Christ. This doctrine pleased the zealous burghers, many of whom felt superior in morality and intellect to their priests, while it gave the itinerant preachers the position of leadership over the new heretical communities. The Latin church had, of course, encountered heretical doctrines before in isolated instances, but since the Donatist heresy of the fourth century, it had not been troubled by any such doctrine that had a large popular following and that was associated with mass social and intellectual discontent. Before the end of the twelfth century the papacy did not discover how to deal with this grave threat to the unity of the church and the authority of the priest-hood.

By the nature of its doctrine, antisacerdotalism implied a sectarian rather than an ecumenical religion. A number of sects were devoted to their saintly leaders, but there was little or no cooperation among them. The only one of the late twelfth-century antisacerdotal sects that took on the character of more than an isolated local movement was the Waldensians, who took their name from Peter Waldo, a saintly merchant of Lyons in southeastern France. Lyons and its environs had for a long time been distinguished by extremely ascetic religious leaders. Near Lyons in the 1040s was established the first anti-Cluniac monastery to be founded north of the Alps. The archbishop of Lyons in the 1080s and the 1090s was the most devoted disciple that Gregory VII had in northern Europe. Waldo and his disciples called themselves the Poor Men of Lyons. They preached not only antisacerdotal, antisacramental, and Donatist doctrines, but the corollary theory of the apostolic poverty of the church that influenced the policy of the radical Gregorian pope, Paschal II, in the second decade of the twelfth century. The church, as seen by the Waldensians, was not the prevailing Catholic institution, but the purely spiritual fellowship of saintly men and women who had experienced divine love and grace.

The Waldensian sect spread to the cities of northern Italy, where it had the greater part of its adherents by the later twelfth century. The followers of Peter Waldo were proto-Protestants, who, for the first time, clearly presented the doctrines to which the more radical Protestant sects of the sixteenth and seventeenth centuries subscribed. And their doctrines contain the same combination of freedom and authoritarianism, of personal religious experience and the rule of the saints, that distinguished the sixteenth-century Anabaptists and the seventeenth-century English Puritan sects who were their ultimate disciples. Although later driven from the cities of northern Italy by the church, they survived in small numbers in Alpine valleys until the seventeenth century; they were the "slaughtered saints" of whom John Milton speaks in his famous sonnet.

The apocalyptic and eschatological tone of the antisacerdotal move-

ments was given emphasis and greater content by the prolific speculations at the end of the twelfth century of a southern Italian abbot,
Joachim of Flora, whose treatises received remarkably wide and rapid circulation. Following suggestions already made by St. Bernard, Joachim
claimed that the world had entered the age of Antichrist, which immediately preceded the Second Coming and the Last Judgment. But whereas
Bernard had satisfied himself with denouncing archbishops and bishops
as the captives of the devil, Joachim identified the papacy itself with
Antichrist. This revolutionary doctrine, which turned hierocratic theory on
its head, proved to be enormously popular with all heretical movements
up to and including the Protestant leaders of the sixteenth century. It
made simpler the heretics' denunciation of the church and allowed them
to indulge in an unqualified hatred of the Catholic priesthood. Subscribers to this doctrine could dismiss even the most zealous and moral
acts of the papacy as merely the treacherous wiles of Antichrist. Their
eschatological convictions gave the adherents of Joachimism the strength
to withstand any counterattack by the church. They alone were the true
disciples of the Lord who would gain their triumph at His imminent coming. Men who held convictions such as these were not liable to be moved
by appeals to tradition, reason, or common sense.

The dualism implicit in Joachim's speculations comes out much
stronger and in an absolute form in the heretical movement that won an
enormous number of adherents in southern France: the religion of the
Cathari (Pure Ones, Saints), or the Albigensian religion (after the town of
Albi in Toulouse, where the heretics were particularly strong), or
medieval Manicheanism, as it is sometimes called. At the end of the
twelfth century the wealthy bourgeois and many of the nobility of
Toulouse and Provence, and perhaps even the count of Toulouse and his
family, were members of an heretical church whose doctrines closely
resembled, and perhaps were the perpetuation of, that fourth-century
Manicheanism to which St. Augustine had for a time subscribed and then,
after he became a Christian, denounced in the severest terms. Many of
the people of southern France who were not actually members of the
Albigensian church seem nevertheless to have admired its saintly leaders;
the count of Toulouse most likely fell into this category. Considering the
wealth of this part of Europe and the vitality of its culture, its increasing
defection from the Catholic church threatened a schism in the Christian
world of the greatest significance. In the eyes of the papacy and other
orthodox believers everywhere in 1200, the Albigensian domination of
southern France constituted a cancer in the body of European civilization
that had to be rooted out at all costs.

The origins of the Cathari movement are not known for certain. In the late eleventh century the movement made a dim appearance in the towns of both northern Italy and southern France. It mostly disappeared in the former but slowly gained adherents in the latter, and after 1150 it came out in the open and brazenly and successfully challenged the church. The clergy of southern France were notoriously incompetent and corrupt; this situation provided fertile ground for the growth of popular heresy and accounts for the initially perfunctory and inadequate efforts made to stop the steady expansion of the Albigensian church. The twelfth-century papacy may be regarded as ignoring too long the Albigensian threat and of being too conservative and timid in its remedy, which was simply to preach against the Cathari. A heretical movement that struck such deep roots in society was not likely to be destroyed by even the most eloquent homiletics and apologetics. Yet the appearance of a popular schismatic church on such a great scale was a new thing in Latin Christianity. The well-meaning lawyers who dominated papal government did not realize until after 1200 that novel and radical methods would be needed to destroy the Albigensian heresy.

Some historians see a direct line of transference of ideas stretching from the twelfth-century Cathari to the fourth-century Manichees. This view holds that although Manichean doctrines disappeared in the Latin world, they invaded the Byzantine empire from their place of origin in Persia and were carried into Bulgaria in the tenth and eleventh centuries. There was indeed a Manichean sect called the Bogomils in the Balkans, and it has been suggested that its doctrines were spread to western Europe along trade routes in the late eleventh and twelfth centuries. It was possible, however, to derive the dualist theology, which is the heart of Manicheanism, from the neoplatonism that dominated early-medieval philosophy and theology. The Manichees believed that there are two gods, the god of good and the god of evil, of light and of darkness, who struggle for victory in the world. Man is a mixture of good spirit and evil matter. The Cathari believed they were the ascetic "perfects" who achieved a pure spirituality, and those who did not live the fully ascetic life might nevertheless assure themselves of salvation by recognizing their leadership. These "auditors" of the true faith received a sacrament on their deathbed that wiped away their previous sin and allowed the reunion of their souls with the Divine Spirit. Assuming that the possibility of receiving the grace of God through the ministry of the Catholic priesthood is denied, the Christian would have to conclude that catharsis is the only approach to God and would have to posit the mystic's sharp antithesis of spirit and matter. The Albigensian theology, then, seems to have been the result of the combination of antisacerdotalism with neoplaton-ism, and even if some pristine Manichean ideas did filter into Europe from the Balkans or Byzantium, it was the strength of these two doctrines in twelfth-century Europe that prepared the ground for the eastern heresy and provided the intellectual stimulation for its growth.

The thirteenth-century persecutors of the Albigensian sect attributed to them several other beliefs aside from this basic dualist theology. It was claimed that they rejected the Incarnation of Christ because it involved the imprisonment of the deity in evil matter. And it was asserted that the Catharist conviction that matter was evil led to bizarre ideas and social mores. The Albigensians were said to be opposed to marriage, believing that marriage perpetuated the monstrosity of the human race in which the divine spirit was encased in the gross and evil body. They were said, however, to permit any kind of sexual promiscuity, presumably as long as procreation was avoided. They advocated as virtuous both racial and individual suicide. They were also accused of exposing babies (a not-uncommon postnatal abortion practice in overpopulated European soci-ety), of allowing their "perfect" saints to starve themselves to death, and of believing that whatever the auditors (laity of the Albigensian church) did before they received the final purifying sacrament was of no account. Consequently it was claimed that the Albigensian laity engaged in the most profligate and dissolute living, for no morality is necessary if the human body is innately evil and a sacrament suffices to free the spirit.

Much of this orthodox polemic sounds like old libels dredged up against any radical and separatist religion in premodern society. Charges of sexual promiscuity covered up by hypocrisy were leveled against Christians in the pagan Roman Empire. From what is known about the mass of Catharist laity, they were a quiet, devout, and hard-working group. While noble and bourgeois families provided leadership, the majority of Cathars appear to have been poor peasants. Family bonds were strong in Catharism, and the indoctrination of children into the faith was pursued with great care. If the center of Catholicism in southern France, says Malcom Lambert, was the church, the center of Catharism was the household. The determinism at the center of Catharist doctrine—an evil god creates evil—appealed to illiterate peasants, for whom the canonical Augustinian explanation of evil as the falling away from God was too difficult.

The Catharists' central figure of the ascetic leader was common to all the popular heresies. Of course saints were the focus of popular belief in the Catholic church. The Catharist saints impressed because they were ready at hand, eager to communicate and help, always on call as it were.

In peasant villages and the less salubrious streets of medieval cities such personal contact was important, as it still is today with respect to the impact of religious leaders.

Arno Borst, another prominent historian of Catharism, points to the peaceful dialogue between Catharists and Catholics in the closing decades of the twelfth century and regrets, as any liberal scholar would, the fury and the violence that was to follow after the turn of the century. Yet whatever the Catharists taught and no matter how pious and benign they were, they formed a counterchurch: They had withdrawn their presence and support from the Latin church. When Latin bishops and priests observed the thinning attendance of their churches and the decline of revenue from their flocks, whatever the theological niceties or ethical subtleties, they were afraid.

Fear leads to anxiety and, in certain contexts, to conflict and violence. That is the tragedy of what happened among the religious communities in southern France between 1180 and 1220. The story of Catharism is both an inspiring and heartbreaking one. Europe was not ready to tolerate separatist communities that were an apparent threat to the established church. Many centuries would pass before such toleration was practiced.

There is another side to the story—the Catharist connection with feminism and the Jews that inflamed bad feeling and fanaticism on the Catholic side. The more closely the Catharist movement is studied, and it has been intensely examined in recent decades, the more it appears, either for reasons of continuity or because of fortuitous coincidence, to resemble the doctrine of a powerful antiorthodox church group in the eastern Mediterranean in the late first and second centuries A.D. that has come to be referred to as Gnosticism (from its claims to *Gnosis,* true knowledge). The Gnostic church was heavily infected by dualistic ideas adapted from Persian Manicheanism. As Elaine Pagels stressed, Gnosticism aroused the ire of the Catholic bishops by another characteristic—its proclivity to give women positions of leadership in its community at a time when the mainline church was becoming ever more male dominated and prone to marginalizing women's capacity to lead or even to speak in ecclesiastical assemblies. Southern French Catharism of the early thirteenth century appeared to be not only heretically dualistic in its theology but more inclined than the Roman church to find a place of prominence or at least easy participation for women, and the latter quality probably made it attractive to nobility of Languedoc, who were more equitable in their attitude toward women (of their own class) than were the nobility of the north.

We do not know whether Gnosticism was perpetuated all through the early Middle Ages in Europe as an underground movement in Latin Christianity. In southern France it is more likely that the Christians picked up Gnostic ideas from the wealthy Jewish community. The great authority on the history of medieval Jewish mysticism, Gershom Scholem, identified a significant Gnostic strain in the Kabbalah, the Jewish mystical culture that emerged in Provence in the early thirteenth century. Both the Catharists and the Kabbalists believed in metempsychosis (the transmigration of souls). Therefore from one perspective, the rise of Catharism is a consequence of cultural transference from the Jewish to the Christian world in southern France. This Judaizing background of Catharism helps to explain the fury with which the papacy struggled against it and the increased tempo of the condemnation of the Jews by Rome in the early thirteenth century.

Catharism came to arouse more fear and hate in the papacy and the church hierarchy than these authorities themselves could fully articulate and explain. It revived (or continued in a highly visible form) the specter of ancient Gnosticism, early Christianity's gravest threat and most formidable enemy. And the Catharists gave off intimations of the feminizing and Judaizing of the traditional Catholic faith that the hierarchy eventually came to realize that they had to encounter with every conceivable means at their disposal. It was a struggle for the soul of Europe.

CHAPTER SEVENTEEN

The Entrenchment of Secular Leadership

I. Power and Charisma

The investiture controversy had shattered the early-medieval equilibrium and ended the interpenetration of ecclesia and mundus. Medieval kingship, which had been largely the creation of ecclesiastical ideals and personnel, was forced to develop new institutions and sanctions. The result, during the late eleventh and early twelfth centuries, was the first instance of a secular bureaucratic state whose essential components appeared in the Anglo-Norman monarchy. The intellectual expansion of Europe in the twelfth century, which was largely the work of churchmen, was in some ways more beneficial to the growth of secular power than to ecclesiastical leadership. The improvements in education, law, and even the increase in piety all came to serve the aims of monarchy. The rise of the universities produced a new kind of administrative personnel for royal government. The great increase in legal knowledge gave kings a way of implementing their control over society. It also gave them a juristic ideology to replace the early-medieval tradition of theocratic kingship, which had been divested of its effectiveness by the attacks of the Gregorian reformers. The explosive effects of the new piety also contributed to the entrenchment of secular power. The widespread criticism of the clergy made it easier for royal government to assert its own leadership in society. The many problems arising from the new piety also distracted the hierarchy from paying close attention to what was happening in political life and gave kings greater freedom to pursue their own interests without ecclesiastical interference.

The twelfth-century Roman curia had only one firm policy with regard to the kings of western Europe: The northern rulers were not to threaten the independence of the papacy by invading Italy. Otherwise the popes took a flexible and pragmatic attitude toward the European kings, trying to win from them limited concessions, such as recognition of the papal curia as the central appellate court of the church. The calm in church-state relations allowed the monarchy to make use of the new learning to improve its administrative techniques, bureaucratic personnel, and ideology and to entrench its leadership in society. Especially in England and Capetian France, by 1200 all classes and groups were becoming accustomed to the regular exercise of royal power in law and taxation. The central importance of the royal government in the lives of nobles, bourgeois, and the higher clergy was becoming routinized. Given a dramatic and strong personality on the throne, the engine of royal power would become an extremely formidable one that would be difficult for the papacy to control. Two such charismatic royal figures appeared in the second half of the twelfth century, namely, Henry II of England and Frederick Barbarossa of Germany. By the last decade of the century the advance of royal power was a matter of deep concern to the Roman curia. On all sides the success of monarchy was being demonstrated, and the papacy was now faced with the problem of learning to deal with the kings who, in one way or another, had established vast reserves of wealth and military strength and in some cases inspired an emotional loyalty in their subjects.

The strength of the medieval state was determined by three essentials: the personal qualities of the ruler; the ideology of kingship; and the effectiveness of the administrative, legal, and financial institutions. In the earliest stage of medieval monarchy the king's power had depended almost exclusively on his own personality. If he was a formidable warrior, he commanded loyalty, at least within his immediate circle, and if he did not exhibit the characteristics that the warrior class admired, royal property and power were usurped with impunity by local lords, and the king was neglected and insulted. From the eighth until the end of the eleventh century the church buttressed the inadequate foundations of monarchy with moral and religious sanctions, and the kings of the period had come to depend heavily on ideology to sustain the loyalty of lay and ecclesiastical lords, with various degrees of success. They also made painful experiments in the development of effective administrative institutions, and after the Gregorian papacy had delivered a mortal blow to the old doctrine of sacred kingship, the institutional basis of royal power was accentuated, while the kings also sought to find new moral and theoretical sanctions for their power. The twelfth-century monarchies made use of administrative institutions and ideology in varying degrees, but the personal qualities of the king could still contribute strongly to the growth of royal power. Where a self-perpetuating and self-conscious bureaucracy existed, governments could now sometimes get by with little or no decrease in authority for a considerable period, even if the throne's occupant did not make an impressive and attractive figure. But the effectiveness of even the most skilled bureaucracy would be weakened by the long reign of a king who was inept in war and government. The personality of the king still counted for much in the affairs of states. And if the king was a charismatic figure, great in the arts of war and peace, an admired leader in the eyes of the landed classes, then royal power would enjoy an immediate growth. A king of charismatic qualities, even without the assistance of centralized administrative traditions, could make a profound impression upon society.

For four decades after 1150 political life was dominated by two charismatic figures, Henry II of England and Frederick Barbarossa of Germany. Both kings exhibited a rare combination of qualities that made them appear almost superhuman figures to contemporaries: longevity, boundless ambition, extraordinary organizing skill, and greatness on the battlefield. They both came to the throne in the prime of manhood; they were handsome and proficient in courtly gestures, which some members of the nobility now found attractive, without being in any way softened by courtly ideals. They were both benefited at critical points in their careers by outstanding strokes of good luck. Henry and Frederick were men of active, not scholarly, disposition. But they keenly appreciated the potential uses of the new learning, especially in the field of law, to royal government. They were adept at selecting educated men who served them with intense loyalty. Henry and Frederick were formally devout, but they were not greatly moved by the piety of the twelfth century. They were ruthless in pursuit of their aims, and they were not charitable toward their enemies. They believed mostly in themselves and never questioned the identity of the amelioration of society with the advancement of their own power.

When Henry II (1154–1189), the first of the Angevin line, became king of England, he was already duke of Normandy, count of Anjou, and the most powerful prince in northern France. The condition of England in 1154 was favorable for the achievement of Henry's ambitions. The feudal lords had just experienced two decades of exhausting civil war, and they wanted the restoration of the peace and good government of the Anglo-Norman kings. This Henry gave them. He completed the work of his grandfather, Henry I, making the shire court into a royal court presided over by an itinerant justice who carried the king's commission. He effectively destroyed the jurisdiction of the private feudal courts and brought the civil cases involving land disputes, which had previously been tried in the feudal courts, before his own justices. He greatly expanded the use of the sworn inquest, or jury, in civil suits, and he introduced the indicting grand jury in criminal cases. The reign of Henry II constitutes the most important era in the creation of the institutions of the common law. It was therefore fashionable among Victorian writers to hail Henry II as the founder of liberal English institutions and constitutional monarchy. Nothing could have been further from his mind. His aims were no different from those of contemporary rulers, such as Frederick Barbarossa of Germany and Philip Augustus of France: He wanted as much power for himself as possible. Henry and his judges did not make much use of Roman law, and he did not formulate a theory of juristic absolutism on the basis of the Justinian code. But he did not do so because English legal institutions had already gone in a different direction from those on the Continent, and Henry found it cheaper and more convenient to preserve the prevailing system, systematizing and improving it. In accordance with political traditions that he found in existence in England. Henry recognized that he had to rule, at least formally, with the advice and consent of the lay and ecclesiastical magnates. He introduced his improvements in the English common law not by royal decree but by "assizes" (establishments), that is, improvements in the prevailing law with the consent of the magnates, in accordance with the Germanic ideal of legislation that still prevailed in England. Some of Henry's courtiers addressed him in terms of Roman absolutism and even those of the archaic traditions of theocratic monarchy, but he made no attempt to formulate an ideology of royal absolutism in England. He was satisfied with the exercise of an effective control over society through royal, legal, and financial institutions and through his position as feudal liege lord; his was a practical absolutism.

Henry's marriage to Eleanor of Aquitaine brought him a principality that, when joined to his other possessions, made him the ruler of most of the western half of France. He was an extremely energetic man who spent a great deal of time attending to the affairs of his continental principalities. In England he was content to achieve order, wealth, and power; he did not concern himself deeply with the ideological foundations of his rule. The tone and efficiency of Henry's government can be seen in *The Dialogue on the Course of the Exchequer,* the first great administrative treatise written in the Middle Ages. It was the work of Richard FitzNeal, the head of Henry's exchequer, and, as a reward for his services, bishop of London. Richard's treatise is an admirably organized and informative work written in the dialogue form so popular in the twelfth century. The philosophy of administration set forth in its preface is highly significant. FitzNeal tells the novice in the exchequer, for whom his treatise was especially intended, that it is the function of the exchequer officials to exercise royal policy, not to decide on its merit. Here is already, full blown, the secular bureaucratic attitude that knows no sanction beyond the king's will.

The advance of royal power in England in Henry II's reign was facilitated by the absence of any organized opposition. The lesser members of the feudal class, who were called knights in England, benefited from the increase in royal power because they were more likely to get justice in the king's court than in the private feudal courts of their lords. The great nobles were loath to quarrel with a king who commanded such vast resources and who could simply destroy them with the twin engines of law and taxation. Henry was popular with the English bishops, who had, for the most part, begun their careers as royal clerks and were personally grateful to the king. The attention of the papacy was completely distracted from English affairs by its struggle with the German emperor. The only opposition that Henry ever experienced came from an unexpected source: his own appointee as archbishop of Canterbury, the former royal chancellor Thomas Becket. The archbishop's motives in trying to limit the king's authority over the English church and his willingness to engage in a bitter quarrel with his former patron and friend were the cause of much speculation by contemporary writers, as well as by modern historians and dramatists. Clearly, Becket was a psychologically disturbed person, but his neurotic tendencies do not detract from the significance of his struggle against the advance of secular power and his position as the first martyr to the Leviathan state.

Becket was the son of a poor knight who had gone into trade in London. He was therefore a bourgeois who rose to a high position in ecclesiastical and royal government, which was as yet unheard of in his day north of the Alps. His father had great ambitions for his precocious son and sent him to be educated in the new French schools. On his return to England Becket became the principal secretary of the archbishop of Canterbury; then royal chancellor; and finally, on the archbishop's death, he was made the primate of the English church by Henry II. He proceeded to struggle against royal power in as vehement a manner as he had previously served it, much to Henry's surprise and chagrin. As a bourgeois who had risen high in circles that were as yet open only to the landed classes, Becket had a strong feeling of insecurity and inferiority, for which he compensated by the most zealous fulfillment of his duties. He determined to become as great a servant of the church as he had been of the monarchy. But this determination led him to take a stand that ran contrary to the long tradition of royal control over the English church. He began to propound doctrines that had not been heard in Europe since the time of Gregory VII and that were regarded as archaic even in Rome. His colleagues in the English episcopate were as annoyed as the king by the archbishop's stand. The bishop of London, an excellent scholar and administrator, made cruel allusions to Becket's bourgeois background, and the bishops generally regarded the archbishop as either a fool or a madman. The issue upon which Henry II and Becket quarreled most bitterly was whether clergymen who were accused of crimes should be tried in royal or ecclesiastical courts; Becket saw this as part of the larger issue of whether the English church should be subjected to the legal supremacy that the royal government was imposing on the whole realm. He refused to surrender on this issue and, receiving no support from his ecclesiastical colleagues, fled to exile in France and appealed to Rome for help. Becket's conduct greatly embarrassed the pope. It was hard to deny the theoretical validity of the archbishop's argument, but the papacy had no inclination to arouse the ire of one of the two strongest kings in Europe, especially while it was engaged in a struggle against the other.

Becket finally returned to England and pursued his quarrel in a reckless manner that could end only in disaster for himself. He proceeded to excommunicate some of his opponents among the English bishops, and finally the exasperated king remarked to his court that he wished someone would rid him of this nuisance. Four knights who overheard this careless statement, wishing to court Henry's favor, took him at his word and rode off to Canterbury to slay the archbishop. Becket appears to have expected this end, and he certainly welcomed his martyrdom, which would be an unusual achievement for a bourgeois and would fulfill his desire to be an ideal churchman. He waited calmly for his executioners at the high altar of Canterbury cathedral, objecting only that one of his assassins happened to be his vassal and was therefore violating his oath of homage in killing his lord.

Becket was far more useful to the church dead than alive. The querulous archbishop immediately became the Canterbury martyr, whose shrine attracted thousands of pilgrims over the next three centuries. The papacy, which had largely ignored Becket when he was alive, found his martyrdom to be useful as a lever for winning concessions from the dismayed English king. To gain absolution for his part in Becket's death, Henry had to surrender on the issue of criminous clerks. The result was the peculiar institution of "benefit of clergy," which lasted until the Reformation. If a man, indicted in a royal court, could prove that he was a member of the clergy, the case was transferred to the jurisdiction of an ecclesiastical court; in practice, however, the royal judges frequently proceeded to try the case before the defendant could prove his clerical status. The most important concession that Henry made to Rome was to recognize that all English churchmen could have freedom of appeal to the papal court in ecclesiastical disputes, including cases of disputed elections of bishops and abbots. This was the first instance of the penetration of some form of effective papal jurisdiction over the English higher clergy. The fact that it took the assassination of the archbishop of Canterbury to achieve it indicates the degree of royal control over the English church since the time of William the Conqueror. Henry's concession was the entering wedge of papal influence in English ecclesiastical affairs, but by and large, royal power suffered little from reactions to Becket's death. During the next three decades the king continued to appoint bishops and abbots as before, to receive the homage of these spiritual lords, and to tax the English church heavily. The loyalty of the English higher clergy to the crown was unaffected by the Becket interlude.

Henry II's power was based on the combination of a charismatic personality with administrative skill. His two sons who followed him on the English throne, Richard I the Lionhearted (1189–1199) and John (1199–1216), exhibited only one or the other of their father's qualities, and even then only to a limited degree. Richard had the reputation as the greatest chivalric warrior in Christendom, which made him personally popular with the nobility, but he was inept in government and law. It is probably fortunate for English royal power that he spent nearly all his reign in overseas ventures and left the government in the capable hands of his father's bureaucrats. John, on the other hand, was something of an administrative genius and made some important contributions to the technique of royal administration. He was, however, a paranoiac who suspected treachery everywhere and flagrantly abused the processes of the common law to vent his hatred against certain noble families whom he suspected of treason. Eventually these families were driven to become rebels as the only way of saving themselves from ruin. He was furthermore susceptible to manic-depressive tendencies, at times exhibiting frenetic energy and then, particularly at crucial moments when his presence was required on the battlefield, becoming totally incapable of action. The third weakness of John's personality, his lecherous proclivities, inaugurated the chain of events that brought about his crushing defeat by the Capetian monarchy. He took as his queen the daughter of a minor French count, whose father had already betrothed her to another obscure feuda-tory. The enraged lord, whose intended had been stolen from him in vio-lation of contemporary custom by the English king, appealed to the king of France. Since John was technically the vassal of the king of France for Normandy, Anjou, and Aquitaine, Philip Augustus was the mutual over-lord of both parties to the dispute. John was in one of his deep funks, and he refused to answer the summons to the French court. He was declared a contumacious vassal by Philip Augustus's court and held to have forfeited Normandy and Anjou to the French crown. Had John quickly put his army into the field, he would likely have prevented Philip from seizing Normandy and Anjou. But John did nothing—did not even give instructions to his captains in Normandy. Thus the original homeland of the English kings fell to the Capetian monarch with scarcely a blow being struck.

The loss of Normandy was a disaster not only for the Angevin family, but for many of the English nobility who had held fiefs across the chan-nel. They henceforth had to confine their interests to England, and they necessarily became more and more concerned with John's use of royal, legal, and financial institutions. Any medieval king who was defeated on the battlefield was bound to lose the respect of his people and find his authority challenged at home. John was simply employing in a more relentless and severe manner the institutions of royal power that had developed in his father's day. But his lack of an attractive and imposing personality removed from the English political situation the factor that had previously compensated for the stringency of Angevin institutions.

The charismatic personal qualities of the king, which contributed to the growth of royal power in England during the reign of Henry II, was the chief resource of monarchy during the same period in Germany. The reign of Frederick I Barbarossa (1152–1190) was a magnificent perfor-mance, a fantastic juggling act in which the king tried to overcome the enormous obstacles to the revival of imperial authority. Frederick's formidable enemies defeated him on almost every side, yet in the end, by what appeared to be an incredible stroke of good luck but was partly the consequence of his unceasing efforts, he emerged triumphant. When Fred-erick came to the throne, the prospects for the revival of German imperial power were extremely thin. During the previous half century, the great German princes had steadily increased their territorial sovereignty, and the king was left with only his family domains and the vestige of control over some bishoprics and abbeys. For a quarter century before Frederick's accession the holders of the German throne had done nothing to reverse the disastrous consequences of the investiture controversy. They were too involved in the great feud that had broken out between the descendants of the Salians; the Hohenstaufen dukes of Swabia; and the Welfs, first dukes of Bavaria and then, as a result of a marriage alliance, also dukes of Saxony. When the Salian line died out with Henry V in 1125, the princes refused to give the crown to his nephew, the duke of Swabia, fearing that he would try to regain the power that the German monarch had lost during the investiture controversy. Their choice, Lothair, the duke of Saxony (1125–1137), found himself embroiled in a bitter feud with the Hohenstaufens, and for protection he allied himself by marriage with the Welfs. On Lothair's death, one of the Hohenstaufen princes gained the throne as Conrad III (1137–1152), but the struggle between the two great dynasties continued unabated.

When Frederick Barbarossa succeeded his uncle in 1152, there seemed to be excellent prospects for ending the feud, since Frederick was a Welf on his mother's side. But the Welf duke of Saxony, Henry the Lion, could not be appeased; he remained the implacable enemy of the Hohenstaufen monarchy. Barbarossa had the force of his own personality, the duchies of Swabia and Franconia, and very little else to begin with. The German crown still enjoyed some vestiges of its former control over the German bishoprics and abbeys, but this control could not provide the additional resources that Frederick needed to crush the Welfs and the other great princes. He tried for a time to make additions to his family holdings and to build up a royal domain in the Rhineland, but he quickly realized that it would be a long task and would not in the end give him the resources he needed. His only hope lay in asserting his effective control over northern Italy and taxing the Italian communes heavily. Only then would he have the wealth to defeat the great princes. It was a risky plan, since the Italian cities were bound to put up stiff resistance to real, instead of merely nominal, imperial control, and such a plan might arouse the pope's fears. But Frederick could find no alternative if he wished to regain royal power in Germany. The prospect of asserting imperial domination in Italy also appealed to Frederick's personal inclinations. He had a high sense of the dignity and potential powers of his office, as set down in Roman law, and he tended to envision himself as a successor to the Roman emperors. He was strongly under the influence of the new juristic absolutism, and he could not bear to see the perpetuation of the discrepancy between the prevailing weakness and the potential glory and autocracy implicit in his office.

Frederick made his first expedition to Italy in 1154–55. He wanted to make a show of strength, to assert German hegemony personally, and to get himself crowned emperor by the pope. He accomplished all these aims, partly because the pope was having trouble with the communal movement in Rome led by a fiery disciple of Abelard, Arnold of Brescia, who combined intellectual and social radicalism. Arnold and the commune proclaimed the independence of the city and appealed for support to the German king. But Frederick had no sympathy with the Italian urban leaders and their ideal of the city-state; the latter was contrary to the achievement of his ultimate aim to rule northern Italy. Frederick captured Arnold of Brescia, had him burned, and had his ashes scattered into the Tiber.

There were three parties in the northern Italian situation: the emperor, the communes, and the papacy. On his visit to Rome Frederick had been disturbed by the pope's insistence that he officially perform the office of papal groom in accordance with the Donation of Constantine. But Barbarossa's first expedition to Italy indicated to him that he and the pope were natural allies against the city-states and their principles of self-government. He returned to Germany to prepare for a great expedition that would bring the riches of northern Italy under his control. Meanwhile, a great debate was waged in papal circles as to whether the papacy ought to ally itself with Frederick against the communal movement or to join ranks with the city-states and revert to the traditional papal policy of trying to keep the emperor out of Italy. It was a hard decision to make. The northern Italian burghers were notorious for their frequent quarrels with bishops and for their anticlerical and even antisacerdotal views. The pope certainly did not want a commune in Rome. Should the papacy throw in its lot with the scurvy bourgeois? It was a difficult choice to make, and there was a division among the cardinals. Those who opposed Frederick tried to foment a split between emperor and pope by means of provocative tactics. A papal legate addressing Frederick's court in 1157 claimed that the emperors received their power from the pope, which he knew would greatly anger the young and ambitious ruler. Adrian IV, the only English pope, slowly moved toward an alliance with the communes against the German ambassador, and when the cardinal who had intentionally aroused the emperor's wrath was elected to the throne of Peter as Alexander III in 1159, it became evident that the die was cast and that another great imperial-papal struggle was inevitable.

During the next two decades Frederick made three great expeditions against the northern Italian cities. He won some initial victories, including the defeat and humiliation of the obstreperous burghers of Milan. The professors of the law school in Bologna proclaimed at a diet, or assembly, on the Roncaglian plain in 1158 that the emperor's claims to appoint the chief officials of each city and to impose taxes were in accordance with Roman law. Frederick was helped at first by the fact that there were deep divisions among the oligarchs who ruled the Italian cities. Some, called the Ghibellines, after the Italianized form of Waiblingen, one of the Hohenstaufen possessions, were willing to surrender to Frederick's demands and the juristic arguments of the civil lawyers, but the majority, who came to be called the Guelphs, after the Hohenstaufen enemy in Germany, determined to devote all their resources to a struggle to retain their independence. For a few years the emperor managed to subject some of the Italian cities to his absolute authority, but after two decades it became apparent that the alliance of the papacy and the commune was too much for him. The pope contributed organizing ability and leadership and managed to unite most of the cities, which had always fought each other with delicious hatred, into the Lombard League (1167). In 1174 the armies of the Lombard League inflicted a complete defeat on the imperial forces at the battle of Legnano, and Frederick decided to cut his losses and sue for peace. Alexander III, having achieved his aim of keeping the emperor out of Italy, could afford to be generous; he forgave the emperor for setting up an antipope in accordance with the traditional technique of imperial-papal struggles. The peace of Constance of 1183 allowed Barbarossa to save face, but nothing more. His loose suzerainty over northern Italy was recognized, but he was denied the right to appoint the city officials and to collect taxes. In other words, after two decades of war Frederick had failed to gain control over northern Italy, which he felt was the first great step toward the restoration of imperial authority over the German princes.

When Frederick returned to Germany after his defeat in northern Italy, he was a bitter and exhausted man. The princes, far from being subordinated to royal control, were intensifying their hold on wealth and power in Germany and entrenching their positions as the leaders of society by their direction of the great eastward movement of the German people. In the 1130s the Germans again, for the first time since Otto II's reign, began to press against the Slavic world to the east. They crossed the Elbe and in the twelfth century created a "new Germany" stretching eastward to the Oder and even beyond. They opened up the Baltic seacoast and founded great commercial centers, such as Lübeck. The "old Germany" west of the Elbe was the creation of the church and the German monarchy, but the new Germany was largely settled and civilized at the direction of great princes who had understood the significance of the colonization movement and had rushed to put themselves at the head of it. Dukes and margraves who already had great fiefs in the old Germany now carved out vast domains in the east, thereby completely upsetting the balance of power in Germany and making the existing Hohenstaufen power relatively less significant. The dukes' direction of the *Drang nach Osten* involved no consideration for the Slavs, who were massacred or subjugated, but it was clever and efficient. The princes attracted peasants from the Low Countries and western Germany, especially those experienced in the new techniques of colonization, by offering favorable terms of settlement. The immigrants of the eastern frontier were promised freedom from the old manorial dues and services and large blocks of land instead of the meager manorial strips. These attractive offers, when combined with the fertility of the soil and the protection the peasants received from the princes, induced a steady eastward movement in the twelfth century, resulting in the creation of the new Germany. Frederick Barbarossa played no part in this development. He allowed it to go on without making any attempt to intervene, and the princes greatly increased their domains and power by default. Modern writers have criticized Frederick for his blindness in getting involved in the morass of Italian politics while ignoring the opening up of eastern Germany, where the Hohenstaufens would have been able to create the royal domain they needed if they had early assumed the direction of the movement. In retrospect this was a grave miscalculation that, in the long run, greatly conditioned the future history of the German monarchy. But it is hard to be severe with Frederick for making this fatal error. At the beginning of his reign the eastward movement was still a modest development; Frederick believed that he needed an immediate increase in his resources, and Italy appeared to be the only place he could obtain it; the creation of new, wealthy domains in the east seemed a far-off prospect. Frederick's gamble failed, and by the end of the 1170s he was in some ways worse off than when he started, but under the circumstances he had made the most plausible choice of the alternatives open to him.

When the aging and disappointed king returned to Germany, he vented his anger on his old Guelph enemy, Henry the Lion. One slim hope of victory seemed open to Frederick: the use of the feudal resources of the crown in the manner that the Norman and Angevin rulers of England had done for more than a century and that the Capetian kings were to follow just a quarter of a century later. German feudalism was by no means English feudalism. The feudal pyramid in the empire was truncated, and although the great dukes were the emperor's vassals, their subvassals did not recognize the king as their liege lord. But Henry the Lion, as Frederick's vassal, could still be impleaded in his lord's court and, if found guilty by his peers, declared in forfeit of his feudal duchies of Saxony and Bavaria. On this legal basis Frederick inaugurated his great feudal trial against his Guelph enemy, charging him with failure to render his lord military service in the Italian campaigns and with other felonies. The princes were not reluctant to see the great duke of Saxony brought low, and when Henry refused to appear in Frederick's court to answer the indictment brought against him, they declared his fiefs forfeit. Frederick was able to drive Henry out of Saxony and Bavaria and leave him only his eastern principalities, which were not fiefs of the crown, but the princes would not let the emperor absorb the forfeited duchies into his own domain; he had to infeudate the Guelph principalities to other princes. The trial of Henry the Lion was the decisive moment in German feudalism; Frederick's failure to gain the lands of his Guelph enemies meant that the emperor could not use feudal law to increase his power, which had been the case in England for more than a century and was also soon to be attempted successfully in France.

In the last years of his life the aging emperor finally had to abandon the prodigious efforts and great wars of his younger days. He took the cross and died en route to the Holy Land in 1190. But the great emperor was able to die with the comforting knowledge that his son would have the resources to achieve the triumph of imperial power that he had lacked. By an incredible combination of circumstances Frederick's son, who had already been crowned Henry VI before Barbarossa's departure on the third crusade, found himself the ruler of the Norman kingdom of Sicily, one of the wealthiest countries in the Mediterranean world. Four years previously Barbarossa had married his son to the Norman Sicilian princess Constance, but this union did not appear significant because Constance's chances of inheriting the throne were slim; if her chances had been good, the pope would never have allowed the marriage. The year before Barbarossa's death Constance, because of unexpected deaths in her family, inherited the Norman Sicilian crown, and her husband came into possession of the kind of domain that Barbarossa had striven unsuccessfully for three decades to obtain. Yet the decisions of fortune had been prepared by the indomitable will of the emperor. He had tried one method after another to achieve his grand design, and all had failed. His last effort, a dynastic union with the Norman house in the hope that someday one of his successors might gain the throne, had an almost immediate result in the ascendancy of the Hohenstaufens.

It was Frederick's enormous reputation as one of the greatest men in Christendom that induced the Norman Sicilian king, the traditional ally of the papacy against the German emperor, to agree to an alliance of the northern and southern ruling dynasties. Barbarossa's long struggle with the pope did not in any way lessen the intense popular admiration that he evoked. The sort of enthusiasm with which he had been greeted by his uncle, Bishop Otto of Freising, in the early part of his reign, continued all through his life and long afterward. He became a folk hero, a kind of messianic figure who, it was said, would return some day and lead the Germans to new glories. This emotional response transcended the severe institutional limitations of the German monarchy and gave the Hohenstaufens the aura of majesty and virtue that, it seemed in 1190, had brought them to the threshold of the power they had sought for so long.

But Henry VI's temperament and character differed even more strongly from Barbarossa's than Richard's and John's did from Henry II's. Barbarossa appeared to contemporaries to be a man with greatness of soul; Henry IV was singularly lacking in this quality. He was pompous, calculating, and ruthless, a schemer and a bully. It took him until 1194 to enter fully into possession of southern Italy. Almost immediately he began an attack on the cities of northern Italy and scored initial successes. Henry could not refrain from making extravagant announcements of how the Hohenstaufen family would achieve western and, in fact, world supremacy. He terrified the German princes; the northern Italian cities; and, above all, the papacy, which found itself on the verge of being surrounded by the Hohenstaufen power it had fought twenty years to keep out of Italy. Henry VI's only miscalculation was not to take into account the effects of the unsalubrious Italian climate, which had carried off some of his wife's family in their prime and had made him king of Sicily. Henry died suddenly in 1197, leaving a three-year-old child as his heir and the affairs of Germany and Italy in turmoil. This act of God favored the enemies of the Hohenstaufens even more than a similar stroke of fortune, eight years previously, had given Barbarossa most of what he had wanted. It is difficult for a modern German historian to write a book on the twelfth or thirteenth centuries without expatiating on the misfortune of Henry VI's early death and attributing to this one event the subsequent troubles and final collapse of the medieval German empire. Yet, the fact that Henry VI's death was such a great calamity demonstrates the almost exclusive reliance that the German monarchy had to place on the person of the king because of its lack of administrative institutions. Nothing in medieval history illustrates more graphically both the value and the limitations of charisma than does the history of the German empire in the second half of the twelfth century.

II. The Capetian Ascendancy

The seizure of Normandy and Anjou in 1204 and their incorporation into the royal domain of the French monarchy was a great turning point in the history not only of France but generally of Europe. The kingdom of France, which was ruled by the Capetians in a direct line of succession until 1328 and then by the cadet branches of the family, the Valois and the Bourbons, until the nineteenth century, was to be the most important European state at least until 1700 and, in the opinion of some historians, until 1870. If the lands lying between Flanders and the Pyrenees and between the Atlantic and the Rhine could be brought under an effective central government, the result was bound to have a profound impact on European civilization, for this government would then have at its command a larger population and more intellectual, economic, and military resources than any other state in Europe. The conquest of Normandy signaled the emergence of such a state, but a century before there was no France; it was merely a geographic expression. It was a large, diverse land with neither topographical, political, economic, linguistic, nor cultural unity.

The people of the north and the south spoke different Romance dialects. Northern France was the classic land of feudalism and was largely a rural area; its dominant figure was the feudal baron. The culture, society, and language of southern France had much more in common with Christian Spain and Italy than with northern France. Languedoc, the region of the southern dialect, had a vibrant urban civilization and a literate bourgeois class. Its aristocracy was also becoming urbanized; like the northern Italian nobility they had town houses, and they enjoyed the intellectual benefits of town life. The third area of what later became France, the Rhineland region, tended to look eastward toward the German empire, to which many of its bishoprics, principalities, and cities technically belonged, and many of the people in this area spoke German rather than one of the French dialects. In central France there was a mountainous region that served as a hangout for robber barons and made travel between the north and the south difficult. Thus, in 1100 France was not naturally or even potentially one country. It was the Capetian monarchy of the twelfth and thirteenth centuries that created France, which need not have existed; there was no national destiny of France before the rise of the French monarchy. But if the country could ultimately be subjected to royal power, then the kings would have at their disposal wealthy cities, a large feudal warrior class, and universities and their graduates—a formidable combination.

The history of the Capetians before the twelfth century gave no promise of the later success of the dynasty. The Capetians gained the French crown in 987, but until 1108 the French kings were nonentities who had no control over the great dukes and counts who were their nominal vassals. They did not even have unchallenged power in their own domain of the Ile-de-France. Paris was surrounded by the castles of robber barons, and the French king was sometimes afraid to go outside the walls of the city. The first Capetian monarch to contribute to the institutional foundation of royal power was Louis VI the Fat, or the Wideawake (1108–1137). Because of the information provided by Louis' biography, written by his chief minister Abbot Suger of St. Denis, he is much more of a real person to us than any of his predecessors, who are faceless men, renowned only for piety or personal scandal. One of the mistakes of the early Capetians was their involvement in grandiose attempts to expand their authority when they were not even strong in the Ile-de-France. Under the wise and patient guidance of Suger, Louis VI generally pursued a policy that was both much more limited and more effective. He was not free from his predecessors' delusions of grandeur; he made a stab at conquering Flanders, which ended in humiliation when his army was routed by the Flemish burghers. But usually he stayed close to home and succeeded in destroying the power of the petty lords and robber barons in the Ile-de-France, thereby providing a secure base of operations for his successors.

The long reign of his son Louis VII (1137–1180) was the turning point in the development of Capetian institutions and the beginning of the exercise of some royal jurisdiction over the great feudal princes. Louis VII was a devout, hard-working, and colorless figure who suffered the terrible humiliation and great loss attendant upon his divorce from Eleanor of Aquitaine. Some historians have said that Louis VI made such an impression by his work of building royal power in the Ile-de-France that the extremely wealthy duke of Aquitaine deigned to marry his daughter to the heir of the French throne. This is a possibility, but it may have been simply the result of whimsy by the troubadour duke of Aquitaine. In any case, Louis VII lost the vast accretion in the territory of the royal domain that Eleanor had brought with her, and this duchy passed under the rule of Henry II, Eleanor's second husband. As a consequence, Louis faced the grim fact that his nominal vassal ruled the western half of France and, even without England, was immensely more powerful than Louis himself. Yet, by the end of Louis's reign the Capetian king was beginning to exercise some leadership among the great princes who were his nominal vassals.

The court of the French king, as the overlord of the great feudatories, was technically the high court of the realm. But before the reign of Louis VII it was merely a theoretical possibility. The dukes and counts ignored the king's court in their dealings with each other, and the king had no power to compel his vassals to give him suit at court in accordance with feudal law. In the latter half of Louis's reign the great vassals began to bring cases in the royal court for the first time. They did so partly because by the middle of the twelfth century there was a balance of power among the great feudatories and therefore little possibility of set-tling their disputes by the old method of feudal warfare. They knew that they would receive a fair judgment in the court of the peaceful and pious Capetian king. The French feudal princes also turned toward Paris for the first time because of their fear of the overwhelming power of Henry II. By his vast holdings the Angevin ruler had made himself the most obvi-ous threat to the future independence and security of the other dukes and counts, and as a reaction they looked with greater favor on the Capetian king as a counterbalance to Henry II. In the long run Louis VII benefited greatly from Eleanor of Aquitaine's marriage to Henry II. For the first time the value of the Capetian monarchy in the affairs of France became evident to the great feudatories.

The French royal demesne had been traditionally administered by *prévôts,* local lords who paid the king a lump sum for the privilege of farming the demesne in his area. This primitive system was indicative of the general ineptitude of the early Capetians. The prévôts cheated the king, ruthlessly abused the populace, and tried to turn their jurisdictions into hereditary patrimonies. Furthermore, by delegating his local authority in this way, the king lost the opportunity to impress the local areas with the tradition of royal leadership. Louis VI by and large continued this ruinous system of local administration, but in the latter part of his reign there are indications that he was experimenting with sending officials directly from the royal court to supervise the local administration of the royal demesne.

Louis VII's son Philip II Augustus (1180–1223) turned these experi-ments into the creation of a distinctive local administrative system, whose essentials were perpetuated to the end of the *ancien régime.* The third of the great rulers of the later twelfth century, alongside Henry II and Fred-erick Barbarossa, Philip was singularly lacking in their glamorous and attractive qualities. He was a miserable, crafty hunchback totally without scruples. His high-sounding appellation was probably intended to mean "the augmentor" rather than to associate him with the Roman emperors. Yet Philip's devious qualities were the only ones that could have led to a great increase in the French royal demesne. By the late twelfth century the political borders of Europe had been drawn, and in France the division of the country among the feudatories had a long tradition behind it. The rearrangement of the political map of France could not be accomplished without craft and guile, qualities in which Philip excelled. But Philip was also an extremely industrious and ingenious administrator who prepared for the expansion of the royal demesne by creating the *bailli,* the local financial, legal, administrative, and military representative of the French monarchy. In England the local officials of the royal government were the sheriff, who acted as the general administrative officer and was in charge of tax collection in the shire, and the itinerant justices who presided over the county courts. The bailli combined both these offices, carrying out all the administrative, judicial, and financial services on behalf of the king. The English sheriff and his assistants were wealthy members of the local landed classes with strong interests in the shire where they worked, which meant that in the long run the monarchy had to preserve the goodwill of the county families who were its agents or suffer the paralysis of local government. This problem was not so evident in the reign of Henry II because of his overwhelming popularity and power, but after 1200 it became more and more apparent in England that royal government could be effectively carried on only with the assent and cooperation of the leading families of the county. The social and political characteristics of the bailli were different. He was a paid official sent out by the royal government, and he had no roots in his area of jurisdiction. He was a true bureaucrat whose whole income and social status depended on his position as a royal servant. He was therefore fanatically loyal to the king and was concerned only with the full exercise of royal power.

Unlike the English county families from whose ranks were drawn the sheriffs and other local officials, the bailli never took it into his head to question the merit of the royal policy. The difference between the French bailli and the English sheriff was not so much the result of the prescient wisdom of the French monarchy; rather it was determined by geographic and social circumstances. The territory that Philip Augustus initially had to administer was only the size of one of the larger English counties. He did not need many officials to govern this small area, and he could afford to dispatch reliable and experienced men directly from his court. In fact, the institutional term designating the French local official was simply that of bailiff, a generic word used all over Europe to mean a personal agent or steward. In the beginning the bailli only differed in degree from the bailiff who managed the estate of a great manorial lord. But by the end of the twelfth century the bailli had become more of a public than a private institution of the monarchy. It would have been difficult for the Capetian kings to perpetuate this institution and to apply it to the new areas they conquered if it had not been for the educational revolution of the twelfth century. It was the universities that provided them with the clerks and lawyers who filled the office of bailli, and these were the ideal personnel to serve as local bureaucrats. They were intelligent, industrious, and well educated, and few of them had any prospects in life other than what they could gain in the royal service.

During the reign of Philip Augustus several of the baillis were already magistri, university graduates who were sent to administer the new areas that were absorbed into the French royal domain and to incorporate them fully into the royal jurisdiction. The same institution was extended in the thirteenth century to Languedoc when the southern principalities came under French rule. In southern France the bailli was called the seneschal, another old generic term for the agent of a feudal lord that was now given a new meaning as the local paid representative of the French monarchy. By the middle of the thirteenth century the baillis and seneschals had become a self-sustaining corporate group and in some ways were more fanatical supporters of the extension of royal power than was the king himself. It was they who subordinated local customs and institutions and brought the disparate regions of France under a common government. It is no exaggeration to say that France was the creation of a bureaucracy that began to assume its characteristic form at the beginning of the reign of Philip Augustus, perhaps even a little earlier.

The advance of royal power in France was conditioned by the king's relations with the bourgeois and the church. It is a nineteenth-century myth that the king of France realized the importance of the new urban development and that he allied himself with the new class against the feudal nobility. Even if this were true, it would not have secured his triumph because the towns of northern France were too few and, aside from Paris, too small in size and wealth to affect profoundly the power structure. In reality Louis VII and Philip Augustus were not much more sympathetic to the ambitions of the burghers than were the lay and ecclesiastical princes. The towns on the royal domain received only meager communal privileges, and even then only after a long struggle and heavy payments to the royal treasury. But the townsmen generally favored the advance of royal power as a counterbalance to the feudal lords and because they were able to win more concessions of urban self-government from the king than from the local magnates, even though they had to pay dearly for them.

The relation between the Capetian monarchy and the church played a much more important part in the eventual Capetian triumph. The backwardness and insignificance of the eleventh-century Capetian monarchy is demonstrated by the fact that the French king held on to some of the accoutrements of theocratic monarchy long after the papacy had forced the abandonment of such traditions in the much more powerful monarchies of Germany and England. From the late eleventh century the papacy generally looked on the French monarchy as its ally and supporter, if for no other reason than that the pope had to have some support among the kings of Europe. The pope was intermittently embroiled with the German emperor and feared the consequences of his claims over northern Italy. In view of the power of the English monarch, his hold over the church in his territory, and the distance of England from Rome, the papacy could not ally itself with the Norman and Angevin kings. The French king remained the only possible candidate, and he appeared so weak and innocuous that it seemed impossible that he would ever threaten the authority of the papacy. The Capetian kings, furthermore, had a great reputation for piety; even in the twelfth century they were known as the "very Christian" kings. Therefore Gregory VII was unusually moderate in his relations with the Capetian monarch. During the late eleventh and twelfth centuries, France became a common place of refuge for the popes driven from Rome by the German emperor. Urban II went to France to get away from the armies of Henry IV and to preach the first crusade, and Alexander III sought the protection of Louis VII in the 1160s when Frederick Barbarossa held Rome for a short time. The sympathetic attitude of the papacy allowed the French kings to perpetuate some of the archaic traditions and rituals of early-medieval kingship. There was a close association between the Capetian dynasty and the royal abbey of St. Denis. The regalia of the French crown were kept there, and much later than monastic statesmen played a leading role in other European governments, abbot Suger of St. Denis, in the reigns of Louis VI and VII, continued to be the chief minister of the royal administration. Whereas the ceremony of anointment was becoming a mere formality in Germany and in England, the religious and emotional qualities of this ceremony were still accentuated in France.

The association of the church with the French monarchy was particularly emphasized during the long reign of Louis VII. Louis, who was personally devout, exhibited great friendship for both the pope and the higher clergy all over France. He received Alexander III with the greatest deference, and he took the side of bishops and abbots in their struggles with local lords. In so doing, he was, of course, helping to advance royal power as well as satisfying his own devout inclinations. Louis's attempts to aid the higher clergy were part of his general effort to expand the jurisdiction of the royal court. The Capetian king's reputation as the friend and ally of the papacy could not but help contribute to his prestige in France and might eventually prove useful in his relations with the great feudatories and the other kings of western Europe.

The moral and religious traditions of the very Christian Capetian monarchy were valuable to Philip Augustus. They provided the necessary façade behind which he could undertake his depredations and pursue his crooked schemes. He gained the northern county of Artois by his marriage and then turned upon the vast domains of the Angevin ruler in northern France. He fomented the rebellion of Henry II's sons against their father and made the great king's last years miserable. He was continually plotting against Richard and John, and by 1204 he had achieved his great triumph. He had incorporated all northwestern France into the royal domain, leaving the English king with only Gascony and part of Poitou, the most distant of the former French possessions of the Angevin house. In the first two decades of his reign Philip clearly demonstrated for his successors how the territory of the French crown might be expanded: by dynastic marriage, by political and diplomatic chicanery, by feudal forfeiture, and by outright conquest. The old innocuous royal ally of the church had suddenly become a great power in northern Europe, and not the least of the problems facing the thirteenth-century papacy was the kind of adjustment it should make to this new situation.

CHAPTER EIGHTEEN

The Peace of Innocent III

I. The Reaffirmation of Papal Leadership

It is a tradition in the history of the papacy that the cardinals often oscillate between choosing strong and weak popes to obtain alternate cycles of aggressive, reforming and then calm, conservative pontificates. Since the death of Alexander III in 1181, the papal throne had been held by a succession of well-meaning but weak men who seemed to have been paralyzed into a state of immobility by the vast problems affecting the church as a consequence of the twelfth-century changes in learning, piety, and power. Papal leadership was becoming such a negligible factor in European life that the cardinals went to the other extreme in 1198. They chose the ablest member of the college of cardinals, Lothario Conti, who took the title of Innocent III (1198–1216). At the time of his accession Innocent was only thirty-seven years old, phenomenally young for a pope. Innocent III came from one of the leading families of the Roman aristocracy. He was a man of limitless energy, high intellectual capacity, and unusual gifts as a leader and administrator. He was a canon lawyer of great ability, and he could have gained a distinguished reputation as a theologian if he had had the time or inclination. He was fully aware of the problems that the papacy faced on all sides, and he had no doubt that he could find ways to deal with them. The unusually high degree of self-confidence that characterizes men of his superior qualities was combined in Innocent's case with his high sense of the traditions and power of the papal office. He believed that "everything in the world is the province of the pope," that St. Peter had been commissioned by Christ "to govern not only the universal Church but all the secular world." Innocent was fond of alluding to hierocratic theory, in which the spiritual sword was superior to the earthly sword, in which the subordination of monarchy to the priesthood was likened to the moon's dependence on the sun. Innocent's was not a revolutionary temperament, however, but that of a constructive conservative; he was not another Gregory VII. He did not intend to launch an apocalyptic attack on the forces that threatened to terminate the leadership of the church in medieval society; rather, by a great variety of methods he intended to exert papal influence on the changed society of western Europe and to control the effects of twelfth-century learning, piety, and power. He wished to direct these new forces into channels that would restore ecclesiastical influence in Europe. Innocent wanted a new equilibrium between the church and the world that would bring political, intellectual, and religious order to a society seething under the impact of new ideas and institutions. The greatest tribute to his ability, good judgment, and inflexible determination is the high degree of success he had. When he died, exhausted from his labors, papal leadership in Europe had been reaffirmed and the church was counterattacking on every front against heresy, intellectual disorder, and secular power. By the end of the 1230s a new consensus and optimism had entered European life. The forces dissolving the medieval world order seemed to have been stopped and turned aside by the peace of Innocent III.

The necessary foundation of all the other achievements of his pontificate, according to Innocent, was the reconstruction of the administration of the church. This reconstruction involved a general rationalization and tightening of central control to make more real the canonist's doctrines of the plenitude of power of the absolute papal monarchy in the church. The reforms that Innocent introduced all through his pontificate were summed up and confirmed by the decrees of the Fourth Lateran Council of 1215, one of the three most important ecumenical councils of the Catholic church, the other two being the Council of Nicaea in 325 and the Council of Trent in the sixteenth century. The Lateran Council set the number of Christian sacraments at the seven that still obtain in the Roman church: baptism, confirmation, marriage, and extreme unction (which mark the stages in the life of man) and the Eucharist or mass, confession, and the ordination of priests (the ones that are at the heart of sacerdotal Christianity). Only a bishop can confirm and ordain priests. The early-medieval church had never clearly defined the number of the sacraments. Damiani had at one point listed eleven, including the ordination of kings. The twelfth-century standard textbook on theology, Peter Lombard's *Sentences,* had listen seven, and this view was accepted by the Lateran Council. The council decreed that every member of the church was to confess his sins to a priest and to receive the Eucharist at least once a year and as often as possible. This was a reassertion of the authority of the priest-hood over the laity and was intended as a direct challenge to the doc-trines of the antisacerdotal heretics. As a way of further inhibiting the cor-rosive effects of the new piety, the Lateran Council announced that there were to be no new saints and relics without papal canonization and that the proliferation of religious orders was to cease.

The Fourth Lateran Council's listing of marriage as a sacrament was an important step in a trend that had been gaining momentum in the pre-vious century—demanding a church ceremony for legitimation of a mar-riage. In the year 1000 the majority of people in Christian Europe were not married in a church ceremony. Marriage involved Germanic-style cohabitation, frequently signified by the giving of a ring. By 1200 perhaps half the people in Western Europe, particularly among the wealthier and more literate classes, were married by a priest. After the Fourth Lateran Council, sacramental marriage in the church became the prescribed norm, although in 1500 there were still many peasants who were married by the simple rite of cohabitation. If the family involved had property, church marriage was now a necessity in order to assure legitimacy of offspring and uncontested inheritance. This was a way of increasing the impor-tance of the priesthood in everyday life.

The more general practice of marriage as a sacrament also increased the church's control over divorce. What the representative of God had joined could now also be dissolved only by the church. It is a myth that the medieval church did not allow divorce. Until the Fourth Lateran Council, if you married within the seventh degree of consanguinity (someone who was your cousin seven times removed), you needed church approval. The common practice was to do this without license from the church. The cousinhood could later be conveniently discovered and an annulment obtained. The Fourth Lateran Council narrowed the ban to the third degree of consanguinity. This still allowed for heavy traf-fic in divorce proceedings through annulment (even if there were chil-dren of the marriage) from bishop's courts all the way to Rome. In effect, divorce was not hard to get in the medieval church if you could afford the legal fees. Innocent's bringing of marriage within much closer ecclesi-astical jurisdiction thereby increased the church's capacity to interfere in individual lives. Today in New York City thousands of Catholics first give close attention to the Cardinal Archbishop when they seek a church divorce. That was also true in medieval Europe after the Fourth Lateran Council.

Innocent greatly expanded the system of papal legates as a way of bringing the bishops of western Europe under closer control by Rome, and whereas the twelfth-century popes had frequently appointed the metropolitans in various countries as legates so as not to offend national feelings, Innocent chose Italian cardinals as his representatives to the territorial churches. In turn, the bishops were to give much greater attention to the affairs of their dioceses, particularly to the quality of the clergy under their rule. The bishops and their adjutants were to engage in annual visitation of the monasteries in their dioceses and to inspect carefully the cathedral and parish clergy to make sure they merited their offices. Innocent asserted with a high degree of success the right of the pope to appoint bishops in special cases: in the event of a disputed election whose resolution was appealed to Rome, if an episcopal or other church office was vacant for six months, and if the previous bishop died while on a visit to Rome. The frequent disputes over episcopal elections and the notoriously unsalubrious climate of Rome gave the thirteenth-century papacy many occasions to claim that the power of appointment had "devolved" upon the Roman curia.

The pontificate of Innocent III thus witnessed a general increase in the legal powers of the papacy as the high court of Christendom and the refinement of the legal institutions of the church. This general tightening of the administrative system of the church and the increase of centralized control had the immediate effect of improving the quality of both the higher and the lower clergy. Thirteenth-century episcopal visitation turned up hundreds of cases of incompetence and dereliction of duty by the monastic and parish clergy, and in turn the episcopate came under constant pressure and scrutiny from Rome to fulfill its pastorate. Innocent demonstrated that the effects of the new piety had gotten out of control in large part because of lax administration and that the best way to wean men away from their enthusiasm for heretic saints was by presenting to the world a Catholic clergy that was conscientious, zealous, and well informed.

The vast administrative structure of the papal monarchy, like that of any other government in Europe, needed a large amount of money to keep the machine going. The cardinals were furthermore princes of the church; they often came from prominent families of the Italian aristocracy and were accustomed to living well; and in any case the papal court, as one that claimed to be the most important in Christendom, could not appear impoverished and niggardly in comparison with the establishments of rulers north of the Alps. In addition, the pope had to find the money for the support of diplomatic and military ventures if he was to deal effectively with the entrenched secular powers of Europe.

Where was the money for these purposes to come from? Like any king, the pope had his demesne in the form of the papal states, but this was not enough to maintain the papal administration, diplomacy, court, and army. Like the kings of western Europe, he had to devise new forms of taxation. Special papal tithes levied for the third crusade had demonstrated both the vast wealth that could be obtained by a general tax on the clergy and how relatively easy it was to administer the tax, in view of the subordination of the clergy to papal authority and the church's supply of loyal and literate tax officials. Accordingly, in 1199 Innocent levied the first general income tax on European churchmen for papal needs. Its great success made it the first of a variety of taxes levied by the thirteenth-century papacy on the clergy. This steady income not only facilitated the improvement of the papal administration, it gave the pope the added resources that were needed for his complex involvement in European politics.

A prime necessity for the freedom of papal action with regard to the kings of northern Europe had always been the security of the papacy in Rome. From the beginning of his pontificate Innocent worked hard to strengthen papal control over the city of Rome and over the papal states, which he sought to expand, while the power of the emperor to intervene was rendered negligible by the sudden death of Henry VI and the consequent dispute over the German throne. Innocent had a hard time asserting his complete control over the government of the Eternal City; the jealous nobility and the commune fought him step by step, but by 1205 he had firmly established his authority in his own city. Since Rome lived largely off the business of the curia, it could not long withstand the demand of the pope to control its municipal government. Innocent had even greater success with the patrimony of St. Peter, and during his pontificate the papal states attained the dimensions that they retained until the middle of the nineteenth century.

Secure at home, Innocent was able to devote his superb political talents to defining the pope's relations with the great northern monarchies. "The imperial business," as it was called in papal circles, was the most pressing political matter. Henry VI had terrified the papacy, and it was Innocent's intention to separate the kingdom of Sicily from Germany once more and to preclude the papacy's ever again being faced with the threat to its independence that Henry VI had presented. Innocent was given a great opportunity to achieve this aim by the renewal of the feud over the German throne between the Hohenstaufens and the Guelphs that plunged Germany into civil war after Henry's death. The Hohenstaufens and their supporters chose Henry's brother Philip of Swabia as king, while some of the German nobility who had come to fear the

Hohenstaufen family joined in the election of Otto IV of Brunswick, the son of Henry the Lion. Both parties ignored the rights of the child Frederick II, Henry's son, who remained in Sicily with his mother. Both parties tried to gain Innocent's support because only the pope had the authority to make one of the rival kings emperor. Innocent waited three years to render his decision, intentionally allowing the civil war to deplete the power of the German crown further. Finally, in 1200, he rendered his decision, to no one's surprise, in favor of Otto, who recognized the boundaries of the papal states, surrendered what remained of royal authority over the German church, and promised not to intervene in Italy.

Innocent appeared to have completely removed the German threat to the papacy, but in 1208 Philip was assassinated in a personal quarrel, and Otto married his daughter and established an unchallenged claim to the German throne. Almost immediately Otto took up the traditional policy of the German kings and moved upon northern Italy. Innocent was angry and disappointed, but not dismayed, for the Welf king was a colorless and incompetent leader who was no match for the pope. In 1212 Innocent recognized young Frederick II as king of Germany, after first extorting from Frederick the promise that he would abdicate as king of Naples and Sicily when he established his effective rule in Germany. Innocent then devoted himself to organizing a great coalition between the papacy, Frederick II, and Philip Augustus of France against Otto and King John of England, who was allied by marriage with the Welf house. This was the first great example of the clash of international alliances in European history. The conflict was decided at the battle of Bouvines in 1214, which had a profound effect on the political development of thirteenth-century Europe. Philip Augustus inflicted a crushing defeat on Otto and thereby opened the way for Frederick to gain the German throne.

At the time of Innocent's death in 1216 the pope was again firmly convinced that he had permanently solved the German problem. Frederick II, whom Innocent personally admired and trusted, was obtaining the support of the German nobility, and Frederick had promised to abdicate the Sicilian crown as soon as he fully gained their loyalty. Furthermore, it did not appear that the German emperor would be much of a threat to the papacy in the future. Two decades of civil war and sweeping concessions of territorial sovereignty made to the German princes by the various claimants to the throne had further diminished the power and resources of the monarchy and had undone all the work of Frederick I and Henry VI.

Innocent's triumphs in the imperial business were paralleled by his relations with the English and French monarchies. He humiliated the powerful Angevin king and improved the prospects of the French papal ally. The papacy had always been extremely wary of becoming involved in a struggle with the English king, but Innocent pressed such a contest and won a complete victory. The quarrel between the pope and King John arose over a disputed election to the see of Canterbury that, in accordance with the new provisions of canon law, was appealed to Rome. Innocent rejected the candidates offered him and appointed instead Stephen Langton, an Englishman who had been a theologian at Paris and was at the time a cardinal in the Roman curia. John regarded this appointment as a gross violation of the traditional royal authority over the English church; he furthermore regarded Langton as a papal agent, and he refused to recognize the archbishop-elect and forbade him to enter England. A bitter conflict ensued in which both pope and king used extreme measures. Innocent placed England under an interdict, which suspended church services, and John seized a great part of the landed wealth of the English church. Finally Innocent encouraged Philip Augustus to prepare for the invasion of England under the papal banner, and John, terrified that he would lose England to his great enemy as he had lost most of his continental possessions, abnegated himself before the pope. He not only accepted Langton as archbishop, but he became the pope's vassal and made England the fief of the papacy. These sensational events seemed to demonstrate that no king could withstand for long the will of the papacy.

Even the pope's ally, Philip Augustus, incurred Innocent's wrath. They disputed a private matter, but Innocent, as the guardian of the faith and morals of Europe, used all the moral and religious powers at his command to force Philip's accedence to the papal will. Philip had entered into a marriage contract with a Danish princess named Ingeborg to obtain the assistance of the Danish fleet for one of his ventures against the Angevins. When the titanic northern princess arrived in France, Philip changed his mind and refused to accept her as his wife. The affair dragged on for years until Innocent became pope and adopted his accustomed drastic measures, including the leveling of a papal interdict on France that forced Philip to give way. Eventually a compromise settlement favorable to all parties was reached. This strange incident demonstrates Innocent's supreme self-confidence in the power of the papacy and his willingness to use all the weapons at the pope's command even in minor matters. In general, Innocent's relations with France were greatly to the benefit of the Capetian monarchy. The alliance he established with Philip Augustus against Otto IV and John intensified the long association of the papacy with the Capetian monarchy and cloaked Philip's expansionist policies and devious methods in an aura of morality. The greatest boon that the French monarchy received from the papacy, however, was the Albigensian crusade, which opened up southern France to penetration by the north and eventual incorporation into the French crown. Philip Augustus did not participate in the Albigensian crusade, and it is possible that he did not fully perceive its significance. But the crusade destroyed the power of the nobility of Languedoc and made inevitable the subjection of southeastern France to the Capetian king.

Innocent had originally hoped to bring the Albigensian heretics back into the church by sending in outstanding preachers to demonstrate the Cathari errors. This approach had little success; the Albigensian doctrines had penetrated the social and intellectual milieu of southern France too deeply. The murder of a papal legate in 1208, in which the count of Toulouse was thought to be implicated, induced Innocent to take a more drastic measure, namely, the launching of a crusade against the heretics. Innocent had already become familiar with the use of the crusading ideal for some special purpose favorable to the Roman church. The fourth crusade of 1204, which Innocent had proclaimed, had been turned by the Venetians from its initial aim of fighting the Moslems to the attack and capture of Constantinople. Innocent readily accepted the change in plans because he saw the Latin Kingdom of Constantinople as the means of bringing the Greeks back into union with the Latin church and under the authority of the papacy. If a crusade could be directed against Constantinople, then assuredly it could be directed against heretics whose insidious doctrines, perverse morality, and stronghold in southern France threatened the unity of Latin Christendom. The northern French barons enthusiastically responded to Innocent's proclamation of the Albigensian crusade. They looked upon it as a heaven-sent opportunity to carve out fiefs for themselves in the rich lands of the Languedoc. The Albigensian crusade took on the qualities of a land grab. The northern barons, led by one Simon de Montfort, a lord from the Ile-de-France, indiscriminately attacked the heretics and the orthodox and perpetrated bloodbaths in the southern cities. As a consequence the southern nobility, whether or not it sympathized with the Cathari doctrine, bitterly resisted the crusaders, and the king of Aragon, who was far from being a heretic, came to the assistance of the count of Toulouse.

At the battle of Muret in 1213 the southern forces were decisively defeated, and although it took another dozen years to end all resistance, the victory of the north was assured in the long run. By his launching of the Albigensian crusade Innocent prepared the way for the French crown to gain the wealthy lands of Languedoc, which finally took place in the 1220s. Innocent was criticized by the southern nobility in his own day and by many modern writers, for preaching this crusade against the Cathari. It has been said that he perverted the crusading movement and that he destroyed a brilliant civilization in the south of France. There is some truth to both indictments, but he had no alternative if he was to cut the cancerous sore of Catharism out of the body politic of Christendom.

With his typical thoroughness Innocent could not leave the heretics to be rooted out and judged by diocesan officials in southern France, whom he greatly distrusted anyway. He sent in legates commissioned to establish courts for dealing with heretics.

Out of these precedents developed the general papal mandate for judicial Inquisition officially prescribed in 1233, but well operative in the time of Innocent III. Panels of designated churchmen under the papal rules of Inquisition were to investigate reports of heresy and counter-churches in particular areas. The Inquisitors did not have to reveal to suspects called before them who had informed on them, nor could the accused confront the informers. The first and main aim of the court of Inquisition was to persuade and pressure defendants to confess and recant. For those who did so, on first offense, the normal penalty was mild. But those who refused to confess and who remained under suspicion of heresy and subversion of the Roman church were put to torture in Roman law's traditional manner of getting at the truth. Those who confessed and then recanted were discovered by the Inquisitors to have relapsed into heresy and would on the second offense be subject to a much more severe penalty, such as ritualized public humiliation, imprisonment, and loss of property. Those with an established record of heretical resistance or repeated relapses from orthodoxy would be "relaxed to the secular arm," to suffer death by burning.

Contrary to the widespread belief in the nineteenth and early twentieth centuries, the Inquisitors were, with few exceptions, not psychotic sadists who were insatiably seeking vengeance upon heretics through death penalties. The Inquisitors were normally well-trained canon lawyers and frequently Dominican friars or members of another religious order. Recent research has shown that they were sufficiently astute to be skeptical of the witchcraft craze of the fifteenth and sixteenth centuries and to find the vast majority of the accusations against old women and similar marginal people who were alleged to be witches to be without substance.

Therefore, the courts of the papal mandated Inquisition should never be considered in the same category as the Nazi holocaust or Stalinist purges. Surviving Inquisitorial records are sparse. But it is a good guess that even including the Spanish Inquisition of the late fifteenth and sixteenth centuries, which in more Draconian fashion operated directly under the aegis of the Spanish crown rather than the papacy, the total number of people who died at the hands of all Catholic Inquisitions did not exceed five figures and probably did not total more than ten thousand people.

No one would claim that the Inquisitorial courts were liberal institutions. These courts used torture in the Roman manner, did not allow defendants to confront or often even to know the names of their accusers, sorely harassed and frightened people, and confiscated substantial property of the wealthy and high-born. The Inquisitorial process was not predicated on liberal doctrines of freedom of thought, such as had occasionally been expressed by pagan Roman aristocrats and that became central in western culture in the eighteenth century. Innocent III and his successor were opposed to a doctrine of religious and intellectual freedom. The heretics were enemies of Christian civilization and had to be eliminated—by persuasion, if possible, or by force, if necessary. St. Augustine had propounded such a doctrine, and it became much more meaningful when the Latin church was confronted with the mass movement of popular heresy around 1200. For Innocent III the gravest kind of crisis threatened the unity and security of the Latin church and not to proceed against the heretics with every means at the disposal of Christian society was not only weak and foolish, it was a betrayal of the Lord. Yet the Inquisitors wanted to kill nobody. They wanted to embrace everybody within the one and true Catholic church. They were eager to welcome dissenters and schismatics into the Roman community. They exulted in the conversion of Jews, and, in fact, some of the early Inquisitors were converted Jews who had joined the Dominican order.

Nothing, as Innocent said, was outside the province of the papacy, and he felt compelled to legislate not only on the matter of heretics, but on the treatment of the Jews. He forbade attempts to convert them to Christianity by force, but he advocated ghettoization—their exclusion as social pariahs from European society. The Fourth Latern Council decreed that Jews should wear a yellow label so they could easily be distinguished as outcasts. This requirement was to have a long and illustrious history in western Europe. Some writers have attempted to whitewash Innocent's Jewish policy; they claim that he wanted to ostracize the Jews to save them from further pogroms, which were becoming endemic in European life as a result of the dissemination of the blood libels. It seems unlikely that Innocent was motivated by humanitarian reasons. He shared in the militant Christianity of his time, and the threat to the church from the great wave of antisacerdotalism tended to make ecclesiastical leaders even more intolerant and severe in their dealings with those who dissented from the Catholic faith. Innocent would not have been flattered by attempts to make him out to be a liberal. He had an unmitigated belief in the truth of the Catholic faith and the validity of the hierocratic tradition, the Petrine theory, and the Donation of Constantine. Both his doctrine and his personality were authoritarian. For eighteen years Innocent devoted his magnificent administrative and leadership qualities to furthering these doctrines, with far-reaching results.

For Innocent and his successors in the thirteenth-century papacy the Jews assumed a more threatening image for Roman Christianity than ever before. For Innocent III and his cardinals and Inquisitors, the Jews were associated with other enemies of the church—heretics, magicians, and witches against whom the church had to wage war and persecute with all the powers it could command. Even lepers (not only people with the communicable skin disease but a catchall category for social deviants) and liberated women sometimes fitted into this "other" of anti-Catholic demonized enemies of the church.

Was this a paranoid, papal hysteria, or was there some substance to it? The spread of Catharism and Waldensianism certainly generated a fierce anxiety in Rome. Like all anxieties, it fed upon itself and perhaps exaggerated the threat to the church, but it was not a paranoid delusion. It was grounded in reality even if it distorted that reality at the margin. Even the tendency of Innocent III, his immediate successors, and the papal Inquisitors to associate Jews and heretics had a segment of plausibility. Catharism sprouted in southern France where there was a large, wealthy Jewish population, whose rabbis were developing the mystical literature of the Kabbalah. And the Kabbalah had at its core the dualist theology of ancient Gnosticism, which had been a great threat to the mainline church in the second century A.D. So if Innocent III enunciated a greatly increased papal hostility to Jews and sought their full segregation from Christian society, illiberal as this policy appears from our point of view, it was not removed from thirteenth-century reality or contrary to its cultural assumptions.

Yet Innocent realized that his own methods could have only a limited impact on the problems of piety and learning. He had reorganized the church, humiliated kings, and caused the taking up of the sword against the worst of the heretics, but none of these approaches could resolve the struggle in men's minds that followed from the effects of the new piety and the challenge of Aristotelian science. It is not the least of Innocent's accomplishments as an administrator and leader that he was sensitive to the need for a more positive kind of approach than he himself could take and that he realized the significance and value of the work of St. Dominic and St. Francis.

II. The Dominican and Franciscan Ideals

The founding of the Dominican and Franciscan orders demonstrates the continued vitality of medieval civilization in the early thirteenth century. The product of the institutionalization of asceticism in the twelfth century—the religious orders working in the world—was used to meet the consequences of the new piety and the new learning and to reassert the leadership of the church in European society, thereby completing the bases of the new consensus that Innocent had set out to construct. The Dominican order met the forces that challenged the medieval order by teaching the truths of Catholic dogma and demonstrating their compatibility with science; the Franciscan approach was emotional, not intellectual. It appealed to men's hearts rather than to their reason. It was founded on the premise that profound individual religious experience could strengthen faith. The development of thought, religion, and culture in the thirteenth century was largely the working out of the implications of the Dominican and Franciscan ideals.

The Order of Preachers, to give its official name, was a product of the struggle against the Albigensians. A Spanish priest named Dominic, working as a preacher against the heretics in Languedoc, gathered around him a group of like-minded disciples who aimed to live saintly lives, to be as ascetic as Cathari prefects, and to engage in homiletics and apologetics. In 1216 St. Dominic secured the pope's approval of a new order that would follow rules derived from the Austin canons and the Premonstratensians. The order attracted from the first a steady stream of young men who fitted its high standards: The candidates had to be men of both ascetic persuasion and first-class intellectual powers. In the Dominican order ability counted for everything and overrode even the prescriptions of seniority. The officials of the order were responsible to meetings of the general chapter, and the representatives sent to these meetings were elected to ensure that the best man would most likely be chosen, irrespective of his age or length of time in the order. Like Dominic himself, the members of the preaching order were men who subordinated their own personalities and characteristics so that their talents could be fully put to the service of the church. The Dominicans were the intellectual shock troops of the thirteenth-century church. These were the ideal clergy to administer the new courts directed against heresy, and in the thirteenth century the Inquisition was largely a Dominican institution. Similarly, the aims, organization, and personnel of the new order made it eminently suitable for undertaking the task of meeting the Aristotelian challenge.

For three or four decades the Aristotelian texts had steadily been coming in from the Arabic world, and the philosophy and theology faculties of the University of Paris and, to a lesser degree, of other institutions had been deeply involved in trying to relate this new science to the older biblical-patristic tradition, with indifferent results. The Dominicans assumed this task eagerly, and by the middle of the century they had come to dominate the University of Paris. As scholars and intellectuals they were convinced that revelation and science were ultimately one truth. As the official apologists for church doctrine, they deeply sensed the necessity for a philosophical defense of Christian doctrine, and it was one of the Dominican professors at Paris, Thomas Aquinas, who definitively formulated this kind of intellectual system in the third quarter of the thirteenth century.

The Dominican message was addressed to educated people; it was the Franciscans who undertook the hardest task of trying to come to terms with the impact of piety on the ordinary townsman, of trying to control the direction of the urban religiosity that produced the great anti-sacerdotal movement. It was not the idea of St. Francis of Assisi (1182–1226) that his disciples should be organized into a corporate order along the lines of the Dominicans. He simply called on all men to live the life of Christ as fully as they could. And the saintly lives of his disciples, the *fratres minores,* "the little brothers," would suffice to stir men's hearts by example and convert them to better ways. It was the most direct possible approach to the problem of converting society. The walls of pride and hatred that had been created by the complexities of social life could be breached only by manifestations of Christian love. It was both the simplest and the most profound message possible, and its implications troubled the leaders of the church as much as they admired the greatest saint whom medieval civilization produced, the man who most perfectly followed in the steps of the Lord.

St. Francis's life was as simple and pure as his teaching. His father was a wealthy merchant of Assisi in northern Italy, and his mother came from the urbanized nobility. He was a rich, spoiled youth who read chivalric romances and dreamed of himself as another Lancelot. But when he tried to become a knight, he was wounded and disgraced. He passed through one of those great conversions that other great religious minds of Christianity have experienced—St. Paul, Augustine, Ignatius Loyola, and Luther; he felt the grace of God coming unto him, and instead of mundane love, the most exalted kind of religious love became the inspiration of his life. He determined to live as Christ had lived—a mendicant, a teacher, a healer, the friend of all creatures, the preacher of the simplest and the most sublime truths. He wandered around the cities and villages of northern Italy existing solely as a beggar, and yet with the most complete faith in God's grace to provide for him. He ministered to the poor, the sick, even the lepers, whom no one else would approach. He tried to lead the rich and the powerful to live more fully Christian lives, and he was never discouraged by the insults directed at him. He celebrated the glories of God's creation with a magnificent lyric addressed to the sun, and he preached to the birds, whom he also regarded as his brothers.

The figure of the itinerant preaching saint had been familiar in the cities of northern Italy for two centuries, and such men had played a great role in fomenting the heretical movements of the twelfth century. But St. Francis seemed to go beyond any of these previous saints by the perfection of his life. His complete fulfillment of the life of Christ was confirmed by the appearance on his body of the stigmata, the wounds of Christ, it was said. He soon gathered men and women around him, whom he sent out along the dusty roads of Italy to bring the Christian gospel to the laity in the way that he had done. The rules he set down for his Little Brothers were general statements of principles, not the specific code of a corporate order. Francis's basic requirement of his disciples was that they live and preach Christ and pursue their pilgrimage to the City of God with complete faith in divine beneficence, "taking nothing for the way." The Little Brothers were to be poor in every sense of the word: poor in spirit, in possessions, in offices, and in learning. The kingdom of God within man was all they needed. The friars were, in accordance with the example of the apostolic church, to hold no property either individually or corporately. They were to live in abandoned churches, caves, or anywhere they could find shelter. Their physical labor was to earn them their keep, and if this did not suffice, they were to be mendicants. They were to obtain no privileges from the pope, and they were not to be ordained priests. They were not to seek learning because it was a snare and a distraction; to know that they should adore and serve God was enough.

These ideals bore some striking similarities to the attitudes of the Waldensian heretics, and Innocent and other ecclesiastical leaders were at first deeply concerned by the implications of what St. Francis was teaching. But there was something more, and this made all the difference: St.

Francis was not an antisacerdotalist, but a firm believer in the authority of the priesthood and the efficacy of the sacraments, and he fully subordinated himself and his Little Brothers to the hierarchy. The priests alone, Francis told his followers, could minister the Eucharist that made salvation possible. He said that he had such faith in the priesthood and the sacraments that he would have faith even in the ministration of the sacraments by a bad priest. This constituted an explicit negation of the Donatist heresy and allowed Innocent to give his approval to Francis to continue his work and to found his little society of Friars Minor. Innocent shrewdly perceived that St. Francis was supplying the necessary supplement to the pope's own work of restoring the prestige and leadership of the church. The Franciscan movement would make the positive contribution of inspiring the religious feelings of Europe, which could not be done by cardinal legates and Inquisitors. Innocent, who was a different kind of man from the saint of Assisi, nevertheless glimpsed how useful Francis's work was to the church.

The Franciscan movement was the rallying point for all those laymen who were no longer satisfied with the church hierarchy but who did not want to break with the church and go off into the uncharted wastes of heresy. The teaching of St. Francis allowed those who wanted an intense personal religious experience to remain within the church. This was the best of all possible spiritual worlds, and it profoundly satisfied the religious yearning of the thirteenth century. The great enthusiasm that greeted St. Francis and his disciples, so deeply moved the laity of the thirteenth century, revivified their attachment to the church, and brought about the rapid spread of the Franciscan movement over Europe was not simply the result of the saintly disposition of these angelic men. It was because the Franciscans were both saints and Catholics. St. Francis was the product of mass psychology; the laity of his time wanted and needed such a figure, and they were fortunate in finding a man who so perfectly fitted their ideal.

The papacy after Innocent III determined to harness the Franciscan movement more firmly as an agent of clerical leadership by turning it into a corporate order on the model of the Dominicans. St. Francis only reluctantly agreed to these changes, and most of them were carried out while he was absent in the Levant trying to convert the Moslems. After his death the Franciscan order's leaders, with papal encouragement, proceeded to violate some of Francis's most fundamental rules. The Franciscans, and the Dominicans as well, became priests and were given the authority to wander over the countryside and through the towns, hearing confession, and administering the sacraments, much to the chagrin of the jealous parish priests and cathedral clergy. The Friars Minor came to hold property corporately, and Franciscan scholars became as outstanding as Dominicans for their work in philosophy and science. By the last quarter of the thirteenth century Franciscan professors dominated Oxford as much as Dominicans took the lead at the University of Paris. These changes were to produce grave disputes within the order, but did not detract from the new devotion and respect for the church that the Franciscans gained during at least the first half of the thirteenth century. Among Innocent III's many decisions, none was as important as allowing Francis of Assisi to send out his Little Brothers into the cities and villages of Europe.

Just as Arthurian romance proclaimed the self-image of the aristocracy, Franciscan piety expressed the outlook of the thirteenth-century townsmen. The whole tenor of Franciscan teaching replaced traditional sacramentalism with a religion centered on personal experience. This was the kind of religion that the bourgeoisie demanded; it fitted their whole attitude toward themselves and toward society. The townsman's position in the world was not derived from inherited status and traditional privilege; it was the consequence of his own efforts. Much as his business success was the result of his private striving and a reward for his hard work and self-restraint, he wanted his religion to concentrate upon a personal experience of Christ and the Virgin and to offer salvation as a reward for purity of life. Franciscanism—the ideals of which are directly advertised in the paintings of the late thirteenth-century Italian artist Giotto—satisfied, indeed intentionally catered to, these middle-class attitudes. It was believed that St. Francis, more than any other man, followed perfectly in the steps of the Lord, to the extent that the stigmata (signs) of the Savior's wounds appeared on his body, entirely because of his complete purity and love, not because of any official status.

Sanctity, then, was a matter of personal experience and private devotion, just as social and economic position was (or ought to be) entirely a matter of personal achievement. The bourgeois wanted to believe that if he fastened his devotion on the Virgin and Child and lived an abstemious life, he was as good as the pope, better indeed than any martial aristocrat. Franciscan friars, preaching in the marketplaces of all European cities, allowed the bourgeoisie this self-serving doctrine, dangerous as it was for the stability and authority of the church.

The style of Franciscan preaching—again paralleled exactly by Giotto's painting—was at one with the content of the friar's sermons. The Franciscans abandoned the elaborate allegorical explication of biblical texts that had been the form of all previous medieval preaching. Instead, they told simple moralistic stories and described events drawn from common experiences of middle-class life, and their stories were told in a highly realistic manner. Again, the intention was to gratify the bourgeoisie, who thereby gained instruction in Christian morality without having to bother about arcane or learned traditions of biblical exegesis. Giotto's style, which departed from medieval impressionism and nonrepresentational iconography toward a commonsense naturalism, was part of this Franciscan involvement in bourgeois culture—the inspiring story plainly told for plain men who want to be inspired. If the High Middle Ages produced the code of the gentleman and an ideology of aristocratic leadership in society, bourgeois Franciscan puritanism and naturalism sanctified and nourished the sentiments of the common man—a crucial precondition for modern democracy and mass culture.

CHAPTER NINETEEN

The New Consensus and Its Limitations

I. The Cathedral of Intellect

The pontificate of Innocent III initiated a half century of renewed peace and apparent stability in European life. There were no important wars from the battle of Bouvines in 1214 until the 1290s. The first three quarters of the thirteenth century were the concluding stage in the long period of population growth and economic boom that had marked European economic history since the middle of the tenth century. Innocent III's success in dealing with the kings of western Europe was continued by the popes who followed him. The rulers of France and England were saintly men who appeared deferential toward the papacy, and the renewed struggle with the Hohenstaufen house ended in the complete triumph of the church. The half century that followed Innocent's death was also the period of balance and consensus in intellectual life, a period when the thinkers of western Europe tried to work out the implications of twelfth-century creativity and to demonstrate the relationship between revelation and science as part of a single body of truth. The resulting ambitious constructions of the mind were paralleled by a new consensus in the realm of piety. The attack of the Inquisition on heresy, reinforced strongly by enthusiasm for the Franciscan ideal, brought about a sharp decline in the influence of the antisacerdotal movement that had shaken the medieval world order to its foundations at the end of the twelfth century. By 1260 popular heresy seemed to be a negligible factor in European life. The Franciscans and their followers succeeded in channeling the intense spirituality that now characterized all groups in society, but especially the townsmen, toward the enriching and fulfilling of Catholic

Christianity. Some of the greatest achievements of medieval art and literature remain as monuments to the new harnessing of popular piety in the interests of the church.

The new architectural style that originated in the middle of the twelfth century in the Ile-de-France and that later, by a pejorative misnomer, came to be called Gothic had gone on from triumph to triumph since its experimental beginnings in Abbot Suger's day. The great bishops of northern France—of Chartres, Paris, Orleans, Amiens, Sens—in the century after Suger engaged in a great competition to erect vast cathedrals in the new style, with wide portals, high clerestories, soaring buttresses, pointed arches, ribbed vaulting, rose windows, and magnificent sculptured façades. They strained the vast resources of their sees and the architectural ingenuity of Europe to create yet greater and higher edifices, and they ended by erecting, in the shape of crosses, buildings that had the greatest amount of uninterrupted and undivided interior space that western man had ever known. The new French style spread rapidly to England and Germany and even influenced Italian architecture, where the previously dominant Romanesque form had originated. It was in the Ile-de-France, however, that Gothic architecture achieved its greatest triumphs.

The lord, bourgeois, or peasant who entered Notre Dame or Chartres was given his most effective impression of the nature of heaven. All arts were employed, all senses were stirred, to render a momentary insight into the indescribable glory of the heavenly life. The stained glass refracted the Divine Light and bathed the altar in a myriad of miraculous colors. The worshippers, standing in their thousands to see and hear the celebration of the mass with all the visual and musical pomp of an imperial church, could not tell from inside the cathedral how its walls were held up. As the choir intoned the complex harmonies of its hymns and chants; as the bishop or his adjutant stood before the altar in his golden vestments; and as the Savior, Virgin, and saints blazed forth from the glass mosaics in the clerestory and stood out below in sculptured roundness from the surrounding gloom by the falling light, it was easy to imagine the angelic host as the supporters of this divine temple.

These supreme moments of faith were made possible only by an enormous amount of planning, money, and labor. It was a great task to build a Gothic cathedral, requiring the best efforts of hundreds of men over many years. The cathedrals of France of the late twelfth and thirteenth centuries were not put together by a few clerics and pious laborers who sang hymns to the Virgin while they worked. They were built by guilds of masons who had to be well paid for their work. The bishop not only used his own income, but raised funds from kings, the nobility, and burghers. The townsmen's municipal pride led them to support the building of the episcopal cathedral, even though they frequently were engaged in a bitter quarrel with the bishops over their communal rights. The bishop was not always inspired by the highest motives; the cathedral was in a sense his monument, and the same prelate who cared nothing for the sufferings of peasant and proletarian and who was stingy in his charity to the sick and the helpless could achieve both contemporary and posthumous renown as a cathedral builder. Even with all this effort, the completion of a Gothic cathedral within thirty years was considered very good time, and in some instances the construction lagged over a century or more. All sorts of obstacles could arise: the original bishop could die and his successor could care less about the work, the money could run out, and the architects and builders could run into technical problems. Erecting a Gothic-style cathedral even today is a very expensive and difficult proposition—there has been one a-building in New York City for sixty years—and it was no less so in the thirteenth century. There was a ready supply of stonecutters then, which is lacking today, but medieval construction machines were simple and the thirteenth-century knowledge of civil engineering was crude.

The Gothic architect worked his plans by geometric proportions. He could not determine exactly the stress at any point in the walls of his building, and he had to take great risks, with not always happy consequences. The more strident the ambitions of his episcopal employer, the greater the chance he had to take, and the larger structures of the thirteenth century had to be supported, as a measure of security, by projecting flying buttresses. Under these conditions it is not surprising that good architects, who rose from the ranks of the master masons, were highly valued and remunerated. They were a small professional elite, the more successful of whom were deluged with commissions and often took on several jobs at the same time.

The architect's task was not only to plan and execute the construction of the cathedral, but to supervise its decoration. The architect was responsible for directing the craftsmen, whose stained-glass windows, sculptured statues, friezes, and ornaments were considered as necessary to a cathedral as were illuminations to a good manuscript. In obscure corners of the cathedral or high on the exterior walls, where the details of decoration were invisible to the viewer on the ground, the craftsmen were sometimes allowed to use their imagination, and they created all sorts of weird and grotesque figures in accordance with vulgar humor or popular myth. But the iconography for the sculpture and stained glass was carefully worked out in advance and designed to the smallest detail by the supervising architect. At times the bishop or abbot who had commissioned the building would make specific suggestions about the motifs and symbols he wanted depicted in his church, or scholars in the patron's service would advise the architect. It is possible that more learned architects worked out motifs themselves. But it is also clear that much of the symbolism in Gothic art was not the result of conscious thought, but merely the adaptation of traditional Christian iconology that can be traced back for centuries through illuminated manuscripts. The often overcommitted and hard-pressed architects borrowed ideas extensively from churches already in existence. The sketchbook of an early thirteenth-century French architect, Villard de Honnecourt, for example, reveals that he had gone around to various cathedrals and made extensive copies of both the architectural and iconographical work he liked.

If all aspects of art were not as much the product of conscious thought as some enthusiastic modern writers believe, the cathedrals of northern France nevertheless remain the monumental symbols of the intellectual tendencies of the first seven decades of the thirteenth century. If the leitmotif of twelfth-century thought was creativity and originality, that of the earlier and mid-thirteenth century was order and discipline. As the Gothic cathedral combined all the artistic and engineering resources of the thirteenth century to create a house for the divine spirit, the thinkers and writers of the period tried to create a cathedral of intellect. The heterogeneous and sometimes conflicting currents of twelfth-century thought were subjected to the scrutiny of ordered intelligence, its bewildering twists and turns straightened out into systematic patterns, and its open ends circumscribed and marked off by visible limits. Thirteenth-century thought resembles the form of the Gothic cathedral in another way, however: The structure is dominated by a central nave and transept open for all to see, spacious, finished, magnificent, but it also contains less prominent and rather obscure side chapels and rooms, and there was a pressure on the walls of this great intellectual edifice that sometimes worried its architects.

Thirteenth-century civilization had a compulsive urge to collect and systematize all forms of knowledge. There was an underlying feeling that if all the known information in a certain field could only be brought together in a regular pattern within the pages of a large book, the gnawing doubts and confusions would go away, and educated men could feel secure and happy. It was a natural reaction against the centrifugal tendencies of twelfth-century culture. Prodigious effort and fine intelligence went into the making of such systematic compendia, which were popular at all levels and in all fields of thought. There was a *summa* for every interest and taste; the most comprehensive, if not the most profound, was the gigantic *Speculum Mains* (Greater Mirror) of Vincent of Beauvais, a French Dominican. Theology and philosophy and law of every kind, whether civil, canon, feudal, or common, had its great systematizers. There were textbooks on cosmology describing the universe on the basis of the theories of Ptolemy, Aristotle, and the Arabic scholars, all presenting variants of an earth-centered universe, which fitted in so well with the book of Genesis and the obvious central place of man in God's creation. For the less learned there were encyclopedias of all knowledge, some of them written in the vernacular, enthusiastically received by nobles of courtly inclination and burghers trying to improve themselves. Bestiaries were popular, not least because they described and pictured animals no one had ever seen.

The thirteenth-century penchant for systematizing all knowledge in summaries and encyclopedias was paralleled by the incorporation of all important intellectual activity within the life of academic institutions. Not again until the twentieth century would the universities of the western world so dominate the life of the mind, and the academics held an even greater monopoly in the thirteenth century. Thirteenth-century thought was "scholastic," that is, academic. All the important writers on theology, philosophy, law, and science were "scholastics," that is, they were professors in the schools, the universities, and they were devoted to the use of the dialectical method of reasoning and exposition that had become common in the twelfth century. The institutional milieu in which they worked inevitably conditioned their outlook in other ways. It was an intensely serious, competitive, and confined environment, one that was probably better for refining the prevailing doctrines than for breaking away from accepted patterns and opening up new lines of thought. Medieval professors and students have sometimes been depicted as jovial and serene characters; this was generally not the case. It would be more accurate to typify them as unhappy, compulsive, and aggressive.

The medieval university, which grew out of the early twelfth-century French cathedral schools and the Italian municipal schools, was a distinctive and original contribution to the institutionalization of higher education. It was organized for the dissemination of many branches of knowledge to a large number of students as cheaply and as systematically as possible, and as such, it was superior to the academies and schools of rhetoric of the ancient world. The medieval system was designed to get students through prescribed programs and to give them degrees certifying a minimum proficiency; this is still the basic idea of a university in western civilization. The medieval university also developed a new teaching method involving lectures and the use of textbooks that is still, for better or worse, substantially in use today. The medieval lecture was literally "a reading"; the professor read a passage from a text, such as the Justinian code, the Bible, or one of Aristotle's works, and developed his interpretation by glossing the text. Since books could be produced only by manuscript, they were extremely expensive, and only the wealthier students could buy standard editions of the textbooks. Three or four students would get together to buy a book and to write down the professors' glosses on the text. There was little or no discussion between the professor and the students. The only Socratic dialogue in the medieval university was among the professors, who occasionally offered competing courses on the same text and engaged in great public debates on disputed theses.

The universities were organized as special guilds for manufacturing learned men. North of the Alps the teachers acted like the masters of any other guild; they set the length of time a student had to serve as an apprentice and journeyman, and they established the conditions under which he could enter the ranks of the master-teachers and receive his final degree. All such degrees, whether the graduate was called master or doctor, were technically licenses to teach, even though most university graduates did not become teachers; they were certificates of competence in the craft pursued by the corporation. The intellectual standards and length of study required by the undergraduate were severe. (A medieval student took as long, or longer, to train for a learned profession as students in American universities take today.) In the schools of Italy, which specialized in civil law in the north and medicine in the south, the guild was in the hands of the undergraduates, or bachelors, who hired the teachers and set rules requiring the lecturers to finish the commentary on the prescribed texts before the end of the term of study. This was the bourgeois attitude toward education at work. Examinations in the medieval university were given orally; they were comprehensive and difficult.

The guilds of masters in the northern universities were licensed by the bishop in whose city they taught. Occasionally the bishop intervened in the university if he was concerned by the doctrinal implications of what was being said or written by one of the professors. The papacy and the king also exercised supervision over the universities. As a consequence, professors were occasionally silenced, and their doctrines were condemned. But what is remarkable is the great degree of freedom that the thirteenth-century professor had, even in the fields of theology and philosophy. The discipline and control to which the professor was subjected were largely intramural. His colleagues constantly competed with him for intellectual distinction, the best professorships, and the devotion and sometimes the fees of the students. Any slipshod or revolutionary thinking would be stiffly challenged. Furthermore, many of the professors were members of religious orders, particularly the Dominican and Franciscan, which exercised a further control over their work.

It is a myth that most students in a medieval university were zealots who wanted to become theologians. Actually there was not a much greater proportion of the thirteenth-century university students studying theology than there is today. Among the students the most popular faculty by far was law, and for the same reasons that this study attracts large numbers today. Law was the road to good jobs in the church and the state. On the other hand, the study of theology, although it might be hailed as the queen of the sciences, was long and difficult and offered little employment opportunity on completion of the degree.

The medieval student's life was always hard and frequently desperate. Most of the students came from families of lesser knights, who could offer their children little in the way of a patrimony, or from the burghers, for whom the system presented a way of escaping from their class and entering the service of the church or the state. The students' impecunious condition was made worse by the exorbitant prices and the inadequacy of the food and lodging available in university towns such as Paris and Oxford. Occasional fights between townsmen and students, and even large-scale riots, were the natural result. The king and bishop were supposed to protect the students from exploitation, but they were not very effective in this regard. The University of Cambridge was founded in the early thirteenth century by masters and students who left Oxford in disgust after a particularly violent "town and gown" riot. During the thirteenth century certain wealthy benefactors, including a Robert de Sorbon at Paris, began to establish communal houses, or "colleges," for the students. At Oxford the colleges became more and more important in the teaching life of the university. It was also traditional at Paris to divide the students into certain "nations" according to their provenance. Because a student found his studies long and hard, the cost of living high, and the discipline to which he was subjected severe, it is not surprising that he occasionally vented his unhappiness in drinking, gambling, and street fighting. It is also not surprising that some of the most illustrious thinkers in thirteenth- and fourteenth-century academic life were querulous and disagreeable men and rather unstable personalities.

The arts faculty provided the basic preliminary studies in the medieval university, from which the students proceeded, as rapidly as possible, to their advanced work in law, theology, or medicine. The teachers in the arts faculty were generally not the better minds in the medieval university, and their treatment of the classics lacked the humane values that John of Salisbury had found in the cultivation of the liberal arts. John had feared that humanism could not prevail in the dialectical atmosphere of the university, and the subsequent development of the study of the liberal arts proved the keenness of his intuition. The thirteenth-century scholastics wanted to find the truth, but they did not appreciate great literature either for its esthetic qualities or as a teacher of morality. The teachers in the arts faculty approached the classics analytically, looking on the ancient texts as a body of knowledge to be subjected to the tools of dialectic; that is, the word structure and rhetoric of the texts were to be dissected and then systematized. But the teachers' narrowly utilitarian approach left no room for either the ideas or values of the classical tradition. The ancient world meant nothing to them; they were self-consciously separated from it. In its antihumanist attitude thirteenth-century thought was at its weakest, and this failure was to be important in later medieval culture. The perpetuation of the classical tradition, which had been the task of ecclesiastical schools since the sixth century, moved out of the university and was joined with the romantic literary tradition. It was the Italian poets of the late thirteenth and early fourteenth centuries who revived humanist values and were the true successors of John of Salisbury. The hostility that the Renaissance humanists frequently expressed toward scholasticism and the universities, even though many of them were university graduates, was the result of the rejection of the humanist tradition by the thirteenth-century schoolmen.

The scholastics believed that their dialectical method and great store of Christian and Greek learning prepared them to answer all problems. For instance, they devoted considerable time and ingenuity debating whether the taking of usury was compatible with Christian doctrine and what was the "just price" that the ecclesiastical authorities should permit the merchant to charge. Although the scholastics concluded that there were moral limitations to capitalist enterprise, they nevertheless allowed the business entrepreneur a comfortable return on his investment and labor. In actual practice the scholastic limitations on profit taking were generally ignored with impunity by the merchants and bankers.

The greatest demand that society, particularly the church, placed upon the scholastics fell in the areas of logic, metaphysics, epistemology, and theology. The intellectual problems that were left over from the twelfth century and that became even more pressing and crucial as a result of the absorption of the Aristotelian corpus and its Arabic commentators were the ones that fully exercised the dialectical skill and unsurpassed mental powers of the thirteenth-century scholastics. By the middle of the century there was great confusion and controversy among the philosophers and theologians as competing and sharply different intellectual systems contended against one another. There were still those who supported the older Augustinianism and neoplatonism and a strongly realist position. A member of the arts faculty of Paris, Siger of Brabant, openly advocated the Averroist position, whose strict determinism and denial of creation *ex nihilo* and the individuality of the soul were as much a contradiction of Christian as of Arabic revelation. A German Dominican at Paris, Albertus Magnus, was attempting to establish a Christian Aristotelian position, but with little success.

At this point another Paris Dominican, Thomas Aquinas (1225–1272), began to work out his distinctive system. The completion of his work in the *Summa Theologica* was the major turning point in thirteenth-century thought, a breakthrough of first importance. But it was one that startled and disturbed as many of his contemporaries as it satisfied. Nothing is further from the reality of thirteenth-century culture than to imagine that Thomism was immediately acclaimed by all as the answer to the intellectual problems of the church. Modern Catholicism may regard Thomism as the official philosophy of the church, but this is far from the attitude that prevailed in St. Thomas's day and for the next two centuries. Thomas was regarded by many as a radical, highly speculative, and tendentious thinker. Yet the importance of his work was recognized from the first even by those who criticized it. Thomas had created a vast, complex, subtle, and ordered system that integrated to the fullest possible degree Aristotelian science and the Christian revelation. The question remained, however, whether such a system was philosophically valid or theologically desirable.

Aquinas was not disturbed. The criticism he received from within and outside his university did not upset his usual serenity. He was attacked not only by some of his colleagues, but by the bishop of Paris and the leading contemporary Dominican philosopher at Oxford. But he went on with his teaching and writing, adding bit by bit to his intellectual structure, which the art historian Erwin Panofsky said exhibits all the qualities of a Gothic cathedral, and fully earning his reputation as the "angelic doctor." Thomas Aquinas's personality, remarkable for self-confidence, serenity, and moderation in debate, has often been regarded as typical of the medieval scholastic, but on the contrary, these qualities made him the great exception. His intellectual preeminence partly accounted for his serenity, but this quality must also be attributed to his famous obesity and, above all, to his class background. Whereas most of the schoolmen came from modest and even obscure backgrounds, Thomas was the scion of an aristocratic Neapolitan family, and he retained in his intellectual work the unshakable self-confidence of the highborn.

The Christian philosophy of Thomas Aquinas may be said to be founded on a magnificent paradox: He tried to arrive at most of the conclusions of Augustine and the neoplatonists by using most of the science and logic of the Averroists. This was an extremely bold and risky undertaking, and it is no surprise that he startled and stunned his contemporaries by daring and completing it in a vast systematic treatise. Thomas's basic assumption was that Aristotelianism need not lead to the conclusions that Averroes, "the Commentator," had derived from Aristotle, "the Philosopher." Although his critics unjustly accused him of being close to Averroism because of his use of Aristotelian science as the basis of his philosophy, he wanted above all to negate the double-truth theory of the great Arabic thinker. There was not one truth in science and another in faith; it was possible to prove the essential doctrines of Christian theology by rational logic.

It was his Aristotelian epistemology that allowed Aquinas to work his way to this conclusion. His whole system rests on the principle that knowledge comes not from the illuminating participation of the mind in pure and divine ideas, as was held by Augustinian Platonism, but that it is primarily built up out of sensory experience. As an Aristotelian he could not accept the Platonic theory of forms; to him it was not scientific, and any Christian philosophy that was based on this false epistemology would fail, as the twelfth-century realists had failed, in the face of the nominalist attack. If the origin of human knowledge is in the senses, however, then the constructions of the mind would have a secure foundation, and we could proceed by reason to consider the nature of reality. Therefore, Aquinas arrived at a conclusion that may be termed "moderate realism," but he got there from an Aristotelian, non-Platonic starting point. He admitted that there are certain ultimate areas of the Christian faith to which reason cannot penetrate: it is impossible to prove the miracle of Incarnation or the Trinity. But it is possible to prove rationally the existence and many of the attributes of God. Aquinas presented five proofs for the existence of God, all of which were based on the Aristotelian argument for the existence of a first cause. There cannot be an infinity of causation; there must be an original, unmoved mover, which Aquinas identified with God. Thus far, however, he only proved the existence of the deterministic deity of Aristotle and Averroes, not the Christian providential God. He proceeded to argue, with a validity that was doubted by many, that from this premise could be derived the Christian attributes of God as perfect, omniscient, omnipotent, and free. Similarly, he proceeded from Aristotelian causality by way of logical argument to prove creation ex nihilo, and similarly from Aristotelian psychology to the human soul, and from Aristotelian ethics to Christian virtue.

Aquinas believed that he had come close to the ultimate principles of Augustinian teaching. He had arrived there, however, by a new route; the discredited trail of Platonism had been replaced by the new and secure highway of Aristotelian science. The critics of Thomism fell into two groups. The Averroists and other keen students of Aristotle claimed that he had misused the work of the philosopher and had perverted Aristotelian causality and logic. Those who were inclined to the older neoplatonist and Augustinian position denied that he had come out at the Augustinian deity at all. Rather, they claimed that Aquinas had blundered into the dead end of Aristotelian determinism. They said that the Thomistic deity was mechanistic and not omnipotent and free—a machine, not Christ. They claimed that the Thomist-ordered universe had been achieved at the price of rejecting Augustine for Aristotle and that Thomas was undermining the distinction between the Greek and Christian worldviews that Augustine had drawn. Augustine had emphasized the primacy of will over intellect; Thomas had achieved his ordered world by subverting will to the supremacy of intellect.

The latter criticism of Thomism was presented by the Franciscan philosophers who, at the time of Aquinas's death, were coming to dominate the theology faculty at Oxford. Already Thomas's contemporary, the Italian philosopher St. Bonaventura (1221–1274), who was also the head of the order of the Friars Minor, had published a great treatise that reasserted the Platonic-Augustinian position against the new Aristotelianism. In Bonaventura's system the Platonic realist theory that universals individuate matter was joined with a strongly Augustinian theology that was compatible with the outlook of the disciples of St. Francis. The primacy of will, and therefore of love, over intellect was again predicated, and the majesty and grace of God were emphasized against the mechanistic deity of Aristotle.

St. Bonaventura's attempt to present a philosophical statement of the Franciscan ideal was an expression of a deep anti-intellectual current in thirteenth-century culture that could not long remain quiet in the face of the implications of Thomism. The Franciscan movement had brought back within the church the current of piety that had overflowed ecclesiastical banks and threatened to destroy sacerdotal supremacy in the twelfth century. But if piety once again recognized the authority of the church, it nevertheless had a definite conception of God, and it was not the conception that appears in the *Summa Theologica*. Even when Thomas wrote a hymn on *Corpus Christi*, it was an old-fashioned celebration of "the everlasting Father, and the Son who reigns on high, With the Holy Ghost proceeding forth from Each eternally." The spirit of the two great Franciscan hymns of the thirteenth century, Jacopone da Todi's *Stabat Mater* and Thomas of Celano's *Dies Irae*, was profoundly different. Between them they illustrate the twin themes of the Franciscan worldview: religious love and the majesty of God:

> O thou Mother, fount of love,
> Touch my spirit from above,
>   Make my heart with thine accord!
> Make me feel as thou hast felt;
> Make my soul to glow and melt
>   With the love of Christ my Lord.

> Thou giv'st leave, dread Lord, that we
> Take shelter from Thyself in Thee,
>   And with the wings of Thine own dove
>   Fly to the sceptre of soft love.

The influence of the Franciscan movement in the mid-thirteenth century was amply demonstrated by the tremendous popularity of the cult of the Poor Man of Assisi, as expressed in the *Little Flowers*, the biographical and legendary accounts that circulated immediately after his death, and in many other ways. The importance of the Franciscan movement was also illustrated by the number of outstanding minds it attracted, although St. Francis himself had opposed learning as a dangerous temptation. By 1270 the intellectual life of Europe, in which the incomparable edifice of Thomism loomed so large, was also marked by the rise of a group of Franciscan philosophers who were beginning to put into philosophical form their dissatisfaction with the Dominican integration of science and revelation. In other words, a dangerous dichotomy was just beginning to make its appearance in the ordered thought-world of the thirteenth century.

As an offshoot of mid-thirteenth-century Franciscan thought, like a flying buttress projecting from a French cathedral, is the dim beginning of modern science. The subject is made more obscure by our lack of unanimity on what constitutes the essential nature of modern science. Can science be defined as the observation of nature? It can be said that this definition is too vague and fails to distinguish the novel factor that separates modern from earlier science. Then is it the quantification of nature, the expression of natural phenomena in mathematical terms? This seems to be a good definition, except for the fact that mathematics does lie about nature sometimes; it posits relationships that do not always exist in nature. One may identify modern science with the experimental method. There is, however, some confusion about the nature of the experimental method, although it may be accepted that it has something to do with inductive reasoning and the capability of disproving ("falsifying") a paradigm.

Whatever may be regarded as the proper definition of the nature of science, the work of Robert Grosseteste (1170–1253), bishop of Lincoln and protector of the English Franciscans, and the Oxford friar Roger Bacon (died 1292) may be said to apply. In both cases there was a gain of new knowledge through observation in such fields as optics and astronomy, where little equipment was needed, and some understanding of the value of the inductive, as well as the deductive method. Grosseteste further asserted the need to express natural phenomena in terms of mathematical propositions. The penetration of Arabic mathematics into western Europe was for the first time opening up to European thinkers the mathematical dimension in human thought. Bacon's writings are furthermore distinguished by a tone of intellectual aggressiveness and independence that may be associated with the general attitude of the modern scientist.

The most important question that rises from the work of these two men is why the first steps to modern science should have come from the Franciscan movement and not from Thomism. The answer lies partly in the nature of Aristotelianism and partly in the tendencies of the Franciscan intellectual movement. The Aristotelian science was the best yet known in the world, and that is why Thomas thought it was necessary to integrate it with Christian revelation. But since it was based on a system of deductive reasoning from certain premises, it was fundamentally an intellectual cul-de-sac, as Bacon was the first to see clearly. By his integration of Aristotelian science with revelation, Thomas in any case made it into a closed system that could not move in new directions. The Franciscan movement, with its emotional religiosity, might seem an odd starting point for modern science, but it had certain characteristics that proved fruitful in this regard. It was Plato who had claimed that the cosmos operated in terms of ideal mathematically proportioned forms, and the early Platonic cast of the Franciscan philosophy, as expressed in

Bonaventura's work, led Grosseteste to his theory of the quantification of nature. Bacon, writing a little later, was already under the influence of the general Franciscan revolt against Aristotelianism that threatened to break apart the scholastic cathedral of intellect in the late decades of the thirteenth century.

II. The Moral Authority of the State

St. Thomas Aquinas's attempt to bring all the problems of the human mind within an ordered system led him to develop a political theory that was as significant and as bold as his philosophy and theology. Just as he broke definitively with the Platonic tradition of the early Middle Ages in his interpretation of divine and human nature, so also, he created a revolution in political thought. The political doctrine of the early-medieval thinkers was strongly conditioned by Augustine's hostility to the state and by his denial of independent moral sanction to political authority. Augustinian philosophy had established the primacy of will over intellect in defiance of the Socratic teaching; similarly, political Augustinianism had negated the Greek view of the state as a moral being whose existence was necessary for the fulfillment of human potentialities. The Greeks could not conceive of man living apart from the state, but to Augustine it was only the interior and not the social man that counted, only the relationship between the human soul and the all-powerful deity that gave meaning to human life. In the Augustinian view the state in and for itself was only a band of robbers, without moral quality, and the state received sanction only insofar as it furthered the ends of the City of God. Turned into a more specific doctrine, Augustinianism became the political theory of the church before the twelfth century, which made the state the servant of the church and gave the state a moral sanction only insofar as monarchy subjected itself to the commands of the hierarchy, particularly the papacy. Political Augustinianism reached its fullest form in the radical aspects of the Gelasian doctrine, in the Donation of Constantine, and in the pronouncements of Gregory VII. In the twelfth and thirteenth centuries the canon lawyers, who worked under papal auspices, perpetuated this ecclesiastical political theory, giving it a new format by their juristic doctrines of the plenitude of absolute papal power.

The actual entrenchment of secular leadership in society more and more contradicted the established hierocratic tradition, however, and from the middle of the twelfth century a new current in political speculation among the leading thinkers of Europe began to come slowly to the fore. Without abandoning the theory of the ultimate supremacy of the church, these thinkers tried to delineate a theory of the state that would conform more realistically to actual social conditions, in which the leadership of royal government was rapidly becoming indispensable. John of Salisbury and Otto of Freising, in the twelfth century, took the first steps in this new direction, and it remained for Thomas Aquinas, in this as in other fields of thought, to fulfill and formulate in a precisely defined doctrine the novel tendencies of twelfth-century speculation.

As was the case with his philosophical and theological work, Thomas found the starting point for his political doctrine in Aristotelian science. He was as impressed with the merits of the philosopher's *Politics* as he was with his metaphysics, epistemology, and ethics. Consequently he was prepared to accept the Greek view of the moral necessity of the state and Aristotle's doctrine that man was a political being whose potentialities could be fulfilled only in political society. The political doctrine of Aquinas, therefore, constituted a revolution against the tradition of political Augustinianism and a reversion to the Greek idea of the moral integrity of the authority of the state. But as he attempted to do in his theological works, while rejecting the spirit and methodology of Augustinianism, Thomas did not want to throw aside the authoritative church father's conclusions. He wanted to arrive in political thought at a point not far distant from the Augustinian tradition, but only by making use of the truths of Aristotelian science. In other words, Aquinas wanted to maintain both the moral quality of the state, in conformity with the teachings of Aristotle, and the continued ultimate supremacy of the church in society. Aquinas attempted to achieve this extremely bold and provocative integration of the old and the new in medieval political thought through his philosophy of law. He asserted that the law of the state had to be in conformity with natural law, which, in turn, was a reflection of divine law, and when the positive law of the state was in conformity with the law of God in this way, its moral sanction was complete and unmitigated. By this legal doctrine Aquinas thought that he had given to political authority its necessary moral quality and had subordinated it to the hierocratic agency of divine will. He believed that he had recognized the value of secular leadership in Christian society and yet had maintained fundamentally inviolate the traditional Gelasian doctrine.

The delicate balance and integration of hierocratic and secular authority that distinguishes political Thomism conformed in many ways to the relations between the monarchy and the church in the mid-thirteenth century. Undoubtedly the realities of contemporary political life encouraged Aquinas to formulate his departure from the Augustinian theory of the state; what was happening in England, France, and Germany in his day seemed to confirm his political philosophy to a marked degree. The English king, Henry III, was a saintly and docile man who continued the deferential attitude toward Rome that his father, King John, had been forced to adopt in his later years. An even more impressive confirmation of Thomist doctrine could be found closer to home, in Paris itself, in the personality and attitudes of Louis IX, who must have seemed to Thomas the incarnation of his political ideal. Louis was renowned as a self-sacrificing crusader and a righteous persecutor of heretics and hater of Jews. His popular image is revealed in the biography of the king written by a prominent Champagne nobleman, the lord of Joinville, which was the first medieval royal life produced by a layman. In Joinville's account Louis is a saintly but brave man who has no other ambitions than service to God and the furtherance of the welfare of his people. He endures without complaint great suffering during his ill-fated crusade in Egypt and ends his life in martyrdom in Tunis while attempting, like St. Francis, to convert the infidel. In France Louis bears without rancor ill treatment by his mother when she is regent of the kingdom and turns aside the rebellion of obstreperous barons without a thought of vengeance. He insists that his government fulfill the highest ideals of Christian justice, and to assure this the king sits under an oak tree and personally renders his judgment in cases brought by his adoring subjects. The angelic doctor and the saintly king were almost exact contemporaries, and in both instances strong movements for their canonization were already under way before their deaths. St. Louis seemed to be political Thomism in action.

Aquinas's ideal of church-state relations was confirmed in other ways as well. The German emperor Frederick II warred against the papacy in Italy, but the hierocratic representative of divine law emerged completely triumphant from this struggle, and during Aquinas's lifetime the contumacious Hohenstaufen family, as befitted tyrants, was wiped from the face of the Earth and their Italian possessions handed over by the pope to the brother of the ideal Christian monarch Louis IX. The integration of papal and royal authority was amply demonstrated during the thirteenth century by grants to royal governments of a share of clerical taxation when the kings undertook some venture favored and encouraged by Rome. It was also illustrated by the increasing involvement of the papacy in clerical appointments all over western Europe on the basis of a maze of canon-law precedents. To maintain unchallenged their own predominant control over clerical appointments, secular rulers found it expedient to give the pope the right to designate and make "provision" for the filling of certain clerical offices within their realms.

Thomas's political philosophy, while in some ways radical and pro-vocative, thus seemed to be an expression of a new political consensus in European life that fulfilled the work of Innocent III during the half century following his death. The policy of the great pope with regard to the European monarchies was perpetuated by his able successors, particularly Gregory IX (1227–1241) and Innocent IV (1243–1254), who resembled Innocent in their legal background, diplomatic and administrative expertise, and intransigent defense of papal interests. These popes had some remarkable triumphs and generally strengthened the edifice of papal power that Innocent had delineated. There were, however, certain aspects of Rome's relations with the English, French, and German monarchies that the papal curia found deeply disturbing even during the lifetimes of Thomas Aquinas and St. Louis. The new political consensus, so imposing in many respects, was not without definite limitations and weaknesses. There were discrepancies between the Thomistic ideal order and the realities of political life that the angelic doctor could not well perceive from the vantage point of the Paris schools. Changes were occurring in the institutions and ideology of thirteenth-century kingship whose significance was not fully apparent until the later decades of the century.

The English political situation from the last years of John was one that was peculiarly exasperating to the papacy. The English king had finally been brought low, but the Italian cardinals were puzzled and annoyed to discover that royal power no longer seemed to dominate English life. The papacy now had a vassal in the person of the English king, but one who could not keep order in his own house. Instead, the English barons, with the encouragement and assistance of some churchmen, engaged in revolts aimed at establishing institutional controls over the king's government. They propounded legal theories subjecting the king to the due processes of law, which, they claimed, could be changed only by consent of what was called "the community of the realm." To the leaders of the papal curia, steeped in the Roman-canonical traditions of absolutism, news of these political experiments and constitutional ideas made strange reading. Not only was the cardinals' sense of right order offended, but the power of the papal vassal and therefore, indirectly, the effectiveness of Roman intervention in England, was threatened. As a consequence, for six decades after John made his subservience to the papacy, the curia was invariably in favor of royal authority in England and hostile to the novel constitutional experiments and ideas, with profound consequences for Anglo-papal relations.

In 1214 John suffered his second great humiliation and defeat at the hands of his archenemy Philip Augustus of France. He had allied himself with his relative, Otto IV, to foment a two-front attack on the Capetian kingdom. Otto was supposed to come down from Germany through Flanders by a route that would become familiar to German armies in the nineteenth and twentieth centuries, while John pushed upward from Poitou to complete a great pincers movement. John won some initial successes, but he was overcome by one of his periodic fits of depression. He stood idly by while Philip deployed most of the French army against Otto and inflicted a crushing defeat on the German emperor at Bouvines. This second military disaster was the signal for the crystallization of baronial revolt against Angevin power in England. John had for a long time been using the prerogatives of the crown, such as relief, wardship, and scutage, in an unusually severe manner to increase the royal income from taxation. John's government was hard-pressed; the king had a growing administration, and he was engaged in far-flung diplomatic and military ventures, and with the general introduction of heavy plate armor and other improvements in military technology, the costs of warfare were steadily increasing. The baronial leaders did not sympathize with John's predicament, however; they did not want to be subjected to heavy taxation for the support of a king who was a failure on the battlefield; who had lost them their hands in Normandy; and who had corrupted the law courts to obtain judgments against baronial families whom John suspected, in many cases on little or no grounds, of disloyalty. Furthermore, the king had been defeated and humiliated by the pope, and he had entered into a position of vassalage to the papacy, which was a flagrant turnabout in Anglo-papal relations as they had existed since the time of William the Conqueror.

The majority of the great barons, led by members of certain northern families who had particularly suffered from arbitrary procedures in the royal courts, prepared the first real rebellion against the royal liege lord in England since the Norman invasion. The baronial movement appears to have been given defined and conscious aims by the archbishop of Canterbury, Stephen Langton, who, far from being the papal sycophant who had been expected, turned out to be a man of strong and independent opinion. Ignoring the fact that John was the pope's vassal, Stephen aligned the English church alongside the lay magnates in what was a little later to be called the community of the English realm. It appears to have been Stephen who suggested to the barons that they stipulate their grievances in the form of a "great charter," which they forced the king to approve and seal in 1215. Stephen took as a precedent for Magna Carta the coronation charter of promises made to the English church and people by Henry I in 1100. Magna Carta contained a long list of baronial rights and privileges that the king promised not to infringe. It was, of course, a document that was biased in favor of the interests of the baronial class, but it was a class that claimed, and on the whole had the right, to speak for the "whole people of England."

Magna Carta placed severe limitations on the exercise of the financial powers of the Angevin monarchy, although many such provisions were eliminated in the final issuance of the document by the government of Henry III in 1225. It is highly significant, however, that the barons did not try to destroy the common-law system that Henry II had perfected or to regain from the royal courts the independent powers and jurisdictions of the private feudal courts that had been lost to royal justice. Nor did any of the great nobles try to gain special concessions for themselves; they spoke as a group whose liberties were homogeneous throughout the realm. This was a consequence of 150 years of powerful central government in England that had so unified the country that the great magnates, while they wanted to limit royal authority, could not conceive of depriving themselves of the benefits of efficient royal administration and law. It did not even enter their minds to establish autonomous principalities.

The greatest importance of Magna Carta lies in the theory of law implied in the statement that the king should observe "the law of the land" and that he cannot proceed against anyone without following the due processes of the common law. If the king wished to do something beyond the prevailing law of the land, such as impose a new tax, he could do so only with the consent of the community of the realm. Magna Carta thus reasserted the Germanic constitutional principle that had been incorporated into the common law; as a great thirteenth-century English lawyer later expressed it, "in England law rules and not will." It is because it expresses the ideal of the supremacy of the law over the will of the king that Magna Carta became such an important rallying cry for later generations of Englishmen who were struggling against royal power. During the thirteenth and fourteenth centuries, dissatisfaction with the arbitrary quality of royal government came to be expressed in demands for royal confirmations of Magna Carta. The seventeenth-century English common lawyers saw in Magna Carta the bastion of English liberty against royal despotism. They even said that Magna Carta confirmed trial by jury in the full meaning of the term. Although the jury of verdict was not actually developed until the later thirteenth century as a result of the Fourth Lateran Council's prohibition of ordeals as a method of proof, the seventeenth-century interpretation of Magna Carta was not as absurd as many modern critics have said. The fundamental doctrine of Magna Carta was that the king could not proceed against any freeman in the realm except by the prevailing due process of the common law, whatever its institutions might be.

Magna Carta did not provide for any generic liberty; it only set forth—for all freemen—the right to enjoy what the law gives. The only universal right is the procedural one of due process, a protection available (in different forms, to be sure) to all men. What due process guards in any case may in fact be most unequal. Nevertheless, the fundamental idea of common law liberty is due process. "The law of the land" merely confirms to every man his own liberties and possessions. The common law envisages a hierarchical society in which every man carries with him certain privileges. The law protects these privileges, but by no means equalizes them. Specific liberties will belong to you according to your status in society.

A great lord will possess vast liberties along with his acreage, but as far as a man of lesser status is concerned, the law of the land may say he has nothing—except, of course, freedom from arbitrary proceeding. Due process is simply a procedural technique enlarged into a principle, but it is a principle that acknowledges no theoretical limits; it is a principle concerned only with means, not ends. Due process can itself be the vehicle for depriving a man of his life and property, even if he is a duke. Does due process, then, not know any constraints? Yes, in the sense that it contains a strong principle of self-preservation. The due process that the law affords must itself be changed by due process.

The common law idea of liberty is antithetic to equality. In Magna Carta, where the idea is resoundingly enunciated, liberty and property are virtually synonymous. Liberty is what one possesses—tenure, or franchise, but even the man who owns nothing has the right to the due process suitable to his status in society—however unenviable that may be. Due process is a superb protection for what you already have, though it is innocent of any criteria for evaluating the justice by which possessions are divided. Dukes and peasants own quite different things, but each has judicial liberty. The common law assumes that the rights granted to men are very disparate, but among them there is one universal right—the right to have what belongs to you under the law.

The last clause of Magna Carta provided for a general feudal *diffidatio* and barons' revolt against the king if he failed to keep his promises. The barons almost immediately had cause to make this provision operative. John appealed to his overlord, Innocent III, to absolve him from his vows to the barons, which he claimed he had made under duress, and the pope, who did not like the theoretical implications of the great charter or the diminution of his vassal's power, immediately complied. Innocent furthermore censured Langton for his participation in the drafting of Magna Carta and suspended the archbishop from the exercise of his office. The barons took up arms against the king and called in the son of Philip Augustus to help them, but John's death made possible the restoration of peace between the royal government and the magnates. However, John's heir, Henry III (1216–1272), who was still a minor at the time of his father's death, was not any more successful in the exercise of royal leadership. After he came of age in the 1220s, crisis after crisis developed in his relations with the leaders of the community of the realm until, in 1258, a committee of barons took over the management of the royal administration. In 1264 Henry tried to resume control over the royal administration, but he was defeated in open battle by the barons and captured.

The constitutional crisis of Henry III's reign was a product of both his weakness as a king and the further development of the constitutional ideas reflected in the provisions of Magna Carta. Henry was an extremely devout man with fine esthetic tastes, and he was largely responsible for the building of Westminster Abbey in its present form. But he was a failure as a soldier; he lost Poitou to Louis IX, his wife's brother-in-law, whom he greatly respected and treated with deference. Henry was even more subservient to the pope and allowed himself to be involved in papal plans for replacing the Hohenstaufen ruler with a more pliant king. The pope offered Sicily to one of Henry's sons in return for huge payments, which the king supplied out of the royal revenue. The only way the royal government could obtain extraordinary revenue for this and other purposes was by developing new forms of taxation. John's administration had already experimented with the exploitation of the old principle of the feudal "gracious aid"—a special tax that vassals might give to their lord for a certain purpose, but only with their specific consent. As the liege lord of all the English magnates, John was able to obtain consent for an aid to fight the French king, and this precedent was used several times by Henry III's government to obtain consent for a tax on the revenue and property of the magnates and their subvassals. The unpaid county officials were made responsible for assessing and collecting the tax, and the techniques they used were modeled on those used to implement a tithe levied by the church in 1188 to support the third crusade.

As the magnates became more and more dissatisfied with Henry's government, the king was unable to obtain their consent to the imposition of new taxes, and he had to default on his payments to Rome, whereupon the pope handed Sicily over to the brother of the French king. This move placed Henry in a most disadvantageous position. His treasury was bankrupt, and the baronial class was strongly critical of his administration; they were angry at his deferential attitude to Rome and his gifts of royal and ecclesiastical offices to his French relatives and their supporters. As in 1215, baronial discontent in England was given direction by some churchmen, including the head of the Franciscan order in England. Many ecclesiastical leaders felt neglected, deprived, and mistreated by the Roman curia, which had struck bargains with the king for the taxation of the clergy and which filled lucrative offices in the English church with Italians.

The barons and the discontented churchmen were inspired by an incipient nationalist feeling that took the form of both xenophobia and a greater emphasis on the need to control the royal government by the representatives of the community of the realm. But the magnates alone could no longer presume to speak for the whole country. The lesser nobility, the knights of the shire (or the gentry, as they were called in later centuries), were now taking the leading part in the administration and taxation of the shire. They were becoming a distinct group, or estate, in the realm, and the great barons could no longer claim to represent them. Similarly, the burgesses, particularly in London, made distinctive commercial contributions to the life of the country. Although their legal and social status was still inferior to that of landholders, it was useful because of their wealth to associate them with the baronial movement.

In 1265 the leader of the barons, probably with the advice of his Franciscan friends, summoned representatives of the knights of the shire and the burgesses for a meeting of the great council of the realm, which heretofore had been attended exclusively by the lay and ecclesiastical magnates. This was the first joint assembly of the groups who, by the end of the thirteenth century, regularly came together in those occasional meetings of the great council of the realm called "parliaments." In 1265 the knights and burgesses were summoned merely for propaganda purposes, but the fact that they were invited at all indicates a new consciousness by the barons that they could not speak for the whole community of the realm. The baronial constitutional doctrine was that, in matters that concerned the whole realm—taxation, legislation, foreign policy—the king had to act with the consent of the whole realm, and the knights and burgesses were summoned to give verisimilitude to this view.

Representative institutions were common all over western Europe in the thirteenth century. They were used in provincial meetings of magnates in France; in the Spanish Cortes, or assembly of estates; and in town government. It has been suggested that this development was the result of the dissemination of the Roman-law idea of proctorship and attorneyship. England was the country in which representative institutions, beginning in the 1260s, played their most important role in political life; yet England was precisely the country that remained outside the area of Roman-law influence. The English judges before the end of the thirteenth century were mostly churchmen who were familiar with civil and canon law, and it is possible that the idea of representation filtered into the realm through these legists. But while the idea of attorneyship may have helped give more formal shape to English representation, it is apparent that this institution had strong indigenous roots in England. In the workings of the common law the grand jury was supposed to speak for the whole "country" of the shire, and juries brought the record of cases from the shire to the central royal courts and similarly represented the county before the royal judges. A meeting of the great council of the realm was technically an expanded meeting of the Curia Regis. Hence, when the baronial leaders in 1265 wanted to hold an augmented meeting of the great council, they had both the idea and the experience of representation in the workings of the common law ready at hand. A parliament in the thirteenth century was a special meeting of the royal court to deal with great matters of state, and to it could be summoned representatives of the knights of the shire and of the burgesses to use this grand occasion to gain the approval of all groups in the community of the realm for the policy of the central government.

The leader of the barons in 1265 was Simon de Montfort, a son of the French lord of the same name who had led the Albigensian crusade. Simon had become an English earl by inheritance through his grandmother; he married the king's sister; and his intelligence, ability, and friendship with the Franciscans qualified him to be the leader of the baronial movement. Many of the other magnates, however, lacked his superior qualities, and once they had gained control of the central administration, they found the work hard and boring. The baronial movement therefore began to break up almost on the morrow of its victory, as several of the magnates turned away from the affairs of the central government to pursue more private interests. In 1265 a royal army led by Henry III's heir, Edward, defeated and killed Simon de Montfort, and Henry regained control of his administration. His troubles, however, had constituted a salutary lesson to his son, who came to the throne as Edward I in 1272. Edward had seen what failure as a military leader and servility to Rome had done to ruin his father. He also had become conscious of the corporate and national feelings of the country, and he determined to channel these attitudes toward the reconstruction of royal authority in England.

In the half century after Innocent III the papacy had enjoyed the unfailing devotion and loyalty of the English king, which stood in sharp contrast with Anglo-papal relations during the previous 150 years. But the curia was disappointed to discover that this great advantage was rendered nugatory, in large part, by the peculiar internal conditions of England, in which all groups in society, including many of the churchmen, wanted the great limitation of royal authority. The pope's relations with the empire during this period differed in almost every way. In this direction the curia had to struggle against an extremely able enemy in the person of an emperor who brought back the terrifying days of Henry VI. This struggle terminated in the most complete victory over monarchy that the medieval papacy ever attained.

The settlement of the imperial problem that Innocent III had regarded as definitive did not last very long. Innocent had given Frederick II (1215–1250) the imperial crown upon the condition that he would abdicate his kingdom of Sicily when he gained the full recognition of the German princes. This recognition was achieved in 1218, when Otto IV, who had been Innocent's original candidate for the German throne, finally died. But Frederick had no intention of giving up Naples and Sicily, which were the real strongholds of his power. He was, in fact, uninterested in Germany, and he visited it only to make sweeping concessions to the German princes, bishops, and towns, recognizing their full territorial sovereignty and completely undoing what was left of the centralizing work of Frederick Barbarossa and Henry VI. Frederick was an Italian, and he wanted to make himself the ruler of all Italy, to bring the great cities of the north, which had successfully resisted his grandfather, under his full domination. He was vague about whether he would recognize the integrity of the papal states, and, by the middle of the 1220s, the Roman curia found itself again facing the prospect of the papacy being swallowed up in a Hohenstaufen Italy.

Frederick claimed that his aim of conquering northern Italy would not endanger the independence of the papacy, and he may have been sincere in his profession. But the Roman curia did not intend to put it to an empirical test, for Frederick was a strange man, the "wonder of the world," who seemed to stand outside the moral order of his day. He had been raised as an orphan in Sicily by various princes, and he had been badly treated as a youth. Innocent III had been his official guardian, but the pope had done little to protect the personal welfare of his ward. Frederick grew up to be a handsome and extremely talented man: a great soldier, a patron of the arts and sciences, the author of a formidable treatise on falconry. But he was a megalomaniac who considered himself beyond the ethical standards of Latin Christianity. It is appropriate that

Frederick was idolized by the Nazis in the 1920s and 1930s and that the most popular and probably best modern biography of him, published in Germany in 1927, had a swastika on its cover. Frederick II was a sort of intellectual Fascist, a man of learning and fastidious tastes, but a brute and a bully nevertheless. The organization and atmosphere of his court and administration were conditioned by oriental despotism. He had been strongly influenced by Arabs and Greeks, who lived in great numbers in his kingdom, and the flattery and subservience with which rulers were traditionally greeted in the Moslem countries went to his head. Frederick envisioned himself not only as the reincarnation of the Roman emperors, but as a leader of messianic qualities. He and his court propagandists did not refrain from the sacrilege of drawing parallels between Frederick's life and that of Christ.

Given these attitudes, personality, and resources, Frederick was bound to be a formidable enemy, and by the 1240s, the papacy, after moving slowly for two decades, had been plunged into a maelstrom of violence in its attempts to deal with him. The initial skirmishing between Frederick and the papacy was on a peripheral matter and was not free from elements of farce. To gain Innocent III's support, Frederick had taken the cross, but he was reluctant to carry out his vow because he was eager to inaugurate his campaign in northern Italy. Finally, in 1227, he actually did go to the Holy Land while he was under excommunication from Rome for his previous failure to fulfill his crusading vows. He merely went through the motions of fighting the Moslems and then hurried back to southern Italy, where a papal army had invaded his lands, although with little success. A truce was patched up between the emperor and the pope, but it broke down after Frederick won a great victory over the Lombard League in 1239, and his mastery of the whole peninsula became a grim possibility.

The Italian cities were no longer as united against imperial domination as they had been in Frederick Barbarossa's time. In many cities there were oligarchic families who were Ghibellines, as the proimperial party in the Italian cities was called. Faced with this danger, Gregory IX put to work all the resources that the papacy commanded. He excommunicated the emperor and denounced him as a heretic, for which there was plausible grounds, and he summoned a church council in Rome to give greater effect to this denunciation. An emperor who regarded himself as standing beyond good and evil was not one to be greatly worried by religious sanctions. He commanded his admiral to sink or capture many of the ships bringing churchmen to Rome from other parts of Europe.

This monstrous act convinced the papacy that only the most extreme measures would succeed against Frederick. In 1245 Innocent IV held a council at Lyons, on safe ground just outside the border of Louis IX's kingdom, and preached a crusade against the emperor. This was a departure from the original idea of a crusade, but it was not quite, as it has sometimes been called, "a political crusade." Frederick had murdered churchmen and offended the moral sensibility of Christendom, and his personal beliefs were certainly close to heresy if they were not, indeed, outside the Christian faith altogether. Innocent IV's preaching of a crusade against Frederick was an extreme measure, but under the circumstances there appeared to be no alternative, and it could be doctrinally justified.

It was one thing, however, to declare a crusade against Frederick; it was another to get any important ruler in Europe to risk his armies against the emperor, who controlled a great part of the resources of Italy. In the remaining five years of Frederick's life the crusade against him was largely a desultory affair, for the most part a propaganda war. When the superman of the thirteenth century finally passed from the scene in 1250, the papacy determined to continue the crusade and make it into a war against the whole Hohenstaufen family so that such a monster as Frederick should never again arise to threaten the vicar of Christ. Frederick's only legitimate son, Conrad IV (1250–1254), put up stiff resistance, however. His premature death, leaving only a child as his heir, terminated the Hohenstaufen line on the imperial throne. There was an unseemly squabble for a few decades among the German princes and various other European rulers who also offered themselves as candidates for the elective German throne. The interregnum was finally terminated in 1273 with the election of Count Rudolph of Hapsburg as king. Rudolph was a minor prince with modest ambitions. For all practical purposes Germany during the next two centuries was to consist of a variety of independent states.

In Sicily the Hohenstaufen line was perpetuated by Frederick II's illegitimate son Manfred (1254–1266), who turned out to be as able a leader as his father. Finally, the papacy, in desperation, offered the Sicilian crown to the brother of Louis IX, Charles of Anjou, who arrived in Italy with a formidable army and in a swift campaign defeated and killed Manfred, the last of the Hohenstaufen rulers in Sicily. Two years later, in 1268, Conrad IV's young son Conradin appeared in southern Italy with a small army, which was easily routed by the new French ruler. Conradin was captured and, with papal permission, publicly executed in Naples.

The papal struggle against Frederick II and the last of the Hohenstaufens is significant in several ways. In the first place, it ended with a dramatic and total victory that demonstrated the power of the papacy to destroy a monarchy that violated the moral law and flouted the supremacy of the church. In this respect it confirmed political Thomism by seeming to demonstrate that even the most powerful royal families that challenged the vicar of Christ would go down to defeat before the combined spiritual and material swords, which, in accordance with the Gelasian doctrine, were both ultimately in the hands of the pope. But some men could draw another implication from the same series of events. For twenty-five years a king had withstood every kind of weapon at the disposal of the papacy. Was the imposing structure of papal monarchy that Innocent III and his successors had created vulnerable to royal power after all? The third consequence of the struggle between empire and papacy in the thirteenth century was the injection of a new attitude of reckless violence into contemporary life that began to poison the moral atmosphere of Europe. First, the emperor and then the pope had used the most extreme and morally dubious methods, which even their most eager partisans had difficulty justifying. The emperor had murdered bishops, and the pope had hunted down Frederick's descendants to the man and had exercised a blood vengeance on the last youthful remnant of the house of Hohenstaufen. As is often the case in long and desperate wars, the defender, in his harassed struggle for survival, came to employ the ruthless methods of the aggressor.

The designation by the papacy of Charles of Anjou as ruler of southern Italy and Sicily was the second boon that the Roman curia gave to its ally, the French monarchy, in the thirteenth century. The first had been the gift of nearly all southern France, which was a consequence of Innocent III's Albigensian crusade—the greatest turning point in the history of the Capetian monarchy. Philip Augustus, by his own efforts, had made himself the ruler of northern France, but without the papal crusade against Languedoc it would have been an enormous and probably impossible task for the Capetians to conquer the wealthiest and most thickly populated part of France. Philip had not participated in the crusade itself, but the need for royal leadership arose in 1218 when the leader of the northern barons who were carving out fiefs for themselves in Languedoc, the elder Simon de Montfort, was killed and the force of the crusading movement momentarily faltered. The nobility of southern France, who were now fighting more for personal and national reasons than for religious ones, made their last important stand. This brought into the war Prince Louis, heir to the French throne, whose army immediately carried out an atrocious massacre in one of the southern cities. During his short reign as Louis VIII, from 1223 to 1226, this fierce warrior inaugurated the incorporation of the southern provinces under the French crown. The

Dominican inquisitors and the French seneschals arrived together, and in the following quarter of a century destroyed whatever was left of the independent spirit of the once great culture of southern France. In 1249 a brother of the French king became the count of Toulouse, and the Capetian monarchy, which a century before had not even been strong in the Ile-de-France, fulfilled its self-appointed destiny of extending to the Mediterranean.

The last opportunity for the French feudatories to stop the advance of Capetian power in the thirteenth century came during the early years of the reign of Louis IX (1226–1270), when the king was still a minor and the government was under the regency of his mother, Blanche of Castile, the first of that incomparable breed of Spanish princesses who influenced the political life of Europe over the following five centuries. The young Henry III of England joined the rebellious dukes and counts of the north of France in a feeble attempt to undo the work of the previous half century. They were no match for Blanche and her son. For his pains Henry lost more French territory, and, with the exception of the wild duke of Brittany, the French princes, including the leader of the rebellion, the courtly count of Champagne, demonstrated that even when they had the Capetians at a disadvantage, they did not have the will to stem the advance of royal power.

The saintly mien of Louis IX was what the royal government needed during the following half century to develop its institutions and to entrench its control over the remaining pockets of feudal power in both the north and the south. By the middle of the thirteenth century the French Curia Regis had begun to differentiate into distinct financial and legal branches. Out of the latter developed the Parlement of Paris, which consisted of a professional judiciary that encouraged appeals from all over the realm, thereby extending royal legal jurisdiction and further diminishing the importance of baronial courts. The Parlement similarly asserted its superiority over the ecclesiastical courts. The royal bureaucrats also worked hard to decrease the autonomy of the French towns, whose number and wealth had greatly increased as a result of the southern conquests. The dissatisfaction in many cities with the narrow and corrupt oligarchies who dominated the communal governments gave the royal administration the pretext for intervention and closer subordination to the central authority.

The characteristic personnel of the French bureaucracy, who had already made their appearance in the reign of Philip Augustus, were perpetuated as their responsibilities and size increased. They were a largely self-sustaining group of lawyers whose sole guiding principle was the expansion of the royal power with which they identified themselves and that they furthered by every legal subterfuge that their learning and ingenuity could devise. This astringent attitude was probably the only way to build the French state. The many provinces that had been rapidly appended to the French crown contained such an amalgam of provincial traditions, conflicting feudal jurisdictions, local laws and customs, and episcopal and bourgeois privileges that the only common rationale for constructing the semblance of a political entity was that right always ran with the king.

A saint on the throne was the ideal moral façade behind which the guile and force of the royal clerks worked to create the most powerful despotism in Europe. The baron, the bishop, and the burgher, who experienced the incessant evaporation of their old privileges, could always feel comforted by the fact that St. Louis was sitting under an oak tree and dispensing justice. Did the king ordain or even understand what his ministers were doing? It appears that he was by no means entirely a figurehead. He sent out "investigators," among whom Franciscan friars were prominent, to find out what his baillis and their assistants were doing in his name and to record the complaints of the people they ruled. These investigations turned up almost every kind of subtle chicanery and ruthless severity known to human ingenuity. St. Louis appears to have sympathized with his subjects, but the methods of the royal servants did not change.

If the expansion of Capetian power over the whole realm was largely the work of harsh magistri over whom St. Louis appears not to have exercised close supervision, Louis's personal direction of royal policy toward the church and the papacy is readily apparent. It was a policy that, although it allied the French government ever more closely with the Roman curia, by no means made the French monarchy the deferential servant of Rome. Louis IX's relative, Henry III of England, was far more pliable in his relations with the papacy. In no instance did St. Louis ever sacrifice the interests of the French monarchy in his ecclesiastical policy. He strongly asserted the rights of jurisdiction of the French crown over the clergy. He refused to help bishops confiscate the property of barons who had been excommunicated. He spoke sharply to prominent members of the higher clergy whom he regarded as having failed to fulfill the duties of their office. For his crusade against Egypt he made heavy demands for financial support from the pope and the French church. He did not answer Innocent IV's appeal for a crusade against Frederick II. It was an ominous sign of St. Louis's conception of church-state relations that he was made uneasy by this use of the crusading ideal to attack a duly constituted monarch. He even protested against papal taxation of the French clergy to support the crusade. He allowed his brother to invade southern Italy only after obtaining his own terms for such a venture. The pope who conceded to Charles of Anjou full rights over what had been Frederick II's kingdom was a Frenchman, as was his immediate predecessor on the papal throne. By the end of Louis's reign there was a strong French party among the cardinals, who inevitably looked to Paris for leadership.

The Angevin domination of southern Italy was the concluding stage in the rise of French power in Europe that had begun with Philip Augustus's conquest of Normandy in 1204. A change of fundamental importance had taken place in the European balance of power by 1270. The German monarchy had been totally eliminated as a factor in European politics. Its place was taken by the old ally of the papacy, the Capetian kingdom. The papacy, who had fought so long to keep the German emperor out of Italy, had eagerly established the brother of the most powerful king in Europe in the Italian realm in place of the hated Hohenstaufens. With the resources of the wealthiest state in Europe, the loyalty of the French clergy, a French stronghold in Sicily, and with a French party in the college of cardinals itself, the Capetian ruler had the power to dominate the papacy more thoroughly than any king since the middle of the eleventh century. But in 1270 the papacy was not concerned about its potential vulnerability. On the contrary, it led the universal acclaim for a king who seemed the perfect Christian monarch. There was no cause to fear a ruler who confirmed the Thomistic confidence in the moral quality of the state.

III. The Interests of Society

While the intellectual, ecclesiastical, and political leaders of thirteenth-century Europe sought to meet the challenge of twelfth-century creativity, lord, burgher, and peasant also sought to adjust as best they could their private interests and destinies to social change.

All classes and groups in all regions of thirteenth-century Europe found their lives conditioned by four common factors. The first was a great increase in social control because of the expansion of government and of legal institutions. The second was the transition from a society based on status to one based on money. Birth still counted a great deal in determining a man's life; it was hard in many parts of Europe for even the wealthiest burgher to enjoy certain privileges that the son of a lord took for granted. But, on the other hand, status was not enough for a happy and secure life; no matter how impressive a man's pedigree might be, bad financial management resulted in hard times. The third factor was related to the second. The first seven or eight decades of the thirteenth century marked the final stage in a long period of boom, population growth, and inflation that had characterized the European economy since the middle of the tenth century, and this general economic condition profoundly affected the interests of all groups in society. Finally, the thirteenth century was the age of the long peace, which would not be experienced again for many centuries. From the Battle of Bouvines in 1214 until the beginning of the long and ruinous struggle between England and France in the 1290s there was no major war in western Europe, and this condition of peace had important and varying consequences for the classes of society.

Neither in government nor in economy nor in war were the nobility, the landed class descended from the feudal lords of the tenth century, as important as they had been before 1100. But taking everything into account, they were still easily the dominant class in society, a position they were to retain in Europe until the nineteenth century. There was a growing heterogeneity in the life and organization of the nobility, both horizontally and vertically, and it is possible to establish definite regional types. In Italy and southern France the nobility was marked by its high degree of urbanization and involvement in city life. The German lords were, as a group, closer to the early-medieval warrior class: The disintegration of Germany into a maze of petty principalities gave the German nobility many opportunities to act independently and to serve in local wars. Urbanization had had no appreciable effect on the landed classes of northern France and England, who held themselves completely aloof from the burgher class, whom they condemned as social inferiors. There was a growing polarization between the great aristocrats and the nobility of more modest means. The former were becoming a closed caste of superior blood and self-conscious mores and rituals, while the latter were becoming local gentlemen, in many cases as rustic and ignorant as the peasants among whom they lived.

The thirteenth-century lord was circumscribed, especially in England and France, by ever more efficient systems of government, law, and taxation. He was a different person from the thugs of the tenth century, and even from most of the men who fought in the first crusade. This was, of course, especially true of the upper strata of the nobility. These noblemen frequently had a limited amount of literacy and education—enough to write letters in the vernacular and to read chivalric romances or little treatises on the life of a gentleman or on estate management. Most of this noble literature was written in French, which had become the international language of the aristocracy, as it was to remain until the twentieth century. At least three members of the thirteenth-century French nobility were highly literate and sophisticated men. William de Lorris wrote the first half of the *Romance of the Rose,* a sort of encyclopedia of romantic allegory that was popular with aristocratic readers and is still regarded by some people as a great work of literature. Another French nobleman, Villehardouin, wrote a graphic and honest account of the ill-fated fourth crusade, in which he was a participant. Joinville's *Life of St. Louis* is a personal memoir by an intimate of the great king. In some respects it is almost as idealized as previous medieval royal biographies written by ecclesiastics, but it presents a large number of circumstantial details, and it is still the only biography of Louis IX worth reading. A minor lord of mid-thirteenth century England, Sir Walter of Henley, produced a treatise on estate management for the benefit of his son. It is well organized and full of common sense about crops, sheep raising, and manorial administration.

The thirteenth-century lords were educated at home for the most part. But some of the urbanized nobility of northern Italy and southern France received a university education and became civil lawyers. From the end of the thirteenth century in England it became fashionable for county families to send their sons to the schools of common law in London, called the Inns of Court, to obtain a rudimentary knowledge of law, which would later stand them in good stead in their almost incessant lawsuits over proprietary rights. Many younger sons of the nobility, of course, were destined for the church and were sent to the universities; a few became great scholars and professors.

Fighting was the original raison d'être of the nobility, but during the long peace of the thirteenth century, there were limited opportunities inside Europe for the exhibition of military skill. A slow revolution was taking place in military life. The cavalryman, the armored knight on horseback, was becoming a more and more expensive commodity as plate armor formed an increasing proportion of his equipment. Consequently, the knight who could afford to equip himself was much in demand. When a king had to fit out a whole army, he found it a great drain on his resources. As a result, the practice of calling out the feudal vassals declined and the hiring of professional mercenaries increased. At the beginning of the thirteenth century the heavily armored knight was the almost exclusive staple of warfare. By the end of the century, although the knight was still the backbone of any army, his strategic importance was being challenged by the increased use of massed infantry. The appearance of new weapons began the slow process of obsolescence that steadily diminished the value of the knight over the following two centuries. Flemish and Swiss mercenaries showed in the late decades of the century that well-disciplined peasants armed with pikes could break a feudal charge. In the thirteenth century it was also demonstrated that armor could be penetrated by a metal bolt fired from a crossbow. All over the Continent military leaders added contingents of crossbowmen to their armies. The great weakness of the crossbow, however, was that it had to be mechanically loaded and that once the crossbowman had "shot his bolt," he was usually out of the battle; the effect of this terrifying new weapon, in some ways the ancestor of the gun, was also diminished by its short range and poor accuracy. In the mid-thirteenth century English armies, fighting in Wales, came up against the longbow, a rapid-fire and long-range weapon that they adapted for their own use against the French in the fourteenth century. The shaft fired from the longbow did not often penetrate armor, but it made possible a massive salvo that created havoc among knights charging into battle. In response to these changes in military technology, armor became heavier and horses larger, but they did not maintain the previous exclusive military importance of the knight. By the end of the thirteenth century the knight was rendered immobile, after being thrown from his horse, by the sheer weight of his armor.

Although a decline was under way in the military importance of the knight, it was still unthinkable to go to war without having the nobility as officers. The nobility, in spite of technological change, maintained their stranglehold on war because of social traditions and values. The old feudal sub-vassals were becoming obsolete; it was a risky proposition to go to war with an army composed of men who owed only forty days' service a year and who in any case might be ill equipped and ill trained. The mercenary had, by the middle of the thirteenth century, become the staple unit in European military life. But it was the more prominent nobility whom the king commissioned to raise and equip his mercenary contingents. Because of the long peace of the thirteenth century, however, there was no great demand for aristocratic services of this kind before the 1290s, a situation that the aristocrat found frustrating and inhibiting. He knew a little bit about a great many things—government, law, literature, agriculture—but only in warfare was he an expert.

The inability of the greater nobility of the thirteenth century to demonstrate their military superiority over other groups in society encouraged them to find social and ceremonial expressions of their status. By the end of the thirteenth century the aristocracy had become a closed, self-conscious class with specific conventions and rituals in which the rustic lords and common knights could not participate. A whole science of heraldry and genealogy developed, expressing the belief that nobility was a matter of blood and not of service. The ritual of knighthood and chivalry became steadily more elaborate and a code of gentility became more universal among the great lords. The boy of gentle birth was sent off at the age of seven or eight to be a page in the household of a great aristocrat, where he was given his rudimentary education. Seven years later he became a squire and was trained in arms, and finally, if he could afford the expense, he "took on him the order of knighthood" in a great ceremony during which he made chivalric vows and was dubbed by the great lord. These and similar rituals, which have been so often associated with feudalism in the popular mind, were actually the products of its declining stage. They are the means by which an old ruling class, whose importance in society was atrophying, attempted to preserve its former status, substituting class exclusiveness for social utility.

The rise in the population curve and the inflationary cycle that prevailed during most of the thirteenth century made it a good period for landlords. However, the landed classes were plagued by personal indebtedness, and this was particularly true among the great nobles. The maintenance of an aristocratic household and the extravagant style of living expected of a great lord was beyond even his lavish resources in many cases. In a sense, monarchy corrupted the nobility. The king had great means, he could use income from taxation as well as his private estates to maintain his household, and he was able to put on a splendid show. The nobility ran into debt trying to imitate the monarchy, and lesser lords, imitating the great aristocrats, ruined themselves trying to keep up establishments that were beyond their means. Another cause of the economic troubles of the nobility was simply poor management of their resources. Some of them were very good at husbandry, but most of the great nobility were too caught up in the diurnal round of court and tournament to give close attention to how their stewards were maintaining their vast holdings. It seems probable that many of the hard-pressed nobility of the thirteenth century were mining their already unfertilized and nearly exhausted lands in a desperate effort to meet their financial obligations. This expedient only intensified their economic problems. By the end of the thirteenth century, in England, Germany, and France, once-fertile agricultural lands had been played out and could no longer be cultivated.

The political interests of the thirteenth-century nobility varied greatly from country to country. In Italy the political life of the great aristocracy was inevitably involved with urban development. When, at the end of the thirteenth century, the burghers discovered that they could not effectively administer their own governments, they were often willing to pay the price of calling in members of the nobility and accepting them as despots to achieve a modicum of peace and order. This is the origin of the famous "Renaissance princes." The political disintegration of Germany provided many opportunities for the advancement of great and even petty lords. There was always some small court where an intelligent, literate, and aggressive nobleman of even modest means could find an important place. This remained the prevailing political and social condition of Germany until the nineteenth century. In France and in England the lives of the nobility were more and more dominated by the institutions of national monarchy.

The thirteenth-century French nobility found their feudal jurisdictions evaporating and themselves circumscribed at every turn by the relentless royal administration. But royal taxation was not heavy, and the crown established a greatly increased measure of peace, order, and security that lords who were less proficient in warfare found advantageous to their interests. For the more aggressive kind of thirteenth-century French nobleman there were outlets for his energy, particularly the Albigensian crusade and the conquest of Sicily. Because of the size and provincial traditions of the country, the French aristocracy never became a politically homogeneous group. It was the royal government that was able to envision the unity of the realm, but the nobility continued to think of themselves as Normans, Bretons, Burgundians, etc. There were no general assemblies of the French nobility until the first meeting of the Estates General in the early fourteenth century, and this was merely a propaganda show, not the beginning of an effective institution. The only important assemblies of the French nobility were local, provincial, and regional. The Capetian government did not bring the nobility together to obtain their consent to taxation; it dealt with them in this fragmented way, which was a reflection of the fact that the nobility tended to think in terms of their own problems, rather than those of the realm.

The situation in England was different. Partly because it was a much smaller country and partly because of the much longer tradition of the unity and homogeneity of royal power and common law over the whole realm, and partly because the greater nobles frequently held estates in two or even more counties, the English nobility thought of themselves not so much as the men of Kent or Devon or Yorkshire, but as the leaders of the community of the whole realm. From the time of the Norman Conquest they had been summoned from every corner of the kingdom to attend great meetings of the Curia Regis, and this tradition naturally led to advice and common consent on taxation and legislation by the higher nobility in the thirteenth century. The English aristocracy knew much more about the workings of royal government than did members of the same class across the channel, and this knowledge accounted, in part, for their attempts to take over the direction of the royal administration in the reign of Henry III.

The bourgeois of England and northern France were embittered by the continued domination of the nobility in society and by the continued exclusive political and legal privileges of the great lords. Their literature is marked by cynical and critical pictures of the nobility and churchmen who enjoyed the advantages of traditional status that, in bourgeois eyes, they did not deserve. Thinly disguised allegories, such as the extremely popular fables concerned with Reynard the Fox, bitterly vented the burghers' feeling that they had been ill used. Their outlook on life was necessarily more rational and less romanticized than that which prevailed in chivalric literature. This rationalism and cynicism distinguishes the second part of the *Romance of the Rose*, written by Jean de Meun, a university-educated French bourgeois, from the courtly idealism of the earlier part of the work. The thirteenth-century bourgeois generally could not afford to take a romantic view of life; he had to depend on his own talents and energy to avoid helpless poverty. The walls of the medieval town enclosed a society that was extremely competitive, in spite of the efforts made by the old craft guilds to control economic life, and in which there was little charity for the weak and the incompetent. Yet the same merchant or craftsman who was critical, skeptical, and without illusion was intensely pious and emotional in his religious attitudes. This was the means of escape from the restraint and disappointments of urban life. The burgher supported the construction of great municipal churches, and he was intensely devoted to the religious leadership of the Franciscan friars. He stood for hours listening to the friars' harangues or watching miracle and morality plays, whose leading characters and plots were based on biblical stories. He made crude jokes about the clergy, but heaven and hell were extremely real and concretized places for him. The crowded and unsalubrious medieval cities and the political and legal limitations against which the burgher struggled made for repressed people who oscillated between the extremes of cynicism and religious devotion.

During the thirteenth century, there was a continued increase in urban wealth and institutions, but these brought in their wake new problems to plague bourgeois life. In the cities of Flanders and in northern Italy, which were engaged in large-scale production and international trade in woolen textiles, there was an increasing polarization of wealth and the intensification of a class struggle. In every guild there was hard feeling between the masters who controlled the corporation and the subordinate journeymen and apprentices. There was hostility between the wealthier guilds devoted to the international cloth trade and the more ordinary guilds that produced goods for local consumption. In the Flemish textile cities, such as Ghent, and in the Italian industrial centers, particularly Florence, a large proletariat had emerged by the thirteenth century. At the other end of the social scale were great entrepreneurial oligarchs who endeavored to dominate the town governments and to secure regulations suitable to their own interests, and finally there was a bitter struggle for power among these ruling families. The larger the medieval city, the more bitter became its class and political struggles. The atmosphere was one of continual distrust and mutual hatred.

The bourgeois of the thirteenth century made great progress in strictly economic development. The volume of trade in the Mediterranean; in the Baltic; and with the Middle East, central Asia, and Russia was steadily increasing. The merchants of northern Italy used their experience in international exchange to develop banking institutions, and they became even wealthier as the financial agents of the papacy. In the middle of the thirteenth century Europe revived the extensive use of gold coinage in international trade, and the gold florin first minted in 1252 to serve the needs of Florentine merchants became a monetary standard for Europe. The burghers achieved a high level of general literacy, which was reflected not only in belletristic literature, first in France and then in Italy, but in the development of the professional notary to draft the myriad of documents necessary in a highly literate and commercial society.

But the burghers could not solve their political problems, and the cities suffered from continual internal instability. Because the cities were so faction- and class-ridden, their electoral systems became extremely indirect; nobody trusted anybody else to cast an honest vote. By the end of the thirteenth century many of the Italian towns were giving up their communal freedom, which they had struggled for centuries to obtain, a development that has been much bemoaned by modern liberal historians. Political power was surrendered by the burghers to a *podestà,* a dictator who came from the ranks of the local aristocracy and whose family became hereditary princes in the wealthy commercial centers.

In some parts of Europe the communes maintained their independence. There were still "free cities" in the German Rhineland in the fourteenth century. The most outstanding group of independent communes were the German Baltic commercial cities that made up the Hanseatic

League. The north German merchants not only engaged in far-flung trade stretching from Russia to England, but they formed political and military alliances and fought Scandinavian kings for hegemony in the Baltic. Wherever there was strong royal power, the burghers had little political autonomy. The French towns in the thirteenth century, including some in the south and along the Rhine, which had enjoyed communal privileges, were brought under the expanding royal administration. In England the political and legal privileges of the bourgeois lagged behind those on the Continent. The London merchants, until almost the end of the thirteenth century, were exasperated by the exchequer's insistence that their legal status was scarcely different from that of peasants on the royal demesne and that all burgesses were subject to arbitrary taxation.

One of the fundamental facts of thirteenth-century civilization was the failure of the industrial and commercial classes to make use of their economic and intellectual importance to achieve a measure of political leadership in society. By 1300 even the Italian communes were losing their political freedom. The governments of the emerging national monarchies were in the hands of the landed classes and university graduates, who, although in many cases were of bourgeois provenance, had no interest save that of their royal masters. It was still kings, lords, churchmen, and scholars who were the leaders of European society. The economic importance of the bourgeois was not translated into political and social leadership until the late eighteenth and nineteenth centuries.

The largest class in medieval society, comprising certainly a majority of the total population, was mute. There is no thirteenth-century peasant literature, and it is only in the fourteenth century that there is any kind of writing that we can identify as representing the peasants' outlook. *Piers Plowman* was probably written by one of the poor English parish priests, who were themselves often drawn from the peasant class. Its anguished, bitter, and apocalyptic tone indicates that the peasant was conscious of his exploitation by the ruling classes in society, but was devoted to the teachings of the church, which had been brought to him by the spread of the parish system and the preaching of itinerant friars.

Economic historians tell us, from their study of manorial and legal records, that the economic condition of the peasants was improving in most parts of Europe in the thirteenth century, particularly in France and Germany. The combined impact of a money economy and the colonization movement allowed the peasants to escape from the servile dues and services of the old manorialism. Some carved out "new villages" from former wastelands, while others joined the movement to the eastern frontier, where the German lords gave them favorable terms of settlement. Those who remained in their old open-field villages were often able to reach an agreement with their usually hard-pressed lords to commute the old manorial services into money rents. Thus, in England, France, and Germany the serf was becoming a small, independent farmer. He was still exploited and abused by the local lords, contemned by the bourgeois, and ignored by prelates, but he was better off than he was two centuries before. In Italy the peasantry suffered from the economic domination of the bourgeois capitalists, who bought up land and exploited them mercilessly. Everywhere there was an extensive gradation within the peasant class itself—from wealthy peasants with their own plows, animals, and farms to landless day laborers whose existence was always marginal.

The concerted effort of medieval social historians, beginning with Marc Bloch in the 1930s down to the recent writings of E. LeRoy Ladurie and Natalie Zemon Davis, has been in the direction of according the peasant a significant degree of rationality; his family life, attributes of caring and compassion; and his community, a degree of autonomy and class consciousness. After reading Ladurie, one perceives that the late medieval peasant had the same positive and negative qualities as did the early twentieth-century French farmer. The peasant cultures of rural France changed little between 1300 and 1950 in this reading. After reading Zemon Davis (or watching the film she was instrumental in making) one anticipates that the wealthier French peasant around 1500 had the affluence and intellect to do just about anything a modern middle-class family would do and that the young men in the village through their boisterous conduct expressed a symbolic rebellion against the institutions of social control.

Yet even the wealthy peasant had no surcease from the endless round of birth, death, disease, and labor, alleviated only by many saints' days and other church holidays on the calendar, by drunkenness, by the Sunday morning service conducted by a semiliterate parish priest, and by the more intriguing sermons of an itinerant friar. If the hundreds of thousands of peasants who trooped across the pages of English legal court rolls were typical, the one thing that characterized the more hardworking, skillful, or lucky peasant family was the insatiable love of land, not just as a source of wealth, but as an anchoring force in their lives and as the vehicle for perpetuating the family in and beyond the emerging generation.

CHAPTER TWENTY

The Search for Order

I. An Old Land

By the late thirteenth century western Europe was an old land. Whereas early medieval Europe had been pitifully short of manpower, by the late eleventh century some areas seem to have had an excess of people in relation to available land. After 1050 the prolific Norman French aristocrats could not provide enough land for their many sons. One result was the Norman expansion into Sicily and Britain; another, the eager participation of Norman knights in the crusades. Intensive cultivation in the eleventh and twelfth centuries produced a shortage of land in western Germany and gave impetus to the eastward drive of German aristocrats in the thirteenth century. In England the population pressure and land hunger were so great by the late thirteenth century that marginal land was brought under cultivation. Much of this land was abandoned a century later and not cultivated again until the sixteenth-century boom, and some of it was never cultivated again.

A traveler through the European countryside in 1300 would have found much the same conditions of intensive cultivation and rural prosperity that exist there today. There was a thriving market for grain, mutton and beef, wool, and grapes for wine, and landlords took pains to get the largest possible yield from their estates. The more enlightened were well aware of the advantages of manure for fertilizer and the rudiments of animal husbandry. The peasant, fast moving out of his servile status, was becoming either a rent-paying free tenant or a small landowner himself. Sir Walter of Henley, an English gentleman of the mid-thirteenth century, remarked in a treatise on successful farming that "great wealth" will come to whose who "know how to keep all the points of husbandry, as the tillage of land and the keeping of cattle." The petty lord or country gentleman, smelling of the barn and fields, and the ambitious peasant, squeezing every possible ounce of profit from his land, were central figures in European rural society and have remained so, especially in France, down to the present day, while the captains and kings have come and gone.

In 1300, however, the great lords—the high nobility—still dominated rural Europe. In all countries their castles and chateaus loomed triumphant on the horizon. The booming agricultural market and the favors gained at the royal court enriched the aristocracy as never before, while literacy and the chivalric code gave them a heightened consciousness of their superior status. The great lords looked down upon the simple country gentleman with arrogant disdain. They were contemptuous, as always, of the peasantry and profligate with the blood of common folk as they pursued their endless raids and wars.

Yet by 1300 aristocratic mayhem and pillage usually had to be justified as serving the interests of the national monarchies. From 1214 to 1294 there were no major wars in Europe; this was the century of the long peace, and the nobles were frustrated and restless. Even so, they acted differently from the barbaric lords of Charlemagne's times. Many exhibited fastidious taste in furnishing and decorating the enormous drafty castles and chateaus in which they lived. The castle was now a home, as well as a fortress. In this time of peace the aristocrat enjoyed the pleasures of court ritual and satisfied his compulsive taste for violence in the hunt.

The most obvious difference between the world of Charlemagne and the European environment in the thirteenth century was the existence in the latter era of many towns and cities, most of which had only a few thousand inhabitants, engaged in local trade and heavily dependent on the castle or cathedral that loomed over them. But there were a handful of urban centers—London, Paris, and Florence, for example—with populations of 50,000 to 100,000. And though burghers did not constitute more than 10 percent of Europe's population, their economic, religious, and cultural influence was profoundly important in shaping high and late medieval civilization. Already these cities had both the attractions and disadvantages of the urban environment. The economic and cultural opportunities they offered were counterbalanced by bad housing, inadequate sanitation, and overcrowding. Destructive fires and drunken violence in the streets were everyday occurrences. William Fitz-Stephen, writing a chamber-of-commerce brochure for London in 1173, boasted that "the only pests . . . are the immoderate drinking of fools and frequency of fires." In the fourteenth century a new pest—the Black Death (bubonic plague)—carried off a third of Europe's population in twenty years.

In 1300 the main structural feature of a town north of the Alps was the huge wall that had been laboriously erected—often over a period of centuries—to protect the burghers from the depredation of raiding nobles. And although the wall served its purpose until the fifteenth century, when gunpowder made it possible for cannon balls to breach its thickness, the physical security was gained at a heavy social and psychological price. The wall that kept the robber barons out also crammed the houses of the town together along crooked, filthy streets and exacerbated the burghers' proclivity to mass paranoia.

In northern Italy the urban environment had more to offer than it did beyond the Alps. Here, monarchy had failed to subdue urban autonomy, and the aristocracy had been absorbed into city life. High bourgeois families, grown fabulously rich from commerce and banking, imitated and embellished the French aristocratic style. Freeing themselves of the smell of warehouse and countinghouse, they became the first urban aristocracy in Europe since the heyday of the Roman Empire. Civic pride inspired them to adorn their cities with public buildings, squares, and monuments that provided a worthy setting for their own palazzos.

Many parts of cities like Venice and Florence stand today much as they were in the later Middle Ages, and we can see for ourselves that no urban environment has ever been more gracious and delightful, no urban oligarchy more enlightened. Here also were instability and violence; here also were dreadful poverty and miserable slums. But the amenities that the urban environment of late medieval Italy had to offer were among the best that city life has ever offered. The Italian cities made the most of the promise held out by the medieval saying, "Urban air makes free."

Whatever the strength of national, regional, and urban institutions, the family household still remained the most important institution in the lives of western European people in the later Middle Ages. Who the king was and what he did or did not do could at times deeply affect personal lives, and the composition and policy of an aristocratic parliament or of a town council could have a similar impact. These were elements of modernization in medieval society, looking toward the national and bureaucratic state of the modern world. But who your father, your siblings, and your cousins were normally served as the prime determinants of people's lives in the later Middle Ages, much more so than today. One can posit this rule: The more important your family as the shaper of your life, the more medieval the nature of a society.

In the fourteenth and fifteenth centuries, statistical data become available—fragmentary, of course, and still highly circumstantial but illuminating—on the size of family households. Nineteenth- and early twentieth-century social historians imagined that the standard medieval household was occupied by the extended family involving three generations and many siblings and servants. We know now that for middle-class and working-class families in the later Middle Ages, the norm was close to the modern nuclear, rather than extended family: the husband; the wife (often the second or third wife in a series because of the high mortality rate in childbirth); children; perhaps one aging parent; perhaps one unmarried sibling; and from zero to four or so servants, depending on economic circumstances. Given the low life expectancy of medieval people—on average, outside monastic havens, in the mid-30s—it is not surprising that the three-generation extended family was the aberration, not the norm. Old folks didn't survive long in that world. Where there were large, extended family households, we are looking at wealthy people, the top 2–3 percent of the population—the higher nobility and the great merchant families. Only these families could afford to sustain many layers of relatives and droves of servants. Indeed the capacity to finance this high-consumption household was a hallmark of being in the top layer of the social order. The life-style of the rich and powerful in the later Middle Ages meant not only material things and patronage of the arts and clergy, but the ability to maintain extended households.

The medieval household, like households today, made efforts to regulate its size. The male head of the household normally remarried when his wife died and continued to produce progeny with a younger wife. Widows, unless they were wealthy, usually did not remarry if they were above the age of thirty. Adolescent daughters were married off young—around fourteen or fifteen—and among middle-class as well as wealthy and noble families this practice could be expensive, since a dowry was required to effect a marriage. Therefore, having a lot of daughters was a liability in the medieval household, and the exposure of surplus infant daughters, in effect aborting them shortly after birth, was widely practiced. If the family already had several sons, male infants would also be exposed. The medieval world had no effective means of contraception, although some historians believe that the ancient world did have the effective use of vaginal diaphragms and that science was lost in early medieval times. Abortion was practiced but sparingly because the feebleness of medieval medicine meant that abortions were life-threatening ventures. That is why exposure of infants was preferred. That the killing of newborn babies was condemned by the church did not seem to impede this manner of limiting the size of families.

On the other hand, a shorter biological clock for females limited procreation. Woman's fertility after the age of thirty was uncommon, and menopause came about a dozen years earlier in the medieval world than it does today. Families might want to preserve infant life rather extinguish it, especially in the case of the more valued sons, and the problem on this side was breast-feeding, the only form of transmitting nourishment to infants in the medieval world. When the mother's milk was insufficient, the solution was to use wet nurses—neighborhood women who had recently given birth and had a surplus of milk.

The diet of the ancient Mediterranean world conformed to modern nutritional standards. It was low in cholesterol and consisted of rice or some other grain topped off with a bit of fish or fowl. The Mediterranean people were horrified to see the German invaders eating slabs of cow meat. The more northern part of medieval Europe became, in Germanic tradition, a carnivorous society. Until the thirteenth century there was so much wild game in the ubiquitous European forests that a high-protein diet was possible for all classes. If the nobility feasted on venison, the peasants could always eat pig and rabbit. As the forests shrank in the late Middle Ages, game became more scarce and restrictions on forest hunting were widely imposed on the peasantry. Large tracts of woodland became game preserves for the upper classes (even in the eleventh century William the Conqueror had set aside more than a million acres for his hunting). The staple diet of the late medieval peasant was oatmeal, which nutritionists now tell us is much healthier than is a high-protein diet of red meat. At the end of the Middle Ages, if the nutritionists are right, the incidence of heart disease among the peasantry should have been lower than among the nobility. Since sugar was still rare and expensive, medieval teeth were normally free of cavities.

The nobility and the great merchants were no longer satisfied with simply eating sides of red meat. Wealthy households in the fifteenth century began to hire fancy chefs who could prepare elaborate feasts with highly spiced dishes, the components being imported from the Far East. By 1500 the cuisine of Florence had become the most admired in Europe, and shortly thereafter it was exported to Paris and became the foundation of French cuisine. Meanwhile, the intrepid Florentine traveler Marco Polo had been to China and brought back with him a noodle dish that became Italian pasta (much lower in cholesterol than Germanic steaks), and Jewish refugees from militantly Christian Spain brought into southern Italy a dish that we would recognize as pizza.

With regard to entertainment, late medieval households in noble courts and in cities appreciated the innovative development of popular drama performed by professional companies. Various kinds of ball games were popular as well. In larger urban areas prostitution thrived and was closely regulated by city governments. It is a safe guess that 10 percent of young women in a medieval city were whores, but this was still true of London in 1850.

One side of medieval household life that was changed in northern Europe by the sixteenth-century Protestant Reformation was the increased number of work days. In the medieval calendar, there were only about 250 full work days a year because of the large number of saints' days and other church festivals.

Alcoholic beverages were a diversion and comfort to households among all classes. Everyone drank beer, even for breakfast, and the alcoholic content was three to four times higher that today's suds. Mead, a kind of beer made from fermented honey, was popular in northern Europe, and also had a powerful kick. Wine was the favorite drink of the nobility and wealthier middle class. Besides royal vanity, the reason why the English fought so hard to hold on to vestiges of Eleanor of Aquitaine's lands in western France was that these lands were the source of the Bordeaux wine they loved so much ("claret" was the biggest import item in medieval England). The only hard liquor in the medieval world was expensive brandy. Brandy was invented by monks, and the French produced most of it, from cognac around Bordeaux (after 1450, when the English were driven out, an Irish mercenary named Hennessey stayed in Bordeaux and founded a family cognac industry that is still going strong) to Normandy's calvados, the white lightning of the medieval world.

II. The Crisis of the Late Middle Ages

Despite vast social and economic changes in the thirteenth century, the medieval mind remained essentially conservative. Piecemeal improvements in technique greatly increased the efficiency of age-old methods of cultivation and transportation, but labor-saving devices did not lead to a scientific revolution. Medieval society struggled to incorporate Aristotelian scientific principles into the traditional theological system and had little desire for basic change. The same was true in social relationships and concepts. The town and the bourgeoisie appeared, but the still-predominant view was that there were but three orders in the divine arrangement of society: warrior, priest, and peasant. Even the use of money did not force a change in the medieval belief that theoretically usury was a sin and that the only true wealth was in land and agriculture. It did not occur to medieval men to seek an alternative social, economic, and political framework—the very attempt would have seemed both futile and blasphemous.

Conflict was incipient in twelfth- and thirteenth-century Europe. Mass heretical movements appeared for the first time. The unrest of the bourgeoisie, the financial problems of the nobility, the power struggle between the German emperor and the pope—all were potentially explosive phenomena. But an expanding society can absorb and contain conflict; by and large, European society in the High Middle Ages provided outlets for the energies of its divergent elements.

In the fourteenth and fifteenth centuries, however, European society suddenly stopped expanding. Economic depression was accompanied by political chaos and social disorder, in which competing forces engaged in a struggle to the death. The medieval world order, which had become fully developed only in the thirteenth century, was fundamentally shaken. The struggles among dynasties, nations, and classes brought the medieval world to its knees.

The fourteenth and fifteenth centuries were a period of crisis and dissolution. Plagues and wars were more frequent and more severe, and an exhausted and demoralized society did not easily recover from the repeated blows it received. Instability and decline are not merely tags that historians have attached to the late Middle Ages; the men and women living at the time were themselves aware that theirs was a troubled world. Violence and extremism in human affairs accompanied a wide variety of natural disasters and social dislocations.

From the close of the thirteenth century to the middle of the fifteenth, Europe suffered a general economic depression. Few, if any, towns increased in size, and many decreased considerably. The great banking houses in Italy were in eclipse; even the Medici banking house that flourished in the early fifteenth century declined in wealth. Although prices remained stationary, unemployment increased sharply in the industrial centers. In Flanders the workers demanded that a minimum annual production of cloth be guaranteed. The gap between rich and poor widened everywhere as trade declined. Yet this depression in the late Middle Ages was not as severe as the depression at the beginning of the medieval period. Although trade diminished, it was not destroyed, and by the end of the fifteenth century a gradual recovery was under way.

Both trade and agriculture suffered a labor shortage after 1350, caused, in part, by the devastation of the plague in all parts of Europe. In the towns, rapidly rising wages were returned to their former low level by legislation. In agriculture the drop in manpower meant that the total amount of land under cultivation decreased. Many of the lands that were brought under cultivation in the twelfth and thirteenth centuries were allowed to fall into disuse, and the profits of the landlords dropped accordingly.

In some cases, resources that had been discovered at the height of expansion merely dried up, leaving a gap that the medieval world, with its limited techniques, could not fill. The supply of new metal, especially silver—the basic metal of exchange in northern Europe—was drastically curtailed by the petering out of the rich silver mines in the north. The Goslar mines in Saxony filled with water, and there were no technological means of overcoming this difficulty.

A worsening climate was another natural obstacle to prosperity in Europe. Europe entered its "little Ice Age." Various indicators, including the activities of glaciers in the late thirteenth and fourteenth centuries, show that winters all over Europe became colder and longer. This trend in climate probably shortened the growing season and reduced the abundance of the harvests. Records show that Venice was having trouble finding timber for its flourishing shipbuilding industry; this problem may have been related to the recession of the timber line in the Alps, which resulted from the general drop in temperature.

A more dramatic and direct factor in the economic depression in Europe was the Black Death. During the High Middle Ages an epidemic of the plague had decimated the population in many places, but within a generation or two the normally high birthrate had repaired the damage. The effects of the plague that struck in 1348–49 were not mitigated by a rising birthrate. Epidemic disease, certainly bubonic plague but possibly also a rare strain of murrain that in this rare instance affected humans as well as domestic animals, swept over Europe, killing at least a quarter and as much as 40 percent of the population in some areas. Many flourishing cities became virtual ghost towns for a time. The clergy was especially hard hit, losing perhaps a third of its most dedicated servants.

The plague was much more severe in the cities than in the countryside, but its psychological impact penetrated all areas of society. No one—peasant or aristocrat—was safe from the disease, and once it was contracted, a horrible and painful death was almost a certainty. The dead and dying lay in the streets, abandoned by frightened friends and relatives. The effect of this devastating epidemic, in the middle of the fourteenth century, was reinforced by recurrences several times in the ensuing half century. The bubonic plague was caused by a bite from a parasite carried by rats, but European medicine in the Middle Ages did not know that.

The incidence of the absolute decline in European economic life was heightened by shifts and dislocations in the balance of trade. In northern Europe, Flemish predominance faded as England began to use its wool to manufacture its own cloth, and Dutch ports were increasingly able to capture international traffic at the expense of the ports of Flanders. Though Flanders was still relatively rich, its days of preeminence in the northern European economy were over.

The Hanseatic League of northern German cities suffered a similar fate. At the height of their power in the 1360s, the Hanseatic merchants were able to establish a virtual monopoly on East-West trade in northern Europe and to defeat the king of Denmark to secure a trade route across the southern part of the Danish peninsula. By the fifteenth century, however, a number of factors combined to destroy their unity and power. The league lost the herring trade to Holland because the herring changed their spawning patterns, and it lost a major part of the East-West trade to the cities of southern Germany.

Even the apparently unchallengeable position of the Italian cities declined in the fourteenth and fifteenth centuries. The general problems that beset trade and banking were complicated by specific problems in the Orient, where Italy purchased the luxury goods that were the staples of its trade with Europe. The loss of Eastern sources was made almost complete by the conquest of the remnants of the Byzantine Empire in the mid-fifteenth century by the Ottoman Turks. Portugal and then Spain—not Italy—led the search for new routes to the East, which were to revolutionize European trade. Soon the Mediterranean would be relegated to a position second to the Atlantic Ocean as a European trade route. By the end of the fifteenth century, the approaching Italian eclipse was already apparent.

The era stretching from the later decades of the thirteenth century to about 1480 was marked by recurrent institutional collapse, inept political leadership, natural disasters, warfare, economic decline, and social upheaval. Yet this same period saw progress in the definition of political and legal concepts and great achievements in intellectual life and visual arts. It was also marked by both the steady entrenchment of secular attitudes and the proliferariton of forms of mysticism. Historians have come to regard the fourteenth and fifteenth centuries as an age of transition in which an old world was dying and a new world was struggling to be born.

In the fourteenth century the discontent of urban workers and the peasants led to serious rebellions. In general the conditions of peasants were improving; by the end of the fifteenth century, few serfs were left in western Europe. But the advantages of freedom were counterbalanced, at least in part, by the new responsibilities that it entailed. Freedom did not necessarily bring prosperity, and it did not greatly enhance the social status of the peasant. Urban workers suffered as the worsening of economic conditions struck directly at the manufacturing industries in Flanders and Italy. The lower classes were the first to feel the effects of depression in the form of fewer jobs and lower salaries.

Increased taxation, which was an inevitable result of frequent wars, was a tremendous burden to workers, and as the cost of war kept rising, discontent became profound and widespread. Agrarian and urban revolts were many and violent. The most severe were the late fourteenth-century rising of the French peasantry, called the Jacquerie; the Peasant's Revolt of 1381 in England; and the repeated rebellions of the Flemish and Florentine textile workers against the oligarchic guild masters. But the results of these working-class revolts were meager—at best, a few promises that were quickly broken once order had been restored; at worst, cruel suppression of the leaders and the massacre of their followers. In the fifteenth century the rebels were often heretics, and the church joined the monarchy and the nobility to subdue the rebellious.

The increase in warfare meant that the noble warrior played an indispensable role in politics. In Germany the fourteenth and fifteenth centuries were the heyday of princely power; effective national and imperial authority was negligible. In Italy also, no national power could break down the resistance of the cities or the pope, and in Spain the national monarchy was only slowly consolidating its territory. In England and France, however, the idea of national monarchy was well established by the end of the thirteenth century, and increasingly the authority of the crown became a prize to be sought, rather than an alien force to be abolished. In England and France, nobles attempted to exercise the powers of the crown as regents or through baronial councils and tried to use the legal and fiscal institutions of national government to their own advantage.

The increasing influence of the nobles as warriors and governors in a period of governmental chaos was paradoxically accompanied by a real weakening of the economic and political position of the nobility. As serfs became free peasants who were responsible only for the payment of rent on their land, the services due on the lord's demesne were gradually abolished, and the lord was forced to hire labor. Because of the shortage of agricultural labor in the fourteenth and early fifteenth centuries, many lords found it profitable to let out a substantial part of their land to small peasant farmers, and the great estate increasingly gave way to a multitude of small farms from which the lord received a fixed rent. With a decreasing amount of land under cultivation, the dependence upon fixed rents in an inflationary period reduced the income of the nobility. Inevitably the noble tried to make up this loss by seizing the royal taxes collected on his estates. By meddling in national politics, the higher nobility intended to expropriate additional portions of crown income and authority for their personal advantage. The lesser nobles, who were unable to appropriate royal revenues, became more dependent on the crown.

The division within the nobility became increasingly apparent during the fourteenth and fifteenth centuries, as the great magnates gained in wealth and influence while the lower nobility became much more readily the subjects of a national power. In England the title of nobility could pass only to the eldest son of a noble, so that the number of nobles was always closely restricted. The rest of landed society consisted of the gentry, who depended upon the income from their estates and satisfied themselves with monopolizing local politics. Occasionally, the gentry mingled with rich burgesses of the towns, who bought land or married into the aristocratic families of the countryside. In France and the rest of Europe, the title of nobility passed to all sons, and thus the nobility was a relatively large class, jealous of its separate status and loath to intermarry with the bourgeoisie unless economic contingencies dictated union with a rich bourgeois family.

Dislocations within the nobility and within society as a whole were dramatically indicated by bands of mercenary soldiers, products of the incessant wars of the period, who roamed the countryside. In the fourteenth and fifteenth centuries, kings, princes, popes, and Italian cities resorted to purchasing the services of mercenary soldiers. Organized into bands under a leader, these mercenaries hired themselves out to the highest bidder; sometimes a higher price offered in the middle of a campaign induced them to change sides. The worst evil the mercenaries brought, however, was not their lack of loyalty, but their constant plundering of the countryside. The mercenary bands were permanent bodies organized for the profit of their members, and when unemployed, they lived off the countryside, taking whatever they could find. A besieged noble or monastery could usually buy them off with tribute and send them on to the next county, but the peasants had no defense. The disorder that followed from mercenary depredations was a strong argument in favor of the reestablishment of the order and security of the King's Peace in the countryside.

The barbarity of the mercenary bands contrasted with the growing niceties of courtly life. The highest level of culture and the greatest splendor were achieved in the elegant courts of the Italian nobility (although an Italian noble might, in fact, be a fat bourgeois merchant, rather than the stereotype of the Christian knight). Standards of dress became increasingly lavish, and courtly manners became exceedingly elaborate. Especially in Italy, the courtier was an educated man of refined tastes. Courtly society in northern Europe lagged behind its Italian counterpart, but it, too, became more and more elaborate, in spite of the decreased income of most of the nobility. Orders of knighthood abounded in the circles of great nobles, as well as of kings. Tournaments lost their rough-and-tumble character and became ceremonial; jousting became a gentle-manly sport. In fact, more and more knights were little acquainted with the art of wielding a lance. In time knighthood became a purely heredi-tary status, and the noble began to distinguish himself from the com-moner not by his accomplishments in battle, but by his coat of arms, his dress, and his behavior.

The attempts of the nobility to govern revealed the impracticality of the noble way of life. The barons paid little attention to the necessary details of government, and their constant infighting for personal advan-tage made the failure of baronial government inevitable. If the baronial council did not adjourn to the hunt at a crucial juncture, its members ignored a crisis while bitterly engaged in factional strife. The nobility's normal lack of concern for governmental affairs and their almost exclu-sive devotion to the interests of their families ill fitted them to be leaders of the troubled society of fourteenth-and fifteenth-century Europe.

The wars of the fourteenth and fifteenth centuries were both a cause of the problems that beset national governments and the result of royal attempts to expand the authority of the crown. The Hundred Years' War between France and England was only the most severe and protracted of the conflicts of the period, but it aptly illustrates the fundamental charac-ter of later medieval wars: it was both dynastic and national in origin. In its early stages the war was fought over the feudal obligations of the English king in France, the claims of the English king to the French throne, and the ambitions of both monarchs to control the rich wine-growing regions of Gascony and the prosperous industrial cities of Flan-ders. By the fifteenth century, however, national feeling in both countries had escalated to such an extent that public opinion was almost as opposed to ending the conflict without a decisive victory as it was to granting the taxes necessary to continue the war.

The new institutions developed by the late medieval monarchy to consolidate its power and authority proved too weak to remain effective in the face of long and bitter wars. While the king attempted to extend his power, he was forced to strain the resources of the crown to the maximum. Society could accept and even welcome the royal judges who represented order and stability, but the tax collector was obstinately and often successfully resisted by all elements of the population. The king was still expected to finance the government out of his personal income—he was supposed "to live of his own." High nobles were usually exempt from taxation (theoretically because of their military services). The bulk of taxation therefore fell upon the gentry, the peasantry, and the burgesses, and even their taxes might be appropriated by a local magnate. The use of national or provincial assemblies to approve new taxation enabled the monarchy to close the gap between the crown and public opinion. More often than not, the king actually received only a fraction of the taxes owed in any given levy.

The vicissitudes of heredity also hampered the expansion of royal power in the fourteenth and fifteenth centuries. The problems that arose when the king left a minor heir or no heir at all were serious enough in a society where the power of the ruling house was never securely established, but these problems were aggravated by the accession of physically weak or even demented kings. When a king was sickly or feebleminded, or when the throne was in dispute, the chaos of baronial politics descended upon the institutions of the state. By the fourteenth century the concept of the crown was so firmly established in France and England that kingship could not cease to exist, but the royal government was often reduced to a façade for the worst manifestations of baronial politics. It remained for future centuries to establish the institutions of national government so firmly that they could continue to operate in the absence of strong royal leadership.

III. Papacy and Clergy

Medieval Christian society, at least in theory, was universal in extent. On the political side, the Holy Roman Empire proclaimed its own universality, ignoring local and dynastic particularism. In reality, of course, the Holy Roman Empire was German, and at times Italian, in its makeup and policy, and other kingdoms in Europe were uneasy and defensive about its claims to universal authority. But while the tendency to divide into national states grew stronger with the rise of monarchy in France and England and other parts of Europe, the church remained universal: All men were at least potentially Christian and therefore fell somehow within the purview of the universal Christian church.

The papacy reached the height of its power in the thirteenth century. Administrative, legal, and fiscal refinements made the Roman curia a vast, effective machine that increasingly implemented the authority of the pope in the farthest reaches of Christendom. Having defeated the last of the Hohenstaufens, the popes had nothing to fear from the Holy Roman emperor. Popes like Innocent III and Innocent IV voiced papal claims in extreme terms and behaved like most prominent sovereigns in Europe. At the same time, thirteenth-century popes knew how to compromise and shared the vast income from church lands with secular overlords. Pious kings listened to the pope with respect and dealt with him in a spirit of compromise; recalcitrant kings, such as Frederick II, were likely to find that the spiritual power of the pope was accompanied by earthly power asserted with force of arms.

The power of the pope was heavily based upon his personal ability and his alliances with powerful secular rulers. In the fourteenth and fifteenth centuries the growth of national states dwarfed the power of the papacy, and the popes often became tools of royal policy instead of the reverse. The power of the papacy was one of the first casualties of the growth of national monarchies and the entrenchment of lay and secular interests that characterized the fourteenth and fifteenth centuries.

The greatest work of thirteenth-century French literature, the second part of *The Romance of the Rose,* written in the late 1270s by a university-educated French bourgeois, Jean de Muen, demonstrates on every page that the peace of Innocent III and the compromise of Thomas Aquinas did not satisfy the intellectuals of his generation. The romantic idealism of the twelfth century has turned cold and sour: "So degenerate is all the world that it has put up love for sale." On all sides de Muen saw greed, corruption, and rottenness. Scholars and lawyers, he said, "sell their skill for cash." Although he was a bourgeois, de Muen saw no redemptive qualities in his own class: "No merchant ever lives at ease; he has for life enlisted in the war of gain, and never will acquire enough." De Muen had only contempt for the leadership of medieval society. Kings and princes have "brought despotism to pinch and rob the folk," he said. On all sides he saw "bad divines who overrun the earth, preaching to gain favor, honor, wealth." The Franciscan ideal had also failed miserably: "Poverty . . . is unloved and vilified by all." In de Muen's eyes all the efforts to achieve a Christian commonwealth that were made in the twelfth and thirteenth centuries had proved futile. His poem heralds the frustration, bitterness, anger, and dismay of the late thirteenth century, which was soon to be articulated in the monumental struggle between the French monarchy and the papacy and that contemporaries assumed marked an end of an era and the demise of medieval papacy.

French kings and nobles in the thirteenth century had provided the bulk of the manpower needed by the popes in crusades against the Muslims and within Europe, and France had more than once provided a haven to protect the pope from the wrath of the German emperor. Yet at the end of the thirteenth century it was the French king Philip IV who struck a devastating blow to the power and prestige of the pope.

The enormous power that the French monarchy enjoyed at the accession of Philip IV the Fair (1285–1314) had a corrupting effect on the personnel of the royal bureaucracy, especially the chief ministers of the crown. These ministers were men of modest background, of knightly or bourgeois provenance, who had made their way in the world because of their legal knowledge and administrative ability after a hard early struggle in life. The vast resources that they controlled in the king's name and their almost unlimited power to ruin men born to a much higher social status made them into arrogant and unprincipled scoundrels. Since the time of Philip Augustus, the French bureaucracy had been known for its harsh attitudes, and this was to some degree a political necessity if the country was ever to be really united under the crown. But the megalomania of Philip the Fair's ministers was something new. To severity and chicanery were now added slander, blackmail, and extortion. The government of late thirteenth-century France discovered the technique of the "big lie": the more fantastic the accusation, the easier it would be to destroy helpless opponents. It learned how the processes of law could be easily perverted into an invincible agency of despotism. The royal administration always acted against its helpless victims with a parade of legal formalities; it discovered that if governments will only use a façade of juristic institutions, the most extreme and groundless accusations will begin to take on the coloration of truth in the dim minds of the populace. It is not easy to discern what part the king played in all this—to what extent he actually directed this vicious policy or was merely the dupe of his ministers. The latter is the more probable. Personally devout and brave, Philip was also silent and stupid, the perfect façade behind which the bureaucracy could work its plans. His ministers were monsters of cynicism, but the king seems actually to have believed their big lies. They had no trouble convincing him of the legality of their attacks on anyone who stood in their way, including the vicar of Christ himself.

After the death of St. Louis the papacy found itself in greater and greater difficulties. Its legal and financial institutions were the object of criticism all over Europe, and not least by churchmen who found themselves heavily taxed by Rome and frequently impleaded in the papal courts. The cardinals were well educated and good administrators, but they had gained a bad reputation for nepotism and venality. The extreme measures taken against the Hohenstaufens had disturbed sensitive minds, who doubted that the keeper of the keys of heaven should use methods that better suited petty Italian despots. The Spiritual Franciscans sowed confusion by raising the claim that the papacy had failed to emulate the poverty of the apostolic church. Once again anticlericalism, this time directed chiefly against the papal "wolf," became a leitmotif of western literature. There were, in addition, grave problems within the curia itself. Intermittently since the tenth century the throne of Peter had been embroiled in the feuds of the ambitious Roman families, who regarded the papal tiara and the cardinal's hat as the entry to new dynastic riches. In addition to the parties maintained by leading families of the Roman aristocracy within the college of cardinals, there was also a minority group of French cardinals who were sensitive to the demands of the Capetian government and the Angevin ruler of southern Italy. Under these conditions of a faction-ridden cardinalate, every papal election produced a minor crisis and scandalous rumors. By the early 1280s the papacy was in an extremely vulnerable position if any major issue arose in Europe that affected its interests and tested the mettle of the curia. Such an issue arose out of a strange and mysterious series of events in Sicily, and the papacy was found wanting in the effectiveness of its reaction to this crisis.

Angevin rule in southern Italy and Sicily was from the first unpopular with the native population. Charles of Anjou, unlike the previous Hohenstaufen rulers, had no claim to descent from the original Norman house, albeit he had seized this wealthy land with papal authorization. His treatment of the people he had conquered was not much better than that which the northern French nobility had accorded to Languedoc early in the century. It was another land grab by the French nobility, who had no concern for the welfare and the dignity of the people they had conquered. Angevin rule in southern Italy marked the beginning of the long descent of this previously prosperous region into miserable poverty. It is unlikely that anything would have come out of the Italian hatred for the French if it had not been for Charles of Anjou's ambitions against Constantinople. In 1261 the Latin Kingdom of Constantinople, which was the creation of the fourth crusade, finally tottered to its demise, and the princely Byzantine dynasty of Palaeologus gained the throne of Constantinople. The resources of the revived Byzantine state were meager, and it was all the Greeks could do to hold off the Turks until the Moslems finally took the Golden City on the Bosporus in 1453. Innocent III's plan for the reunion of the Roman and Greek churches, as a result of the Latin conquest of Constantinople, thereby ended in failure. For another two decades the Byzantine ruler bought protection against a western counterattack by agreeing to a formal union of the two churches, but in 1281 this pretense was renounced by Charles of Anjou, who made plans to attack Constantinople.

The Greeks had forgotten how to fight, but not how to conspire. Byzantine agents and gold gave direction to the bitter hatred of the Sicilians, and in 1282 they arose and massacred the French garrison in a savage rebellion that came to be known as the Sicilian Vespers. The exact details of the organization of the Sicilian Vespers have baffled historical researchers; the conspiratorial genius of the Sicilian people was first clearly demonstrated in 1282. But it is apparent that the Byzantines had taken the lead in fomenting the uprising. The Sicilians gave their loyalty, however, to the king of Aragon, whose wife was the daughter of Manfred, Frederick II's illegitimate son and the last Hohenstaufen ruler. The Spanish king accepted the crown of Sicily, and after landing on the island prevented Charles of Anjou from reconquering it.

The papal throne at the time of the Sicilian Vespers was occupied by a Frenchman who was the tool of Charles of Anjou. He not only devoted the financial resources of the papacy to helping Charles in his war of reconquest, but he announced that the throne of Aragon was forfeit and proclaimed a crusade against its ruler. There was no moral or religious justification for this extreme measure. It had been one thing to launch a crusade against the Albigensian heretics—and even the crusade against the Hohenstaufens had plausible grounds—but the crusade against Aragon was purely political and manifested the grossest debasement of the crusading ideal. The kings of Aragon had always been among the foremost Christian soldiers; now the Aragonese ruler found himself, for purely political reasons, treated as though he were an enemy of the church. To ensure French response to the political crusade against the Spanish ruler, the pope conferred the title to the throne of Aragon on the son of Philip III and offered the Capetian king the income from a crusading tax levied on the French clergy. Philip III advanced on Aragon while Charles warred against the Sicilians and Spaniards to regain Sicily. Partly because of the effectiveness of the Sicilian and Spanish fleets; disease that broke out in Philip's army; and, above all, the courage and military skill of the Spaniards, the French suffered ignominious defeat on both fronts.

The crusade against Aragon was the second act of the tragedy that led to the destruction of the medieval papacy. In the following two decades the papacy exhausted its finances in its desperate effort to regain Sicily for its Angevin ally. And finally it had to acknowledge the separation of southern Italy into the two kingdoms of Aragonese Sicily and Angevin Naples. Philip III had died on his way back from the ill-fated crusade against Aragon, and his son's ministers, chagrined at the first defeat of Capetian arms in the thirteenth century, decided to make the papacy the scapegoat. They claimed that the curia had failed to fulfill its obligation to support the French enterprise, and they convinced Philip the Fair of the truth of these allegations. After 1285 the attitude of the French government toward Rome became more and more severe and intransigent; it appears that the royal ministers were waiting only for a suitable opportunity to crush the papacy as they had subordinated everything in their own country.

They did not have long to wait. The feuds between the Roman aristocratic families in the college of cardinals made every papal election increasingly difficult and scandalous. Finally, in 1292, when the papal throne was vacant, the factions in the college of cardinals canceled each other out, and no candidate could gain the necessary two-thirds majority. For two years, while Christendom looked on in dismay, the cardinals quarreled and plotted and the see of Peter remained unfilled. A temporary compromise was reached in 1294 when all factions agreed to the election, as Celestine V, of a famous Italian hermit and spiritual leader. Celestine was completely bewildered by the duties of his office, and after a few months of confusion in the papal curia he abdicated. Celestine's "great refusal," as Dante called it, was a sensational scandal and the cause of bitter controversy, for no pope had ever abdicated, and many sincere people claimed that the heir of St. Peter could not resign his office, since theoretically the pope had been designated by divine grace. Celestine said that he had been told to abdicate by an angelic voice, although it was rumored that this message really came from Cardinal Benedict Gaetani, the leader of one of the factions in the cardinalate, by means of a secret speaking tube. Substance was given to this rumor by Gaetani's election as Pope Boniface VIII (1294–1303), and when Celestine died shortly afterward, it was claimed that he had been poisoned at Gaetani's order.

The scandal that marked the beginning of the pontificate of Boniface VIII was exceeded only by the outrage that brought it to an end. The papacy in 1294 was in an extremely vulnerable position. Its moral authority in Christendom had been greatly vitiated, and the monarchies of northern Europe had developed to the point where any disagreement with the pope would be translated immediately into animosity and violence toward Rome. But Boniface was so mesmerized by the theory of plenitude of papal power and by the institutions of Roman autocracy that he could not bring himself to face the realities of the situation and restrain himself from provocative action. In many ways he was as extreme and irresponsible as any minister of the king of France. He was a skilled lawyer and an excellent administrator and sincere in his devotion to the authority of the church. His conception of the papal office was not fundamentally different from that of Innocent III, but he lacked Innocent's political skill and diplomatic tact, and he actually faced a situation that was potentially more dangerous to the papacy in some respects than that with which Innocent had to cope. Neither in his own time nor since has Boniface had a good reputation, and some of the criticisms directed against him have been unfair. It is not exactly his fault that the French government was dominated by cynical and ruthless men whose amorality was something new in the Christian world. But he was at fault for failing to recognize the existence of this new situation and to adjust papal policy to meet it. Instead he pushed recklessly forward, making the most extreme claims (although not by any means unprecedented ones) for papal authority, and he suffered terrible defeat.

In 1294 the inevitable war between the expansionist French and English monarchies had begun. No major war had been fought in Europe in eight decades, and both governments soon discovered that they had underestimated their military expenditures and their financial resources were severely strained. They looked around for expedients to increase royal income. The most obvious source was taxation of the clergy, for which there was a dubious precedent in the several occasions on which the church had given royal governments large shares of the income from crusading taxes. Both the English and the French royal governments claimed that this precedent gave them the right to tax the clergy for any war purpose whatsoever, and there was a plausible argument for this view. There seemed, after all, to be little difference between taxing French churchmen for a war against Aragon and requiring them to support a war against England. The big difference was, however, that the pope did not authorize the new tax, and Boniface regarded it as a flagrant violation of canon law. He published the bull *Clericis Laicos,* which prohibited all clerical taxation by lay rulers without papal permission on pain of excommunication. The bull was marked throughout by an extremely bellicose and intransigent tone. Its opening statement asserted that "the laity have been from the most ancient times hostile to the clergy," a palpable untruth in view of the enormous enthusiasm and devotion that laymen had shown and were still showing to many clergymen.

Boniface's lack of restraint and moderation conclusively drew the lines between papal authority and royal sovereignty, and the kings of England and France proceeded to reply to his challenge in a similarly definitive manner. Edward I terrified the English clergy by withdrawing from them the protection of the common law, and Philip the Fair's ministers demonstrated their mettle by a full-scale campaign of harassment and vituperation in which they were so experienced. They banished the Italian bankers from France and cut off the export of money from the realm to deprive the papacy of a considerable part of its resources. They launched a shower of pamphlets against Boniface, asserting the sovereign power of the king over his subjects and the obligation of the clergy to contribute their share for the defense of the kingdom. The French episcopate was suborned into telling the pope that the clergy would be regarded as enemies of the state if they did not pay taxes to support a national war. Boniface was bewildered and frightened, and he rapidly gave way, acknowledging that the king of France, and by implication all secular rulers, had the right to tax their clergy for the defense of the realm. This was a clear admission by the papacy of the sovereign power. of the state over the national church. It was Boniface's second mistake, for it showed Philip the Fair's ministers that the pope could easily be forced into submission, and it gave them a taste for even more extreme measures.

The opportunity for new violence came in 1301. The previous year had been a great jubilee year for the church. Thousands of pilgrims had made their way to Rome and acclaimed the pope in religious festivals. These demonstrations restored Boniface's confidence and arrogance. If the people of Europe were so loyal to the vicar of Christ, what did he have to fear from mere kings? He was ready to engage in a new struggle with the French monarchy, and this time he would not give in. The royal administration had found one of the bishops of Languedoc recalcitrant and troublesome; this prelate was a fiery southerner who hated the men of the north for subjugating his land. Philip's ministers decided to make an example of the dissident bishop. Using their accustomed methods of extravagant slander and legal niceties, they had him arrested on a charge of treason, and with their usual cynical audacity they demanded that the pope remove their prisoner from his episcopal office so he might be punished for his alleged crime.

Boniface replied to the provocations in an equally extreme manner. He suspended his previous concession to the French king on clerical taxation, severely criticized Philip for the immoral conduct of his administration, and summoned the meeting of a council of French clergy to Rome to reform the church in Philip's realm. In 1302 he issued another inflexible statement of hierocratic doctrine, the bull *Unam Sanctam,* claiming that both the spiritual and temporal swords were ultimately held by Christ's vicar on Earth; that if a king did not rightly use the temporal sword that had been lent him, he could be deposed by the pope; and concluded with an unmitigated assertion of papal authority: "We declare, proclaim, and define that subjection to the Roman Pontiff is absolutely necessary for the salvation of every human creature."

One of Philip the Fair's ministers is said to have remarked, on reading Boniface's latest pronouncement, that "my master's sword is of steel, the pope's is made of verbiage." The king himself appears to have been momentarily shaken by Boniface's salvo, but his ministers were not frightened. They had complete confidence in the effectiveness of their techniques of despotism, which had crushed so many opponents of state power in the previous two decades, and they now directed the venomous method of the big lie against the pope. The leading force in the royal administration was now William de Nogaret, a violently anticlerical lawyer from Languedoc who seems to have reacted against the work of the Inquisition in his home country with impassioned hatred for the church. At what later came to be regarded as the first meeting of the Estates General, he read a long list of charges against Boniface, accusing him of every crime from heresy and murder to personal immorality and black magic. The pope was depicted as the enemy of the church, and it was asserted that it was the duty of the "very Christian king" of France to rescue the church from this monster. The lay population believed Nogaret's charges, and the clergy went along with these fantastic lies, partly because they were bewildered by the violence of the accusation and partly because they were frightened.

For half a century Europe had become more and more inured to the intemperate language and extravagant denunciations that were exchanged between secular rulers and the papacy and even among churchmen themselves. This legacy of reckless charges had so increased the credulity of even sincere and intelligent men, and the incessant use of slander and calumny in debate had so debased the moral currency of Europe, that men were prepared to accept the most outlandish accusations, even against the pope. When Nogaret said that he had evidence for his claim that Boniface was a heretic in the fact that the pope had once declared that he would rather be a dog than a Frenchman, implying that Boniface did not believe in the soul, devout and honest men gravely nodded their assent.

Boniface was driven to the wall by the French government; he had left only the ultimate weapon in the spiritual armory of the papacy. He

repaired to his family's palace at Anagni to prepare a bull of excommunication and deposition against the king of France. But he had not anticipated the physical violence that the royal government was prepared to
bring against him. Nogaret had been dispatched on a secret mission to
Italy to capture the pope and bring him back to France for trial. With the
support of personal enemies of Boniface and his family among the Italian
nobility and the secret connivance of some cardinals, Nogaret took the
pope prisoner at Anagni and started northward. It is difficult to see how
Nogaret could have hoped to get Boniface back to France, but in any
case the people of Anagni and the pope's aristocratic relatives freed Boniface and escorted him back to Rome, where he died a broken man
almost immediately. The poet Dante, who had condemned Boniface and
refused to regard his election as legal, perceived that the events at Anagni
were a momentous turning point in the history of civilization. "The new
Pilate," he said, had imprisoned Christ in the person of His Vicar and
allowed him to be done to death. All Europe waited anxiously for the
next act of this fantastic tragedy.

The pope had been defeated by the kings or princes many times
before, but the prestige of the Holy See had been restored by able successors. In this case, however, the other difficulties surrounding the
papacy precluded such a possibility. Papal succession rested in the hands
of the college of cardinals, which elected each new pope. The influence
of the French cardinals had increased during the thirteenth century; they
had steadily gained ground on the Italians who had always controlled the
institution. The trend was reflected in the election of a French archbishop, who took the name Clement V, to succeed Boniface and in
Clement's decision to remain outside Italy. Clement settled in Avignon, a
city that was just across the Rhone River from French territory. There was
nothing unusual about a pope's choosing to live beyond the reach of the
turmoil of Roman politics, but the subservience of Clement V to the
French king was a radical change in papal policy. Clement's temporary
residence at Avignon became the permanent home of the papacy for the
next seventy years in "Babylonian captivity" of the Roman pontiff.

Clement allowed the government of Philip the Fair to carry out
another act of bold aggression—the victorious assault on the Order of the
Templars. The Templars had begun in the twelfth century as a service
order to provide support for the crusaders. From this function they came
to specialize in banking services for the crusaders and eventually for the
papacy. By the mid-thirteenth century the Templars had become international financiers who were charged with transferring the large amounts of
cash collected by the papacy from the clergy, upon whom Rome had

imposed an income tax in 1198. Of course, kings had to be bought off with a share of clerical taxation, but the annual transmittal to Rome by the Templars was immense. The Templars had set up the headquarters of their bank in Paris, and in the early years of the thirteenth century, Philip the Fair's government, hard-pressed by the expenses of war with England, determined to alleviate its fiscal problems by expropriating the reserves of the Templar bank. To achieve this end, it brought charges of heresy and sodomy (secret Arab vices both intellectual and sexual, it was alleged) against the Templars. Clement was pressured into appointing an inquisitorial court that sustained the charges. In the resulting scandal and uproar, culminating in the dissolution of the Order of the Templars, the French monarchy, with the pope's acquiescence, seized the assets of the Templar bank.

Clement's successors were not as subservient to the French monarchy as he had been, but his concessions did lasting damage to the prestige of his office. The French bureaucracy continued to manufacture charges against Boniface after his death, and Clement was forced to compromise on the issue of clerical taxation and to retract many of the claims of his predecessor. These concessions advertised the weakness of the Avignon papacy and gave credence to the general belief that the popes at Avignon were tools of the French monarch.

The college of cardinals was unable to rectify the situation and restore order in the church. The cardinals were often more concerned about protecting their extravagant way of life and their national and family interests than about promoting the long-term interests of the papacy. Papal appointments did not guarantee able and qualified men to fill the offices of the church. Sons, relatives, and political allies of popes and cardinals were spread throughout the church in Europe, frequently with little regard for the demands of the office or the qualities of its recipient. Many churchmen held more than one office; simony and absenteeism were common.

The end of the "Babylonian Captivity" and the return of the popes to Rome in 1377 did not signal an end to abuses within the church. Instead, national divisions within the college of cardinals resulted within a few months in the "Great Schism." The cardinals who followed the pope to Rome elected an Italian pope, Urban VI, expecting that his Italian background would pacify the Romans while his subservience to the college of cardinals would protect their own interests. Instead, Urban VI shed his sheep's clothing and began a vigorous and uncompromising vendetta against corruption in high places. The cardinals protested, but Urban was resolute. Finally, a portion of the college withdrew back to Avignon, where its members charged that the cardinals had elected Urban VI under duress and that his election was therefore invalid. They elected a new pope, who took up residence at Avignon. Since Urban VI, supported by the Italians in the college of cardinals, refused to resign, there were now two heads of Christendom, two Holy Sees, two colleges of cardinals, and two papal curiae.

While there was a general division along national lines in support of one or the other popes, the church organization was split at every level. Some monasteries often had two abbots, one loyal to each pope, and in many places priests of differing loyalties conducted competing masses. The support of the pope at Avignon by the University of Paris only complicated the insoluble legal puzzle. Attempts were made to induce one of the popes to resign, but neither would do so without the simultaneous resignation of his rival, and proposed meetings of the two pontiffs for its purpose always encountered some insurmountable obstacle.

Councils had been used throughout the history of the church to solve difficult problems. The conciliar movement that became prominent in the late fourteenth century was an expression of the belief held by certain reformers that the authority of a general council was superior to that of the pope. The Council of Pisa, held in 1408, not only failed to end the schism but added a third pope to the confusion. When its demands that the two popes should resign met with refusal, the newly elected third pope continued to press his claims.

The solution to the schism and the high point of the medieval conciliar movement came at the Council of Constance in 1414. The council, summoned by the German emperor, undertook to settle not only the schism but the more general issues that concerned those who supported a conciliar solution to the church's difficulties. The council delayed in electing a pope because it feared that a new pope would restrict the further discussions of the council, but finally two of the popes were eliminated, and a third, the successor of Urban VI, resigned. The new pope soon asserted the absolute authority of the papal office, and the claim that the council was superior to the pope was thereby set aside. Progress in reform was thus prevented by the power of the papacy, the conflicting claims of national interests, and the general resistance of the vast and cumbersome church organization to any radical changes in its makeup.

Although the restoration of the unity of the papacy did not result in reform of the church, the voices demanding reform were not silenced. The conciliar movement was only one form these demands assumed. Even the Franciscan and Dominican orders—the mainstays of papal influence in much of Europe—were sources of criticism of the papacy and of the clergy in general. The Spiritual Franciscans, who believed that absolute poverty was imperative for their order and the ideal way of life for all servants of the church, broke away from the main body of Franciscans. They objected to the legal circumvention of the Franciscan vow of poverty, whereby the pope held property in his own name that was actually used by the order. The wealthy and worldly popes, cardinals, bishops, and abbots found the demands of the Spiritual Franciscans singularly unappealing.

Laymen in Italy and northern Europe did not lag behind the most extreme elements in the clergy, but echoed their demands for a return to piety and honesty in the Holy See and in the church at large. The Brethren of the Common Life were the most important reform group in northern Europe. They were organized into houses of men or women who labored and lived together, practicing a communistic way of life. The members of the Brethren could choose to leave at any time. Models of piety, they became the primary agents for the education of laymen in northern Europe, thus exercising tremendous influence on public opinion.

Frequently affiliated with the Brethren of the Common Life were women's associations called Beguines. Some of the Beguines took monastic vows, but most of the Beguine groups were informal associations of laywomen, usually of middle-class urban background, who devoted themselves to social improvements and the support of popular preachers. The Brethren of the Common Life and the Beguines were prominent facets of the general movement of reform and piety called *Modern Devotion*.

A radical wing of the Spiritual Franciscans, the Fraticelli, demanded poverty not only for their own order, but immediately also for the church as a whole. This doctrine was condemned as heretical by the papacy in 1322, and the Fraticelli were prosecuted by the Inquisition. In general, however, neither the Spiritual Franciscans nor the Brethren of the Common Life lapsed into heresy or openly opposed the organization and doctrine of the church. While the papacy was uneasy living under their scrutiny, no measures were introduced to suppress these movements.

Yet heretics who condemned pope and clergy with uncanonical arguments multiplied and found a ready audience, especially among the urban bourgeoisie but among nobles and peasants as well. In Italy the radical monk Savonarola amassed a large following, many of whom remained loyal to his memory even after he was burned at the stake, while in England the Oxford professor John Wyclif expounded heretical views on the sacraments, condemned the priesthood for its corruption, and claimed that the ultimate authority in religious matters was not the pope but the Bible. He also advocated that laymen should expropriate church property, which gained for him protection by the royal family. Wyclif's followers, the Lollards, spread their doctrines by preaching and promoting the reading of the Bible; they provided a faith built on personal experience. The Lollard movement in England helped to inspire the Peasant's Revolt of 1381, which plagued the monarchy and nobility, as well as the church. Although the Lollards were cruelly put down, their doctrines spread, both in England and on the Continent.

The most important heresy of the fifteenth century, the Hussite movement in Bohemia, took many of its doctrines from Wyclif and his followers, particularly those concerning reform of the church. In Bohemia the heresy was connected with a national rebellion against Germany. For this reason it was more widespread and longer lasting than other heresies. John Hus was rector of the University of Prague when he began to expound his heretical doctrines. He soon received the dual recognition of a wide following and of ecclesiastical condemnation as a heretic. He was summoned to the Council of Constance to answer for his beliefs and agreed to appear when he was guaranteed safe conduct. His examiners were willing to pardon him if he would recant, but when Hus remained intransigent, he was seized without regard for his safe conduct, on the grounds that the church could not be held to an agreement that damaged God's interests. Hus was burned at the stake.

The death of Hus did not end the Hussite heresy, however. The conversion of another Bohemian national leader to the Hussite doctrine sparked resistance to a German invasion aimed at subjugating the heretics. Even after Bohemian resistance collapsed, the heresy survived. Today it forms the basis for the teachings of the Moravian Church.

Although the church, with the help of the German nobility was able to subdue the Hussites, the repression of demands for reform offered no lasting solutions. The Renaissance papacy of the fifteenth century perpetuated the faults of its predecessors behind the façade of brilliant humanist culture. Many popes were scholars and leading patrons of the arts. Yet the conspicuous consumption of the Renaissance popes further weakened the prestige of the papacy.

The growing power of national states in the late fifteenth century led to further domination of the church by national governments. Henceforth the pope could not effectively intervene in ecclesiastical affairs within the states of Europe, nor could he play a decisive role in international politics. Many of the higher clergy shared the general desire for reform, but the papacy was caught between pressures from church councils, on the one hand, and the European monarchs, on the other, and it could not or would not take an effective lead in reform. The papacy and the college of cardinals remained preoccupied with Italian politics and dynastic struggles, while growing nationalistic feelings added fuel to the fires of religious discontent in northern Europe. All this precluded the recovery of the glories of the thirteenth-century papacy. It also set the stage for the final blow to the universal authority of the church, the Reformation of the sixteenth century.

The word most often associated with the late medieval church is *corruption*. There was much criticism at the time and stereotyping in the literature of greed, careerism, incompetence, sellouts, and other unscrupulous dealings from the pope and the college of cardinals down through bishops and friars to village priests. The Protestant reformers of the sixteenth century highlighted late medieval ecclesiastical corruption as the justification for their separation from the Roman church. Late medieval corruption in the church was a dogma of nineteenth- and early twentieth-century liberal historiography, and the picture of the late medieval church presented in college textbooks has remained highly critical. What is the degree of truth in this standard view of heavy corruption in the late medieval church? We are dealing here with a matter of perception, and there is not likely to be a consensus on such an issue. This is, however, an issue that should be addressed.

First, to the extent that there was corruption, it was at least in part the result of the decline of the medieval papacy after the onslaught upon it by the French monarchy in the early fourteenth century and the Avignon episode and Great Schism that followed. Innocent III had tried hard to improve church discipline and to root out corruption down to the local level. He was deeply concerned about unprofessional and unethical behavior in the clergy. He called the bishops of southern France "dumb dogs who do not bark" and viewed laxity and indiscipline as the seedbed of heresy. Innocent III's Fourth Lateran Council mandated a system of frequent visitations (inspections) of their dioceses by bishops down to the most obscure parish. This was a wearying and expensive task, not relished by the aristocrats who filled most episcopal sees, but the visitation system was carried out quite effectively in the thirteenth century. Papal legates in each country, meanwhile, were supposed to keep the bishops in line. Here the problem was an age-old one and not resolved by the thirteenth-century papacy. The bishops were largely political appointments; they normally came from prominent families and were politically well connected. It was extremely difficult to discipline a bishop under such circumstances, and the pope rarely tried.

After the collapse of the medieval papacy in the fourteenth century, the visitation system lacked strong impetus from the pope, and it slowly disintegrated. Unless a particular bishop was particularly zealous (and there were some), by the late fourteenth century visitation had lapsed, and the consequence was a relaxation of supervision over the lower ranks of the clergy that resulted in petty greed and incompetence that were particularly offensive to the highly literate middle class. It was the middle class's resentment of the clergy's slovenliness that is reflected in the literary stereotype of avaricious friar and ignorant priest.

The second impetus to corruption in the late medieval church was that now as always the property and offices of the church were eagerly sought by lay people, from the king and duke down to city fathers and the local gentry. Everyone thought that churchmen should be saints and scholars, but at the same time laity of all ranks sought ways to dip into church property and get their relatives jobs in the church. This practice eroded the fiscal base that the church needed to perform its spiritual, educational, and charitable responsibilities and often filled the ranks of the clergy, from the college of cardinals down to village vicars, with not the best candidates or blatantly unsuitable ones. The duke who used law or force to seize church property and insisted on a bishopric for his undereducated third son, the merchant capitalist who trafficked in ecclesiastical finance and collected exorbitant fees for his services, and the local squire who engaged an abbey in a decades-long harassment for a share of its income and property were liable then to turn around and complain viciously about the corruption of the church. Who was doing the corruption?

The powerful heretical movements of the late Middle Ages, which were indeed partly caused by ecclesiastical laxity and indiscipline, also contributed to the general enfeeblement of the church. The heretical groups portrayed the traditional church as hopelessly corrupt, even if the problem was often underfunding rather than peculation. At a given time in the late Middle Ages anywhere from 10 to 25 percent of the population of western Europe had effectively separated themselves from the Roman Catholic church; they stopped paying tithes and other dues for church services and set up counterchurches. The loss was not only in funding, but in personnel because the clergy of these heretical churches were frequently religious people of high commitment and considerable learning and not rarely charismatic personality—precisely the kind of clergy the orthodox church badly needed to counterbalance the incompetents, the selfish careerists, and the outrageously corrupt.

There was one area of behavior in which the late medieval church was probably less corrupt than in earlier centuries—in the enforcement of clerical celibacy. Since the Gregorian reform of the eleventh century, the Latin church had made concerted efforts to make all the clergy, not just monks, friars, and nuns, "eunuchs of heaven." By the fourteenth century the campaign to divest the clergy of concubines was having a visible impact. Bishops, even cardinals, might still have occasional mistresses or resort to prostitutes, but it seems a safe estimate that by 1400 the great majority of the bishops did not have what were later called common-law marriages, that is, concubines with whom they regularly cohabitated and produced families.

A significant proportion even of the parish clergy was probably celibate most of the time during the fifteenth century. Gregory VII would have been pleased and perhaps surprised to witness the relative success of the radical program of sacerdotal celibacy that he instituted—uniquely among all Christian denominations, the Greek church demanding celibacy only of bishops and allowing priests to marry legally—not only because St. Paul urged it, but because Gregory thought that an unmarried clergy without families would be able to separate itself from the corrupting effects of family obligations.

Yet the church got surprisingly little credit for this change in the marital status and sexual behavior of its clergy. The Protestant reformers of the early sixteenth century turned things around and said that clerical celibacy was one of the downsides of Catholicism. Whether it was or was not is an interesting question. Today we look at the psychological and eugenic sides of the question. Sexual deprivation is not entirely healthy for most people, we believe. And by eliminating the progeny of so many of the most intelligent and learned people in European society (think of the whole faculty of Paris and Oxford universities, for instance), the church was engaging in reverse eugenics. The Jews did just the opposite. Not only did the rabbis condemn celibacy, but they were encouraged to marry young and produce lots of children—Jewish couples who followed rabbinical law were supposed to celebrate the Sabbath with copulation. The Protestant reformers leaned to the Jewish, rather than the Catholic, attitude in this matter.

The late medieval church in retrospect should inspire sympathy more than condemnation. Even when it achieved what was then considered a good and religious thing to do, clerical celibacy, it was condemned, just as the very people among the powerful laity who ravaged its resources were the first to raise the specter of corruption.

Except for the proclivity of a late fifteenth-century pope to cultivate mistresses and produce children, no aspect of the later medieval church has been as severely castigated as has the selling of paper (or parchment) indulgence certificates as equivalents to penance for the remission of sins. This was indeed a widespread practice in the late medieval church. Sellers of indulgence certificates were as common a fixture on the ecclesiastical scene of 1500 as stock and bond salesmen are today, and Martin Luther dramatized his revolt against Rome in 1517 (predicated upon much more complex and doctrinal issues) by making a fuss about a particularly aggressive local indulgence seller, as if we would want to abandon capitalism today because a brash Wall Street salesman phoned us during the dinner hour.

Indulgences arose this way: To obtain the remission of a sin in the Catholic system requires sincere contrition ("I am sorry, and I mean it"), confession to a priest as the representative of Christ and the church, and the performance of penance (punishment), which could vary from the trivial (leave a coin in the collection box on your way out) to the arduous and expensive (make a pilgrimage a thousand miles to the shrine of St. James of Campastella in Spain) to the actually unpleasant (work as a peasant in monastic lands for two years—very rare). When Pope Urban II preached the first crusade in 1085, he said that joining the crusading army was a plenary indulgence—a maximal form of penance. Then in the twelfth century, the papacy went one step further and introduced vicarious indulgence: You didn't have to go on a crusade, but if you gave money to support crusaders, that was (almost) as good as going to the Holy Land yourself and perilously fighting Moslems, and you got an indulgence certificate to prove that you contributed. Undoubtedly this was a major departure and theologically marginal, but it generated a splendid stream of income for the underfunded church and was immensely popular with the laity.

Fourteenth-century people were living in bad times of biomedical holocaust and deep economic depression. Medicine, whether of the biochemical or social kind, was rare. Thus people found comfort, perhaps even more intensely than in previous medieval centuries, in what anthropologists call magic. They touched relics of saints, went on pilgrimages, consulted astrologers, and (illicitly) in some cases used witchcraft. And they bought indulgences in huge amounts—like buying lottery certificates today, but indulgences were better than lottery tickets because the church told you that they made you a winner in the heavenly sweepstakes. Even more extended vicarious indulgences were introduced—you could buy an indulgence for an already-dead relative and reduce her time in purgatory.

Intellectuals in the universities became increasingly wary of the selling of indulgences, and the newer kind of humanist was highly critical of this practice. Theorists and scholars of the younger generation of 1500 had fastened on a vision of a reformed church that would be as spiritual, immaterial, and ethical as possible. That such a puritanical church was far removed from demotic culture and the faith and temperament of ordinary people did not bother them. The masses would benefit somehow from a puritanical church, and to attain this goal, indulgences were the first of the so-called corrupt practices of the contemporary church that had to be excised.

In early sixteenth-century Europe, whenever the reformers could gain the support of governmental authorities, they actually carried out their antimagic program, the elimination of what they regarded as the corrupt heritage of the late medieval church. The indulgence system was eliminated; relic worship was proscribed; church architecture was made much more austere; the elaborate gold cross was simplified and moved closer to the worshippers; and, in some cases, even the exquisite stained-glass windows were replaced with plain glass. Were the people happier to be saved from the notorious manifestations of late medieval "papist" corruption? There was no agreement on that point then, and there is none now.

IV. The European States

If the power of the papacy generally declined in the fourteenth and fifteenth centuries, the position of the Holy Roman emperor, who had been the main threat to papal power in the first half of the thirteenth century, was even worse. Throughout the third quarter of the century there was no German emperor, as the national politics of Germany was submerged in a morass of internal wars and disputes. This interregnum served to accelerate the feudalization of German society and to turn the concerns of Germany to the north and east.

The development of German trade in the area around the Baltic Sea was accompanied by the intensification of a great movement of eastward colonization that had begun in the late twelfth century. The initial agents of colonization were the monasteries, but the main beneficiaries were the princes. In western Germany, princely holdings usually consisted of a series of enclaves surrounded by lands of the church and of lesser lords, but in the east the princes could firmly establish their authority in the virgin territory from which they carved out their vast estates. By the fourteenth century the center of Germany had moved noticeably eastward, and the magnates at the top of the feudal hierarchy were more powerful than ever.

Even so, the princes had good reasons for desiring the reestablishment of the imperial throne, if they could rely on the subservience of the emperor to their own interests. In dealings with the French and the papacy a strong German emperor could be useful, and the continued disorder within Germany also called for the establishment of some central authority. In the eyes of the German magnates, then, the emperor should be able to assert the rights of Germany in international affairs while at home he served the interests of the princes who elected him. Such a conception of the emperorship was, of course, contradictory, and when Rudolf of Habsburg became emperor in 1273, he devoted his energies to the aggrandizement of his dynasty instead of German foreign relations— much to the dismay of his princely electors. The electors' fear of the accumulation of overwhelming power in the hands of one family led to frequent changes in dynasties before the Habsburgs were firmly established as hereditary possessors of the Holy Roman emperorship in the fifteenth century.

The emperorship itself continued to be primarily a formal title: The emperors exercised real power only in their family duchies and were unable to construct the instruments of a truly national government. There was nothing inevitable about the failure of Germany to develop national institutions in the late Middle Ages as did France, England, and Spain, but a number of factors combined to prevent the emperors from consolidating their gains. The internal resistance of the princes was aided, and indeed often manipulated, by foreign powers that were opposed to the establishment of a strong German monarchy. The papacy continued the policy it had followed in the thirteenth century to prevent the emperor from renewing his challenge to papal power in Italy.

The most powerful threat to Germany and the emperorship in the fourteenth and fifteenth centuries, however, was the eastward expansion of France. The area that had been the Carolingian middle kingdom along the Rhine River fell under German sovereignty in the High Middle Ages. Now France launched a program of continuous encroachment upon German territory in the Rhineland. In addition, France intermittently put forward claims to the Roman imperial title itself, on the grounds that predominance in Europe had passed into French hands. Continual papal and French intervention did not achieve a French Holy Roman emperor, but their meddling in German politics precluded united German resistance to French expansion into western Germany. If Germany was too weak to work the situation to its advantage, at least the misfortunes of its enemies left it autonomous and free to wallow in political chaos.

It was impossible for the German emperors to establish a strong national or international policy under the prevailing circumstances, and for the most part they preferred to devote themselves to the much more realistic task of personal and dynastic aggrandizement. Since all land that was left without a legal heir passed into the hands of the emperor, a family could become a great power in one generation if it could secure election to the emperorship. Frederick II's grand dreams of a world monarchy gave way to realistic policies designed to increase the power of the emperor among the princes to gain an advantage in the continual princely infighting.

The realities were formally recognized by the emperor in the Golden Bull of 1356, which attempted to introduce order into the election of the emperor and to define clearly the powers of the princes. The status of elector and the electoral process had hitherto been vaguely defined. Now the number of electors was set at seven—three bishops and four princes—who were clearly identified; the right of election was attached to the lands of the electors, and the division of these lands was forbidden; and the rights of the princes were clearly set down. In this way, although the emperor did not diminish the power of the electors, he was able to introduce an orderly system that would not provide easy openings for papal or French intervention or result in disputed elections. At the same time the Golden Bull recognized the fundamental territorial divisions in the empire and, in effect, the sovereign powers of the princes.

Although the princes were successful in removing the threat of imperial hegemony in Germany, they were left with the problem of consolidating their own power. Their lands, like those of the emperor, lacked territorial unity, and the chaos of feudal relations that had developed in preceding centuries left Germany a patchwork of overlapping and competing jurisdictions. In addition, the subjects of the princes were as wary of the expansion of princely power as their princely overlords were of imperial power. Numerous combinations of social, economic, and political groups confronted the attempts of the princes to bring all their subjects under their jurisdiction.

Among the groups that sought to inhibit the rise of princely authority, the most enduring combination was the League of Upper Germany, later known as the Swiss Confederation. Rural and urban cantons under a republican form of government entered into an agreement for mutual defense. Although they disagreed constantly about everything else, the cantons were united in their fear of foreign overlordship, and the Swiss fighting force became the most renowned in Europe. The poverty of their mountainous homeland encouraged Swiss soldiers to grasp the opportunity to become foreign mercenaries, and many of the armies of Europe depended henceforth upon a hard core of Swiss fighting men. The rather nebulous nationalism of the Swiss was surpassed by that of other emerging nationalities, such as the Poles and Bohemians, who sustained concerted and prolonged opposition to German overlordships.

The Hanseatic League was just one of several leagues of German cities that were formed to defend their mutual interests, often against the demands of the princes. Even the knights whose small holdings nestled among those of the great princes combined to demand concessions and to protect themselves against the princes, whose position was complicated by their lack of money. The princes' vast expenses had to be met from private sources and from whatever taxes could be wrung from their tight-fisted subjects. Although a prince could occasionally wipe out his debts by debasing the currency, in the long run inflation only worsened his financial difficulties.

Not until the latter part of the fifteenth century were the princes able to make the concept of territorial sovereignty work effectively as the basis of government. They learned to use meetings of estates (assemblies of the representatives of various social groups or classes) as English kings used the Parliament—to justify their need for money for the public good and to secure general consent among all their subjects. Gradually they were able to overcome the claims of cities and knights to special exemptions. The extension of princely jurisdiction to all subjects was greatly aided by the introduction of the principles of Roman law into the administration of justice, replacing the chaos of local custom with a coherent body of legal practice that consistently favored judicial and administrative centralization.

The improvement of the fortunes of the princes in the late fifteenth century was paralleled by the multiplication of the Habsburg domains under Maximilian I. When Maximilian came to the imperial throne in 1477, the Habsburgs were merely one of the more powerful German families, but through fortunate marriages and clever diplomacy, Maximilian was able to acquire an impressive list of dynastic holdings in eastern and western Germany; in Italy; and most important, in Spain and the Netherlands. In spite of his success, however, the position of the emperor was little changed in Germany. The rising power of the Habsburgs depended, to a large extent, upon their foreign holdings.

Germany at the end of the fifteenth century remained a geographic, rather than a political, designation. Even the consolidation of the holdings of the princes left a vast number of smaller states that were not amalgamated until modern times. The development of German states helped to stabilize and rationalize German politics, but German particularism left a number of unsolved problems that contributed to continued disorders in sixteenth-century Germany. In Germany alone in western Europe, serfdom continued to prevail after 1500, and the discontent of the peasantry led to repeated revolts in the fifteenth and sixteenth centuries. German power in international relations was hampered by internal divisions and by the lack of a consistent and forceful policy. Most important, the German church, unlike the churches in France, England, and Spain, was unable to develop a measure of national autonomy; it remained an easily exploitable source of revenue for the extravagances of the Renaissance papacy. All these conditions helped to lay the groundwork for the Protestant Reformation in Germany.

During the early Middle Ages the Muslim conquest introduced the Arabic language and Arabic institutions to the Roman-Visigothic society that had prevailed in the Iberian peninsula. In Muslim Spain, Arab, Jew, and Christian contributed to the vibrant culture. The first rebirth of classical learning in western Europe was on the Iberian peninsula.

To the north of Muslim Spain, in the mountainous regions of the peninsula, obscure and minute Spanish Christian kingdoms existed through the early Middle Ages. In the eleventh century, the Christian princes began the movement of expansion into Muslim territory known as the Reconquista. For two centuries the Spanish Christian kings, the nobility, and the church cooperated in a battle against the Muslims for control of Spain. The princes provided the unity and direction of the movement, while the church preached a crusade against the infidel. In the course of the Reconquista the Spanish nobility gained renown for its preeminence in combat: The Spanish noble was a Christian knight distinguished from the rest of society by his prowess and religious zeal.

By concentrating the fighting energies of the Spanish nobility on a holy war against Islam, the Reconquista gave direction to what was essentially a turbulent period of political readjustment in Spain. Particularism characterized the political structure of medieval Spain just as it did that of medieval Germany. Much of the constant warfare of the twelfth and thirteenth centuries involved attempts by one noble or another to advance his own interests and had little to do with defeating the infidel per se. The career of the great hero of the Reconquista, known to history as the Cid, provides a good example of this aspect of Iberian development. The Cid, like most other nobles, was primarily a warlord seeking personal advantage; his idealized image as a Christian knight ignores the fact that he fought on the side of the Moors, as well as of the Christians, choosing the side that was most to his advantage.

By the fourteenth century most of Spain had been conquered for

Christendom. Only the small kingdom of Granada on the southern coast of Spain remained in the hands of the infidels. The rest of the peninsula had gradually been gathered into a few kingdoms that had to struggle to maintain their independence while they enlarged and enriched themselves through war, marriage, and diplomacy. The three greatest kingdoms of the fourteenth and fifteenth centuries were Castile, Aragon, and Portugal.

Castile, located in the center of Spain, controlled the largest amount of territory. Like the other Spanish kingdoms, it was forged out of several smaller principalities. Castile provided most of the manpower and energy for the Reconquista and benefited most from it. Territorial aggrandizement was a mixed blessing, however. The land of central Spain was difficult to farm under normal circumstances, and the devastation that accompanied the Reconquista, abetted by natural disasters, reduced the productivity of the land even below its former level.

The economic and social problems that beset Europe in the fourteenth century were particularly severe throughout Spain and especially in Castile. The Spanish peasants revolted several times in the fourteenth and fifteenth centuries, with little result. The nobles, no longer distracted by the Reconquista and not restrained by a highly developed feudal system, were a constant threat to the development of a centralized political system. The great magnates, as well as the lesser nobility, shared legal and extralegal privileges that made them difficult to control. The cities and the clergy also formed separate social and political elements, jealous of their autonomy and aggressive in the pursuit of privileges and immunities.

Parliamentary institutions appeared in Spain earlier than in the rest of continental Europe, but they did not effectively limit the power of the sovereign. The composition of the Cortes, as the estates were known, depended upon the king, who could call as many or as few of the nobles, clergy, and burgesses as he wished. Although the Cortes granted extraordinary taxes to the king, this did not lead to the practice of demanding and receiving concessions in return for financial aid to the crown, as occurred in England.

Despite the strong tradition of hereditary monarchy in Castile, the exercise of monarchical power was hampered by the vicissitudes of hereditary succession and the dearth of strong, centralized governmental institutions. When Alonso X the Learned introduced a uniform law code based on the principles of Roman law, its acceptance was greatly delayed by resistance from the nobility and the towns. The power of the monarch, even more than in northern Europe, depended on his personality; the Castilians were unfortunate in producing a great number of unfit rulers.

The kingdom of Aragon, in the northeast corner of the Iberian peninsula, was distinguished from Castile by its geographic position and its political traditions. The unification of landlocked Aragon with Catalonia gave the kingdom an outlet to Mediterranean trade that allowed it to benefit from the commercial revolution of the High Middle Ages. Trade established the prestige and power of Aragon; Barcelona became one of the richest cities in Europe. The geographic position of Aragon, which lies contiguous to southern France and faces Italy across the sea, naturally involved it in European politics much more than its Castilian neighbor.

Although the Cortes had more clearly defined powers in Aragon than in Castile and might act as a check on royal power, the kings of Aragon were often effective and powerful monarchs. Aragon joined the Reconquista, but its location dictated that its main expansion should be not on the Iberian peninsula but on the islands of the Mediterranean. After the Sicilian Vespers in 1282—a revolution against the French overlords of the Sicilian kingdom—the king of Aragon was able to take over the island of Sicily, which was finally separated from the southern Italian kingdom of Naples. Through a combination of war and diplomacy, Aragon also gained control of the Balearic Islands, Sardinia, and Corsica.

Only the tiny kingdom of Navarre in the north, Portugal in the west, and Muslim Granada in the south remained outside the united jurisdiction created by the marriage of Ferdinand of Aragon and Isabella of Castile in 1479. The reign of these two monarchs had a decisive influence on the institutions of sixteenth-century Spain and Latin America. Through their efforts the territorial aggrandizement of Spain was accompanied by the development of national political institutions and by economic expansion that placed Spain in the front rank of European states.

The conquest of Granada, which was completed in 1492, removed the Muslims from Spain as an independent political force. It also served to develop an effective national army under the control of the pikemen and other foot soldiers who were armed with early firearms supplemented by light cavalry and artillery to form a powerful fighting force that could have challenged even the Swiss infantry. In addition, Ferdinand became grand master of the three knightly military orders that had been responsible for the independent power of the nobility. Henceforth, the military and financial resources of these orders could be used by the crown.

Just as the military orders were taken over by the crown and used for its own ends, the local judicial bodies of the towns were manipulated by the monarchy until they could be replaced by a royal judiciary. The two monarchs refrained from introducing revolutionary principles of taxation, preferring instead to make full use of a lucrative tax on all commercial transactions. Although this tax greatly enhanced the royal treasury, it also discouraged commerce and was therefore damaging to Spanish interests in the long run. The Cortes were also used to extend the power of the monarchy; after they had served their purpose—granting money to the king—they were called with less and less frequency until they practically ceased to exist. A bureaucracy similar in operation to that developed by the French in the thirteenth and fourteenth centuries further extended the authority of the monarchy. The rapid expansion of royal power greatly decreased the autonomy of all particularized forces in the kingdom: the nobility, the cities, and the clergy.

Ferdinand and Isabella asserted their authority in religious as well as political matters. They carried out a full-scale reformation of the church within their realms to root out corruption and to bring the church more firmly under the authority of the crown. Their attempts at reform were remarkably successful.

The most extreme effects of the alliance between the crown and the clergy were exhibited in the Spanish Inquisition, begun by the monarchy around 1480. During the fourteenth and fifteenth centuries, the spirit of toleration that had characterized medieval Spain steadily diminished. The three communities—Christians, Jews, and Moors—had always been separate but not necessarily hostile. Now antagonism produced legal liabilities for Jews and Muslims, and open hostilities occurred, especially against the Jews, who formed a substantial part of the prosperous trading and money-lending classes in Spain. Still, the Jews and the Muslims were obviously essential to the economic prosperity of Spain, and therefore the laws that placed disabilities on them were usually ignored. By the reign of Ferdinand and Isabella, however, growing popular antipathy toward the Muslim and Jewish minorities provided solid support for the religious fanaticism exhibited by the two sovereigns.

Many of the Jews and Muslims had found it convenient to convert to Christianity, at least formally, in view of the growing persecution of non-Christians. The first impetus of the Inquisition was directed against these new Christians, often with the overzealous aid of other recent converts. The Inquisition used all the standard techniques of Roman law, including torture and informers; the accused had few rights, and accusation was presumptive evidence of guilt. The impact on Spanish society of the prolonged reign of terror was increased by the final expulsion of unconverted Jews and Muslims from Spain in the late fifteenth and early sixteenth centuries. The expulsion resulted in the loss of a sizable portion of the productive element of the population, although the majority of Jews became new Christians and stayed in Spain and Portugal.

The results of the Inquisition were dwarfed for the time being by the expansion of Spanish wealth and power that accompanied the age of exploration. Economic prosperity, stemming from the exploitation of the Spanish overseas empire, internal unity, and religious homogeneity, characterized sixteenth-century Spain. When Christopher Columbus, flying the Spanish flag, landed in the islands off the coast of America on October 12, 1492, Spain possessed only the Canary Islands and the remnants of the Mediterranean empire of Aragon. Within a few decades it had the largest overseas empire among the European states. At the moment when the economy of the Mediterranean world was entering its last decades of prosperity, Spain was in the forefront of the expansion of Europe into the unknown lands of America and the Orient.

Spain's only rival was Portugal, which had survived the unification of the Iberian peninsula to remain an independent state. Portugal had spent the last half of the fifteenth century exploring the west coast of Africa. The original impetus given to Portuguese exploration by Prince Henry the Navigator had made Portuguese seamen the most advanced in geographic and maritime knowledge in Europe. Soon after Columbus landed in America, Vasco de Gama rounded the Cape of Good Hope and completed the voyage to India by the eastern route. His successors established the Portuguese empire. By the end of the fifteenth century, the first steps had been taken that were to expand European interests around the globe. The location of the Iberian peninsula and the policies of the strong monarchies that developed in Spain and Portugal placed these states in an ideal position to exploit the new opportunities.

The most highly developed national states in the fourteenth and fifteenth centuries were England and France, where the foundation of monarchical government had been laid in the thirteenth century and earlier. The two countries were similar in form of government, and until the middle of the fifteenth century much of what became western France was held by the English king. Contact between the two kingdoms had been close since the reign of William the Conqueror in the eleventh century. In the fourteenth and fifteenth centuries, however, England became more and more distinctive in its culture. The great war between the two countries encouraged nationalism and finally eliminated English territorial holdings in France. By the end of the fifteenth century, the English language had replaced French in the government and among the nobility of England. At the same time, the menace of English invasion had heightened French national consciousness, and the consolidation of royal power made the French nation more of a territorial and governmental reality.

During the course of the fourteenth and fifteenth centuries, the institutions of monarchy in France and England were sorely tested. Intractable barons, economic depression, lawlessness, problems of dynastic succession, and the incessant warfare that marked the relations of the two countries revealed that a centralized national government was often no more than an aspiration.

The events of the thirteenth, fourteenth, and fifteenth centuries proved that the effective power of the English crown was still dependent upon the personality and ability of the monarch. With the accession of Edward I (1272–1307), England found itself again under the leadership of a popular and ambitious monarch. Edward, like his French contemporary Philip IV the Fair, was an aggressive and successful king. He produced legislation dealing with every aspect of government, including his legislation that opened up the market in land to free exploitation by ambitious families. He also established a national customs system.

In foreign as well as domestic affairs, Edward I tried to expand the domain of English government. Wales proved a much easier prey than did Scotland, where English aggression only aroused Scottish nationalism. To the north, Edward's heavy investment in men and arms brought only occasional and fleeting victory and eventually inspired a Scottish-French alliance that rendered England's northern neighbor more dangerous than ever.

As usual, military ventures demanded increased taxation. Edward found the calling of a general Parliament the most effective way to publicize his need for money and to gain the commitment of the nation to an increase in royal revenue. And his attempts to get additional revenue were successful; Parliament instituted an export duty on the wool trade with the Low Countries.

Parliament served royal purposes, but it also allowed the subjects to make demands upon the king. In the English Parliament, unlike the Spanish Cortes, the practice finally developed of presenting a common petition to the king that had to be answered before money could be granted. Thereby the knights and burgesses (who after 1340 joined together in the House of Commons) could make their corporate voice heard not only on financial issues, but through requests and statements of grievances to which the king had to respond.

In the reign of Edward I, Parliament was called into session only occasionally, and its governmental role was only vaguely outlined. But the strength of the precedents set during the reign of Edward I became apparent during the reign of his successor, Edward II (1307–27). The second Edward was personally unattractive and incompetent. Consequently, another unsuccessful experiment in baronial government spanned the years 1311 to 1322, with the weak government relying heavily on Parliament. As Parliament met more frequently—almost annually—its prerogatives increased: Henceforth, a law made in Parliament could not be questioned, and eventually any law that lacked Parliament's sanction might be suspect. Also, it became increasingly necessary to secure the approval of Parliament for general taxation. Thus in the early fourteenth century Parliament became more self-conscious with regard to its rights and responsibilities and more important in the general workings of the English government.

Edward III (1327–77) successfully returned to the aggressive policies of Edward I. A paragon of the chivalric virtues, he continued armed involvement in Scotland and on the Continent and completed the transformation of the royal army. From a feudal force based on the mounted knight, the royal army became a professional army utilizing both cavalry and an infantry armed with the longbow. The expansionist policies of Edward III involved England in the Hundred Years' War, which was to dominate the next century and half of English and French history.

The reign of Philip IV the Fair of France (1285–1314), like that of his contemporary, Edward I of England, marked a high point in the development of national monarchy. Philip the Fair built upon the territorial and institutional base left by his predecessors to extend the royal domain and to increase the powers of the monarch in the nation at large. After the arrest and subsequent death of Pope Boniface VIII, Philip continued to tax the French clergy and to exercise other customary forms of jurisdiction over the tangible assets of the church.

Philip was not satisfied to tax his subjects only when the realm was endangered. Before Philip's time, the king was expected to live upon the income from the royal domains, supplemented by special income from his vassals on specific occasions and by occasional taxation of the clergy. Philip and his ministers were able to expand the right of the king to tax his subjects when the realm was in danger into a general right of taxation that far surpassed the scope of the original forms of royal revenue.

Since regional particularism was much stronger in France than in England, a national parliament for the purpose of levying taxes was not as practical as were local and provincial assemblies, which could be persuaded or forced to guarantee the payment of the tax. Even when a session of the Estates General was called, it often had to be supplemented by local estates. These assemblies were essentially bargaining agencies that defended the legal fiscal privileges of the region and attempted to get still more fiscal concessions in return for assenting to the tax being levied. Local assemblies could be called into session or dismissed virtually at the will of the king. The particularism of the French estates made them less useful to the monarch and less influential in the development of centralized parliamentary institutions than were their English counterparts.

Governmental institutions advanced in efficiency and sophistication under Philip the Fair and his ministers. Previously all royal officials—executive, judicial, salaried bureaucrats, and lay and ecclesiastical vassals—had been dealt with collectively as the Curia Regis. Under Philip the Fair the household was separated from the king's council, which assisted in the formation of policy. Furthermore, the parlement—the royal council in judicial session—became a distinct organ of government, entrusted with the function of a supreme court of appeals. In the following century the monopoly of this function by the Parlement of Paris was broken by regional parliaments that exercised similar functions. Gradually the parliaments gained power in the realm, especially through their right to promulgate royal legislation. Their resistance to royal law became a powerful weapon in later centuries. The financial aspects of government, like the judicial, were entrusted to a special branch of government located in Paris.

Philip's success was due, to a large extent, to his outstanding ministers. These men were completely dedicated to the monarchy, and if they were unscrupulous in its defense, they made effective public servants for an aggressive king. By the end of Philip's reign in 1314, powerful and efficient institutions of government provided the arms with which the monarchy could reach out to every part of the kingdom.

The aggressive nature of the French monarchy and the Continental ambitions of the English king brought on the long conflict known as the Hundred Years' War. Much of the basis of the conflict rested in the feudal relationship that brought the two sovereigns face to face in the duchy of Aquitaine. Aquitaine was the possession of the king of England, but he held it as a vassal of the French king. This relationship meant that the English king had to do homage to his French neighbor and that the French king had the usual feudal rights within the duchy. The French bureaucrats enforced these rights with their customary bias in favor of their king, but the victim of their encroachments in this case was the king of England. The English kings had a great interest in Aquitaine: it was the home of the excellent Bordeaux wines, a popular import for the English nobility, and foreign possessions suited the territorial ambitions of Edward I and Edward III. The English kings, however, were lax in their feudal duties; the French kings were quick to invade and confiscate portions of their fief, and the result was a series of wars and confrontations in the late thirteenth and early fourteenth centuries.

After the death of Philip the Fair, the situation grew more complicated as the issue of dynastic succession became crucial in France for the first time in centuries. The Capetian kings had almost always been fortunate enough to leave capable male heirs. Unfortunately for France, the three sons of Philip the Fair each served a short reign and died without a male heir, and in 1328 there was no Capetian successor to the throne. Since Edward I had married the daughter of Philip the Fair, Edward III of England could claim the throne as Philip's grandson. For the French this would have meant a king who, although French in culture, was English in interests and had been a notoriously disobedient vassal of the French king. In addition, Edward was a minor and was still controlled by his disreputable mother and her lover. The French nobility eagerly chose as their king Philip of Valois, a member of a cadet branch of the Capetian house, stating that the succession could not pass through the female line—an innovation in French practice.

In the years following the accession of Philip VI, the English and French monarchs clashed over the performance of homage, and Edward III set about building alliances and raising an army to invade France. Edward had a natural ally in the leader of the Flemish rebels, who had thrown off the rule of their French-born count. He was also able to buy, for a handsome sum, the support of German princes and the German emperor. War broke out in 1337, but as was to be the case for most of the Hundred Years' War, the results were inconclusive.

The very circumstances of the war almost precluded clear victory by one side or the other. France was the most powerful country in Europe, with a population three times that of its English adversary. The English king had to raise an invading force with no more financial backing than the fragmentary income derived from fourteenth-century methods of taxation. He was heavily dependent upon alliances, which were often conditional upon his ability to pay. Edward's army was sufficient for a successful invasion of France, but it could never hold the entire country. France, on the other hand, while clearly superior in resources to its smaller and poorer opponent, could not invade England or prevent the English from crossing the channel, having lost its entire fleet early in the conflict.

In the first half century of war, the English confined themselves to raids on the French countryside that decimated the peasantry but yielded a relatively small amount of booty and did little direct damage to the French military effort. They were, however, able to take and hold the port of Calais, and in the first two major military engagements of the war, a small force of English invaders succeeded in defeating a much more numerous body of French knights. Tactics and superior weapons—the longbow—allowed the English to carry the day. In the second encounter, the Battle of Poitiers in 1356, the English captured the French king.

The Treaty of Bretigny, which followed the English victory, awarded the English a large ransom for the captured king and made Edward III the nominal sovereign of one third of France. First the king and then a number of important French lords were held as security for the ransom. When one of the hostages escaped from captivity, the French king chivalrously surrendered himself to the English. He died in captivity.

Under his successor, Charles V (1364–80), the French gradually began to recover from their misfortunes. Charles V worked hard to fulfill the Treaty of Bretigny, but the payment of the ransom did not solve the more basic issues between the two countries, and the war continued. To field an effective fighting force against the English, Charles V reformed the French army. Feudal levies to meet each emergency were given up in favor of a paid permanent force under a professional commander. Instead of leading the army, as was customary for French kings before and after his time, Charles appointed the pompous but effective general Bertrand du Guesclin to command it in his place. The French army began a long campaign in which it avoided great battles and engaged in guerilla tactics. The result was that the English could not hold the territories they invaded, and limitations in money and manpower enforced a gradual constriction of their effort, until by 1380 they again held only Calais and part of Aquitaine.

By 1380 Edward III, Charles V, and du Guesclin were dead, and the following years saw both countries plunged into political chaos. In England there were intense struggles for control of the royal government, while in France the minority of Charles VI allowed full play to baronial politics. The French king no sooner came of age than he became subject to periodic fits of insanity. At first annual interludes in his reign, these periods grew longer and more frequent until Charles was merely a useless figurehead, ignored or forgotten in the contest for control of the French government.

The alienation of powerful elements within France was as damaging to the nation as was its loss of a strong central leader. Eventually a faction led by the powerful duke of Burgundy formed an alliance with the English. This alliance and the aggressive policies of Henry V (1413–22) of

England precipitated a vigorous renewal of the war. The English, buttressed now by troops from Burgundy, met the knights of France at Agincourt in 1415. Again, French knights charged against a smaller English force and were decisively defeated. The culmination of the English advance was the Treaty of Troyes of 1420, which left the English and their Burgundian allies in possession of the northern part of France. The son of Charles VI was declared illegitimate, and his daughter was married to Henry V of England, who thereby became heir to the throne of France.

French resistance after the Treaty of Troyes centered on the son of Charles VI, the future Charles VII. After the deaths of Charles VI and Henry V, the infant Henry VI of England was crowned king of France. Ruling in his name, the regency continued to press English interests, while Charles struck a vacillating and unattractive pose in his attempts to defend his rights. At this point Joan of Arc emerged from her native province and her father's farm to declare that heavenly voices had commanded her to don knight's attire and defend France against the wicked Englishmen.

In a day when magic and miracles were commonly accepted, Joan's story was not prima facie untrue, and a panel of theologians found no reason to regard her as a charlatan. Joan was accepted by several of the leaders of the French army and finally by Charles himself, whom she convinced of the justice of his claims. Joan's prestige rose to its greatest height when she led the successful attempt to break the siege of Orleans in 1429. In the same year she induced the king to force his way through English territory to Rheims, where he was properly crowned in the traditional place and manner of French monarchs. Joan's naive aggressiveness finally led to her capture by the Burgundians, who turned her over to the English. Subjected to a trial that used the traditional methods of the Inquisition, Joan recanted in a moment of weakness. She regained her strength, however, put on masculine attire once again, and finally was burned at the stake as a relapsed heretic.

Eventually Joan was retried posthumously, exonerated, and canonized. Her dedication to the French nation symbolized the spirit of the French effort to drive the English out of France. England lost the Burgundian alliance and was gradually forced to yield most of the territory it had won. By 1453 only Calais remained in English hands.

The French victory was at least partly due to advances in weaponry that allowed the French army to win on the battlefield. The English longbow could not match the new French artillery. Town and castle walls, no matter how strong, could not withstand heavy cannon, which also had devastating effects on the ranks of an advancing army.

The departure of the English army from France did not bring peace, but the beginning of a civil war among the English royal family for possession of the throne turned the nation's attention to domestic problems. By 1453 the war between England and France, which had lasted for over a century, was at an end. The two countries were exhausted by taxation to meet war costs, and much of the western French countryside was devastated. Both countries welcomed the reassertion of peace and order in whatever form.

In France, Charles VII remained weak and personally unappealing, but the monarchy gained a great deal of prestige from the expulsion of the English. The king's contemporaries called him Charles the Well-Served for good reason: The great constitutional and institutional reconstruction of France was not so much the work of Charles VII as of the ministers who worked on his behalf. The king emerged from the Hundred Years' War with no constitutional limitation on his authority; with new sources of taxation—such as the general tax on salt—which freed him from dependence upon the estates; and with a powerful, nonfeudal standing army. The Pragmatic Sanction of 1438 reaffirmed the king's control over the income and personnel of the national church, removing the problem of ecclesiastical autonomy.

The major problem that remained to the French monarchy was that of territorial consolidation. The most formidable independent section of the kingdom was the duchy of Burgundy, which had allied itself with England with such disastrous results for France. Louis XI (1460–1483), successor to Charles VII, was just the right king to amalgamate Burgundy into the royal domain. He was clever and unscrupulous and reveled in diplomatic intrigue. His paid spies were everywhere in Europe, and just as he bought support in foreign kingdoms, he lavished gifts upon the church and offerings to the saints to be assured of God's favor. In the long run, Louis XI was able to add Burgundy to the royal domain and to further the advance of a strong and stable government in France.

When Louis's successor brought Brittany into the royal domain through a fortunate marriage, all the major areas in France were under the control of the king. It remained, however, to eradicate that local particularism that had been a constant feature of French politics. The royal courts and administration could bring some sort of uniformity to the kingdom, but regional cultural differences gave each province a sanction against national power that was difficult to break down. Concessions wrung from the king in time of stress gave legal backing to local privileges.

The king was able to dissipate the effects of localism by restricting the nobles' independent sources of power. The great magnates were opportunists first of all, and their particularism and selfishness tended to turn them against each other. An attractive and energetic king could readily exploit this aristocratic weakness and win important nobles over to his side by gifts of honors and offices. In this way the barons themselves were gradually attached to and made dependent upon the wealth of power of the crown. Nobles, no longer the indispensable backbone of the military, became the king's servants and beneficiaries. By the end of the fifteenth century, the royal court was the center of aristocratic existence, monarchy was supreme in France, and the ground was prepared for the royal absolutism of the sixteenth and seventeenth centuries.

For the English, the last half of the fifteenth century merely marked a change from foreign war to domestic strife. The great nobles, through the practice known as livery and maintenance, kept in their pay small private armies that made them and their clients immune to control by a local or national government. Aristocratic brutality and the corruption exhibited by royal officials helped to bring about popular revolts, such as that led by Jack Cade in 1450. The revolts only worsened the lawlessness rampant in the land.

With a restless nobility and a superabundance of claimants to the throne, England was plunged into a protracted civil war. When King Henry VI (1422–61) became insane in 1453—he inherited the Valois' bad gene through his mother—the prevailing turmoil was exacerbated as the Yorkist and Lancastrian branches of the royal family contended for the throne—a conflict that modern writers have called the Wars of the Roses.

From 1471, when Edward IV (1461–83) was able to establish his position firmly, his reign proved to be the first step out of the political morass in which England was floundering. Edward's policies were not revolutionary in themselves, but his forceful application of the principles of medieval monarchy and his careful control of Parliament and other institutions of government that had been maturing beneath the noisy surface of political life, gave his government an innovative appearance. The antipathy with which the English gentry viewed continued civil war was buttressed by the gradual decimation of the belligerent. For almost a century the English nobility had been killing each other off, until by the last quarter of the fifteenth century the power of the once-great noble families had been greatly diminished.

When Edward IV died in 1483, his brother murdered Edward's infant sons and became Richard III, only to lose his crown and his life two years later at the Battle of Bosworth Field. Henry VII (1485–1509), whose hereditary right to the throne was questionable, was king by right of conquest at the end of the battle. Henry was the first Tudor ruler of England.

He established a dynasty that would last for over a hundred years and preside over greatly enhanced national power, unity, and prosperity.

Italy had been an exception to the pattern of political and social development that existed in medieval Europe. Italian urban life never disappeared, even in the early Middle Ages, and Italy never became as exclusively rural as did the rest of Europe. Italian town and country life had a fluid character, as opposed to the sharp demarcation between city and countryside in the north. Even feudalism, the most characteristic medieval institution, developed only partially in Italy. The commercial revolution in Europe in the High Middle Ages came first to Italy. In northern Europe, it arrived gradually and introduced a new urban element into rural society. In Italy, urban centers soon came to predominate in both economic and political affairs. The cities first asserted their autonomy and then expanded to bring the surrounding countryside under their jurisdiction.

The predominant economic, social, and political class in medieval Italy was not a feudal landed nobility, but an aristocracy based on money and wealth amassed through trade and finance. As the cities surpassed the countryside, the landed nobility was either pressed downward to an inferior position through the lack of money or amalgamated with the moneyed classes of the city. At the same time, the highest ranks of the merchant class became indistinguishable from the nobility in status and way of life.

The most sustained attempt to bring some overriding unity to the entire Italian peninsula was undertaken by the house of Hohenstaufen which had the tragic good fortune in the last decade of the twelfth century to inherit both the kingdom of Sicily in southern Italy and the Holy Roman emperorship. The northern cities and the popes, who ruled the Papal States in central Italy, desperately resisted the attempts of the Hohenstaufen family to establish hegemony over the peninsula. The protracted conflict had a lasting impact on Italian politics; two parties emerged—the Guelphs and the Ghibellines—the former favoring the papacy and the independent communes, the latter favoring the empire. The demise of the Hohenstaufens, and with them the issue of imperial hegemony, left in the Italian cities two factions whose irreconcilable hostility continued for more than a century after the original issue dividing them had vanished.

The other lasting result of the attempt of the Hohenstaufens to unify and control Italy was the introduction of the French house of Anjou into the kingdom of Sicily, which comprised the island of Sicily and the southern part of the Italian peninsula. To drive the Hohenstaufens from its southern flank, the papacy had to call in foreign help—a standard tactic for the papacy and the Italian cities. Consequently Charles of Anjou, the brother of Louis IX of France, received Sicily as his reward for driving out the Hohenstaufens. The kingdom, established by the Normans two centuries earlier, was now restored to French domination. It remained the only major part of Italy under a centralized political authority, but the spread of its political control was precluded by the insecurity of the ruling house and by its dependence on papal support.

After the Sicilian Vespers, the national rebellion of 1282 against French rule, the kingdom was divided into two parts: the island of Sicily under Aragonese domination and the mainland kingdom of Naples under the French. Sovereignty changed hands several times in the fourteenth and fifteenth centuries as the Spanish and the French continued to struggle for control, and southern Italy, one of the most prosperous and culturally advanced parts of the peninsula, fell far behind its wealthier northern neighbors.

The center of Italian vitality in the fourteenth and fifteenth centuries was in the northern cities. In the thirteenth century their characteristic political form was the commune, a republic governed by an oligarchy. In these cities the rise of a civil bureaucracy, as well as a diplomatic corps, provided some stability in the business of government even under the ever-present conditions of social disturbance and class conflict. The chief concern of the city governments was usually directed toward the commercial interests of the city, and the bureaucracies kept business going even during incessant changes of leadership.

In most cities Guelphs and Ghibellines existed side by side in enduring hatred, and factional rivalry was complicated by a maze of family alliances and feuds. There were also serious class conflicts within the Italian cities. The "best" families, whose wealth and prestige were centuries old, met constant competition from the "new men," who often surpassed them in wealth. There was also a strong middle class in most of the cities—skilled artisans and shopkeepers who were organized into guilds to press their common interests and to regulate trade. Below them were the unorganized and therefore perpetually exploited workers, employed in industry or on the docks. The dissatisfaction of the workers took the form of riots and revolts that might bring them a new oppressor but seldom gained them any permanent advantage. Beyond the walls of the city were the peasants, subject to highly efficient bourgeois landlords.

The vast number of interests and conflicts resulting from the economic and social complexities of Italian life make the political history of Italy in the fourteenth and fifteenth centuries a morass of alliances, wars, and intrigues. A political faction or party was rarely stable enough to hold power for long. Family feuds and personal jealousies were constantly at work to undermine political stability and the social order. The style and methods of Italian politics were personal and vindictive. The other European peoples certainly could not boast about the high moral character of their political life, but they found Italian politics shocking in its brutality and lack of scruples. In northern Europe a more stable political tradition allowed hereditary or legal rights to exercise a binding force most of the time, but in the smaller states of Italy, murder or bribery could with impunity overturn both legality and convention. The loser in any conflict or quarrel had an infinite variety of devious political means at his disposal. A protracted development of political power, such as the Reconquista in Spain or the gradual aggrandizement of the domains of the crown in France, was precluded in Italy by the very instability of political life. A grand alliance, easily built, vanished just as quickly with another turn of the political wheel of fortune.

The communes were unable to find a constitutional or political solution to their problems. Lawlessness became a constant fact of life. Mob riots characterized the political activities of the middle and lower classes, while the *grandi*—the urban nobility—lived in fortified towers in the cities, the urban counterparts of the castle. They and their armed retainers could be bound by no law, and the constant conflicts among the nobility threatened any kind of order in the life of the city.

A typical solution to the endemic problems of the Italian city was the summoning of a foreigner to act as podestà (the high magistrate and sometimes temporary dictator). Since he was not involved in any of the factions of the city, he could be trusted with the absolute power that was the only means of keeping order. Gradually, in the fourteenth and fifteenth centuries, these tyrants established their power on a permanent and hereditary basis in most cities. In some cases the podestà, whose term was limited, was able to extend his rule for life and to pass it on his heirs. Another powerful figure was the captain of a mercenary band; more than one city found itself subject to the leader of its hired defenders.

As the leading cities expanded, their former competitors and dozens of smaller towns were swallowed up in larger territorial units. In most of the cities of Italy the institution of the hereditary dictatorship was at least partly responsible for the territorial aggrandizement of the city. The exception to this general rule was the republic of Venice, where a merchant oligarchy directed the affairs of the city in a manner at least as absolute as that of any dictator. Venice, built on marshes at the head of the Adriatic Sea, was spared much of the class conflict and political complexity of other cities by its inhabitants' unity of economic interests. Venice was almost exclusively built on trade and shipping, and the furthering of its commercial interests was the constant aim of Venetian policy.

The government of Venice was unique not only for its republican constitution, but for the state control of economic life that marked its public policy. Public works on a large scale were always essential because of the necessity of maintaining the canals. The Venetian fleet was built and manned by the city; merchants rented space in the vessels as they needed it. Every phase of commercial life was closely controlled by the ruling oligarchy. Venetian diplomatic policy revolved around the control of trade routes to the Black Sea area. In the fourteenth and fifteenth centuries a party that favored territorial aggrandizement gained control in the city and began a policy of expansion around the Adriatic Sea to safeguard crucial passes across the Alps and routes to the timber essential to the shipbuilding industry.

The major liability in Venetian political life was the republic's long wars with competitors. Venetian interest in the eastern Mediterranean had led to many years of hostilities with Genoa, which ruined the Genoese and in the long run weakened both cities. Venice's policy of expansion brought it into conflict with eastern European countries, such as Hungary. Finally, in the late fifteenth century, Venice engaged in a long war with the Turks that left the city exhausted and defeated.

Florentine politics, infinitely complex, were more representative of the development of Italian cities. The constitution was complicated and constantly changing. Florence's large working class revolted more than once, and the aristocratic factions plunged the city into constant turmoil. The power structure of the Guelph party acted as an extralegal governing force in the city, suppressing its enemies by exiling or execution them as Ghibellines.

In 1434, after years of political maneuvering, Cosimo de'Medici, the head of the prominent banking and mercantile family, was able to gain complete control of the government of Florence: The Medici remained political bosses, scrupulous in their regard for at least the letter of the law. Although his power was exercised through informal channels, Cosimo was able to dominate the Florentine government: He had the vast resources of the Medici bank, along with the usual means of ruining his enemies. Thus an opponent who was overtaxed and hounded by officials might find credit refused to him as well.

The Medici government did succeed in maintaining order in Florence, and most of the time it governed in the public interest. The most famous Medici ruler, Lorenzo the Magnificent, departed from the unassuming ways of his predecessors but was no less popular. When his enemies plotted to kill him, arranging to have him stabbed at mass, the plot failed. The public refused to be aroused against him and instead lynched many of the leaders of the revolt, including the bishop.

After Lorenzo's death there was an interlude in Medici rule during which the monk Savonarola attempted to institute a reign of piety and virtue in the city. Savonarola and the subsequent republican regime failed, and Florence returned to Medici rule in 1512 in spite of the decline of the Medici banking house. The greatest days of the Medici family and of Florence occurred in the late fifteenth century, when an heir of the Medici ascended to the papal apogee of power among the Italian cities.

The greatest city in the northern Lombard plain was Milan. When the house of Visconti ascended to power in the early part of the fourteenth century, Milan began a steady expansion that eventually brought much of northern Italy under its control. Thus, while it did not have the commercial predominance of Venice or the industrial activity of Florence, Milan remained one of the most powerful Italian cities.

The Visconti left no heirs in the mid-fifteenth century, and Milan unsuccessfully attempted to establish a republic. Instead, Francesco Sforza, the commander of a mercenary army in the employ of the Visconti, was able to return as their successor. Since Milan, like most Italian cities, had no citizen defense against the mercenaries, Sforza's military power was a sure means of gaining political control. In the later part of the fifteenth century the Sforza and Medici families cooperated to prevent any one state from upsetting the balance of power among the cities of northern Italy.

It was not until the pope was firmly established in Rome after the Great Schism that the papacy reestablished its hold over the Papal States. The task of holding these territories in check was especially difficult for the popes because there could be no possibility of hereditary rule. Each pope had to formulate his own policy, often hampered by the nepotism of his own and his predecessors' families, who demanded offices and privileges in his domains. In spite of their difficulties, the popes of the later fifteenth century returned to an influential role in Italian politics. They were an important factor in the diplomatic intrigues that characterized intercity rivalries, and they tried to expand their power into new territories. The ambitions of the papacy became one of the major factors militating against stability in Italian politics.

From the end of the Hohenstaufen dynasty in the thirteenth century until the last decade of the fifteenth century, Italy had been relatively free from foreign invasion and intervention in Italian politics. Italian wars had been isolated from developments in the rest of the period in every respect, and the Italians did not have to face foreign armies. Wars between the Italian cities had been fought not by their citizens, but by hired mercenary soldiers.

At first, foreigners made up the bulk of these adventurers, but gradually the Italians used their own mercenary captains, who went to war for a profit and found it much more efficient to stay with the traditional form of calvary warfare. Furthermore, to attempt to annihilate an enemy meant risking annihilation in return, so there was a tacit agreement that bloodshed would be kept to a minimum. Captives were taken and ransomed for a moderate amount. Warfare in fourteenth- and fifteenth-century Italy was a gentleman's affair, with endless maneuvering and a minimum of actual armed conflict. When the armies of northern Europe came over the Alps in the late fifteenth and sixteenth centuries, the Italians found that they had been bypassed in the techniques and technology of warfare, and they could not stand against the invaders.

The political division and controversy that were customary among Italian cities took on a new color when the northern countries recovered from the wars and disasters of the fourteenth and early fifteenth centuries. A number of powerful cities had developed in Italy, but in northern Europe the era of the national state had begun. By the last decade of the fifteenth century, the French monarchy was an adversary whose resources dwarfed those of any power in Italy. Italian predominance in the economic sphere was challenged, as trade routes moved from the Mediterranean to the Atlantic. In the High Middle Ages, northern kings had been greatly dependent upon their Italian creditors; now they had their own resources upon which to draw for revenue.

When an Italian city called in the French monarchy to intervene in an Italian quarrel in 1494, the French king, Charles VIII, was in a position to take effective action. He entered Italy with a powerful army whose Swiss pikemen and artillery completely outclassed the Italian mercenaries. Most cities simply submitted without battle. Although Charles's invasion did not result in the permanent subjugation of Italy, it did reveal that Italy was vulnerable to invasion.

The reaction of the Italian cities to invasion was to form a league under the leadership of the Medici and Sforza rulers of Florence and Milan that was designed to prevent any state from upsetting the Italian balance of power. In case of foreign invasion or when any one state attacked another, all the states in the league would unite in defense of the victim of the attack. The principle of collective security could be only a temporary emergency measure, however, and it was rendered futile by the realities of Italian particularism and the predominant power of France and Spain. In Italy there was no common political basis that could turn division and rivalry into a firmly established national power capable of meeting the monarchies of northern Europe on equal terms. The sixteenth century revealed that the invasion of Charles VIII was not a temporary threat from which Italy had been delivered but, rather, a foreshadowing of things to come.

All the wealth and culture of Italy was useless in the face of the rising national monarchies. By 1500 the monarchical, bureaucratic, national state had become the prime force for order in European life.

CHAPTER TWENTY-ONE

Late Medieval and Renaissance Culture

I. The Harvest of Medieval Thought

The crisis of the later Middle Ages did not distract the intellectuals and artists of Latin Christendom from theory and creativity. On the contrary, the gloom and doom of the times made them think all the more deeply about the nature of God, the universe, mankind, and society. In the midst of devastation from pandemics, war, climatic deterioration, and economic depression, they exhibited a passion for learning of all kinds—for linguistic and literary innovation, for philosophical and scientific inquiry, for massive productivity and creativity in the visual arts. No era in western civilization left a heritage of more masterpieces in literature and painting or seminal works of philosophy and theology.

A long series of great historians in the past century and half has sought to articulate the cultural dynamics of the period between 1270 and 1500 that generated so much intellectual, literary, and artistic innovation. Some have seen the cultural development of the period 1270–1500 as fitting into a pattern of intellectual and artistic revolution, of breakthrough renaissance. This was the thesis that Jacob Burckhardt propounded with regard to Italy in 1860, and others extended this interpretation more generally to all Europe. It was only a question of precisely when particular cultures were, like Burckhardt's Renaissance Italy, freed from the "faith, illusion, and childish prepossession" of medieval society and the modern world was ushered in, signified by a full consciousness of individual human personality that broke the bonds of "race, people, party, family, or corporation"—that is, modernist individualism replaced medieval collectivity.

Another group of historians have seen in the fourteenth and fifteenth centuries, at least outside northern Italy, not a brilliant cultural dawning, but a rich autumnal glow, the maturation and fulfillment of the long medieval centuries. They have viewed late medieval culture as bringing to a conclusion the cultural revolution of the twelfth century, with its twin facets of classical recovery and romantic intensification. Some have emphasized a novel laicized spirit breaking through medieval religious structure, while others have focused on the revamping of medieval religiosity in the direction of personal piety resulting in the augmentation of ordinary people's faith. "The diapason of life has not changed," Johan Huizinga wrote in 1919 about the fifteenth century in France and the Netherlands. "Scholastic thought with symbolism and strong formalism, the thoroughly dualistic conception of life and the world still dominated. The two poles of the mind continued to be chivalry and hierarchy."

Inevitably many historians have concluded that the period 1270–1500 was marked by two distinct cultures whose trends contradicted each other—Italy was breaking through to a cultural revolution, while northern Europe was bringing to term the ideas and sensibilities of the twelfth and thirteenth centuries, extending the implications and trying to resolve some of the conflicts of the great intellectual advances of that era. In this view, there was some interaction between the late medieval cultures of northern Europe and the Italian Renaissance, but they were going each their own way. It was not until the end of the fifteenth century that intense efforts were made to reconcile the two cultures, and these efforts produced a monumental intellectual and moral crisis around 1500 that brought on the Protestant Reformation.

Symbolically it is easy to relive the primary significance of the late medieval cultures because they are still active. In the span of a few hours an academic at Columbia or New York University can role-play two constants of the culturally upscale fifteenth-century experience. In the morning she can be a member of an examining panel giving an oral exam to a doctoral student in the humanities. In the afternoon (after lunch in a French or Italian restaurant whose cuisine as we know it goes back to the late fifteenth century), she can visit the Frick Museum or the Morgan Library of Art or a gallery at the Metropolitan Museum and enjoy the fabulous collection of art that a billionaire put together for his own edification. These are both reruns of cultural scenes of late medieval Europe— the doctoral oral replicated from the universities of Paris or Oxford or Padua, and the splendid private art collection replicated from many places, but especially Florence. Let us begin by looking at the implications of the scholastic exercise.

At the University of Paris in the late thirteenth and the fourteenth centuries, and soon at other centers such as Oxford and Cologne, scholastic theology reached the height of its development. The focal point of Christian thought and higher education was indisputably the University of Paris, where St. Thomas Aquinas and other great theologians taught and wrote. The university's authority in matters of doctrine led kings and popes alike to appeal to its faculty for support in political and doctrinal controversies. Paris certainly was the leader in scholastic thought, but scholasticism itself was universal. St. Thomas and St. Bonaventura were Italians, and Italian universities were among the successors to Paris as centers of scholasticism. During the late fourteenth and the fifteenth centuries, the universities at Padua, Bologna, and Pavia flourished as centers for the study of Aristotelian natural philosophy, making full use of the comments and writings of the Arab philosopher Averroes. Between 1280 and 1320 Oxford was the most innovative center of philosophy.

Ultimately medieval theologians were unable to establish a common view of either the divine or the natural aspects of the Christian universe. The attempt by Thomas Aquinas to argue from the natural to the divine and thus to reconcile Aristotelian metaphysics with the Christian concept of God found opponents on every side. St. Bonaventura and his followers rejected Aquinas's argument that man can arrive at a rational, if imperfect, knowledge of God by analogy from the natural world, arguing that knowledge of God comes from mystical communion with the divine, not from nature. On the other hand, the Christian followers of Averroes—the most distinguished Muslim commentator on the Aristotelian corpus—argued that man's only sure knowledge comes from nature and that consequently he can have no secure knowledge of God by exercising reason. The most extreme Christian followers of Averroes held, as did Averroes himself, that philosophy and theology could contradict each other. The implication of this doctrine—that matters of faith could not be proved and were in fact contradicted by philosophy—was viewed as heretical by the more conservative churchmen.

The major outcome of the great Thomist age of synthesis was a reaction against it that shook scholastic philosophy to its foundations. As the fluid and even amorphous body of Christian doctrine that existed in the twelfth and thirteenth centuries was subjected to the dual impact of Aristotle and the social and political disorders of the fourteenth century, the medieval worldview began gradually to break down. The philosophical issues bequeathed by the thirteenth century to the fourteenth proved impossible to solve. Philosophical schools, roughly divided between the

Franciscan followers of St. Bonaventura and the Dominican followers of Aquinas, formulated precise and rigid definitions of orthodoxy. In 1277 the bishop of Paris declared that Aristotle could not be publicly taught or read at the university. Even while he was alive, Aquinas had incurred the disapproval of ecclesiastical authorities.

The study of Aristotle continued, however. Oxford was outside the ban, and even in Paris the prohibition could not be enforced. Censorship continued in the fourteenth century, with the objects of condemnation varying with the philosophical inclination of the censors. The prohibition of deviant opinions was unsuccessful, but it tended to harden doctrinal controversy. The late thirteenth-century academic controversies were mainly responsible for the separation of theology from philosophy and science. Philosophers and scientists continued to work within the framework of Christian doctrine, and their preoccupations were often ultimately theological, but the tensions between the different intellectual commitments grew more apparent.

The Oxford philosopher Duns Scotus (1266–1308) stressed the unknowability of God and the inaccessibility of His nature. Man's knowledge of the natural world might come from sensory perception, but not his knowledge of the divine will or his own will to do good. Scotus thus tried to reconcile the Aristotelian view of knowledge derived from sensory perception with the orthodox Christian conception of a free and unlimited deity.

Duns Scotus was the greatest medieval logician. As his name implies, he was born in Scotland; he joined the Franciscan order, studied at Paris, and taught theology at Oxford. He began with an extremely searching inquiry into the power of the human intellect to abstract from sensory data and arrived at a conclusion contradicting Thomist optimism, which believed it possible to build up a rational knowledge of God on an epistemological foundation of sensory experience. Scotus concluded that the human mind cannot penetrate God's being through ratiocination. God is infinite, but human reason is finite. God is absolutely omnipotent and free to follow His own will; the human mind cannot work out a train of causation to be able to know rationally the inner being of God. Scotus was not trying to undermine faith but to enhance its exclusive importance; he was trying to make revelation the only source of the knowledge of divine being. He thought that he had protected the majesty of God and the freedom of the will from the limiting effect of Thomistic determinism.

Duns Scotus died at the height of his intellectual powers and before he could complete his work. The major implications of his doctrine were worked out by William of Occam (died 1350), another Oxford Franciscan of extreme precocity who developed his system by 1320, when he was not more than thirty years old. Occam effected a revolution in scholastic philosophy by a complete separation of logic and metaphysics. This separation had already been suggested by Scotus, but Occam made the distinction absolute. He maintained that logic does not deal with being as such, with propositions from the standpoint of the accordance with fact or existence. Intellectual propositions are purely forms of thought divested of all metaphysical content, of any connection with ultimate truth. "Their being is their being understood." Logic, then, deals only with the analysis of modes of signification, or "terms," but when we ask if metaphysical knowledge is possible, if man can know ultimate truth rationally, Occam's reply is negative. Universals are merely intellectual symbols, far removed from ultimate reality, that are formed by the mind out of repeated sensations and confused memory and that only dimly stand for individual things. Our conceptions of causality are contingent upon this mental process and have no reality outside the mind. Occam thereby arrived at an extreme nominalism that is close to the radical empiricism of Hume and Wittgenstein.

Occam's purpose was the same as that of Scotus: He wanted to uphold the Franciscan claim that knowledge of God can come only through revelation and intuition and that divine being cannot be known rationally, which for him would imply a limitation of divine being. He used philosophy to destroy the importance of philosophy and to uphold the Franciscan approach to the deity as the only way. His extreme nominalism, or "terminalism," argued with enormous subtlety and force, immediately had a powerful effect on the schools that, by the 1330s, were the scene of a great debate between the Occamist "modernists," as they were called, and the supporters of the Thomist "ancient way."

Occam believed that he had used the dialectical weapons of the schools against the schoolmen. He had demonstrated that philosophy itself supported the teachings of St. Francis concerning the intuitive knowledge of God. Occam's devotion to St. Francis made him susceptible to the doctrines of the radical wing of the Friars Minor. At the end of the thirteenth century the Spirituals had again become active, and they openly preached the apostolic poverty of the church and the apocalyptic heresies of Joachim of Flora. Not satisfied with his onslaught on Thomism, Occam began to attack the temporal power of the papacy and to demand the apostolic poverty of the church. He fell under the censure of Pope John XXII and spent the last years of his life at the court of the German king Louis of Bavaria, who was also at odds with the pope. Occam was joined in his flight to seek royal protection by the minister-general of the Franciscans, who had sided with the Spirituals and thereby finally opened the split within the order that had been threatening since the middle of the thirteenth century. In 1322 the papacy condemned the doctrine of the apostolic poverty of the church as a heresy, and the more extreme members of the Spirituals in Italy, known as the Fraticelli, were hunted down by the Inquisition. These conflicts inaugurated a sharp decline in the vitality of the Franciscan order and its leadership of European piety.

In the realm of science, Occam's preference for the specific over the general gave great impetus to the development of a modern view of the investigation of nature. Observation had been recognized as the basis of scientific conclusions since the work of Robert Grosseteste and Roger Bacon in the thirteenth century. Grosseteste and his disciple Bacon stressed the importance of sensory perception and thus of observation and experiment. Their careers at Oxford were among the first to distinguish the English university—which was free from many of the harsh conflicts that limited the pursuit of scientific investigation at Paris—as the prime center of medieval scientific thought. During the early fourteenth century, Merton College at Oxford developed a school of mathematics unparalleled in Europe.

Early fourteenth-century scientists devoted themselves to pointing out and attempting to correct the manifest inaccuracies of Aristotelian physics. For all his empiricism, Aristotle's conclusions often did not correspond with discernible facts. In the Aristotelian universe general cause—of motion, for example—was inherent in the nature of any object or force. In a hierarchically ordered universe, every object and every element (earth, water, air, and fire) sought its natural place. Occam, on the other hand, held that the only valid source of knowledge about the world is what is observable. Motion, for instance, cannot be said to exist; it is only a convenient term to express the fact that we see a thing first in one place and then in another. Therefore motion—and, indeed, general cause in the Aristotelian sense—was invalidly conceived.

The successors of Occam helped to set the stage for the scientific revolution of the sixteenth century, but they were separated from the achievements of Galileo, Copernicus, and Newton by their distinctly limited methods of experimentation and inadequate knowledge of quantification. Their assertions too often were shots in the dark—brilliant attempts at valid explanations that were neither refutable nor verifiable by the methods at their disposal. The bonds of the Aristotelian universe had been broken, but the new methods did not as yet lead to definitive results. No coherent scientific view of the universe, no paradigm, could be molded to replace the Aristotelian synthesis.

Occam concluded that while relations between individual things are mental products, the individual things themselves do exist and are knowable. Through simple sensory data the human mind can learn to perceive these individual, permanent things in nature, which are extended, quantitative, and measurable. Occam thus glimpsed that universe of discourse, based on the quantification of nature, that made the thought-world of Galileo, Copernicus, and Newton possible. The Oxford Franciscan himself suggested the law of inertia, although among his contemporaries only the small group of natural philosophers at Merton College, Oxford, could understand what he was saying. In the latter half of the fourteenth century the Parisian Occamist school, following their master's rejection of metaphysics and advocacy of the observation and analysis of individual things, advanced to the threshold of modern mechanics, physics, and analytic geometry. Nicholas of Oresme, undoubtedly the most outstanding member of this school, suggested the principle of the daily rotation of the Earth before Copernicus and proposed the law of falling bodies before Galileo.

Occam's disciples thus had all the intellectual equipment to achieve the great scientific breakthrough of the sixteenth and seventeenth centuries. Why did they not proceed with their work? Why did these scientific studies decline so completely in the fifteenth century that it has taken the most thorough research of modern scholarship to discover the work of Nicholas of Oresme and his colleagues? The answer lies in the social background in which these men worked. No one in the fourteenth century, not even the scholastic scientists themselves, perceived the empirical value and social utility of the law of falling bodies. The men who pursued these new studies did so on their own time; they had no social encouragement. There were no chairs in science in the universities, but there were many in dialectic and theology; it was much more profitable to pursue the latter disciplines than to engage in scientific research that no one, outside a small circle, appreciated. It was a change in military technology that eventually made mechanics a socially useful subject and encouraged the revival of research in the sixteenth century. Gunpowder was just coming into use in the fourteenth century, and Europeans were still unskilled and amateurish in its use. By the sixteenth century armies had become sufficiently adept at firing cannonballs so that someone who could devise a formula for falling projectiles could make a contribution whose empirical value could be understood.

The second factor that frustrated the great scientific movement of the fourteenth century was a deficiency in mathematical knowledge, particularly algebra. The late medieval thinkers knew that natural science required the quantification of natural phenomena, but they could implement this goal only in a fragmentary way.

Without a breakthrough to modern science, what were liable to be the more innovative kinds of intellectual pursuits in northern Europe in the late fourteenth and fifteenth centuries? Prominently mysticism, which came in several varieties. One was the philosophical approach in the early fourteenth century of Nicholas of Cusa, derived from Occamism and Averroism: God was completely free and outside nature. Only the direct communion of the individual with God would reveal to him the divine will. Nicholas of Cusa called this doctrine appropriately "learned unknowing."

A second kind of practical mysticism, popular in Germany and evoked in the writings of Master Eckhardt and Johannes Tauler, was a humble but firm expression of a puritanical, hard-working, prayerful, and quiet private life. The Pennsylvania Amish are direct heirs of this German quietism.

A third stream in late medieval northern mysticism is found in Thomas à Kempis's the *Imitation of Christ,* the classic text of the Modern Devotion movement in the Netherlands, founded by Gerhard Groote. The *Imitation of Christ,* a popular Christian homily, is a variance of experiential New Age Christianity. The taking of the sacrament of the Eucharist in an expectant mental state of upbeat piety and prayerfulness engenders a conviction of union with Christ. Kempis commanded obedience to prelates so he aroused no concern of counterorthodoxy. But he was diluting the sacramental nature of Christianity through a doing and feeling kind of middle-class sentimentality. No doubt this is the kind of faith that many ordinary people were seeking in the fifteenth century, and this current in late medieval religion flowed easily into the evangelical wing of Protestantism in the next century.

A much-cultivated intellectual pursuit in the late medieval world was elaborate criticism of the clergy, not infrequently written by a priest himself. If this criticism was cultivated intensively and imaginatively enough, it became a subculture of its own, the center of a quasi-paranoid worldview by which everything else could be understood. When the Jews were expelled from western Europe and driven eastward into the Slavic cauldron, the Latin clergy themselves became the demonic scapegoats of European culture.

The most febrile text of late medieval anticlericalism was *Piers Plow-*

man, attributed to a London cleric, William Langland. This long poem, which has survived in three different versions, has all sorts of apocalyptic dimensions, but bitter and circumstantial criticism of the clergy is what makes it a compelling work of literature.

> I saw the Friars there too—all four Orders of them—preaching to the people for what they could get. In their greed for fine clothes, they interpreted the Scriptures to suit themselves and their patrons. . . .
>
> There was also a Pardoner, preaching like a priest. He produced a document covered with Bishops' seals, and claimed to have power to absolve all the people from broken fasts and vows of every kind. The ignorant fold believed him and were delighted. They came up and knelt to kiss his documents, while he, blinding them with letters of indulgence thrust in their faces, raked in their rings and jewelry with his roll of parchment!—So the people give their gold to support these gluttons, and put their trust in dirty-minded scoundrels. . . .
>
> Then I hear parish priests complaining to the Bishop that since the Plague their parishes were too poor to live in; so they asked permission to live in London, where they could traffic in Masses, and chime their voices to the sweet jingling of silver. [Trans. S. F. Goodridge]

Another popular cultural current in the late Middle Ages was cultivation of the old traditions of romantic chivalry. Aristocratic court life in the fifteenth century became extremely stylized and immensely more expensive with the obsessive profileration of rituals, games, pageants, and feasts. On the imagined model of King Arthur's Knights of the Round Table, kings and dukes established tightly selected orders of chivalry carrying titles like Order of the Garter and Knights of the Golden Fleece. A great deal of time, money and artistic, costuming, and cuisinary ingenuity was devoted to the ceremonial activities of these privileged orders. Tournaments were no longer loosely organized war games. They were now minutely choreographed exhibitions of individual prowess and refined sadistic taste.

The aristocratic chivalric displays of the latter Middle Ages were intended to give to the life-style of the higher nobility an intrinsic social value so that the vast expense, thought, and imagination and the best artistic skills lavished on their life-style were justifiably expended. This was the way the nobility blocked status declension in the face of the disposable capital and leisure time of the great merchants and some governmental officials of plebeian lineage.

The affluent and highly literate class of country and town gentry, merchants, and lesser clergy were not, however, willing to allow the aristocracy to reserve neoromantic traditions exclusively for themselves. As much as they could, middle-class people sought to participate in chivalric culture. This desire accounts for the immense resurgence in the popularity of Arthurian literature. Ordinary people could at least read about King Arthur, Queen Geneviere, and Sir Lancelot even if they lacked the resources and the status to dress and behave like these models of nobility. A retired English mercenary soldier and sometime professional bandit, Sir Thomas Mallory, retold the old stories in a rousing Camelot synthesis, *Morte d'Arthur,* that was the most popular book in the English language in the late fifteenth century and one of the first to come off the new London printing press.

The chivalric enthusiasm of the latter Middle Ages made the devastating and ruinously expensive Hundred Years' War socially palatable, glazing it over with romantic motifs, both in the conduct of the war and in the official history of it written by Froissart, an English courtier. Froissart glamorized terrorism and massacres as a series of Camelot encounters and turned blue-blooded thugs like Edward the Black Prince into golden heroes of the Lancelot mold.

Yet another intellectual pursuit in a culturally deadlocked context wherein theological-philosophical syntheses had disintegrated and the quantified paradigms of modern science had not yet been determined, was low level social criticism—descriptions and commentaries about the lives, foibles, and petty triumphs and tragedies of men and women in various social groups and occupations. Today we call it tabloid journalism. It was immensely popular both with the middle class (it was instructive as well as amusing) and the nobility (they could look down with disdain on what the little people were doing).

The bestseller in this genre was the long book in English rhyme, Geoffrey Chaucer's *The Canterbury Tales,* written in London about 1380. Chaucer was a high-level customs official, a member of the entourage of the richest duke, and a well-traveled royal diplomat. He witnessed the lives of all sorts of people, from the grandees of the royal court down to dockside workers. He had an active sex life himself and a keen interest in women's lives. Among his array of characters are the very perfect, gentle knight; the poor scholar and teacher; the prioress who spoke bad French and sang through her nose; and, as the audience demanded, a wide retinue of scrofulous and greedy clerics. Chaucer's most successful character, today worth a sitcom of her own, was the Wife of Bath, married five times and a perpetual pilgrim because she enjoyed the touring ambience.

Chaucer was a skillful poet and a master of European literary traditions—he was immensely learned and he drew upon this learning and literary mastery in his writing. But essentially he had the mind and temperament of a journalist. Within a framework of ostensible rigid affirmation of traditional ethics, he was interested in depicting the diversity and idiosyncracies of people's lives and how they operated at the margins of traditional ethics. He sensed that this is what the literary marketplace demanded.

A writer of similar journalistic instincts and another insightful social commentator was Christine de Pizan, who lived in Paris in the early fifteenth century in the gloomy time of the Hundred Years' War. Christine was the daughter of an Italian astrologer whom the French king had hired, but had to become a career woman after her father's untimely death. Her steady job was as a manuscript copyist, but she was also successful in pioneering women's journalism. Her best book was *The City of Woman,* in which the life of women in various social groups is minutely described. The book is written with a subtle tongue in cheek and delicate fake piety and a subliminal feminist mindset.

Chaucer's and Christine's literary achievements were paralleled by the Flemish painters of the fourteenth and fifteenth centuries, who worked on commission from their patrons among the nobility and great merchants. Like Chaucer's and Christine's writing, the art of the Flemish painters was fundamentally a secular enterprise that aimed to satisfy a market.

The two greatest early Flemish masters were Jan van Eyck and Roger van der Weyden, who—along with their predecessors, the Master of Flemalle and Hubert van Eyck—were responsible for developing the Flemish style. Detailed realism characterizes the work of Jan van Eyck. His "Madonna of Chancellor Rollin" shows the chancellor kneeling before the Madonna and Child. A window behind the central figures looks out on a city depicted in minute detail. Jan van Eyck's preoccupation with detail gave his work a static, serene quality that contrasts with the structural dynamism and emotion in the paintings of Roger van der Weyden. Oil had been used in paints before, but Jan van Eyck contributed the technique of applying layers of translucent oil paint over the base colors, which allowed the full exploitation of highlights and provided an impression of depth that heightened the color. Although their work was largely free from Italian influence, the great Flemish artists exploited the principles of perspective, which had been transmitted from Italy to the Franco-Flemish manuscript illuminators of the fourteenth century.

The subject matter of the Flemish masters ranged from the traditional religious themes found in manuscript illumination to portraiture, which allowed them to concentrate on the individual personality. Portraits became a popular and most lucrative art form; by the end of the fifteenth century the renowned portrait painter Hans Memling had become one of the richest men in his city through the generosity of his patrons.

II. The Italian Renaissance

The philosophers, writers, and artists of northern Europe in the fourteenth and early fifteenth centuries were significantly influenced by the Italians. But Italy was still special, still different. Its culture was unique and in some regards revolutionary.

The essentials of the Italian cultural style of the fourteenth, fifteenth, and sixteenth centuries are closely identified with the movement known as humanism. The term *humanism* has been used to denote many kinds of ideas and activities, but it has two major (and compatible) meanings. First, there is social (sometimes called civic) humanism, which describes the outlook of the upper middle class in the Italian cities during the Renaissance. The upper bourgeoisie, glorying in its new political power, expressed its independence by placing great emphasis on human autonomy and on the value and grandeur of the city-state. The new class imitated the French aristocracy of the thirteenth century, taking up the aristocratic education, style, and courtly life that they considered suitable to their own emancipation and to their equality with the northern aristocrats. Social humanism inspired a passionate civic patriotism, a belief that all urban resources should be applied to the defense and beautification of the republican commune.

The second major aspect of humanism was the intellectual movement, based on Platonic philosophy, which emphasized the primacy of human values and individual creativity over feudal and ecclesiastical traditions and institutions. Humanist philosophers believed that the human mind was capable of deciding for itself without relying on traditional authority. In both its social and intellectual aspects, humanism drew strength and inspiration from the Greek and Roman classics, which taught the value of the city-state and its self-governing urban elite and upheld the critical powers of the individual human mind.

Both northern and Italian humanists applied their learning and philosophy to the study of the Scriptures, as well as the ancient classics. Most Italian humanists were devout Christians, enthusiastic about the possibility of applying critical methods to biblical studies. Many of them aimed at some form of Christian Platonism. The humanist emphasis on individualism did not necessarily result in secularism; it was also directed toward mysticism, an individual, personal relationship to God. Humanists were not necessarily antipapal; in fact, Rome became an intellectual and artistic center during the Renaissance. In the late fifteenth and sixteenth centuries, several popes—notably Pius II—were humanists themselves, as well as patrons of the arts.

Thus the term *humanism,* which is used to characterize an international intellectual and philosophical movement that was particularly suited to the Italian elite, denotes not only the study of the humanities, but certain assumptions about man's place in the universe and the proper direction of human moral and rational capacities. Scholars in the Middle Ages became familiar with the classical tradition, but saw it ultimately as an alien and pagan view of the world. The men of the Renaissance were able to study that tradition with complete empathy for the first time. Humanism advocated an educational system in which classical studies were the curriculum for moral as well as intellectual training.

The culture of the Italian Renaissance was closely tied to conditions in fourteenth- and fifteenth-century Italy. The wealth of Italy, the matrix of social relationships, the character of political life in the Italian city-state, and the more remote impact of Roman cultural traditions all played important roles in shaping the character of the Italian cultural revolution. The structure of Italian society allowed the Renaissance to develop as a pervasive cultural mode, rather than the isolated expression of a few geniuses. For every Petrarch or Giotto, there were hundreds of lesser men who studied and imitated their works or served as patrons of art and letters.

The two aspects of Italian society that most clearly distinguished Italy from the rest of Europe were wealth—its quantity and the means by which it was amassed—and the political structure of the city-state. By the latter part of the thirteenth century, Italy had a money economy based on trade and finance. The late thirteenth and early fourteenth centuries saw the rise of the great banking houses. The pope was the bankers' largest single customer in Europe, since he needed an agency for the deposit and transfer of vast church funds. Money was lent in sometimes staggering sums to kings and merchants and nobles. The surest investment was provided by merchants' enterprises, since impecunious kings and nobles were a notoriously bad risk. Often the banks had widespread trading connections in addition to their purely financial interests.

Next to the bankers in magnitude of wealth were the international merchants, and below them were the lesser traders and merchants. The merchant-artisan was in a separate and lower class, and a frequent source of disorder. The man of means invested in land—often extensively—but land was not a primary source of the fortunes of the wealthy Italian families of the fourteenth and fifteenth centuries.

The elite of Italian society differed in many ways from the feudal nobility of northern Europe. Neither a life of leisure nor the security of heredity played as pervasive a role among the upper class in Italy as it did in northern Europe. French noblemen had for centuries lived as courtiers on the income from landed estates and offices, but Italian wealth was not so stable. One generation, or even a few years, could destroy a mercantile enterprise that had been built up with endless pains. The vicissitudes of business had a powerful impact on the income of wealthy Italian families—economic disasters were common liabilities in Italian life. Thus even the wealthiest families needed heirs with the ability to handle family finances, and sons of great magnates were trained for business enterprise. Careers in civil or canon law or international commerce were not frowned upon; they were the necessary foundation for economic and social prominence.

The fluid and sometimes fragile nature of wealth had a profound impact upon social relationships. Although only a few great families held sway at the top of Italian society at any one time, there was a fair amount of social mobility in Italian life. The oldest families were not always the wealthiest and often traded their good breeding for the cold cash of the nouveaux riches through marriage. Every city had its share of self-made men who, in a single lifetime, were able to amass wealth and power through ability and energy. There might also be a vast disparity between the wealth and prestige of different branches of the same family. Few men felt secure enough to consume the family fortunes placidly: The life of an Italian noble was filled with activity and struggle.

The political structure of the Italian cities also had a significant effect on social and cultural life. In the tyrannies established in the late fourteenth and the fifteenth centuries, effective political and military power in the city-state rested in the hands of one man, the podestà, the holder of power. The political stability so essential to the well-being of the merchant could collapse overnight with the podestà's death or defeat. At the same time, the ordinary merchant was isolated from political life. Policy and power were the domain of the prince and his personal associates—in his court. The prince gathered around him those who were useful because of their practical abilities or desirable because of the luster they could add to his image.

The tenor of Italian courtly life has been preserved in Castiglione's *The Book of the Courtier*. The courtier was supposed to be, above all, a gentleman: a man of good breeding, physically attractive, and accomplished in all things. He was to be a good warrior, proficient at games and tournaments, a man of art and letters. Good at everything, he yet must refrain from obvious effort, from an excess of enthusiasm, and from boasting. It was quite respectable to finish the race in the middle of the field, though never last. The search for honor and glory must not mar the effect of graceful speech and conduct.

The Renaissance gentleman of Castiglione's portrait differs from the chivalric knight of medieval tradition (and of northern Europe in the fourteenth and fifteenth centuries) in his intellectual pursuits; the careful rhetorical style of his speech; his easy references to Cicero, Aristotle, and the ancient heroes; and his sophisticated opinions on the writings of Petrarch and Dante and on contemporary paintings and sculptures. He differed from the ideal Christian knight in his preoccupation with finite rewards: his own glory and advancement and that of his patron. The ultimate function of the courtier was to guide his patron by personal excellence and sound advice.

The late fifteenth-century popes, many of whom were noted humanists, established great Renaissance courts that were peopled with leading writers and artists. St. Peter's Church and the papal library, among the other Roman monuments, attest to the wealth and the exquisite taste of popes who were poets and patrons, rather than saints.

Both the princely courts and the Italian republics regarded themselves as continuers of the Roman political tradition: Whereas the princes were the heirs of the Caesars, bringing peace and civilization out of chaos and ignorance, the republics sought to restore the glories of the Roman Republic, so beautifully idealized in the writings of Cicero. The greatest flowering of the Renaissance came not in the princely states, nor even in the papal court with its vast resources, but in republican Florence.

In the fourteenth century, Florence survived the ravages of plague, civil war, the fall of the major banking houses, and the revolt of the lower classes to rebuild republican institutions and expand its trade once again. The old oligarchy lost leadership to newer wealth—to bankers, lawyers, and international merchants in the greater guilds. The offices of government were placed in the hands of a series of councils, in which membership was restricted primarily to members of the guilds. The lower middle class and the old nobility were given minor roles in government, where they were neither so frustrated as to rebel nor so powerful as to hinder seriously the new oligarchy. In practice, the offices of government rotated among the members of a hundred or so wealthy and respectable families, the precise position of any family depending upon its wealth, ability, and political connections at any given time.

In the early fifteenth century, diplomatically and militarily isolated, Florence stood alone against the attempts of the dictator of Milan to reduce all northern and central Italy to subjection. The members of the ruling oligarchy restrained their habitual factional bickering to meet the threat and imposed a system of direct, graduated taxes on themselves. Workers who lived off their wages were classed as paupers and not taxed. The result of the struggle was the victorious assertion of the republican institutions and ideology of Florence.

Civic patriotism and humanist ideals characterized political and intellectual life in Florence in the first half of the fifteenth century. Participation in government was a necessary concomitant to economic success because the unrepresented or unpopular family found that it bore the full burden of taxation. The sons of the oligarchies sought to excel in business, government, or church administration, and for success in any one of these fields, the tastes of the time required a humanist man of letters with the proper oratorical style. Leading artists and writers were public heroes.

The houses of wealthy Florentine humanists were tangible proof of the wealth and refinement of their owners. Artistic masterpieces, classical and modern, were supplemented by manuscript libraries with beautiful copies of Cicero, Seneca, Aristotle, and other great classical authors. The household staff was often adorned by a Greek or Latin tutor, a highly respected addition to the usual array of servants. Wealthy private citizens and the city government commissioned works of art to commemorate great persons and events. This was the great age of ecclesiastical building in Florence, as well as in Rome and other Italian cities. Civic patriotism demanded beautiful buildings, the finest Latin style in public documents, and literary works describing the long and glorious history of the city. Professional scholars of the highest renown taught at the university in Florence, which was known throughout Europe as a great center of the New Learning.

The height of the Renaissance spirit in Florence was reached during the reign of the Medici family, whose wealth came from the famous Medici bank, which was founded in the late fourteenth century and had branches all over Europe. The Medici were able to obtain the banking business of the papacy, which had been left without an adequate banker by the fall of the great Florentine banks earlier in the century. At that time the Medici were known as supporters of the popular party in Florence and were thus political enemies of powerful houses in the ruling oligarchy. For many years the Medici family was forced to pay outrageously high taxes, and opposition to the Medici continued to grow—but so did their power.

The outstanding manager of the bank and the architect of the political takeover of the government of Florence was Cosimo de'Medici. After a year in exile Cosimo returned to Florence as the effective power behind the workings of the Florentine government. Commissions and councils continued to sit, and new officials continued to be drawn from a rigid lottery. The difference was that no man could rise in office nor any family continue in prosperity without the sufferance of Cosimo de'Medici. Families who had once used the taxing power of government to lash the Medici found themselves taxed into ruin and denied the credit essential for their commercial enterprises.

The rule of the Medici fostered Florentine humanism. Cosimo was the patron par excellence; cultural life reached new heights under his sponsorship. And if Cosimo was liberal, his grandson Lorenzo the Magnificent, the last great Medici ruler of Florence, was lavish. Lorenzo was not the banker or the statesman that Cosimo had been, however. He was unable to reverse the decline in the fortunes of the family bank—although he covered it for a time with funds drawn from the public treasury (a not entirely unjustified action in view of the public expenditures made from Medici funds). In the early sixteenth century, a Medici pope continued the tradition of patronage begun by his predecessors, but the wealth and finally the real power of the Medici had disappeared by the end of the fifteenth century. In 1500, Renaissance culture had just begun to suffer from the economic decline of the Mediterranean world that eventually would relegate Italy to a secondary place in European life.

The situation in Florence was, in many ways, a concentrated example of the Renaissance environment of all Italian cities. Professional and amateur humanists existed side by side. Professors, tutors, and professional artists were inseparable from Renaissance gentlemen, who often made outstanding contributions of art and letters while conducting their more mundane political and mercantile affairs. Although a large part of the Italian contribution to classical studies, art, and letters was absorbed by the academic circles in northern Europe, the Renaissance as a comprehensive cultural mode found its full expression only in the Italian cities.

The Italian Renaissance was a diversified cultural outpouring that extended to every facet of the intellectual and artistic life of the Italian elite. It was a cultural movement, rather than an intellectual revolution as such. It did not contribute to western civilization a new paradigm for ordering man's conception of the universe or his experience, as did the scientific revolution of the sixteenth century. Rather it contributed a new style of life and a new educational ideal. By reemphasizing certain aspects of the western tradition, the Renaissance created a new cultural mode that was to dominate the ideas of the European elite for centuries and that accelerated the erosion of the medieval worldview. The particular character and direction of the Renaissance were due, in large measure, to the formative influence of a few great men, such as Dante, Petrarch, and Boccaccio.

These men's scholarly achievements and experiments in literary form and style exerted an enormous influence on the development of humanist letters. Dante Alighieri (1265–1321) was in many ways a transitional figure. Dante has often been depicted as the poet who put the *Summa Theologica* in verse, as a fervent disciple of Thomas Aquinas. There are plausible grounds for this view; undoubtedly Dante was heavily influenced by Thomistic doctrine. But he was also sympathetic to some of the views of the Averroists, and in his approach to political thought there is a new note of radical voluntarism that strongly contradicts Thomistic political doctrine. Dante was a man of prodigious learning and deep piety. But the radicalism of the northern Italian communes is also manifested in his work. He was reaching out to new intellectual horizons that were not yet clearly perceptible. He oscillated between the extremes of traditional medieval doctrine and audacious radicalism, signifying the dilemma of the new generation of late medieval thinkers.

Dante was a Florentine who spent the last twenty years of his life in exile from his native city, which he loved deeply, as a consequence of one of those interminable political feuds that poisoned the life of the northern Italian communes. He was the creator of the Italian vernacular as a literary language. He brought into Italian literature the romantic motifs that had prevailed in French poetry for over a century, and in his lyrics there is that same subtle intertwining of mundane and spiritual love upon which the French and German romances had already been built. He venerated Virgil and the great names of classic Latin literature and was a pioneer in uniting humanism with romanticism.

Dante's most ambitious work, *The Divine Comedy,* has generally been regarded as the greatest medieval poem. It is an allegorical epic based upon prodigious learning and almost incomparable literary craftsmanship. It has been viewed as the summation of medieval orthodox religious thought and as a presentation in allegorical and poetical form of the chief tenets of Thomism. There is much to commend this interpretation. Dante describes how he was led on a journey from the depths of Hell, through Purgatory and Heaven, to the glory of the beatific vision. His three guides on this journey symbolize the three ascending stages of knowledge. Virgil takes him through the circles of Hell to the lower stages of Purgatory; the Roman poet whom Dante idolized is meant to represent reason, which by its own efforts can sufficiently educate men in the good life to escape damnation. Dante is guided through the higher stages of Purgatory and all but the highest circles of Heaven by a certain Beatrice. A woman of this name did play an important part in Dante's life, although they seldom met and she became the wife of a wealthy Florentine banker. Beatrice came to symbolize for Dante the romantic ideal of secular and spiritual love, and in *The Divine Comedy* she is meant to represent Grace or Divine Love, that is, revelation or the church, whose sacraments are the only way to salvation and admission to Heaven. Finally, to come face to face with the Divine Spirit, the guidance of St. Bernard, who symbolizes the mystical experience, is necessary. There is a rough parallel between this scheme of religious pilgrimage and Thomistic doctrine. At least St. Thomas and Dante agreed on the ability of reason to show men the rudiments of the good life and the necessity of the church for fulfilling this potentiality and for understanding the higher truths. Dante's designation of Bernardine mysticism as the highest form of knowledge is derived from Franciscan teaching much more than from Dominican Thomism. Appropriately, St. Francis and St. Dominic appear in the same circle of Heaven, and the poem ends with a prayer to the Virgin.

There are some aspects of *The Divine Comedy*, however, that are sharply at variance with its generally orthodox and traditional teaching. Siger of Brabant, the Averroist antagonist of St. Thomas Aquinas, turns up in Dante's Heaven. There are many expressions of hostility to the claims of the papacy. Dante puts into the mouth of St. Peter a bitter condemnation of the "rapacious wolves, in garb of shepherd" who have betrayed their office, and he was particularly uncomplimentary to his contemporary Boniface VIII, whom he consigned to Hell. In Dante's view it is regrettable that Constantine ever made his Donation to the pope and thereby involved the vicar of Christ in worldly matters. There is a more profound limitation to Dante's orthodoxy, and it lies in the scheme of salvation that he presents. His literary concretization of traditional medieval religiosity, its vision of Hell, Purgatory, and Heaven, reflects an overfamiliarity with this doctrine of salvation and the beginnings of its ultimate exhaustion. The poetic construction of such a detailed picture of religious cosmology indicates that the traditional doctrines have lost their freshness and vitality and have become conventional stereotypes. That is not to say that Dante did not believe in the Catholic view of salvation, but he so internalized these doctrines that the line between literary imagination and theological reality became indistinct.

The radical implications of Dante's thought are more pronounced in his treatise on *Monarchy*, which was ostensibly written to advocate the rights and powers of the emperor in Italy, to whom Dante looked as the rightful ruler of Italy and as the restorer of his personal fortunes. As a matter of fact, the German king Henry VII did come down into Italy during Dante's lifetime, but he immediately turned around and went back again without doing anything to end Dante's exile from his beloved Florence. The significance of the work does not lie in its traditional arguments from law and historical tradition on the superior authority of the Roman emperor in the world, but rather in its novel attitude. Dante makes favorable allusions to the Averroist doctrine of the collective immortality of the soul, which stand in strange contradiction to his view of personal immortality upon which *The Divine Comedy* is based. He debates the traditional papal interpretation of the Petrine biblical text, claiming that from Christ's words to Peter "it does not follow that the pope can loose or bind the decrees of the empire." He denies the validity of papal claims based on the Donation of Constantine because "Constantine had no power to alienate the imperial dignity, nor had the church power to receive it." Most significant is Dante's argument for imperial authority, not only on the basis of tradition, law, and biblical texts, but from a simple and radical doctrine of pragmatic necessity: The welfare of the human race, he says, is best advanced under monarchical rule. This represents a new departure in medieval political thought. The implication of Dante's argument is that political power is based upon the sanction not only of divine and natural law but of social necessity.

Francesco Petrarch (1304–74), much more than Dante, was a man of the high Renaissance. His love sonnets were written to Laura, the object of his unending but unrequited love, but they deal above all with his own state of mind. Petrarch was constantly concerned with his soul, his emotions, his intellect, and his reputation. He epitomized the self-consciousness of the Renaissance man. Yet Petrarch was also deeply religious, concerned about his own salvation and the defense of orthodoxy. His writings were often marked by reference to Christian literature— Augustine's *Confessions* was one of his favorite works—and Christian dogma. For Petrarch, however, piety did not mean self-denial or self-abasement before the mystery and mastery of God; he saw self-fulfillment as a Christian duty. Petrarch did not consider the things of the world to be works of the devil. He valued worldly things and man himself as evidences of the divine on Earth. For Petrarch, concern with himself and with humanity was truly Christian.

As a classicist Petrarch gained an unparalleled reputation in his own day, and although by the refined standards of the later Renaissance his Latin was less than pure Ciceronian, he was the foremost man of letters in fourteenth-century Italy. He was an avid manuscript hunter and had an impressive library. Unable to learn Greek for lack of a teacher, he nonetheless valued his manuscripts of Plato's writings and was active in the search for translators and teachers of Greek. Petrarch was not merely concerned with the language and style of the classics, however; he found the Stoicism and civic patriotism of Cicero and other great Romans wholly in keeping with the ideal behavior of a Christian gentleman and citizen.

The greatest of Petrarch's associates was Giovanni Boccaccio (1313–75), another eager manuscript hunter and Latin stylist. Like Petrarch and Dante, Boccaccio had his perpetually unsuccessful love affair. But Boccaccio's love, even more than Petrarch's, was a love of frustrated desire involving little idealization. His passion was expressed not only in admiration of his beloved but in the bitterness of betrayal.

Boccaccio thought of himself as primarily a Latin poet, but his greatest contribution to European literature was the *Decameron*. Written in vernacular prose, the *Decameron* is a series of stories told by a group of young women and gentlemen who have gone to the hills outside Florence to escape the plague. There is little apparent didactic purpose to the tales. Some are funny, some are sad, and many are marked with satire or ribaldry. Their major purpose was not to educate but to entertain.

Writings in the vernacular did not play the major role in the literature of the time. Both Petrarch and Boccaccio spent the greater part of their energies cultivating their Latin and their knowledge of classical literature. Throughout the fourteenth and fifteenth centuries the main drive of Italian culture was in the direction of classical studies. In the universities, chairs of rhetoric were established so that scholars might lecture on the classical masterpieces, on the style and grace of the language and the worthiness of the ideas set forth by the great classical authors. The ability to speak and write properly was the distinctive mark of an educated man, and in the hands of men like Petrarch, classical Latin once more became a supple and graceful vehicle of expression.

The study of Greek was more difficult for the Italians, since teachers were rare and complete Greek texts almost unknown at the beginning of the Renaissance. After 1400, chairs for the study of Greek were established in most Italian universities, and subsequently good Latin translations of Greek works began to appear. Later, after Constantinople fell to the Turks in 1453, many Greek scholars migrated to Italy. Their learning and the manuscripts they brought with them made a substantial contribution to classical studies.

The rarity of complete and accurate manuscripts of the most important works of antiquity led to a search for manuscripts that took scholars to Byzantium and to monasteries all over Europe. When manuscripts were located, they were often in poor condition. Classical scholars were forced to become experts in textual criticism, collecting and collating available manuscripts to put together as complete and accurate a text as possible. Perhaps the greatest expert on the critical evaluation of manuscripts was Lorenzo Valla (died 1457), who brooked no compromise with the evidence presented in the texts. He proved conclusively, for example, that the Donation of Constantine was a medieval forgery. Even the rage of ecclesiastical officials did not deter Valla from publishing the conclusions derived from his study of textual evidence. The groundwork of modern philology and textual criticism was laid by the scholars of the Renaissance.

Classical literature as we know it today was first assembled by Renaissance scholars. The possession of complete and accurate manuscripts of many ancient thinkers, including Cicero, Plato, and Aristotle, had a profound impact on the study of the classical authors. Many writers had previously been known to the Middle Ages only through one or two of their works, and even Aristotle, whose major works had been translated in the thirteenth century, now became better known as the full corpus of his writing was made available. With full texts at hand, it was possible for the first time for scholars to evaluate critically the writings of the great authors of antiquity. The result was often a revolutionary change in attitude toward their works.

A consequence of the impact of the New Learning was the enhancement of the reputation of Plato. In the mid-fifteenth century, the Platonic corpus was successfully assimilated into humanist thought through the work of Marsilio Ficino (died 1499). Under the patronage of Cosimo de'Medici, Ficino founded the Florentine Academy, an informal school of writers and artists that was devoted to the full comprehension and assimilation of the works of Plato. Ficino himself made the most successful synthesis of the philosophy of Plato, asserting that there was one universal truth and that all valid philosophies partook of at least a part of it. Ficino's interpretation of the Platonic universe was ideally suited to give a philosophical underpinning to the humanistic view of man. Ficino believed that the human soul lay midway between the carnal and the divine and could choose between the lower and the higher course.

The greatest follower of Ficino, Pico della Mirandola (died 1494), carried his teacher's belief in the compatibility of all great philosophical and theological systems to a new extreme. Pico lived only thirty-one years, but became one of the most learned men of his day, mastering Hebrew as well as Greek and Latin. He then embarked upon a synthesis of all knowledge into one system, asserting that Christian, Jewish, and pagan thought did not contradict one another in essentials. Pico was a keen student of the Jewish Kabbalah.

The humanist philosophy was wholly compatible with the outlook of the Italian upper class. The secular educational system developing in Italian cities was directed toward education in the humanities—that is, in art and letters—to prepare the young man of good family to take his place in society. The young man's goal was not to become a highly trained scholar, but to develop the proper social values and the right forms of expression. He was more concerned with ethics than with philosophy or theology. The search for truth was an accepted value, but it was not isolated from secular concerns. Rather, the student was supposed to become a man of affairs, a citizen who took an active part in public matters. With a few notable exceptions, even professional scholars and teachers did not exclude themselves from public life; they were in great demand as secretaries and ambassadors.

The secular and classical attitudes that characterized humanist thought, and the examples of the Italian city-states, exerted a profound influence on the development of political theory in the fourteenth and fifteenth centuries. Thomas Aquinas had asserted a fundamental harmony between the temporal state and the divine. Renaissance thinkers amended Aquinas to perceive the state as an end in itself, with its own purpose. The first treatise on political theory by a Renaissance thinker was the *Monarchy* of Dante. Dante saw the state as an essentially secular institution whose independence from spiritual authority was essential to its well-being.

In 1324 the appearance of the *Defender of the Peace* of Marsilio of Padua brought forth a storm of controversy that did not die down for over a century. Marsilio's beliefs were tinged with Averroism (which he imbibed while a student and teacher at the University of Paris), leading him to assert the absolute separation of the secular and the spiritual, and he was vehemently anticlerical. He denied the authority of the pope and of the church in secular affairs on the ground that these were purely temporal concerns, outside the jurisdiction of the papacy. He further held that the absolute authority of the pope was a tyrannous usurpation and that the supreme authority in the church lay with the entire community of believers.

In the more positive aspects of his work, Marsilio relied heavily upon Aristotle, asserting that the proper end of the state was the provision of peace and security for its citizens. Marsilio was a thoroughgoing republican, defining the law as the expression of the will of the weightier (that is, worthier, wealthier) part of the citizenry and the true expression of the common good. Men as individuals were prone to evil, but the collective opinion of the citizens must necessarily result in the common good. In his voluntarist concept of law, Marsilio recognized the need to provide some other principle upon which the state could demand obedience if it did not claim to be the expression of divine will. He asserted that the transcendent end of the state—the common good—commanded the obedience of the citizens and that the consent of the citizens bound them to obey the laws, in theory and in practice. Thus Marsilio laid the foundation for the modern doctrine of sovereignty.

Although the departure from the clerical view of the state preoccupied much of Renaissance thought, the political experience of the Italian city-states was another important influence on the Renaissance concept of government. After Florence had successfully withstood the invasion of the Milanese tyrants, for example, the Florentine Republic became the subject of numerous works that glorified its history and propounded the political principles of republican Rome. Florentine writers believed that the public spirit of the citizens—inherited from their distant ancestors in the Roman Republic—and the excellence of the republican constitution were responsible for the political strength and cultural glories of Florence. The writing of Cicero and the example set by Brutus and Cassius, the murderers of the tyrant Caesar, were woven into the political ideology of the Florentine government. This concept of the high moral aim of the state in republican Florence had its parallel in the political ideology of the podestàs of Italy, who claimed to be the perpetuators of the Pax Romana of the age of Augustus. The tyrants held that only a universal monarch (or at least a national Italian monarchy) could ensure the peace necessary for the earthly well-being of mankind. Neither Florence nor the tyrannies, however, consistently practiced their high-sounding principles.

Despite the theoretical pronouncements of humanist writers, the political life of the Italian city-states was as sordid as any in Europe, and a much more pessimistic view of the state dominated the writings of the greatest political thinker of the Renaissance, Niccolo Machiavelli (1469–1527). Machiavelli wrote about politics from firsthand experience as a Florentine diplomat and administrator. In addition, he had read the works of Aristotle and the writings of Latin authors on the history of Rome and the political ideals of republican Rome. His works—among them *The Prince,* dedicated to Lorenzo the Magnificent as a manual of government; the *Discourses,* a commentary on Roman history written to illustrate the political principles that could be learned from the past; and the *History of*

Florence—express a purely secular attitude. Beyond that, they show Machiavelli as a man who distrusted all ideals. He strove to show things as they were, not as they ought to be, "for how we live is so far removed from how we ought to live, that he who abandons what is done for what ought to be done, will rather learn to bring about his own ruin than his preservation."

Machiavelli thought that religion was necessary in the state to secure the obedience of subjects and that the corrupt example of the papal court had destroyed the morals of the Italian people. For Machiavelli, the struggle for power was the essence of politics. The only constant in human affairs was perpetual change. The most adaptable political organism was the most durable. The state was not a reflection of hierarchical order or theological principles; its appropriateness and durability depended not upon moral purpose, but on the successful monopoly of power.

Machiavelli had a fundamentally pessimistic—or realistic—view of human nature, tempered by a firm belief that man was the most creative force in the universe and, in fact, the only force for effecting change. He did not commit himself on the ideal form of government any more than on its moral end, since any government was only a transient organism that eventually would disintegrate through its own weakness or the challenge of a superior force. In *The Prince* he asserted that only the strong government of a single man could save Italy from the throes of political chaos, but in the *Discourses* he seemed to favor a republican form of government, suggesting that government by the people was more likely to be free from abuse than was government by a prince.

To Machiavelli, it was not the form of authority but its techniques that determined the durability of a state. Governmental decisions must be based solely on the interest of the state. Whereas one was morally bound in private affairs, in matters of state no moral considerations could be allowed. Machiavelli's open advocacy of the use of harsh methods, if necessary, to preserve the state brought him notoriety as a political thinker, but more important for the development of political theory was his conception of the state as an independent entity with its own principles of operation.

New attitudes, ideas, and techniques poured forth from Italy in the fourteenth and fifteenth centuries in the visual arts. As in philosophy, the general cultural currents of the Italian Renaissance and the genius of a number of artists gave rise to new styles and themes that represented a break with the medieval past. The first major departure from the medieval tradition was the concept of a painting as a window through which a three-dimensional scene is visible, rather than as an opaque surface offering only two-dimensional effects. The Florentine artist Giotto (died 1336) moved significantly away from two-dimensional symbols, representing his figures not as flat images but as rounded beings related to each other in space. The Florentine school of painters soon leaped ahead of the rest of Italy in artistic production, and some of the artists made significant technical contributions, but Giotto had no outstanding immediate successor. In fact, in the latter part of the fourteenth century there was a marked reversion to a more medieval type of perspective and theme, perhaps in reaction to the Black Death and the financial crisis of that period. At the end of the century, after a definite interruption, painters again took up the new style where Giotto had left it and advanced Giotto's experiments.

The concept of depth, or perspective, was developed in Italy and passed on to the miniature painters of France and the Low Countries, to become one of the elements of the International Gothic style that predominated throughout Europe in the mid-fourteenth century. In the first half of the fifteenth century a more far-reaching departure from medieval style took place with the formalization of the mathematical theory of perspective by another generation of great artists. This step was first taken by Filippo Brunelleschi (1377–1446) and further developed by Leon Battista Alberti (died 1472), who used the theories of classical art and architecture as the basis for extensive writings on the techniques of composition and construction. Henceforth, perspective was considered a mathematical problem that could be solved in a precise manner. For the approximation of perspective by the ancients and the crude attempts at representing depth by Byzantine and Romanesque artists, the Renaissance artists substituted theoretical and technical knowledge that allowed them to represent perspective accurately. Romanesque and Byzantine traditions retained an important place in Renaissance art, and the innovations of great Flemish painters like the Master of Flemalle, Jan van Eyck, and Roger van der Weyden were assimilated by the Italian artists.

Renaissance classicism in art was a complex phenomenon whose contours were shaped by the interaction of the genius of a number of great artists and by various currents of classical and contemporary influence. The interrelationship between the different forms of artistic endeavor—architecture, sculpture, and painting—had a profound impact on the course of this development. The impact of the classical conception of form and subject was first seen in sculpture and architecture. The figures in Ghiberti's east doors of the baptistery in Florence (later called *The Gates of Paradise*) are scriptural in subject but genuinely classical in style and mood. The statue of David by Donatello (1386–1466) is in many ways a monument to the spirit of classicism. *David* is one of many statues of the hero who slew Goliath—an extremely popular theme in Florentine art—but it is revolutionary as a study of the nude human form, a masterful example of the ideal of natural grace, realistically portrayed, which characterized ancient sculpture.

As architects, Brunellischi and Alberti, whose works on perspective had such an important impact on Italian art, studied ancient writings, as well as the ruins of the ancient world that were omnipresent in Rome. Developments in architecture were characterized by the incorporation of classical forms, such as the dome of the cathedral at Florence by Brunelleschi and the use of the triumphal arch in the façade of the cathedral at Rimmini by Alberti. Renaissance architects worked within carefully established principles of proportion and construction, based upon classical models. Gothic cathedrals were in a sense never finished; succeeding generations continued to make whatever accretions they found useful and desirable, and the result was often the juxtaposition of several different architectural styles and a huge building whose general outlines obeyed no set rules of proportion or construction. The Renaissance church, on the other hand, was a unified structure in which the principles of symmetry and harmony precluded the miscellany of Gothic architecture.

Much of the early influence of classicism in painting came as a result of the incorporation of concepts borrowed from sculpture. Masaccio's portrayal of St. John disrobing in the desert is an example of a representation of the human figure which is fundamentally sculptural and classical in conception. The increasing realism that characterized the treatment of the human form and face found its inspiration in the examples provided by sculpture and by the Flemish painters, who developed the techniques of portraiture.

The most important step toward the assimilation of an overriding classical spirit into painting was taken not in Rome or Florence, but in the northern part of Italy. The painter Andrea Mantegna (1431–1506) moved away from the Gothic and Netherlandish tradition to a harsh naturalism. The background to his figures is filled not with delicate detail, but with barren rocks and leafless trees. In his painting of the Crucifixion, the harsh, rocky background reinforces the agony of Christ on the cross and the desolation of the mourners below.

The high point of the development of Renaissance painting did not come until the late fifteenth century in the work of Leonardo da Vinci (1452–1519). Leonardo was a kind of universal genius who dabbled in almost every aspect of learning. To his patrons he advertised his proficiency in painting, in the construction of siege machines, and in many other fields. His notebooks contain speculations on anatomy, biology, and aeronautics, as well as on new techniques of painting. His experimental bent led him to try new ways of producing paint, but the medium he used was not durable, and a number of his paintings deteriorated. However, his experiments also resulted in the development of the technique of blending light and dark colors known as *sfumato,* so beautifully exhibited in the *Virgin of the Rocks.*

Leonardo's genius extended far beyond the technical aspects of his art. The subtle shades of expression on the faces he portrayed first made his work outstanding. His *Mona Lisa* is only the most famous example of his ability to portray human character. In *The Last Supper,* Leonardo took a decisive step forward in his solution of the problem of composition. In most paintings of that famous scene, the impression is simply one of a group of holy men, usually with Judas sitting across the table to symbolize his separation from the rest of the apostles. Leonardo's *Last Supper* is composed of groups of figures whose facial expressions illustrate their relationship to the central figure, Christ. For example, Judas sits beside Christ, his posture and expression revealing the horror with which he contemplates the crime he will commit.

Leonardo articulated the underlying spirit of Renaissance art by asserting that a painting ought to be judged by its verisimilitude with the object or scene portrayed. His anatomical studies gave him a new understanding of the structure of the human body, and unlike most of his contemporaries, he used real models to portray accurately the folds of garments and other details.

The achievements of Renaissance art cannot be delineated by a description of the work of its greatest artists; it was the scope and volume of artistic endeavor that marked the era as paramount in the history of art. The names of hundreds of artists fill in the contours of the complex development that took place in the fourteenth, fifteenth, and early sixteenth centuries. Many who would have stood out from their contemporaries as artistic giants in any other period appear as minor figures in the Renaissance. Concomitant to the expansion of artistic endeavor was the vastly increased demand for all kinds of art by cities, rich men, and popes in fourteenth- and fifteenth-century Italy. The artist had hitherto been an anonymous craftsman in the service of the church, possibly with some patronage from nobles or kings. The Italian artist of the Renaissance remained a craftsman in many respects, often working as a painter, sculptor, or architect upon demand and even producing more marginal artistic works, such as decorative pieces; but the value that the Renaissance placed upon art and artistic achievement elevated his social position. The successful artist became a man of wealth and fame who could take his place in the upper ranks of society.

It is difficult to find in Renaissance culture a particular theory or principle that is wholly original. The leading tenets of the Renaissance view of man, society, and the universe can be found in various strains of the classical and medieval traditions. But this derivative quality of the particular ingredients of Renaissance culture does not detract from the achievement of the Italian city-states of the fourteenth and fifteenth centuries. The Renaissance artists and writers sifted and scrutinized the classical and medieval traditions for the best that had been thought and said in the world and synthesized the ideas that seemed most in accordance with the nature of humanity into an integrated philosophy and style of life that dominated the culture of the early modern world. During the three centuries after 1500, western civilization lived off the intellectual capital of the Italian Renaissance, and the philosophy, political theory, art, and literature of the early modern world were extrapolations from one or another aspect of Renaissance culture.

Even in the modern industrial society of the past century, the humanist tradition that was crystallized in Renaissance Italy had been the essential core of the higher culture of the West. Modern society has spawned a mass culture that departs from Renaissance humanism in significant ways, and modern thought in the realms of science, social theory, and psychology has opened vistas that were largely beyond the ken of fifteenth-century Italian thinkers. But these new doctrines have not been integrated into a systematic theory and style of life that can compete with the humanist tradition in unity and completeness.

The most significant achievement of the Italian Renaissance was its establishment of a culture that suited the way of life of the now-literate nobility and the now-leisured high bourgeoisie while perpetuating most of what was valuable in classical and medieval civilization. Put another way, Renaissance culture allowed the lord or businessman to believe that his pursuit of power, status, and wealth was justified, that he had a right to indulge his feelings. But at the same time it placed these private interests and individual sensibilities within the context of a universal and political order and directed them to social needs. This was no mean achievement: Indeed, this balance—tense or even awkward as it may often be—is fundamental to modern life and is why the Italian Renaissance may rightly be regarded as the dawn of the modern world, even though the humanist scholars failed to reach modern science and the Italian merchants and entrepreneurs did not attain the Industrial Revolution.

Looked at from the other direction, classical culture and medieval culture both fell short of harmonizing private interests and personal sensibilities with social concerns and the natural order, although they included all these ingredients. Faced with individualism, both classical and medieval society tended to panic, to try to force the individual back into the community or subject him to hierarchical authority. The Athenians executed Socrates, and medieval society abused Abelard, but Renaissance Italians lionized Petrarch and Lorenzo de'Medici. This bald contrast is justified insofar as we may conclude from it that Renaissance culture was not necessarily more productive of individuality and sensibility than was classical or medieval culture, but that it was more prepared to come to terms with individualism; to accord it an impregnable value; and to believe optimistically that it could enrich society and illuminate natural order, rather than threaten them.

Renaissance culture deserves to be termed "secular," although not in the sense that the humanists were unbelievers or anticlerical even in fundamental matters. The humanists were critical of "the shallow Churchman," as Aeneas Silvius (Pope Pius II), himself a great humanist, said. The humanists were themselves generally well trained in theology and scholasticism. They thought that the intellectuals of the church had become abstract and narrow, divorced from the reality of human love for God. They believed that many bishops were corrupt and disgracefully ignorant. However, this belief did not make them enemies of the church; it made them passionate advocates of the renewal and modernization of the church.

Yet Renaissance culture must be termed secular because it gave value to man's secular concerns and finally justified worldly endeavor not as a regrettable weakness, but as something fundamental to and glorious in human life. Modernity required this celebration of man's involvement with his feelings and his participation in nature and society. Medieval men could never quite escape from a sense of guilt, or at least regret, about their natural, secular actions; Renaissance culture was a liberation from this guilt and restraint.

The advance toward a new secular culture that liberated and justified sensibility was inaugurated by the romantic revolution of the twelfth century. But there is certainly a heightened and more explicit expression of this attitude in Dante's writings. Petrarch confronted the antagonism between soul and body, between the spiritual and secular worlds, between the Christian and classical traditions, more directly than did Dante. Although he described this conflict in apologetic and guilt-ridden terms, he could not deny that he was intensely conscious of his total humanity:

> My incorruptible treasure and the superior part of my soul is with Christ; but because of the frailties and burdens of mortal life. . . . I cannot, I confess, lift up, however ardently I should wish, the inferior parts of my soul . . . and cannot make them cease to cling to earth. [Trans. E. Cassirer]

For Petrarch, classical culture was the road to emancipation from the trammels that medieval theology placed upon human nature. For him, ancient Rome was the generator and symbol of a better society and a more humane philosophy than that which prevailed in his own day. His desire for a fuller and finer appreciation of human life is expressed in a longing for return of the Golden Age of the Roman Empire:

> Verily Rome was greater, and its remains are greater, than I had supposed. I marvel now, not that the world was conquered by this city, but that it was conquered so late. [Trans. E. H. Tatham]

By the fifteenth century the philosophy of humanism, expressed paradoxically by Dante and defensively by Petrarch, was unequivocally enunciated in Florence's intellectual circles. Never before or since has the dignity of man been more emphatically stressed than in Pico's oration on this theme:

> I have come to understand why man is the most fortunate of creatures and consequently worthy of all admiration and what precisely is that rank which is his lot in the universal chain of Being—a rank to be envied not only by the brutes but even by the stars and by minds beyond this world. . . . Man is rightly called and judged a great miracle and a wonderful creature indeed. . . . The saying . . . "know thyself" urges and encourages us to the investigation of all nature, of which the nature of man is both the connecting link and, so to speak, the "mixed bowl." For he who knows himself knows all things. . . . [Trans. E. Cassirer]

Pico retained the ancient and medieval doctrine of the great chain of being, but he rejected the implication of that doctrine by using it to point not to man's limitations, but to just the opposite. Since man stands at the center of the chain of being, he combines all things in the universe in himself. Man is the most wonderful and complete of all creatures. To understand human nature is to know all things. Man is not only the measure of all things; he is an end in himself, and to cultivate human qualities is to feel and understand the universe. No more radical celebration of humanity has ever been made.

We have arrived at the theory of liberal humanism, which holds that the resources of human society are so vast as to be virtually unlimited. There is no need for violence, poverty, and misery in society because the human mind is powerful enough to devise remedies for these ills and to establish a community in which all men will have the freedom to cultivate the sublime and beautiful that are potential in every human being.

If one looks for the essence of Italian Renaissance humanism, one finds it in the field of education. Both the pedagogical theory and the curriculum that prevailed in Italian humanist circles in the fifteenth century exclusively dominated European education to the end of the nineteenth century, and the humanist influence is still crucial in our better schools and universities. As against the medieval university, the humanists contended that the liberal arts should be not a cursory preparation for advanced professional studies, but the main concern of any educational institution. Through the development of the mind in literary—chiefly classical—studies, the student would be so equipped with broad knowledge and wisdom, and his reason and feelings would be so finely tuned, that he could undertake any further investigation he wanted.

Put in today's terms, the humanist view of education is that universities should be concerned with teaching and communicating with undergraduates. Professors should be excellent teachers, with broad interests. The curriculum should be concerned with the culture of the past and problems of the present and should be directly relevant to the student's professional experience and social commitment. Research and professional training should either be assigned a decidedly secondary role on the campus, relegated to separate institutes or professional schools, or abandoned as socially useless or reactionary. The struggle in the universities between the humanists and the "scholastics," as Petrarch called them, still goes on.

The Renaissance humanists often despaired of reforming the universities with their entrenched faculty devoted to specialized research and narrow professional training. They turned their attention to secondary education and reformed or newly established preparatory schools—nearly always for boys only—for students aged eight to sixteen. These schools were where the mind of the new generation could be molded in language and literature, in ethics and history, and prepared for leadership in diverse careers and callings.

The curriculum and pedagogy that the Renaissance humanists had established all over western Europe by 1500 was the foundation of the French lycée, the German gymnasium, and the English "public" (nonclerical) school of modern times. In these schools was crystallized the cultural heritage of the classical and medieval worlds that achieved a universe of discourse, a common language (usually Latin and French), and a standardized symbolic culture in which the European elite from Edinburgh to Warsaw, from Stockholm to Naples, was trained in the next half millennium. Combined with continued faith in the Christian tradition as articulated by Augustine, as communicated in Jerome's Bible, as rationalized by Thomism, as synthesized by Dante, this was to be the essence of western civilization down to the early decades of the twentieth century. Although eroded at the edges, challenged by radical political and cultural ideals, damaged by materialism and democracy, this medieval heritage, transmitted through Renaissance humanism and its educational and literate traditions, had not lost its intrinsic vitality and social value at the end of the second Christian millennium.

III. Medievalism and the Middle Ages

The cultivation of the Italian Renaissance in the age of Machiavelli and Leonardo da Vinci, around 1500, has traditionally been regarded as the endpoint of the Middle Ages. There are several additional justifications for viewing 1500 as the termination of the medieval era. The "splitting of the faith," as the Germans call it, the outbreak of the Protestant Reformation, and the permanent division of the western Church, was also about to begin. By 1500 the transatlantic colonial penetration of the Americas by the Iberian peoples was under way. Following upon their successful circumnavigation of Africa and the opening up of India and the Far East to European trade, it meant a radical turning away from a cultural and mercantile focus on the Mediterranean and a drastic alteration in the pattern of the European economy. By 1500 the printing press with movable type, which had been introduced in Germany around 1470, was being widely employed. A revolution in communication was under way.

These are all good reasons to regard the end of the fifteenth century as the end of the Middle Ages, just as the accession of a Christian Roman emperor in the early fourth century marks the beginning of medieval times. But just as the medieval beginning can also be claimed to lie with the barbarian invasions of the early fifth century, so can not-absurd arguments be made for other dates to mark the end of the Middle Ages, all the way from the French monarchy's destruction of the papacy in the early fourteenth century to the political and industrial revolutions of the eighteenth century.

In determining the start and end of eras, there is room for diverse judgments. But all things considered, there are grounds for thinking of 1500 as the most conceptually persuasive medieval terminus. The increased secularism of Renaissance learning, coupled with the reivified monarchial states and their ruthless exercise of the balance of power, the Protestant Reformation, the introduction of the printing press, the migrations, imperialism, and economic changes attendant upon overseas ventures to the Americas and East Asia, determined structural and cultural changes of major proportions that deeply penetrated the institutional formation and the mentality of the European peoples. What Johan Huizinga said in 1919 of the end of the fifteenth century remains true:

> A high and strong culture is declining, but at the same time and in the same sphere new things are being born. The tide is turning, the tone of life is about to change.

In the past three decades, aside from much attention to family and woman's history, research and publication in the medieval field concentrated primarily on the fourteenth and fifteenth centuries. This focus has been partly for professional reasons. In European archives are several tons of unpublished manuscripts, records, and books of the period 1270–1500, and provided that they can read the difficult script of the period, Ph.D. candidates who are seeking subjects for dissertations or untenured assistant professors who need to write a quick second book, working from unpublished materials is prudent because anything coherent reported in them meets academic requirements of a contribution to knowledge. Furthermore, those who conduct research in Florence, Venice, Paris, or London can get research grants to live in a desirable place for a year or two.

There are, however, intrinsic intellectual reasons for this recent intensive work on the late Middle Ages. So little was known three decades ago about that era, and it seemed so important as a transition to the culture and society of the sixteenth century that was widely assumed to be the start of the modern world (an assumption no longer secure), that the sinking of deep research shafts in one, often relatively narrow aspect of the late Middle Ages was amply justified.

The quality of detailed research on the late Middle Ages is high, but the overall result has been disappointing. No paradigm or overall interpretation of the period 1270–1500 has yet been offered that integrates the multiple facets of the culture and society of western Europe. Even in the richly explored Italian Renaissance, historians are still mulling over the paradigms propounded by Jacob Burckhardt in 1860 and Erwin Panofsky in the 1950s, rather than formulating new models. The two most interesting general views on the late Middle Ages (neither translated into English) remain the books of Rudolf Stadelman (1928) and Augustin Renaudet (1939). Perhaps the comprehensive overview propounded in these older books was attainable precisely because their authors were not distracted by a flood of detailed monographs and could reflect on the general perspectives.

Without a new paradigm that integrates diverse aspects of the late Middle Ages, there remain seven obvious paradoxes in the history of that era. The first paradox is in the political sphere. In the late Middle Ages there was plenty of discussion of what we call constitutional liberalism and a much greater visibility of a high bourgeoisie, who were the most persistent advocates and implementors of this progressive doctrine in later centuries. Yet the main trend in late medieval political life was the resurgence of aristocratic power and the high visibility of the great nobles in politics and government. In other words, neither the rebellions of peasants and artisans nor middle-class constitutionalism had a significant political outcome. Europe's political system remained hierarchic and oligarchic, and the hierarchies and oligarchs became more prominent on the political scene between 1270 and 1500. At the end of the period, European monarchs were still regularly enriching and yielding power to the high nobility. Even in Italy the great merchant families modeled their political behavior on the northern grandees (and the ancient Roman aristocracy), and far from seeking to introduce constitutional liberalism and a modicum of representative democracy, they turned themselves into hereditary nobility.

The second paradox was in the social sphere. The Black Death, which carried off 25–40 percent of the population, created a labor shortage, ended the vestiges of serfdom in western Europe, and increased the number of wealthy peasant families. The demographic collapse alleviated the slowly developing food shortage that the overpopulated Europe of the early fourteenth century had experienced. But aside from this consequence, the biomedical holocaust had no impact. It should have inspired a vast theological and moral literature probing the meaning of the disaster. There was almost none of that. Instead there was the *Decameron,* in which the Black Death served as the pretext for entertainment and soft-core pornography.

The third paradox of late medieval history concerns the church. There were enormous learning, intelligence, organizational skill, and speculative imagination of all kinds in the late medieval church. Intrinsically the church was *not* in decline. In terms of brainpower, information, and literary and artistic capability, it was on the upswing, if anything. Yet the church could not resolve its basic institutional problems, either at the papal level or at the local level, where a variety of parsons and friars competed intensely with one another and brought lay opprobrium on themselves.

The fourth paradox also involves the church. Never before and rarely since was there such intense evangelical feeling and popular enthusiasm about the Christian message among ordinary people. Instead of exulting in and channeling this piety and devotion, the top structure of European intellectuals in the late fifteenth century chose to condemn it as being infected with superstition and idolatry and formulated programs to eradicate much of it in the name of purifying reforms.

The fifth paradox again refers to the intellectuals and scholars. There was intense cultivation of every aspect of classical learning except the two that would have had the greatest social impact—mathematical literacy and republicanism. The former would have ignited the scientific revolution, the latter a democratic upheaval.

The sixth paradox refers to the learned professions. The legal profession became thoroughly professionalized, and English common law assumed the organizational form and behavior patterns that still exist in the United States and Canada, as well as in Britain, for better or worse. Physicians and surgeons made no progress in their professional standing or in improving their contribution to society. Instead they did a lot of damage. Panicked by the Black Death, whose cause mystified them, they convinced Europeans to close their windows and sheath them with heavy drapes to keep out the "bad air" that, they alleged, brought plague and to stop taking baths, which, they claimed, opened the pores to the dread disease. This quack medicine was not completely revised until the twentieth century.

The seventh paradox was ecological. Europeans had lived in the midst of vast forests throughout the earlier medieval centuries. After 1250 they became so skilled in deforestation that by 1500 they were running short of wood for heating and cooking. They were faced with a nutritional decline because of the elimination of the generous supply of wild game that had inhabited the now-disappearing forests, which throughout medieval times had provided the staple of their carnivorous high-protein diet. By 1500 Europe was on the edge of a fuel and nutritional disaster for which it was saved in the sixteenth century only by the burning of soft coal (which, in turn, started air pollution) and the cultivation of potatoes and maize (Indian corn as fodder for cattle) that were imported from America.

These paradoxes make the late Middle Ages an intriguing but not an edifying sight. They can be viewed, indeed, as the start of "early modern Europe," which continued until the political, industrial, and liberal and scientific revolutions of the eighteenth century. This early Modern Europe continued to be marked by the paradoxes, confusions, and crises that distinguished the fourteenth and fifteenth centuries.

Because of the disorder of the period 1300–1500, those who admire the medieval heritage and seek some kind of revival of medievalism in our time look to the earlier centuries from St. Augustine and St. Benedict to St. Bernard of Clairvaux and St. Thomas Aquinas for inspiration, contrasted with the materialism and decadence of the closing years of the twentieth century. They see in the medieval centuries a society in which people's lives were rarely programmed by the centralizing bureaucratic state and in which people therefore had to make their own decisions, communal and personal, without the dictates of political and legal power. They see a culture that arose out of chaos, violence, and cruelty by the application of learned intelligence to social behavior. They see a world that recognized the capacity of individuals to love God and human beings and turned this love into wonderful artistic and literary expressions. They see a world that used reason and tradition to integrate society with the environment and created prosperous and stable communities. They look to the medievalism of those times for a model of religious devotion and moral commitment that led also to the founding of great universities and the support of learning, art, and imaginative literature.

The medieval world we know was far from perfect. Life expectancy was short, and disease was mostly incontestable. It was a world burdened by royal autocracy and social hierarchy inherited from ancient times. Its piety and devotion were affected by fanaticism and a potential for persecution. Its intellectuals were given to too abstract and not enough practical thinking. But it exhibited as elevated a culture, as peaceful a community, as benign a political system, as high-minded and popular a faith as the world has ever seen.

In the 1990s there is a difference of opinion among scholars as to when this good and beautiful Middle Ages ended. The Austrian liberal

Catholic historian Frederick Heer proposed in the late 1950s that 1200 was the medieval dividing line between expansionary freedom and contracting repression. A younger generation of historians, including R. I. Moore and Jeffrey Richards in Britain and John Boswell in the United States, have confirmed this dividing line on the ground that around 1200 medieval Europe became what Moore dramatically termed a persecuting society. It is asserted that at the beginning of the thirteenth century the repressive marginalization of what are today called minorities—heretics, Jews, women, leapers, witches, and homosexuals—was much intensified and draconically institutionalized.

This book has recognized this contracting aspect of thirteenth-century culture and society. But it has also regarded the effort of Innocent III's papacy politically, Thomas Aquinas intellectually, and the Franciscans emotionally to fashion a new consensus down to around 1270 as still within the continuing parameters of a creative and expansive central era in medieval culture. It is possible that had this consensus been realized and built upon in the late Middle Ages that in time open horizons would have prevailed and the persecuting tendencies would have been mitigated. But after 1270 things fell apart, and the medieval center no longer held. Thus, in spite of remarkable efforts at constitutional liberalism in the late Middle Ages and the progressive qualities of Renaissance humanism, what, from our perspective, was a confrontational and authoritarian intolerance toward minorities did indeed flow out of social anxiety and political rationalization soon after 1200 and was not reversed.

Therefore, arguments that are derived from different criteria can lead, with equal persuasiveness, to the conclusion that the good and beautiful Middle Ages ended either around 1200 or 1270. At some point in the thirteenth century Europe entered a time of disintegration and conflict that, by 1500, had brought about the waning of medieval civilization.

THE MIDDLE AGES ON FILM

Films are not a substitute for history books, but films can evoke the ambience and sensibility, as well as the visual locus, of the Middle Ages, not only in a supplementary reinforcing and entertaining manner, but sometimes in a distinctly perceptive and persuasive way. Here are the ten best films ever made with a medieval context, ranked approximately in order of merit. The story lines of three of them occur outside the conventional medieval era, but nevertheless describe scenes and events that are still medieval. One takes place in Japan, but in a social context that directly parallels the European situation. It will be noted that among the directors of these films are some of the greatest directors of all time: Eisenstein, Bergman, Kurosawa, Olivier, Pasolini, Russell.

1. *The Seventh Seal*
Ingmar Bergman's incomparable masterpiece, set in Sweden at the time of the Black Death, is in a class by itself when it comes to evoking medieval sensibility about life and death.

2. *Ran*
Akira Kurosawa's film is loosely based on Shakespeare's *King Lear* and is set in late medieval Japan. It perfectly captures the violence and beauty of the chivalric world.

3. *Henry V*
Laurence Olivier made this film of Shakespeare's play in 1944 as a patriotic gesture, and hence he cut two scenes in which the Bard accurately indicated the downside of the Hundred Years' War. These scenes were restored in Kenneth Branagh's neo-Brechtian 1989 version. Yet Olivier's version is much closer than Branagh's to the ambience of the fifteenth century, and he had the whole Irish army to fight the Battle of Agincourt.

4. *The Name of the Rose*
This careful and expensive adaptation of Umbert Eco's best-selling novel was a commercial failure despite a wonderful performance by Sean Connery as

a Franciscan friar modeled on William of Occam. If it had been explained to the history-ignorant audience at the beginning of the film that the pope and many Franciscans were at loggerheads in the fourteenth century, the film's plot would have made much more sense.

5. *Alexander Nevsky*

Sergei Eisenstein made this film in 1938 about the prince of Novograd's fight with the Teutonic knights as patriotic anti-German propaganda with Stalin's support. The film had to be suppressed during the era of the Hitler-Soviet pact, but it came back strong after the German invasion of the Soviet Union in 1941. Eisenstein's German expressionist 1920s kind of dramaturgy is a bit off-putting today, but it fits in well with the iconology of Byzantine and late medieval kingship.

6. *The Return of Martin Guerre*

This film depicts a crisis in an affluent peasant family in France in the early sixteenth century, based on the research of Princeton's Natalie Zemon Davis, who acted as historical adviser for this French production. The story closely follows the record of a court trial. The peasants are a bit too articulate for historical accuracy; at times the ambience seems more twentieth than sixteenth century.

7. *The Navigator*

About half this 1988 little-known New Zealand science fiction film is convincingly set in a northern English coal-mining village during the time of the Black Death and is obviously under Bergman's influence. It is closer to the reality of medieval peasant culture than is *The Return of Martin Guerre*.

8. *Black Robe*

This stunning French Canadian film, made in Quebec in 1990, about Jesuit missionaries among the Canadian aborigines in the early seventeenth century, is fiercely accurate and evocative of an important and underwritten segment of medieval church history—missionary work among the heathens on the frontier. Think of St. Boniface and the Frisians in the eighth century.

9. *The Gospel According to St. Matthew*

The life of Jesus, as written by Matthew, is bleakly depicted by the Italian Communist director Pier Pasolini. The result is much closer to late medieval Sicily, it is not surprising, than to ancient Judea.

10. *The Devils*

Ken Russell's characteristically over-the-top version of Aldous Huxley's novel about hysteria and witchcraft in early seventeenth century France nevertheless captures persuasively important aspects of the medieval religious experience. Even its remorseless anticlericalism replicates a prominent ingredient of late medieval culture.

RECOMMENDED READING

If you want to go further in medieval studies, you have an excellent feast before you. The medieval field is replete with masterful and accessible books that can be found in any good college library and are usually available from publishers. My book *Inventing the Middle Ages* (Morrow, 1991) will give you a painless introduction to the historiography of medieval studies and an intellectual roadmap of how twentieth-century medievalists think and why they do so.

A Short List (14 titles)

Here is a short reading program in medieval history that, if mastered, will make you well informed on the subject, so you can more than hold your own in any discussion about the European Middle Ages around the faculty lunch table, in the country club lounge, at a publishing house brainstorming session, in a church study group, or in an undergraduate or adult education seminar.

The full bibliographical listing for each book, including the publisher, is found in the Long List that follows. The books on this short list are all in print, most of them in paperback, and they can be ordered directly from the publisher or through your local bookstore.

The order listed here approximates the chronological sequence of the subjects the books are dealing with.

Peter Brown, *Augustine of Hippo*
Richard Krautheimer, *Rome, Profile of a City, 312–1308*
George Duby, *Early Growth of the European Economy*
John Marenbon, *Early Medieval Philosophy*
Pierre Riché, *Daily Life in the World of Charlemagne*
March Bloch, *Feudal Society*
Jonathan Riley-Smith, *A Short History of the Crusades*
R. W. Southern, *The Making of the Middle Ages*
Frank Barlow, *Thomas Becket*

David Knowles, *The Evolution of Medieval Thought*
Joseph Strayer, *On the Medieval Origins of the Modern State*
Jeffrey Richards, *Sex, Dissidence and Damnation: Minority Groups in the Middle Ages*
E. LeRoy Ladurie, *Montaillou*
Donald Howard, *Chaucer*

The Long List (143 titles)

Here is a core bibliography in medieval studies, expanded and updated from *Inventing the Middle Ages* (1991). A date given in square brackets at the end of the listing is the date of the original publication of the work if it has gone through two or more editions or copyrighted imprints or translations.

Abulafia, David. *Frederick II: A Medieval Emperor.* London: Allen Lane, Penguin Press, 1988.

Barlow, Frank. *Thomas Becket.* London: Widenfeld and Nicolson, 1986.

Baron, Hans. *In Search of Florentine Civic Humanism.* Princeton, N.J: Princeton University Press, 1988.

Baron, Salo Wittmayer. *A Social and Religious History of the Jews,* 2d ed. rev. Philadelphia: Jewish Publication Society, 1965 [vols. III–VIII, 1957]. Vols. III–IX.

Barraclough, Geoffrey. *The Origins of Modern Germany,* 3d ed. Oxford: Basil Blackwell, 1988 [1947].

Bartlett, Robert. *Trial by Fire and Water: The Medieval Judicial Order.* Oxford: Clarendon, 1988.

Bischoff, Bernard. *Latin Palaeography: Antiquity and the Middle Ages.* Translated by Dalbhi O. Croinin and David Ganz. New York: Cambridge University Press, 1990.

Bisson, Thomas N. *Medieval Crown of Aragon.* New York: Oxford University Press, 1986.

Blair, Peter Hunter. *An Introduction to Anglo-Saxon England.* New York: Cambridge University Press, 1966 [1956].

Bloch, Howard, R. *Etymologies and Genealogies: A Literary Anthropology of the French Middle Ages.* Chicago: University of Chicago Press, 1983.

Bloch, Marc. *Feudal Society.* Translated by I. A. Manyon, Andover Routledge, 1989 [1961]. Paperback, 2 vols. Chicago: University of Chicago Press, 1963.

Bolgar, Robert Ralph. *The Classical Heritage and Its Beneficiaries.* New York: Harper & Row, 1964 [1954].

Borst, Arno. *Medieval Worlds.* Chicago: University of Chicago Press, 1992.

Boswell, John. *Christianity, Social Tolerance, and Homosexuality: Gay People in Western Europe from the Beginning of the Christian Era to the Fourteenth Century.* Chicago: University of Chicago Press, 1980.

Brown, Peter Robert Lamont. *Augustine of Hippo: A Biography* New York: Dorset Press, 1986 [1967].

———. *Society and the Holy in Late Antiquity.* Berkeley: University of California Press, 1987.

Brucker, Gene A. *Renaissance Florence*. Berkeley: University of California Press, 1983 [1969].

Brundage, James A. *Law, Sex, and Society in Medieval Europe*. Chicago: University of Chicago Press, 1987.

Bury, John Bagnell. *The Invasion of Europe by the Barbarians*. New York: W. W. Norton, 1967 [1928].

Bynum, Caroline Walker, *Jesus as Mother: Studies in the Spirituality of the High Middle Ages*. Berkeley: University of California Press, 1982.

Caenegem, R. C. van. *The Birth of the English Common Law,* 2d ed. New York: Cambridge University Press, 1988 [1st ed., 1973].

Cambridge Economic History of Europe. Edited by Michael M. Postan et al., vols. I–II. New York: Cambridge University Press, 1966 [1941, 1952].

Cambridge History of Later Medieval Philosophy: From Aristotle to the Disintegration of Scholasticism. 1100–1600. Edited by Norman Kretzmann, Anthony Kenny, and Jan Pinbors. New York: Cambridge University Press, 1982.

Cameron, Evan, *The European Reformation*. New York: Oxford University Press, 1991.

Chenu, Marie Dominique. *Nature, Man, and Society in the Twelfth Century: Essays on the New Theological Perspectives in the Latin West*. Preface by Étienne Gilson. Selected, edited, and translated by Jerome Taylor and Lester K. Little. Chicago: University of Chicago Press, 1968.

Clanchy, Michael T. *From Memory to Written Record, England 1066–1307*. New York: Basil Blackwell, 1992 [1979].

Cochrane, Charles Norris. *Christianity and Classical Culture: A Study of Thought and Action from Augustus to Augustine*. New York: Oxford University Press, 1966 [1940].

Cohn, Norman R. C. *The Pursuit of the Millennium,* rev. and expanded ed. New York: Oxford University Press, 1972 [1957].

Contamine, Philippe. *War in the Middle Ages*. Translated by Michael Jones. New York: Basil Blackwell, 1984 [1980].

Curtius, Ernst Robert. *European Literature and the Latin Middle Ages*. Translated by William R. Trask. Princeton, N.J.: Princeton University Press, 1973 [1953].

Dawson, Christopher. *The Making of Europe: An Introduction to the History of European Unity*. New York: Meridian Books, 1956 [1932].

Douglas, David Charles. *William the Conqueror: The Norman Impact upon England*. Berkeley: University of California Press, 1964.

Dronke, Peter. *Medieval Latin and the Rise of the European Love-Lyric,* 2 vols. Oxford: Clarendon Press, 1968.

———. *Women Writers of the Middle Ages: A Critical Study of Texts from Perpetua (203) to Marguerite Porete (1310)*. New York: Cambridge University Press, 1984.

Du Boulay, F. R. H. *An Age of Ambition: English Society in the Late Middle Ages*. New York: Viking, 1970.

Duby, Georges. *The Early Growth of the European Economy: Warriors and Peasants from the Seventh to the Twelfth Century*. Translated by Howard B. Clark. Ithaca, N.Y.: Cornell University Press, 1974.

————. ed. *A History of Private Life, Vol. II, Revelations of the Medieval World*. Translated by Arnold Goldhammer. Cambridge, Mass.: Harvard University Press, 1988.

Dyer, Christopher. *Standards of Living in the Later Middle Ages*. New York: Cambridge University Press, 1989.

Easton, Stewart C. *Roger Bacon and Search for a Universal Science: A Reconsideration of the Life and Work of Roger Bacon in the Light of His Own Stated Purpose*. Oxford: Basil Blackwell, 1952.

Erdmann, Carl. *The Origin of the Idea of the Crusade*. Translated by Marshall W. Baldwin and Walter Goffart. Foreword and additional notes by Marshall W. Baldwin. Princeton, N.J.: Princeton University Press, 1977 [1936].

Fawtier, Robert. *The Capetian Kings of France: Monarch and Nation, 987–1328*. Translated by Lionel Butler and R. J. Adam. New York: St. Martin's Press, 1960.

Fichtenau, Heinrich. *The Carolingian Empire*. Translated by Peter Munz. Toronto: University of Toronto Press, 1978 [1st English ed. 1957].

Fletcher, Richard. *The Quest for El Cid*. New York: Alfred A. Knopf, 1989.

Fuhrmann, Horst. *Germany in the High Middle Ages c. 1050–1200*. Translated by Timothy Reuter. New York: Cambridge University Press, 1986.

Ganshof, François Louis. *Feudalism*. 3d English ed. New York: Harper & Row, 1964 [original French ed. 1947].

Gilson, Étienne Henry. *A History of Christian Philosophy in the Middle Ages*. New York: Random House, 1956.

Gimpel, Jean. *The Cathedral Builders*. Translated by Teresa Waugh. London: Cresset Library, 1988 [1963].

Gurevich, Aron. *Medieval Popular Culture: Problems of Belief and Perception*. Translated by James M. Bak and Paul A. Hollingsworth. New York: Cambridge University Press, 1990 [1988].

Halphen, Louis. *Charlemagne and the Carolingian Empire*. Translated by Giselle de Nie. New York: North Holland, 1977 [1949].

Hanning, Robert W. *The Individual in Twelfth Century Romance*. New Haven, Conn.: Yale University Press, 1977.

————. *The Vision of History in Early Britain: From Gildas to Geoffrey of Monmouth*. New York: Columbia University Press, 1966.

Haskins, Charles Homer. *The Normans in European History*. New York: F. Ungar, 1959 [1915].

————. *Norman Institutions*. Cambridge, Mass.: Harvard University Press, 1918.

Herlihy, David. *Medieval Households*. Cambridge, Mass.: Harvard University Press, 1985.

Herrin, Judith. *The Formation of Christendom*. Princeton, N.J.: Princeton University Press, 1987.

Hodges, Richard. *Dark Age Economics. The Origins of Towns and Trade A.D. 600–1000*. New York: St. Martin's Press, 1982.

Hodgkin, Robert Howard. *A History of the Anglo-Saxons*, 2 vols., 3d ed. London: Oxford University Press, 1967 [1st ed., 1935].

Howard, Donald R. *Chaucer: His Life, His Works, His World*. New York: E. P. Dutton, 1987.

Huizinga, Johan. *The Waning of the Middle Ages: A Study of the Forms of Life, Thought, and Art in France and the Netherlands in the XIVth and XVth Centuries.* New York: St. Martin's Press, 1969 [1924].

Hyde, John Kenneth. *Society and Politics in Medieval Italy: The Evolution of the Civil Life, 1000–1350.* New York: St. Martin's Press, 1973.

James, Edward. *The Franks.* New York: Basil Blackwell, 1988.

Jones, A. H. *The Later Roman Empire,* 2 vols. Baltimore: Johns Hopkins University Press, 1986 [1964].

Jungman, Josef Andreas. *The Mass of the Roman Rite: Its Origins and Development.* Translated by Francis A. Brunner. New rev. and abridged ed. by Charles K. Riepe. New York: Benziger Bros., 1961.

Kantorowicz, Ernst H. *Frederick the Second, 1194–1250.* Translated by E. O. Lorimer. New York: F. Ungar, 1957 [1931].

————. *The King's Two Bodies: A Study in Medieval Political Theology.* Princeton, N.J.: Princeton University Press, 1957.

Keen, Maurice Hugh. *Chivalry.* New Haven, Conn.: Yale University Press, 1984.

Kelly, Amy Ruth. *Eleanor of Aquitaine and the Four Kings.* Cambridge, Mass.: Harvard University Press, 1978 [1950].

Kern, Fritz. *Kingship and Law in the Middle Ages.* Translated with an introduction by S. B. Chrimes. Oxford: Basil Blackwell, 1968 [1939].

Knowles, David. *The Evolution of Medieval Thought,* 2d ed. Edited by D. E. Luscombe and C. N. L. Brooke. New York: Longman, 1988 [1962].

————. *The Monastic Order in England; A History of Its Development from the Times of St. Dunstan to the Fourth Lateran Council, 940–1216,* 2d ed. Cambridge, England: Cambridge University Press, 1963 [1940].

————. *The Religious Orders in England,* 3 vols. Cambridge, England: Cambridge University Press, 1948–1959.

Krautheimer, Richard. *Rome, Profile of a City, 312–1308.* Princeton, N.J.: Princeton University Press, 1980.

Kuttner, Stephan Georg. *Harmony from Dissonance: An Interpretation of Medieval Canon Law.* Latrobe, Pa.: Archabbey Press, 1960.

Ladner, Gerhart B. *The Idea of Reform, Its Impact on Christian Thought and Action in the Age of the Fathers.* Cambridge, Mass.: Harvard University Press, 1959.

Laistner, Max Ludwig Wolfram. *Thought and Letters in Western Europe, A.D. 500 to 900,* rev. and reset ed., Ithaca, N.Y.: Cornell University Press, 1966 [1931].

Lambert, Malcolm. *Medieval Heresy: Popular Movements from Bogomil to Hus.* New York: Basil Blackwell, 1992 [1976].

Lane Fox, Robin. *Pagans and Christians.* New York: Knopf, 1986.

Leff, Gordon. *Heresy in the Later Middle Ages: The Relation of Heterodoxy to Dissent, 1250–1450,* 2 vols. New York: Barnes & Noble, 1967.

————. *Paris and Oxford Universities in the Thirteenth and Fourteenth Centuries: An Institutional and Intellectual History.* Huntington, N.Y.: R. E. Krieger, 1975 [1968].

Le Goff, Jacques. *Time, Work, and Culture in the Middle Ages.* Translated by Arthur Goldhammer. Chicago: University of Chicago Press, 1980.

Le Roy Ladurie, Emmanuel. *Montaillou: The Promised Land of Error.* Translated by Barbara Bray. New York: G. Braziller, 1978.

Lewis, C. S. *The Discarded Image: An Introduction to Medieval and Renaissance Literature.* Cambridge, England: Cambridge University Press, 1967 [1964].

Lopez, Robert Sabatino. *The Birth of Europe.* Philadelphia: Evans, 1967.

MacFarlane, Alan. *The Origins of English Individualism: The Family, Property and Social Transition.* Oxford: Basil Blackwell, 1978; reprinted with corrections, 1985.

Mango, Cyril A. *Byzantium: The Empire of New Rome.* New York: Scribner's, 1980.

Marenbon, John. *Early Medieval Philosophy (480–1150): An Introduction,* 2d ed. London: Routledge, 1988 [1983].

————. *Later Medieval Philosophy (1150–1350): An Introduction.* London: Routledge, 1987.

McFarlane, Kenneth Bruce. *John Wycliffe and the Beginnings of the English Non-conformity.* New York: Collier Books, 1966 [1953].

McGinn, Bernard. *Visions of the End: Apocalyptic Traditions in the Middle Ages.* New York: Columbia University Press, 1979.

McKittrick, Rosamond. *The Frankish Church Under the Carolingians.* New York: Longman, 1983.

Miller, Edward, and John Hatcher. *Medieval England: Rural Society and Economic Change, 1086–1348.* New York: Longman, 1978.

Milsom, S. F. C. *Historical Foundations of the Common Law,* 2d ed. London: Buttersworth, 1981 [1st. ed. 1969].

Mollat, Michel. *The Poor in the Middle Ages.* Translated by Arthur Goldhammer. New Haven, Conn.: Yale University Press, 1986 [1978].

Mommsen, Theodor E. *Medieval and Renaissance Studies.* Edited by Eugene F. Rice, Jr. Ithaca, N.Y.: Cornell University Press, 1959.

Moore, Robert Ian. *The Formation of a Persecuting Society: Power and Deviance in Western Europe, 950–1250.* New York: Basil Blackwell, 1987.

Morris, Colin. *The Discovery of the Individual, 1050–1200.* Toronto: University of Toronto Press in association with the Medieval Academy of America, 1987 [1972].

Morris, John. *The Age of Arthur: A History of the British Isles from 350–650.* New York: Scribner's, 1973.

Morrison, Karl Frederick. *Tradition and Authority in the Western Church 300–1140.* Princeton, N.J.: Princeton University Press, 1969.

Muir, Lynette R. *Literature and Society in Medieval France: The Mirror and the Image, 1100–1500.* New York: St. Martin's Press, 1985.

Munz, Peter. *Frederick Barbarossa: A Study in Medieval Politics.* Ithaca, N.Y.: Cornell University Press, 1969.

Nichols, Stephen G., et al. *The New Medievalism.* Baltimore: Johns Hopkins University Press, 1991.

Oberman, Heiko Augustinus. *The Harvest of Medieval Theology: Gabriel Biel and Late Medieval Nominalism,* 3d ed. Durham, N.C.: Labyrinth Press, 1983 [1963].

Owst, G. R. *Literature and Pulpit in Medieval England: A Neglected Chapter in the History of English Letters and of the English People,* 2d ed. rev. New York: Barnes & Noble, 1966 [1933].

Painter, Sidney. *The Reign of King John.* New York: Arno Press, 1966 [1949].

Panofsky, Erwin. *Gothic Architecture and Scholasticism.* Latrobe, Pa.: Archabbey Press, 1951.

———. *Renaissance and Renascences in Western Art.* New York: Harper & Row, 1972 [1960].

Patterson, Lee. *Negotiating the Past: The Historical Understanding of Medieval Literature.* Madison: University of Wisconsin Press, 1987.

Peters, Edward. *Inquisition.* New York: Free Press, 1988.

Pirenne, Henri. *Medieval Cities: Their Origins and the Renewal of Trade.* Translated by Frank D. Halsey. Princeton, N.J.: Princeton University Press, 1969 [1925].

Pollock, Frederick, and Frederick William Maitland. *The History of English Law Before the Time of Edward I.* 2d ed. 1898, 2 vols. Reissued with an introduction and select bibliography by S. F. C. Milsom. Cambridge, England: Cambridge University Press, 1968.

Power, Eileen Edna. *Medieval People,* 10th printing. New York: Barnes & Noble, 1963 [1924. The text did not change after the 1924 edition. Paperback edition, Penguin, 1950].

Powicke, Frederick Maurice. *King Henry III and the Lord Edward: The Community of the Realm in the Thirteenth Century,* 2 vols. Oxford: Clarendon Press, 1947.

Prestwich, Michael. *The Three Edwards: War and State in England, 1272–1377.* London: Weidenfeld and Nicolson, 1980.

Richards, Jeffrey. *Sex, Dissidence and Damnation: Minority Groups in the Middle Ages.* New York: Routledge, 1991.

Riché, Pierre. *Daily Life in the World of Charlemagne.* With expanded footnotes and translated with an introduction by Jo Ann McNamara. Philadelphia: University of Pennsylvania Press, 1988 [1978].

Riley-Smith, Jonathan. *The Crusades: A Short History.* New Haven, Conn.: Yale University Press, 1987.

Robertson, D. W. *A Preface to Chaucer: Studies in Medieval Perspectives.* Princeton, N.J.: Princeton University Press, 1962.

Robinson, I. S. *The Papacy 1073–1198: Continuity and Innovation.* Cambridge, England: Cambridge University Press, 1990.

Runciman, Steven. *A History of the Crusades,* 3 vols. New York: Cambridge University Press, 1980 [1951–1954].

Russell, Jeffrey Burton. *Witchcraft in the Middle Ages.* Ithaca, N.Y.: Cornell University Press, 1984 [1972].

Sawyer, P. H. *The Age of the Vikings,* 2d ed. New York: St. Martin's Press, 1972 [1st ed., 1962].

Shahar, Shulamit. *Childhood in the Middle Ages.* New York: Routledge, 1990.

Southern, Richard William. *The Making of the Middle Ages.* New Haven, Conn.: Yale University Press, 1953.

————. *Robert Grosseteste: The Growth of an English Mind in Medieval Europe.* Oxford: Clarendon Press, 1986.

————. *Western Society and the Church in the Middle Ages.* Harmondsworth, England: Penguin, 1970.

Stevens, John E. *Medieval Romance: Themes and Approaches.* London: Hutchinson, 1973.

Stock, Brian. *The Implications of Literacy: Written Language and Models of Interpretation in the Eleventh and Twelfth Centuries.* Princeton, N.J.: Princeton University Press, 1983.

Strayer, Joseph Reese. *On the Medieval Origins of the Modern State.* Princeton, N.J.: Princeton University Press, 1970.

————. *The Reign of Philip the Fair.* Princeton, N.J.: Princeton University Press, 1980.

Stuard, Susan Mosher, ed. *Women in Medieval Society.* Philadelphia: University of Pennsylvania Press, 1976.

Tellenbach, Gerd. *Church, State and Christian Society at the Time of the Investiture Contest.* Translated by R. F. Bennett. Oxford: Basil Blackwell, 1959 [1936].

Temko, Allan. *Notre-Dame of Paris.* New York: Viking Press, 1967 [1955].

Tuchman, Barbara W. *A Distant Mirror: The Calamitous Fourteenth Century.* New York: Alfred A. Knopf, 1978.

Ullmann, Walter. *The Growth of Papal Government in the Middle Ages: A Study in the Ideological Relation of Clerical to Lay Power,* 3d ed. London: Methuen, 1970 [1955].

Vinogradoff, Paul. *Roman Law in Medieval Europe,* 3d ed. Oxford: Oxford University Press, 1961 [1909. The second edition of 1929 is the definitive text].

Von Grunebaum, Gustave E. *Medieval Islam.* Chicago: University of Chicago Press, 1953 [1949].

Weitzmann, Kurt. *Illustrations in Roll and Codex. A Study of the Origin and Case Method of Text Illumination.* Princeton, N.J.: Princeton University Press, 1947.

Wemple, Susanne. *Women in Frankish Society: Marriage and the Cloister.* Philadelphia: University of Pennsylvania Press, 1981.

White, Lynn Townsend. *Medieval Technology and Social Change.* New York: Oxford University Press, 1964 [1962].

Whitney, James Pounder. *Hildebrandine Essays.* Cambridge, England: Cambridge University Press, 1932.

Wilson, Christopher. *The Gothic Cathedral: The Architecture of the Great Church 1130–1530.* New York: Thames and Hudson, 1990.

Wolfson, Harry Austryn. *The Philosophy of the Church Fathers,* 3d ed. rev. Cambridge, Mass.: Harvard University Press, 1970 [1st ed. 1956].

Young, Karl. *The Drama of the Medieval Church.* Oxford: Clarendon Press, 1967 [1933].

INDEX

Abelard, Peter, 50, 319, 330–33, 336–38, 342, 343, 357, 358, 359, 558

Abortion, 478

Absolutism: and the bureaucratic state, 277; and church–state relations, 55; Dante's view of, 548; and early Christianity, 36–37, 79–80; and the intellectual expansion of Europe, 311, 312, 316, 318, 328–29; and the Judaic tradition, 26–27, 36–37; and the Justinian code/Roman Empire, 12, 13, 26, 125–26, 311, 312; and the law, 311, 312, 316, 318; and monasticism, 149–55; and secular leadership, 395–415. *See also* Papal absolutism

Acre, castle at, 301–2

Adrian IV (pope), 324, 326, 404

Adrianople, battle of, 46, 100, 123

Agincourt, battle of (1415), 519

Alaric the Bold (Visigoth king), 101

Alberti, Battista, 554, 555

Albertus Magnus, 443

Albigensians, 300, 389–93, 424–25, 428, 461, 469, 491

Alcoholic beverages, 480

Alcuin, 165, 179, 181–82, 188–89, 190, 192, 320, 322

Alexander II (pope), 313

Alexander III (pope), 404, 405, 414, 417

Alexander the Great, 4, 19

Alexandria, Egypt, 40, 51, 153, 364

Alexius Comnenus (Byzantine emperor), 291, 295

Alfred (Anglo-Saxon king), 95, 166

Alonso X the Learned (Spanish king), 510

Anabaptists, 388

Anaclete II (pope), 339–40

Anchoritism, 147–48

Andrew the Chaplain (Andreas Capellanus), 349, 350

Anglo-Norman monarchy, 277–84, 315–16, 395

Anglo-Saxons, 91, 93–94, 205, 278, 280–81. *See also* England; English law

Anjou, 207, 287–88, 402, 409, 522–23. *See also* Charles of Anjou

Annulments, 235–36

Anointment of kings, 175–76, 178–79, 182, 207, 212, 239, 414

Anonymous of York treatises, 265, 286

Anticlericalism, 384–93, 470, 490, 536–37, 551

Anti-intellectualism, 445–46

Antisacerdotalism, 384–93, 419, 426–27, 429, 430–31, 435, 445–46

Anti-Semitism, 253, 365, 366

Apology of Socrates (Plato), 16

Apostolic poverty, 261–63, 377, 388, 430, 488, 490, 499, 533, 534. *See also* Asceticism

Aquinas, Thomas: Dante as a disciple of, 546; and the dialectical method, 335, 337; disapproval of, 532; as a Dominican, 429; and the Italian Renaissance, 561; and the paradoxes of the middle ages, 566; political theory of, 448–51, 461, 551; and scholasticism, 531, 532; and the systemization of knowledge, 14, 443–45, 446; and the translations of Aristotle, 358, 362, 369

Aquitaine, 113, 207, 348, 349, 352, 410, 480, 516–17, 518. *See also* Eleanor of Aquitaine

Arabs/Arabia, 133, 300–301. *See also* Islam; Moslems; *specific country or person*

Aragon, 491–92, 510, 511, 523

Architecture: in 1050 AD, 237; Byzantine, 554; and church reform, 505; and classical thought, 554, 555; of Cluny, 334; Gothic, 321–22, 323–24, 436–38, 555; and the intellectual expansion of Europe, 306, 321–22, 323–24; and the Italian Renaissance, 544, 554, 555; and the Norman conquest, 285; Romanesque, 222–23, 321, 322, 436, 554

Archpoet, 345

Arianism: and the barbarian invasions, 93, 102, 103, 104, 105, 108, 109, 111, 113, 130–31, 155; basic concepts of, 50–51; and church-state relations, 56; collapse of, 49, 127; and the Council of Nicaea, 50; and the Germanic peoples, 58; and the Moslem invasions, 58; and nationalism, 50–51; and the Roman Empire, 57–58

Aristocracy. *See* Nobility

Aristotelianism: banning of, 532; and the crisis of the late middle ages, 480; and the Dominican order, 429; and education, 20; emergence of,

13–14; and Gregorian reform, 255; and the harvest of medieval thought, 531; influence of, 20; and the intellectual expansion of Europe, 306, 320, 334–38; and the Italian Renaissance, 550, 551; Italian universities as centers of, 531; and Judaism, 360–61, 363–72; and the manuscript search, 550; and the moral authority of the state, 449; and Moslem thought, 138, 140, 360–61, 362–63, 371–72; and papal absolutism, 427; Platonism compared with, 19–20, 360, 362; and politics, 449, 551; preservation of, 83; and scholasticism, 534–35; and the systemization of knowledge, 14, 442–43, 444–48; and theology, 360–61; translations of, 20, 83, 108, 334–35, 357–61. *See also* Dialectical method

Arnold of Brescia, 337, 404

Art, 323, 324, 436, 483, 530, 539–40, 544, 553–57

Art of Love (Ovid), 350

Arthurian legends, 352–54, 537, 538

Asceticism: and the Dominican order, 428; and emotional religiosity, 378–79; and Gregorian reform, 248–49, 262–63, 375; institutionalization of, 380–84, 428; and monks' role in society, 373–84; and popular heresy, 391–92; and popular piety, 373–74, 428; and the proliferation of religious orders, 373–84; purpose of, 146; and the rise of monasticism, 146, 147–48; and the Virgin cult, 378–79. *See also* Benedictine order, Franciscan order

Ataulf (Visigoth king), 101–2, 107

Athanasius, 147

Attila the Hun, 106

Augustinianism: and classical thought, 74–75, 76, 80–81, 448; and the Dominican order, 428; and the intellectual expansion of Europe, 320, 327, 328, 329; and the Italian Renaissance, 548, 561; and justification for the crusades, 290; and liberalism, 75; and monks' role in society, 381; and the moral authority of the state, 448, 449; and mysticism, 79; and Platonism, 75, 78, 81; and popular heresy, 384, 426; and rationality, 75; and salvation, 84–85; and the systemization of knowledge, 443, 444–48. *See also* St. Augustine

Augustus Caesar, 7

Authority: moral, 448–64. *See also* Absolutism; Papal absolutism

Averroes, 359–60, 362–63, 369, 370, 443, 445, 531, 536, 546, 548, 551

Avicebrol, 368

Avicenna, 359–60, 362

Avignon, papacy at, 496, 497–98

Bacon, Roger, 447, 448, 534

Bailli/bailiffs, 412–13

Baldwin of Lorraine, 297

Balkans, 129, 130

Banking: and the decline of the papacy, 494, 496–97; in Italy, 471, 481, 525, 526, 541–42, 544–45; and the Jews, 365–67, 512; and the Knights Templars, 382–83, 496–97; and the Medici family, 525, 526, 544–45

Baptism, 49

Barbarian invasions: as beginning of the middle ages, 561–62; and the Celtic church, 162; and church-state relations, 62–63, 64, 95, 97–98, 102, 104, 105, 107, 109–10, 112–13, 115–16, 118, 145, 155; and the economic unity of the Mediterranean world, 141–42, 143; effects of the, 9; and the fall of the Roman Empire, 41, 44–47, 62; first century of, 99–104; and the Franks, 93, 94, 102, 104, 110–21; and German law, 13; and imperial unity, 57; and nationalism, 89, 91; reasons for the, 89, 90, 99–100. *See also* Germans/Germany: barbarian invasions by the; Huns; Moslems: barbarian invasions by the

Barthes, Roland, 14

Basil II (Byzantine emperor), 226

Beatific vision, 341–42, 349, 546. *See also* Mysticism

Becket, Thomas, 324–25, 399–401

Bede, 162, 164–66, 320

Beguines, 499

Benedictine order: in Britain, 160, 164, 165; criticism of the, 248–49, 374, 376, 377, 378, 379; and education, 160; in France, 160, 170; function of the, 376; in Germany, 167–71; and Gregorian reform, 247, 248–49; Gregory the Great as a prototype of the, 157–58; and the intellectual expansion of Europe, 355; and the medieval equilibrium, 206; and monks' role in society, 374, 376, 377, 378, 379; nuns in the, 121, 154–55, 355; and the papacy, 155; and popular piety, 373. *See also* Cluniacs; St. Benedict of Nursia

Beowulf (Anglo-Saxon poem), 91, 92, 163–64, 194, 197, 345

Berbers, 227, 302, 371

Berengar of Tours, 320

Bestiaries, 439

Bible: as allegory, 40, 370, 432; and Aristotelianism, 360; criticism of the, 22; and the illuminated manuscripts, 190; Jerome's translation of the, 70; as a social document, 22; study of, as primary task of medieval universities, 21; and the Wyclif heresy, 499–500. *See also* Gospels; Higher Criticism; New Testament; Old Testament

Biographies, 331–32, 466

Biscop, Benedict, 164

Bishops, 70, 74, 437, 440, 441, 501

Black Death, 476–77, 481, 482, 563–64

Blanche of Castile, 462

Bloch, Marc, 196, 473

Blood feuds, 94, 96, 208

Blood libels, 365, 426

Boccaccio, Giovanni, 384, 546, 549, 564

Boethius, 82, 83, 108, 110, 320, 334–35, 343, 357

Bohemund, 294, 295, 296

Bologna, Italy, 310, 311, 404–5, 531
Boniface VIII (pope), 492–96, 497, 515, 547
The Book of the Courtier (Castiglione), 542–43
Book of Pastoral Care (Gregory the Great), 158
Borst, Arno, 392
Boswell, John, 566
Bosworth Field, battle of (1485), 521
Bourbon dynasty, 409
Bourgeois: in 1050 AD, 237–38, 240; in 1300 AD, 476, 477; anticlericalism of, 404; and class issues, 470–71; and the crisis of the middle ages, 480, 485, 487; and economic issues, 471, 487; and education, 440, 441, 471; emergence of the, 230–31, 261; and the Franciscan order, 432–33; individualism of the, 432; and the intellectual expansion of Europe, 344, 348; and the Italian Renaissance, 540; and law, 472; and literature, 344, 348; and the nobility, 469, 485; and the peasantry, 473; and politics, 471; and popular heresy, 384, 386–88; and popular piety, 247, 373, 432–33, 470; population of, 476; and the rise of Europe, 230–31; and romanticism, 470; and secular leadership, 413. *See also specific country*
Bouvines, battle of (1214), 422, 435, 452, 465
Brethren of the Common Life, 499
Bretigny, Treaty of, 518
Britain. *See* England; English law; *specific monarch*
Brittany, 520
Brunelleschi, Filippo, 554, 555
Bulgaria, 226, 390
Bultmann, Rudolph, 32–33
Burchard of Worms, 312
Burckhardt, Jacob, 529, 563
Bureaucracy: and the Carolingian world, 191–92; criticism of the, 326; and early Christianity, 74; emergence of the, 277–88, 395; and the intellectual expansion of

Europe, 326; and the law, 310, 314–15, 316, 318; and monks' role in society, 376; papacy as a, 263, 273, 314–15, 418–28. *See also* England; France; *specific country or monarchy*
Burghers. *See* Bourgeois
Burgundy, 91, 93, 102, 105, 113, 518, 519, 520
Bury, J. B., 56, 128, 130
Byzantine Empire: in 1050 AD, 237; architecture in the, 554; and the barbarian invasions, 106–7, 109–10, 123–24; and church–state relations, 56–57, 109–10, 126, 127–28, 130–31, 156, 159, 173–74; contributions of the, 225–28; decline of the, 225–28; and dissent, 69; and early Christianity, 186; and the fall of the Roman Empire, 41; and feudalism, 291; influence on first Europe of, 190; and Islam, 136–37; limitations of the, 225–28; lordship in the, 226; and the Macedonian Renaissance, 226; and the medieval equilibrium, 215; and nationalism, 127; and North Africa, 128; and the Ottonian Empire, 215; reconquest of Italy by the, 105, 107, 110, 124–31; and the rise of Europe, 232; and Roman law, 124; and the Turks, 483. *See also* Constantinople; Crusades; Greek Orthodoxy; Justinian

Caesaropapism, 56–57, 87, 128
Calixtus II (pope), 273
Camaldoli order, 374
Cambridge University, 441
Canon law: authoritative sources for, 312; and the Carolingian world, 194–95; and church-state relations, 175, 423, 450; codification of, 244, 258, 308, 312–14; emergence of, 62; Germany as a center for study of, 276; and Gregorian reform, 244, 258, 312–14; and heresy, 314; and the intellectual expansion of Europe,

308, 312–14; and the Italian scholars, 312–14; and the Justinian code, 312–14; Leo I's contribution to promotion of, 64; and the moral authority of the state, 450; and papal absolutism, 258, 312–14, 420, 423, 448; and Roman law, 244

Canonization, 419

Canterbury, 159, 164, 236, 279, 423

The Canterbury Tales (Chaucer), 292–93, 538–39

Canute (Anglo–Saxon king), 166, 278

Capet, Hugh, 207, 208

Capetian monarchy: and Aragon, 491; and church–state relations, 413–15, 423–24, 461–64, 490–92; and England, 401, 402, 410–11, 415; and the intellectual expansion of Europe, 322; and the law, 311–12, 316; and the medieval equilibrium, 205, 207, 208, 222; and the moral authority of the state, 461–64; power of the, 266, 282, 461–64; and St. Denis Abbey, 239; and secular leadership, 396, 409–15; and succession questions, 517–18. *See also specific monarch*

Cardinals: and canon law, 312; and church-state relations, 404; and the decline of papal power, 496, 497–98; domination of papal government by, 273; and the election of the pope, 417, 492, 496; and the essentials of a Christian society, 249–50, 254; French, 464, 496; function of, 249–50; and the moral authority of the state, 451; reputation of the, 489; and the Roman nobility, 490; social class of, 420

Carloman (Frank king), 169–70

Carolingian world: and Anglo–Irish culture, 166–71; and bureaucracy, 191–92; and the Carolingian Renaissance, 190; and church–state relations, 171–83, 186–87, 194–95; and classical thought, 81, 84; and colonialism, 166–71; culture and society in

the, 185–95; decline of the, 186, 189, 206–7, 212; enigma of the, 171–73; and feudalism, 199, 200; and Germanic institutions, 172–73; leadership by the, 171–73; and the medieval equilibrium, 205–6, 217; military system of the, 192; and monasticism, 218; and the Ottonian Empire, 217; partition of the, 193; rise of the, 166–83; and the succession question, 175; and Viking invasions, 189, 193–94. *See also specific person*

Carthusian order, 378

Cassiodorus, 82–83, 107–8, 109, 152, 190

Castile, 510–11

Castles, 476

Cathari. *See* Albigensians

Cathedral schools, 319, 321, 324, 325, 376, 439

Cathedrals, architecture of the, 435–38

Celestine V (pope), 492

Celibacy, 71–73, 251–52, 503–4

Celtic church, 156, 159, 161–66

Chadwick, H., 91

Chain of being, 559–60

Chalcedon, Council of (451), 64, 127

Champagne, 207, 349, 352, 462

Chanson de geste, 346–47, 352

Charlemagne cycle, 348, 352

Charlemagne (French king), 141, 143, 165, 171, 178–82, 190, 191–92, 214–15, 260

Charles of Anjou, 460, 461, 464, 490, 491, 523

Charles the Bald (Carolingian monarch), 182, 186, 190

Charles V (French king), 518

Charles VI (French king), 518, 519

Charles VII (French king), 519, 520, 527

Charles VIII (French king), 528

Charters, medieval, 201

Chartres, University of, 319, 320, 324, 325, 330

Chaucer, Geoffrey, 292–93, 538–39

Childebert II (Merovingian king), 159

Chivalry, 348–49, 468, 476, 537–38, 543

Chomsky, Noam, 14

Chrétien de Troyes, 352, 353

Christian humanism, 82, 321, 326

Cities. See Bourgeois

Christianitas, 249, 261. See also Gregorian reform

Christianity: ambiguities in, 68, 79; evolutionary development of, 29–40; and the fall of the Roman Empire, 47; Judaism compared with, 29–37; and the Old Testament, 39–40; origins of, 29–40; and political monotheism, 55–66. See also Church

Chronicle (Jocelyn of Brakelond), 379

Church: as a bridge between the ancient and medieval worlds, 6–7; corruption of the, 492–505; development of the, 38–39; divisiveness in the, 49–66; hierarchy in the, 26–27, 37, 38–39; as an illegal organization, 37, 68; institutionalization of the, 66–88; as the mystical Body of Christ, 206–23; and the paradoxes of the middle ages, 564; reform of the, 497–505; St. Paul as founder of the, 37; schism between Greek Orthodoxy and the Latin, 86–87, 254, 291, 299, 424, 490–91; special privileges of the, 62; as a state, 62, 63; as a temporary institution, 80; universality of the, 78–79, 487–88. See also Heresy; Monasticism; Papacy

Church fathers, 66–88, 337, 449. See also specific person

Cicero, 9, 11, 190, 326, 549, 550, 552

Cid, El, 509

Circumcision, 35–36

Cistercian order, 248, 339, 377–80

Cities: in 1300 AD, 476–77; and class issues, 471; and the crisis of the late middle ages, 480, 483; piety in the, 435–36; plague in the, 482; problems of the, 471. See also specific country or city

The City of God (St. Augustine), 53, 74–75

The City of Woman (Christine de Pizan), 539

Class issues: in 1050 AD, 237–38; and birth vs. money, 464–65; and the

cities, 471; and class consciousness, 7–8; and the crisis of the late middle ages, 480; and the crusades, 293–94; and early Christianity, 38; and economic issues, 483–84, 541–42; and English law, 317, 472; and Gregorian reform, 260–62; and the Italian Renaissance, 541–42; and monasticism, 154–55; and nuns, 378; and paganism, 59. See also specific civilization, country, empire, or class

Classical thought: and art/architecture, 554–55; and Augustinianism, 74–75, 76, 80–81, 448; as a bridge between cultures, 81; and church–state relations, 60; and the crusades, 296; and early Christianity, 38–39, 60, 84; and the harvest of medieval thought, 530; as an ideal, 8; and the intellectual expansion of Europe, 306, 320, 325–26; and the Italian Renaissance, 540, 541, 543, 544, 548–49, 559; and Judaism, 366; medieval suspicion of, 8; and the moral authority of the state, 449; and the paradoxes of the middle ages, 564; translations of, 296, 357–61; transmission of, 81–88; and universities, 442, 549. See also Aristotelianism; Neoplatonism; Platonism

Clement V (pope), 496, 497

Clergy: appointments of the, 450; and the Black Death, 482; corruption of the, 492–505; development of the, 38–39; and Gregorian reform, 255–56, 260; and the law, 400–401, 494; taxation of the, 493–96; and women, 72. See also Anticlericalism; Celibacy; Church; Donatism; Investiture controversy; specific person

Clericis Laicos (papal bull), 493

Clermont, Council at (1095), 292, 293

Clovis I (Frank king), 105, 107, 112–14, 115

Cluniacs: in 1050 AD, 239; and Abelard at Cluny, 330; and the architecture of Cluny, 334; and asceticism, 373, 374, 375; and church–state relations, 218–23, 233; and the Cluniac Ideal, 218–23; dissatisfaction/criticisms of the, 240, 334, 373, 374, 375, 377; and Gregorian reform, 246, 247, 250–51, 253, 270; importance of the, 239; and the intellectual expansion of Europe, 322, 330, 334; and medieval equilibrium, 218–23; and monks' role in society, 373, 374, 375, 377, 378; and popular piety, 373

Collations (Cassian), 148–49, 151

Collections (Gregory IX), 313

Colonization: and the Carolingian world, 166–71; of Europe, 229–30, 236, 375, 378; and the peasantry, 472. *See also* Crusades; Germany: eastward movement in

Comitatus, 95, 197

Communes, 231, 404, 405, 471–72, 522, 523, 524

Compurgation, 96–97, 98

Conciliar movement, 498, 500–501

The Concordance of Discordant Canons (Gratian), 313

Concordat of 1111, 262–63

Concordat of London (1107), 286

Concordat of Worms (1122), 273–74, 286

Confession, 418–19, 425

Confessions (St. Augustine), 331, 548

Conrad I (German emperor), 212

Conrad II (German emperor), 220

Conrad III (German emperor), 298, 403

Conrad IV (German emperor), 460

Conradin (Sicilian king), 460

The Consolation of Philosophy (Boethius), 83

Constance, Council of (1414), 498, 500

Constance, peace of (1183), 405

Constantine: biography of, 331; and church-state relations, 37, 40, 48–50, 52, 53–55, 56, 59, 63, 260; conversion of, 37, 40, 48–49, 57, 67; and the Council of Nicaea, 50; as a divine monarch, 7; and Donatism, 52; importance of, 47; and Italy, 48–50; military reforms of, 46; personal background of, 47–48; pope as true successor of, 258. *See also* Donation of Constantine

Constantinople: Charles of Anjou's attack on, 490–91; and the crusades, 41, 293, 295, 299–300; fall of, 41, 549; and the fall of the Roman Empire, 54; as a fortress, 54, 123–24; and Islam, 136; Latin Kingdom of, 299–300, 424, 490–91; Moslem conquest of, 490; and the Moslem invasions, 54; papal relations with, 254; as a second Rome, 53–55, 59; as a trading center, 124, 232; wealth of, 226

Constitutional liberalism, 563, 566

Cordoba, Spain, 138–39, 140, 233, 359, 362

Corpus Christi (Aquinas), 446

Coulton, G. G., 385–86

Council of Chalcedon (451), 64

Council of Clermont (1095), 292, 293

Council of Constance (1414), 498, 500

Council of Lyons (1245), 460

Council of Nicaea (325), 50, 56, 418

Council of Pisa (1408), 498

Council of Trent (sixteenth century), 292, 418

Courcelle, P., 93

Court life, 485–86, 542–43

Courtiers, 486, 542–43

Covenant theology, 24–25, 26–27

Crossbow, 467

Crusades: against the Albigensians, 300, 389–93, 424–25, 428, 461, 469, 491; against Aragon, 491–92; and church–state relations, 450, 461, 463–64; and the conquest of Constantinople, 41; and the crusading ideal, 289–97, 298, 301, 424, 463–64, 491; and economic issues, 294, 296, 298, 299, 424; effects of the, 301–3; Egyptian, 300, 302, 450, 463; and the English investiture controversy, 286; first, 232, 253, 272, 289, 293–97, 302, 414, 504; forces in

Crusades (*cont.*)
the, 295–96; fourth, 299–300, 424,
466; against Frederick II, 460,
463–64; and Gregorian reform,
262, 272; and indulgences, 504;
leadership in the, 294–95, 407,
424–25; and militarism, 289–303;
and monks' role in society,
382–83; and the moral authority
of the state, 460, 461, 463–64; as
outmoded, 301; and the people's
crusade, 293–94; as a political
institution, 300; rationale for the,
290–94, 298; and the rise of
Europe, 232; route of the, 295;
second, 298, 334; third, 298–99,
383, 407, 421
Cur Deus Homo (St. Anselm), 338–39
Curthose, Robert (duke of Normandy),
294, 350

Damiani, Peter: and the dialectical
method, 320, 325, 335; and the
essentials of a Christian society,
250–53, 255, 256, 257, 261; and
Gregorian reform, 245, 246–47,
248; influence of, 338; and popu-
lar heresy, 387; and the sacra-
ments, 418
Dante Alighieri, 250, 341, 492, 496,
546–48, 551, 558, 559, 561
David (Donatello), 554–55
Davis, Natalie Zemon, 473
Dead Sea Scrolls, 33, 147
Death of the Persecutors (Lactantius),
48
Decameron (Boccaccio), 549, 564
*The Decline and Fall of the Roman
Empire* (Gibbon), 41, 42
Decretists, 313
Decretum (Gratian), 313, 337
The Deeds of Frederick Barbarossa (Otto
of Freising), 329
Defender of the Peace (Marsilio of
Padua), 551–52
Deforestation, 564–65
de Pizan, Christine, 539
Descartes, Rene, 14, 335
Deurbanization, 128, 143, 152

Dialectical method, 19–20, 313, 320,
321, 325, 330, 331, 335, 337, 439,
442–43
*The Dialogue on the Course of the
Exchequer* (FitzNeal), 398–99
Dialogues (Plato), 15, 16
Dictatus Papae (Gregory VII), 258–59
Dies Irae (Thomas of Celano), 446
Diet, 479
Diocletian (Roman emperor), 46, 47–48,
54
Dionysius (monk), 190
Discourses (Machiavelli), 552, 553
The Divine Comedy (Dante), 250, 341,
546–47
Divine law, 449
Divine monarchy, 6–7, 12, 55. *See also*
Theocratic monarchy
Divorce, 419
Domesday Book, 284
Dominican order: and asceticism, 428;
and the decline of papal power,
498–99; founding of the, 428–29;
and the harvest of medieval
thought, 531–32; and itinerant
priests, 421–32; Jews in the, 426;
and monks' role in society, 381;
and popular heresy, 425, 428–29,
461–62; as scholars, 428–29, 432;
and scholasticism, 531–32; selection of men for the, 428; and the
systemization of knowledge, 441,
446
Donatello, 554–55
Donation of Constantine, 176–78, 180,
182, 194–95, 216, 258–59, 285,
404, 427, 448, 547, 548, 550
Donation of Pepin, 178
Donatism, 49, 51–52, 58, 63, 78, 80,
255–56, 263, 343, 384, 387, 388,
431
Dooms (Anglo-Saxon law), 91
Dopsch, Alfons, 92, 93
Dualism, 40, 72, 147, 389–91, 392, 427,
530
Due process, 453–54
Duns Scotus, 532, 533
Durham cathedral (England),
285

Ecclesiastical History (Eusebius), 48
Ecclesiastical History of the English People (Bede), 165
Ecclesiastical leadership: advance of, 145–60; and church-state relations, 155–60; and monasticism, 145–55. *See also* Leadership; Papacy; Papal absolutism; *specific person*
Eckhardt, Master, 536
Ecology, 564–65. *See also* Bourgeois; Manorialism; Nobility; Peasants
Economic issues: and class issues, 483–84, 541–42; and the crisis of the middle ages, 481–83; and the crusades, 294, 296, 298, 299, 424; and the Italian Renaissance, 541–42; and the rise of Europe, 229–32; and the unity of the Mediterranean world, 141–43. *See also* Merchants; Trade; *specific country, monarchy, or class*
Education: aim/function of, 82, 325, 551; and Aristotelianism, 20; and biblical study, 21; and the bourgeois, 440, 441, 471; and the decline of papal power, 499; and deurbanization, 152; and early Christianity, 38, 60; in the first Europe, 188–90; and Gregorian reform, 244; and the intellectual expansion of Europe, 343; and the Italian Renaissance, 551, 560–61; and leadership, 395, 409; for the medieval church, 11; and the monarchy, 441; and monasticism, 82–83, 152–53, 160, 163–71, 179, 188–90, 208, 233, 375–76; and the nobility, 465, 466, 468, 476; Plato's concept of, 17; in the Roman Empire, 10–11, 81. *See also* Universities; *specific university, person, or country*
Edward the Confessor (Anglo–Saxon king), 220, 236, 247, 278
Edward I (English king), 457, 494, 514–15, 517
Edward II (English king), 515
Edward III (English king), 515, 517, 518
Edward IV (English king), 521
Egypt: in the ancient world, 3, 4, 5, 22; Arab/Islamic domination of, 127, 129–30, 132–33, 135, 136; and the Byzantine Empire, 127, 130; and the crusades, 300, 302, 450, 463; economic issues in, 139; and the Moslem invasion, 51; nationalism in, 51; and the oriental culture, 132; religion in, 5, 22, 51, 58, 127, 129, 132, 135; rulership in, 5
Einhard, 179, 181, 192
Eleanor of Aquitaine, 298, 349, 398, 410, 411
Emotional religiosity: and asceticism, 378–79; and the Franciscan order, 428, 431, 447; and Gregorian reform, 252–53, 261–62; and the intellectual expansion of Europe, 306, 314, 341, 343; and the papacy, 314
Encyclopedists, 81–88
The End of the Ancient World (Lot), 41–42
England: in 1050 AD, 235–36; army of, 376, 467, 515, 517–18; backwardness of, 166, 278; and the barbarian invasions, 103; baronial government in, 515; baronial revolt in, 452–58; Benedictine order in, 164, 165; bourgeois in, 470; as a bureaucracy, 281–84, 287, 316, 318, 395; canon law in, 313; church–state relations in, 166, 259, 262, 279–80, 282, 284–88, 399–401, 414, 422–23, 435, 449–50, 451–58, 463, 493–94; civil war in, 520, 521; class issues in, 317; colonization of, 378; conversion of, 149, 156, 159–60, 162, 164, 165; decline of medieval, 166; demographics of, 277–78; economic issues in, 483, 514, 517; feudalism in, 196, 198, 203, 281, 282–83, 307, 316, 317, 398, 399, 407, 454–55, 517; feuds in, 96; and France, 401, 402, 410–11, 415, 423, 451–52, 455, 462, 493–94, 513–14, 516–18; Franciscan order

England (*cont.*)
in, 456; and Gregorian reform,
265–66; and the intellectual
expansion of Europe, 305–6, 307,
308, 315–18, 346; investiture controversy in, 273–74, 284–88; Jews
in, 366; literature in, 346; lordship
in, 166, 211; and the Magna Carta,
452–55; monarchy in, 95, 164,
211, 278–79, 287–88, 327,
397–402, 469–70, 513–15, 518–19,
520; monasticism in, 219, 376,
378, 379; and the moral authority
of the state, 449–50, 451–58, 463;
nationalism in, 456, 486, 513, 514;
as a national state, 484, 513–21;
nobility in, 465, 466, 469–70, 484,
485, 521; Norman conquest of,
211, 277–81, 346, 475;
peasantry/serfs in, 164, 188, 472,
473, 484; population pressures in,
475; power in, 514–15; and representative government, 456, 457,
514–15; slaves in, 163; and the
Viking invasions, 166, 236, 283;
women in, 120. *See also* English
Law; Hundred Years' War
English law: and the adversary system,
12–13; and the barbarian invasions, 97, 98–99; and class issues,
317, 472; and the clergy, 400–401,
494; codification of the, 307–8,
315–18, 397–98; and German law,
308, 315–18, 398, 453; and the
intellectual expansion of Europe,
307–8, 315–18; and the Magna
Carta, 453–55; and the monarchy,
191, 283–84, 397–98; and the
moral authority of the state, 457;
and the nobility, 469–70; and the
Norman conquest, 191, 283–84;
and the paradoxes of the middle
ages, 564; and the Parliament,
515; and Roman law, 12–13, 126,
315, 317, 318, 398, 457; weaknesses of the, 317
Entertainment, 479–80
Epictetus, 20
Erdmann, Carl, 290
Eschenbach, Wolfram von, 353

Essenes, 33, 147
Etymologies (Isidore of Seville), 83
Europe: in 1050 AD, 235–41; in 1300
AD, 475–80; balance of power in,
464; colonization of, 229–30, 236,
375, 378; countries included in
the first, 185; culture and society
in the first, 185–204; deforestation
of, 236; demographics of, 475,
563; emergence of the first,
185–95; factors creating the first,
161–62, 170, 171–73; geography
of the first, 187–88; Latin as dominant language in the first, 185–86;
as a new civilization, 185; rise of,
228–33; as two cultures, 530
Eusebius of Caesarea, 7, 48, 52, 53, 54,
56, 66, 67–68, 75, 136, 331
Exchequer, 287, 398–99, 472
Excommunication, 86, 254, 269, 400,
459, 463, 495–96
Experimentalism, 447, 534–35
Explorations, 483, 513

Family, structure of, 477–79
Feminism, 539
Ferdinand of Aragon, 511, 512
Feudalism: and church-state relations,
200–203, 209, 211, 282, 454–55,
462; and the crisis of the middle
ages, 486; definition of, 195–96;
emergence of, 197–204; and the
Hundred Years' War, 486; importance of, 204; and Judaism, 365;
and the law, 200, 307, 308,
311–12, 316, 317; and lordship,
195, 196–204; and manorialism,
196; and the medieval equilibrium, 206–11; and military service, 198–99, 201, 209, 281, 283;
and monarchy, 202–3; and
monasticism, 153–54; and monks'
role in society, 376; and the
moral authority of the state,
454–55, 462; and the nobility,
467, 468; and the Peace of God
movement, 202; and secular leadership, 398, 399, 406–7, 409,
411–15. *See also* Vassalage; *specific country or monarchy*

Ficino, Marsilio, 550
Filioque controversy, 291
FitzNeal, Richard, 398–99
Fitz-Stephen, William, 476
Flanders, 207, 231–32, 237–38, 248, 410, 467, 470–71, 481, 483, 484, 486, 517
Flemalle, Master of, 539, 554
Flemish painters, 539–40, 554, 555
Florence, Italy, 471, 477, 479, 484, 525–26, 527, 530, 543–45, 552, 559
Florentine Academy, 550
Florentine painters, 554
Fontrevault order, 378
The Fountain of Life (Avicebrol), 368
Four Doctors, 311
France: alcoholic beverages in, 480; army of, 467, 517, 518; banking in, 493–96; and the barbarian invasions, 93, 94, 101, 102–3, 105–21; bourgeois in, 470; bureaucracy in, 462–63, 489, 516; cathedrals of, 436; church–state relations in, 65, 155, 159, 167, 168, 170, 173–83, 239, 259, 291–92, 413–15, 422, 423–24, 435, 449–50, 451, 461–64, 488–92, 493–97, 501, 515, 520; communes in, 472; and the crusades, 291–92, 294, 295, 300, 302, 450, 461, 463–64, 488–89; economic issues in, 141–42, 143, 515–16, 518, 520; education in, 170, 179, 244, 276, 321, 324, 376, 409, 471; and England, 401, 402, 410–11, 415, 423, 451–52, 455, 462, 493–94, 513–14, 516–18; feudalism in, 196, 198, 202–3, 307, 407, 409, 411–15, 462, 517, 518; Franciscan order in, 463; and Germany, 506; and the intellectual expansion of Europe, 305–6, 311–12, 316, 321, 345–51; and Islam, 136; and Italy, 490, 527; Jews in, 364, 366; law in, 91, 311–12, 316, 489, 516; literature of, 345–51; manorialism in, 188; monarchy in, 202–3, 469, 513–14, 515–16, 517–18, 521; monasticism in, 145–46, 149, 170, 233, 248,
374, 375, 377, 383; and the moral authority of the state, 449–50, 451, 461–64; nationalism in, 486, 513–14; as a national state, 484, 513–21; nobility in, 465, 466, 469, 484, 485, 520–21; peasantry in, 472, 473, 476, 484, 517–18; popular heresy in, 389, 392, 393; representative government in, 456, 469, 515–16; Roman influence in, 93; scholarship in, 276; and Sicily, 460, 461, 464, 469, 511, 522–23; and the Viking invasions, 193–94. *See also* Capetian monarchy; Carolingian world; Hundred Years' War; Merovingian world; University of Paris; *specific region or monarch*
Franciscan order: and asceticism/poverty, 248, 263, 428, 430, 488, 499, 534; and church–state relations, 456, 463; and the crusades, 300–301; and the decline of papal power, 498–99; and education, 441; and emotional religiosity, 428, 429, 431, 432–33, 447; and the Fraticelli, 499, 534; and the harvest of medieval thought, 531–32, 533–34; hymns of the, 446; as itinerant priests, 431–32; and monks' role in society, 381; and the moral authority of the state, 456, 463; papal reactions to the, 430–31; and the paradoxes of the middle ages, 566; and popular heresy, 435; and popular piety, 428, 429–33; as scholars, 432; and scholasticism, 531–32, 533–34; and the Spiritual Franciscans, 490, 499, 533–34; and the systemization of knowledge, 445–46, 447–48
Franks, 105–21. *See also* France; *specific person*
Fraticelli, 499, 534
Frederick I Barbarossa (German emperor), 275–76, 298, 311, 329, 337, 396, 397, 398, 402–8, 414
Frederick II (German emperor), 300, 422, 450, 458–61, 463–64, 488, 507

Free will, 23, 84, 260–61
Friars Minor, 533
Fulda, monastery at, 168–69, 271

Gaetani, Benedict, 492. *See also* Boniface VIII
Gaiseric the Lame, 102
Ganshof, F. L., 198
Gaul. *See* Carolingian world; France; Merovingian world
Gefolge, 95, 197
Gelasian doctrine, 86–87, 158, 177, 186, 258, 448, 449, 461
Gelasius I (pope), 86, 109, 127, 155, 177
Genealogy, 468
Genoa, Italy, 525
Geoffrey of Monmouth, 352
Gerard of York, 286
Gerbert of Aurillac (aka Sylvestr II), 140, 215–16, 217, 384
German law: and the barbarian invasions, 13, 91–92, 96–99, 108; and English law, 308, 315–18, 398, 453; and French law, 311–12; and the intellectual expansion of Europe, 307, 308, 309, 311–12, 315–18; and the medieval equilibrium, 213; and the Ottonian Empire, 213; and Roman law, 307, 309, 508
Germania (Tacitus), 91
Germans/Germany: barbarian invasions by the, 41, 44–47, 62, 89–110, 123–24, 145, 155, 162, 479; bourgeoisie in, 266; and the Carolingian world, 190–91; church-state relations in, 158–59, 168–71, 211–17, 259, 403–8, 414, 421–22, 449–50, 451–52, 458–61, 463–64, 506, 509; cities in, 483, 508; civil war in, 402–8, 421–22; communes in, 471–72; conversion of, 167–71; and early Christianity, 93, 167–71; early political institutions of, 95–96; eastward movement in, 100, 378, 383, 405–6, 472, 475, 505; economic issues in, 230, 483, 505, 508; feudalism in, 196, 203, 274–75, 406–7, 505, 507; folk poetry of, 91; and France, 506;

"free cities" in, 471–72; as a geographical designation, 508–9; and Gregorian reform, 265–76; and the Hussite movement, 500; and the intellectual expansion of Europe, 305–6, 307, 308, 309, 311–12, 315–18, 346, 352–53; interregnum in, 460, 505; investiture controversy in, 395, 402–3; and Italy, 311, 403–5, 407, 408, 414, 422, 450, 458–61, 506, 522–23; Jews in, 366; literature in, 346, 352–53; and the medieval equilibrium, 211–17; merchants in, 472; monarchy in, 10, 180–82, 183, 203, 273–76, 408, 464, 506–9; monasticism in, 168–69, 276, 378, 383; and the moral authority of the state, 449–50, 451–52, 458–61, 463–64; mysticism in, 536; and nationalism, 500, 508; nobility in, 465, 484, 505; particularism in, 505–9; peasantry/serfs in, 188, 266, 472, 473, 509; political disintegration of, 464, 469; power in, 506–7, 508; and representative government, 508; and republicanism, 507–8; Roman influence on the, 93; Scandinavian origins of the, 90, 93; and Sicily, 421, 422, 458, 522; sources about early history of, 91–92; universality of, 487; vassalage in, 274–75; women in, 120. *See also* Carolingian world; Hohenstaufen dynasty; Ottonian Empire; *specific emperor*
Ghibellines, 405, 459, 522, 523, 525
Gibbon, Edward, 41, 42
Giotto, 432, 433, 554
Gnosticism, 72, 73, 392–93, 427
Godfrey of Lorraine, 294, 297
Golden Bull (1356), 507
Goliardic poetry, 345
Gospels, 32, 33, 35, 40, 64–65, 147, 262
Gothic architecture, 321–22, 323–24, 436–38, 555
Goths, 93, 104, 106–7, 109. *See also* Ostrogoths; Visigoths
Gottfried of Strassburg, 353
Granada, 510, 511

Gratian, 60–61, 313, 337
Greece/Greeks, 7, 8–9, 147–48, 149, 162–63, 549. *See also* Classical thought; Hellenistic civilization
Greek Orthodoxy: and celibacy, 251, 503; and dissent, 69; and the fall of the Roman Empire, 47; and papal authority, 173–74; and the Petrine doctrine, 65; schism between the Latin church and, 86–87, 254, 291, 299, 424, 490–91
Gregorian reform: and Aristotelianism, 255; and asceticism, 248–49, 262–63, 375; authoritative sources for, 262; and the Benedictine/Cluniac order, 246, 247, 248–49, 250–51, 253, 270; and canon law, 244, 258, 312–14; and celibacy, 251–52; and the Cistercian movement, 248; and class issues, 260–62; criticisms of, 265–66; and the crusades, 262, 272; divisions in, 245–46; and Donatism, 255–56, 263; and economic issues, 243–44; and education, 244; and emotional religiosity, 252–53, 261–62; and the essentials of Christian society, 249–65; and God's role, 253; and heresy, 262; importance of, 250; intellectual consequences of, 263–65; and the investiture controversy, 243, 244, 246, 262–63, 266–76; leadership of, 245–46, 249–65; and the medieval equilibrium, 246, 249, 255, 260, 272; and monasticism, 247–49, 375; and mysticism, 253; nature/origin of, 243–49; outcomes of, 375; and papal absolutism, 258–59, 263, 273, 327, 328, 448; and papal bureaucracy, 263, 273; and popular piety, 246–47, 261; and poverty, 261–63; and the social gospel, 261, 262, 263; and theocratic monarchy, 260–61, 265–66, 273, 395, 396
Gregory I the Great (pope), 66, 85–86, 118, 155–60, 165, 169, 174, 177, 205, 257
Gregory II (pope), 174

Gregory VII (pope): and the Anglo-Norman monarchy, 277, 279–80; background of, 257–58; and canon law, 308; and celibacy, 503; and the crusades, 290–91; death of, 272; and the English investiture controversy, 284, 285, 286; and papal absolutism, 87, 327, 328, 448; personality of, 257; and popular heresy, 388; role in Gregorian reform of, 256–62; and secular leadership, 414; and social criticism, 260–62, 263; stature of, 256–57; and theocratic monarchy, 260–61. *See also* Gregorian reform
Gregory IX (pope), 313, 451, 459
Gregory of Tours, 111, 112, 113, 115–16, 117, 141–42, 148, 155, 157, 177, 185
Groote, Gerhard, 536
Grosseteste, Robert, 447–48, 534
Guelphs, 405, 407, 421–22, 522, 523, 525
Guesclin, Bertrand du, 518
The Guide for the Perplexed (Maimonides), 369–70
Guilds, 231, 365, 436, 440, 471, 523, 543

Hagiography, 53
Halevi, Judah, 368–69
Hanseatic League, 471–72, 483, 508
Hapsburg dynasty, 506, 508. *See also specific monarch*
Harding, Stephen, 377, 380
Harold Godwinson (king of England), 278–79, 280
Haskins, C. H., 278–79
Hastings, Battle of, 280
Hebrew Bible. *See* Old Testament
Heer, Frederick, 565–66
Hellenistic civilization, 8–9, 10
Henry I (English king), 286–87, 307–8, 315, 350, 397, 452
Henry I (German emperor), 212
Henry II (English king): ascension of, 288; charisma of, 396, 397–402; and church–state relations, 324–25, 332, 399–401; and France, 298, 410, 411, 415; and the intellectual expansion of Europe, 315,

Henry II (*cont.*)
  316, 317–18, 324–25, 332, 351; and the law, 315, 316, 317–18, 397–98; marriage of, 298; power of, 396, 397–402, 412
Henry II (German Emperor), 216–17
Henry III (English king), 450, 453, 455–58, 462, 463, 470
Henry III (German emperor), 220–22, 239, 240, 247, 254, 260, 265–66
Henry IV (English king), 285
Henry IV (German emperor), 254–55, 266–76, 291, 414
Henry V (English king), 273, 518–19
Henry V (German emperor), 262–63, 271, 287, 403
Henry VI (English king), 519, 521
Henry VI (German emperor), 299, 407, 408, 421
Henry VII (English king), 521–22
Henry VII (German emperor), 548
Henry of Bracton, 318
Henry the Lion (duke of Saxony), 403, 406–7
Heraclitus, 16
Heraclius I (Byzantine emperor), 129, 132
Heraldry, 468
Heresy: and absolutism, 79; and Augustinism, 426; and canon law, 314; and church corruption, 502; and the crisis of the middle ages, 481, 484; and the decline of papal power, 499–500; and the Dominican order, 428–29; and Gregorian reform, 263; and the intellectual expansion of Europe, 314, 320, 343; and popular piety, 374; romantic love as, 349; and scholasticism, 531; and women, 427. *See also* Anticlericalism; Antisacerdotalism; Crusades; Inquisition; Popular heresy; *specific heresy*
Hermit-saints, 248, 374
Hierocratic theory. *See* Papal absolutism
Higher Criticism, 22, 32
Hildebrand. *See* Gregory VII (pope); Gregorian reform
Hildegard of Bingen, 355–56

Hincmar of Rheims, 186
Hippo (city), 102
History: Christian views of, 23, 26; Greek/Roman views of, 23, 24, 77; Judaic views of, 23–24, 25, 77; Otto of Freising's views of, 328; St. Augustine's views of, 76–78
History of Florence (Machiavelli), 552–53
History of the Franks (Gregory of Tours), 111, 115–16, 177
History of the Goths (Cassiodorus), 108
History of the Kings of Britain (Geoffrey of Monmouth), 352
History of My Calamities (Abelard), 331, 332
Hohenstaufen dynasty: and anticlericalism, 384; and church–state relations, 421–22, 435, 450, 455, 458–61, 489–90 491; and the civil war, 421–22; demise of the, 522; and the intellectual expansion of Europe, 328, 353; and Italy, 522–23; and the moral authority of the state, 455, 458–61. *See also specific monarch*
Holy Roman Empire. *See* Germans/Germany; Hohenstaufen dynasty; *specific emperor*
"The House of God," 375
Hugh of Cluny, 257, 270
Hugh of Fleury, 265
Hugh the Great, 219
Huizinga, Johan, 530, 562
Humanism, 190, 505, 540, 560. *See also* Christian humanism; Renaissance humanism
Humbert of Silva Candida, 245, 250, 253–56, 259, 387
Hundred Years' War, 486, 513, 515, 516–18, 538
Huns, 64, 89, 99–100, 103, 106, 300–301
Hussite movement, 500

"Ice Age, little," 482
Iconoclastic controversy, 69, 173–74, 226
Ile-de-France, 322, 410
Illuminated manuscripts, 190, 226, 437
Imitation of Christ (Thomas a Kempis), 536

Immortality, 40, 360, 362, 370, 548

Imperial ideals, 173–83

Imperial title, 180–82, 183, 214–15

Imperial unity, 57

Incarnation, 29–30, 32, 40, 77, 127, 165, 391, 444

Individualism, 331–32, 352, 353–54, 374, 428, 432, 540–41, 558

Indulgences, 86, 292–93, 504–5

Innocent II (pope), 339–40

Innocent III (pope): and anticlericalism, 384; and asceticism, 382; background of, 417; and church corruption, 501; and church-state relations, 421–22, 435, 451, 454–55, 458–61; and the crusades, 299, 300; death of, 418, 422; election of, 417; and the Jews, 426–27; as a leader, 493; and the moral authority of the state, 451, 454–55, 458–61; and papal absolutism, 313, 417–28, 451, 458–61; and the paradoxes of the middle ages, 566; peace of, 435; and popular heresy, 384; power of, 488; stature of, 257. See also Lateran Council, Fourth

Innocent IV (pope), 451, 460, 463–64, 488

Inquisition, 79, 314, 370, 372, 425–26, 427, 429, 435, 461–62, 495, 499, 512–13, 534

Intellectual freedom, 440–41

International Gothic style, 554

Introduction to Divine and Human Readings (Cassiodorus), 152

Investiture controversy: aim of the, 245; in England, 273–74, 284–88; in Germany, 243, 244, 246, 262–63, 266–76, 395, 402–3; and Gregorian reform, 243, 244, 246, 262–63, 266–76; importance of the, 246; and the intellectual expansion of Europe, 311, 329; and the law, 311; and leadership, 402–3; and the medieval equilibrium, 272, 395; and the Ottonian Empire, 213; outcomes of the, 245, 246; and the Turkish conquest of Byzantium, 291; as a world revolution, 244

Ireland, 90, 103, 149, 161–71. See also Celtic church

Irnerius, 310–11

Irrigation systems, 6, 139, 227–28

Isabella of Castile, 511, 512

Isaiah (biblical), 31

Isidore of Seville, 83, 105, 165, 194–95, 312

Islam: and Aristotelianism, 362–63, 371–72; and the Byzantine Empire, 136–37; decline of, 371; divisions within, 137–38; and early Christianity, 133, 135, 136, 140, 142; economic issues in, 139–43; expansion of, 131–43; and the Jews, 132, 133, 134–35; limitations/weaknesses of, 225–28, 289; messianic/mystical aspects of, 138, 361, 371; oriental traditions of, 132, 139; and Platonism, 362; political institutions of, 227–28; and the reason and revelation controversy, 361–63, 371–72; religious teachers of, 137–38; Roman influence on, 132, 140; theology of, 134–35; as a universal religion, 133–34. See also Crusades

Italy: and the barbarian invasions, 101, 103, 104–10; bourgeois in, 404, 470–71, 477, 523, 540; bureaucracy in, 523; cities in, 471, 477, 483, 522, 523, 524–25, 527, 542, 552–53; class issues in, 522, 523, 524, 525, 541–42; communes in, 231, 404, 405, 472, 522, 523, 524; court life in, 542–43; economic issues in, 231, 471, 481, 522, 523, 524–25, 527, 541–42, 544–45; education in, 244, 276, 376, 440, 471, 551; feudalism in, 196, 522; and France, 490, 527; and Germany, 311, 403–5, 407, 408, 414, 422, 450, 458–61, 506, 522–23; and Gregorian reform, 275–76; and the Hapsburg dynasty, 508; and the intellectual expansion of Europe, 305–6, 308–10, 312, 346; invasions of, 526–28; and the investiture controversy,

Italy (*cont.*)

275–76; Justinian's reconquest of, 105, 107, 110, 124–31; legal studies/law in, 308–10, 312, 524; literature in, 346; merchants in, 276, 471, 524–25, 541–42, 557, 563; monasticism in, 247–49, 374–75; nobility in, 465, 466, 468–69, 477, 484, 485–86, 524, 542, 557; particularism in, 522–28; peasantry in, 473, 523; politics in, 542, 543–45; popular heresy in, 388; Renaissance in, 530, 540–61, 563, 566; republicanism in, 525, 526, 543–45, 552; social structure in, 541–42; universities in, 531, 549. *See also specific city*

Itinerant preachers, 387–88, 430, 431–32, 472

Itinerant scholars, 233

Ivo of Chartres, 265, 312

Jacopone da Todi, 446

Jacquerie, 484

Jarrow (monastery), 164, 166

Jean de Meun, 470, 488

Jerusalem, 136, 296, 297–98, 300

Jesus Christ, 31–35, 36, 39, 64–65

Jews/Judaism: and the Albigensians, 392–93; and Aristotelianism, 360–61, 363–72; assimilation of the, 371–72; basic concepts in, 29–37; and celibacy, 253, 503; Christianity compared with, 29–37; and classical thought, 358, 359–61, 363–72; conversion of the, 302–3, 366, 372, 426, 512; and covenant theology, 24–25, 26–27; and the crusades, 293, 295, 296, 301, 365; deterioration of position of, 365–72; diets of the, 479; in the Dominican order, 426; eastward migration of the, 366; and economic issues, 139, 364, 365–66, 512; in England, 366; expulsion of the, 512–13, 536; and feudalism, 365; as a foundation of medieval culture, 21–27; founding of, 22–23; in France, 364, 366; in Germany, 366; ghettoization of the, 366, 371, 426; and history, 23–24, 25; and the Inquisition, 427; and Islam, 132, 133, 134–35; and the law, 364, 365–66, 372; massacre of (1096), 253; and monasticism, 147; and moral theory, 24; and mysticism, 138, 370–71, 427; and nationalism, 368–69; and neoplatonism, 368, 370; origins of, 22, 23; and papal absolutism, 426–27; persecution of the, 79, 132, 293, 295, 296, 301, 302–3, 364, 365, 367, 369, 512; and Platonism, 18, 364; political traditions in, 24; postexile period of, 30–40; progressive tradition in, 77–78; and radicalism, 25–27; and reason and revelation, 363–72; reform tradition in, 24–27; and the Roman Empire, 33–34, 39–40, 46, 363; as slaves, 2; in Spain, 302–3, 364, 367–72, 512–13; and trade, 139, 143. *See also* Anti-Semitism

Joachim of Flora, 343, 389, 533

Joan of Arc, 519

Job, Book of, 30–31

Jocelyn of Brakelond, 379

John the Baptist, 33, 147

John (English king), 95, 401–2, 415, 422, 423, 450, 451–52, 455

John of Salisbury, 306, 319, 324–28, 329, 330, 442, 449

John the Scot, 190

John XXII (pope), 533

Judaism. *See* Jews/Judaism

Judges, law, 309, 312, 314, 315, 318, 457, 487

Julian the Apostate (Byzantine emperor), 59–60, 111

Julius Caesar (Roman ruler), 44, 90

Jury system, 191, 283, 309, 317, 318, 453, 457

Justices, legal, 316, 317

Justin I (Byzantine emperor), 109–10, 124, 127

Justinian (Byzantine emperor), 47, 105, 107, 110, 123, 124–31, 143

Justinian code, 54, 125–26, 130, 131, 308–14, 315, 398

Kabbalah, 370–71, 393, 427, 551
Kempis, Thomas à, 536
Kingship. *See* Monarchy; *specific monarchy/dynasty or monarch*
Knighthood, 468, 486, 543
Knights of the Golden Fleece, 537
Knights Hospitalers, 382
Knights Templars, 382–83, 496–97
Knowledge, systemization of, 438–48
Knowles, David, 151
Koran, 360, 361, 362–63
The Kuzari (Halevi), 368

Lactantius, 48
Ladurie, E. LeRoy, 473
Lambert, Malcolm, 391
Landlords, 8. *See also* Feudalism; Lordship
Lanfranc, 210, 280, 284, 285, 320, 322
Langland, William, 536–37
Langton, Stephen, 423, 452, 454–55
Las Navas de Tolosa, battle of (1212), 302
The Last Supper (Leonardo da Vinci), 556
Lateran Council, Fourth (1215), 318, 366, 384, 418–19, 426, 453, 501
Latin (language): domination of, 185–86, 344
Latin transmitters, 81–88
Latouche, R., 93, 112
Law: and absolutism, 311, 312, 316, 318; aim of, 309; and the bourgeois, 472; and bureaucracy, 310, 314–15, 316, 318; and the Carolingian world, 191; and the crisis of the middle ages, 483; divine, 449; and feudalism, 200, 307, 308, 311–12, 316, 317; and forged documents, 177; and the intellectual expansion of Europe, 306–18; and the Italian Renaissance, 551–52, 564; and Judaism, 364, 365–66, 372; and leadership, 395; and the moral authority of the state, 449; natural, 11, 309, 449; and the peasantry, 472; as a profession, 564; and rationality, 309, 310; and "royal law," 309; and the systemization of knowledge, 439, 441;

and urbanization, 308. *See also* Canon law; English law; France: law in; German law; Judges, law; Jury system; Justinian code; Roman law
Lawyers, 306–18, 425, 462–63, 466
Leadership: and the bourgeois, 413; and charisma, 395–408; criticisms of, 488; and the crusades, 294–95, 407; in early Christianity, 36–37; and education, 395, 409; and the fall of the Roman Empire, 44; and feudalism, 398, 399, 406–7, 409, 411–15; and the investiture controversy, 402–3; and the Judaic tradition, 26, 36–37; and the law, 395; and monasticism, 145–55; and popular piety, 395; and power, 395–408; and the Roman curia, 395–96; secular, 395–415; and the theocratic monarchy, 395, 398, 414. *See also* Ecclesiastical leadership; Papacy; Papal absolutism; *specific person or group*
League of Upper Germany, 507–8
Lechfeld, battle of the, 214
Legnano, battle of (1174), 405
Lennard, Reginald, 277
Leo I the Great (pope), 63–65, 66, 104, 127
Leo III (pope), 180–81
Leo IX (pope), 220, 235, 240, 251, 253, 254
Leonardo da Vinci, 555–56
Letter to Hermann of Metz (Gregory VII), 260–62
Lévi-Strauss, Claude, 14
Liberal arts, 82–83, 325, 326, 338, 442, 560
Liberal humanism, 560
Liberalism, 14, 75
Life of Constantine (Eusebius), 48, 52, 331
Life of St. Anthony (Athanasius), 147
Life of St. Louis (Joinville), 450, 466
Literacy. *See* Education
Literature: and anticlericalism, 384; and the intellectual expansion of Europe, 343–56; and the Italian Renaissance, 546–49; and the

Literature (*cont.*)
nobility, 465–66; and the peasantry, 472; and popular piety, 436; romantic, 346, 352–54, 442; and scholasticism, 442; and vernacular languages, 344–56. *See also* Writers; *specific writers*
Little Flowers (St. Francis biography), 446
Liudprand of Cremona, 225, 295
Lives of the Twelve Caesars (Suetonius), 179
Localism: and the Carolingian world, 192–93; emergence of, 182; in the first Europe, 188
Lollards, 500
Lombard, Peter, 337, 418
Lombard League, 405, 459
Lombards, 130–31, 156, 157, 174, 178, 214
London, England, 278, 286, 480
Long peace, 467, 476
Longbow, 467, 519
Lopez, Robert, 142
Lordship, 166, 172, 182, 195, 196–204, 211, 217, 226
Lot, Ferdinand, 41–42
Lothair (duke of Saxony), 403
Louis VI the Fat (French king), 322, 323, 410, 411, 414
Louis VII (French king), 298, 322, 323, 410–11, 413, 414–15
Louis VIII (French king), 461–62
Louis the Pious (French emperor), 182, 190, 193, 218
Louis IX (French king and saint), 300, 302, 450, 462, 463–64, 466
Louis XI (French king), 520
Louis of Bavaria, 533
Low Countries, 166–71, 514
Love. *See* Marriage; Romanticism; Sexual issues; Women
Loyalty, 94, 197–204, 396
Luther, Martin, 86, 292, 504
Lyons, council at (1245), 460

Macedonian Renaissance, 226
Machiavelli, Niccolò, 552–53
Magic, 118, 504–5
Magistri, 310

Magna Carta, 452–55
Maimonides, 359–60, 363, 369–70, 371
Maitland, F. W., 195
Mallory, Thomas, 538
Manegold of Lautenbach, 275
Manfred (Sicilian king), 460
Manicheanism, 389, 390–91, 392
Manorialism, 172, 188, 196, 211, 472, 473. *See also* Peasants; Serfs
Mantegna, Andrea, 555
Manuscript search, 549–50
Manzikert, battle of (1071), 291
Marco Polo, 479
Marcus Aurelius, 20
Marranos, 372
Marriage, 418, 419
The Marriage of Philology and Mercury (Martianus Capella), 82
Marshal, William, 351
Marsilio of Padua, 551–52
Martel, Charles, 168, 169, 174, 199
Martianus Capella, 81–82
Marx, Karl, 14, 195
Mathematics, 82, 139, 447, 554, 564
Matilda (English queen), 287–88
Matilda of Tuscany, 268, 269, 270
Maximilian I (German emperor), 508
Medici family, 481, 525–26, 527, 544–45, 550, 552, 558
Medicine, 139, 229. *See also* Black Death
Medieval Cities (Pirenne), 230
Medieval equilibrium: and the Cluniac Ideal, 218–23; and feudalism, 206–11; and Gregorian reform, 246, 249, 255, 260, 272; and the investiture controversy, 272, 395; nature of early, 205–6; and Normandy, 206–11; and the Ottonian Empire, 211–17; and the reaffirmation of papal absolutism, 417–28
Medievalism, 565–66
Memling, Hans, 540
Mercenaries, 467, 485, 524, 526, 527
Merchants: and the ancient world, 2; and chivalry, 537–38; and class issues, 537–38; and the crisis of the middle ages, 483; criticisms of, 488; in Germany, 472; in Italy, 276, 471, 524–25, 541–42, 557, 563; and the law, 308; as nobility,

522; and the papacy, 276; and politics, 542, 563; and popular heresy, 386; and the rise of Europe, 231–32; and scholasticism, 442. *See also* Trade

Merovingian world, 111–21, 141–42, 145, 155, 167, 192–93, 198, 205

Mesopotamia, 3, 4, 5, 22, 363, 364

Middle ages: beginning/ending of the, 561–66; crisis of the, 480–87; modern interest in, 561–66; paradoxes in the, 563–65; revival of the, 565

Milan, Italy, 70, 128, 231, 240, 267, 293–94, 404, 526, 527

Military religious orders, 381, 382–83

Military service: and the Carolingian world, 192; and the crusades, 289–303; and feudalism, 198–99, 201, 209, 281, 283; and the medieval equilibrium, 210; and monks' role in society, 376, 381, 382–83; and the nobility, 466–67, 484; in the Roman Empire, 44–46. *See also* Mercenaries; *specific country*

Milton, John, 388

Milvian Bridge, battle of the, 48, 49

Ministerialis, 221–22, 274, 376

Minnesingers, 352–53

Mirandola, Pico della, 550–51, 559–60

Missi system, 192–93

Modern Devotion movement, 499, 536

Mohammed, 123, 133–43

Mona Lisa (Leonardo da Vinci), 556

Monarchy: and the barbarian invasions, 94, 95; beginnings of, 6–13; and the bureaucratic state, 277–84; criticisms of the, 488; divine, 6–7, 12, 55; and education, 441; and Eusebius's views of the ideal life of a medieval king, 52–53; and feudalism, 202–3; Germanic view of, 10; and German law, 98–99; and ideology, 396–97; and the imperial title, 180–82, 183; and intellectual freedom, 440–41; and the nobility, 469; and Platonism, 53; and succession questions, 487. *See also*

Absolutism; Caesaropapism; Leadership; Theocratic monarchy; *specific monarchy/dynasty, monarch, or country*

Monarchy (Dante), 547–48, 551

Monasticism: in 1050 AD, 239–40; and absolutism, 149–55; and the Carolingian world, 218; and class issues, 154–55; and the Cluniac Ideal, 218–23; communal, 148–55, 248; and ecclesiastical leadership, 145–55; and education, 82–83, 152–53, 163, 170, 179, 188–90, 208, 233, 375–76; and feudalism, 153–54; and Gregorian reform, 247–49, 375; and the hermit–saints, 374; and individualism, 374; and Judaism, 33, 147; and monks' role in society, 375–84; and papal absolutism, 420; and the proliferation of orders, 373–84; rise of, 145–55; and scholarship, 82; and wealth of monasteries, 153–54; and women, 154–55. *See also* Asceticism; *specific order or country*

Mongolians. *See* Huns

Monophysite heresy, 50, 51, 127, 129

Monte Cassino, monastery of, 248

Montpellier, University of, 311

Moore, R. I., 566

Morality: and the Donatist heresy, 52; and early Christianity, 37–38; and the fall of the Roman Empire, 47; and Judaism, 24; and Platonism, 18; and the state, 448–64

Morte d'Arthur (Mallory), 538

Moslems: in 1050 AD, 237; and Aristotelianism, 138, 140, 360–61, 362–63, 371–72; barbarian invasions by the, 51, 52, 54, 58, 89, 105, 155; and the Byzantine Empire, 129–30; conversion of the, 431; and Frederick II, 459; Justinian's policies toward the, 129–30; in Spain, 512–13; translations of classical thought by the, 359–61, 362–63. *See also* Crusades; Islam

Muret, battle of (1213), 424

Mysticism: and Augustinianism, 79; and the barbarian invasions, 118; and the Carolingian world, 187; and church corruption, 504–5; and the crisis of the middle ages, 483; and early Christianity, 145, 146; and Greek Orthodoxy, 69; and Gregorian reform, 253; and the harvest of medieval thought, 536; and the Hundred Years' War, 519; and the intellectual expansion of Europe, 322, 325, 341–42, 353, 355–56; and Islam, 361, 371; and the Italian Renaissance, 540–41, 547; and Judaism, 370–71, 427; and popular heresy, 393; and the reason and revelation controversy, 361; and scientific thought, 536; and social structure, 118

Naples, Italy, 128, 458, 492, 511, 523
National state: emergence of the, 487; growth of the, 488; power of the, 500–501, 528. *See also specific state*
Nationalism, 50–51, 89, 91, 127, 355, 368–69, 456, 486, 500, 501, 508
Natural law, 11, 309, 449
Navarre, 511
Neoplatonism: and art, 324; and the Carolingian Renaissance, 190; and the intellectual expansion of Europe, 321, 322, 324; and Judaism, 368, 370; and paganism, 59; and popular heresy, 390–91; and the systemization of knowledge, 443, 444, 445
Netherlands, 483, 508, 536
Neustria, monasteries in, 207
New Learning, 544, 549–51
New Testament, 32–33, 36, 64–65, 68, 253
Nibelungenlied (Germanic folk poetry), 91, 102
Nicaea, Council of (325), 418
Nicene Creed, 57
Nicholas of Cusa, 536
Nicholas I (pope), 182, 258–59
Nicholas of Oresme, 535
Nobility: in 1300 AD, 475–76, 477, 479; in the ancient world, 2–21; and the bourgeois, 469, 485; and class issues, 476; and the crisis of the middle ages, 484–86; diets of, 479; divisions within the, 485; and economic issues, 468, 484; and education, 465, 466, 468, 476; and feudalism, 467, 468; and the harvest of medieval thought, 537–38; and the intellectual expansion of Europe, 344, 346–56; and the Italian Renaissance, 542, 557; as lawyers, 466; merchants as, 522; and military service, 466–67, 484; and the monarchy, 469; and the peasantry, 484; and politics, 468–69, 484, 486, 563; power of the, 484–85; status among the, 467–68, 476; in the thirteenth century, 465–70; and urbanism, 465, 468–69; as writers, 344, 465–66. *See also* Chivalry; Feudalism; Lordship; Roman nobility; *specific country*
Nogaret, William de, 495, 496
Nominalism, 336–38, 444, 533
Normandy: in 1050 AD, 236–37; and the Capetian monarchy, 409; and church-state relations, 268, 272, 279–80, 407–8; and the Cluniac Ideal, 219, 222; and the conquest of England, 211, 277–81, 346, 475; and the crusades, 475; education in, 210; England forfeits, 402; feudalism in, 281; and Gregorian reform, 268; importance of, 236–37; and the investiture controversy, 268; and the medieval equilibrium, 205–11, 219; military service in, 376; monasticism in, 376; and Sicily, 407, 475; and the Viking invasions, 208. *See also* Anglo-Norman monarchy
North Africa, 51, 58, 65, 101, 102–3, 128, 135, 136, 139
Nuns/nunneries, 72, 120–21, 154–55, 355, 378, 380

Oath of Strasbourg (842), 186
Old Testament, 21–27, 39–40, 84, 253, 366, 369–70

Orange, Synod of (529), 85
Ordeals, 96–98, 316, 318, 453
Order of Bridgebuilders, 383
Order of the Garter, 537
Ordination of kings, 418
Orosius, 328
Ostrogoths, 90, 100, 104–10, 113, 124, 126, 127, 128
Otto I the Great (German emperor), 212–17, 225, 260, 266
Otto II (German emperor), 215, 217
Otto III (German emperor), 215–16, 217
Otto IV (German emperor), 451–52, 458
Otto IV of Brunswick, 422
Otto of Freising, 272, 319, 328–29, 330, 408, 449
Ottonian Empire, 205–6, 211–17. See also specific emperor
Oxford University, 432, 441, 445, 530, 531, 532, 534, 535

Paganism, 58–61, 65–66. See also Arianism
Pagels, Elaine, 392
Painting, 553–57
Palaeologus family, 490
Palestine, 135, 295, 363
Panofsky, Erwin, 443, 563
Papacy: in 1050 AD, 235; and abdication of the pope, 492; as the Antichrist, 343, 389; at Avignon, 496, 497–98; bureaucratic nature of the, 263, 273, 314–15, 418–28; corruption/scandals of the, 492–505; criticisms of the, 489–505; and Dante's Divine Comedy, 547; decline of power of the, 488–505; and the election of the pope, 254, 267, 339–40, 417, 490, 492, 496, 497–98; emergence of the, 63–66; financing of the, 158, 420–21; height of power of the, 487–88; importance of the, 65; and intellectual freedom, 440–41; and the Italian Renaissance, 543; and the patristic culture, 66–88; and popular piety, 314; reformation of the, 220, 240, 488–505; and the Roman nobility, 180–81, 183, 195, 268, 421, 490,

492; schism about the, 497–98, 526; and secular absolutism, 329; as true successor of Constantine, 258; and vassalage, 452, 454–55. See also Church; Ecclesiastical leadership; Papal absolutism; Papal Curia; specific pope
Papal absolutism: and Aristotelianism, 427; and canon law, 258, 312–14, 420, 423, 448; and the Carolingian world, 173–83; and the church fathers, 67–88; and church-state relations, 493–96; and corruption, 492–96; and the crusading ideal, 424; and Gregorian reform, 258–59, 263, 273, 327, 328, 448; and the Inquisition, 425–26; and the intellectual expansion of Europe, 312–14, 327, 328, 343; and the Italian Renaissance, 551; and the Jews, 426–27; and monasticism, 158; and the moral authority of the state, 448–64; and the papal schism, 498; and popular heresy, 426–27; and popular piety, 419, 420, 427; and the Protestant Reformation, 501; reaffirmation of, 417–28; and Roman law, 12, 87; and secular leadership, 395–415. See also Donation of Constantine; Gelasian doctrine; specific pope
Papal Curia, 273, 313, 314, 383–84, 395–96, 420, 451, 458, 461, 487–88. See also Cardinals
Papal infallibility, 258–59, 263. See also Papal absolutism
Papal legates, 419–20, 501
Papal power. See Papal absolutism
Papal States, 170, 522, 526
Paris, France, 113, 238–39, 410, 479. See also University of Paris
Parish system, 373, 472
Parzifal (Eschenbach), 353
Paschal II (pope), 250, 262–63, 273, 286, 388
Patristic thought. See Church fathers; specific person
Peace of God movement, 202, 210, 247

Peasantry: in 1300 AD, 475–76, 479; and the ancient world, 2; and the bourgeois, 473; and colonization, 472; and the crisis of the middle ages, 484, 487; diets of, 479; and economic issues, 472–73, 487; and the Hundred Years' War, 517–18; and the law, 472; and literature, 472; as mute, 472–73; and the nobility, 484; and the paradoxes of the middle ages, 563; and popular heresy, 391; and popular piety, 373, 472; rationality of, 473; rebellions by the, 483–84, 500; and warfare, 467; wealth of, 473. *See also* Serfs; *specific country*

Peasant's Revolt (1381), 500

Penances, 85–86

People's crusade, 293–94

Pepin II (Carolingian king), 166–67

Pepin III (Carolingian king), 168, 169, 170, 174–76, 178

Persia, 22, 129–30, 132, 136, 137, 139

Peter the Hermit, 293

Petrarch, Francesco, 546, 548–49, 558–59, 560

Petrine doctrine, 64–65, 158, 186, 427, 548

Philip II Augustus (French king), 298–99, 398, 401, 402, 411–13, 415, 422, 423, 451–52, 461

Philip III (French king), 300, 491, 492

Philip IV the Fair (French king), 489, 492, 493–97, 514, 515–16, 517

Philip VI (French king), 517

Philip of Macedon, 19

Philip of Swabia, 421–22

Philo, 136, 364, 366, 370

Philo Judaeus, 40

Philosophy, 13–27, 439, 532, 533. *See also* Aristotelianism; Platonism; Scholasticism

Piers Plowman (Langland), 472, 536–37

Piety. *See* Popular piety

Pirenne, Henri, 92, 140–41, 142, 143, 230

Pisa, Council of (1408), 498

Pius II (pope), 541, 558

Platonism: Aristotelianism compared with, 19–20, 360, 362; and Augustinianism, 75, 78, 81; and the background of Plato, 14–15; as a dominant philosophical system, 13–19, 20; and early Christianity, 18, 38, 40, 147; and the early church hierarchy, 39; and education, 17; emergence of, 13–19; and the Gospels, 32; and the intellectual expansion of Europe, 331, 332, 333–38; and the Italian Renaissance, 540, 549, 550; and Judaism, 18, 364; and the manuscript search, 550; and the Monophysite heresy, 127; and moral theory, 18; and Moslem thought, 134, 362; and papal views of sexuality, 72; and politics, 53; preservation of, 83; and the Socratic dialogue, 15–16; and Stoicism, 20; and the systemization of knowledge, 444–48; as a system of thought, 14; translations of, 108; and universals, 16–17, 23. *See also* Neoplatonism

Podesta, 471, 524, 552

Poetry/poems: and love sonnets, 548

Poetry/poets: Anglo–Saxon, 91; and anticlericalism, 384; and the *chanson de geste*, 346–47, 352; Germanic, 91; Goliardic, 345; and humanism, 442; and the intellectual expansion of Europe, 344–45, 346–54; and the romantic epics, 346, 352–54; and the troubadours, 346, 348–52; by university students, 344–45; in the vernacular, 345–54

Poitiers, battle of (1356), 518

Policraticus (John of Salisbury), 326–28, 329

Politics: in the ancient world, 5–13; of Aquinas, 448–51, 461, 551; and Aristotelianism, 449, 551; and the barbarian invasions, 91, 94, 95–96; and the bourgeois, 471; and early Christianity, 55–66, 86–87; and the fall of the Roman Empire, 41; and the intellectual expansion of Europe, 326–28; and the Italian Renaissance, 551–53; and merchants, 542, 563; and the nobility, 468–69, 563; and the paradoxes of the middle ages, 563; and Platonism, 53. *See also* Church–state relations; *specific civilization, country, or empire*

Politics (Aristotle), 449

Popular heresy: and Augustinianism, 384, 426; and church corruption, 502; dimensions of, 384–93; as negligible, 435; and papal absolutism, 426–27. *See also* Anticlericalism; Antisacerdotalism; Inquisition

Popular piety: and art, 436; and asceticism, 373–74, 428; and the bourgeois, 432–33, 470; and the Franciscan order, 429–33, 445–46; and Gregorian reform, 246–47, 261; and the harvest of medieval thought, 530; and heresy, 374, 387; and the intellectual expansion of Europe, 306, 314, 321, 323, 328, 334, 338, 342, 343, 345, 348, 350; and literature, 345, 348, 350, 436; and monks' role in society, 373–84; new consensus about, 435; and the papacy, 314, 381; and papal absolutism, 419, 420, 427; and the peasantry, 472; and persecution of Jews, 365; and secular leadership, 395; and the systemization of knowledge, 445–46. *See also* Investiture controversy

Portraits, 539–40, 555

Portugal, 483, 510, 511, 513

Poverty, apostolic, 261–63, 377, 388, 430, 488, 490, 499, 533, 534. *See also* Asceticism

Pragmatic Sanction (1438), 520

Prebend, 381

Predestination, 84

Premonstratensian order, 381, 428

Pre-Socratics, 15–16

Primate, 345

Primitivism, 145

The Prince (Machiavelli), 552, 553

Procopius, 129

Professorships, 439–41

Proletariat, 240, 261, 483–84

Prophets: Christian, 36; Jewish, 22–24, 25–27, 36

Proprietary churches, 213, 275

Protestantism, 23, 52, 388, 389, 480, 501, 503, 509, 530, 536, 561, 562

Provence, 348, 358, 359, 370, 389, 393

Psalms, 151

Pseudo-Isidorian Decretals, 312

Psuedo-Dionysius, 322, 323

Pullan, Robert, 324

Puritans, English, 146, 388

Raoul de Cambrai (feudal epic), 200

Rashi, 366

Rationality/reason: and Augustinianism, 75; and the intellectual expansion of Europe, 331; and the Italian Renaissance, 546–47; and Judaism, 363–72; and the law, 309, 310; and Moslem thought, 361–63, 371–72; of peasantry, 473; and Roman law, 11, 12, 13. *See also* Aristotelianism; Scholasticism

Ravenna, Italy, 63, 101, 106, 107, 124, 130

Raymond of St. Giles, 292

Raymond of Toulouse, 294

Realism, 334, 335, 336–38, 443, 444, 445

Reason. *See* Rationality/reason; Scholasticism

Religious orders: proliferation of, 373–84, 419

Renaissance, Italian, 540–61, 563, 566

Renaissance humanism, 442, 500, 540–61, 566

Renaudet, Augustin, 563

Representative government, 456–57, 487, 508, 514–15. *See also specific country*

Republic (Plato), 15

Republicanism, 7, 11–12, 507–8, 543–45, 552, 564

Revelation. *See* Aristotelianism; Bible; Church fathers; Scholasticism; *specific person*

Richard III (English king), 521

Richard the Lion–hearted, 298, 299, 350–51, 401, 415

Richards, Jeffrey, 566

Rollo (Viking), 208

Roman Empire: and absolutism, 12, 13, 26; administration of the, 46–47, 114–15, 130, 132; ancient world influences on the, 5; and the Byzantine Empire, 130, 132; and Christianity, 37–40, 53, 67; and class issues, 38; creation of the, 9–13; decline and fall of the, 40–47, 54, 62, 66, 197; disintegration of the, 75; and early Christianity, 54, 55–66; economic issues in the, 42–43; and education, 81; and Judaism, 33–34, 39–40, 46, 363; military service in the, 44–46; politics in the, 9–13; and republicanism, 7, 11–12; and the Roman destiny, 47–66; St. Augustine's views of the, 76–77; social issues in the, 9–13; unity in the, 46–47; women in the, 71, 119–20. *See also* Barbarian invasions; Roman law

Roman law: and absolutism, 12, 13; and the barbarian invasions, 98, 99, 103, 108–9; and the Byzantine Empire, 124, 130, 132; and canon law, 244; and Christianity, 38; as dominant in Europe, 11; and English law, 12–13, 315, 317, 318, 398, 457; and equity, 13; and French law, 311–12; and German law, 307, 309, 508; and Gregorian reform, 244; and the Inquisition, 512; and the intellectual expansion of Europe, 307, 309, 311–12, 315, 317, 318; and papal absolutism, 12, 87; process/procedures in the, 12–13; and reason, 11, 12, 13; and representative government, 456–57; and social structure, 11–13; and Spanish law, 510; weaknesses of the, 309; and women, 120. *See also* Justinian code

Roman nobility, and the papacy, 180–81, 183, 195, 268, 421, 490, 492

Romance of the Rose (Jean de Meun), 470, 488

Romance of the Rose (William de Lorris), 466

Romanesque architecture, 321, 322, 436, 554

Romanticism, 349–54, 470, 488, 530, 537–38, 547, 548, 549, 558–59

Romantic literature, 346, 352–54, 442

Rome, Italy: in 1050 AD, 240–41; and the barbarian invasions, 101; and Constantinople as the second Rome, 53–55; deurbanization of, 128; and the Gothic War, 128; and the Ottonian Empire, 215–16; papacy returns to, 497; papal control of, 421; sack of, 101; as a symbol, 216. *See also* Papacy

Roscelin, 336

"Royal law," 309

Rudolf of Hapsburg, 460, 506

Sacraments, number of, 418–19

St. Ambrose of Milan, 61, 66, 68, 70–74, 86, 87, 104, 119, 155, 261

St. Anselm of Canterbury, 285–86, 332, 335, 336, 338–39, 341, 384

St. Antony, 153

St. Augustine of Canterbury, and the conversion of England, 159–60, 165

St. Augustine of Hippo: autobiography of, 331; background of, 74; and the barbarian invasions, 101, 102, 104, 118; and the church, 78–80, 155; *City of God* by, 53, 74–75; decline of interest in writings of, 260; and Donatism, 51–52, 78, 255; and human nature, 75–76, 84–85; influence of, 74, 75, 76, 81, 84, 119, 136; and Manicheanism, 389; and the patristic culture, 66, 68; political theory of, 86, 87, 155; social/historical vision of, 76–78; study of works of, 189, 190; systemization of thought of, 14; views about women of, 71, 72; as a writer, 343. *See also* Augustinianism

St. Basil, 148

St. Benedict of Aniane, 218, 219

St. Benedict of Nursia, 149–55, 157, 158

St. Bernard of Clairvaux: and asceticism, 377; and the crusades, 298, 334; and Dante's *Divine Comedy*, 547;

and Donatism, 343; and the intellectual expansion of Europe, 319, 325, 330, 334, 338–43, 344; and the Knights Templars, 382; papal views of, 343; and popular heresy, 384, 387, 389; and popular piety, 334, 387

St. Bonaventura, 445, 447–48, 531–32

St. Boniface, 167–71, 174, 175, 179, 205, 322

St. Columban, 156

St. Denis, 113–14, 322

St. Denis, Abbey of, 178, 239, 321–22, 323–24, 414

St. Dominic, 428–29, 547. *See also* Dominican order

St. Dunstan, 219

St. Francis of Assisi, 250, 339, 429–33, 446, 450, 533, 547. *See also* Franciscan order

St. Gregory. *See* Gregory I the Great (pope)

St. Ignatius Loyola, 339

St. Jerome, 66, 68, 69–70, 80, 104

St. John Cassian, 148–49, 151

St. Leo. *See* Leo I the Great (pope)

St. Louis. *See* Louis IX (king)

St. Martin, 148

St. Patrick, 162

St. Paul (aka Saul of Tarsus), 13, 21, 31, 35–37, 40, 67, 68, 71, 72, 84, 113–14, 120, 136, 251, 503

St. Peter, 65, 547

St. Peter, basilica of, 240

St. Sophia, cathedral of (Constantinople), 125, 126

St. Sylvester, 177

St. Thomas Aquinas. *See* Aquinas, Thomas

St. Victor, monastery of (Paris), 341

Saladin, 297, 298, 299

Salic law, 91, 112

Salin, E., 92–93

Salvation, 31, 36, 84–86, 146, 147, 341–42, 432, 547

San Vitale, church of (Ravenna), 125

Sanctuary, right of, 62

Savonarola, 499, 526

Saxony, 265–66

Scandinavia, 90, 93, 472

Schism: between the Latin and Greek churches, 86–87, 254, 291, 299, 424, 490–91; and the papacy, 497–98, 526

Scholasticism, 439–48, 530, 531–36, 560

Scholem, Gershom, 393

Scientific thought, 428, 429, 432, 435, 443, 444–48, 449, 534–36, 564

Scythians, 108

Secularism: emergence of, 277, 287; and the Italian Renaissance, 558–59, 562; and leadership, 395–415. *See also* National state

Seneschals, 413, 461–62

Sentences (Lombard), 337, 418

Serfs, 4, 117–18, 188, 483, 509, 563. *See also* Feudalism; Peasantry; Vassalage

Sermon on the Mount, 261

Seven Books Against the Pagans (Orosius), 328

Sexual issues: and the double standard, 354–55; patristic attitudes toward, 71–73; and popular heresy, 391. *See also* Romanticism

Sforza family, 526, 527

Sheriffs, 281–82, 412

Shiites, 138

Sic et Non (Abelard), 337

Sicily: and church-state relations, 455, 458, 460, 461, 464; and the crusades, 300; and the French, 268, 300, 407, 460, 461, 464, 469, 475, 491, 511, 522–23; and Germany, 407, 421, 422, 458, 522; and Gregorian reform, 268; and Islam, 130, 136, 140; and the moral authority of the state, 455, 458, 460, 461, 464; Plato in, 15; as a scholarly center, 296, 358, 359; and the Sicilian Vespers, 491, 511, 523; and Spain, 491, 511, 523

Siger of Brabant, 443, 547

Simon de Montfort (the elder), 424, 461

Simon de Montfort (the younger), 457

Slavery, 2, 38, 43, 163

Slavs, 215, 216, 217, 405–6

Social criticism, 538–39

Social gospel, 261, 262, 263

Social issues: and the ancient world, 1–13; and the fall of the Roman Empire, 41; and the Germanic invasions, 91, 94; and Stoicism, 21. *See also* Class issues; *specific civilization, country, or empire*

Social justice, 25

Spain: and Aristotelianism, 20; and the barbarian invasions, 101, 102–3, 105; Berber domination of, 227; bureaucracy in, 512; as a center of scholarship, 138–39, 140, 296, 358, 359, 362, 363; and church-state relations, 65, 155; class issues in, 510; and the crusades, 289–90, 302–3, 509; economic issues in, 510, 511, 512, 513; explorations by, 483, 513; and Gregorian reform, 262; and the Hapsburg dynasty, 508; Inquisition in, 372, 425–26, 512–13; and the intellectual expansion of Europe, 346; and Islam, 136, 137, 138–39, 140; Jews in, 302–3, 364, 376–72, 512–13; law in, 510, 511–12; literature in, 346; military in, 511; monarchy in, 510–11; Moslems in, 155, 511, 512–13; as a national state, 484, 509–13; nobility in, 509; peasantry in, 510; and the Petrine doctrine, 65; power in, 510–11; *Reconquista* in, 262, 289–90, 302–3, 509, 510, 511; and representative government, 456, 510; and the rise of Europe, 232; and Sicily, 491, 511, 523. *See also specific region*

Spinoza, Benedict, 22

Spiritual Franciscans, 490, 499, 533–34

Stabat Mater (Jacopone da Todi), 446

Stadelman, Rudolf, 563

State: Augustinian views of the, 448; Germanic concept of the, 95–96; and moral issues, 326–27, 329, 448–64; Roman concept of the, 9–13. *See also* National state

Stephen of Blois, 288, 294, 350

Stirrup, invention of the, 228

Stoicism, 13–14, 20–21, 59, 83, 549

Strayer, J. R., 195

Stylites, Simon, 147–48

Succession questions. *See specific person or country*

Suetonius, 179

Suffering, 31, 36, 38, 78

Sufists, 138, 361

Suger (abbot of St. Denis), 319, 321, 322–24, 330, 410, 414, 436

Summa Theologica (Aquinas), 337, 443, 446, 546

Sunnis, 138

Sutri, synod of (1045), 220

Sutton Hoo ship, 92

Swiss, 467, 507–8, 527

Sylvester I (pope), 177

Sylvester II (pope), 216, 384

Symmachus, 61, 73–74, 119

Synod of Orange (529), 85

Synod of Sutri (1045), 220

Syria, 58, 127, 129–30, 132–33, 135, 136, 138, 139, 295, 296, 362

Systemization of knowledge, 438–48

Tacitus, 9, 91, 163–64, 197

Talmud, 364, 366, 368, 370

Tauler, Johannes, 536

Technology: and the fall of the Roman Empire, 42–44; and the rise of Europe, 228–29; and warfare, 467, 477, 519, 527, 535

Tertullian, 38, 67, 80, 84

Teutonic Knights, 383

Theobald of Canterbury, 324

Theocratic monarchy: in 1050 AD, 239; and the Carolingian world, 173–83; and the Cluniac Ideal, 220; and the creation of the first Europe, 170, 175–76, 179; in Germany, 217, 220; and Gregorian reform, 260–61, 265–66, 273, 395, 396; and leadership, 395, 398, 414; and the medieval equilibrium, 207, 217

Theodora (empress), 47, 125

Theodore of Tarsus, 164

Theodoric I (Byzantine emperor), 82, 102, 105, 106–10, 131

Theodosius I the Great (Byzantine emperor), 58, 60, 61, 62, 63, 73, 100, 111, 116, 119, 127, 128, 260

Theodosius II (Byzantine emperor), 124

Theology, and the systemization of knowledge, 439, 441, 442–48

Thomas of Celano, 446

The Three Books Against the Simoniacs (Humbert), 254–55, 256

Torah, 36. *See also* Old Testament

Torture, 309, 314, 425, 426, 512

Toulouse, 113, 207, 292, 300, 348, 389, 424, 462

Tournaments, 351, 486, 537

Tours, 136, 148

Trade: and the Anglo–Saxons, 278; and the bourgeois, 471; and the crisis of the middle ages, 481, 482–83; and explorations, 483; and Gregorian reform, 244; and Islam, 139–43; and the Jews, 364; and the rise of Europe, 230, 231–32; and the Roman Empire, 42–43. *See also* Merchants

Trappist order, 380

Treatise on Royal and Sacerdotal Power (Hugh of Fleury), 265

Treaty of Bretigny, 518

Treaty of Troyes (1420), 519

Treaty of Verdun (843), 193

Treitschke, Heinrich, 383

Trent, Council of, 292, 418

Trinity, 40, 50, 64, 337, 444

Troubadours, 346, 348–53, 355

Troyes, Treaty of (1420), 519

Turks, 100, 226, 227, 291, 292, 293, 296, 483, 490, 525

The Two Cities (Otto of Freising), 328

Unam Sanctam (papal bull), 494–95

Universals, debate about, 333–38, 445

Universities: and biblical study, 21; and classical thought, 359, 442, 549; college system at, 441; emergence of, 244, 276, 310, 319–20, 324, 439–40; faculty of the, 441–42; as guilds, 440; and the harvest of medieval thought, 530; and indulgences, 504–5; and the intellectual expansion of Europe, 306, 310, 319–20, 321, 324, 325, 326, 332–33, 344–45; and the Italian Renaissance, 531, 549, 560–61; and the liberal arts, 82; and literature, 344–45; and secular leadership, 395, 409; students at, 344–45, 384, 439, 441; and the systemization of knowledge, 439–48; teaching methods at, 440; and urbanization, 332–33. *See also specific university*

University of Paris: and Averroism, 551; criticism of the, 325, 338; and the Dominican order, 429, 432; experimentalism at, 534; and the harvest of medieval thought, 530; and the intellectual expansion of Europe, 318–20, 324, 325, 328, 330, 338; and the papal schism, 498; and scholasticism, 531, 534, 535; stature of the, 318–19; students at the, 318–20, 324, 325, 328, 330, 441

Urban II (pope), 246, 272–73, 286, 414, 504

Urban (pope), and the crusades, 291–94

Urban VI (pope), 497–98

Urbanization: decline in, 128, 143, 152; in the first Europe, 187; and the intellectual expansion of Europe, 308, 332–33, 348; and the law, 308; and monks' role in society, 374; and the nobility, 465, 468–69; and popular heresy, 386–88; and the rise of Europe, 187, 230–31; and universities, 332–33

Usury, 365–66, 442, 480

Valla, Lorenzo, 550

Vallombrosa order, 374–75

Valois dynasty, 409

Vandals, 64, 102–3, 104, 128

Van der Weyden, Roger, 539, 554

Van Eyck, Hubert, 539

Van Eyck, Jan, 539, 554

Vassalage, 195, 197–204, 209–10, 221, 229, 365, 452, 454–55

Venice, Italy, 143, 232, 294, 295, 299, 424, 477, 482, 524–25

Verdun, Treaty of (843), 193

Vernacular languages: and the intellectual expansion of Europe, 344–56; and the Italian Renaissance, 546,

Vernacular languages (*cont.*)
549; and literature, 344–56; and
the systemization of knowledge,
439
Viking invasions, 163, 166, 189, 193–94,
208, 236, 283
Villard de Honnecourt, 437
Villehardouin, 466
Vincent of Beauvais, 439
Virgin, cult of the, 339, 341, 349,
378–39, 432, 436
Virgin: and Dante's *Divine Comedy*, 547
Virgin of the Rock (Leonardo da Vinci),
556
Virginity, 71, 72
Visigoths, 90, 99, 100–102, 103, 105,
113, 136, 155, 302, 364
Visitation system, 420, 501, 502
Vitalis, Ordericus, 279
Vogelweide, Walther von der, 353, 384

Wagner, Richard, 91
Waldensians, 388, 427, 430
Walter of Henley, 466, 475
Warfare: and the crisis of the middle
ages, 486; and technology, 467,
477, 519, 527, 535. *See also* Feu-
dalism: and lordship; Mercenaries
Welf, 422
Westminster Abbey, 239, 455
William the Bastard. *See* William the
Conqueror
William the Conqueror, 191, 209–11,
236–37, 277–84, 317, 479, 513
William de Lorris, 466
William II, Rufus (English king), 285–86

William of Malmesbury, 332
William of Occam, 532–35
Witchcraft, 425, 504
Women: and the barbarian invasions,
119–21; and Christianity, 37–38;
and the double standard, 354–55;
emancipation of, 354; in England,
120; and family issues, 478–79;
and the Frankish kingdoms,
119–21; in Germany, 120; and the
harvest of medieval thought, 539;
as heretics, 427; and the Inquisition, 425; and the intellectual
expansion of Europe, 349–50,
354–56; and monasticism, 154–55;
patristic attitudes toward, 71–73;
and popular heresy, 392, 393; and
the priesthood, 72; in the Roman
Empire, 37–38, 71; and Roman
law, 120; and romanticism,
349–50, 354, 547; and succession
questions, 287–88; as writers,
355–56, 539
World revolutions: aim of, 245; characteristics of, 244–45. *See also*
Investiture controversy
Worms, Concordat of (1122), 273–74,
286
Writers: and anticlericalism, 384; and the
intellectual expansion of Europe,
343–56; nobility as, 465–66; and
vernacular languages, 344–56;
women as, 355–56, 539. *See also*
Church fathers; Renaissance
humanism
Wyclif, John, 499–500

(continued from front flap)

lighting of prominent medieval personalities through dozens of biographical sketches, which has been retained.

Although it draws upon a century of detailed research on the medieval world and is authoritative in its learning, from first page to last Cantor's book tells an exciting and compelling story.

NORMAN F. CANTOR is professor of history, sociology, and comparative literature at New York University (where in 1991 he was selected as one of the dozen best teachers in the university by the students). He is the author of numerous books, including *Inventing the Middle Ages*, which was nominated for a National Book Critics Circle Award, *Twentieth-Century Culture*, and the forthcoming *Medieval Lives*. He is currently writing a history of the Jews entitled *The Sacred Chain*. He lives in New York City and Sag Harbor, Long Island.